Portable Video

Portable Video

ENG & EFP

Fifth Edition

Norman J. Medoff
Edward J. Fink
Tom Tanquary

AMSTERDAM • BOSTON • HEIDELBERG • LONDON
NEW YORK • OXFORD • PARIS • SAN DIEGO
SAN FRANCISCO • SINGAPORE • SYDNEY • TOKYO

Focal Press is an imprint of Elsevier

ELSEVIER

Acquisitions Editor:	Elinor Actipis
Publishing Services Manager:	George Morrison
Senior Project Manager:	Brandy Lilly
Assistant Editor:	Robin Weston
Marketing Manager:	Christine Degon Veroulis
Cover Design:	Louis Forgione
Interior Design:	Multiscience Press, Inc.

Focal Press is an imprint of Elsevier
30 Corporate Drive, Suite 400, Burlington, MA 01803, USA
Linacre House, Jordan Hill, Oxford OX2 8DP, UK

Library of Congress Cataloging-in-Publication Data
Application submitted.

British Library Cataloguing-in-Publication Data
A catalogue record for this book is available from the British Library.

ISBN 13: 978-0-240-80797-3
ISBN 10: 0-240-80797-9

For information on all Focal Press publications
visit our website at www.books.elsevier.com

07 08 09 10 11   5 4 3 2 1

Printed in the United States of America

To my wife, Friederike, and my children, Anna and Liam.
—Edward J. Fink

Lynn, Sarah, and Natalie Medoff
—Norman J. Medoff

Contents

Foreword

For me, the terms Electronic News Gathering and Electronic Field Production are still as exciting as the day I first learned them in a class at Rutgers University in 1976. For many people coming into this exciting arena today, everything that they know about video is indeed portable. Today's youth grew up with a small camcorder and they have never used anything but a laptop to edit their video. For these kids, this book could simply be named VIDEO.

Opportunities in television news are no longer confined to television. We now watch news on *other screens* including our computers, portable media players, mobile phones and probably on our wristwatches someday soon. With so many places to view video news, more people are viewing news (including sports) than ever before. However, we are not just seeing a simple up scaling of the *old news* audience. Indeed many are viewing TV network news on these *other screens* but more people are viewing video news that was produced by medium, small and even tiny companies. The modern news audience is watching niche news.

There's an audience for technology video news. Video production costs are now low enough to cost justify the existence of a weekly show named *This Week In Technology* or *TWiT* and they have several competitors. In the future, perhaps by the time that you read this, there will be news programs for dozens and hundreds of niches. If you have a love for local real estate, I am sure that you can pursue this love but you can expect some income from your role on the Local Real Estate News Show. This income will either be a paycheck from an employer or a payment check from an advertiser if you launch your own entrepreneurial video real estate news venture.

The number of hours per week that are being recorded on video is increasing dramatically. In a typical city there are video shoots going on all over the place. Not just the politicians and the sporting events, but the computer users and the yoga instructors are also being recorded on video. It seems that more and more of life needs to be recorded, reviewed, reflected upon and/or analyzed. Opportunities in video news are growing as fast as YouTube did in 2006. Learning how to shoot and/or edit video in the field has never been more compelling. Hundreds of thousands of people are dreaming of video fieldwork but you are one step ahead of them because you are reading a book about how to do this well.

It may seem funny, but paper books are still very good learning tools. I first met Norm in the late 1980's when he contacted me because he was happy to learn about Videomaker Magazine. Our relationship is about video but is reliant upon our use of paper (my magazine and his book). You have an excellent book in your hands that will help you to become a great video shooter, editor and/or field producer. I am certain that you will have an interesting time continuing this pursuit!

—Matt York
Publisher/Editor, Videomaker Magazine

Preface

The first edition of this book was written more than 20 years ago. Since that time, the number of people who shoot video professionally has grown considerably. There are more television stations, cable and satellite operations, corporate video users, and producers who create programs for a variety of traditional and new exhibition outlets. The Internet continues to offer opportunities to place streaming video or podcasts on sites available to everyone. Even corporations that have been print-oriented for many years, such as large newspaper conglomerates, are hiring videographers to shoot news stories for their Web sites. The wireless telephone industry is now making video content available directly to cell phones. Viewers want choices and the ability to get programming on demand—on their terms, not just when the broadcast, cable, or satellite channel decides to air it.

Television viewers in the 1950s and 1960s often had three or four television viewing choices. In the 1970s, cable television increased the viewing channels to at least 12 and sometimes 30 channels or more. The number of viewing choices continued to grow, but the growth curve flattened out in the 1980s and 1990s as the cable industry went through consolidation and shakeout. However, applications of video are going to dramatically increase once again because of the new technologies that use video.

Advances in video compression combined with faster Internet connections will eventually lead to the Internet as a source of video that will rival other delivery systems. Broadband connections have replaced dial-up connections, and many cities are considering city-wide WiFi accessibility. Amateur videographers can easily upload their videos to the Web on the YouTube site.

As the technology to put full-frame, full-motion video on Web sites becomes more accessible, more sites with video will appear. When portable video first became accessible to corporate, educational, and institutional entities, the demand grew rapidly for people to create professional-quality video images. This demand created many jobs for videographers. Now the electronic media industry is creating numerous ways of distributing video to its audience. Many industry leaders admit that "content is king," meaning that more and more programs will be made to fill the many traditional channels and for those that are just getting started.

In the fifth edition, we again find that although technology has changed (for the better), the basic ingredients for shooting professional-quality video are not necessarily technology-based. Consumer and prosumer cameras are becoming more like computers that can also shoot video, which sometimes creates problems with numerous menus and settings. Although a better camera will help a skilled videographer get better video in a wider variety of situations, the real keys to good video are variables like lighting, composition, framing, and exposure. Lens technology hasn't changed that much. However, lighting devices have gotten better (more light from less power), and there are a few new designs, like fluorescents that help videographers. What's more important is what has not changed at all. While cameras and tape and digital recorders are creating digital images, and editing can be accomplished on a consumer laptop computer, it's still the *content* of the pictures that creates the story or product. Most of the advances in the technology deal with the manipulation of the video images *after* the images are shot. Once stored, the video images can be edited quickly and with tremendous creative flexibility. Most importantly, digital technology is becoming accessible to lower-end users. As video processing becomes easier and more robust using computers in the digital environment, we recall a saying that was rampant in the early days of computer programming: "Garbage in, garbage out." If input to the computer is meaningless or of low quality, the output is meaningless or of low quality. The same is true in video. The best digital editor in the world can only do so much to improve bad video. The key to the production of high-quality video images lies in a thorough knowledge of the basics, which allows the videographer to capture good images on any camera that, when edited together on any system, tell a good story. Your computer can't do that for you. Your video camera will only be as good as you are. The best and most successful videographers are those who have "a good eye" and are skillful in shooting and recording video. It is our hope that after reading the fifth edition of this book, you will have the skills needed to create video for traditional outlets, the new digital media, and whatever follows.

Acknowledgments

Many people contributed to this edition with advice, suggestions, pictures, and other materials. Our sincere thanks to the following people: Steve Paskay, Hank Bargine, Chris Wooley, Alan Lifton, Mara Alper, Chris Strobel, Price Hicks, Courtney Connell, Brandon Neuman, Marvin Seligman, and Stacy Moore. We also wish to thank Elinor Actipis and Robin Weston. We'd also like to thank our reviewers, Hank Bargine, Joey Goodsell, William Snead, Mario Esquer, Bettina Fabos, and Jackie Layng.

1 Introduction

Welcome to the world of portable video! So you have access to a camera, a tripod, some lights, a microphone or two, and some editing software on a computer. What do you do? Where do you start? What do you need to know? This book is designed to give you the basics of portable video production. We hope this text will guide you as you create better and better video stories for news, entertainment, and nonbroadcast uses.

Experiments using electricity to transmit video began back in 1884. In 1926, English experimenter John Logie Baird developed a system for transmitting live video images using a **mechanical system**. The mechanical system was primitive by today's standards, and other methods were tried to achieve a better picture. Beginning in the 1920s, other experimenters attempted to use an **electrical system** for television. Philo T. Farnsworth and Vladimir Zworykin both developed systems that eventually were combined to create the working television system that debuted at the 1939 World's Fair in New York.

The television cameras developed for electrical television were large, heavy, clumsy, and expensive. The demand for sports, news, entertainment, and nonbroadcast applications encouraged companies to attempt to design television cameras that could be easily used by one person in the field. The need for portable video systems was apparent early.

Figure 1-1   Philo T. Farnsworth and his model Mabel with a 1935 portable video camera.

ENG AND EFP: THE WORLD OF PROFESSIONAL VIDEO

Portable video systems have been around for a long time. In 1965, Sony released a video system called the Porta-pak that recorded black-and-white pictures on a reel-to-reel videotape recorder. The quality was bad and the video was almost impossible to edit. Some educational, government, medical, and experimental users (video artists) found the Porta-pak helpful in conveying ideas where film would be too expensive. Mostly, however, it was thought of as a toy with limited appeal. Even as color was introduced, the idea of shooting field video with a portable camera was not feasible. The equipment was just too big and cumbersome, and the video was lacking in quality.

The appearance of the U-Matic videocassette by Sony in 1971, coupled with the introduction of higher resolution color cameras, suddenly gave portable video a new appeal. This self-threading cassette system, in a machine small enough to be carried around and operated by battery, replaced the Porta-pak's reel-to-reel system and greatly improved the quality of the recording. The camera was in two pieces—the **camera head** and the **camera control unit** (**CCU**)—both of which could be powered by a battery. Two people could easily walk around with the gear and record video. With the equipment mounted on a small cart, one person could operate the system.

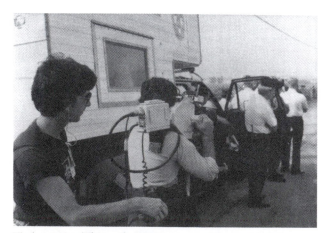

Figure 1-2   This early ENG camera, Thompson Micro-CAM, required two persons to operate it in the field. (Courtesy of Larry Greene, KCBS-TV)

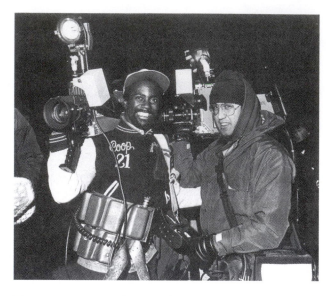

Figure 1-3   News photographer in 1980. Each full set of gear weighed about 80 pounds. (Photo by Joe Vitti)

Knowing the power of video cameras in news and sports coverage—even though their use was limited by their size, miles of cables, and often days of setup time—the TV networks began to experiment with this new portable technology. Companies like Sony, Thomson, RCA, and Ikegami worked closely with the networks to deliver a smaller, higher quality camera that could meet their needs. Their primary focus of use was live TV and, in particular, sports. Having a smaller battery-powered camera could increase the coverage of a sporting event dramatically. One of the earliest uses of portable video in network news was President Nixon's historic visit to China in 1974. CBS decided to use video instead of 16mm film to cover the event. The **electronic news gathering** (**ENG**) revolution had begun. The 1976 CBS coverage of the presidential campaign put the video camera in the mainstream of news coverage. Reporters no longer had to wait for the 16mm film to be developed to air the story. They could now report live from the campaign stop with the use of these new camera units, or shoot tape and have it aired almost immediately. But an even more dramatic change was already under way.

Starting with early experiments at stations such as the CBS-owned and -operated (O&O) KNXT in Los Angeles in 1974, video slowly began to create a foothold in daily news coverage. In 1974, KMOX-TV (now KMOV-TV) in St. Louis became the first all-video, or all ENG, newsroom in the country, using the Ikegami HL-35 two-piece camera. This novel approach to covering local events became an important factor in the competitiveness of the station's news ratings. By the second half of the 1970s, the video revolution began sweeping local television stations across the country.

Fueled by the new realization that there was money in news because news had a big and growing audience, more and more stations started news shows or began aggressively expanding their news operations. At the local level, it no longer mattered whether a network's programming was the highest rated; what mattered was how big the audience—and therefore the advertising dollars—was for the local news show. The competition became fierce. Station and network management looked for any means to gain a competitive edge in news. The ability to get a breaking story on the air first epitomized the race in every way. Suddenly, that newly downsized video camera and its videotape recorder were just what the doctor (or station owner) ordered.

The newfound portability of both the video camera and the videotape recorder, which was being demonstrated at CBS and local stations like KNXT, KMOX, and WBBM in Chicago, was now revolutionizing the film-dominated daily television newscasts in two very important ways. First, it was possible for a videocassette of a breaking news story to be delivered to the station and, after just a few minutes of editing, be played on the air. Faster yet, the raw or unedited tape—which didn't have to be developed—could be put directly on the air, allowing the viewer to see a live-to-tape presentation only minutes after it was shot. Second, because the camera was now electronic instead of mechanical, its video signal could be broadcast live from the field with little setup or fuss, aided by newly developed microwave technology to send the video to the station for broadcasting. Live TV news on location was suddenly available to almost any station at a low price. That changed not only the look of the industry, but the various ways in which stories were covered, forever.

This new form of acquiring pictures—and consequently the whole business of television news—became known as **electronic news gathering**, or **ENG**. As the news ratings race continued at an ever-

increasing pace, the demand for better, lighter, and more reliable camera gear also grew. Companies rushing to supply news departments with the latest advance in equipment began finding new outlets for their products. Mass production, better technology, and competition within their own industry had made video equipment cheaper and therefore more accessible to a wide range of users. Hospitals, government agencies, corporations, educational institutions, and independent production houses began to replace their film cameras with video cameras. Organizations that didn't have any production capabilities suddenly found that producing their own projects on video was cost effective because of the decreasing price of video equipment and its ever-increasing quality. From hospital teaching tapes to TV commercials, any use of a single video camera with a portable videotape recorder that wasn't for a newscast became known as **electronic field production**, or **EFP**. The similarities between ENG and EFP are many. Generally, the equipment and its operation are the same. Only the style of shooting and the production goals often separate the two.

By the 1990s, high-quality video **camcorders** (camera and videotape recorders in one unit) had not only become affordable to the general public but had become commonplace. This invention created a world where almost no event goes unrecorded. Whenever something important or newsworthy happens anywhere in the world, it is usually captured on video by someone. One of the most famous—or infamous— events was the police beating of Rodney King, which was captured by an amateur videographer trying out his new camera from the balcony of his apartment. That home video began a chain of events that led to one of the worst civil disturbances in the history of the United States. It also secured the video camera's place as a powerful tool for a free society's ability to communicate. Some might say that single moment was the culmination of the TV revolution: the fullest realization of the power of television and its profound effect on society.

It is with this power in mind that the video professional sets about the job of creating both news and commercial product. Used properly and with ethical guidance, video can be the most persuasive means of communication, regardless of the delivery system. Video is no longer only for broadcasting and industrial/educational uses; it can be used by anyone in society. With the broadening opportunities for streaming video on the Internet, podcasting, and vlogging, anyone can have his or her own TV station. Learning and understanding the tools and techniques of the trade can make the videographer an integral part of any modern communication medium, whether it is a commercial broadcast television network, cable, satellite, the Internet, or an as-yet unimagined delivery system.

Figure 1-4   Shooting home video has been a common activity in millions of homes since the 1980s.

Figure 1-5   Home video–captured scenes can sometimes be sold to local TV stations, network news programs, or other TV production companies.

ELECTRONIC NEWS GATHERING: CAPTURING THE EVENT

A Brief History

In its purest form, ENG is the art of shooting news—photojournalism for television. It is the descendent of a long tradition of documenting events with moving pictures. As with the still camera, one of the first uses of the motion picture camera was recording historic events. Cameras rolled as trench warfare consumed the European continent in World War I. Later, a more organized effort by news services would show World War II to moviegoing audiences via the newsreel. With the advent of television and its growing acceptance in the 1950s, newsreels were replaced by newscasts. The style of shooting had changed little from the fields of France to Edward R. Murrow's reports beaming into 1950's living rooms. The camera operators were a very select group of people who followed a tradition from generation to generation.

TV news grew as an industry in the 1960s, and the style of shooting began to change. Up until then, the film cameras used were rather large and heavy, so most shooting was done from a tripod in controlled situations. Small handheld cameras had no audio recording capabilities and were used mostly in hard-to-get-to places, such as in airplanes or on battlefields. The lighter sound-on-film cameras of the 1960s, such as the Cinema Products CP-16, allowed the camera operators greater freedom of movement without having to leave sound or quality behind. The handheld shot became more important. The cameraperson could now be closer to the action than ever before. The introduction of color-reversal film, which could be developed as fast as black-and-white film, added a new sense of reality to every newscast. But it was video that upended decades of tradition.

At the broadcast network level and at most of the large local stations, video cameras came in and film cameras left, as did many of the film camera operators. People who were trained in the art of cinema and experienced in the business of journalism were suddenly replaced by engineers from the studio who knew how the electronics worked in the camera but not much about "shooting" or journalism. News events couldn't wait for these people to learn the craft, so stations and networks had to accept the new priority: just get any shot that helps tell the story. The video revolution was painful not only to the displaced workers and confused managers, but also to the viewing public. Pictures on the evening news went from sharp clear images in realistic color to dull muddy visions with smears lagging behind moving objects and colors ranging from orange to bright green. Sometimes it seemed that the operators were trying to master the technology first and find a good shot—or any shot—second. A lot of the respect for the visual part of TV news was lost when the film/video changeover occurred.

Figure 1-6 A two, person ENG crew on location at a military installation. (Courtesy of Hank Bargine)

TV News Videography Today

By the late 1980s, after more than a decade of struggling for acceptance, **the news videographer (also known as a TV photojournalist)** had come into his and her own. Many people still believe film looks better than video, but the people shooting the video are finally on the same creative level as their counterparts in film. Tune in to any network news magazine show, and you will see state-of-the-art creative photography that just happens to be shot on video. There are still plenty of examples of bad videography in local (especially small market) TV news programs. Their unavoidable inclusion in the newscasts stems more from the changing nature of the news business than any-

thing else. The proliferation of news outlets, the relentless competition, and the almost unrealistic deadline pressures of live TV have allowed quality standards to become a secondary concern at times.

If there is one driving maxim in the ENG world today, it is this: "Any image that can be recorded is better than no image at all." To understand this statement, you must understand the nature of modern TV photojournalism. Yes, quality is important—very important—but nothing is as important as capturing the event. Bringing back the story is the ultimate goal. Because news cannot be planned or controlled—that is, staged—each news story on location is different. Decisions have to be made on a case-by-case basis, and often on a second-by-second basis. This book will provide guidance for using a video camera in almost any application, but, specifically for the future news videographer, it will be a guide to making those quick decisions as well as to making creative choices that will set the videographer apart from the competition.

Many concepts differentiate ENG videography from any other form of shooting. The primary one is mentioned above: the event being covered is the most import thing. You can't go to the fire and not bring something back. A news shooter's mandate is to find any way to bring back the story. Beg, borrow, or buy whatever you need to get the shots necessary to tell the story (within ethical considerations). There are five other areas in which a news shooter has a unique concern:

- Time

- Control

- Preparation

- Story line

- Responsibility

Time

People who work in TV news have the sound of the clock pounding in their ears. On a normal day, the pressure builds as the time of the newscast draws closer. The show goes on at exactly 5:00 or 6:00, whether you're ready or not. And not being ready is a crime with a stiff penalty—one that can easily include termination of employment. A videographer's entire day revolves around when things take place, how long they last, and how long it takes to get to the next locale or back to the station. The press conference will take place at 10:00 A.M. sharp. The noon interview at the school lasted one hour. The 3:00 story about illegal immigrants has to be shot one hour away from the station. How everything fits into the day, and what can be done at each location, is determined not only by its importance, but also by the time involved.

The situation is doubly confounded when the story is breaking at the moment, such as a plane crash. A news shooter must be constantly aware of the time he or she is spending getting to the location, making the shots, and getting them on the air. It may involve driving them back to the station, driving to meet a microwave van to "feed" the pictures back to the station, or waiting in one spot for the van to arrive. Which method gets the pictures on the air the fastest? How far away is the station, the van, another videographer? On top of the pressure to shoot good video, the videographer must always be apprised of the time it takes to get the footage back to the station.

Control

The next factor that sets a news shooter apart from other videographers is the idea of control: basically, there is none. News videography, with very few exceptions, must follow the mandates of good journalistic ethics. At the heart of those ethics is the rule against manufacturing an event or scene. In other words, you don't cause anything to happen that would not normally be happening. You can't go to a protest gathering and tell the participants that it would make better pictures if they marched around the building chanting. You can only show up and shoot what's there. If it's dull, then it's dull. Period.

Applying this rule, as well as working with an entire code of ethics (discussed later in this book) can make shooting even the simplest story difficult.

What it all comes down to is this: you do not have, nor should you have, any control over your subjects. Even telling a housewife, whom you're shooting as part of a story on stay-at-home moms, to make a pot of coffee can be wrong. If you're asking her to do something

she wouldn't normally be doing at that time of day just to give her something to do so you can have some action to shoot, then it's a violation. It may seem silly, but if you make an exception here and there, you simply push the line farther away from what is an accurate representation of the truth. If you get into the habit of arbitrarily drawing the line, then you tend to forget where the line was supposed to be in the first place.

Preparation

Video projects of any kind require preparation. What sets the news videographer apart from other (EFP) videographers is that he or she needs to be prepared for anything. You may haul a full set of lights up to a senator's office ready to do a three-light formal sit-down interview only to find out the senator is late for a vote and you must shoot the politician in the dark hallway while he walks to place his vote. Having a battery-powered light (sometimes called a sungun) mounted on top of the camera will save the day. You hadn't planned on using that unflattering light source, but having the correct exposure, as opposed to a dark, low-contrast shot, is far better when seeing the senator answer important questions on camera. No matter how much planning goes into an upcoming news shoot, anything can change because of the concept mentioned above: you have no control.

Since you have no control, you must be prepared for anything. News videographers must have a full and complete understanding of the equipment and techniques available to them. Another thing this book will do is make sure the prospective shooter is up to speed on both of those points. The last thing necessary for good preparation is practice. Unfortunately, this book can't create that experience, but it will instruct the student about to how to get it.

Story Line

A typical assignment in TV news is to cover an event where little is known about the nature of the subject. A press conference has been called, but the information is vague as to what it's about—only that it's important. The videographer working in concert with the reporter, producer, or assignment editor must not only film the event but also understand the event. The script for the story being covered won't be written until after all the shooting is complete—sometimes hours after the shoot. To obtain the necessary pictures and sound bites that will provide viewers with a clear and concise presentation and fit with the script, the videographer needs to have as much knowledge and detail as possible about the story he or she is covering before and during the shooting. The videographer is the one primarily responsible for visualizing the story.

If, for example, the press conference was about a dangerous toxic chemical that was found in the local landfill, then the first thing to be considered is getting pictures of that landfill. Paying close attention to all the details of the story can make a big difference in what gets shot and how. It may be that the source of the contamination is from liquid deposits to the dump. So, in shooting the landfill, most of the effort would be put into finding trucks dumping liquid waste, chemical drums, or any other evidence visible at the site. Even with that knowledge, the videographer needs more information. Which companies are doing it? If no one knows, then the shots of trucks dumping liquid waste must be made so that the identity of the company is hidden. You cannot imply wrongdoing by any one company unless they have been accused. One hopes that the writer of the on-air segment will convey the fact that the video seen is not the actual dumping but simply represents the kind of dumping responsible for the problem. You can easily see how shooting without the fullest understanding of the story can lead to more problems (like lawsuits) than just pictures that don't match the story.

News videographers never shoot in a vacuum. The video will have to be assembled into an edited story at some point. Having the correct mix and variety of shots that cover every aspect of the event or story can make the difference between a visual story line that is hard to follow, or one that speaks for itself. Each picture, every scene, must accurately depict what the videographer wants to convey. Before the videographer begins recording, these questions must be asked:

Why am I shooting this?
What does it mean?
What else do I need to go with this footage to make it a complete story?
Where will this footage be shown?

Responsibility

Despite the fact that a news videographer often works as part of a much larger team—the newsroom—the videographer is often the only person responsible for getting the story. A shooter working alone in a smaller market may be the only one near a major story when it occurs. An event such as a plane crash can put that videographer on the front line of coverage with no reporter or other assistance for minutes or even hours—crucial time when the story must be fully covered. The videographer must not only gather the shots necessary but also gather information, find witnesses and/or survivors who can tell their stories on camera, make contact with the authorities on the scene, and figure out a way to get all this back to the station to be the first on the air with it. That's why shooters are called photojournalists. It is now common for news footage to appear not only on the nightly newscast, but also to be **repurposed**. News footage may be used for a two-minute story at the 6:00 and 10:00 P.M. newscasts on one station, and then it may air as part of a larger story in another market, possibly at a station owned by the same station that aired your story. Sometimes footage is requested by a national news service like CNN or Fox News. NBC might use some news footage at a local affiliate station, then in the Nightly News, then again on CNBC, MSNBC, or even Dateline NBC. The footage might also be edited and compressed into a small, digital file for streaming on a news Web site.

Even at the network level, a cameraperson must be able to do all the jobs needed in the field, including being on camera. If you are the witness to a major event as well as its videographer, then you may be called on to give your firsthand accounts to the audience, perhaps even live from the field. No job in the news business should ever be considered strictly someone else's. But more than anyone else, the videographer is in the position to do it all. After all, television without pictures is called radio.

This certainly doesn't preclude the videographer from being a team player. The overwhelming majority of time, it really does take all those people to put a good show on the air. It makes for a better product when each member of the team concentrates on being the best at what he or she does and lets others be the best at doing their jobs. However, as with so many

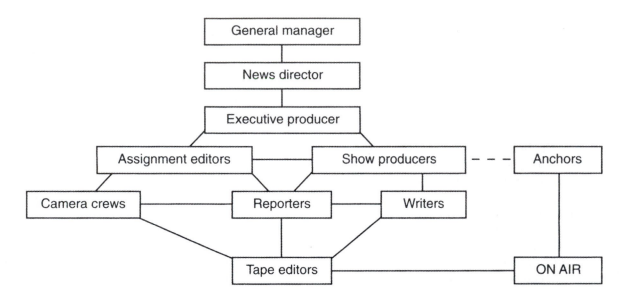

Figure 1-7   Typical newsroom chain-of-command flowchart.

other aspects of news, you must also plan for the worst-case scenario. For the videographer, that means being prepared to go it alone.

Being a news videographer can be the greatest job in the world. It involves seeing history as it is made, experiencing the drama of life up close in a way that very few in this society will ever do, going places that few will ever get to see—and being paid to do it.

ELECTRONIC FIELD PRODUCTION: VIDEO PRODUCTION ON LOCATION

Birth of an Industry

The techniques used in portable or field video were not invented by those who began to shoot ENG in the late 1970s. Starting in the early days of filmmaking, a single (film) camera was used by cinematographers to record drama or comedy to create feature films. This style of shooting became known as **film style** or **single camera** shooting. These cinematographers developed the technique of shooting a scene from one camera angle, then shooting the same scene from one or more different camera locations or camera angles. After the film was processed, a film editor would edit various parts of the different **takes** together to make one ver-

sion of the scene. The scene would have smooth action, and it would appear as if there were numerous cameras all shooting the same scene at the same time.

The need for doing the production in this fashion was much the same then as it is now. An aesthetically pleasing scene that appears to have been shot by multiple cameras can be achieved by one camera and one camera operator. Then as now, good cameras were expensive, and multiple camera productions were not cost effective. A good filmmaker could create a film that had a big-budget look by using a small-budget crew and camera.

As news evolved from documentation to newsreels, only a few others outside the movie industry were making use of the moving picture. Making films of any kind was expensive, time consuming, and had relatively few practitioners. With the advent of television and smaller film formats like 16mm and 8mm, more organizations and even consumers began to use the medium. Health and science films produced by the government and shown on chattering 16mm projectors became common in the classroom. Home movies became a symbol of middle-class success.

But it was the video revolution started by the news competition that sparked a whole new industry. Based entirely on the new portable video systems, electronic field production, or EFP, was born. Suddenly, for a slightly larger initial investment, the cost of shooting a minute's worth of moving pictures went from being measured in dollars to being measured in pennies. Without the punishing conditions of news coverage, the equipment could be easily maintained and, therefore, last longer, so its reliability was no longer a question. Video productions that were once confined to and constricted in the studio suddenly broke free to take place in almost any location imaginable. This freedom from high-cost and limited locations allowed anyone with the desire to communicate a message the method of doing it.

Video Production Today: The Process

The process of producing an ENG story differs from producing an EFP project. Since ENG is mostly shot on the day the story is assigned, little time is available for preparing for the location and the shoot. The shoot occurs where and when the event is happening. Preparation for ENG is discussed in Chapters 2 and 6.

In EFP, much more time is available to the videographer to prepare for the shoot. The process is discussed both in Chapters 3 and 6. For non-news production, the general process and stages of production are the same three phases they have been for many years: preproduction, production and postproduction.

The Three Phases of Production

The first phase of production, preproduction, is perhaps the most important for the success of the project. At this stage, a client contacts a company or producer who can produce video projects. The project is discussed and client goals are decided. A producer then begins research for the project and a script by creating a script outline, a **treatment** (a synopsis of the project), a **storyboard** (individual pictures or drawings of the scenes in the project), then the script. A crew is selected that includes people who will perform the functions of producer, director, videographer, actor(s), and production assistants (also known as PAs or grips). In large productions, there may also be people selected to do makeup, set lights, collect audio, and perform other necessary functions. A video editor is also selected. Once the script is written (and approved by the client), the location(s) is selected, schedules are created, and rehearsals can begin. This phase takes 60 to 80% of the total time spent on the project.

The second phase is production—the actual recording of the video for the project. Once all of the decisions have been made about the script, location, equipment, and crew, the actual shooting can begin. The talent rehearses, the equipment is setup, the crew takes their places at the shoot location, and once the director is satisfied that all variables are correct and under control, the shooting can begin. This includes not only shooting the main action and characters, but also shooting additional shots, such as **cutaways** (shots relating to the main action), that might be helpful in the editing process. A good producer will not leave the location until he or she is sure that all the shots needed at that location have been recorded.

The third phase of production is postproduction. This is the phase when the "raw footage" or unedited video is combined to make the project that was planned. It involves putting the shots and scenes together to tell the story, and making sure that the shots look right and sound right. The key person in this phase is the video editor who does the actual combining of the shots to make the story come together properly. The script is the blueprint for the project, and the editor, along with the producer, works to make the video match the script. Although some creative choices might differ from the original script, the video project should follow the script as written. The client sees the project after it is edited and either approves it or suggests the changes necessary to make sure that the project meets the client's goals. We will discuss more on this stage of the production process in Chapter 7.

As you go through this book you will notice the similarities between ENG and EFP. The equipment is basically the same. The shooting aesthetics are the same. The basic principles are very similar. Ideas and concepts in one discipline can easily be applied to the other in many cases. Learning news videography prepares you for doing production work, and vice versa. But there are differences that must be understood. The two production styles are derived from very different goals. In news, the event is of paramount importance, while in EFP, the overriding importance is placed on what the client (who in the case of entertainment is the producer) wants. The sole purpose of the production is to serve the client's goals, whatever they are. It may be as simple as showing all the new Fords for sale, or as complex as teaching a group of teenagers that violence is not the answer to life's problems or giving instructions about how to install a new component into your computer. In entertainment programming, the goal may be to scare, mystify, or get the audience to laugh or otherwise enjoy the program. Whatever the subject, the goal is to communicate the message of the client.

ENG has many differences when compared to EFP. Most of these differences simply involve the reordering of priorities. Some involve approaching a situation from the exact opposite point of view. The following areas are of concern to a production videographer:

Budget
Planning
Script
Authority

Budget

If time is the driving force behind the news videographer, money is what drives the production videographer. Before any work is done, a budget is set in place. Going over budget can result in people and bills not being paid—not the kind of thing you want to happen in the business world. In EFP, you can say that time is money. This is especially true when it comes to the hours it takes to get something done. If a flat rate of $1000 is allotted to pay the members of the crew, then each member should have a reasonable expectation of how much work is involved for that amount of money. If the shoot starts to run longer than anticipated, then the hourly salary for those crew members begins to decline. That makes for unhappy workers and, in some cases, workers who walk away from the job in disgust. The producer, the person with the responsibility for getting the project done, has two choices: go to the client and ask for more money, or cut other items from the budget to make up the difference.

Generating an accurate budget can be one of the most difficult tasks in EFP. As the example above illustrates, a miscalculation can cause the entire project to fail. Unlike news, every aspect of the production process must be accounted for in that project's budget. That means figuring in the cost of everything from

duct tape to wear and tear on the camera. Chapter 11, *Budgeting and Pricing,* will explain how to create an accurate budget that will keep you in your job and out of hot water—and possibly bankruptcy court.

Planning

The factor that allows budgets to be drawn up accurately is the extensive planning that goes into any EFP shoot. To control the budget, every aspect of the production must be planned well in advance. An accurate assessment of what must be done, how many people will be needed for the crew, what equipment will be used, and any other items needed for the production must be compiled before the shooting begins. Most EFP projects also include editing as part of the overall job. How long will it take in the edit room? Are you going to need special effects?

In the real world, nothing ever goes quite as planned. A good production videographer should be intimately involved in the planning process. If the videographer makes up the entire crew, then he or she takes on the responsibility of being prepared for those unforeseen problems. On larger productions, the

Figure 1-8 This EFP crew is shooting a documentary while dealing with extreme weather and an inquisitive (and dangerous) onlooker. (Courtesy of Hank Bargine)

videographer may be working for a production manager but still should be included in any planning process. The best planning also includes what to do if things go wrong. What if it rains? Can the shoot be rescheduled? The EFP videographer must always be able

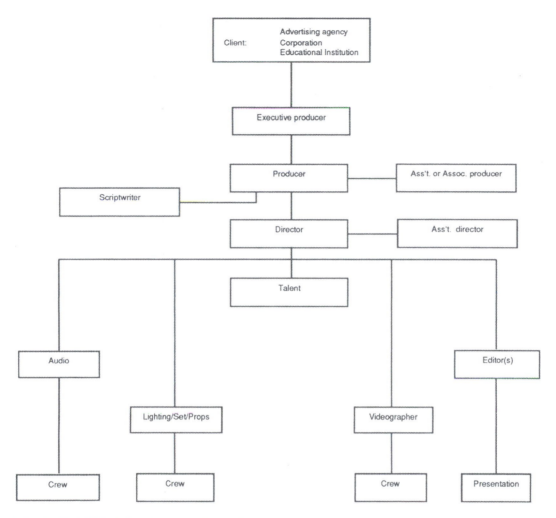

Figure 1-9   Typical EFP chain-of command flowchart.

to assess each situation and problem and offer constructive alternatives that meet not only the budget but the client's goals as well.

Script

The blueprint for what will take place in the field and in the edit room is the script. Nothing gets done without one. The script, just like the blueprint for a new building, gives everyone the guidance they require to get the job done. In larger budgets and more sophisticated productions, the script is visualized in a series of drawings called the **storyboard**. Each shot is sketched out so that every member of the production team knows what the finished product should look like. In smaller production crews the videographer director,

should have a well-defined image of what the look should be. How the shots are made, their framing, the camera movement, the action within the frame, and the lighting are all determined by the script, either directly or by interpretation.

A public service announcement (PSA) on boating safety may have a script calling for scenes of a boating accident. The producer and/or the director with the cameraperson will go over each sentence, indeed every word, of the script to find ways of illustrating the message being conveyed. Within the confines of the proposed budget, they will design shots and scenes that depict what the script is saying. They will identify locations for the shooting to take place, determine how and where the camera is to be positioned, and determine what kinds of actors are needed, all the props necessary, and how the action will be framed. If the script includes a concept that, for whatever reason, can't be depicted directly by a specific shot (for example, the emotions of a victim's family), then visualizing it can be a creative challenge. That's when the production team and the talents of the videographer are stretched. The shots must now be symbolic of the message being delivered. They must convey the emotion of the script without showing exactly what the script is talking about. Seeing a hand toss a wreath onto the water may be all that's necessary to cover the narration describing a family's grief.

Authority

The final word on all aspects of a production shoot comes from the client. The client can reject the script, the actors, a particular shot, and even the videographer. The producer acts as the representative of the client in the client's absence. The producer makes all the decisions before, during, and after the shoot on authority of the client. The production videographer must understand her responsibility within that framework. It can be considerable or minimal. The EFP shooter needs to determine the shooter's level of authority as soon as possible when a production starts.

In a large organization, the videographer's duties are generally limited to work associated with the camera: designing and setting up shots, lighting, and executing the shot. The videographer won't have the burden of total responsibility for the project. In smaller productions, the videographer may be the producer, writer, sound tech, and even actor. Here the shooter-as-producer will have to get the entire job done. What the EFP cameraperson must be able to do in any size organization is offer help and assistance whenever necessary. If the producer can't solve the problem of a shot that just doesn't fit the script, the videographer must be ready to step forward and offer a possible solution based on his knowledge of production skills and creative solutions.

Being a production shooter in today's ever-changing field of video can be both exciting and challenging. As multimedia becomes more common in our communications with each other, there will always be a growing demand for a video product. Unencumbered by the constraints of journalism, EFP videographers can explore the outermost limits of their creativity. They can reach into the highest realms of visual art.

Knowing the Basics

At this point, you should know about some of the differences between ENG and EFP—and also know the similarities. In the real world, almost any job you get involving portable video will include a combination of both disciplines. The news shooter might also work on commercials and PSAs done by the in-house production department at the station. The production shooter will be assigned a shoot that the client wants done ENG-style or perhaps to shoot a documentary-style program. In today's marketplace, most working videographers are freelancers—they work for themselves. The phone rings and they're off to a job that may last one day or one week. One day they work for ABC World News Tonight, the next day they're shooting a commercial for the local candidate for governor, and the day after that they're doing a training video on a new assembly line at an electronics plant. They could also be shooting a segment for a show on HGTV on any given day. The type of shooting depends on who is paying them that day.

As the Internet and other forms of delivery continue to expand, the demand for videographers will grow just as fast. As the world of digital video grows, the potential uses of that video also grow. Streaming video, webcasting, TV-on-demand, DVDs, interactive TV, podcasting, vlogging (video blogging), video to cell phones, and broadcasting are all slowly becoming one and the same. But no matter what the format, no matter what the recording media, no matter what the delivery system, one thing will never change: it will always be videography, capturing images electronically and storing them for later use.

In the following chapters, this book will give you a complete course in the basics of videography. Since all forms of shooting share the common goal of telling a story, the methods and principles of storytelling are the same no matter how the story will be sent or viewed. By learning the basics, students or beginning-level TV photojournalists can quickly learn to provide a certain level of quality in their work. Recipes for success come from the rules and formulas established over the years in news and production videography. They are a guide to get the novice cameraperson on the road to finding that elusive thing called style. Individual style is what creates truly unique views that make videography an art.

SUMMARY

ENG and EFP shooting have a long and rich tradition. Film cameras were used to record news events and to create narrative stories from the early to the late 1900s. Beginning in earnest in the 1970s, videotape (which had been invented earlier but needed to become smaller and more reliable for day-to-day use) replaced film for news and other small-budget videos, because of its lower cost and because it could be played back instantly without first having to be developed like film. In this new millennium, tapeless recording—recording digital video files directly on solid-state recording devices with microchips—is replacing videotape.

Whatever the technology of portable video, the demand for more and more video content will only increase as the means of distributing news, information, and entertainment increases. Vlogs, podcasts, webcasts, and video phones, as well as more traditional satellite, cable, and terrestrial broadcasting all require video product. With the size and price of cameras continually decreasing, along with the higher sophistication and lower price of editing software, just about anyone can create video content today.

Whether creating news or non-news projects, the video producer must be trained in an arsenal of skills if he or she is to communicate the desired message of the video effectively to the intended audience. Each chapter in this book will address an area within that arsenal. These chapters are organized into four parts or clusters:

Shooting Video on Location
1. Introduction
2. ENG
3. EFP

The Process
4. Basic Shots
5. Scriptwriting
6. Preproduction and Production
7. Post Production

The Tools
8. Video
9. Audio
10. Lighting

The Business of Video
11. Budget and Pricing
12. Copyrights
13. New Trends

The first section, *Shooting Video on Location*, introduces you to the profession, business, and art of portable video. Chapters 2 and 3 define and discuss the two major styles of portable video, electronic news gathering and electronic field production.

The second section, *The Process*, introduces you to the language of video using basic shots (Chapter 4) and scriptwriting (Chapter 5) needed to build video programs. Chapters 6 and 7 describe the steps needed to plan, shoot, and edit a video project.

The third section, *The Tools*, gives you in-depth information about the equipment and techniques that you need to know to create high-quality video using consumer or professional equipment.

The final section, *The Business of Video*, informs you about how projects are budgeted and priced, legal issues that all videographers and producers should know about, and new developments in the industry that change the equipment and how the industry operates.

After reading and applying this text, it is hoped that you will be equipped with the full arsenal of skills necessary to create effective video projects, whether news (ENG) or non-news (EFP).

2 Electronic News Gathering Style

PART ONE: RECORDED COVERAGE

The decisions you make in the field while shooting any story will give your video a look or a particular style. Because no two people see the same scene in the same way, your vision of what is possible with the camera becomes your style. Within the world of TV news, documentary work, and reality-based programs, you must operate under certain constants while shooting. These constants help the viewer identify the type of story being told; they also act as an overlay to your individual style, not replacing it but limiting it to certain parameters.

In electronic news gathering, stories tend to fall into one of several categories: spot news, general news, feature news, and sports news. Each of these areas requires a unique approach on the part of the videographer, and each has its own guidelines that define a certain look. When a story is assigned to you, the nature of that story sets up certain expectations about how it will look and how you will approach the shooting.

Spot News

Although spot news is the reason most photographers come to TV news, it is the hardest ENG style to mas-

ter. It is truly what shooting news is all about. Whether it's a gunfight between law enforcement and a cult group, a raging war in the Middle East, or the attempted assassination of the president, you—because of your presence—are recording history. Even the most mundane event can suddenly become a moment in time that will live forever.

How well you do your job will also live forever. If you fail, generations to come will miss seeing that dramatic moment. Think for a moment how many events in history you remember by the pictures you saw; think how much less impact the events would have had if they had not been recorded on film or tape. If we never saw an atomic explosion, would we be as awed by its power? If no camera had recorded the first man stepping onto the moon, would that step have had the same historical impact? If we would not see stories of war on the news, would we really grasp the death and suffering?

News photography lets the viewer see and hear things as if he or she were actually present. (See Figure 2-1.) An ENG photographer's job is to bring the event to the viewer so that the viewer can react to what is happening. It is not the photographer's job to tell someone that a war is immoral but rather to show what a war is like, what is taking place, and the effect it has on those involved. Most news shooters will never be in a position to record a major part of history, but

Figure 2-1   Many reporters, such as this student videographer, take a small camera to shoot both video and still images to "repurpose" the story for different media, such as broadcast TV, the Internet, and print.

some will be, often solely because they were at the right place at the right time. Therefore, each videographer must be prepared to rise to the occasion.

When shooting spot news, the photographer will be in one of three situations: (1) in the middle of what is happening, (2) in the middle of the aftermath, or (3) stuck on the perimeter while the event is happening or just after it has happened.

Shooting in the Middle of the Action

One of the most famous examples of this situation is the assassination attempt on President Ronald Reagan in 1981. The camera crews assigned to shoot every move the president makes had no idea what was about to occur on that fateful morning. Within a few seconds, the calm scene was transformed into one of utter chaos. The photographers had to operate on instinct and training to capture that moment of history. Some did better than others at capturing the event. The best shooting came from an NBC cameraman, who held his shot wide until he could tell what was going on and then decided what was most important to show. He moved the camera and used the zoom lens to take viewers from one horrible section of the scene to the next, pausing just long enough to show what was happening before moving to the next area of action. No shaky zooms or wild pans whipping around to distort

what the picture contained. The cameraman found and held the shot on each element in the story in the order of its importance.

You can imagine the amount of self-control it took to do his job under these circumstances. Not many people could have done it, but this is the situation you must always anticipate if you work in news. It does not have to be the president; it could happen at a simple court hearing or as you follow a mail carrier on his route. Sometimes unexpected events happen when a camera is there. A simple demonstration by a student group might escalate into a full-scale riot with you at the center.

If you find yourself in the middle of an unfolding situation, keep your lens at its widest setting and keep your camera recording. It sounds simple, but it is surprising how many good pieces of news have been lost because this rule was not followed. If the story is breaking around you, you must shoot it as you would see it. Don't zoom in to one element and exclude the others that are still happening. Pan if you have to, or walk to a better vantage point, but save the zoom for later when you feel more in control of the elements.

Keep Recording   Above all, keep recording. From the moment the camera is turned on, keep shooting and don't stop for any reason. After things settle down or you gain control of the situation, you can be more selective about what to shoot. Remove the lens cap and zoom wide *after* you hit the record button; run from your car or van while already in the record mode; try to make every second viable. Even when you are running with the camera to get a better position, keep the camera on the action and as steady as possible. By keeping the camera on, you cover yourself in the event something unexpected takes place while you are at the location. Many times, the biggest moment of drama comes from seemingly nowhere.

Some of the most dramatic footage from the great Indian Ocean tsunami of 2005 came from amateur shooters who kept recording from their balconies or hotel rooms even as the water swelled beneath their feet. Obviously, if you find yourself in actual danger, you should get out of harm's way quickly. If possible, zoom wide and run or drive with the camera pointed in the direction of the action. Once you are safe, you can frame and compose shots more carefully. In the case of the tsunami, much of the footage reveals that the shooters could not have run to any higher ground before the waves hit, so they recorded from their vantage points as the water roiled around them. One photographer noticed a person clinging to a tree and was able to record one of the most memorable images of that historic disaster.

Keep the Lens Setting Wide The previous point—record continuously—is one of the reasons to stay wide. Camera movement is less noticeable when the shot is wide, and you also have a smaller chance of missing some important action. These are events you will not be able to get later; once they are missed, they are gone forever. Use the camera as you use your eyes—let the viewer see as much as possible of what you see. Let it all take place before you. Use the zoom only to maintain the field of action. Go in only as tight as is necessary to eliminate areas of "dead" space.

Look as You Shoot It may seem silly to say this, but you have to tell yourself to look up once in a while. With the lens wide, you can easily take your face away from the viewfinder and look around as you shoot. Watch your back. Look out for danger, and make sure you aren't getting in the way of emergency personnel. Above all, look for any elements you might be missing because your eye is glued to the ones in the viewfinder. When covering an event such as a riot, this technique could save your life.

Hold the Shots You must learn to count in your head while you shoot. In the middle of a breaking story, time will become very distorted. When you think you have a long enough shot of one particular element, you probably do not. Ten is a great number to use. Unless you must change shots to capture something that is leaving the scene or providing a more dramatic element, count to 10 before making any changes in your shot. This technique allows the viewer time to perceive the shot and gives the editor the ability to cut out pans and walking shots to condense the event for presentation.

Get Static Shots Don't forget to get **set shots** or **statics**. If the action slows for a moment, look for a good composition that you can make near where you are positioned. Don't stop recording, but slide to the next camera angle and hold the shot as if on a tripod. Try to find the most dramatic angle you can—one that shows the totality of the event either literally or symbolically. Use this moment to catch your breath and organize

your thoughts as to where you should be next. Just take in the scene, read it, and try to anticipate the next area of likely action. These statics will probably be some of your best shots.

Check Your Gear Often Don't panic in the middle of an action scene. Move to your first shot and count it out, go to the next shot and count it out, and keep recording. Check the camera often to make sure it is indeed in the record mode, and check your audio often to make sure the sound is there and not too low or overmodulated. Stay wide, keep shooting, time your shots by counting in your head, and look for the most important elements to photograph. Stay with the action, and check all of your systems as often as possible.

Shooting in the Aftermath

The second example of a spot news situation is one in which the main action is over and all that remains is the aftermath. For example, you arrive at the scene of a gas explosion shortly after the firefighters have begun to aid the victims. This situation can also be very intense with quite a bit of pressure, but for the most part things are under control. While you should still follow many of the same principles as when shooting in the middle of the action, a situation like this usually gives a photographer more time to make shots. Shooting in the aftermath is the most common type of spot news. It still requires hustle to get all the elements, but nothing new is going to happen. All the fire equipment is in place, the medical personnel are attending the injured, or the police have subdued the gunman.

In this type of aftermath situation, you do not need to record the entire time, but the situation does demand fast decision-making nonetheless. You are still trying to present the story as the viewers would see and hear it if they were present. Because the events are under more control than in the first situation, your shooting can be more controlled.

Look for a Variety of Shots Look for a good opening wide shot, and try to stay wide for most of the action shots. Because things are not moving as quickly, you have the time to look for medium shots and, above all, close-ups. With the zoom lens, you can pursue the tight shots of faces that really tell the stories of the individuals involved, without fear of losing other elements of the story.

Look for the Action   With your knowledge of sequencing and storytelling elements, you should know what shots to get and be out there getting them while staying out of the way. The key is always to look for the action—shoot what moves, but keep with the story. Do not get sidetracked with unimportant things like shooting the crowd of onlookers. As when shooting in the middle of the action, this type of shooting is often off the shoulder, so use your feet as much as possible to get close to each element.

Focus on the Story   Do not include extraneous shots in what you shoot; you are merely wasting time and tape or file space. If the spectators are not part of the story, do not shoot them. If the police are having a hard time moving them back, then they are part of the story. If the story has enough action in it, there is no need for a cutaway, and you should look for transition shots instead. By varying angles and focal lengths, the piece should fit together without the useless shot of uninvolved people watching.

In many cases, it will be obvious that the main element of the story is happening when you arrive. It might be as simple as flames shooting from a building's windows or as subtle as a single person lying on the ground surrounded by a few people. Generally, a quick look around at the people involved will give you a clue as to where the main action is. If firefighters are rushing to the back of a building, maybe you should, too, if you can.

The thing you must never forget is to focus on the people involved. If there is a rescue unit at the scene of the fire, then look for the injured. Stop by the ambulance first, as it will soon be leaving for the hospital; the building will be there for quite awhile. You might miss some of the best flames, but without the people the story would be lacking even more. A quick soundbite from a victim on the way to the hospital, describing a narrow escape, can sink the competition's shot of the flames you missed. Do not spend too much time on any one element. Keep moving. Look for those small but potentially powerful human elements that can take your story above and beyond the rest. Look for the elements that will not last long, and get them as soon as you can. Decide which things will move and which will be there later when things are calmer or you have more time.

As the story is winding down, look for a good closing shot. The typical one for a fire story is that of a lone firefighter sitting on the curb, with smoldering ashes in the background, removing an air mask and wiping away the sweat. Or, it might be a person quietly grieving at the site of the fire or the water to the hoses being turned off. It might be literal, such as the ambulance driving off. It might be symbolic, such as a tight shot of the police yellow or red tape blowing in the wind. You want to leave the viewer with a sense that the story is over. The closing shot should say "The End."

If the story is only going to run as a 20-second voiceover, there will be no air time to use such shots. For this type of presentation, you simply need the best 20 seconds of the event with the most action possible and that all-important human element. (See Figure 2-2.)

Shooting on the Perimeter of the Action

In the third example of spot news, you are restricted from close access to the action. If you are held blocks away from a chemical leak or hostage situation, you must be prepared to use the tripod and shoot at the longest focal length possible. This situation is the reason most cameras have a lens with a 2× extender that doubles the focal length. It is impossible to shoot at those focal lengths from off your shoulder—they're just too shaky. If the tripod is not available, rest the camera on the ground or on anything else that will steady the picture.

Look for Movement   Because of your distance from the location of the actual event, you need to keep a sharp eye peeled for any movement. The action might be simple, such as people moving around police cars or fire engines, but any movement is better than none at all. In this situation more than any other, you need to shoot anything that moves: additional equipment arriving at the scene, officials talking on two-way radios, or SWAT team members suiting up. Any movement can become symbolic action.

Remember the Edit Room   You might encounter a situation in which you will not get a shot of the real story, but you must have pictures of some sort to show on the air. In this case, you must come as close as you can to depicting the story with your shots. Sometimes this means just a shot of the police tape used at a crime

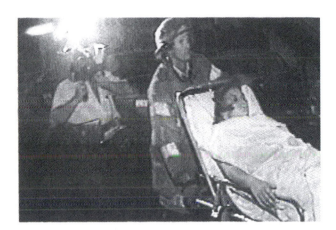

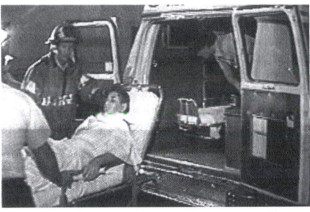

Figure 2-2   When shooting spot news, the ENG photographer tries to get shots of the action that tell a story: (1) the visual intensity of the fire; (2) and (3) the human element—how the fire affects people; and (4) the action taken by the firefighters to bring the fire under control.

scene to keep out unauthorized persons and a police officer standing next to it. Or it might be just the police car used for the roadblock keeping you out.

Never walk away from anything without enough video to cover a one-minute story without shooting the same shot over and over. This can really tax your creative skills, but you have to think like an editor: What am I going to use to cover this script? In a situation where the pertinent pictures are few and far between, a shot of onlookers could be useful; they still have nothing to do with the story, but they can help pad a piece that is already visually weak.

Stay Near the Center of Information   In most cases in which you are restricted from the scene and held far from any direct action, you will usually be able to be at or near the command center set up by the controlling agency. This will become your major source of pictures

for the story. You might get better shots later on, but you cannot count on that. This is why you should shoot everything you can until you have exhausted the possibilities. Police officers looking at a map, conferring with each other, or even just walking from one place to another will do. If the event goes on for quite awhile, the station will either ask for some footage to be fed back or ask for a live update with a video insert. You had better have some footage to give them, and you certainly better be carrying more than one tape or memory card with you.

Don't Overshoot   When real pictures are scarce, be selective in the amount of footage you shoot. After you have that initial group of shots to cover a short script, fall back, observe, and conserve batteries and tape or file space for a chance at some real action. You shouldn't have to record more than four to six minutes of video if you are making every shot really count. There is no point in getting volumes of generic video that look like the same shots over and over.

Use the Tripod The sticks allow you to use the longest focal lengths to reach into any scene visually, picking out shots your shoulder-mounted competition cannot get. They might also be the *only* shots you can get. Without the tripod—and with two to three hours of waiting—your shoulder will not be able to perform later when you might really need it. If you're on the sticks, you can always pull the camera off them quickly and run with it, should the need arise.

Dealing with the Authorities

Before shooting any spot news, you should have a **press pass**, or ID card, issued by the law enforcement agencies of your city, county, and state. This identifies you as a bona fide member of a news organization. Without this pass, shooting spot news can be a risky and sometimes impossible job. A press pass sometimes even gets you across police and fire lines to gain better access to the event. Sometimes the pass is worthless, and at other times it can get you into more trouble than it keeps you out of. However, without it you do not stand a chance. The press pass involves some serious responsibilities. If the authorities let you into or close to the scene, you cannot interfere with what they are doing or disobey any special requests they have. Such requests might include not showing a certain area of a fire scene that is part of an arson investigation, or not showing the face of an undercover agent. If you violate the trust given you, your future dealings with that agency are jeopardized, as well as those of your employer and other members of the press—not to mention the harm you can do to the agency or the investigation.

It is not a good idea to try to outwit the authorities. It is quite impossible to shoot the rest of the story from the backseat of a police car. In some cases, the risk involved in going around authority can be life threatening. You would not want to be in a deranged sniper's line of fire! Police/media relations are always strained at best, but the only good course of action is to play by the rules. Sometimes there will be a need to circumvent the authorities to get at the really good pictures of the story. These decisions can only be made on a case-

by-case basis and must be made with the clear understanding that what you are doing is illegal and may harm you or someone else. Just like a combat photographer, if you are willing to accept the ultimate responsibility, then you do as you think best. If you do get into trouble disobeying an authority, your employer will most likely *not* help you out of it. This is similar to getting a speeding ticket on your way to a story—you are on your own when breaking the law.

Flexibility and creativity are key when shooting in protected situations. For example, one reviewer of this text reported that he was the news photographer for a small crew covering the aftermath of Hurricane Katrina on the Gulf Coast. Even with their press credentials, the authorities were not inclined to let the crew members into restricted areas. So each morning, they bought a few hundred dollars' worth of bottled water. When they arrived at the closed-off scene, they showed both their press passes and their stacks of water. The water did the trick: they were allowed access to cover the story while also bringing water to hurricane victims.

Going Live

On any major spot news story, there will likely be a voice on your two-way radio or cell phone screaming for a live shot even before you arrive on the scene. The pressure to get on the air first can be so great that actually shooting the story becomes a secondary consideration. Often, the situation requires you to be in two places and do two things at the same time. You have to decide what to do. Shoot the pending dramatic rescue, or pull cables for the live shot? This might seem like a simple choice, but the voice on the mobile phone can make it a very hard decision. Most of the time you'll know what to do by instinct.

You will also most likely not be alone for long. Any big story is going to have all the resources of the station thrown at it. You might be able to shoot footage because the second videographer arriving will do the live. Try to coordinate on the radio or phone even before you get to the location. If you're the second to arrive from your station, you should be thinking *live shot*. Let the first in be the primary for shooting coverage, and you can set up the system for getting the footage out to the world. The assignment desk might coordinate all this, but in any leadership vacuum, be ready to step in with a plan to get the story on the air with the best coverage you can and the quickest way you can. That *is* spot news.

Be Prepared

Spot news requires instinct and a great deal of luck. You can increase the luck factor by always being prepared. If your equipment is organized, easy to get to, and well maintained, and you know what is required to make a good story, then when the big one comes your way, the Emmy is yours. Shoot with both eyes open, always looking for the next shot, impending danger, or anything else that might be about to happen. Keep your eyes moving but your camera steady. And check your systems: if you aren't recording, you won't get the shot; and if you don't have audio, that's what people will remember about you for years to come—"So-and-so had the pictures and not one peep of audio; it could have been a career-making story."

General News

This category of news stories, as the label implies, is very general. Most stories fall under this heading. These are stories about the city council, the plans to build a new housing development for the elderly, or the strike by local bus drivers. Most storytelling techniques apply directly to this form of news. The main concept in general news, sometimes called **hard news**, is to communicate ideas or information to the viewer. The story must be very understandable, with a good beginning, middle, and end. On this type of story, the reporter and videographer must work closely to produce the maximum impact on the viewer.

Presentation is of utmost importance. The subject matter might be the dullest in the world, but if the information is important (or if the boss demands the story), the story must be done and done well. As they say, "There's no such thing as a boring story, only a boring approach." The idea is never to lose a viewer; never give a viewer the opportunity to say "so what" or "who cares" to what you are presenting—or, worse yet, switch channels.

Get a Good First Shot

Always make the first shot of the story count. More than likely, it will be your best shot, and it should be. Grab the viewers' attention immediately to get them into the rest of the story. As a general rule, it is bad form to open a story with a talking head or a reporter stand-up. This opening looks too much like the people on the news set—that is, a person talking without showing you anything. If television news becomes the same as radio, why watch?

Sound is also important in the first shot. A natural sound clip is a good opening for almost any story. A dramatic soundbite can also be a good opening, but good ones do not occur that often. In an opening shot of a street construction story, the sound of the jackhammer (if one is in the shot), turned up full for about two seconds, can set the story's tone and topic. "Get ready, Seattle, the streets are being torn up."

Create Visual Soundbites

The worst thing about general news stories is the lengthy talking head shots that can make up the bulk of the video. While interviews are the bread and butter of TV news, they do not have to be the most boring part of the story. As with anything in TV news, the talking head can be overused. Most reporters use two basic styles of talking heads: one to make the stories they have written more credible, and the other to let the subjects tell their own stories. The former is a traditional journalistic style, in which importance is placed on the reporter's ability to interpret and analyze; the latter is a style of simply allowing subjects to present their points at length, with little additional comment from the reporter. Both styles have their place, although letting subjects tell their own story is better suited to feature reports.

In either case, the talking head should be well shot. If the subject is to be on camera for a long time (maybe as much as two minutes in a three-minute story), then the interview had better be pleasing and interesting to watch for the entire time. By shooting each answer during the interview at a different focal length (changing focal lengths during the question) or maybe doing some answers in a reporter-subject two-shot, the parts used for the edited interview

Figure 2-3   To make this interview for a school-related story look interesting, the shooter: (1) placed the subject in front of a background that adds context—a school bus; (2) keystoned the background, using diagonal lines that run along the z-axis, converging toward an out-of-frame vanishing point, to add depth perspective; (3) used selective focus to add additional depth and to draw attention to the in-focus subject by defocusing the background; and (4) canted the camera—tilted the horizon line—to add a youthful feel to the youthful subject.

might vary enough to add some interest beyond nice framing. (See Figure 2-3.)

You may sometimes opt to do parts of the same interview at different times and different locations. If the same subject is to be heard many times within the story, it might be possible to shoot in more than one location. One bite might have the subject behind a desk; another might come from a walking conversation with the reporter; and still another might have the subject on a balcony overlooking the factory. It takes a little more time to do the interview, but the results are far better.

Another way that can work in certain situations is simply different perspectives or angles within the same basic setting. By moving the camera to different points of view within the room for different sections of the interview, the edited piece can look like a multicamera shoot. A good idea is to shoot a **master shot**, or establishing shot, followed by a series of **setups**, or different camera positions, including **over-the-shoulder (O/S)** shots, medium shots, and close-ups. An important guideline in this situation is the **30-degree rule**: each camera setup should be at least 30 degrees or more from the other setups, without "crossing the line"—

the action axis or 180-degree rule. (See Figure 2-4). If the camera setups are too close to each other, the shots do not vary much from one to the next, making the story less interesting visually, and possibly causing the editor to make jump cuts between shots with similar framing. The important thing is to work with the reporter or producer to find creative ways of avoiding long stretches of static talking heads.

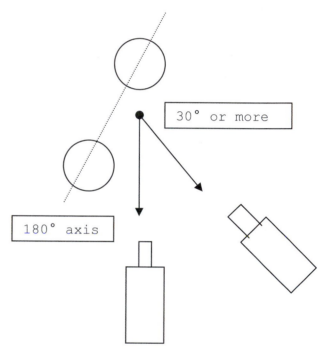

Figure 2-4   Diagram of the 30-degree rule for camera setups. The circles represent two subjects, with the 180-degree line between them. The two camera positions are on the same side of that line, with at least 30 degrees of separation.

Cover Long Soundbites with Video

When a piece does have long stretches of talking heads or long soundbites, try to cover as much of them as possible with **B-roll**—all the shots other than the interviews or talking heads (which are the A-roll). These might be establishing shots, close-ups, inserts, cutaways, or anything else that includes images and action relevant to the story. If you are going to use several bites or one long-running bite from a subject, the audience only needs to see that individual for about 5 seconds. In that time, the voice is established with a name and a face so the picture portion is free to show what he or she is talking about—the B-roll footage.

A 20-second soundbite of the builder of a new housing project could have the last 15 seconds or so covered by related video (plans of the building, construction underway, etc.). Try also to make this video lead into the next audio, whether it is another talking head or a reporter voiceover. The sequence you started over the interview continues, if ever so slightly, over the beginning of the next section of script.

The same can be done in reverse. If the reporter's track is about housing construction, and it leads into a soundbite from the builder, let the video of construction overlap the first 5 to 10 seconds of the builder's 20-second bite. The builder's face then appears and connects with the voice, but the length of the talking head has been reduced in favor of more interesting video.

If the builder is to appear twice fairly close together in a piece—two bites separated by a brief reporter's comment—the second bite need not have the builder on camera at all; that entire bite can be covered by B-roll. This assumes that you have enough video to cover all the soundbites and that your video is appropriate to go over the audio.

Keep the Story Moving

Often you will not have enough video (or any appropriate video) to use in or around talking heads. Say the construction project story is done on a day where the workers are off. In these situations, you need to provide a large variety of two-shots, cutaways, and setup shots to help fill the time. Remember, any story looks better when people are in the shots. Instead of using only unpopulated shots of the site, try to find a variety of ways of working in the subject and the reporter— the only people you have. An example of a setup shot getting into a soundbite might be a zoom-out from the plans on the wall to a wide two-shot of the builder and reporter talking, or shots of them walking around the site. Taken from many angles and distances to them, you can use these shots to cover both the script and long soundbites. Shots like these fill the time and keep the video moving.

Illustrate the Topic

The hardest thing to do in general news stories is to find pictures that go with the topic. If the story is about illegal campaign funds, the challenge will be to find pictures. By working closely with the reporter or producer, a videographer should begin early in the shooting process to visualize the unfolding story. There might be nothing to shoot but leaked memos that are nothing more than pieces of paper. If that's the case, make them into a piece of art. Place them on a desktop, light them up nicely (perhaps use a gobo pattern), and try some slow pans or tilts. (See Figure 2-5.)

Whatever the topic of the story, you must start thinking of ways to cover the future script with video. Be creative. Think symbolism. A story on the hay fever season might make use of tight shots of pollen-producing weeds blowing in the breeze. Better yet, use tight shots of them in the foreground with people in the background. Or, try just a tight shot of a tissue box with a hand pulling out a tissue. The shot is symbolic of the sneezing that's associated with the pollen without finding someone doing it or staging the shot (a big no-no). The bottom line is that every story has pictures. The earlier you start thinking about which ones to get, the better.

General news stories are serious and businesslike in subject matter and approach. Your photography should reflect the same characteristics. There is no staging of events or the subject's actions. Your job is to represent the subject or event as accurately, simply, and clearly as possible, while at the same time making it interesting or at least pleasing to watch. This type of story can be the greatest challenge to the news shooter. It is the place where names are made in this industry. If you can make a city council story come alive and be visually interesting as a feature without staging the shots, then the rest of what you do in this business will be easy.

Feature News

This category is perhaps the most freeform of all. Feature stories are usually lighthearted looks at people and events, or involved pieces about lighter or more personal, intimate subjects. They are not hard news by

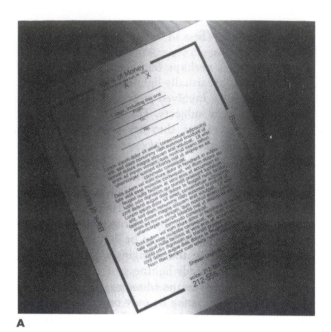

A

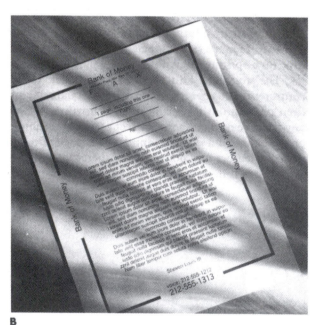

B

Figure 2-5   Two alternatives to shooting this document square and flat: (1) the paper is at an angle and highlighted with a shaft of light; (2) the light is shining through a water glass to create a pattern across the paper.

any means; rather, they are referred to as **soft news**. That doesn't mean they are comedies, but simply stories told more like essays than news reports. The stories in this category should entertain, touch, or somehow connect with the viewer on a personal level. Approach

feature news with an emphasis on creativity; this type of story is a rare chance for both reporter and news photographer to be as wild and imaginative, or as inspiring and engaging, as possible.

Music usually adds lightness or emotion to feature stories and allows the editor to do some creative cutting. While there might be only one such story in a newscast, the feature piece can be the most memorable in the show. In what can be a very depressing news day, people like to feel good about something or feel touched by another human being's experience. The feature gives viewers the chance to end the news time on a spiritual high note.

The story might be a picture essay on a skydiving contest with no reporter, or a simple story about children picking out pumpkins for Halloween. Almost any positive or good-news subject can be made into a good feature if a creative approach is used. Do not treat the feature as a nonstory and therefore a throwaway, even if it seems like an ad for some company. The audience feels this type of story is important. It is your job to make it work creatively. The feature can also be a profile of the town's oldest volunteer, struggling to teach poor kids how to read, or the personal story of one mother's fight to change the laws after losing her only child to a drunk driver. Whether you are showing a two-year-old rolling a pumpkin home or the tears of one person's crusade for a better society, the feature aims at the heart of the viewer.

It can take a whole day, a week, or even a month to do a good feature story. Or it can take an hour. The idea can be mapped out well in advance and shot a little at a time until the piece comes together. Features need not be timely, so they can air at any time. They have a longer "shelf life" than general or hard news. Soft news stories allow more work to be put into them. However, you will not always be given that time.

Try Different Techniques

Feature news provides a chance to use all the tricks of shooting and editing: odd angles, dramatic camera moves, unusual lighting, quick edits, wipes, and other special effects. (See Figures 2-6 and 2-7.) Features are the perfect place to use dissolves. No approach or technique is too unusual for the feature story as long as it *fits* the story. Try whatever you can to make your piece

Figure 2-6 Shooting extreme close-ups (XCUs) and layering shots, such as this frame from a feature story on hummingbirds, can enhance the visual experience.

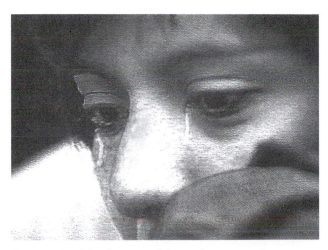

Figure 2-7 The framing of this audience member at a memorial service uses selective focus and foreground to give added emphasis to the tears on her cheeks.

stand out and touch your audience. Good lighting, beautifully framed shots, slow zooms, dissolves, and symbolic images can come together in a feature story to touch even the most hardened news watcher. If you can feel with your camera and your editing, then the viewer will also feel. The audience should come away from the piece affected by what you have shown.

Many feature stories take on the air of a Hollywood movie. They might be a parody of a harder story, such as a tongue-in-cheek piece on a professional baseball league strike. The production of the story might become just as involved as any commer-

cial shoot. The thing that separates pure journalism from this style of TV news is its goals. A general news story on the success of this year's must-have Christmas toy would discuss the toy's creator, sales, and so forth. A feature on the toy might simply be about a character (perhaps the reporter) trying to understand how this unlikely toy became this year's Christmas bestseller, with people camping outside stores to get it. The character might demonstrate other tongue-in-cheek uses for the toy, such as a door stop, and end with the toy being run over by a steamroller. The first piece informs; the second entertains with little regard for information other than to point out that the toy is popular.

Do not mislead the viewer. If the piece is to entertain, make sure it is obvious that is what's happening. Blending fact and fiction can be a dangerous game. Make sure that what you are doing has clearly defined goals and that facts are never lumped in with staged material—keep them separate in the viewer's mind. A feature on a new private fishing lake might be mostly fact, but a shot of the reporter pulling a three-foot shark out of the water might lead some viewers to think sharks are in the lake. Make sure there is only one possible interpretation of what you are doing in the story and that any jokes are clearly understood to be just that.

Sports News

Many videographers love to shoot sports. If there is a slot on the staff for a full-time sports shooter, it's never without a waiting list to fill it. Shooting sports has become an art form all its own. Sports video falls into two categories: features and competition.

Features

The ENG photographer shoots a sports feature much like the news feature—with the maximum amount of creativity and involvement. If you are doing a piece on a boxer training for a fight, get in the ring (if they let you) and have the boxer spar right at the camera lens. This type of involvement can bring the subject up close for the viewer and give a perspective not available during a match.

You can do something similar for any sport. Use the fact that it is only practice to get the camera involved in places where it normally could not be used. Gymnastics is a good sport for features: put the camera under the gymnasts, let them jump over the camera, or put the camera right on the balance beam. Make these stories fun to do and fun to watch, while trying to show the hard work taking place.

Competition

As an ENG photographer, you will shoot sports competition mainly for highlights or to capture a very short portion of the event, whereas competition coverage for EFP is often live coverage of the entire event. Almost all sporting events should be shot from a tripod, unless other footage is being obtained from the company covering the event. Choose a good vantage point from which all the action is visible.

The public is used to seeing sports shot with many cameras. Most of the time you will have only one camera, but be required to do just as good a job and not miss any of the action. The best location for almost any sport is from above and as much to the center of the action as possible.

Basketball and Football   For basketball, the ideal location is on the half-court line, about one-third of the way up the rows of seats. Floor angles are nice, and you should get some if they let you, but if a major play is at the far end of the court you stand a good chance of missing it or having your view blocked by the referee or other players. The high shot gets all the action clearly and allows you to zoom in or out to include as much of the action as you want. The same is the case with football. Field-level shooting is very exciting, especially from the end zone, but the best view is always from the press box or the equivalent.

If many plays are to be used as highlights, it is impractical to use a cutaway between each of these plays. Good football plays usually end with a long run, or pass, or the score itself. The ending shot should look sufficiently different from the beginning of the next highlight, and there is little worry of a jump cut. In basketball, the field of action is much smaller, and therefore most of the players tend to be in the shot most of the time. For this sport it is a good idea to zoom in on the playmaker just after the points

are scored. Besides emphasizing that player, this technique allows the editor to cut from that tight shot to the next highlight (which might be at the same end of the court), or to allow time for the reporter-anchor's voiceover to talk about that player. Even in football, it is a good idea to zoom in to the key player as the play ends, unless you are already on a tight shot of that player.

Sideline photography, usually done off your shoulder, is a way to add a closer, more dramatic feel to your highlight shots. Field-level perspectives can really distort distance and speed (remember the "half-the-distance, twice-the-size" concept). The big risks are missing something or being run over. If you are covered by being able to take video from another source, such as the company broadcasting the game, then anything you might miss on the sidelines can be obtained elsewhere. The biggest problem with ground-level shooting is the perspective of the camera. It is hard to tell relative distances between players, which makes some plays actually look rather nondramatic. When you are learning how to shoot these two sports, it is better to master the high shot before moving to ground level.

Races   Races of every kind—human, car, horse—involve tracks. As with basketball and football, the best angle is usually above the action at the center. This position allows you to see everyone in the race and to have the action pass in front of your camera. (See Figure 2-8.) If you are allowed, you might also set up a camera at the far end of a straight track or at the end of a straightaway on a circular track. From this perspective, you can shoot the racers head-on as they approach. Keep in mind, however, that you obviously cannot be on the track, so you have to use a telephoto (zoom) lens from far away. Because this compresses distance and makes moving objects appear slower, this angle causes the racers to seem closer together and moving at a slower speed than they actually are.

Baseball   This sport is difficult to shoot with only one camera. Action is taking place in two areas at the same time, and it seems you should be following both the ball and the runners. Usually it is best to follow the ball until it is caught, then you can pan quickly to the runners. Just following the ball often gives you all the action anyway, but if it is a long double and a runner is headed for home, it can be difficult to show both. Do

Figure 2-8   A photographer captures a racehorse and rider as they pass in front of the camera position.

not take the easy way out and just go wide to show the whole field. A TV screen is too small for any of the real action to show up at all. If you miss the runner scoring, you can use a shot of the runner walking to the dugout as the run-scored shot.

If you are above and directly behind home plate, you should see all the plays nicely. Start on a two-shot of the pitcher and batter (top and bottom of the picture from this camera position), and zoom in to follow the ball when it's hit. If you lose the ball, zoom out wide and pan in the direction it went until you regain sight of it. (You will see the players running to where the ball is going.) Stay with it as you use your left eye to scan the infield for other action. If a runner is making it to home with little chance of being thrown out, quickly pan to that shot. Otherwise, stick with the ball. By making all of your moves as smooth as possible, even when you lose sight of the ball, no one will notice any errors on your part.

Golf and Hockey   Golf balls and hockey pucks are difficult to follow: a golf ball is too small, and a hockey puck moves too fast. Staying fairly wide in hockey is the best way to avoid missing the play entirely. As you become familiar with the game, it is easier to anticipate where the puck is going. For golf, it takes a lot of practice to keep your eye glued to the ball.

Hockey is similar to basketball in how it is shot, except that it moves much faster. A good sports videographer can shoot hockey fairly tight, but most people cannot. It is best to be high up and at center ice to do

the shooting and zoom in to the playmaker at the score. Golf is obviously a much slower game to shoot, but it can be the most strenuous to do because of all the walking between shots. It is best to be either directly behind or directly in front of the golfer. In front means way down the fairway, farther than it is possible to hit the ball. From behind, you can start wide and zoom in to follow the ball; from in front, you can start tight on the golfer and widen out to keep the ball from leaving the frame. Trying to **whip-pan** (pan the camera very fast) with the ball as it flies by you is not a good idea.

General Sports Tips

A good rule of thumb when shooting any sport with which you are not familiar is to stay wide at first and slowly shoot it tighter as you become more comfortable with the game. Shooting too tightly at first can leave you faked out, causing you to miss the play, so choose your focal length carefully. If too many plays are getting away from you, widen out until you have better control. Above all, make it smooth. Do not jerk the camera or hesitate in a zoom or pan; make every movement seem like it is purposeful, whether it is or not.

Watch network or cable TV's coverage of the sport that you are going to shoot. See how the experienced professionals do it; see the kinds of shots they get and how they follow the ball. Try to take what they are doing and adapt it to a one-camera shoot. The cuts that are done live on the network may have to be done in editing for you, but if you record the right elements, you can make it look pretty close to network coverage. The main thing is to follow the ball or stay with the leader. It takes practice and much concentration, but it is the only way to get professional results.

Summary

ENG photographers are assigned to shoot a variety of formats, including spot, feature, general, and sports news. Understanding what's expected of you for any assignment is a great advantage. By knowing the type of story you are assigned, you have a head start on achieving what's expected. Like many jobs, TV news is fairly predictable in the type of work that is done. The story on the city council meeting has been done the same basic way for decades. Making a radical change in that approach might not go over big with the boss or the public. Adding a touch of your personal style and a little creative thought, however, can garner the attention of the above two benefactors.

Basketball free throws are an example of changing style. Televised basketball used to stay on a fairly wide shot from the sidelines during free throws. Eventually, camera operators and directors tried a close-up on the player's face, cutting to the wide shot with matched action just as the player began the free throw—the wide shot being necessary to follow the ball. Viewers liked seeing the concentration on the free-thrower's face before the shot, so this is now the way most free throws are covered. Whatever the shots and whatever the edits, the number-one goal is always effective communication. With a good working knowledge of how each type of story is done, you can carefully take the viewer to your personal vision of that story.

PART TWO: LIVE COVERAGE

With today's high-quality portable cameras, live news coverage is possible from just about anywhere. Live coverage is one reason why television news soared to such high levels of popularity. Just as an earlier generation listened to Edward R. Murrow giving live radio accounts of the bombings of London during World War II, today's generation has *watched* U.S. forces in Iraq, evacuees at the New Orleans Superdome after Hurricane Katrina, and so on. While TV newscasts have lost some viewers in recent years due to competition from other news sources, such as the Internet and podcasts, many people still turn to TV news for their primary source of information. For example, on September 11, 2001, while many people learned of the horrific events of that morning on the radio or via a computer or from family or friends, almost all turned on their full-screen TV sets to watch the story unfold, witnessing the collapse of the twin towers of the World Trade Center as it happened.

There can be no greater drama and no greater use of the medium than to see history being made live on the screen. Even on local news stations, the use of live TV has led to the same mesmerizing effect on viewers during events of great regional importance or curiosity, which are often picked up by national and international news sources. An Internet cannibal in Germany, Russian sailors trapped in a submarine, and a mine collapse in Kentucky have all riveted local audiences, and then national and international audiences, as living dramas unfolded before them just as for the people actually present.

Live TV has power of enormous proportion, which is accompanied by social responsibility. The use of live TV in the Iraq War is criticized both for elevating the reporter's personal experience above that of the overall events and for possibly revealing too much information of use to the enemy. The only certainty is that millions watch. A reporter who panics or gives misinformation during a major story could have a profound effect around the world. On another level, local TV news is accused of reducing live TV to just another gimmick to attract viewers. For example, after the nation watched live coverage of O. J. Simpson in a white Ford Bronco, just about anyone on a freeway trying to elude police is likely to make a live story, even if the story lacks newsworthiness. Despite its drawbacks and misuses, live TV is the pinnacle of broadcast journalism when news breaks out anywhere in the world.

Live TV can also be of considerable importance to the business world through teleconferences. Just as local news stations use live cameras to hype ratings, companies and educators can use live TV to add a new sense of immediacy to the information they convey. This section discusses the tools of live TV, its typical formats and uses, some tricks of the trade, and some common problems.

Getting the Picture Out

The starting point of live TV transmission is the camera. Any broadcast-quality video camera with a composite NTSC output can feed a transmitter. Often, the output of the camera is fed through a **distribution amplifier (DA)** to maintain proper video levels. A low video signal might not transmit well and will come across muddy, with increased noise or poor color. A high, or hot, video signal might transmit as a washed-out picture, possibly causing a breakup in the transmission or noise in the audio portion. The most common faults in these two examples are either an improperly exposed camera or signal loss due to a long cable run from the camera to the transmitter. If these problems are not too extreme, the DA can correct them by its gain and equalizing functions. To operate, the DA must be connected to a waveform monitor to display the effects of any adjustments.

The four basic ways of transmitting a live picture from the field are by means of the following:

Telephone lines
Fiber-optic lines
Microwaves
Satellites

Telephone Lines

The local telephone company can set up a video-feed point from just about anywhere using a balanced line (different from a regular phone line). Because of the time necessary to set up this type of transmission, it is rarely used except for events such as election returns where there is plenty of lead time for installation. Because of deregulation in the telephone industry, it can be a challenge to find the right company or unit to deliver such a line, but most phone companies have experience with this method of delivery. The lines can be run to just about anywhere that has phone service.

Fiber-Optic Lines

Similar to regular phone lines, newer phone systems have light-transmitting cables already in place. These fiber-optic lines carry light-encoded video and audio information to distant distribution centers with little loss of signal. This system's benefits are best seen when using digital signals. Special encoders and decoders are needed at each end of the fiber line to change video and audio signals into laser light and back again.

Microwaves

Microwave equipment is relatively small and usually owned by the TV station using it. The most common placement of a microwave system is in a van (some-

times called a live truck, RF truck, or feeder) that has an antenna at the top of a telescoping mast that may go as high as 50 feet. (See Figure 2-9.) The truck usually has a reel of multiline cable (two video and four audio lines in one cable) that can stretch about 300 feet. A normal video cable allows up to a 1,000-foot run before the loss of signal becomes too great for the DA to compensate.

Figure 2-9 Satellite and microwave trucks (feeders) are a common sight wherever major news events occur.

Microwave transmitters work in a spectrum of radio-frequencies measured in gigahertz (GHz) and have specific channels assigned by the Federal Communications Commission (FCC). The standard ENG channels have always been 2, 7, and 13 GHz. Each channel can be subdivided further into parts simply called A, B, C, D, and Center, with the option of the microwaves going clockwise or counterclockwise. These variations allow many stations in the same market, or many transmitters at one station, to transmit at the same time. With the increased use of this technology, more channels have been opened up, including 2.5, 6, 6.5, 10, 12, and 40 GHz. Generally, the lower the channel number, the easier it is to transmit over long distances.

A microwave link can transmit up to 50 miles if there are no obstructions. Microwaves need a clear line of sight from transmitter to receiver to work. This is why the antenna (either a dish or golden rods) is on a mast and the receiver is usually on a mountaintop or the tallest building; the signal can then go from there to the station by a secondary microwave link or hard line (telephone lines). Because the microwave beam is very narrow, it is essential that the transmitting and receiving antennas be pointed precisely at each other. (See Figure 2-10.) When they are many miles apart, this is not an easy task. Experienced people at each end can accomplish this in a very short period of time—sometimes in seconds, if the operators are very good.

While the truck-mounted microwaves are usually on channels 2 or 7, a portable system called a mini-mic uses channels 13, 18, and 40 GHz. This shoebox-size transmitter can be placed in a backpack for the camera operator to wear; it can also be mounted on a small tripod near the camera to take the place of what might be a hard or impossible cable-run back to the live truck. Because the range of this small transmitter is limited, a mini-mic is primarily used in sports coverage or to replace a cable where mobility is the critical factor (e.g., from a high floor of a skyscraper). The receiver is at the live van where the signal is retransmitted to the station.

Satellites

With so many satellites in orbit today, almost anyone who has an uplink or downlink (a ground-to-satellite transmitter or receiver) can buy satellite time. With the advent of 24-hour news channels, such as CNN, transmitting breaking stories live to the whole country has become a must. While microwaves are limited to less than 50 miles and line of sight (although they can be relayed or hopped to greater distances), a portable satellite uplink mounted on a truck can go anywhere there is a road and sky. (See Figure 2-11.) Today, most stations in the top 100 markets have satellite trucks.

Figure 2-10 A microwave truck with its transmitter atop an extended mast for a clear line of sight with the receiver.

Many memorable TV moments have reached our eyes and ears via satellite. Some events allow for planning, including time and space to set up large-scale feeds, such as Princess Diana's wedding and funeral in London, or the World Cup soccer tournament in Germany. Other events do not provide the luxury of time and space, such as reports from journalists in Afghanistan and Iraq who are "embedded" with military units, giving them unprecedented access to war coverage but no lead time and no luxuries. In these latter cases, the reporter usually uses an uplink system called a fly-away that is small enough to be folded down and shipped as airline baggage. (See Figure 2-12.) Powered by batteries, a fly-away system can be used in any remote area without any utilities. The batteries can be recharged by

Figure 2-11   Satellite news gathering (SNG) trucks make it possible to feed live pictures and reports from just about anywhere in the world.

solar devices if necessary. Live TV can literally be done from any spot on the face of the Earth as soon as the crew arrives and sets up. Travel time is the only limit to getting it on the air.

Figure 2-12   Workers set up a fly-away satellite uplink. (Courtesy of Earth Stations)

Communications

None of this would be possible without a top-rate communications package. This usually means a good two-way radio system or a cell phone or both. As mentioned earlier, it is critical that the transmitter and receiver of both microwave and satellite systems be pointed directly at each other. Being off by as much as one degree can mean the difference in getting the signal or not. Microwave systems are one-way transmissions. When you are in the field, you cannot tell if you are lined up with the receiver; someone at the receiving point must tell you when you have it right. Microwave receivers are generally controlled remotely from the TV station by an ENG coordinator. He or she watches a digital readout of the incoming signal's strength, pans the receiver to get the strongest reading, then has the transmitter operator pan the truck's antenna until the strongest signal is found. The truck operator usually has a map with the receive site(s) on it and can aim the antenna fairly accurately with a compass or a good guess. The fine-tuning should be an easy process with good communication.

Satellite setups are much more technical but can be done without talking to anyone. Because a satellite also sends a return signal, it is possible for the operator to see the quality of the signal as it is returned and tell how well in line the two are. The concern here is knowing which satellite, which channel, and what time to set up. Because people from all over the country might be trying to use the same satellite, there has to be a coordinator who tells each uplink what to do and when. Unlike a microwave system, this coordinator is usually at the headquarters of the satellite company, which might be on the other side of the country. Having a cell phone is sometimes the only answer, but having some type of phone is mandatory.

The receiver dish must be lined up with the satellite in use and tuned to the channel of video and audio; these are two separate systems within the transmission. The exact times of transmission must be confirmed. Satellite time can be bought on the spot or can be arranged in advance to ensure availability. Satellite time is purchased in multiples of five minutes and often cannot be extended. If you buy five minutes of time for 12:00:00 P.M., at 12:05:02 P.M. you are off the air; the satellite owner pulls the plug. For ENG work, this means you either buy more time than you think you need, or have someone on the phone constantly with the satellite company to okay purchasing more time if it looks like the shot is going to run long. It is also possible that the next time block has already been sold and is unavailable to you. For major news events, a network might buy up all the time available and share the time with others, using a local coordinator at a single feed point. The coordinating network feeds its material first, and all others literally line up on a first-come, first-served basis to feed their material. Because of the time factors involved with satellites, most recorded material is edited before sending, and live shots are locked into specific times so local producers must slide everything else in their program to accommodate the satellite. This is one reason most satellite trucks contain edit systems.

The use of satellite trucks for EFP is generally much less hectic. These situations are usually planned well in advance, and the satellite time is booked with much spare time to work out any bugs or in case things run long.

Interrupted Feedback

Interrupted feedback (IFB) is just as essential as the communications needed to set up the transmissions. The on-camera talent needs to be able to hear the cue that they are on the air. IFB systems offer small earphones for the talent to wear, thereby allowing them to receive directions in one ear while they are on camera.

Portable TV

The most primitive way of doing this in live news is to have a portable TV set tuned to your station; the talent can simply see when they are on the air. An earphone run from the TV set lets them hear the introduction and any questions that may follow. The camera operator usually has the same two-way radio used to set up the microwave signal with an earphone to listen for any instructions from the station. If the regular speaker in the TV is used when the reporter's mic is live, it can cause an audio feedback (a high-pitched screech) that would ruin the shot. Using this type of IFB setup does not have the interrupt part of the sys-

tem, because the audio is right off the TV. Any instructions from the show director, producer, or assignment desk must be relayed to the reporter by the photographer listening to the two-way radio. It is a good idea to be sure everyone understands the basic hand signals of TV production in case things need to be communicated while on air.

Mix-Minus

The more common form of IFB is a separate off-air audio feed called **mix-minus.** This feed is from the on-air audio board with the audio from the remote or live shot taken out or subtracted. Talent can be annoyed by their own voices coming back in their ears while they are talking. Because of the time delays involved in the signal transmission, particularly with a two-second satellite delay, the talent hear their voices as strange echoes. A mix-minus feed is usually patched into a telephone line or a two-way radio. Some TV stations have a radio channel dedicated to broadcasting nothing but off-air or program audio 24 hours a day. In this way, an IFB system is always in place. Other stations with multiple channels on their two-ways might simply give one channel over to IFB for the short time needed to do the shot and use it for other traffic the rest of the time. This mix-minus system allows the producer or other needed participants to interrupt the program audio and give special instructions, cues, a countdown to hit a soundbite, or whatever else is necessary, over the radio or phone IFB (hence the name "interrupted feedback"). Just like the dedicated radio channel for IFB, many stations have dedicated phone lines that, when called, automatically hook up to the mix-minus feed. In large markets, where there can be as many as six or seven different live shots back to back, the radio and phone systems can be quite complex.

Form and Style

Essentially, live shots are just like stand-ups. They are generally short and are done in a controlled manner. The biggest difference is that they occur at a very specific point in time and there can be no second take.

Live Spot News

In this age of instant information, the ability to go live from any major breaking story is essential. Breaking stories that usually get live coverage include major fires, shootings, car-bus-train-plane crashes, natural disasters (e.g., earthquakes, hurricanes, tsunamis), and so on. Most stations have extensive plans for how to cover big stories such as these, but they all follow two basic rules.

1. If more than one crew is being sent to the event, the first crew is responsible for shooting to document the event, and the second crew on the scene is there to set up for the live shot.
2. If only one crew is available, it quickly records enough footage to air about one minute of edited video, and then returns to the van to set up the live shot.

The pressure to do two things at the same time can be intense; the desire to cover the story has to be weighed against the need to get the story out first to beat the competition. This is one of the great moral dilemmas in TV journalism. The ultimate success or failure to balance these two concerns rides on the location of the live van at the scene. If the news photographer can anticipate the situation on arrival and know whether any particular parking spot will allow for a signal to be set up, then the story can be shown live or recorded from the same location. The ideal situation is to set up where you can see the event or disaster area and leave the camera on the tripod rolling while you set up the signal and run the cables. Even though this is a two-person job, most stations only staff a live truck with one shooter-engineer. Once hooked up, the camera feeds the event live to the studio where it can be recorded as well as taken live at the producer's call.

If the van is parked under power lines, or thick trees or tall buildings are between it and the only receiver available, then the station could be at a serious disadvantage. In extreme cases, jobs could be lost over the failure to get a signal out. The greatest pressure in television comes during setting up a live shot from a major spot news story. Without a clear battle plan as to how to pull it off, the story can turn into a nightmare. However, if you can get set up in record time and get good pictures as well, then you will most certainly be a hero.

Another concern in the location of the van is proximity to the story. You need to ask yourself questions such as these:

1. Can I safely raise the mast from this spot (any overhead power lines)?
2. If I have only 300 feet of cable, can I get the camera to a good vantage point?
3. Am I blocking a roadway or emergency vehicle route?
4. Am I too close and likely to be caught in a dangerous situation (such as a brush fire) so that I will have to move quickly?
5. Are the authorities going to let me stay here?

The wrong answer to any of these questions can ruin your shoot or even cost you your life in the case of the power lines; always have a backup plan.

What the producer wants to see is the event or location itself. Sometimes this might mean being on a hilltop overlooking the site. At other times, you might have to settle for just seeing the SWAT team suiting up, because the street is closed and access is denied. The main thing is to see action. If you cannot show the actual story, show the next best thing. Most of the time, the live shot is a subject in front of the camera. You should be able to zoom past the subject into anything happening in the background as the reporter talks about it. Be prepared to ride both the iris (try never to use auto-iris) and the focus. The lighting will probably be of little concern as long as the subject is visible. If the lighting is particularly bad, it might be necessary to place the subject in better lighting with a worse background and simply pan to the action.

The use of the tripod is generally determined by proximity to the action. If you are in the middle of things, it is probably best to hand-hold the camera. If you are at a distance, then you should use sticks. Handholding the camera can add to the drama of a live shot. The reporter can be talking to eyewitnesses or authorities; the freedom to move around can make the background interesting regardless of where the guest stands. Keep in mind that handheld shots look best at wider focal lengths. Doing spot news live is the ultimate in news coverage. Every bit of talent, experience, and training comes to bear in this situation.

Scheduled Events

Most live shots for news are done at events planned well in advance. Parades, city council meetings, and demonstrations are typical live situations. In fact, many organizers purposely schedule their events to co-incide with the news time to get live coverage. In situations like these, there is usually sufficient time to set up in a more relaxed manner, or even site-survey the location well in advance for the best spot to set up. With more prep time, it is possible to get just the shot you want. You might have to run extra cable or use a 13-GHz short hop back to the van, but you have the time to do it.

For these types of live situations, the basic rules for doing a simple stand-up apply. Find a location where there will be some action in the background, but not action that would interfere with what you are doing. The shot should convey the event easily and quickly to the viewer. Some identifiable aspect of the event should be included in the shot.

Two aspects of these types of live shots need special consideration: graphics and guests. Most TV stations tend to add a lot of written information on the screen during a live shot. Not only is the bottom third of the picture taken up with the location, reporter's name, and station call letters or slogans, but the upper corners of the picture might be filled with words reminding the viewer that the picture is live. The shooter needs to be aware of where this information will appear and when it will be in the picture. You can spend a lot of time lining up a background, only to have it covered by a graphic. This can be particularly troublesome when the reporter has a guest. In a two-shot, their heads tend to be at the two upper corners of the picture; if the live graphic is also there, it will cover one of the subjects' faces. Your shots must be designed around the graphics as well as the scene. (See Figure 2-13.)

The best technique for shooting guests during a live shot is to have them on camera only when they are introduced or talking. One way to set up such a shot is to block it before you go live by having the guest and reporter stand side by side at a comfortable distance. The reporter should already be in the best place for the

Figure 2-13   This XCU of a model's face would not be appropriate for a telecast that places text onto the screen; the text interferes with the essential facial features.

background. The guest should then take one large step to the side away from the reporter and one step back away from the camera. The guest should maintain this position throughout the live shot. This allows the videographer to start the shot on a single shot of the reporter without being zoomed in too closely. As the reporter introduces the guest, the camera can widen out to reveal the guest; the reporter then turns on the foot closest to the guest and faces him or her in an over-the-shoulder shot. This puts the two in a more traditional position for an interview, so that the camera can zoom in to the guest as a single shot without the reporter and not have a one-eye or profile view of the guest. As the interview is wrapping up, the camera can zoom back out to a two-shot and the reporter can pivot back to face the camera. The camera can now zoom in to the reporter; the guest is free to leave.

Live for the Sake of Live

Many times in local news, shooters and reporters are asked to do live shots from places where nothing is going on. The location can be an empty field, a house where a shooting happened the night before, or just a street corner. Many stations feel it is necessary to use the live technology just to show the viewers that they have it. Even though it serves no journalistic purpose, it can be seen as a good method to train for the more important times and to experiment with different styles and techniques. You should always be looking for ways to make live shots look like they are live. For live-for-the-sake-of-live situations, this might not be easy. Try to include some action indicative of the time of day, such as a setting sun, rush-hour traffic, or maybe totally empty streets if it is for the late news.

The weather and sports segments are other examples of this type of live TV. With these two segments, it is possible to be more creative and possibly practice handholding the camera during live shots. The sports segment might come from a pregame warm-up, in which the sports anchor walks around among the players asking how their spirits are. The weather segment might be from a cultural fair where the weatherperson walks to a few booths to sample food before giving the weather. Maybe these situations aren't hard news, but they are chances to hone some skills that can come in handy at another time.

Electronic Field Production

More and more non-news productions are being done live. From the early days of teleconferencing to the expanding use of TV on the Internet, live television is becoming a common way to communicate. Stodgy studio teleconferences are giving way to individual managers doing their segments live from the plant floor or inside a research lab. Viewers from all over the country can ask questions of the manager and key workers as they work. Live TV for corporate, business, and educational use continues to increase. Video arraignments take place in courthouses so that prisoners do not have to leave jail to go downtown. Instructional classes are sent live to remote classrooms so that two campuses can be served by one teacher. These are just two examples of two-way, interactive, live EFP. The possibilities are endless.

What Can Go Wrong?

At almost every step of the process of portable video production, problems can occur and cause delays, resulting in shots missed, time wasted, and money lost. When something goes wrong on a live shot from the field, a newscast can become chaotic. Understanding the basic elements of live production can at least reduce the chances of something going wrong, and at best can provide you with a backup plan when the inevitable happens.

Know the System

Live TV has the most pressure of any form of this business. It is also the time when the most things usually go wrong: the station does not have your picture or audio; the talent cannot hear the cues; or the signal is full of breakup. The easiest way to deal with any of these problems is to know how the system works. If you work with a live truck (microwave or satellite), you must know the elements that make up the system and the order in which they are connected. You should be able to trace the signal from the camera to the antenna through every tiny part of the truck. If the receiver gets the color bars from the truck but not the picture from the camera, then you know the problem is not with the transmitter. You should have a checklist for the entire system within the van. The color bar generator-switcher, waveform monitor, tone generator-audio mixer, transmitter, power amp, and TV monitor are all clues to where any problem can be. If color bars are okay at the other end, and your waveform says that the video is correct, then any problem might be at the other end and not with you. The last resort is to bypass everything in the truck and put the video and audio directly into the transmitter (note that transmitters usually require line-level audio, so the mic will likely still have to run through a mixer). By eliminating possibilities, you can narrow any problem down to the piece of equipment or section of the truck. (See Figure 2-14.)

Power in the Truck

All live trucks have a gas-powered generator to supply electricity to the video-audio racks and the transmitter. Larger generators can also provide enough power for lights as well; many are as strong as 20 amps for outside use (called **tech power**). A backup system, and sometimes the main system of power in small vans, is an inverter that runs off the truck's engine. This small device converts the DC power from the engine's alternator and turns it into AC power for use in the rack.

Figure 2-14   In a remote setup like the inside of this production van, a live operator must know how all the equipment works; troubleshooting is part of the daily routine.

Most large vans actually run all equipment off a battery system that is continually charged by the generator. In case of generator failure, this battery system can allow you to keep transmitting for a short period of time if the power load is kept to a minimum. Make

sure you understand the power system in the truck and know what to do if any one element fails.

Lighting

If the live shot is indoors, the lighting will be similar to that used for most stand-ups. Time, of course, is always a factor in how fancy you can get and how many lights you can set up. One consideration in doing live shots is matching the studio style of lighting. While in some cases you might do a stand-up in available light to make it fit with the rest of the story, a live shot should match more to the studio than to the story it introduces, when possible. That means a high-key flat style with little shadow or modeling detail. You must also take into account any guests who might be interviewed and the light level of the background. It would look silly to have the reporter brightly lit and the background almost black by comparison, although that is often the case when only one light is used. (See Figure 2-15.) Try always to set the light up on a stand and not on top of the camera, unless the camera must be panned beyond the range of the stand light.

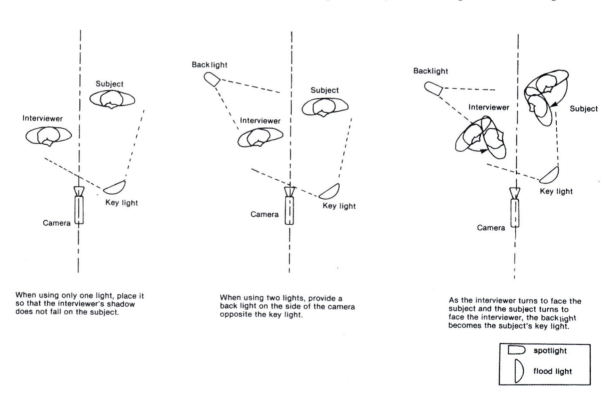

Figure 2-15   Light placement for a live interview with one or two lights, anticipating shadows.

Typical field interviews can be lit with as little as one or two lights. If you have one light, place it in the position of the key on the reporter, making sure that the reporter's shadow does not fall on the subject being interviewed. If you have two lights, place the second light as a backlight opposite the key light. (See Figure 2.15.)

Outdoor live shots might look easy when being set up, but the sun can move to the wrong place in the sky, such as directly behind the talent or below the horizon. You must always be conscious of what time of day the live shot will go, unless it is spot news. It might be daylight when you are setting up for the high-tide story, but at 5:30 P.M. when the live shot happens, it might be pitch dark because it is no longer Daylight Savings Time. If you have not set up some powerful background lights to show the surf, the live shot location could come off looking like the parking lot at the station.

Live shots should always have backgrounds, and at night this can be very difficult. You cannot light up the great outdoors. A good 1,000-watt focusing spotlight can be used to punch up a detail in the background just enough to be visible over the talent's shoulder. Most of the time, you want to light the talent at a level where the camera's lens is wide open to get the most exposure from the background. This offers the best chance to get something in the background to show up at night. Keep in mind the power limits of your generator if you do not have a reliable source of electricity. It is possible to blow an overloaded circuit anywhere. If you use battery lights, make sure they are not going to go dead in the middle of your shot.

Cables

The minimum cable to do a live shot is one video and one audio line. Many shooters keep a 100-foot bundle of twin-lead, or **Siamese** (an audio and video line in one cable), to use whenever they're in a big hurry. They can simply throw it out on the ground, hook up the camera and mic, and be ready to go. More complex shots make use of the multiline cable, which contains two video lines and four audio lines. This heavy cable, usually stored on a power reel, makes use of the full capabilities in the van. One video line is for the camera signal to the truck, another for an off-air TV signal from the truck's antenna to be used for the talent's monitor. One audio line is for the talent's mic to the truck, two lines are for IFB to the talent and camera operator being fed from the van, and one spare audio line can be used for a separate guest mic. A good live van should be able to send any audio down the cable from inside the van, including the two-way radio. Always make sure you have a backup cable in case any one of the primary cables fails. It is better to go live from next to the truck than not to go live at all because of a broken cable.

Wireless

Some remote productions are set up to go wireless. This has the obvious advantage of not needing to cable the camera and microphone back to the van. Instead, each has a transmitter that sends its signal via **radio frequency (RF)** signals to a receiver in the van. This allows for greater portability than cabled systems. The big disadvantage of wireless systems is the same disadvantage you experience with your cell phone: **interference**. The airwaves are filled with wireless communication, from cell phones to garage door openers to traditional broadcast signals. When two signals using the same or nearly the same frequency get close enough to cross paths, static and breakup can occur. Additionally, certain physical elements can interfere with wireless communication, such as buildings with lots of steel in their construction. A great wireless remote broadcast can suddenly go south when the reporter's audio turns to a staticy truck driver warning others of a speed trap as he drives by with his CB radio at the same frequency; or the image suddenly becomes snowy because someone in the adjacent hotel room begins using a hair dryer. For this reason, seasoned television technicians often prefer cabled systems to wireless, even if the reporters prefer the flexibility of wireless over cable.

Batteries

Everything needed to go live should be able to be powered by battery. The rack and transmitter should function off the tech battery in the van for at least an hour without recharge, in case the generator fails. The camera will most likely be powered by battery unless the shot is required for a very long time and AC is available. It can be very embarrassing if your battery fails while you are on the air. Always change to a fresh, fully-charged battery several minutes before the live shot. The off-air TV monitor should also be battery powered, and a battery-powered light should be available in case the power fails for any AC lights you are using.

Live TV is the perfect case for knowing the condition and performance level of each of your batteries. A misjudgment here could cost the station dramatic coverage of a big story. Always have a backup battery handy. Some companies make a battery belt that uses two camera batteries in series, allowing one to be taken off the belt and replaced with a fresh one while not disrupting power to the camera. This type of battery system would be a good investment for any live van.

Crowds

Nothing can ruin a live shot faster than the talent being swallowed up by an overly anxious crowd of onlookers. Not only is this bad TV, but it can be dangerous as well. A live shot from an area with large crowds of angry young people can quickly get out of control. It is not unusual for such a group to turn violent, assaulting the reporter and crew. The type of people and the size of the crowd must be taken into consideration when setting up the shot. A nice quiet plaza at 3:00 P.M. might seem like a good place to do a simple live shot, except that at 5:00 P.M. the plaza is jammed with workers heading home. Perhaps you want that look, but sometimes you do not; it can get dangerous without some form of crowd control.

Many stations like to assign St. Patrick's Day live shots from inside bars. The most dangerous crowds are drunk crowds. Do not let the station's desire for flashy live shots push you into a situation that can cost you a camera or an injury. If the crowd cannot be controlled to your liking, then find a situation that will protect you. At times this can mean doing the live shot from the roof of the van or from behind a homemade barricade. Look at the traffic patterns of the area in which you are setting up. Do not try to do a live shot from the busiest hallway in the building. Leave room for people to walk around you and stand and watch from behind you, the videographer, and not behind the reporter. Nothing looks worse than some idiot making

faces behind the talent who is talking about what a horrible tragedy has taken place. Sometimes it might be necessary to tape off an area with duct tape to keep people out (some people will walk right between you and the reporter as if you're not there). If the situation is really bad, like a spring break story, it might even be necessary to have the police there to protect you.

Permission

Another nightmare that is quite common is to set up for a live shot and then find out the owner of the property is demanding you get out. This can happen at any time you are not on public property if you have not secured permission beforehand. In spot news, the situation is usually too chaotic for anyone to care, but if the shot does not come until after things have settled down, you might be in for a fight with an upset property owner. Police can do the same thing to you. You might set up in an area open to the press only to find that same area closed just before you are to go live. Pleading with them to give you just a few more minutes sometimes works, but you should not rely on this technique. Be prepared to move and have an alternative site picked out.

Summary

Live coverage involves considerations of how to get the picture out, communicate between the field and the news desk, handle interrupted feedback (IFB), apply appropriate form and style, and anticipate everything that can go wrong. We cannot emphasize enough the fact that you have little control over when your shot will be taken live. Whether it is the satellite time that has been booked or the producer's sense of flow within the show, it is someone else who will decide, "You're hot." If you were hoping for a certain background, it can disappear just as the director comes to you. Unless you have total control of the picture's contents, you must live with the fact that things change.

The only way to cover yourself is to be flexible. Never totally rely on any one thing to be there. Assume complications and obstacles. A problem can be as simple as a fire truck pulling in behind the reporter and blocking the view of the fire, or as annoying as all of the people leaving the room 30 seconds before you go live. The only safe approach to live TV is to assume everything will go wrong—because it usually does. If you consider all the factors mentioned, plan for the contingencies, and always stay two steps ahead of yourself, you should be able to surmount any obstacle to doing live TV.

3

Electronic Field Production Style

EFP style encompasses many different types and applications of portable video. An easy definition of EFP is simply that it is professional portable video *not* for broadcast journalism or ENG. While this definition tells us what it is not, it does not give us a sense of what EFP is, or of what style is necessary to produce good-quality EFP work. A better approach to understanding EFP style is to look at the various applications of portable video, the conditions under which productions are made, and the audience for whom the video work is intended.

Unlike ENG, where the audience is the general broadcast viewer, much of EFP work, especially corporate work, often has a very specific audience. Whereas ENG concerns an event that is about to or has already occurred; EFP has a very specific purpose, such as a commercial or public service announcement, the promotion of a new product line, or training for a new procedure. However, quite a bit of the entertainment programs we see on commercial television are shot in EFP. Specifically, many shows are shot in film style, using one camera in the field that shoots the same shot (or action) several times, each from a different angle or focal length. Some of these shows include reality shows, music videos, features/magazine shows, home improvement shows, sports highlight shows, and other entertainment shows. Although most 60-minute narrative drama shows on network television (e.g., *CSI* and *Law and Order*) are shot on film, the style is similar to shooting single camera video. Commercial entertainment is a

special category of EFP, because it attempts to attract a large and diverse audience. Non-broadcast EFP, such as corporate video projects, is produced for a very specific audience.

In EFP, the key is planning. Careful preproduction and scripting help ensure that the final product is purposeful, effective, and affordable. In a corporate setting, the choice of EFP depends on whether it is the best way to get a message across; that is, whether it is cheaper or better than other methods, such as face-to-face communication. There is a sequence of planning in any EFP project that closely follows the sequence of events in writing a script. When the decision is made to embark on a video project, the first questions that must be asked are, "What do we hope to achieve by this project?" and "What are the objectives?"

In corporate work, the objective most often is to inform the audience of something, such as a new or old product, a new benefit to employees, a reiteration of an existing policy, or an introduction of a new corporate executive.

Another very common objective is to help create an attitude or stimulate motivation. A motivational video may be created to inspire salespeople to promote and sell a new line of cosmetics or a new attachment to farm tractors. The project may include sales techniques, product information, or a demonstration of how the product is used. The goal for this type of project is to inform, create, or change an attitude and evoke a certain type of behavior. Corporate video is aimed at a *specific audience* to achieve a *specific purpose.* Rarely is it produced just for entertainment purposes.

Television programs, performance video, music video, nature and documentary video, and video art are generally produced for entertainment purposes. These styles are often carefully preproduced and scripted, but do not always have very specific objectives beyond entertainment; the audience targeted is often more general. Outlets for exhibition are also more general; this type of video may be shown on broadcast, satellite, or cable TV, in classrooms, theaters, festivals, or contests. In addition, the video may be part of a multimedia presentation or even be part of an Internet site or available as a **podcast** or even a **video web log**, or **vlog**. The audience often selects itself. The showing of the video is publicized in broadcast TV listings in the newspaper, in a flyer about a festival, on the Internet, or even in a class syllabus. The audience decides whether it wants to view the video.

This chapter covers eight common categories of EFP style:

1. Corporate and professional videos.
2. Entertainment.
3. Public service announcements and commercials.
4. Performance videos.
5. Sports videos.
6. Music videos.
7. Nature and documentary videos.
8. Video art.

In addition, video for multimedia and video for use on the Internet will also be discussed.

CORPORATE AND PROFESSIONAL VIDEOS

The term *corporate video* has become a popular catch-all term for a number of types of EFP video. This category can include almost all professional non-broadcast users of portable video whose purposes are not entertainment. Some users of this EFP style are not necessarily members of corporations; in fact, many are not. Educational institutions, governmental agencies, labor unions, professional associations, clubs, and civic organizations are common users of this type of video production.

Numerous types of video fit into the category of corporate video; news, information, and public relations videos are very common. Especially popular in large and/or decentralized organizations where face-to-face contact among members is difficult or unusual, these videos are used as a means of disseminating information efficiently and maintaining cohesiveness among members. Another consideration is the availability of information in-house for corporations whose employees' computers are tied together with a local-area network (LAN). These corporations are making Web-type pages available in-house with information that can be seen by employees only. These Web pages have the capability to show video as well as audio and other graphic material. This is similar to the Internet, except that these pages are not available to people outside the organization. The term for this in-house multimedia use of video is **intranet**.

Corporate News Show

Corporate video often takes the form of a company news show. The show consists of several common elements: messages from or profiles of top management; company-wide news such as recent achievements in sales, profits, safety, or growth; branch or regional news; and employee news. Although this communication is called news, it almost never includes hard news (for example, auto wrecks, burglary, or fires) and is never investigative in an adversarial way. This type of video is purely for internal public relations. It is a way of making a large organization seem more personal and familiar.

The host or reporter on an internal company news show conducts on-location interviews, reads news copy over video, or gives lead-ins to packages of stories about the company and its employees. The shooting style is more like a magazine show (with features) than a news show. There is no sense of urgency, and the videographer can usually control what is happening in front of the camera.

Most of the rules mentioned for shooting general news and reporter stand-ups in previous chapters ap-

Figure 3-1 In this corporate news show for a hospital, anchors discuss an innovative surgical technique recently performed by doctors affiliated with the hospital. (Courtesy of VAS Communications)

ply to this EFP style. The goal is to make the organization seem friendly and personal. Your style should reflect this goal. You may use wide shots to quickly establish your location, but close-up shots help convey a friendly mood.

Instruction, Training, and Demonstration

This general category includes instructional video production in classrooms designed to be viewed by persons other than those physically present in the classroom. This can mean a recorded lecture for absent students, or a recorded production of an entire course for students viewing the recording rather than attending live lectures. It also may mean **distance learning,** in which TV is used for live, real-time interaction between two classrooms separated by distance. In corporate and other professional settings, training videos have become so common that they are an expected part of employee orientation and training. Using video for training purposes is the single most common use of portable video in the corporate world. A good, properly produced training video can save many hours of boring repetition by an instructor. It can also provide location shots and event shots that could not otherwise be viewed by the audience.

While instructional video for distant learning may not have a verbatim script, it most often has a very carefully prepared outline for the instructor to follow, with graphic material specially prepared in a form conducive to good video. For example, graphic material should conform to analog TV's 4:3 aspect ratio or the 16:9 digital TV aspect ratio.

Instructional corporate video is used to convey very specific information to the intended audience. Its goal is to have the audience learn something specific, such as a procedure, a task, or a safety rule.

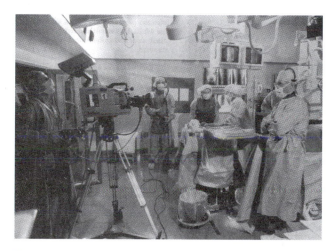

Figure 3-2 This instructional video is being shot in a medical operating room. The surgeon who will be performing the surgery gives an introduction about the procedure about to be performed. (Courtesy of the Arizona Heart Institute)

Instructional video requires a very accurate and organized script and storyboard. Two shooting rules are standard:

1. Each shot must be clear, accurate, and supported by explanatory audio when appropriate.
2. Close-up shots are critical for demonstrating procedures and showing small equipment or controls on larger equipment.

Extreme close-ups (XCUs) may be necessary. When shooting XCUs, make sure they are rehearsed. Because XCUs require high magnification, slight movement by either the camera or the subject may give your shot an amateurish look. Also, shots at high magnification often have a shallow depth of field.

Small movement of the object can cause a loss of focus. During a rehearsal of a shot, mark off the area that defines your sharp focus area, keep the camera still and the object in the focus area. Handholding small objects for XCU shots is not recommended.

Teleconferencing

A significant growth area for corporate video or nonbroadcast video is teleconferencing. Although teleconferencing refers more to a method of distribution than a style of shooting, it became an enormous part of corporate and nonbroadcast TV in the 1990s. There are numerous reasons for this, but the most important are that teleconferencing saved a lot of money by eliminating travel costs, and that the technology needed became available at a reasonable cost. The methods of distribution for teleconferencing have changed, but the usefulness of teleconferencing remains the same. In the 1980s and 1990s, executives of a given national organization in Boston and San Francisco met "face to face" through two-way TV, utilizing a satellite-distributed teleconference. A small university campus reached out to employees of an engineering firm off campus with a graduate course in engineering through microwave distribution and audio call-in. Universities also distributed courses to branch campuses by using a two-way microwave TV system. Students at both locations were able to ask the professor questions and get immediate answers. Although microwave distribution of video for this purpose still exists, the vast majority of common uses for teleconferencing now use the World Wide Web to distribute the video. Inexpensive Web cameras (Webcams) make two-way video cost effective and easy to set up.

The professional or industrial style of this type of video is a hybrid of studio and portable video. Most teleconferences occur in a room or location specially adapted for the purpose or in some type of TV studio. Teleconferences can be shot in various formats that can include elements of a news show, demonstration, motivational video, panel discussion, and lecture.

Sales, Promotion, and Motivation

Public relations videos are shot with the intention of delivering information, but the desired effects are also behavioral and attitudinal. Corporations shoot these videos because they want their salespeople to know about the products and services that they must sell and also because they want to instill in the sales force the positive attitude and energy necessary to get the sales job done. Sales, promotion, and motivational videos are characterized by high energy and dynamism. Enthusiasm is the key word.

As with the demonstration video, these videos require tight scripting to allow the control necessary to keep the tempo of the video upbeat. Camera shots are dynamic, showing much movement. Soundtracks are crisp and lively; the music is upbeat. Lighting is usually bright, with strong direction and modeling (not flat). Often, strong backlighting is used to separate the subject or the product from the background. Colors are often bright.

If editing is noticeable at all, it usually consists of quick cuts rather than slow dissolves to enhance the dynamic energy. Special effects are often employed to enhance the feeling that the product, service, or concept has special merit. These effects can be as simple as a star effect from a star filter on a camera lens, or a computer-generated special effect or animation costing thousands of dollars.

Entertainment

Many of the shows presented on broadcast, cable, and satellite television are not shot in television studios. Scripted, narrative drama shows like *CSI* and *Law and Order* are shot in a sound studio (similar to the way feature films are shot) and on location. These shows are still shot on film and use the film style, or single-camera style of shooting. This technique is similar to video shooting in the field: a single camera is used for multiple takes of a shot or scene. The best takes are selected and then combined in the editing process to construct the show. Other shows (e.g., *Reno 911*) are also shot in this style, but because of budgetary reasons or aesthetic reasons (to give a live feel to the show), they are shot with video cameras instead of film cameras. As video cameras get better, more and more shows will be shot in video instead of film. The newer video cameras that can shoot in 24p (24 frames per second, progressive scanning) give a picture with film-like quality and are beginning to replace film cameras in some shows.

Many shows are shot in a video documentary style. These shows include *Blind Date*, *Fear Factor*, *Survivor*, and home remodeling shows such as HGTV's *Curb Appeal*. These reality shows use the cameras to record the action. Usually, the cameras just try to capture what is happening in front of the camera, and the directors do not have the luxury of retaking shots. Some shows are shot inside a television studio with large studio-configured video cameras, but also use a hand-held camera so that the director can have the freedom to get unusual angles or extreme close-up shots that will add dynamism and excitement to the show.

Many types of performances simply cannot be brought to the TV studio and still retain the mood or energy intended by the performers, directors, or choreographers. Part of the reason for this is that the TV studio is rarely large enough to permit an audience. Many performers accustomed to having audiences present strongly prefer having the audience there for feedback and energy. Also, TV studios can rarely duplicate the space or specific lighting, floor, or sound characteristics of a theatrical stage or auditorium. Because of these limitations, many performers have been recorded in EFP style. If a good postproduction facility is available, a simple multiple-camera EFP shoot can yield a high-quality performance video suitable for broadcasting or showing to an in-house audience. As mentioned earlier, many television shows in a variety of formats are now being shot EFP style, both in and out of the studio. As the cameras get better and more and more shows are shot on smaller budgets for the non-network program providers like The Travel Channel or HGTV, the use of portable video will continue to increase.

COMMERCIALS AND PUBLIC SERVICE ANNOUNCEMENTS

Commercials and public service announcements (PSAs) for broadcast and cable TV probably include every conceivable style of shooting. Styles vary by mar-

Figure 3-3   Most home improvement shows are shot on location with portable video equipment. This can often be accomplished with one camera.

ket size—usually in relation to the budget, which is directly related to market size and type of product—or by the issue to be discussed. Most videographers who shoot these short-format projects do so on a local level (for example, a local car dealership or the local United Way campaign).

Commercials

In broadcasting, all TV stations except those with educational or public broadcasting affiliations rely on commercials to pay for their operating costs. All non-premium cable programming services, such as ESPN, CNN, or MTV, also rely on paid commercials to keep them profitable. This presents an enormous opportunity for aspiring videographers to practice their skills. On the local level, tens of thousands of commercials are produced for airing.

Formats

Just about every style of video has probably been tried in a commercial. There are, however, a number of standard formats that have been used during the past 50 years that encompass most of the TV commercials produced.

Announcement In the days before computer graphics and affordable yet powerful character generators, this commercial was of two general types: an announcer doing a stand-up with the product or in front of the store, and a series of still photos, shot on slides and fed through a device called a telecine that created video from the slides. New technology has made this type of commercial more sophisticated by allowing more complicated and sophisticated manipulation of video images.

Demonstration The introduction of a new product often requires that the use of the product be shown to the audience. Close-up work is common when the product is small or a very close look is needed by the audience, such as a new safety feature on the dashboard of a new model car or a new stamp issued by the post office. If the shot looks best at a very short object-to-camera distance, the shot may need to be done with the lens in the macro mode. This type of shot also requires special lighting. As the camera lens gets very close to the object, the object size grows, but the lens and camera often block some or all of the light needed for proper exposure. Light aimed at 45-degree angles, similar to those on a copy stand, will illuminate the object without causing harsh shadows.

Testimonial This type of commercial is often done in a local grocery store, car dealership, or restaurant. Customers (nonperformers) are interviewed at the location and are asked questions that are intended to yield complimentary responses. Often several of these favorable soundbites are edited together to create the main body of the commercial.

Celebrity Spokesperson Famous people are often paid to go to a new store, attend an event like the county fair, or promote a product or service. The face and voice of the person help the commercial get the desired audience attention. Obviously, medium and close-up shots of the celebrity are needed to make sure that the audience's recognizes the person. High-quality audio in the field is needed for this type of performer, because the audience knows the sound of the famous person's voice.

Dialogue This commercial is often shot on location in familiar settings, such as an ordinary kitchen. Two people might be discussing the pros and cons of an upcoming referendum. An establishing shot of the location is held long enough to show where the discussion is taking place. The technique often includes several over-the-shoulder shots that show the person speaking from over the shoulder of the other person. A child in a conversation with her mother would show shots from the perspective of the listener; a low-angle shot when the mother speaks, a high-angle shot down on the child when the child speaks.

Dramatization Often similar to a dialogue, this commercial is often told as a brief story. This type of commercial often uses natural settings and therefore is shot on location. This could take the familiar before-and-after form—before using the product and after using the product. Humor or exaggeration is common with this format.

Institutional This format is often semi-documentary in form. It may show what a major oil company is doing to clean up the environment while producing a better grade of gasoline. This format is most often used by large corporations to promote goodwill toward the corporation.

Shooting Styles

Stand-up Presentation This format is an attempt at interpersonal communication by an announcer; actually, it is usually a simple and direct sales talk. The performer is shot straight on, with direct eye contact with the audience. This can be shot anywhere and is often done in an auto sales lot or grocery store.

Hidden-Camera Testimonials This format is the typical "yes, this coffee does taste great" spot, in which real people are the stars of the commercial. The camera may not be visible to the real people, thus yielding a more natural response.

Music Orientation Often a musical piece is composed to sell a product and becomes almost more important than any other selling points. In this case, the visuals serve to accentuate the music. Producers of these shots hope that the music becomes closely linked to the product. This is especially helpful if the video spots are used in combination with radio spots.

Visual Orientation Commercials are sometimes produced with very little, if any, emphasis placed on the audio. In this case, the audio merely supplements the video; the message is almost completely visual. National spots for autos often show the auto on the road and keep the factual information minimal.

Figure 3-4   These stills are from typical stand-up presentation commercials. Note the direct eye contact with the camera that enhances interpersonal communication. (Courtesy of John Wade)

Comparative Demonstration   This style often requires quite a bit of pre- and postproduction. In a very short time frame, the producer tries to show how a product is used or compares two products' performance and cost. A typical example would be the grease-cutting ability of two dishwashing liquids. Props such as glass kitchen sinks are needed to show how the product works. Another popular version has a split screen with shots of the two products, for example, Ford versus Chevy trucks. The screens show superimposed facts about price, horsepower, load capacity, or other simple, numerically, oriented comparisons over the shots of the trucks. The shots of the products are usually identical, but subtle lighting or other differences might be used to enhance the sponsor's product.

Animation   Animation is used to create a visual not possible in reality, or to draw attention to the product. Toy and cereal manufacturers have long believed that animation attracts and holds children's attention better than many real announcers. Obviously, this is a time-consuming and expensive approach and therefore is rarely used locally. Advances in personal computers and software designed for computer graphics and animation may change this in the near future.

In addition to the above general categories, numerous combinations of formats and exotic variations of these are used. A celebrity spokesperson may by joined by an animated spokesperson for a theme park. A slice-of-life commercial may include a family trying two different products for comparison. A stand-up presenter may introduce a strongly visually-oriented spot.

All the above approaches can be and often are accomplished in the field. Before high-quality, competitively-priced ENG/EFP cameras were generally available, on-location local commercials for TV were usually shot on 16mm movie film or 35mm slide film. Low-budget commercials were shot on slides. Some slides (usually two to eight) from the shoot were loaded into the slide chain (telecine) at the studio and a soundtrack was added. Many commercials and PSAs are still done in this way, although the slides are often replaced with static video shots of the business doing the advertising.

It is easy to do better than that. Avoid static shots. Without overusing the zoom, add some dynamics to your shots with camera movement. If you have an on-camera announcer or subject, add interest to the shot by placing the subject in an unusual spot; for example, in a car lifted high above the ground with a crane, start on a close-up shot, then zoom out to reveal the exact location. If you add music, try to make some of your edits coincide with the beat of the music to draw your viewers into the message.

When producing a commercial or PSA, keep your time frame in mind. You will probably have only 30 seconds to convey your idea and the needed information. This calls for careful scripting and storyboarding. Commercials and PSAs offer excellent ways of sharpening your creative skills, both with the camera and in scriptwriting. Do not settle for the ordinary; use these short-format projects as a challenge to your ability to interest audiences and tell a complete and interesting story in a short time frame.

Public Service Announcements

Public service announcements (PSAs) are short (usually 30- to 60-second) announcements created and broadcast or cablecast for the benefit of the viewing audience. The sponsor is often a local nonprofit agency, such as the library, humane society, or fundraising effort. Many PSA campaigns are produced for nationwide broadcast by national groups, such as the Ad Council, American Dental Association, American Cancer Society, religious organizations, and the U.S. government. The national campaigns often discuss themes of national concern, such as drug abuse, literacy, environmental safety, and health issues. Usually well financed and shot on film, these campaigns are distributed on DVD, satellite, or through a broadband connection to broadcast and cable/satellite outlets throughout the country.

On a local level, state agencies and nonprofit institutions often attempt to create and produce PSA campaigns with donated help and small budgets. This need often provides students and beginning professionals with an opportunity to produce creative work that will be aired (sometimes repeatedly) on local or regional stations or cable systems.

Budgets

Budgets for PSAs and commercials are usually quite small, limiting your alternatives for creativity and experimentation to those you do not have to buy. Forget about renting the helicopter for your aerial shot, but offer to trade-out with the local emergency health helicopter service—offer to shoot a public service spot or commercial for them in exchange for a free ride. If this does not work, try to get your bird's-eye view from the roof of the tallest adjacent building. Sometimes a wide-angle shot from above gives the desired aerial shot effect. Conveying the notion of acres of gleaming new and used autos may be easier from 100 feet than from a helicopter at 300 feet.

Instead of flashy digital effects, low-budget retail commercials may force you to inject excitement and action with unusual camera angles and some dynamic editing. The point here is that network style and quality commercials require network-sized budgets. Ninety percent of video commercials are *low budget;* this is most likely what you will have to face, especially if you are a beginner. There is hope, however, for the aspiring producer. Computer programs that can manipulate video for special effects and editing are becoming more common and more affordable. These programs allow the low-budget producer to perform three-dimensional effects, such as rotation, or image-to-image changes, such as morphing (for example, a smooth transition from one shape to another, such as an old, boxy-looking car becoming a sleek race car). The nonlinear editors allow an editor to make several versions of a commercial or PSA in less time than it takes a linear editor to complete one version.

PERFORMANCE VIDEOS

Two major types of performance video use EFP. The first is performance video for entertainment purposes, done on location by one or more EFP cameras for later presentation to an audience. The other major type of performance video is shot for historical purposes; an event is captured on video and archived for future reference.

Two methods are used in practice for shooting on-location performance videos: (1) the **switchable camera field shoot**, and (2) the **isolated camera field shoot**.

The switchable camera field shoot uses multiple cameras with a field switcher that selects one camera to be the "taking" or online camera. This system mimics the TV studio, where a director makes real-time switching decisions to select which camera will supply the program video for any given shot. This system is convenient if the director is very familiar with the script of the performance and the look that the performance should have as a finished video product.

This configuration of equipment commonly has three cameras tied to one switcher and a recorder con-

Figure 3-5   Some reality shows (such as *Big Brother, Surreal Life,* or *Real World*) are recorded in the style of a switchable camera field shoot. Numerous cameras are located in the house to record the everyday behaviors of the residents. Outside the house, a production trailer enables the crew to view all cameras and decide which video sequences will be used in the program.

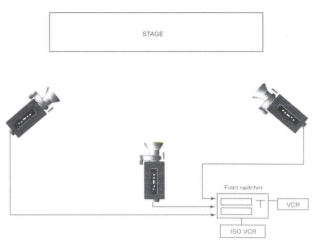

Figure 3-6   Three-camera remote shoot for a performance video. Switching is done in real time, yielding one finished project at the end of the performance. An isolated VCR may also be used for close-up shots taken by one of the cameras.

nected to the program or outgoing line from the switcher. Because only one recording is made, the director decides on the spot which camera will be online. If the wrong decision is made, or if the technical director pushes the wrong button, the recording usually contains the bad decision or error, with virtually no way to fix it.

Two ways exist to avoid the problem of having to live with your mistakes on a "live-to-tape" (now also known simply as "recorded live") multiple-camera switched recording. The easiest is to have one wild camera not hooked to the switcher that shoots cutaway shots during the show, such as audience reactions, extreme wide shots, extreme tight shots, or any shot that could be considered nonsynchronous. Later these can be inserted to cover any mistakes made by the director, technical director (TD), or subject on the master recording, with a minimum of editing time and without a jump cut or loss of continuity.

The second way is to have one of the switched cameras on an isolated line to its own VCR. Most switchers are capable of feeding an isolated (ISO) line from any of the cameras coming into the switcher. If the switcher cannot do this, then a separate deck can be hooked up to one of the cameras. This can be a small

price to pay and a minor hassle to ensure that the finished product meets the highest standards and does not look amateurish. The ISO camera is generally either the least-used camera, the most stable camera of the group, or the one that gives a good wide shot. Very few big-time experienced directors would work without a safety net (that is, an ISO camera) unless the production is going to be aired live.

Whenever two or more cameras are brought together in the manner described above, they must be timed to avoid a glitch when the picture is cut from one of them to another. This method of timing is called **genlock**; there are two methods of doing this. Most professional multiple-camera setups make use of a special camera cable connection on the back of the camera called a **triax adapter** that allows most camera functions to be done at a remote location wherever the cables come together—generally near the switcher. A video control person can **shade** the cameras (control the iris and manipulate the color so that each camera looks as good as the other) as well as time them to each other. In lower budget productions, only a **coax** cable that attaches to the BNC connector on the side or back of the camera is used. Each camera must be matched manually before the shooting starts. To time them, a second coax cable must be run to each camera. This cable is attached to the genlock port on the camera and comes from the switcher, which is feeding a reference signal to each of the cameras that allows the cameras to synchronize their video scan rates. Without this timing function, nothing in a multiple-camera setup will work properly.

Isolated Camera Field Shoot The alternative method for a multiple-camera shoot uses the same number of cameras, usually three, but they are not tied to a switcher. Instead, each has its own independent recorder. The director's job using this method is more one of guidance, rather than final decision making, until the postproduction stage. This is because the director does not have a camera monitor for each camera. The director suggests certain shots to each camera operator, such as "Camera 1, look for Mr. X to enter from stage left, and make sure you get a CU of his face as he sees Ms. Y." If camera 1 misses the shot, the other two cameras may get it.

This method relies very strongly on postproduction. After the shoot, there are three complete versions of the performance, one from each camera. One version is commonly a master shot from the center camera; the other two versions are from the side cameras situated somewhat closer to the stage.

When two cameras are being used to shoot one scene or event for professional use, it is recommended that the cameras be genlocked. On a two-camera interview, even without a switcher (each camera has its own

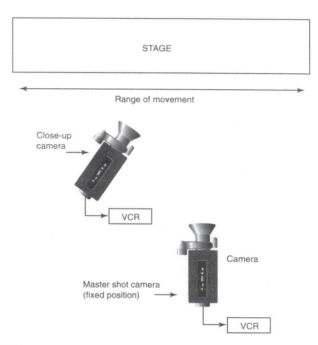

Figure 3-8   Two-camera remote shoot for a performance video. Video from each camera can be mixed, or each may be used unedited.

deck), a genlock cable should be run between the cameras. One simple coax cable from the genlock-out port of one camera to the genlock-in port of the other will lock the two cameras together. Any number of cameras can be hooked together in series this way. This precaution allows an edit machine to synchronize the two recordings or clips in the edit process.

The easiest way to synchronize the recordings of a multiple-camera shoot is by using time code (providing the cameras are genlocked), a method called **jam sync**. A recorder that has a time code–out port, or a stand alone time code generator, can be used as the master. A coax cable from the master's time code–out port can be run to the time code–in port of any deck. Just like genlock, this process can be done in series so that a separate cable does not have to run from the master to every single machine, but each machine needs to be connected to another. The time code master machine can be set to internal time code, and all slaved machines need to be set to external time code on their control switches. Whatever time code is set on the master, each slave machine will record. If another deck is used as the master and the time code is in the record run position, it must be recording before it will

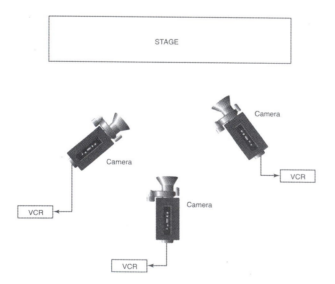

Figure 3-7   Three-camera remote shoot for a performance video. Each camera is isolated and has its own recorder. Video from each camera will be mixed in postproduction to yield a finished product.

send time code to the slave machines. This setup can make it easy to put a multiple-camera show together in the edit room.

Historical Archive

One of the most sensible and efficient uses of video is the historical archive. Unique events, such as celebrations, special performances, and groundbreaking ceremonies, are good reasons to use the inexpensive historical document that can be provided by a quality recording shot on location. The archive video is not the same as a performance-quality or entertainment video intended for later broadcast. It is a low-budget record of an occurrence worth keeping for future reference.

Choreographers and Directors For the dance choreographer, archive video provides a representation of a creation as interpreted by the choreographer at a certain point in time and by the dancers available at that time. Video captures the movement and the staging for the choreographer to use during a later interpretation or reconstruction.

Figure 3-9 An archive video was shot for the choreographer of this dance to provide a record of how the space on stage was used and how the dancers performed.

In the same way, the theater director can obtain a record of a particular performance by the cast at a particular time, using the archive video. It creates a point of reference that a written script, review, or summary

could never provide. The director can obtain a DVD copy and show it just about anywhere on a DVD player.

Another very common use of video for archiving is done by sports teams. Almost every college and university varsity team in a major sport uses video in some way to give feedback to the coaches and players. The techniques vary widely, as do the budgets, with budgets often dictating styles. In college football videographers record practices and games, often from a variety of angles, to provide information for the coaches to use when critiquing player performance and to plan for future opponents. In some cases, the video is used in highlight shows. For example, in a coach's show, footage of a future star practicing might be used when a coach is explaining why that player got playing time. Footage of a player could also be exhibited to show progress after an injury. High school players who aspire to play at the college level (and win athletic scholarships) often hire video producers to use archival footage of their high school performance and other footage to gain the attention of college recruiters and coaches. Even if archive video is not seen by a large audience, it is often a very important coaching tool. In addition, archive sports video can provide jobs for entry-level videographers.

Event Dictates Style The style of the archive video is dictated by the event being recorded and the desires of the choreographer, director, or interested group that will use the video. Choreographers and directors often want to have the entire stage visible to show not just the performers, but also the relationship between the performers and the space in which they are performing. This requires that the videographer avoid the temptation of zooming in on the action and framing it tightly. For both choreographers and directors, the expression of the performer on stage is not the only important aspect of the performance.

In dance, body positioning and articulation of the extremities should be included in all shots. Since dancers often move quickly, they can dance entirely out of the frame if the shot is too tight. Even cutting off the toes or hands in a shot of a dancer can lose what the choreographer needs to see. Directors often want to see entrances of characters while others are on stage. This also calls for a wide shot.

These types of requirements translate into a simple, static one-camera style. Use your tripod and set the camera on a wide master shot of the stage. Make sure that your shot is not so wide that it allows any stage lights to shine directly into your lens. If you are able to use two cameras, use the first camera for a master shot and the second for following action and close-ups of the main performers. You may want to edit these together into your final project or simply provide two versions, one of the wide shot and one of the close-ups.

This type of video may seem boring to you, or it may seem like unimaginative shooting. But keep in mind that the archive is *not* a commercial program to be viewed on broadcast TV; rather, it is a tool used by professionals and scholars to preserve an historically significant event or creative endeavor.

SPORTS VIDEOS

One of the reasons that sports are so popular is that they represent one of the few real live dramas available on television. Keep this in mind when you are planning to shoot any kind of sports coverage. As with any kind of video, make sure that you realize that sports coverage requires that a story be told. Because sports contests can be dramatic, remember the elements of known characters (well known sports names); conflict (a history of hard fought battles between two teams); and suspense (the best games are those where the outcome is uncertain). These elements pull the audience into your video story; in this case, it is a game story. This requires some background work, such as a recounting of the events of the last meeting between the two teams or two competitors. One of the best examples of this kind of dramatic buildup can be seen on a pregame show for the National Football League. Often you will see highlights from a previous game (footage usually supplied by NFL Films), and interviews with the coaches, the players, or even highly partisan fans. This pregame information helps orient the viewer to the drama of the game.

The two main types of sports EFP work are competition and features. Sports features are generally shot for use in pregame or highlight shows. EFP coverage of actual sports competition has two main purposes:

Figure 3-10   Cameras used for professional location video work are usually more like studio cameras. The large, heavy lens and the need for steady telephoto shots require a heavy support system. The camera operator can receive directions via an intercom system.

1. Live coverage of the event for airing.
2. Coverage for replay at a later time, usually in a highlights show.

Live coverage of a sports event is a complex, expensive undertaking that requires numerous cameras; a truck or van with camera control, storage media, switching, and other technical equipment; miles of camera cable; and a group of hardworking professionals.

Figure 3-11   This sports interview could be shot for a pregame show segment or as part of a highlight program. Two cameras are used to let the director in the remote production van choose a shot of the interviewer or the interviewees.

Each sport has a particular sequence of shots compiled from the various cameras to give the viewer a comprehensive and complete view of the event as it occurs. Features usually consist of four elements:

1. Interview with an athlete or participant (for example, the coach or auto racing pit crew member).
2. Shots of this person preparing for the sport or event (for example, lacing running shoes, changing a racing tire, taping a baseball bat).
3. Shots of an athletic performance, competition, or game.
4. Shots of some type of previous success or future challenge.

These are all easy to shoot with one portable camera and can be easily edited together.

Competition Coverage

The basic camera setup for a football game consists of six or more cameras. These cameras and the associated equipment are often brought to a big sports shoot in a large specially-designed production trailer.

Cameras 1, 2, and 3 are located in the stands about one-half to two-thirds of the way up to the top of the stadium. These cameras are used to orient the viewer as to the field location and direction.

One of these three cameras will be used for the line of scrimmage, depending on the location of the ball. The camera closest to the line of scrimmage will be used to show the offensive team's huddle and one wide shot of their lineup at the line of scrimmage. Frame this shot so that about two-thirds to three-quarters of the screen is filled with the offensive team. (See Figure 3-13.) This allows screen space for the quarterback to move into when he drops back to pass or hand-off. (See Figure 3-14.)

Just before the center snaps the ball to the quarterback, the taking camera zooms in tighter on the quarterback. This camera will zoom in and follow the ball from the time the ball is snapped until the play is over. After the play has stopped and the players start to get back on their feet, the director will usually switch to the trucktop-mounted camera, which should have a close-

Figure 3-12   Vehicles like this one are custom designed and equipped for remote video work. It houses all necessary cameras, decks, switches, cables, and so forth, and provides the control room and hardware needed to shoot a remote event such as football or election coverage.

up shot of the ball carrier and the tackler or key defensive person involved in the play. If the play was a good offensive play, the shot will follow the offensive ball carrier. On a good defensive play, the camera might follow the defensive player as he returns to his huddle.

At this point, the director can choose one of several alternatives:

1. A replay, sometimes with slow motion from the on-air camera or any one of the ISO cameras.
2. A graphic superimposed over the real action as the players return to the huddle.
3. A special graphic of the key player—his statistics or picture, or a short piece recorded before the game showing the player responding to a question.
4. A wide shot from the end-zone camera or one of the other cameras (usually over a wide crowd shot), often used to frame statistics or a promotional graphic that is superimposed over the shot.
5. A shot from the sideline camera, either of the coach, key players waiting to come into the game, an injured player, or some other color

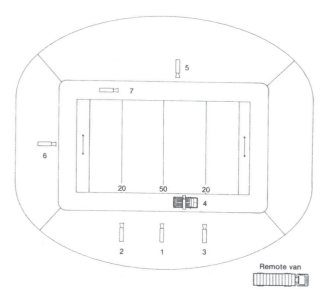

Figure 3-13   Multiple-camera remote professional sports shoot. Cameras 1, 2, and 3 are in the seating areas on the platform, one-half to two-thirds of the way up to the top of the stadium. Camera 4 is mounted on top of the truck. Camera 5 is in the seating area on the platform used for reverse angle shots. Camera 6 is in the seating area behind either goalpost. Camera 7 is the roaming portable camera. Sometimes additional cameras are attached to the goalposts to get shots of attempted field goals. In addition to the cameras shown on the diagram, it is now common for a Skycam to be added. The Skycam actually "flies" over the field and can get shots that aren't available from other cameras.

Figure 3-14   Line-of-scrimmage shot at the beginning of football play. Note how the framing gives the quarterback room to move into for a hand-off or passing.

shot of cheerleaders, fans, mascots or the typical "Hi Mom" or "We're Number 1" shot of a player on the sidelines.

6. As the end of the half or the game approaches, a shot of the clock or scoreboard.

If normal play is continuing, the sequence begins again with a wide shot from camera 1, 2, or 3.

This sequence changes for each type of sports coverage. Soccer coverage is challenging because it is non-stop. Unlike American football, soccer action is almost continuous, with few interruptions. The director has few stops in the action to replay camera angles that were not shown in the first coverage. Penalty kicks and other actions that cause a stop in the time clock allow the director to show, sometimes repeatedly, the action that caused the stop in play. For the most part, however, all cameras in soccer coverage focus on the ball and the players near it. The technique of camera placement can be very similar, however, because the shape of a soccer field is similar to a football field.

Skycam

In the past few years, more and more sporting events feature a special camera suspended above the playing field for a bird's-eye view of the action. Most commonly used for football games, the Skycam sytem from CF InFlight, Ltd. (Malvern, PA) is virtually a flying Steadicam, a broadcast-quality, robotic camera suspended from a cable-driven, computerized transport system. Its unique design makes the Skycam a stabilized camera system that can unobtrusively fly anywhere at up to 25 mph in a defined three-dimensional space—right in the middle of a sporting event.

Feature Coverage

Highlight shows are common to most professional and major college sports teams. These shows consist of past matchups between the teams; a chronology of game footage with replays of key plays; coach and player interviews; and previews of upcoming opponents. You may not have the equipment, personnel, or budget for

Figure 3-15   The Skycam provides a bird's-eye view of the action in sports events.

live coverage of a football game, but one or two EFP cameras with competent camera operators can do a decent job of covering the game for a highlights show.

If only one camera is available for a football game, it should be the one placed at the 50-yard line, one-half to two-thirds of the way up to the top part of the stadium, or even on top of the press box if there is one. Many fields provide a designated space for video cameras. This camera will have a good view of the line of scrimmage for a high percentage of the plays. If the ball is followed closely, a viewer should be able to follow the entire game from the video of that one camera. The trick is to always stay with the ball.

Keep the framing loose until you are sure where the ball is and the play has already developed. Then you can zoom in as the running back crosses the line of scrimmage or the wide receiver pulls in the long pass. Obviously, a camera with a high zoom ratio or range extender is best. The biggest mistake you can make is to zoom in to follow a running back who has been faked a hand-off and does not have the ball.

A second camera would be best placed on a truck mount, but that requires additional personnel, a truck, and lots of expensive cable. A platform about 10 feet above the field at the 50-yard line is a possible second choice. Most likely, the only alternative for a second camera is a handheld one on the sidelines. This camera can provide very dramatic close-ups of the action but can also be blocked by players or referees—or even be run over by the play itself. This camera is most effective when it can shoot from the end zone and get close-ups of scoring plays. For midfield coverage, the camera is best placed about 10 yards in front of the line of scrimmage. This is, however, far from ideal, since the field is often crowned with a center higher than the sidelines, yielding a low camera angle.

Other sports have slightly different requirements and camera placements (for example, golf and tennis, which are shot from the end of the green or court), but a few simple rules usually apply:

1. Get above and in the middle of the action (for example, midcourt in basketball or hockey).
2. Follow the ball (or race car).
3. Frame loosely to avoid losing the object you are following.

MUSIC VIDEOS

Music videos have been popular since the early 1980s. Since the introduction of MTV (Music Television) in 1981, the viewing world has become highly aware of the mixture of songs with visuals. This radio-to-TV product stimulated enormous interest in music video style, as evidenced by the industry opinion from the early 1980s until recently that a band (unless it is a firmly established popular band) must have a music video to have a hit record. Now bands can get exposure through the Internet in a variety of ways, including podcasts that can be made with small budgets. But in general, the demand for music videos have been a boost to the employment potential of aspiring EFP professionals.

The notion of setting visuals to music has been around for a long time. A viewing of Walt Disney's

1940 classic *Fantasia* will convince you of that fact. The idea of having the performers act to their own music has also been around for some time. For example, *A Hard Day's Night* is a mid-1960's Beatles' film in which the Beatles have good-natured fun and sometimes lip-sync to their songs.

Many music videos are still shot on film and then either transferred to video for editing or edited and transferred to video for broadcast. Film, as mentioned in an earlier chapter, has a much better contrast ratio than video, and is better in very low light or very bright conditions. This is changing gradually as video cameras (e.g., the newer 24p cameras) produce film-like quality. Many of the striking digital effects in these videos are accomplished during the editing process. Although traditional music videos can sometimes still be seen on MTV or VH1, music videos are easier to find on cable or satellite channels like CMT (Country Music Television). Music videos are also shown now on broadcast digital subchannels to those who have digital tuners or receive digital cable (e.g., The Tube). Another trend is the availability of music video through cable companies that provide music channels on a video-on-demand basis (e.g., the Harmony Channel). In some music videos, the performers aren't on screen, giving the video producer freedom to select the visuals that convey the mood or story of the music.

Variety of Settings

Despite the drawbacks of video cameras for the big-money music videos, the style of music video is perfect for the EFP videographer. Almost all of these videos have shots done on location outside of the studio. (Just imagine how dull they would be if all music videos only showed the musicians on a stage.) The fun in music videos comes from the unusual locations, camera angles, costumes, and sophisticated transitions between the major elements. Music videos generally are composed of a combination of two elements:

1. The musicians in the studio or on stage performing a song.
2. The musicians on location (somehow suggested by the song), either with instruments or in some dramatic vignette.

The variety of locations both for the performance and the vignette is virtually infinite, since almost anything is acceptable for a few minutes as an accompaniment to a song. Sometimes animation is used to create new locations and effects. Other times, a mundane location such as a supermarket or basement apartment can provide you with the look or mood that you want for your music video. The biggest factor in changing an average setting into something unusual is creative lighting.

Style and Technique

Because the person and personality of the performers are the main interests of the music video, plan on shooting many more tight shots than long shots. You may use a brief long shot to give the viewer a sense of who is performing and where they are, but close-ups will probably be more interesting to the audience. You should also plan on low camera angles to accentuate the presence of the performers. You can shoot a music video in the style of the performance video. Using one camera on a master shot, or using three cameras, record a straight performance version of the song. If this is not a real performance and the performers are lip-syncing, make sure you have the audio to which they are performing recorded on DVD, CD, or videotape. During subsequent takes in various locations, make sure that you play that same version of the song while they lip-sync to it. This allows you to go back to the master version and synchronize your two audio tracks, then insert your video from your location shots. If you have a CD or DVD of the song, use a CD boom box or laptop computer with a CD/DVD drive at each location.

If you are well organized in keeping track of your various versions, putting together a finished composite music video—even from six versions at six different locations—can be relatively easy. Just make sure that your reference audio is on every recording. If numerous locations are not possible or desirable, use the multiple-take style. When using this style, record multiple takes of the song (or portions of the song) while the performers vary their performance, or while the focal length of the camera varies with each take. This style can yield a very respectable music video from an afternoon's shooting.

Music videos are an excellent opportunity for the beginning videographer to experiment with camera technique. Videographers and news photographers who usually have professional style restrictions placed on them can use music videos to loosen up and experiment with the camera. This even helps professionals become more familiar with the versatility and capability of their equipment

NATURE AND DOCUMENTARY VIDEOS

Nature and documentary videos are perfectly suited for the portable video camera, just as they have been suited for the portable film camera for almost a century. This style requires a camera to be where the main characters (or animals or plants) are, or where the main events are occurring. The camera views the events as they actually occur and the characters as they appear, not as they are staged in front of the camera. This is not to say that no editing is done to restructure events. By the use of editing, nature programs have created many encounters between wild animals that never took place. Even documentaries will sometimes use editing to create events that occurred but were missed by the camera.

The point is that the videographer is meant to be a passive participant, not an active one. This is not necessarily intentional in nature programs, but wild animals rarely take cues from directors. Documentaries are meant to present a reality that will enlighten its viewers, not a reality as created by the videographer or director. This style requires an unobtrusive camera to avoid influencing the events that occur in front of the camera. Therefore, retakes of these events are almost impossible, the addition of a large amount of artificial light may be nearly impossible, and getting every shot that you plan is certainly impossible. In addition, the need for safety while shooting becomes very important (See Figure 3-16).

Satellite television, with its enormous array of channels, now offers the Documentary Channel with 24/7 showing of independent documentary program producers. The channel exhibits documentaries of all types, lengths, and styles, both classic and cutting edge.

Although the market for this type of video program is growing rapidly, the beginner should be aware of the fact that documentary or nature video work takes many long hours of shooting and editing. Because of this, the budget for this EFP style is necessarily large—at least in comparison to most commercials, performance videos, and many applications of corporate video. As the number of channels on cable and satellite television increase, with brands like the Discovery Channel continuing to proliferate both in this country and abroad, the market for nature and documentary programs has increased dramatically over the past ten years. In addition to the Discovery family of channels, numerous outlets like PBS, Animal Planet, The Learning Channel, and the National Geographic channel have employed many videographers who are willing to get up close and personal with nature.

VIDEO ART

This EFP style is still a well kept secret. The main reason for this is probably that the number of outlets for this style is quite small. Video art is not the type of on-location video to choose if you need to earn a living doing one style of video work. Video art serves an important role in a democratic society. It allows diverse views to be expressed, even if they are not the dominant ones in the culture. This diversity of viewpoints has a positive effect on a free society by stimulating people to think.

It is impossible to describe video art as a particular style. It is completely free form. It may resemble broadcast TV in length and form, while differing greatly in content. It can be a short piece that violates every known rule about pleasing an audience. Video art is the expression of the artist, who looks at the same things that we do, yet sees something different. It is this difference in vision that makes video art an untapped source of creativity—video art has the capacity to show us the world in a new way.

The process of creating video art is different from other EFP work in several respects. First of all, it is

A

B

Figure 3-16   (A) Shooting a nature program on location can present numerous problems. Nature shooters often must get up close to "nature." Sometimes a single camera operator must cope with rough conditions and sometimes very rough subjects. (Photo courtesy of Ed George) (B) Sometimes a video shoot is difficult because the subject is hard to find. This crew is attempting to find the subject of the shoot, a quail equipped with a radio transmitter, in a corn field in the Midwest. (Courtesy of Lee Vogel, Business Video Solutions, Inc.)

usually not done at a client's request, but because the video artist has the desire to express a topic or concept in a unique form. This means the time frame for creating the work is usually longer. It will generally be created in phases, with arts funding often sought for production and postproduction. Because the work is not being done for a client, the video artist has complete creative control.

Video art can combine EFP production, studio shoots, and complex postproduction techniques. It often entails use of advanced special effects equipment and software that allows the artist to manipulate the electronic signal. This can include digital processing of each pixel of information, varying the frequency of the signal, colorizing and polarizing, using multiple layers of wipes and dissolves, auditory processing, using feedback as a visual effect, and the full range of digital software effects. Software often used includes Photoshop, Illustrator, After Effects, Maya and related plug-ins, and image manipulation software.

Artists gain access to signal-processing equipment through media arts organizations located in diverse areas of the country, including nonmetropolitan areas. In postproduction, the editing rhythm is often a different tempo than conventional TV, either faster, slower, or variable. The video artist has unlimited possibilities. The only constraint is to make choices that stretch and enhance the existing conventions and allow the viewer to experience the world in an imaginative way. Broadcasters show various types of entertainment, nature and documentary programs, commercials, and sports. Corporations use and show training, sales, and demonstration videos. But where do the video artists show their work? In competitions, festivals, art galleries, museums, international festivals, site-specific installations, and on a few programs on cable or public TV. Innovative approaches in video art find their way into the mainstream by influencing approaches used in TV advertising. Many commercials are really a form of applied video art. Other mainstream areas that use video art approaches are promotional IDs used for stations, and the opening graphics and title sequences for all programs. Visual artists comfortable with electronic graphics equipment and software can apply their skills in these areas, as well as in helping create the overall design for these segments. EFP equipment is affordable enough that many college, art school, and university students can gain access to it. But without seeing it themselves, students are often slow in wanting to try this EFP style. The instant gratification of seeing your work on a monitor immediately after it is shot should lure many people to the video art EFP style. Unfortunately, however, with the exception of the very largest cities in this country, video art is virtually unknown.

Perhaps film still attracts so many artistic persons because of its long history and acceptance as an art form. TV, on the other hand, is often regarded as a medium of mediocrity, as evidenced by the constant stream of primetime fare that is usually tasteless, slick, insulting, or all three.

But broadcast TV is merely one method of delivering video; the networks are just some of the many programmers out to attract an audience. Other delivery systems for video exist, and some of them do seek out video art. The Internet and World Wide Web offer tremendous potential for video artists. By creating a home page with video presentation capability, a video artist can have a site that can display the artist's video work to millions with very little cost to either the artist or the viewing audience. Another growing possibility for video artists are alternative methods of distribution that have just recently become "mainstream." Podcasts, downloadable video for mp3 players, and "mobile TV" (video for cellphones) are providing new opportunities for video artists to get their video work to the eyes of interested viewers.

There are tens of millions of camcorders in homes in the United States and in other countries. This can only lead to what some call a "democratization" of portable video. Video can become a form of artistic expression for the masses, not just for the privileged minority with access to professional video equipment and broadcast air time. As portable video becomes more common, available, and easy to produce in years to come, more creative individuals will attempt to use EFP equipment, computer equipment, and the various exhibition outlets like the Internet for art's sake.

MULTIMEDIA

Since video as a means of conveying information became popular in corporations and other non-broadcast entities, videotape has been the dominant means of delivering the video to the viewer, although that is now changing to DVD, streaming, and podcasts. During the 1980s, both video disc and CD-ROM emerged as a means to show video to the intended audience, but both required playback equipment that was not as

Figure 3-17   A frame from a video art work entitled "To Erzulie." (Courtesy of Mara Alper)

common as videocassette machines were then. More recently, computers designed for home and office use are commonly equipped with internal CD-ROM and DVD players, sound cards, and stereo speakers, making these computers excellent playback machines for material produced on CD-ROM and DVD. This capability has further fueled the enormous growth in the use of video for playback in a storage medium other than videotape. Video can now be easily loaded onto an iPod or uploaded to a video sharing site like YouTube.

Multimedia has also grown because of the content of the material. By definition, it is a combination of media: not just video and audio, but all possible media that can be digitized and encoded onto a medium like CD-ROM or DVD. These storage formats are very popular, because they have high storage capacity and are capable of high-quality images and sound. Because they are digital, they have the random access ability to find information anywhere on the disc in a very short period of time. Perhaps most importantly, multimedia allows **interactivity**, so the viewer can easily select information for viewing and input information that prompts the viewing selection. This interactivity can be simple, as in a kiosk in a hotel lobby that lists restaurants in the surrounding area. The viewer touches a TV screen to make choices, such as the type of food preferred from a list of types. The next video that might appear on the screen might be a list of restaurants of that type (e.g., Italian or vegetarian). The viewer can then select from that list and be shown a picture of the restaurant and a sample menu. This type of interactivity is called **reactive** interactivity, where the viewer reacts to questions or choices on the screen.

Another type of interactivity involves the viewer at a higher level. This could be something like game playing, where the viewer is giving feedback to the system regularly. Other videos at this level involve the viewer in complex tasks, such as storytelling, composing, or game-playing. This type of interactivity is known as **proactive** interactivity.

An even more complex level of interactivity is also gaining popularity. This level is differentiated from others because it requires quite a bit of input from the viewer, and this input results in constant change from the game or program being viewed. An example of this type of interactivity is a virtual reality program. This interactivity is called **mutual** interactivity.

Multimedia is distributed in a number of formats, including CD-ROMs and DVDs for personal computers, game cartridges, and laser discs. Enhanced CD-ROMs can play music on an audio system. They also have multimedia material for playback on multimedia computers. The DVD format offers storage and playback of an entire movie with high resolution and excellent sound on one disc. Often a second DVD is included that contains commentary by the director and actors and/or special features. CD-ROM recorders have been common in computer systems since the late 1990s, and DVD recorders have been available since 2001.

INTERNET

Another outlet for video and audio production has emerged in the last 10 years. This outlet allows individuals to access information from places all across the world. It has the capability to provide excellent quality audio and video information. Almost all of this information is free to those who seek it, if you have the appropriate computer equipment. This outlet of course is the Internet. Broadly defined, the Internet is a collection of local networks gathered into a global network.

The Internet allows electronic mail (e-mail), a method of sending text information to other individuals who can access the Internet. The speed of sending the message is faster than any kind of regular mail, even Federal Express, but the same as voice mail. One of the best advantages is that e-mail allows for text that can be a word or two, or chapters from a planned book, or results of a recent experiment. Since the information is sent as text, the receivers can capture the text with their computers, insert it into their word processor, and edit or just store for future reference. They can also delete the message without ever wasting paper.

Users of the Internet can send, download, or upload programs, documents, pictures, or even video. Essentially, anything that can be digitized and stored can be sent via the Internet. The Internet is a storehouse of information that is almost beyond belief in its diversity and depth. Research on almost any topic that can be described in a few words is easy, quick, and can lead to voluminous information. Creating your own location on the Internet is relatively easy; searching for other sites is even easier. If you have an interest in the movies of Angelina Jolie or Brad Pitt, you can go to a search engine featured by one of the popular Internet browsers, type in the name of the actor, and the search engine will list many sites mentioning the name you entered. These sites can be visited through a clever system of links that allows you to travel from site to site by just clicking on your mouse. Your method might involve traveling first to a listing of movies that won Academy Awards and their stars. One of the stars named would be the one you entered for your search. You could scroll down the list and find other stars from that movie. You could click on another movie and that movie site might have a link to a site that has contents of the script for that movie. Clicking on that link will take you to the script site, which would list the name of the scriptwriter and have it as a link to other scripts. It is this method of easy travel that, among other features, makes the Internet so fascinating.

World Wide Web

Since 1992, the World Wide Web has become an important part of the way we communicate. The Web offers us the ability for communication with text, high-quality graphics, sound, and video. While audio has been common for over ten years on the Web at locations like Web radio stations and audio services (e.g., Accuradio), it wasn't until 2005 that video distribution has become not only accessible, but user friendly as well.

Major networks like NBC are making downloads of episodes of favorite programs available. iTunes sells episodes of television programs from a variety of sources (e.g., ABC, Comedy Channel, etc.). Perhaps more interesting, though is the ability of amateur videographers to upload their video to a site where many people can view it. YouTube, a site which first came online in February of 2005, became a favorite for people who likes to share video clips, much like the peer-to-peer audio sharing sites for exchanging MP3 audio files. Since that start date, millions have gone to the site to upload their video and watch video uploaded by others. Using Adobe Flash technology, video can be uploaded to the site easily. The site recommends using the MPEG4 video format and currently displays video in 320 x 240 pixel size at 30 frames per second. The result is viewable video that can be seen by almost anyone on the Web. YouTube can also accept video shot on cell phones. The site's slogan is "Broadband Yourself" and encourages everyone to share their video treasures. As of July, 2006 100 million videos were being viewed daily. The popularity of the site led to it being purchased in October of 2006 by Google, for $1.65 billion dollars.

Preparing and Shooting Video for the Web

Video can be placed on the Web and stored for two different types of transfer. The first type of storage is a video file that is downloadable. This file remains on a server's hard drive until a client requests the file. After a request, the server will send a complete copy of the file to the client. Once the copy of the file is completely received by the client, the client can then play the file for viewing. The second type of file transfer is called streaming. Files that are streamed are sent to the client in a continuous stream of data that can be played just after it is received. At the end of the streaming, however, there is no file stored on the client's computer. Streaming, like broadcasting before it, does not leave a copy of the program behind for later viewing. Video for streaming requires software that can accomplish several tasks.

Software programs are available on the market and as shareware that can prepare video for streaming. These programs can be "stand-alone" programs designed to do the tasks required by streaming. Some video editing programs have features that allow the edited video to be converted into a streaming file format. These programs generally have a few features in common. All of the programs must be able to take the video information and change the file format from the acquisition format to the streaming format. These programs should also be able to help videographers adapt the video to the smaller size display screen and lower resolution that will be shown on the Web.

The process of converting video into a file format capable of streaming on the Web begins with connecting a camcorder, player, or other video source to the computer that will be performing the encoding procedure. Raw video footage in a digital format can be loaded into a computer using a FireWire cable from the camcorder into the computer. The new video file is then placed into a Batch Window. At this point, settings are chosen that will select the desired file format for the converted video information.

There are a variety of video file formats to choose from when creating video streams. The most common formats are:

Windows Media
RealMedia
Quicktime
MPEG (in particular MPEG-4)
Macromedia Flash

Obviously, the viewers of streaming video can only view the project if they have a player program capable of reading files in the selected streaming format. Video producers who want to increase their business in production for the Web should be able to use all formats and encoding software.

The next consideration is the screen or frame size. While a standard size like 640 pixels by 480 pixels is comfortable for viewers, it is simply too big for easy streaming. This screen size would require an enormous amount of information that is too large for streaming to be practical. A smaller screen size will require a smaller amount of information, but will yield a smoother picture. This is an important factor because another variable in video quality is frame rate. Normally, standard NTSC video is shown at a rate of 30 frames per second. Most video projects on the Web must slow the frame rate down enough to allow the size of the file to be manageable. Until bandwidth problems lessen, the rate for much of the video on the Web is 5 to 15 frames per second. The rule of thumb for frame rates is simple: the wider the bandwidth, the more frames per second allowable. Video is often prepared in several versions by connection rate: broadband and 56 kbps (dial-up). Typically, 15 frames per second works for broadband and 7.5 to 10 frames per second for 56 kbps. These rates will yield video that is viewable, but a bit choppy. Generally speaking, the higher the data rate possible for streaming, the higher the frame rate. As more and more viewers leave dial-up connections behind and get broadband connections, higher frame rates will become common.

Movement Because of the small screen size and slower frame rate, some adjustments must be made in the shooting of the project. To keep file size manageable, the videographer should avoid shots that have much camera movement. To the computer encoding the video information, movement requires more information for storage than still images. More information to be encoded results in larger file sizes. Avoid unnecessary camera movement, because on-screen movement will be in the action you are recording. Don't add to the movement unless it is unavoidable.

Backgrounds Simple backgrounds should be used instead of cluttered, complicated ones. Too much meaningless detail in the background wastes bandwidth. Save bandwidth for the use of telling the story. Since your screen size is small, the viewer isn't always able to see it anyway. Make sure that you light everything that you want viewers to see. The encoding process often enhances the "grain" found in darkly lit parts of your picture. The smaller screen size demands that close-up shots be used frequently. Viewers need to be able to identify the subject and place it in the proper context. Therefore, wide shots should be used sparingly. Shots that have a canted or unusual angle should be used with great restraint.

Special Effects Although special effects like dramatic wipes or strobe effects are easy to accomplish with any nonlinear editor, using special effects may be detrimental to your streaming project. Because special effects require more information and thus more bandwidth, they can slow down the stream. Another consideration is the reality that special effects are much less discernable on a small screen than on a large screen. It is best not to take up valuable bandwidth with effects that are all but lost on the viewers. An appropriate axiom here would be "Keep it simple!"

A final consideration for preparing video for the Web is to make a decision about the audio that will be used for the project. Each file format used for video streaming treats the audio in slightly different ways. It is prudent to read the manual for the software program and make sure that the audio will be prepared in the appropriate way.

Once all of these variables are considered and choices are made, the video file is then ready to be sent to the processor to be converted from the video format to a streaming format. Some programs allow simultaneous viewing of the file while it is being converted. A split screen is shown with the original video on one side and the converted video on the other side.

Once the file is fully converted, it can be sent to the Web host, the computer that will store the video project information. The Web host is then capable of making the video stream available on request to other computers or clients regardless of their location.

In addition to the conversion process itself, some software will provide some publishing aids: shortcuts to uploading the converted file to the desired host Web site and detailed instructions that are easy for novices to follow.

The host site will sometimes have information on the site to facilitate the transfer process. Often sites will give specific instruction on how to send a file using FTP (file transfer protocol) and how to make the video file available to the audience. Also, the software should have precise instructions that will enable the videographer to prepare the file to be served from a host or server or embedded in a Web page away from the host.

The above-mentioned suggestions will continue to be appropriate at least until a significant portion of the viewing public obtains broadband Internet connections. When this occurs, full-motion, full-frame video will become easier. This translates into shooting video for the Web in a style that is similar to shooting video for typical exhibition on a broadcast station or any large monitor. In other words, as the technology improves, the restrictions on the videographer who shoots for the Web will diminish.

Interest in Internet use among corporations increased dramatically after the World Wide Web was introduced. Because Web sites are capable of high-quality graphics and sound, corporations began to see these sites as promotional opportunities. Products are routinely promoted on the Web in a variety of ways. Corporations are now creating **home pages** for institutional-type promotions. This presents an exciting opportunity for video producers in the future. Because Web home pages are not expensive to create or maintain, most corporations are interested in having them. Soon, full-motion video will be readily available at the home page for any viewer or **Web surfer** to visit. Where the home page once had a picture of the corporate headquarters or the main product of the company, now videos of a chief spokesperson might welcome you to the site and encourage you to check out the company's latest products or services by clicking on a button or linking to another page or site. These sites might contain information like a video brochure, or any of the standard, videotape-delivered corporate video products that have been in use for 20 years.

Vlogging

Vlogging or **video blogging** is found on a Web log that uses video as the primary content; the video is linked to a videoblog post and usually accompanied by text data to provide context. Some vlogs are just video diaries where people choose to chronicle their lives on video and then post the video to the Web for others to see and comment upon. Other vlogs are similar to newscasts. Many are created by one person, not an entire news staff. Vloggers are Web loggers (bloggers) who like to express their opinions in a place that can be seen by others … the Web. Vloggers often use the Web to express their opinions about political issues and to react to the way that traditional news media cover these issues.

Vloggers use **RSS** (really simple syndication) or some similar format to provide Web syndication. Readers and viewers of blogs and vlogs use **aggregator** software to feed them the vlogs and alert them when new material has been added to vlog sites.

Shooting for vlogs is similar to shooting anything for the Web. It is important to conserve bandwidth by keeping unnnecessary background to a minimum and concentrating mainly on the subject or object that is central to the vlog. In many cases, the vlog shows a talking head, similar to a news anchor.

Figure 3-18   Some vloggers create video blogs that are styled to resemble more traditional newscasts, with the vlogger appearing as an anchorperson. Instead of using a studio, vloggers often use their own homes as a set for the shot. (Courtesy of Jeff Jarvis)

Podcasts

Podcasts are audio or video files, such as radio programs or music videos, that are available over the Internet using either RSS or Atom syndication for listening either on mobile devices or personal computers. Atom is an XML (extensible markup language)-based protocol that facilitates data sharing on the Internet.

The term **podcast** can mean both the content and the method of delivery. Podcasters' Web sites may offer direct download of their files, but the subscription feed of automatically delivered new content is what distinguishes a podcast from a simple download or streaming. Usually, the podcast features one type of "show" with new episodes, either sporadically or at planned intervals, such as daily, weekly, etc. In addition to this, there are podcast networks that feature multiple shows on the same feed.

Podcasting's essence is about creating content (audio or video) for an audience that wants to listen when they want, where they want, and how they want. For aspiring videographers and video producers, it is another way of distributing programming that is low cost and relatively simple to achieve.

MOBILE TV

Mobile TV is video that is distributed to audiences via cell phones. This type of distribution is a new but fast-growing way to get video to large audiences. Content can be anything from a typical news show or segment to an entire episode of a TV series. The obvious concerns about mobile TV for videographers are the size and shape of the screen. Since cell phone video screens are commonly as small as 1.25 inch wide by 1.5 inch high, small detail in the picture may not be seen by the viewer. Also, the aspect ratio of cell phone screens is different than that of televisions. Although analog sets are 4 wide by 3 high and digital is 16 wide by 9 high, cell phone screens can be 4 wide by 5 high. This changes how mobile TV may be shot, since the width of the screen is often smaller than the height. As the construction and design of cell phones change, the screen dimensions may change also. One thing is certain, however mobile TV will become more important and almost ubiquitous in the future. Content providers are constantly working with cell phone service providers to work out plans for more and more video for distribution to cell phones. Just ask your friends if they have a cell phone. Chances are all of them have a cell phone that they carry with them most of the day, every day. This is an audience with a huge potential. Stay tuned for more exciting developments about producing video for mobile TV!

Cell phones are not only video "receivers" but can also be video recorders and senders. Some local television stations are encouraging cell phone users to shoot video clips or take still pictures at the scene of events that are newsworthy. Although cell phones don't have the capabilities to record high-quality video, they are capable of getting a shot of the scene long before the news videographer can get there.

Figure 3-19   Mobile TV, video sent to cell phones, is becoming an important revenue stream for program providers like ESPN. More programming outlets can lead to more opportunities for videographers.

SUMMARY

This chapter discusses the various types of video shot in the field for non-news uses. These uses include corporate and professional video, entertainment, commercials and public service announcements, performance videos, music videos, nature and documentary videos, video art, multimedia, and Internet and related videos.

Corporate video (also known as professional or industrial video) is nonbroadcast video created for specific reasons that further the goals of the company or organization requesting the video. This type of production includes corporate in-house news shows, training videos, teleconferencing, and sales videos.

Entertainment video includes video shot for the purpose of putting together programs that could be aired for broadcast, cable, or satellite distribution for a general audience.

Commercial and public service announcements are short projects, often 30 seconds in length, created for businesses and organizations and also meant to be distributed for exhibition to broadcast, cable, and satellite outlets.

Performance videos include video shot both for historical archive and for showing as entertainment. Often, the historical archive provides a record of a performance used by the creator (e.g., director or choreographer) for reference, résumé, etc. Sports video production includes both competition coverage, shot for exhibition to a general audience, and feature coverage for sports shows and highlights for news shows.

Nature and documentary videos are a growing style of video that has become more popular because of channels like Discovery Channel and Animal Planet.

Video art is a video style that cannot be categorized easily, as it encompasses many styles of work. In fact, video art may or may not conform to any established style. Video art is made as an expression of the video artists and may be entertainment or experimental.

Field production is also used when producing multimedia. Video is shot to be included in a presentation that may include text, graphic materials, film, and audio.

The Internet is playing a more important role in the production and distribution of video. Video is shot for streaming on the Web for many purposes, including corporate video and video for entertainment. In addition, many bloggers are using the Web to distribute their own video news programs, often low-budget simple productions that express the vloggers' political viewpoints. Video producers are also using the Web to store podcasts, video projects, and programs that are downloadable to portable devices for viewing by interested audiences. Mobile TV is the term used for video distributed via cell phones, and it is becoming an increasing important method of distributing video for news and entertainment.

The ease of uploading video and viewing video at Web sites like YouTube may revolutionize how we produce, distribute, and receive video programs. Amateur videographers now have an easy way to make their video projects available for viewing by a potentially huge audience. Like the file sharing sites for music has strongly affected the music industry, sites like YouTube will affect the video and broadcast industries.

4

Framing and Composition—The Language of Video

Before beginning any video shoot, you should have a clear objective or objectives in mind. In ENG work, the goal is to represent the reality of an event or story accurately, interestingly, and in an appropriate context. This involves a lot more than simply pointing a camera at a scene or subject. A news shooter must carefully select what to show and what to leave out. The ideal is to depict what he or she sees to be true at the location, both factually and emotionally.

In EFP work, the goal is usually dictated by the client or producer. The videographer is directed to tell a particular story in a way that will be understood by the intended audience. In a corporate video setting, the goal might be to communicate effectively the advantages and disadvantages of a new health plan to the employees. In a music video created for entertainment, the goal might be to capture visually a mood or statement intended by the musician's composition or song. No matter what type of presentation, you must plan all the elements of the story in light of the intended outcome.

Before deciding what type of shot to make—how to frame it, how to move the camera, or what focal length to use—you must know the message that shot is to convey. After all, the camera cannot think for itself. Every aspect of camera placement, focal length, camera height, and composition of the frame plays a part in the audience's ability to understand what they are seeing. Filmmakers spend years in school and even more years on the job developing these skills. Entire books are written to explain the complex relationships of visual elements. But one thing is certain: everything you place in your viewfinder must be there for a reason.

IDENTIFYING THE STORYLINE

Before you begin a shoot, ask yourself what you are trying to do. Reduce the task to its most basic description. If you can encapsulate the story in one sentence, you are well on the way to reaching your goal. A typical ENG example might be: students at a technical school come from other careers to study microelectronics and enhance their employment prospects. Every aspect of this story is contained in this one sentence. By giving yourself this starting point, you can expand the sentence until you have covered all the points in as much detail as is practical. For an average TV news story, length is the factor that determines how much you can put into that story. Because TV news is more of a headline service than an in-depth documentary service, a story such as the technical school would probably last only 90 seconds on the air.

This example can easily be translated into EFP terms. If the owners of the technical school want to make a one-minute commercial for the school, the basic ingredients of the story will be the same. In both cases, because of the limited on-air time, the videographer must make every shot count. Once you have a goal and a relative time constraint in mind, you need the means to reach that goal.

PART ONE: FRAMING—THE RANGE OF SHOTS

Just as a musician uses a finite number of notes to create a finished song, a video shooter uses a finite set of shots to create a story. The musician can vary the way each note is played, and there are infinite ways to combine notes. Similarly, the uniqueness of the videographer's art comes from the execution of camera shots and movements. Each type of image and camera move has a specific purpose and design. Before discussing the composition within any frame, it is helpful to catalog shots as they might be called for by a script or a director. Each type of shot sets a tone for the type of information contained in the frame. After understanding the type of shots required and their position relative to other shots in a story, we will examine their composition.

A photographer has three basic types of shots available for use in any project. The first type is determined by how wide or narrow the perspective is. The second type is described by some type of physical movement of the camera. The third type is a group of shots used to serve specific functions in the production process.

Shots by Perspective

Early television studio cameras were equipped with a turret lens—a round plate that had a selection of lenses (usually four), each with a different focal length (e.g., 10mm, 35mm, 50mm, 100mm). The camera stayed at one position and a crew member simply rotated the turret to use a lens of a different **focal length** to get a closer or wider shot. Today's cameras have variable focal length lenses, or zoom lenses, that effortlessly go to any focal length in the range of the lens. Nevertheless, the old terminology of early film and TV is still used to describe the content of the frame.

The Wide Shot

The **wide shot (WS)** is sometimes called the **establishing shot**, the **master shot**, or the **long shot (LS)**. It is generally the first shot a photographer should take. It is the most important shot in terms of establishing the setting and action. Typically, it shows the subject from head to toe. One variation, the extreme wide shot (EWS) or extreme long shot (ELS), shows the full subject relatively small compared to the surrounding environment.

The wide shot is made with a short focal length and, therefore, a wide angle of view. This shot should include all the visual elements of the story or scene, if possible. In the example of the technical school story, the wide shot would be used to cover or visually explain that original one-sentence description of the story. The wide shot would include the students, instructor, classroom, and electronic equipment. Every key element should be there. The shot should show relationships and activities that yield information: the older-than-expected students, the instructor in an active teaching role, and the equipment that is the subject of the lesson. These visual elements give the viewer information that reinforces the comments of the announcer or newscaster. Usually, each story contains more than one wide shot.

Just as a writer expands a single sentence into several paragraphs to make a complete story, so too a videographer expands a story idea into visual sentences and paragraphs. A story can be broken up into its component parts. It has a beginning, a middle, and an end. These parts are a series of ideas or facts that combine to form the overall statement used to achieve the goal of the project. Visually, the story must be broken down into those same parts. Think of each part or sequence as a story unto itself. In this analogy, the wide shot would serve as the subject of the visual sentence, or as the beginning of the story. There are two characteristics common to any wide shot.

Establishing the Scene   The beginning of any sequence starts with a shot that establishes the idea of that sequence (or paragraph of the script). The wide

Figure 4-1   This wide shot establishes the setting and what the sculptor is doing; it is clear that he is a sculptor in an older building.

shot reveals the relationship among all the key elements of what the viewers will see in the piece. (See Figure 4-1.)

Within a typical sequence of shots, the wide shot should contain every object or subject that will be recorded in the remainder of the sequence. If we are going to see a man using a lathe while the reporter talks about him and his current job, then the first shot should show the man, the lathe, and his location. In the opening shot of the sequence, relate as much information as possible to the viewer. Questions that should be answered in this example's first shot would include:

- What is the setting of this scene?

- How large is the setting or location?

- What are the important objects?

- What is the main character doing in relation to the objects in the setting?

- What is the machinery or equipment doing?

The shots that follow in the sequence further detail the answers to these questions. Without the wide shot, those details could appear unrelated and therefore seemingly irrelevant or even confusing to the viewer. Ideas that must be expressed in a story can often be

said in a very short time, not leaving enough time for a visual sequence to develop. Most of the time, a wide shot takes care of this problem, because it gives a maximum amount of information in a short period of time. Again, a wide shot expresses a complete thought or idea.

At other times, a wide shot can simply be used to establish the location for the sequence that follows, such as showing the outside of the school building. In other storylines it might show the skyline of a city to let the viewers know what part of the country they are seeing. In these cases the WS stands alone and simply says, "Here we are in/at. . . ."

Creating the Third Dimension The information included in a wide shot is only one of several components required for a good image. If the framing is off, or the shot is too busy or otherwise aesthetically unpleasant, you have not maximized the impact it can have on the viewer. Because the TV is a two-dimensional surface similar to a piece of paper or a canvas, the third dimension must be created. The illusion of depth is what makes a two-dimensional picture come alive. The wide shot is the best place to create the **depth** of the scene. More on how to do that a little later.

The Medium Shot

The **medium shot** or **MS** is the workhorse of most TV stories. It can be defined as the development shot. It concentrates on the subject with little attention given to anything else. If a wide shot shows someone from head to toe, then a medium shot shows a person from the waist up. A photographer might use two variations: the medium long shot (MLS) shows a subject from just above or below the knees and up; the medium close-up (MCU) shows him or her from about the chest up.

In most cases, depth and relationships within the frame are brought out with subtleties of lighting or just a portion of other elements in the medium shot. Lighting can play a major role in bringing out the textures in a medium shot to enhance the feeling of three-dimensionality. Medium shots are usually made with a narrowed field of view or a midrange focal length— not wide, but not telephoto either.

As with all shots, you should maximize information when using the medium shot. You do not need to show a subject's relationship to the surroundings, but you must show more detail of who or what the subject is, or what the subject is doing. In the technical school story, one medium shot might be a student assembling a circuit board. The important elements of the shot are the subject's face, arms, hands, and the circuit board. An important difference between the execution of the wide shot and the medium shot is the number of angles available for the medium shot that are not always available for the wide shot. By keeping the same focal length and distance from the subject, the shot can be taken from the front, at a 45° angle from the front, at the side, over the shoulder, at low angles, or at high angles. (See Figure 4-2.)

Where one wide shot will suffice to start off the story or segment of a story, many medium shots are needed to supply the bulk of the storytelling material. The wide shot can contain many elements or subjects. Our tech school scene has the teacher and maybe a dozen students. Each of them can be used for the developing medium shots. Think of the wide shot as a completed jigsaw puzzle. We are now dividing the puzzle up into different sections for closer examination. These sections are the medium shots.

The key element in the medium shot is variety. If you can shoot the subject from several different angles, you can quickly make quite a few medium shots. The more angles and the greater variety of shots you have when the material gets to the editing stage, the more creative choices you have in assembling the finished story.

The Close-up Shot

The **close-up** or **CU** shot gives the intimate details of the subject. If the medium shot shows a person from the waist up, the close-up includes just the head and shoulders. In our jigsaw puzzle analogy, the section of the puzzle that made up the medium shot is now going

Figure 4-2   These three angles are some of the possible medium shots of this sculptor at work.

to be taken apart to its individual pieces. The close-up is made with the lens at a telephoto focal length. Now the individual subject is going to be examined part by part. A close-up shows the emotions in the face, the manipulation of the subject's hands, or the details of a craftsman's work. (See Figure 4-3.)

The close-up can be thought of as the final shot of a sequence or the fully expressed idea initiated in the wide shot. In our technical school example, the close-up might be a shot of the student's hands positioning a chip or some other element onto the circuit board. The elements in the shot are the hands, the board, and the part being fitted to the board.

Depth in a close-up is completely reduced to the texture of the objects being photographed. The detail of the close-up subject usually gives the depth necessary for a good picture. The number of angles from which a close-up can be shot is often more limited than either the wide or the medium shot. The variety lies in shooting the many different elements of a subject in close-ups, such as face, hands, or even feet (they may operate some tool with a foot pedal). Other possible close-ups in the technical school example might be of a supply of parts or a book of instructions. In other words, you can shoot a detailed close-up of every element contained in the medium shot. It is always a good rule to include some form of relationship with the medium shot, however. The CU of the electrical parts works better if a hand comes into the frame and removes a part for use, or in the case of a CU of a textbook, if a hand reaches across it to turn a page. Movement, especially by humans, is always interesting.

The Extreme Close-up

The **extreme close-up** or **XCU** adds drama or extra emphasis to a series of shots. In our example of a person, the XCU would be a shot of the subject's face or even just the eyes. This shot is made at the very far end of the telephoto lens, zoomed all the way in. In many storylines, this shot could be out of place because of its dramatic emphasis, but when used correctly it can greatly improve the quality of the piece. This type of shot brings the viewer into a world not normally seen in such detail. The extreme close-up presents a larger-than-life image that can be extremely interesting for a viewer. (See Figure 4-4.)

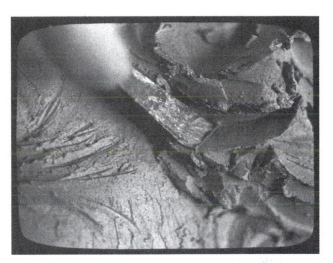

Figure 4-4   This XCU of the sculptor's tool shaping the clay demonstrates the texture and pliability of the clay, which is not normally seen.

The subject should be chosen carefully and the purpose of this shot should be clear. For example, in the technical school story, the XCU could show the tip of the soldering iron as it melts some solder onto the part just put in place during the close-up shot. Seeing the solder actually run and the smoke billow out from around it adds a sense of drama and visual excitement to a rather mundane classroom setting. An XCU of the student's eyes in a story like this might not be appropriate unless the student is wearing glasses and the reflection of the smoking solder can be seen in that reflection (thereby tying the shots together).

The XCU need not be related to the action; it could be simply a detail shot—for example, a single stamp in a story about stamp collecting, or a hole in a leaf as part of a story on crop damage. If used properly, this shot can be the most memorable—and therefore most expressive—in any piece, but it must be used at the correct time, have a good relationship to the surrounding shots, and show an appropriate subject. By using the XCU, video pieces can demand a great deal of attention from the viewer.

Camera Action Shots

This category of shots is defined by moving the camera or changing focal lengths as the shot is recorded. In general, these shots can add dynamics, drama, and interest to the story when the shot's perspective changes as the viewer watches. *Caveat videographer:* avoid moving camera or moving lens shots for the sake of movement alone. Unmotivated movement appears cheesy and fake and grows annoying because it does not stem from the subject. Instead, it is merely slapped onto the shot for no apparent reason—perhaps a failed attempt to cover up for the lack of a dynamic subject in the first place?

The Zoom Shot

For a **zoom**, the glass inside the lens is rotated, either by hand or by an electronic **servo** that operates by the push of a button. As the glass rotates, the image is either magnified to appear to move closer (zoom in), or it appears to move away as it becomes smaller (zoom out). As probably the most overused and misused shot in the field of videography, the zoom is the ruin of many ENG packages and EFP projects. The first thing any new shooter does is work the zoom control until it is worn out. The best way to teach a new photographer to shoot is to tape the zoom servo to *off*. A zoom should be considered a link between two static shots or a means of maintaining proper framing or perspective. Just as in any two individual shots, the ending shot of the zoom should contain different, or at least more or less, information than the beginning shot.

One common mistake many videographers make when starting out is zooming to or from the middle of the frame, keeping equal distance on all sides of the subject as they zoom. To add more visual interest to the movement, try keeping two sides of the frame static in reference to the subject as you make the zoom. (See Figure 4-5.) That means you will zoom into or out of one of the four corners of the screen, while adding a little pan to the movement. This makes the shot pivot on the subject, adding more emphasis to that subject in the frame, which is what you want your viewers to notice.

The two most appropriate uses of a zoom are to show relationships and to emphasize a subject within a larger picture. The first is a zoom-out, and the second a zoom-in. If the topic is a profile of an unemployed worker, you might shoot a scene at the unemployment office. By starting on a tight shot of the subject waiting in line and then zooming out to a wide shot that

Figure 4-5   A zoom from the subject in the field reveals the location. A good zoom always incorporates some panning and tilting of the camera.

reveals the multitude of people waiting in line, you can show the subject's relationship to the surroundings by revealing those surroundings after establishing the subject. This would also give the viewer the perspective of this individual being buried in a mass of people. The relationship between the individual and the rest of the room is well established. Alternately, you might want to emphasize that individual after first establishing the situation. A zoom-in from a wide shot of that room to a tight shot of the very tired-looking subject emphasizes this person. The shot draws the viewer's attention from the overall picture to the plight of one individual who is part of the situation.

The basic "rules" for the zoom shot are as follows:

- Always zoom from something that's important to something else that's important.

- Make sure the beginning and ending shots can stand alone as static shots.

- Zoom out to show a spatial relationship.

- Zoom in to emphasize a particular element contained in the wider picture.

Always keep in mind the time it takes to zoom. A zoom that is too slow might not be able to be used by an editor; a zoom that is too fast might not allow the viewer time to perceive and understand what is taking place. If you have the time and enough tape or gigabytes, shoot a zoom three times: once slow, once medium, once fast. Then choose the zoom with the best speed when the piece is edited. A good rule of thumb is not to make any movement last more than five seconds, and generally to try to limit zooms to about three seconds. This is enough time to execute most shots and still be short enough to fit with almost any editing pace.

When shooting for special effects or for an "artsy" look, a slow zoom can give the feel of gentle movement and can add to the pace and flow of an edited piece. In a faster-moving piece, a snap zoom can be done by putting the auto-zoom servo on *off* and manually wrist-snapping the zoom ring from one extreme to the other (assuming you have a professional-quality camera with a zoom ring). This produces a very dramatic result and should be used with that effect in mind. Too much of any one technique may be bad for the piece. The more noticeable or dramatic the technique, the easier it is to overuse it.

The Pan Shot

A **pan** is the horizontal pivoting of the camera: left and right. In many ways, the pan is like the zoom in how it is used, the two major uses being to show relationships and to show more information than is contained in just one static shot. A pan from a raging brush fire to a nearby house can show the danger the house faces due to its proximity. This type of shot does not work well if the pan lasts too long or if the angle of the pan is too great. If the pan lasts too long, it might not fit into the edited story; if the angle is too great, the relationship might be lost because too much ground is covered between subjects. Panning too fast can blur the picture to the point where nothing is recognizable during the pan. Generally, this is not acceptable. Try to pan slowly enough so that you can obtain a good freeze frame from your video at any point in the pan. You may need to rehearse a pan several times—if you have the time—to find the right speed. Again, try to stick with the three- to five-second rule. There are, of course, many times when a long pan is desirable. (See Figure 4-6.)

For a shot of an extremely long line of people, a long pan can be more effective than several static shots

Figure 4-6   Within this scene, a good pan could be from the composition on the left to the one on the right. Together they form a complete picture of the area.

or a zoom. The same is true for long angles of pans. While about 30° to 90° is as far as you should normally pan, 180° or even 360° can be made to work in the right situation. For instance, when showing how a small town has decorated the entire main street for Christmas, a 180° pan from one end of the street to the other might be very effective. In the middle of a neighborhood totally destroyed by a tornado, a 360° pan could give a viewer a very dramatic overview of the destruction. Again, as with the zoom, the purpose of the pan should be to impart as much information to the viewer as possible in the least amount of time.

The Tilt Shot

A **tilt** is like a pan, but it is the vertical—not horizontal—pivoting of the camera: up and down. The same basic rules apply for its length, speed, and purpose. The shot must start on one properly framed picture and end on another, showing a relationship to, or more information about, the overall subject. For example, an ENG package about earthquake damage might begin with a shot of a reporter at the base of a hill; then, as the reporter speaks, the camera tilts up to reveal a house perched precariously at the top of the hill.

The Dolly and Truck Shots

In all the shots previously discussed, the camera is in a fixed position while shooting. The **dolly** and **trucking**

(a.k.a. tracking) shots require the camera to move while the shot is being recorded. For the dolly shot, the camera moves in closer to, or backs away from, the subject. For the truck or tracking shot, the camera moves left or right, rolling on wheels or sliding on tracks or riding one some kind of truck or cart device.

For EFP work, dollies and trucks should be done on a dolly mechanism or a wheeled tripod. On uneven surfaces, tracks or a platform can be put down for the tripod or pedestal to move. This makes the shot time consuming to set up, rehearse, and execute, not to mention more expensive to the overall production. For ENG work, the use of such extra equipment is usually out of the question. Therefore, dolly and trucking shots become walking shots for most ENG work. Sometimes someone with a bit of ingenuity can improvise a dolly or truck using a grocery cart, wheelchair, bicycle, golf cart, or car if there are crew members to help.

The point to keep in mind when using the dolly or truck shot is that the *perspective* of the shot constantly changes as the camera position changes. This is the purpose of a dolly or truck. These are similar to zooms and pans in that they move from one shot perspective to another in real time, but the difference is the type of perspective change. This change can add a sense of drama by, say, moving closer to the subject in a dolly-in shot, or moving away in a dolly-out shot. The advantage of the dolly shot is that the focal length can stay the same as the shot changes. If the focal length is short, the depth of field will be great; moving the camera in to a closer shot does not lessen that depth of field but exaggerates the perspective. In a zoom, the depth of field steadily decreases (as focal length increases) while you zoom in, and the perspective is compressed. The resulting size of the subject might be similar between a zoom-in and dolly-in, but the visual perspective is quite different.

The dolly or truck can also be a point-of-view shot. In ENG, the walking shot gives the feel of a point of view, if not of a specific character then certainly of the viewer, as if he or she were actually present. This point-of-view idea can work in many stories. For example, in the earlier shot of the long line of people, a trucking shot along the line would give the viewer a firsthand look at what it would be like to be walking along that line.

Another use of the dolly or truck shot is to replace a pan shot to maintain perspective. Instead of panning a long row of TV sets in a showroom, a trucking shot can keep each set in the same proportion (size and angle to the camera). The desired feeling is not so much the relationship of the sets to each other and to the room, but the vast number of sets.

Dolly and truck shots have a beginning, middle, and end, just like all camera movement shots, and each part must be a good shot. For any moving subject, such as a walking on-camera host, the dolly or truck can keep the subject framed while revealing changes in the background that impart new information to the viewer.

To get a feel for the effect of a dolly or truck shot, try dollying a shot for which you would normally zoom, or trucking a shot for which you would normally pan. Often, you will notice that dollies and trucks have greater impact and are more pleasing than zooms and pans. The only drawback is that trucks and dollies require more time and sometimes more skill and equipment than zooms and pans. A walking shot can be too shaky to look good in many segments because it looks out of place with all tripod shots in the rest of the story. While most ENG work should be done on a tripod, spot news is actually a good place to learn the effect and importance of a dolly or truck shot because of its hurried, go-with-the-action nature. Still, you can zoom and pan a lot faster than you can dolly and truck.

The Crane Shot

A **crane (a.k.a. pedestal)** shot is like a dolly or truck, in that the entire camera moves rather than pivots, but instead of moving in and out (dolly) or side to side (truck), the camera moves up and down. For this type of movement, the camera may be mounted on a tripod or pedestal or body rig that allows the camera to be raised or lowered, or it may be mounted on a crane device that allows more dramatic, swooping movement than a simple tripod, pedestal, or body stabilizer. In the absence of a mounting device, the videographer must squat and stand while holding the camera to achieve a pedestal or crane shot. For this shot, the same guidelines apply as for dollies and trucks: keep the movement smooth; move neither too fast nor too slow;

Figure 4-7   For this scene, the shooter could crane or tilt up from the man's shoes to reveal him standing forlornly in the rain, perhaps having missed the bus for a date.

keep the principal subject framed; be aware of the change of perspective on the background; use the movement sparingly—only when motivated for dramatic effect or to reveal the most appropriate visual information in the most effective and timely manner. (See Figure 4-7.)

Special-Use Shots

This category of shots is defined by the function of the shot and not by the focal length, framing, or camera movement. These shots usually serve as transitions from one part of the visual story to another or as aids in the editing process to maintain continuity. The following shots allow the editor to take the viewer smoothly through the flow of the story while not affecting the visual style.

The Cutaway Shot

As its name implies, the **cutaway shot** is used to cut away from the action. When an editor is putting together a series of shots and wants to avoid a **jump cut** (a break in continuity), a cutaway is used to take the viewer to a different subject so that time or subject position can change on the first subject without disturbing the continuity within the overall flow of shots. (See Figure 4-8.)

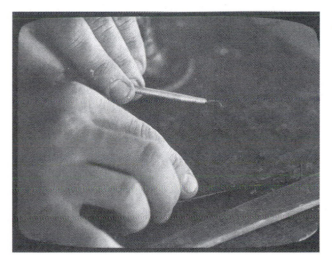

Figure 4-8   In the series of photos of the sculptor, this shot of his hands coming into the frame to exchange one tool for another is a cutaway from the main action of sculpting. It is still part of the story, but does not involve the main action of the subject.

The most basic example of this is during an interview in which two different **soundbites** are **butted** (used back to back). The interviewee's head is not in the same exact position from one shot to the next, and therefore the edit can result in a jump cut: the interviewee's head jumps instantly through space and time to another position. This is a break in continuity for the viewer, who is used to the illusion of real time within a story.

In TV news, the solution to the problem is a cutaway shot to the reporter listening to the interviewee. This shot (picture only) is often called a **reversal**; it reverses the viewer's perspective from the person being interviewed to the reporter. It is inserted over the edit so that the audio is not disturbed and the bridge in time is not noticed by the viewer. This type of shot is often used in an action sequence in which time compression is necessary; that is, when the subject must get from one part of the scene to another in less time (or more) than it really took. In a sports story in which the beginning and end of one boxing round is to be shown, the editor must cut out the middle of that round. To avoid the appearance of the boxer instantly jumping from one part of the ring to another, the editor uses a shot of the crowd for a few seconds between the first and second shots of the fight. The audience's attention is momentarily diverted by the crowd cutaway. This type of cutaway is sometimes called a **reaction shot**; it shows the reaction of a person or persons to the action. Both reaction shots and reversals are specific forms of cutaways.

Another type of cutaway is the **insert shot**. This shot—usually a close-up—reveals some element within the longer shot in a closer perspective. In the boxing example, some tight shots of the boxers' fists flying and feet dancing and faces grimacing would be inserts. As is the case with all edits, continuity should be maintained with insert shots.

The generic cutaway is any shot away from the action or subject but related to it. It can be a wide, medium, or close-up shot. A good cutaway should fit with the other shots, just as all shots in a story should blend together. In the two examples above, the cutaways are shots of people involved in some way with the subject, either listening or watching. These usually make the best cutaways, but sometimes they are not available to record. Often you have to find another related shot. It might be the scoreboard at a sports event, or the clasped hands of a couple being interviewed, but it must always relate to the subject.

The cutaway is used within a sequence of shots involving the same subject in the same location; it is *not* a transition shot. To go from a shot of the mayor in an office to a shot of the mayor at a fundraiser is not necessarily a jump cut. The audience knows there is a change of time with this edit and perceives it as natural. In the movies and higher-quality video productions, very few, if any, cutaways are used, and no one misses them. The reason is that the sequences are so well thought out that the action flows naturally from one shot to the next. Even in shooting news, with a little practice, you can learn which shots to get and how to piece them together so that no cutaways are needed.

In some instances, cutaways slow down the pace of a story without adding any new information to the subject. In many cases, the reporter cutaway can be eliminated by editing in shots of what is being discussed. If the mayor is talking about cutting spending on street maintenance, then why not show shots of the types of maintenance being cut? If you find creative ways not to use cutaways or to use cutaways that illustrate the story, your video pieces will generally look much better and be more interesting.

The Transition Shot

The **transition shot** is an editing tool that allows visual continuity and flow while avoiding abrupt changes in the sequence of shots. Unlike a cutaway, which covers jump cuts in the middle of a single action such as an interview, a transition shot gets the subject or flow of action from one location or action to another. Any two shots edited together that are very similar in composition can create a jump cut. You can't go from the subject talking on the phone to the subject typing at the computer in the same location. A transition such as a tight shot (XCU) of the phone receiver being hung up or an XCU of fingers on the keyboard would bridge the two action shots. The former ends the phone action shot, leaving the subject free to start the next action, and the latter begins a new action. You would use one or the other, not both, because by themselves they are similar shots; they are both XCUs of the same hands.

A subject moved from one location to another in an edit sometimes results in a jump cut if the shots are too similar. The simplest example of a transition shot to use in this case is a **cleared frame**. Keep the camera recording as the subject moves out of the frame. You are left with an empty picture for a second or two and are now free to establish the character anywhere else you wish. The reverse of this is also true. Start with an empty frame for your next location and let your subject walk into the shot. In some cases, it might be easier to pan to or away from the subject to get the subject in or out of the picture.

One very common transition shot in both ENG and EFP is the building or room **exterior shot**. It is usually used to start the next sequence of shots. This is useful as a transition for a subject who is changing geographic locations, because it not only avoids a jump cut across locations but also establishes the setting for the following series of shots. Typically, exterior shots are followed by **interior shots** that reveal the subjects in their new location.

Close-ups make excellent transition shots. Because viewers see so little of the scene or subject in a CU or XCU, it leaves viewers at the end of an expression or thought. Starting a sequence of shots with a CU begins the action or thought before revealing the subject, which also works. The close-up of a sculptor's hands shaping clay, or even the XCU of the tool working the clay, can be the end of one sequence or the beginning of another. If it ends a sequence, you could then cut to a wide shot of the artist placing the sculpture on a shelf at the end of the day. This jump in time is blended into the story by causing the viewer to concentrate on only one small aspect of what the sculptor is doing before coming back to another time in the same location. Use of this method makes it possible to maintain the level of action and information without wasting time on neutral transition shots, such as the subject leaving the frame. Each story has many ways of being told; the style and pacing often determine which type of transition shots work the best. It is a good idea to shoot for many different possibilities and make the final decision in the edit room.

PART TWO: COMPOSITION—AESTHETIC CONSIDERATIONS

Standing back and pointing a camera with the lens at wide angle does not make a wide shot. The image created in the viewfinder must be recognizable by the viewer and contain some form of meaning. A jumble of elements all competing for attention with no unifying theme, direction, balance, or point of interest causes the viewer to look elsewhere.

Many aspects are involved in making a good picture. You can spend an entire college term just learning all the ways to create a well-balanced, pleasing image. Elements such as size, color, relative position, brightness, darkness, and angle all contribute to the aesthetic forces within any frame. Some of these elements will be discussed in the lighting chapter. However, several

rules and guidelines exist that will help you establish a working knowledge of good framing and composition.

Creating the Third Dimension

One of the first things you try to accomplish in any picture is a sense of space. Lighting is a great way to create volume (and it will be covered in the lighting chapter), but any shot you make needs to address this issue. The three ways to avoid a flat picture and create volume are:

- The use of the foreground.

- The use of the vanishing point.

- The use of focus.

Adding dimension or depth is the first tool to improve the viewer's perception of a shot.

Use of the Foreground In the simplest form, the use of the foreground is the establishment of an area or object near the camera and placing the subject in the midground while lining up a good background. The picture has a feeling of depth because the objects are at very different distances from the camera. (See Figures 4-9 and 4-10.) This technique composes the subject along the **z-axis** (depth), in addition to the **x-axis** (horizontal, or width) and **y-axis** (vertical, or height).

Many times it helps to exaggerate this effect (forced perspective) by placing the foreground object extremely close to the camera. Unlike backgrounds, if a foreground is out of focus, it should still be a recognizable form, such as a tree limb or a fence. If the foreground object is too out of focus, it may help in framing but not in adding editorial content or contextual information to the frame. As a general rule, the subject must not be minimized by foreground or overpowered by background. Lighting or, as we shall learn later, placement in the picture can make the subject stand out even with the other elements present. The subject need not be the brightest area of the picture or the largest, if additional factors are present. Other elements can often serve to give the most emphasis to the subject, no matter how small it is.

Use of the Vanishing Point In many shots for which a foreground is not practical or desirable, the use of an-

Figure 4-9   The straight-on shot (left) is flat and uninteresting. All the architectural lines are horizontal and vertical with no foreground or background. Choosing a point of view with foreground (right) gives the picture depth because objects are both near to and far from the camera.

Figure 4-10   While the left shot shows the building clearly, the total picture area is not used to frame the subject. By moving under a nearby tree (right), you can use a branch to frame the picture. The branch not only adds interest and balance to the scene, but also a foreground that increases the depth of the picture.

gles can give the feeling of continuance to the picture. In a drawing or on the screen, diagonal lines seem to converge at some point, implying a third dimension of depth or movement to a distant point. For example, when you look down a straight line of railroad tracks, you can see that, at a certain point, the two rails seem to come together. This is the **vanishing point**. (See Figure 4-11.)

Break the picture down into horizontal, vertical, and diagonal lines. The best examples of this occur when shooting buildings, because the lines are easy to see. As the camera's position and resulting perspective change, so do the lines. When you walk around a rectangular structure, notice that from straight-on at the front, all lines are horizontal (top-bottom) or vertical (sides), with no diagonals. However, as you walk to the side to include both the front and side of the building

Figure 4-11   Even though this railroad track is the same width all the way to the horizon, it appears to narrow as it recedes into the background, thus creating a vanishing point.

Figure 4-12   The angle here causes the train to be keystoned and the other parallel lines to converge on the vanishing point and lead the eye to the central element of the image—the exit to the outside world.

in your perspective, the parallel top and bottom lines of the front and the side appear to be diagonal lines. At the point where the horizontal lines appear diagonal in the field of view, you can easily create depth in a two-dimensional picture. This is called **keystoning**: framing an image, such as a building, so that the parallel top and bottom lines become diagonal, converging toward a vanishing point and creating depth.

Besides creating volume, these converging lines can take the viewer's eye to a subject or important element of the picture. Our eyes naturally follow these **leading lines**, extending them even if they don't continue on their own. By creating a focal point, you can lead the viewer to the main element of the shot. (See Figure 4-12.)

Use of Selective Focus   Another way to create a sense of volume within the frame is to have well-defined areas of focus. This technique is particularly useful when working with longer focal lengths that tend to **flatten** a shot by compressing perspective. A shot of a subject walking down a crowded street, as seen through a telephoto lens, would not highlight the subject if all the faces in the shot were equally in focus. By finding ways to decrease depth of field (shooting with a lower f-stop, perhaps, or standing back and zooming in), you can bring the subject into sharp focus and have both the background and the foreground drop out of focus. This shallow depth of field creates the look of depth and better expresses

the distances between elements in the frame. Even without a foreground, this technique can greatly enhance the three-dimensional qualities of any picture. (See Figure 4-13.)

Figure 4-13   By defocusing the foreground and background, the subject in the midground—the artistic writing—easily dominates the picture.

Effects of Focal Length

As focal length changes—the lens is zoomed in or out—many things change in the resulting picture. The most basic change is the size of the subject: it gets larger as the focal length increases (zooming in). This magnification of the subject also has other effects in the overall picture. As the field of view narrows (the focal length increases), the quantity of background decreases as its size increases. Because the field of view is in the shape of a cone, as you zoom in, the rate of size increase for the background is much faster than either the foreground or midground of the picture. This visual effect is known as **compression.** Objects at different distances from the camera and in line with each other appear to become closer to one another as the field of view narrows (the background seems to be moving forward), even though their sizes relative to each other never change.

This phenomenon can be used to great advantage by the photographer. For example, in a movie where the hero is running down the street toward the camera while being chased by a truck, a telephoto lens (long focal length) makes not only the hero appear large but the truck as well. The compression of perspective in the shot can make it look as though the truck is only inches from the hero when in reality the truck could be 100 feet away. The same shot done with a wide field of view would show the truck's position more clearly and not have the same dramatic effect. The drawback to the zoomed-in shot, however, is the perceived speed at which the truck is closing in on our hero. Because of the compression, even if the truck is rapidly gaining on him, the truck's size barely changes. Image size doubles in reverse proportion to the distance change. For the truck to double in size, it would have to come half again as close to the camera as it is. For a telephoto shot, that could be quite a distance.

In contrast, at a very wide field of view just the opposite effect of compression occurs. In wide-angle shots, things in line with the camera tend to appear much farther apart than they really are. If the object of our truck chase is to see the speed at which the truck is closing in on our hero, the wide shot would do it. With both elements close to the camera (our hero is still the same size in the frame), the oncoming truck could easily double in size within a second or two (halving the already short distance to double in size), thus exaggerating the speed. These effects can be used to bring even static objects closer together or farther apart in a picture. (See Figure 4-14.)

A

B

Figure 4-14   For both pictures, the girl in the foreground is framed in a medium shot and the boy in the background is the same distance from her. Only the photographer's distance and focal length changed. For A, the shooter stood close and used a wide angle to exaggerate distance. For B, the shooter stood farther away and used a telephoto angle to compress distance.

Distance

In place of focal length change, you can substitute camera distance to change the size of the subject. By simply moving the camera closer to the subject, you increase its size in the frame. In the early days of photojournalism, when each lens had one fixed focal length, the shooter had to walk to or from the subject to change the size of the image. Many people still refer to a wide shot as a long shot because you had to walk a long way back to get a wide shot with a fixed focal length lens.

With today's zoom lenses and wider angles of view, you need not walk as far or as much. The thing to keep in mind is the **perspective** of each type of focal length, especially when shooting medium or close-up shots. Zooming in creates less depth of field and less of a three-dimensional view; the perspective is compressed, or flattened. When the videographer walks closer to the subject, the perspective stays the same for the midground and background, but the foreground begins to distort in an effect called **exaggerated** or **forced perspective**. (See Figure 4-15.) The depth of field does not change, but the three-dimensional effect is made more prominent by the rapidly increasing size of the foreground (the opposite effect of zooming in). Again, the objects double in size as the distance to them is cut in half. Unlike zooming, this effect is achieved by moving the camera closer to the subject while maintaining a constant focal length.

Figure 4-15   A wide-angle lens (in this case an extreme wide angle, or fisheye) exaggerates the depth perspective to the point of bending the straight lines of the goal in the foreground and the horizon in the background.

Balancing the Picture

Up to now we have discussed composition as it relates to the camera, lens, and subject size and distance. The final aspect of composition is the arrangement of the elements within the frame. Before you push the record button, you need to ask yourself, "How can I maximize the impact of this shot?" Too many videographers in television never ask that question. Flipping on almost any newscast, you can see the results of "point-and-shoot" news photography. Shots are framed for a subject with no regard for the rest of the picture. A photographer's eye should be trained to look at the entire frame and all the visual elements within it, not just what initially attracts our attention while looking at a scene.

Too often balance is thought of in terms of being centered, or using **symmetrical balance**: having the same amount of space on all sides of the subject. Much of the time this is not the case. Balance is far more complex than that. Often, **asymmetrical balance** makes a better composed image: having objects of different sizes, contrast, and so on balance the image. Imagine two elephants balancing on a seesaw. They are symmetrically balanced; they have the same shape, mass, weight, color, contrast, line, and texture on both sides of the fulcrum. Now consider a balanced seesaw with an elephant on one side and a mosquito on the other. Obviously, the mosquito must be much, much farther away from the fulcrum to balance the elephant. The two sides of the image have different mass, weight, and so on; yet, the seesaw is balanced—asymmetrically.

As we will learn in lighting, a little of something can go a long way. A very small but bright object can upset the balance of a picture quite easily, but can also be positioned to *add* balance to a picture. While there are some basic rules that can lead you to balance the composition of elements within a frame, there is no substitute for what your eye tells you as you look through the viewfinder. Some arrangements just feel better than others when you look at them.

Frame Dynamics   A well-designed garden maze ensures that anyone seeking the center has to make several circuits before they find that center, and they still have to search for an exit once there. A well-designed picture should do the same thing. It has one entrance for the eye, one main subject, and several points of departure away from it. There are three basic patterns to the movement of a viewer's eye.

1. **Circle**—the classic symbol of unity forms the simplest compositions, allowing the eye to circle the image.
2. **Pyramid**—the eye starts at the bottom left, traverses up to the pinnacle, down to the right corner, and finally back to the left to complete a strong and unified composition.
3. **Irregular shape**—allows the eye to move in a dynamic and asymmetrical flow, adding energy and tension to the image.

Western culture has programmed our eyes always to start from the left side of any scene. In theater, the left side of the stage is said to be the strong side for entrances. That does not mean that side of the frame is where the subject should go. The eye starts there, but your composition can take it to wherever the subject is in the frame. It is also possible to have the eye start in other places. A bright sun in the upper right corner of the frame can catch the eye first and then send it down to settle on two surfers in the lower left corner. (See Figure 4-16.)

Figure 4-16 The bright sunset catches the viewer's eye first, and then moves it to the surfers in the foreground.

Lines As we have seen with the vanishing point, where our attention is directed to the point of convergence, lines can play a very large role in leading our eyes. Diagonal lines create vitality with their implied movement. The eye is drawn to anywhere in the frame where two lines cross or one line suddenly changes direction (e.g., a corner). An isolated vertical line, such as a tree, pole, or even a standing person, is noticed first in the picture

and takes precedence over any horizontal or diagonal lines in the scene. (See Figure 4-17.) To achieve a pleasing composition, a horizontal line must cross this vertical element at some point. When a vertical line is not interrupted, it simply splits the screen, creating two disconnected sections of the frame.

Figure 4-17 A lone vertical element—the beachgoer—dominates the picture, intersecting with the horizontal element—the ocean's horizon line.

Color A very important tool in the design of a frame is the color of elements within it. This can be a difficult task for the videographer using a black-and-white viewfinder, though color viewfinders are found on most cameras today. A red rose may stand out as the dominant element in the frame when viewed in color, but in the viewfinder it may be next to impossible to pick it out in the field of grays. In the absence of a color viewfinder or screen, a shooter needs to use one eye to see color and one to look through the viewfinder, combining the two versions to realize the actual outcome of the video. Composition includes giving weight to brighter colors.

Videographers should also know the concept of **complementary colors**, or **contrasting colors**. A color stands out more vividly in relation to its opposite. Continuing the example of a red rose, this flower is seen most vividly when set against cyan elements in the shot because cyan (blue-green) is the opposite of red. A simple way to remember contrasting colors is to create a quick color wheel. (See Figure 4-18.) When you shoot an object, such as a rose, note its dominant color, such as red, and then look for ways to set that

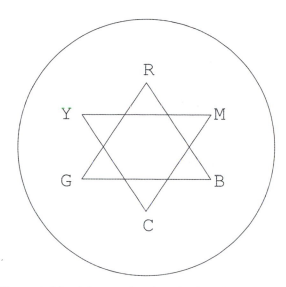

Figure 4-18   This simple color wheel can be easily created by writing the three primary colors of light, RGB (red, green, blue), in a triangle, and then writing the three secondary colors, YMC (yellow, magenta, cyan), in their respective places between the primary colors in an inverted triangle.

object against elements with contrasting colors, in this case cyan leaves or flowers.

The Rule of Thirds   This very important principle of image composition provides an easy way to frame objects by using a nine-square grid as an overlay to the picture. The concept, called the **rule of thirds**, divides the screen by thirds vertically and horizontally. (See Figure 4-19.) It is based on the ancient Greek discovery called the **golden rectangle,** or as Da Vinci called it, the **divine proportion**. An accurate golden rectangle has an aspect ratio of 1.618:1 (the Greek letter **phi** is used for the number 1.618). That ratio is found by dividing the longest side of the rectangle by the shortest side. A true golden rectangle is more like the aspect ratio of a movie screen. The TV aspect ratio of 4:3 (1.333:1) does not contain the same geometric properties as a golden rectangle, but the one-third and two-thirds divisions are a close approximation. As more and more consumers take the plunge into high-definition television, with its movie-like aspect ratio (16:9, or 1.778:1), the TV screen will take on more of the artistic look seen in other forms of Western design.

As you look at any composition, fit the elements of the scene into the grid, positioning them on the four intersections of the lines. Try this idea with a sunset and a very flat horizon, such as the ocean or a large

field. You'll find that long or tall objects, such as the horizon line and maybe a telephone pole, look better lined up along the lines of the grid and not centered in the spaces of the squares. You'll also find that smaller objects like the sun look better placed at the intersection of the lines.

Figure-Ground   One way to organize the elements of the frame is to use the concept of **figure-ground**, figure being the main visual element or subject of the picture—the shape that you notice first—while ground gives it the context in which to exist. Figure can only exist with a ground to place it on. You cannot see figure and ground at the same time. Photographers who point and shoot run afoul of this concept all the time. A figure is any element in the frame that achieves prominence over the rest. By concentrating on just the element you *want* to be the subject of the shot, you cannot see the entire frame—a version of not seeing the forest for the trees.

The best example of this is the infamous tree positioned so it comes perfectly out of the top of someone's head. In another version, a lamp or other object sits atop the subject's hair. (See Figure 4-20.) In these cases, the photographer is so focused on the subject that the other aspects of the frame are literally not seen. But the viewers are not concentrating in the same way; they are just discovering the shot and see it first as simply figure and ground. The tree and head, or lamp and head, appear to be one continuous form. Signs can work the same way. If they are too large or too overpowering in the shot, they become the figure and the person standing in front of them becomes the ground. This is not effective communication.

It is easy to control figure within ground just as you would any object you wish to highlight. Through lighting, color, focus, position, and so on, you determine which object will be figure and which will be ground, despite the complexity of the shot.

Balance   A balanced shot is one in which the elements within the frame are at equilibrium with all the forces of the frame. And there are many. The frame is like a scale; elements and groups of elements have visual weight determined by size, shape, contrast, direction, or just plain interest. Large dominates small; a black bean dominates when seen in a group of all white beans; a regular shape such as a circle dominates within a group of irregular shapes; and certainly a

Figure 4-19 Use of the rule of thirds makes this sailboat and seascape a balanced picture. The sea is in the lower third of the frame; the boat is at B2; and the cloud is at A1.

snake sliding across the floor dominates any picture regardless of composition.

Balance is determined by two factors: the *visual weight* and the visual pattern's *direction of movement*. Position in the frame has a lot to do with an elements' relative weight. A large object near the center of the screen can be balanced by a small object close to the edge of the frame. Objects at the center or on the vertical centerline of the frame have less weight than the same object at the sides of the picture. A face in the left third of the screen can be balanced by **look space** or **lead space** in the right two-thirds of the screen (assuming the person is looking screen right). An element at the top of the frame is heavier than when it is

at the bottom. Because of our left–right conditioning, an object on the left side of the frame has greater visual weight than one on the right side. A picture can be balanced by total symmetry, but these compositions rarely hold visual interest; they are boring. By using a more dynamic framing scheme, such as the rule of thirds and figure-ground, combined with the concepts of eye movement, you can design an image that holds the viewer's interest and therefore imparts more information.

The movement, or implied movement, within the frame is the other part of the balancing act. Converging lines create movement to the point of convergence. Your eye follows a curved line in a field of all straight

Figure 4-20   The subject is composed well in relation to the leading lines (sides of bridge), but the lamp is positioned so it becomes part of the figure instead of ground, appearing to stand atop his head.

lines. One of the most important movements with which you will deal in video is the movement created by the human face. The direction in which a person looks or walks creates a very strong movement in that direction; it is a force that needs to be neutralized in some form within the frame, usually with **lead room**—empty space in the two-thirds of the screen in front of the person.

Composing Specific Shots

Just as shots can be described by their focal lengths to communicate the size of the subject within the frame (WS, MS, CU), there are specific shots that can be called by their common names. Their execution is done by convention. The most common specialty shot is the interview. When a producer or reporter says, "Let's set up for an interview," they have a specific style of framing in mind. The conditions of the location or situation or artistic inspiration can change this, but for the most part an interview shot looks the same from Maine to California, from small town local news to the networks.

The Interview Shot

The basic framing of the interview shot is the head and shoulders of the subject, hence the name **talking**

head. The standard reference point for where the bottom frame line would cut the subject is the "necktie knot." If the subject, man or woman, were wearing a tie, the bottom of the frame would be just below the knot. A looser version of this shot cuts them off at the top of the breast pocket. A shot tighter than the necktie is sometimes called a "choker." To simplify all the compositional information we learned above, there are two basic rules for framing the talking head and having it look good every time.

1. *Never let the subject's eyes go below the horizontal centerline of the screen.* If the focal length changes from the waist up to a close-up of the face, the eyes of the subject should always be in the upper half of the screen, somewhere on or near the upper-third (using the rule of thirds). (See Figure 4-21.)
2. *Keep the tip of the subject's nose on the vertical centerline of the screen.* If the subject is talking to a reporter off camera, you will notice that this rule puts the subject's head slightly off center, somewhere on or near either the left or right third (again applying the rule of thirds). Because the subject is not talking to the viewer directly, this type of framing leaves look space in front of the subject. This space helps balance the shot asymmetrically; it counters the movement created by the direction of the subject's eye line; and it also implies that someone is there just out of the frame. That implication becomes yet another force in the dynamics of the picture. You can start to see how these simple rules support the concepts of composition.

You may at times want to include the interviewer in the shot. If this is the case, you must pay close attention to the balance of the picture; you don't want the reporter to be the figure and the subject to become the ground. If only a portion of the reporter's head is in the frame, make sure the subject is not centered, but off to the other side. As more of the reporter is seen, make sure you are using the tools of composition (e.g., rule of thirds) to keep the subject the main point of interest.

As mentioned above, the standard framing for the talking head should be tight enough to show the sub-

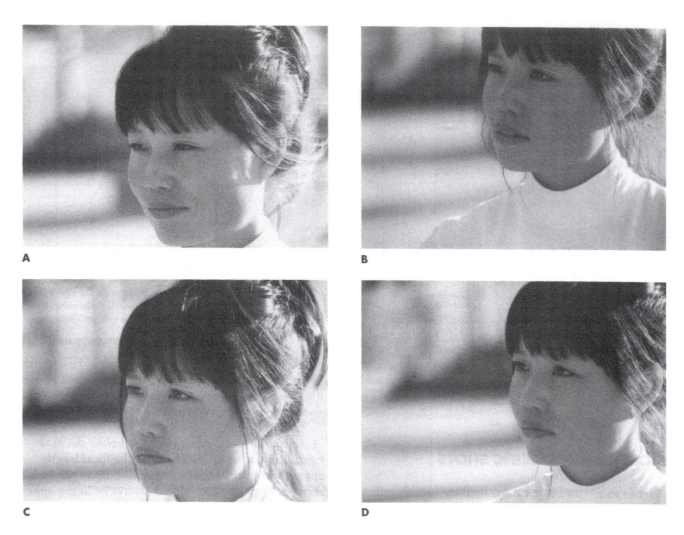

Figure 4-21   (A) The subject is framed with her entire head, placing her face too low—her eyes are not at the upper third. (B) The subject's face is framed too high, as if she is pushing out of the top of the frame. (C) The subject's head is framed dead center, leaving too little room in the direction she is looking. (D) A properly framed head for this focal length—her eyes are at the upper third and the look space in the left two-thirds balances her head in the right third.

ject's face clearly on the average TV screen. In the case of chokers, as on a probing interview on *60 Minutes*, the framing may be extremely tight. You will notice that as the top frame line closes in on the face using the rules stated above, it begins to cut off the top of the head. One of the biggest fights you will ever have over composition with coworkers will be over this effect. Untrained producers will call for **head room** or scream that the top of the head is cut off; they can't see all of the subject's hair. Take refuge in the concepts of good composition. By allowing the face to slip to the bottom half of the frame (eyes below the midpoint) you add weight to the hair of the subject (top

of the screen is heavier) and thereby throw the picture out of balance.

The edges of the frame have a force all their own. As an object begins to near or partially exit any side of the frame, the frame acts as a pull on that object. For a talking head, the face is the center of interest and therefore the main element. When it sinks toward the bottom of the frame, it appears to fall out of that frame. The hair being cut off by the top of the frame produces a feeling of the subject rising, but because the hair is not a major element or focus of the picture, its force carries little weight and is easily countered by the grouping of eyes, nose, and mouth—the figure of the scene.

Be careful when framing subjects too tightly, though. An interview with a welfare mother who has had her food stamps stolen could be a close-up of her face to show the viewer her emotion. However, the same type of shot in an interview with a city official regarding an upcoming change in street signs would not have the same meaning. Reserve the close-up of faces only for emotional or dramatic subjects. Children are the biggest exception to this rule—they almost always look good in close-ups.

Use caution not to overdo the facial close-up. It is basic conditioning to zoom in for a tight face shot when the grieving mother of a dead child starts to cry. While some may argue that the emphasis is needed to convey the full impact of emotion to the viewer, there is also the argument that this type of shot is an uncaring, vulgar invasion of the woman's privacy. It may indeed be more dramatic to zoom out from such a scene to give the subject some space, if only symbolically.

TV is the best medium for conveying emotions, especially in news photography. Ethical principles suggest that the emotions portrayed should be true to your subject (accuracy), but they also should not be offensive to your viewing audience (do no harm). Some subjects deserve more respect than to have their worst moments seen larger than life in everyone's living room. The moral values or degree of good taste you express in your shooting should be the same as you would express any time in your life. The tight head shot can be a powerful tool both artistically and emotionally, but you must be careful how and when you use it.

Effects of Background and Focal Length In some cases, the background can be of such importance that the framing or placement of the subject in the frame is dictated by that background. The best setup for an interview with a farmer about a flooded field may be a wide shot of the field that includes the standing farmer (remember how a single vertical figure can dominate). The farmer may be framed head to toe, and if you place the farmer on the edge of the flooded field (rule of thirds), the impact is enhanced from both a visual and informational point of view. An interview background should add to—*not distract from*—the interviewee (figure–ground principle). If an appropriate

background cannot be found, then choose a neutral one, or use a focal length that produces a depth of field shallow enough to take the background out of focus.

When setting up an interview shot with a specific background, first choose the background. Add the subject to the shot. If the subject does not conform to the framing rules mentioned at the beginning of this section, do not bend the rules, but "tweak" the camera location and/or focal length to satisfy the framing concepts. A very common misuse of background and subject occurs when the photographer tries to put a sign over the shoulder of the subject. If the sign is too high, many new photographers shoot the interview from a low angle or frame the shot so that the subject's eyes are below the middle of the screen. Both generally produce a very uncomfortable shot and overemphasize the sign (again, figure–ground). Never let the eyes of the interviewee or the interviewer go below the horizontal midpoint of the screen. Simply move the camera and subject farther from the sign so that the sign can be placed in the deep background to maintain good framing. Do not force bad framing on your subject just to get a "good" background. A little experimentation usually shows a way to make both satisfactory.

The Reporter Stand-up Shot

The **stand-up** shot is a specialized version of the interview shot used especially in TV news. For EFP, this concept can be used for any on-camera appearance by a narrator who is talking *directly* to the audience. Because of this **direct address** to the audience, the framing of the stand-up is very important. A general rule for this shot is never to frame the subject looser than the waist up or tighter than the breast pocket top. This allows the viewer to have good eye contact with the talent and feel a personal link, which helps establish credibility.

If the shot is framed too loosely, the importance of the subject can be reduced or even lost in the background and the impact is greatly reduced. (See Figure 4-22.) Again, there are ways around this, if careful attention is given to the rules of composition. The talent must be the focus of the shot, or why else have him or her in it? Background is important, but very much a secondary part of the picture. The subject's monologue should help design the shot and determine the type of background used. If the script is general, then the background should be as well. If the script deals with a power plant, however, perhaps the power plant should be in the background.

Figure 4-22   The model in this picture blends into the objects of the scene, becoming part of the background. There is no separation.

Many of the same rules that apply to the interview shot apply also to the stand-up shot, such as placing the subject correctly in relation to the background and keeping the subject's eyes above the middle of the screen. As in the interview, the best camera elevation is a **normal angle**, or **eye level**. One thing this does is place any visible portion of the horizon at the eye level of the subject. The horizon line running through the picture directly behind the eyes of the on-camera subject draws added interest to their face. This is good. (See Figure 4-23.) Any other angle tends to be either unflattering or can add or subtract too much importance from other elements in the picture.

Sometimes, however, a different angle does work for example, if you are shooting a reporter in front of a field of flowers. When the camera is at eye level, the background covers about half of the frame, but the sky might be overcast and "blowing out" (overexposing) the upper portion of the frame behind the top of the head. If you raise the camera above eye level to a **high angle**, or below eye level to a **low angle**, the viewer has a different perspective on the background. In this ex-

Figure 4-23   Any time the camera is at eye level with the subject, the eyes should be at the horizon line. This draw's attention to the subject's eyes, which is desirable.

ample, because of the brightness of the sky, a high angle can place the horizon line at the very top of the frame, leaving the reporter framed against nothing but flowers. This composition can be more dramatic.

The difference between the stand-up and the interview shot is that the subject is talking directly to the camera. The need for the implied second person, the listener, is gone. This allows you more latitude to frame the subject in different areas of the image and to fit the background in around the subject. For any off-center positions, the talent's inside shoulder (closest to the middle of the picture) should be angled slightly away from the camera to help add a three-dimensional quality to the shot and visually direct the viewer's eye to the return journey to the background as part of the overall eye movement. Again, the subject is always the dominant element in the frame, even if he or she is part of the background. A good rule of thumb to simplify stand-up framing is never to let the talent be more than six feet from the camera if you are using wide or medium focal lengths.

The stand-up shot has many variations. The most common is the **walking stand-up**. As with any shot, it should have a purpose. The reason for a walking stand-up shot can be as simple as adding a little movement to an otherwise static composition, or as complex as moving from one animal to another in a story about the county fair. The movement should be slow and comfortable. A relaxed walk not only provides the necessary movement but also visually adds to the conversational tone appropriate for a stand-up. The subject should already be walking when the shot starts and can either stop partway through it or continue to walk throughout the shot. The correct framing needs to be maintained on the walking subject. Depending on other compositional tools, it might be necessary to zoom out as the subject approaches to maintain her in the waist-up framing. Other frame dynamics might work, such as having the reporter grow in size as she approaches the camera, thus drawing the viewer's eye. This works as long as the reporter is the center of attention right from the start of the shot.

As a general rule, the zoom-in is used much more frequently than the zoom-out in the stand-up shot. The zoom-in, or **push**, adds emphasis to a stationary subject, whereas the zoom-out, or **pull**, usually deemphasizes the subject by bringing attention to the ground of the shot. A zoom-out can also be effective when there is some additional information to be imparted by expanding the shot. Keep in mind that doing this generally renders the reporter insignificant, leaving only his words to convey continuity in meaning. His physical presence has been diminished by the new subject of the shot. An example of this is a reporter doing a stand-up in an area that is very dry due to a recent drought. The shot starts as a waist-up shot; as the talent talks, the camera zooms out to show the reporter at the end of a lake's dock with no water in sight. The dry lake bed becomes the new subject of the picture and the reporter fades to ground.

Another factor in stand-ups is direction. The audience is being spoken to, and therefore the direction of the stand-up should always be toward the camera or audience. If the talent is entering the frame from off camera, the direction should still be toward the camera and not at a right angle to it. This usually requires some camera movement to get the talent into the frame in the least amount of time, but the feeling of **positive motion** (motion toward the camera) is worth the movement. Walking into a static shot is time consuming and usually awkward due to the transition period of being half in the frame and half out of the frame. If the transition can't be made quickly, find another way of doing it.

The only time a talent should have **negative motion** (motion away from the camera) is when taking the viewer to another location or showing the viewer something behind the place where the stand-up starts. This can be very effective if the shot is well thought out in advance. The audience does not like to have subjects turn their backs to them without good reason. The main goal is always to communicate—every shot, every subject.

FOLLOWING THE ACTION

Following the action combines all shots and camera moves. Spot news is the best example of this concept, because of the severe time constraints on getting the visual story and the level of action during the shooting. As a story unfolds under the fast-paced conditions of spot news, the shooter tries to stay with the subject or the important aspects of the story. To do this, the news photographer's position and camera zoom must be used to maintain good framing and get all the different shot types necessary to tell the story. Because of the fast pace, the camera should never stop rolling. Often a zoom is necessary or a camera position must change, but the important idea is that the action must always be followed. The action can be allowed to leave the frame (a transition shot), but it must be picked up again with a minimum of lost time.

Sports coverage is the easiest example of following the action (or "staying with the ball"). The action should determine how the shot is framed and what the camera must do. If the action involves more than one subject, such as in basketball, then frame for them all. If it only involves one subject, such as a football running back, then stay with that subject in the best framing to describe the action visually. In some cases it might be best to hold the same focal length and let the action take place while panning to keep the action in the frame. Too much camera movement or zooming can ruin the visual presentation of an event.

All the rules in the previous sections apply to following the action, especially the rule that too much of anything is bad. A videographer needs to do what is necessary to get the shot. But if the piece overuses pans

Centerline of picture

Figure 4-24   As the camera follows the skater, she is left of the centerline (framed on the third), leaving her lead room to the right into which to skate.

and zooms, it might be too annoying to watch while yielding little information to the viewer.

One important rule for composition is always to lead the action in the frame. A runner on a track, an ice skater on an ice rink, or a paramedic rushing a gurney to an ambulance, should not be framed in the center but slightly off center, on or near either the left or right third (again, rule of thirds), with the empty side of the picture in front of them for proper lead room and image balance (asymmetrical). (See Figure 4-24.)

Through the use of the empty space in framing an action, you give the impression that the subject's has someplace to go, and the dynamics of the frame make the figure's movement in that direction seems natural. The subject should not be running into the side of the

frame, creating a look of falling out of the picture. There should always be space left into which the subject can run, even before he or she starts any movement; for example, a runner in the starting blocks should have the space ready to fill before the gun sounds.

BREAKING THE RULES

Rules are simply guidelines to help understand the basics of portable video. Once you become proficient with the basics, you will begin to see the ways you can break the rules and still achieve truly great results. The looking off-camera places the person with eyes at either the top left or right top right third, filling the other two-thirds with look space. Nonconventional framing might place that person's eyes on one of the bottom thirds, but only if the resulting headroom reveals something of importance to the story in the space above the subject's head. Or the frame might place the subject on the "wrong" third—still on a third, but with the look space to the subject's back instead of to the front of the eyes. (See Figure 4-25.) Again, this should only be done if this space behind the subject reveals something of importance to the story.

SUMMARY

Stories can be told with nothing more than the three basic shot perspectives: LS, MS, and CU. Of course, many other shots are available, and experienced videographers know how to use them all. Additionally, shots can involve camera movement, such as a zoom, pan, title, or crane. Some special-use shots include cutaways and transitions.

In addition to framing, the aesthetics of composition are also crucial to successful shooting. These include creating the third dimension, understanding focal lengths and distance, balancing images asymmetrically, applying the rule of thirds and the figure-ground principle, and using appropriate look space or lead room along with not too much head room. These guidelines cover the basic tool chest for recording images for ENG and EFP. By applying these conventions, and by knowing when to break them for effect, you can create video pictures that are both powerful and pleasing, communicating their messages in the most effective ways.

A

B

Figure 4-25   (A) Demonstrates conventional framing with the talent in the left third balanced by look space in the right two-thirds. (B) Demonstrates nonconventional framing with the normally-expected look space behind, rather than in front of, the subject, in this case to draw attention to the building. This suggests the subject had to step outside to get a cell phone signal, further emphasized by the canted camera angle.

talking head is a perfect example. By ignoring the basic rules of framing, it is possible to put the interviewee anywhere in the frame if you know what you are doing. For example, conventional framing of a person

5 Scriptwriting

Portable video projects come in all sizes and shapes. They can be long or short, dramatic or comic, fictional or factual. Whatever form they take, they all begin with a script. Scripts are necessary for ENG and EFP, because they are blueprints or diagrams of the way stories are put together.

Regardless of style, intent, or format, video scripts have something in common: they are all written for the spoken word—for the ear—and for the visual message—for the eye. Writing for video—writing to be seen and heard—is unlike writing for the print media—writing to be read. Readers of the print media can read at their own comfortable pace. They can re-read words or sentences whenever necessary. This puts the burden of comprehension on the reader.

In video, the script must be written in such a way that it is comprehensible to the audience the first time it is viewed and heard (unless it is a training video that can be replayed). All viewers see and hear the video at the same rate. Even if viewers watch a program by themselves and are able to replay it, video scripts should be understandable at the outset.

Writing for any script requires both common sense and talent. A writer needs common sense to realize that writing for the ear requires relatively short sentences, words, and phrases that are easy to pronounce and unambiguous in their meaning, and a conversational style. Writers demonstrate their talent by conveying precise meaning and selecting creative and interesting approaches to the material. This is not always easy—many scripts deal with mundane factual material, such as a piece explaining how a mowing device is connected to a tractor. A talented scriptwriter can take dull, factual material and present it in an interesting way.

ELECTRONIC NEWS GATHERING

Scripts for ENG stories are generally written by the news reporters who cover the events for those stories. These journalists are often trained in broadcast journalism and have certain conventions they have learned to follow. **Hard news** stories, such as major fires, crimes, or elections, require quick turnaround time—the story is often written the day it is broadcast or even just minutes before it airs. **Soft news** features, stories that do not necessarily involve hard news and are not time sensitive, are more like EFP projects, because they can allow for more planning time and need not be aired the day they are shot. They have a longer "shelf life" than hard news stories. (See Figure 5-1.)

W5H and the Inverted Pyramid

Whether hard news stories or soft news features, ENG projects are written to convey precise and understandable material in an informative yet interesting way. The written material should address the well-known "five Ws and an H" questions (W5H) that all journalists are trained to answer: who, what, where, when, why, and how? These questions are often diagrammed

```
Bighorn Sheep pkg

(chopper nat sound up)

Attached by a rope to this helicopter are sheep. . .Rocky Mountain bighorn sheep. .
.animals that were once a natural part of the Southwest.  But today, in northern New
Mexico's Santa Fe and Carson National Forests. . .it is only through efforts like these
that the sheep have returned to their historic rangeland.

SOT AMY  in 40:19  "The operation has been an unbelievable, logistical undertaking,
because this involves working in a wilderness environment, which are very
unpredictable." out 40:29

Amy Fisher, who heads up the bighorn sheep project for the New Mexico Game and
Fish Department, says the goal is to capture and move 20 to 30 adult sheep. . .any
lambs would be a bonus.

(NAT SOT "Watcha doing, huh?")

STAND UP  "Behind me is the Pecos Wilderness Area where the sheep have come
from--they were re-introduced there some 15 years ago.  Now, part of that herd will be
headed to another Wilderness area called Wheeler Peak."

Before heading out to their new home. . .these sheep are weighed. . .examined. .
.inoculated with antibiotics. . .

(NAT SOUND "respiration. . .16. . .16. . .pulse. ..)

. . .all in a very intense outdoor mobil clinic of sorts where seconds matter.

SOT "We gotta keep handling time down, we gotta keep temperatures down and pulse
and respiration down.  They actually could die from the handling procedure."

The sheep are driven by truck to a different forest. . .their new home. . .a place where
their presence is a step toward bringing this ecosystem back to the way it was.

SOT "It represents a real gift to the state of New Mexico."

In northern New Mexico. . .Bonnie Holmes, for CNN."
```

Figure 5-1   This script for a news feature includes natural sound on tape (SOT), footage of sheep being handled and transported, and a reporter's stand-up shot. (Courtesy of Bonnie Holmes)

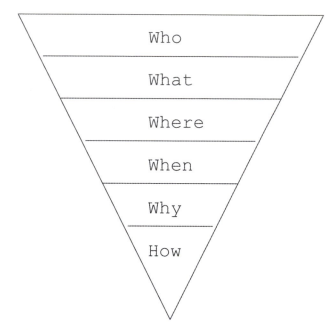

Figure 5-2   The inverted pyramid of journalistic questions.

as an inverted period, with the most important information at the top, or front, of the story and the more detailed, fill-in information at the bottom, or end. (See Figure 5-2.) In this way, if the story has to be cut short to clear airtime for another, breaking story, the end can be cut off without losing the critical information at the start.

While the inverted pyramid is a useful tool that all journalists learn, some choose to arrange the information differently, developing a unique style. A common example is starting a script with a "hook" that might be, say, a "how" question, followed by the basics of who, what, when, and where. A story about a chef, for instance, might begin: "Butter ... that's how Chef Ima Cook keeps her customers coming back. It's her secret ingredient." After that opening, the story could then reveal where she cooks, what her best dishes are, and so on. As with any other craft, it is wise to learn the basics of the W5H and inverted pyramid first and apply them to perfection. Then, once you know how to

change the basics with purpose, you can develop your own "voice."

Writing to the Visuals

The biggest difference between ENG and EFP scriptwriting is that ENG scripts are almost always written after the video has been shot. After an event has been covered, the reporter reviews the footage and writes a script so that the raw shots can be edited into a finished story. This process is sometimes called "writing to the visuals." This includes scripting a brief explanation for the reporter to say in cases where the video is missing some element, but also not overscripting—writing too much when the visuals convey the story. This procedure of scripting after the shoot is necessary because the reporter is often unsure of what is going to happen at the event or what the usable footage will be until after the recording has been made. Keep in mind that a reshoot or second take of an event is often impossible in ENG.

The ENG script is written between the time the event is shot and the time it is broadcast. The word "broadcast" here refers to all possible means of distributing, or "casting," the story to an audience, including over-the-air, cable, satellite, Internet, podcasting, and the like. For traditional television broadcasting, this usually means writing the script during the afternoon just before the evening newscast. The ENG writer has hours or sometimes just minutes to write the script. This is quite different from scriptwriting for EFP.

Writing Interviews

Not all ENG writing occurs after the shoot, however. In the case of interviews, reporters need to script their questions in advance. To be sure, they need to be flexible and adapt to each situation. After starting with the scripted questions, they might discover a more interesting angle during the shoot, in which case veteran reporters know to follow a line of new questions that explores that angle. However, that new angle is only discovered in response to carefully thought-out questions in advance. With well-scripted questions going in, the reporter is ready to follow the script or to adapt and follow a new angle if one presents itself.

You do not want to write **close-ended** questions, those that can be answered by simple "Yes," "No," or "I don't know" responses. These don't give you anything to use in editing the piece. For example, consider a feature about the local dog catcher. A close-ended question, such as "Do you like your job," does not require the dog catcher to speak much. Instead, you want to write **open-ended** questions, those that elicit sentences that can be used as soundbites in the video. An open-ended prompt, such as, "Tell me about your favorite part of this job," is more likely to result in useful soundbites, perhaps the dog catcher enthusiastically relating a story about reuniting a lost pet with its owner. Some writers prefer **two-pronged questions** in which a short, factual answer is followed by a longer, expository response. An example of a two-pronged question is: "How many years have you worked here and what is the most unusual thing you have seen in that time?" This might elicit a nice and usable response such as, "In the 15 years I have worked here, the most unusual thing I ever saw was ..."

Writing Style

Many books cover in detail the writing style for broadcast and electronic news. This text cannot cover every consideration, but the most foundational considerations are presented here. Use these guidelines when you write scripts for ENG. Keep them in mind for EFP writing, as well, because they are generally good points for most kinds of writing.

Primacy and Recency The theory of *primacy* states that we tend to remember first things—images and sounds that we first encounter before others. The theory of *recency* argues that we also tend to remember most recent things—images and sounds that are freshest in our memories. These two theories argue for the importance of a strong open and close in a news script. Begin with a powerful image and soundbite to tease the viewers into the story. The middle should then be brief and should show and tell both. The close, being the most recent in the viewers' minds after the story ends, should go out with a bang: another powerful image and soundbite that give the story closure.

Present Tense, When Possible Be cautious using "today" and "yesterday," because these words are often unnecessary and are implied in each day's news stories. For the immediate past, such as a police rescue in the last few hours, you can use the present (e.g., "Police rescue ..."). For the longer past, such as Abe Lincoln's death, obviously you should use the past tense, but because you're writing for a present audience, look for ways to give your writing a present "spin" (e.g., "A new discovery about Abe Lincoln, who was assassinated in 1865 ...").

Action Words Write action rather than description. Television uses both pictures and sound, so always think of aural and visual imagery in your scripts. For example, write, "Kruschev pounds his shoe on the podium," rather than, "Kruschev gets angry."

Active Voice Write in the active rather than passive voice. For example, write, "She hits him," rather than, "He is hit by her." As with all these guidelines, use common sense. For example, if the person being acted upon is the key to the story, say a celebrity, then you can consider an exception and use the passive (e.g., "Jane Movie Star is struck by a stalker").

Conversational News writing is to be spoken, not read, so write for the ear. For example, write, "Unlock the door," rather than, "Part A, insert key; part B, turn key; part C, push or pull door until open."

Individual Viewer Write for the individual at home watching your story. The audience might be mass, but people tend to consume electronic media alone or in small groups of friends or family. Pretend you're there in the room. For example, write, "Hurricane Xena is heading up the coast. Here are some precautions you might want to take." Do not write, "Ladies and gentlemen, it is my duty to inform you that a hurricane is approaching. Do not panic. Repeat: Do not panic. Listen carefully to the following instructions."

Short Statements Write short, simple, declarative sentences, rather than rambling, run-on sentences. Shorter sentences are easier to read and less confusing. For example, write, "Dick runs. Jane runs. Spot chases Dick and Jane." This is clearer than writing, "As Dick continues running down the street, Jane pursues him at a relatively rapid pace, while Spot, the dog, runs close behind, ever gaining ground."

Brevity Broadcast time is money. Waste no words. Write directly to the point. Always consider ways to cut words *out* of your sentences without losing meaning. Be as concise as you can with no extra words. For example, write, "He falls down," rather than, "He then proceeds to fall down to the ground." The phrase "then proceeds to" is unnecessary, and "to the ground" is assumed in the phrase "falls down." Do you see how three words in the first sentence convey the same meaning as nine words in the second sentence?

Avoid Unnecessary Words People tend to load their talk with lots of unnecessary words. While news writing is conversational, it is also economical and should not waste time with these meaningless and often cliché additions to sentences. Some words to avoid: basically, respectively, latter, former, that. For example, write, "He announces his resignation," rather than, "He basically announces that he is going to resign."

Avoid Redundancy In keeping with the guideline to be brief, avoid words that repeat something already in the sentence or something that can be assumed. For example, consider this sentence: "Right now, firefighters are presently battling a blaze." The phrase "right now" and the word "presently" mean the same thing, so one or the other should be deleted. Another example: "The project is designed to inform community leaders about the objectives of the project." The word

"project" is repeated, so different wording should be used to conclude the sentence.

Source Attribution *Print* news places the source of information at the *end* of a sentence; for example, "The president's health is excellent, according to White House officials." In contrast, *broadcast* news places the source at the *beginning* of a sentence; for example, "White House officials report the president's health is excellent."

KISMIF You already know this one, and it applies to ENG writing as well as to EFP writing: keep it simple, make it fun.

ELECTRONIC FIELD PRODUCTION

Generally, EFP scriptwriters have much more time for the process than scriptwriters in ENG. EFP scripts are often written with enough lead time to allow for careful review and revision. The process allows a script to be evaluated not just for its meaning and effectiveness, but also for its adherence to the budget and capabilities of the production unit.

Scripts for commercials, training videos, entertainment, and so on can be written and rewritten until the scriptwriter, producer, director, and client are satisfied. The scripts usually do not have to reflect the reality of an event or issue as they do in ENG, but they must reflect the concept and intentions of the client and/or producer.

The procedure for EFP scriptwriting is often careful and lengthy:

1. Set goals for the script.
2. Analyze the target audience.
3. Select a format and style.
4. Develop a central visual theme.
5. Research to learn about the concepts to be shown and explained.
6. Write a treatment that conveys the essence of the script.
7. Prepare an outline that lists, in order, all the important aspects of the script.
8. Write the script.

9. Review and revise until all those involved are satisfied.
10. Develop a storyboard to help others visualize your ideas.
11. Develop an editing script in postproduction, making note of any changes in editing that were not part of the shooting script.
12. Throughout the process, pay attention to the basic story structure: beginning, middle, end.

Throughout these 12 steps, you must also keep in mind the budget for the project. You cannot write a script that will require more money to produce than has been allotted. For example, if the script is a commercial with the goal of selling fishing boats, and the manufacturer has budgeted only $1,000, that epic pirate battle you envision will have to give way to small dueling watercraft, provided by the manufacturer, with employees as actors, shot on the local river. Budgets are covered extensively in Chapter 11.

Goals

Once the process of initiating a video project has begun, set your goals at a reasonable and attainable level. Attempting to present the entire history of a large corporation in a comprehensive and detailed fashion might be unrealistic in a 3-minute portion of a 10-minute video presented to stockholders at their annual meeting. It might also destroy your budget. The best way to avoid a problem like this is to set specific goals. Goal outlining should be done on two levels. First, determine the overall purpose of your project. Is it to entertain, inform, educate, demonstrate, or persuade? Then set very specific goals.

An instructional video that attempts to familiarize the sales managers of a farm implement company with a new model tractor might have the following goals:

1. Inform sales managers about the new model: size, weight, performance, and cost.
2. Motivate them to sell the new model by explaining bonuses and incentives.
3. Train them in marketing and sales procedures that will enhance sales of the new model.

Goals should be formulated in terms of their intended outcomes, or effects, on the viewers. Any communication may have three different kinds of effects on an audience: cognitive, emotional, and behavioral. **Cognitive effects** are those that occur when the audience gains knowledge or information. These effects impact what viewers *think* or *know*. **Emotional effects** are those that cause an attitudinal or mode change in the audience. These effects impact the way viewers *feel*. **Behavioral effects** occur when viewers engage in or change actions in some measurable way, such as buying a new brand of detergent or voting for a politician. These effects impact what viewers *do*. In the planning stage, these potential effects can be viewed as obtainable goals or objectives.

Many video projects do not have all three types of desired objectives. Educational videos might be designed only to achieve cognitive effects. Artistic or entertainment videos might only strive for emotional effects. Simulation videos might attempt to teach the audience how to behave in certain situations. Of course, some videos might have goals that impact the audience in all three ways. It is appropriate to consider all three types of effects for your intended audience.

Target Audience

Once you have established the goals for your video, it is time to pay more serious attention to your audience. Your production can be tremendously exciting, visually creative, and perfectly shot, but it might be a total failure if your script is not written for the intended viewers. Consider the difference in a script for a feature that will appear on a local broadcast station's magazine show and a script for a video that will be shown only to volunteers for a charity at their organizational meeting. The topic might be the same, but the style would be quite different.

The magazine show feature is scripted to heighten awareness about the good things the charity does and the need for volunteers or donors to help. The video shown at the organizational meeting would be written to raise the enthusiasm and energy level of the audience and demonstrate or suggest specific behaviors needed to help the charity. This same charity might want to produce a video for use in elementary schools to inform children about the importance of the charity's efforts. Obviously, the language of the script and the pacing and style of the shooting and editing would be different from either the magazine feature or the video made for committed volunteers.

The more you know about your audience, the better. **Demographic** factors are perhaps the best starting points to help you become familiar with the audience. Demographic characteristics are quantitative: they are objective and measurable. Typical demographic categories include age, gender, ethnicity, income, and education level. What is the age range of your viewers? Does your script target males more than females, or vice versa? Is the video intended more for one ethnic group than another? What is the income range of your audience? How much education do the members of your intended audience typically have?

You should also consider **psychographic** factors. These are qualitative: they are subjective and more descriptive than measurable. Typical psychographic categories include lifestyles, values, attitudes, interests, and hobbies. How does your target audience live? What do your intended viewers consider important in life? What are their impressions of your subject likely to be? What captivates their imaginations? What activities do they pursue? Information about both demographic and psychographic factors will help you make some basic decisions about your script. Writing for a small, well-defined audience can be very different from writing for a large, heterogeneous audience.

The exhibition of the final product is also a consideration. Will 10 people see the video? 10,000? Tens of thousands? How will the video actually be shown? On broadcast TV? Cable or satellite? A podcast? A private showing to a small audience using a small TV monitor? A showing to an audience of 100 or more using a large projection TV? Will a frame or even the entire video be part of a World Wide Web page, Internet site, or multimedia presentation? After you have carefully considered the audience and how that audience will watch your project, you can move on to deciding your format.

Format

Video projects can be categorized by their format, which refers to the overall organization and intent of the project. Broadcast-TV programs conform to a limited number of standard formats that provide understanding of the type of entertainment and a time frame for viewers. In broadcast, most programs are written for 30- or 60-minute lengths. The most common formats include:

- Drama

- Newscast

- Game show

- Event (e.g., sports, awards)

- Compilation/video clips

- Action/adventure

- Variety show

- Situation comedy

- Talk show/interview

- Documentary

- Highlight (e.g., sports, awards)

- Magazine/features

- Reality program

- Tabloid entertainment news

Many of these formats have been adapted to non-broadcast situations to get attention and to increase viewer appreciation. For example, a new health benefit could be explained to employees of a large corporation by an executive talking to the camera and using an occasional chart or graphic. Another approach might have employees in a simulated game show, like *Jeopardy,* trying to give answers to questions about changes from old benefits to new. The parody of the game show format gives the writers the opportunity to inject humor into what might be very dull material. Another approach might be to have a TV talk show host interview the company executive, rather than having the executive do a talking head. The show becomes more visually interesting, and the question-and-answer format allows the host to represent the audience and their predictable questions.

Other formats are more appropriate for nonbroadcast TV projects or those that are not fixed program-length. These include:

- Demonstration/how to
- Instruction/classroom topics
- Public service announcement (PSA)
- Music video
- Video art
- Commercial

Choosing one of these formats or a combination can give your project structure and organization that will be helpful to you as a writer and to your audience as viewers.

Style

The style of your writing can vary considerably, but in the context of ENG and EFP we can categorize styles of writing by how the information of your text gets into your program. You can have an announcer give information, usually referred to as narration. You can have dialogue—words delivered by two people at a time—that is either informational, dramatic, comic, or simply entertaining. You can have a combination of either of the above with natural **soundbites**—words delivered by an interviewee in response to prompting or a question.

Narration

Narration is usually a simple, straightforward reading of the script by a narrator or announcer. The narrator is usually not on camera, nor recorded when the video is shot. Narration is also referred to as **voiceover (VO)**. It is common practice to record the narration at a recording session separate from all visual shooting.

Narration should be written to enhance the video and make it more compelling. Good narration guides viewers to a specific time and place that is represented by the video. This can be important when your setting is somewhat generic. For example, an opening shot might be a person in bed sleeping in a darkened room; an alarm clock next to the bed reads 3:10. The audience automatically assumes the setting is at night. Because the intention of the video is to inform the audience about the dangers of sleep deprivation and irregular sleep behavior, the narration could tell the audience that it is 3:10 P.M., not 3:10 A.M. The opening narrative line could be:

> If it were 3:10 A.M., Ralph Salesman would not be shown in this video. The problem is that this video was shot at 3:10 P.M., when Ralph should be meeting with sales clients. Ralph suffers from "nonsleepnia," a condition that is characterized by irregular sleep patterns. In this video we will discuss this vexing behavioral problem and suggest proper methods of treating it.

The narration helps establish the scene and leads the audience into the purpose of the video. In other words, the narration can be a necessary part of the establishing visual shot.

Narration is best when it is succinct and used sparingly. Don't use it unless it adds something to the video. Heavy narration might be necessary for a training video or a video dealing with events that occurred but were not shot (e.g., some historical event before the age of photography), but in all cases, avoid continuous, monotonous narration. Organize your narration in complete thoughts, like paragraphs in the print media. Don't be afraid to break up your narration with periods of silence (assuming you have good video) or to change your narrator or use "sound-bite" type material when appropriate people answer questions relevant to the topic of your video.

Because video projects are written for the ear, the style of narration should be conversational, not overly flowery or stiffly formal. Remember, your video might be viewed by many people at once, but videos are most effective when they reach people as individuals, similar to interpersonal communication.

Dialogue

Dialogue is commonly used for dramatic presentations or when situations are dramatized. To write dialogue, you have to write in more than one voice. Some writers find it best to work with a writing partner so that each can assume a different voice. They then create the dialogue by improvising back-and-forth banter. Although referred to as dialogue, this style of writing obviously also encompasses more than just two people. Most writers strive to achieve economy in their dialogue, writing conversationally but not wastefully. In this way, they create just the dialogue needed to move the story and reveal characters without wasting words and time.

Interview

Many informational programs have a combination of narration and dialogue. The dialogue sometimes consists of responses from persons who are interviewed for the program. For example, a video designed to explore a company's role in preserving the ecological integrity around one of its manufacturing plants could open with narration extolling the virtues of the company's efforts at preservation. It could then include soundbites from credible authorities, such as biologists, who respond to questions about the environmental conditions at the site. When using interviews, keep in mind the guidelines about open-ended questions discussed previously under ENG. The questions should elicit usable soundbites for editing.

Central Visual Theme

Your central visual theme should be stated as a short phrase or sentence that conveys the essence of your visual goal. It summarizes the look of your project. The statement should include the major visual elements of your story.

For example, if the project is a 30-second public service announcement for the local public library, an appropriate phrase might be, "Books are your windows on the world." An appropriate phrase for a 5-minute demonstration video of a new computer workstation could be, "The new Plum III computer fits your desk, your hands, and your mind." A training video for employees of a bakery might have its visual statement, "Dough is our bread and butter."

By stating your visual idea in a short, succinct, central, visual theme at the beginning, you prevent further levels of script and production complexities from obscuring your original intent. Should problems arise during the preproduction phase of your project, it may be helpful to review your initial statement. That statement provides you with an overall visual theme to tie together the shots in your project. As you write the script, you can find creative ways to include this visual theme throughout.

Research

Because producers of EFP video provide their services to many different kinds of clients, EFP projects often require familiarity with technical terms or procedures beyond the realm of the video producer's experience. A complete video project requires fluency in both the video and audio portions of the project, and research is often necessary to attain this fluency. This fluency can be achieved in four ways:

- Interviews with knowledgeable individuals.

- Reading material relevant to the topic.

- Viewing other information previously prepared either by or for the client.

- Searching for information available on the Internet.

Interviews

Interviews with experts may serve two purposes. By discussing the video topic with a person in the know, you will understand the topic better and can write a coherent script that uses appropriate terminology correctly. Additionally, you may be able to record the interview, providing potential source footage for your project, with the permission of the subject, of course.

Reading Material

You should gather as much relevant reading material as you can. You can ask the experts whom you interview for recommendations of items to read. You can also search for books, trade journals, newspaper and magazine articles, newsletters, Web sites, or other sources that explain the topic and provide background information. Books might also be available to give in-depth information for longer projects or for those involving highly technical subject matter.

Client Information

Information that originated from the client is potentially the most helpful, but it is often overlooked. Press releases, marketing information, advertising, sales brochures, or previous video and audio projects can give a quick and accurate overview of the client's goals, techniques, or philosophy.

For example, a few years ago, a sugar manufacturing company needed a video that would give a brief history of the company and describe the steps taken to manufacture sugar from sugar beets. The tape was to be produced for elementary schools and libraries. After checking numerous possible sources, it was found that an old brochure gave much of the historical information and a 20-year-old film had animation sequences in it that helped show and explain the complex technical processes involved. In fact, the animation sequences were still accurate enough that some careful editing allowed them to be transferred to video and used to explain that portion of the company's operation. Needless to say, much time and money was saved as a result of the research for related materials.

Internet Search

Just about any topic, person, or place can be researched through the resources available on the Internet. If you have a good idea regarding what you want in your search, many of the **search engines** available can find very specific information for you in a very short time. (See Figure 5-3.) Just about anything, including audio and video, can be accessed and even downloaded to help give you a better understanding of

Figure 5-3   A screenshot from the popular search engine, Google. (Courtesy of Google).

Treatment

Presentations involving drama, characters, and a plot require a stated **treatment** or brief summary of the project, written in the earliest stages of preproduction to allow the creator (or scriptwriter) to tell the story and better orient the production team, as well as the scriptwriter. The treatment is a short encapsulation of the setting, characters, points of view, and the plot. Major events or changes in characters or characterizations should be mentioned in the treatment. While this step is required in fiction, it is also strongly recommended for nonfiction. The treatment tells the story in narrative form (without dialogue) so that the client or financial backers have a good feeling for what the finished product will look like.

The treatment not only keeps the scriptwriter on track, but it also keeps other members of the creative team and the client on track. The treatment provides firm guidelines for everyone to remember throughout the creative process. For informational projects that have a nonfiction style, the treatment might be quite brief—one to three pages for a short video. This type of treatment should contain three elements: goal, strategy, and content. (See Figure 5-4.)

Treatment for "Heavy-Duty Jack" Corporate Video

<u>Goal</u>

This video is to be shown at trade shows and conventions for suppliers and wholesalers of equipment for industry, construction, farming, hardware stores, and the like. The objective is to persuade these clients to purchase Heavy-Duty Jacks for resale to their customers.

<u>Strategy</u>

The video demonstrates the many uses of the Heavy-Duty Jack. An animated Jack narrates. The central theme is that the Heavy-Duty Jack can be used to accomplish a variety of tasks that involve heavy lifting, pushing, and pulling. The motto might be, "Heavy-Duty Jacks for all your heavy-duty jobs."

<u>Content</u>

The video opens with an SUV getting stuck off-road. The DRIVER takes out a Heavy-Duty Jack and two chains. He fastens one chain to a tree and the other to the SUV; then, he hooks one chain on each end of the jack and begins to ratchet, pulling the SUV free. An animated Heavy-Duty JACK appears in a studio and tells the viewers how the SUV driver never goes anywhere without his Heavy-Duty Jack because it always comes in handy for heavy-duty jobs, like pulling the SUV out of a tight spot.

Animated Jack briefly tells the story of the company that makes "him" as images of the factory and its WORKERS appear, accompanied by upbeat music. Jack emphasizes the high quality, strength, and durability of the all-steel product. Next, Jack cites examples of the many tasks for which the jack can be used. These include: leveling a shed, changing a combine tire, pushing a drill press into place, holding a fence for repair, lifting a piece of concrete sidewalk, and other uses to be determined with the company. Each use is demonstrated on screen as Jack narrates.

The video concludes with studio product shots of each size jack and the jack accessories. Animated Jack reiterates that anyone whose work involves heavy lifting, pushing, and pulling needs the Heavy-Duty Jack. Its versatility and strength make it an ideal companion for all kinds of heavy-duty jobs. Once again the SUV driver appears, Heavy-Duty Jack in tow, heading off to his next heavy-duty adventure.

Figure 5-4   This sample treatment for a sales video for a heavy-duty jack summarizes the goal (including target audience), strategy (including central theme), and content (including beginning, middle, end, setting, characters, plot, and major points).

Goal

The goal of the project should accurately reflect what the originator wants: training, promotion, publicity, or whatever. The goal statement should also include the target viewers to whom this goal is directed. This should be accomplished in a few sentences or a single paragraph.

Strategy

The strategy of the production explains what method will be used to accomplish the goal. If the goal is to teach salespeople how to use a new laptop computer to enter sales data, the strategy might be a step-by-step demonstration showing the computer and the data entry procedure. If the goal is to heighten awareness of a new health benefit, the strategy might be a simulated press conference with the most commonly expressed questions asked and answered. If the goal is to increase sensitivity toward minority groups in the workplace, the strategy might be a series of brief scenarios depicting potential problem situations and how to react to them.

Obviously, your strategy should logically relate to achieving your goal. It is a good idea to state your central theme as part of the strategy, as well. This gives your client an opportunity to visualize your approach. Your client should not be left to wonder how your pure creativity is going to accomplish the objective. If the strategy does not make sense to the client at this stage, you are headed for big problems later.

Content

The content need not be a verbatim script, but a general outline of what will happen and when. This should include at least the beginning, middle, and end, as well as the setting, characters, plot, and any major points to be made. Being too specific is probably as inappropriate as being too vague. It is best to give yourself some creative wiggle room here. Often, some of your original ideas will not pan out. Leave room for slight changes to accommodate ideas that might arise later in the production, or even postproduction, processes. At the same time, avoid being too vague, because the linkage between content, strategy, and goal might not make sense to your client.

For most corporate video projects, a few pages specifying the treatment are sufficient. A complex fiction project with a 30- or 60-minute duration might require a 10- to 15-page treatment to help convey what the final product will look like. This type of treatment may include descriptions of the locations, characters, and some camera direction as well.

Outline

Now all the facts, figures, and visual ideas need to be organized so that they will form the skeleton for the body of your project. An outline should simply and succinctly list the points, facts, comments, and visualizations that will tell your story in the appropriate order. You can easily reshuffle your ideas to form the best story at this stage. Allowing your outline to be reviewed by other production team members, other professionals, and even the client may save hours of rewriting, re-editing, or reshooting. (See Figure 5-5.)

One convenient way to organize your outline is to use index cards. Use one idea, fact, or visualization per index card and include, when possible, a small sketch or photo to clarify the visual idea. Arrange your cards in a logical sequence, then try to tell your story by reading (and embellishing on) each card in the sequence. A few attempts at storytelling in this manner will probably reveal inconsistencies, improper order, and difficult or clumsy transitions that may be hiding in your future outline. Once your cards are in the proper order, construct an outline and allow others to give you some feedback.

Script

Now you are ready to write a **script** that will guide you in shooting the raw footage for your program. At this point your creativity and skill must be fully used. There are some guidelines to keep in mind:

- *Visualize the items on your outline.* Fill in the gaps between each point; visualize the transitions. How do you get from one step to the next? Think visually then allow the audio portion of the script to enhance the video.

- *Make an effort to capture your audience's interest very early in the script.* Try to "hook" your audience with a compelling audio, video, or combined shot in the introductory part of the script. You need this to keep your audience throughout your project. In a video brochure for a new apartment complex, you might have an opening shot of a terrific view of a nearby

NOTE TO REVIEWERS

This is the first draft of the video script for the video introducing the "Choice Program" and First Party Coverage to focus group participants. As reviewed and revised, the script will be used as the basis for recording and editing.

Program Purpose and Use

The primary purpose of this video is to help introduce the Choice Program to participants in focus group research at the Allstate Research Center.

We want the video to provide an easy-to-understand message that will enable the viewer to:

* Understand the coverages provided by the First Party Coverage option and what will happen in various claims situations

* Understand the broad benefits of the First Party Coverage option

* Be able to participate in a focus group discussion and provide their reactions to the First Party Coverage option.

Content

The major content points to be covered in the video are outlined below. The points are listed in the general order in which they will be presented in the video.

I.   About this Tape
    A.   Brief preview
    B.   What's it it for you (the viewer) -- why you should watch this tape

II.   Components of Auto Insurance
    A.   Medical/Personal injury protection (PIP) -- injury to you or your passengers
    B.   Bodily injury -- injury to another person in an accident
    C.   Property damage -- damage to another's property
    D.   Collision -- damage to your vehicle in an accident
    E.   Uninsured motorist -- protection against injury or property damage loss caused by an uninsured motorist
    F.   Under-insured motorist -- protection against injury or property damage loss caused by a motorist with insufficient coverage limits
    G.   Comprehensive -- damage to your vehicle not the result of an accident

III. A Brief Explanation of How Third-Party and First-Party coverage Work
    A.   Third-Party coverage (Tort)
    B.   First-Party coverage (No-fault)

IV.   An Overview of the First Party Coverage option
    A.   Purpose -- to provide a "Choice" in auto insurance coverage
    B.   Differentiation from tort
        1.   No right to sue, except in certain cases
        2.   Others can't sue you, except in certain cases
    C.   Major benefits
    D.   The Choice -- staying with or leaving the tort system

V.   Details of First-Party Coverage
    A.   Compulsory medical coverage -- First Party Injury
        1.   Your own company pays for your medical expenses due to injury
        2.   Limits
        3.   Brings immunity to suits except for:
            a.   drunk driving, criminal negligence, leaving the scene, intentional acts
            b.   uncompensated economic injury damage, uncompensated non-auto economic property damage
            c.   optional coverage can cover these exceptions
    B.   Optional "Residual liability" coverage will handle certain special situations
        1.   Uncompensated economic damages
        2.   Tort immunity exceptions
        3.   Driving out of state
    C.   Other options to First-Party coverage
        1.   Higher limits for the compulsory medical coverage
        2.   Wage loss
        3.   Loss of services
        4.   Funeral benefits
        5.   Coordination of benefits (brings a credit)
    D.   Collision and Comprehensive -- Optional

VI.   Scenarios -- What Happens If You Have First-Party Coverage And...
    A.   You are in an accident caused by another first-party driver
    B.   You cause an accident with a driver with third-party coverage
    C.   A driver with third-party coverage causes an accident with you
    D.   An uninsured motorist causes an accident with you
    E.   Others

VII. Benefits of First-Party Coverage
    A.   Freedom of choice
        1.   Stay in or leave tort system
        2.   Tailor coverage to your needs, resources, preferences
    B.   Potentially lower cost for coverage
    C.   More efficient compensation to accident victims
        1.   Timeliness
        2.   Fairness

VIII. Recap

IX.   Conclusion

Figure 5-5   Objectives and outline for a corporate video script. (Courtesy of Allstate Insurance Company)

mountain peak. Your narration could say something like:

> How would you like a view like this from your apartment? Keep watching and we'll show you a new apartment community where every apartment has a view like this! And if you call the number we'll give you later in this video, you may win a free year's lease!

* *Consider your writing style.* Do not write as if you are lecturing, or writing a technical document or a brochure. Make sure that your writing is conversational. It is best to try to create short sentences. This is the way most people talk to one another therefore, it is appropriate in both dialogue and narration. Another suggestion is to avoid obscure or unfamiliar terminology, unless the narrator explains the terms shortly before or after their use. Make sure that the dialogue or narration is appropriate for the speaker(s). You would not have the president of a corporation say, "Let's get your butts in gear," during a motivational video aimed at company workers. The statement "Let's combine our energies and talents so we can get busy and solve these problems together" would be more appropriate. A five-year-old would not normally say, "I seem to have developed an intense craving for an ice cream cone." More likely, a five-year-old would say, "Mommy, can I have some ice cream?" or "Gimme some ice cream!"

- *Keep in mind that regardless of the specific goal of the video project, it must tell a story.* It should have a beginning, middle, and end, with an appropriate storyline that attempts to meet your objectives. Make sure that your central visual theme is not obscured by overly complex or convoluted plot devices.

- *Know what length of time your video must be and write accordingly.* Assume that about 20 words equals 10 seconds of reading time. Each minute will have about 120 words. After the script is written, read it out loud and time it to make sure you are accurate.

- *Include all necessary directions that explain comprehensively how to translate the written words and ideas into video information.* The style, clarity, and completeness of the script should enable a competent director who may not have been involved with the planning or scriptwriting to take the script and shoot the program as you intended it to be shot. (See Table 5.1 for some common production terms used in TV scriptwriting.)

- *Expect revisions of your script.* No script remains intact in its first version throughout the production process. Your script should be considered a first draft.

Table 5.1   Terms Used in Scriptwriting.

Camera Shots	**Common Abbreviations**
Long shot, wide shot	LS, WS
Medium shot	MS
Close-up, tight shot	CU, TS
Extreme close-up	XCU, ECU
Camera Movement	
Zoom or zoom in	Z or ZI
Pan (left or right)	PL or PR
Dolly (in or out)	DI or DO

Table 5.1   Terms Used in Scriptwriting.(Contin-

Tilt (up or down)	TU or TD
Transitions	
Cut, take	—
Dissolve	Diss
Fade (in or out)	FI or FO

At this point, your script is ready for some fine-tuning in the review process. (See Figure 5-6.) If you feel that your script will be going through many reviews and edits, it might be easier to use some type of scriptwriting program to help you format and edit quickly. Although some word processors have this capability, it may be best to get a program that is designed for writing scripts for electronic media. (See Figure 5-7.)

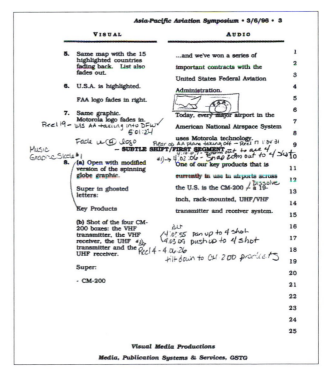

Figure 5-6   A script with typical revisions. (Courtesy of Motorola, Integrated Information Systems Group, Visual Media Communications)

If you're not already familiar with scriptwriting formats, you should read Appendix A and Appendix B at the back of the book. Appendix A provides the bare

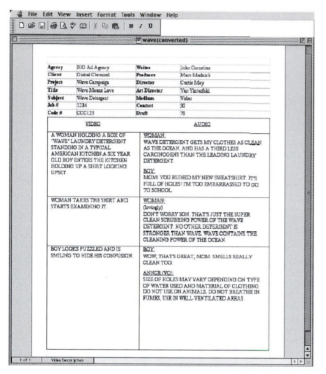

Agency	B10 Ad Agency	Writer	John Cornelius
Client	Global Chemical	Producer	Marc Marbuck
Project	Wave Campaign	Director	Curtis May
Title	Wave Means Love	Art Director	Yan Yinturfski
Subject	Wave Detergent	Medium	Video
Job #	1234	Content	30
Code #	CCC123	Draft	78

VIDEO	AUDIO
A WOMAN HOLDING A BOX OF "WAVE" LAUNDRY DETERGENT STANDING IN A TYPICAL AMERICAN KITCHEN A SIX YEAR OLD BOY ENTERS THE KITCHEN HOLDING UP A SHIRT LOOKING UPSET	WOMAN: WAVE DETERGENT GETS MY CLOTHES AS CLEAN AS THE OCEAN, AND HAS A THIRD LESS CARCINOGENS THAN THE LEADING LAUNDRY DETERGENT. BOY: MOM! YOU RUINED MY NEW SWEATSHIRT. IT'S FULL OF HOLES! I'M TOO EMBARRASSED TO GO TO SCHOOL.
WOMAN TAKES THE SHIRT AND STARTS EXAMINING IT.	WOMAN: (lovingly) DON'T WORRY SON. THAT'S JUST THE SUPER CLEAN SCRUBBING POWER OF THE WAVE DETERGENT. NO OTHER DETERGENT IS STRONGER THAN WAVE. WAVE CONTAINS THE CLEANING POWER OF THE OCEAN.
BOY LOOKS PUZZLED AND IS SMILING TO HIDE HIS CONFUSION.	BOY: WOW, THAT'S GREAT, MOM. SMELLS REALLY CLEAN TOO. ANNCR (VO): SIZE OF HOLES MAY VARY DEPENDING ON TYPE OF WATER USED AND MATERIAL OF CLOTHING. DO NOT USE ON ANIMALS, DO NOT BREATHE IN FUMES, USE IN WELL-VENTILATED AREAS.

Figure 5-7   A screen from the Final Draft A/V scriptwriting program. The program helps create scripts in a variety of formats, including film and TV. (Courtesy of Final Draft, Inc.)

bones of writing single-camera (film-style) scripts or screenplays. Appendix B offers the bare bones of two-column scripts, including a tutorial on how to use the Tables function in Microsoft Word to set up the two-column format.

Review and Revision

After the first draft is written, most scripts are subject to some sort of review process. For a practitioner of video art or a student of video, this review process is internal. The scriptwriter should reread the script a few days after it is written and reassess its merit. Does it depict the desired mood or concepts in the manner intended? Often, some rewriting is necessary.

For scriptwriters in corporate video or any video made for a client, the client generally wants to read the first draft to see if it conveys the desired meaning. In many cases, this review process is not just helpful, it is mandatory. Production often cannot start with-

out client approval of the script. Although it may seem tedious, this review and approval process is a safeguard for the EFP producer and scriptwriter. It often prevents a client from complaining about the scriptwriter's interpretation of the objectives.

The review process leads to a revised second draft and, sometimes, numerous successive drafts. When a draft is finally approved, it becomes a shooting script and acts as the guide for the actual production work. By having a final script approved by the client, the stage is set for shooting to go smoothly and to stay on schedule and on budget. Of course, a few surprises always come up when actual shooting begins; however, a good script can keep these sometimes costly surprises to a minimum.

Storyboard

If there is sufficient time and budget, it is recommended that you create a **storyboard**. This pictorial outline can be drawn up by the writer, director, producer, advertising agency, or even the client. The storyboard is a roughed-out drawing of every scene to be produced in the video. Special pads of paper with blank TV screen outlines on them are usually used to maintain the proper aspect ratio for TV photography. (See Figure 5-8.) With this form, each picture or scene is shown with the dialogue or camera directions to be used directly beneath it. Another layout that requires more detailed information has the description of the scene to the right of the picture. (See Figure 5-9.)

The storyboard allows all crew members and talent to see how the shots should look. This makes it possible for all blocking, props, lighting, special equipment, and special effects to be worked out while the video is still in preproduction. Costs and time can be more closely controlled using the storyboard, because the entire cast and crew know how the finished product should look. Storyboards help eliminate the shocked comment that occurs when the rough-cut version is shown to the client: "That's not at all what we had in mind."

A good storyboard can save time in the long run and help head off serious problems during production. Even if no one involved in the project can draw, stick figures and rough sketches are better than noth-

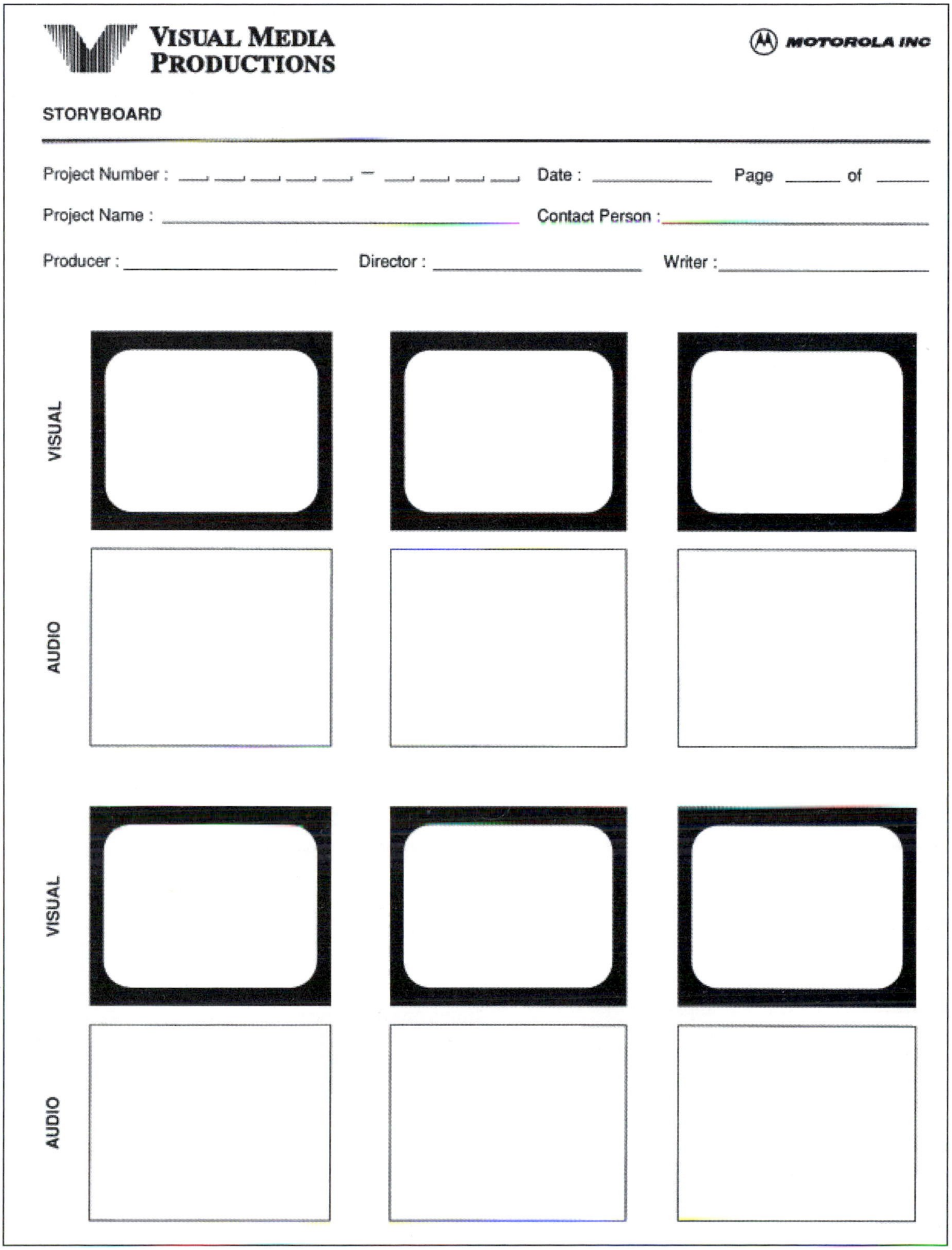

VISUAL MEDIA PRODUCTIONS

MOTOROLA INC

STORYBOARD

Project Number : ___ ___ ___ ___ ___ – ___ ___ ___ ___ Date : ________ Page ____ of ____

Project Name : ____________________ Contact Person : ____________________

Producer : ____________ Director : ____________ Writer : ____________

VISUAL

AUDIO

VISUAL

AUDIO

Figure 5-8 Blanks used for a storyboard by a corporate video operation. (Courtesy of Motorola, Integrated Information Systems Group, Visual Media Communications)

Congress on Endovascular Interventions SPFX Sequence Number3 (FLAME)

1 As the surgeon passes down the empty corridor, he sees a strange light emanating from what used to be OR#2..

2 Frightened and confused, yet entranced by the light, he moves in for a closer examination of this compelling occurrence.

3 We notice strange symbols on the door jam that appears to be made of an unfamiliar metal alloy or resin.

The doorway seems to be filled with clouds of swirling colored gas...oddly two dimensional in appearance.

As he touches the "barrier" he is suddenly drawn in... closer and closer... unable to break free of its pull.

Figure 5-9   This storyboard from a hospital video has descriptions of each shot at the right. (Courtesy of VAS Communications)

ing at all. Alfred Hitchcock never shot a frame of film until it was carefully drawn out in every detail on a storyboard. Steven Spielberg often has drawings of sets and pictures of locations for all scenes before shooting a movie.

If you're not already familiar with storyboard techniques, you should read Appendix C at the back of the book. This appendix provides additional information about storyboarding. It includes the common shorthand and symbols used in constructing the panel drawings and writing the audio descriptions.

Editing Script

After the raw footage has been shot, producers, directors, and writers have another step in the scriptwriting process available to them that is often unavailable to those in studio TV: viewing the footage for editing. This step allows members of the EFP production team

to review all the video for the shooting script and decide if revisions to the original script are needed.

If changes are required or requested, the script can be rewritten to accommodate the editing process. Shot sequences may be changed, some shots or scenes may be deleted, or some new shots may be added. One of the real advantages of EFP television over studio TV becomes especially apparent if new shots are needed. Although equipment and personnel may need to be rescheduled, costly studio space will not have to be rescheduled. The additional EFP work can be done with as few as two or three crew members. If this reshooting does not involve the principal talent, a second unit might even be employed to do the pickup shots at less expense than the first production unit.

The final version of the script, the editing script, is completed at this point. It is the last step in the production process before the final edit of the program is completed. This step usually involves minor changes to fine-tune the most recent draft of the script and the raw footage into a completed program. It is the script that most accurately reflects the shots and dialogue in the raw footage. This script is given to the editor(s) to use as a guide in cutting the final program together.

Story Structure

Throughout the writing process, it is essential to remember that all stories follow the same basic pattern: beginning, middle, end. Screenwriters refer to this as the **three-act structure**. Act 1, the beginning, sets up the story. Act 2, the middle, moves the story forward with more detail, introduces complications, attempts to answer questions, and so on. Act 3, the end, brings the story to its conclusion. Whether it is a 30-second commercial, a 90-second news package, a 10-minute corporate video, or a 2-hour movie, each production starts somewhere, goes somewhere, and finishes somewhere. (See Figure 5-10.)

The Beginning

Each story must start somewhere, so why not at the beginning? What happened first? Where? How? In visual terms, you can generally think of the beginning as the wide shot—the shot that establishes the content of

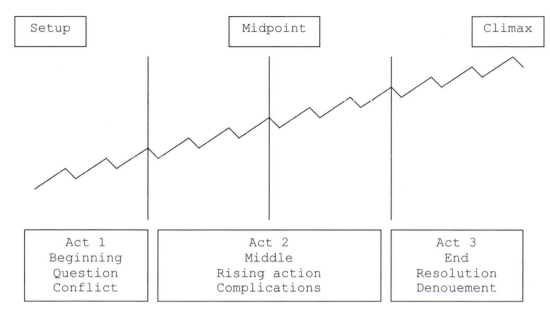

Figure 5-10   Diagram of the basic three-act story structure.

the story, the relationships among the elements, or the feeling and tone of the topic. Most things happen along a timeline; you would not show the outcome of the race and then show some of the racers still running or even starting. Things should be shown in the order in which they occur.

There should be a sense of positive time flow within the story, as if we are seeing an encapsulated version of what took place. The beginning should initiate the story and make the viewer want to see more of it. Aim to spark a viewer's attention, or at least enhance it, by the opening sequence of the story line. The question "What's next?" should always be present. Try not to lose the viewer's attention; the audience should always be anticipating the next element of the story.

A good way of securing a viewer's attention is to establish a sequence of action to follow. A story about a school building that is going to close need not be a collection of building shots. Instead, you can open the story with a shot of children entering the building. By doing this, you have the wide shot of the building, but the added element of kids entering the building within that shot has now started a story line. Very simplistically, you have posed these questions: Where are the kids going? What are they going to do? These are questions that you as editor and photographer can answer visually.

In this example, these questions would not be pressing in the minds of viewers, yet they establish a basic story line. Try to present a situation that needs further information or investigation to satisfy the viewer. Show the subject doing something or moving so that the activity or direction can be explored more fully. The start of a story can have a symbolic opening. The big fire piece could start with the sound of screaming sirens over a tight shot of flames. The scene is set with the elements: fire and firefighters. Audience interest is piqued: What's burning? A beginning must always appear to be headed somewhere. Invite the viewer to follow your lead. Make the viewer consciously or subconsciously ask, "What's next?" or "Why?" or "How?" and then proceed to answer the question. The beginning has to be the grabber, the **hook**. If you lose the viewers' interest at the beginning, they will never make it through the middle.

The Middle

The middle is the guts of the story, the development of the idea started in the beginning. Once the race has begun, how is everyone doing? In visual terms, as the wide shot is to the beginning of the story, so the medium shot is to the middle. The elements established at the start are now explored in greater detail and examined as to how they can further the story. Complications arise. Questions are posed. The story moves forward.

As the middle progresses, use **rising action**, making each segment more dramatic, intense, or gripping than the previous segment. Screenwriters refer to this as **raising the stakes**. In a fully scripted EFP production, for example, this could be sending the main character on a journey in which each scene is more dangerous than the last. In a partially scripted ENG project, for example, this could be revealing facts about the story in a progression that keeps whetting the viewers' appetite for the next segment, much like an appetizer prepares us for the soup, which in turn prepares us for the main course, which might be followed by dessert. The ever-intensifying middle of a story holds the viewers' interest, leading them to anticipate the end.

In our school-closing story line, showing the reasons for this closure would make up the middle. Possible ideas, stated visually as medium shots, are half-full classrooms (low attendance), students sitting amid dilapidated surroundings (disrepair), or city officials arguing over cost (budget). The middle is obviously the longest segment of any story. It develops the ideas. There might be characters for the audience to learn about, situations to understand, or motivations to feel. Write with one eye toward leading the viewers on a journey and the other eye toward segments that videographers can capture with descriptive shots to build interest.

The End

Every story should come to some sort of conclusion. The element that hooked the viewers at the beginning and all the elements that raised the stakes of the story throughout the middle now come together at the **climax**—the moment when your audience receives its **payoff** for watching. All questions are answered. All conflicts are resolved. Typically, the climactic moment is followed by a final shot or two to reduce the intensity and bring closure to the piece. The fancy word for this moment after the climax that brings finality is the **denouement**.

The climax might be a big moment, such as an explosion or car chase, or it might be a more intimate moment, such as two people realizing their love for each other. In the race analogy, the climax is simple: the winner crosses the finish line. The denouement might then be a shot of the winner receiving the trophy. In the school-closing story line, the climactic resolution would be the last answer to the question of why the school is closing, perhaps followed by a final shot of the children leaving the building and the doors closing. A story about taxis could end on a shot of a cab pulling away from the camera and driving off down the street—the old riding off into the sunset idea (negative motion).

Whether it actually comes to an end, or the sun simply sets in the last shot, the story must finish in some way. Even if there is no real conclusion or end, the appearance of one is desirable. The idea started at the beginning must be brought to completion or resolution in some way. The end might be displaying a finished sculpture, sealing up a box, closing a door, the crowd applauding, a skyline shot of the city, or anything that says "The End." The more thought put into how the story will end, the better the chance the viewers will come away with a feeling that the story is complete.

SUMMARY

Scriptwriting is one of the most important steps in the preproduction planning of any video project. Scripts are the blueprints from which videos are made. For news (ENG) and interview projects, the writer is mostly concerned with questions that will elicit good soundbites from the interviewees. Typical open-ended questions begin with the five Ws and H: who, what, where, when, why, how? The resulting soundbites are then edited into the final piece. The information is traditionally arranged in an inverted pyramid, with the most important information first. The actual script for the finished story, including the reporter's exposition, is written after the shoot. Once the footage has been reviewed, the reporter can "write to the visuals," filling in with words where images are incomplete, but not overscripting when the visuals tell the story.

For other types of projects with plots, characters, dialogue, and so on (EFP), the writer creates a full script. Before creating the script, a number of items must be considered and committed to paper: goals, audience, format and style, central visual theme, research, treatment, and outline. Once critical decisions have been made regarding each of these items, the script can be written … and then, of course, reviewed, revised, and rewritten as many times as is necessary for final approval by all concerned: client, producer, director, writer. The final, approved script becomes the shooting script for the project.

If time and budget allow, a storyboard is recommended to give all concerned an idea of how the project will look visually. Also, during and after the shooting phase of production, the footage can be reviewed for editing, and additional script changes can be made, resulting in a final editing script. Throughout this writing process, attention must be given to a satisfying story line that follows the basic story structure: an interesting beginning, an intensifying middle, and a rewarding conclusion.

6

Preproduction and Production

Some clients who ask to have video projects produced think it should take much less time than it actually does. Some think, "We need a 30-minute tape of a performance, so maybe it might take only an hour or two. Enough time to set up, shoot, pack up, and maybe do a little bit of editing." In professional video, a little bit of experience goes a long way. People who have produced video know that shooting is just a part of the three-stage process of making professional videos, which includes preproduction, production, and postproduction.

Making a high-quality video program is not something you can do on the spur of the moment. It takes hours of thinking, planning, writing, rewriting, more planning, and other kinds of hard work. Like painting a picture or writing a story, it takes skill, time, and lots of effort.

This chapter will guide you from the preliminary stages of thinking about a video project through the essential steps needed for preproduction to the day of actual production and shooting. The activities discussed in this chapter will make the difference between success and failure. Preparing for the shoot and actually performing the shoot are phases in the overall production process in which most of the planning and video work is accomplished. Bad planning or a lack of planning leads to video disasters. Overlooking the need for careful planning is a common amateur's mistake. The first section, Preproduction, guides you through all of the steps you will need to plan your project in a professional way. The second section, Production, guides you through the day or days of the shoot and gives you the information you need to begin, execute, and finish a professional style video shoot in the field.

PART ONE: PREPRODUCTION

Between the scriptwriting and the actual production of an EFP video comes the time for preproduction planning and preparation. This part of the production process should account for a majority of the total time spent on the project. Since careful and efficient planning at this stage can save time and money in the actual production phase, it is not unusual for video professionals to spend about 60 to 80% of their time in preproduction activities. The preproduction phase leads to a further divergence in methods between the ENG and EFP styles of portable video.

Electronic News Gathering

ENG style demands that events be covered as soon as they occur—leaving little or no time for careful planning. Preparations for upcoming stories are simply the experiences gained from the previous stories. Events occur on their own schedules, forcing the ENG videographer to cope with whatever difficulties are encountered without the benefit of a second take.

ENG situations call for a more bare-bones style of TV photography. The number one goal is simply to bring back acceptable quality video from every assignment, regardless of conditions or difficulty. What you can do beyond this in the way of quality and content is what makes a news videographer great. Often, all the equipment needed for the entire day must be carried by you at all times during that day—you must literally wear the gear. This limits the complexity of what you can do. It does not, however, limit the creativity of what you can do. Where EFP plans for every contingency and need, ENG plans for how much use can be derived from any one item of gear. The ability to travel quickly without an overload of equipment is essential due to the many deadlines in news gathering. A news videographer learns through experience to anticipate how the story will unfold and what equipment will be useful on any given shoot. The trick is to always have what you need before you need it and not have too much when you do not need it. The ability to improvise is the number one item on the list of things to bring.

Because of the nature of news stories, everything you may ever need for a shoot should be in the van or car with you every day. A return trip to the station may be impossible, and you may not even know what assignments you will have for that day. It becomes incumbent on the videographer, in many newsrooms, to find out what the next assignment is. Often the information given to the videographer is little more than a street address. Sometimes the assignment may require special considerations that the videographer really needs to know about. The first of these considerations is whether the story is to be done live or not. The planning for any event or story starts when the story is assigned. This may be days, hours, or just minutes before the shoot begins. Making more time available for planning gives news crews the opportunity to add more elements to their shooting plan. The result is that the production values of the story are raised. In the case of spot news, you may have only the time it takes to drive to the location to formulate a plan as to how to shoot the scene, how much time to spend doing each task, and how to get a live shot ready for the 5:00 P.M. news. A news videographer always has a plan waiting and ready.

Electronic Field Production

EFP productions are usually shot from a carefully planned script or storyboard that gives the videographer control over much of what is shot. The preparation for EFP work is actually similar to the pre-production process for studio work, but with some important differences. As in studio preproduction, EFP preproduction includes crew and talent organization and selection; a large amount of scheduling, budgeting, graphics planning, and preparation; and the procurement of clearance on copyrighted materials. Studio and EFP preproduction clearly differ, however, because of the added tasks of location selection, travel for talent and crew, and transportation of equipment to the desired location for EFP production. (See Figure 6.1.)

1. In the EFP preproduction checklist, add "Decision about exhibition (e.g., large screen versus mobile TV)" after Budget compilation.
2. Under Postproduction planning and scheduling, change to: Can online editing be done in-house?

Production Crew

The responsibility for selecting the crew is commonly the domain of a person called the executive producer. This person first selects a producer who then helps the executive producer select the other major members of the production crew, including the director, videographer, audio engineer, lighting director, talent, grip, and editor. The number of people assigned to each task depends on the complexity of the project. A small project may require only one person in each area of responsibility or even one person who covers several areas. Larger projects require several people in each area.

News-gathering crews are usually just one or two people: the videographer with or without a reporter. A recent trend has been to have a one-person crew where the videographer and the reporter are the same person.

```
                    PREPRODUCTION CHECKLIST

Client work/general feasibility conversation
Proposal w/script
Specific feasibility decision
Projections of needs: costs, facilities, equipment, personnel
Budget compilation
Preparation of script for shooting
Analysis of script into component parts for final product:
        facilities and locations—studio, showroom, office, plant
        talent
        equipment
        graphics
        props, costumes, set design
        personnel for production
        number and length of shoots required during production
        post-production needs/scheduling
Location selection, survey, analysis, decision
Facilities decision and scheduling
Talent decision and scheduling:
        Is an audition necessary?
Equipment scheduling:
        Is equipment on - hand sufficient?
        Will renting/leasing be necessary?
Graphics, music, sound effects:
        Is artwork needed? Does it require outside work?
        Graphic design or computer graphics?
        Are there any computer/digital special effects?
        Is music required? Are composers/performers needed?
        Are sound effects needed?
        Order graphics, music, sound effects.
Clearance
        Will any copyrighted material be used?
Props, costume, set elements
        Do props need to be purchased or constructed?
Personnel
        How many shoots are there and how long will they be?
        Do you have enough qualified personnel to staff a crew for all shoots?
Post-production planning and scheduling
        Can editing be done in - house?
        Can the necessary editing time be scheduled either in - house or elsewhere?
Preparation for shooting
        Are rehearsals necessary?
        Can they be done on - location?
        Are crew or staff meetings necessary?
```

Figure 6-1   Preproduction checklist.

Reporters are sent out with a small camcorder to cover a story. Today, it's expected that a reporter can write, report, shoot, and edit a story. People who can do this type of one-person reporting are referred to as "backpack journalists."

As market size or the demand for quality increases, a news crew can have a staff that is similar in size to a major EFP shoot. This is especially true in the area of documentary shooting. While technically a news-style product, documentaries are often done more like production work, sometimes having large crews and several layers of creative and financial control. In the sections below, the major crew members and their responsibilities are discussed.

Executive Producer

The production crew begins with the executive producer, who acts as a general supervisor of the project and often serves in this capacity on more than one project at a time. The executive producer initiates selection of the production crew after deciding on project feasibility given all the financial, equipment, personnel, and time constraints. Very often, the executive producer finds the money that funds the project.

A scriptwriter or project creator often seeks for the executive producer position someone who is able to find a funding source as well as the personnel and equipment to produce the script. Once the funding is located, the executive producer often decides generally how the money will be spent. Acting as a liaison between a client and the EFP team, the executive producer frequently selects (or at least suggests) the major members of the production team: the producer, director, and talent. The executive producer may also seek outlets for the exhibition of the project, if appropriate. After initiating the project and selecting a producer, the executive producer often plays a minor role in the day-to-day operation of the project, which is by then delegated to the producer.

Producer

Usually selected by the executive producer, the producer is involved from the very beginning of an EFP project as the overall coordinator and schedule-maker. Although the specifics of scheduling are often the responsibility of others on the team, the producer sets the parameters for the project (for example, the completion date). Having the best overall picture of the specific needs of the current production, the producer also knows the requirements for other projects that involve the production facility. The pivotal person on the video production team, the producer makes the decisions regarding money, personnel selection, and schedule.

For many projects done in-house at TV stations, production companies, or corporations, the team may already be assembled and on staff, simply moving from project to project. Larger companies may have many people in pools of job categories selected on the basis of availability, not ability. While this system works most of the time, it can lead to disaster. It is always

better to hand-pick the production team to get the best working relationships and the best end product.

Director

The director takes a script for a video project and translates it into a visual reality. The director is, therefore, an interpreter of the scriptwriter's words, a translator who takes written communication and transforms it into visual communication, or makes a storyboard come to life. The director must coordinate activities just before and during production, as well as coordinate the activities of the camera operator, talent, and lighting director during rehearsals to create the effect called for by the script or storyboard.

Once the desired aesthetic effect is achieved, the director can begin the actual recording. Because most EFP productions differ from studio TV in that EFP usually involves one portable camera rather than several studio cameras, a good EFP director should know the film style of shooting a scene. The film style of direction does not require one-take production with little or no postproduction editing. Instead, in film style, the director uses one camera to retake the scene from different camera angles and focal lengths to allow selection during postproduction and the freedom to shoot scenes out of sequence for efficiency.

The director must also be able to work with people effectively. This may involve coaching, cajoling, coercing, or otherwise persuading actors and other performers to get the desired performance from them. The director must accomplish this without alienating or demeaning the talent. One disgruntled actor can easily sour the efforts of an entire crew. Since field production involves smaller crews than studio work, each crew member's performance is essential to the success of the shoot. The director is responsible for getting the best possible work from the entire crew.

Production Manager

The production manager is responsible for making sure that the equipment is available and is scheduled properly for shoots. Often, the production manager is the person who understands the needs of the script and translates those needs into specific pieces of equipment and crew members to operate the equipment. The production manager is typically the crew member who, along with the producer, actually schedules the shoots and reserves the needed equipment.

Videographer

The videographer in field TV has a larger responsibility than the videographer in studio TV, primarily because the field director does not sit in front of a monitor bank in a sound-isolated control room and give directions as does the director in studio TV. In the field, the director may have a portable monitor (which may be small or washed out by the sun) but cannot always give direction during a shot, because spoken commands may be picked up by live microphones.

Camera directions are given before a shot, and both director and videographer work together to make each shot look its best. A good videographer takes the director's verbal commands or instructions from a shot list and gets the desired camera shots. A good videographer also finds additional shots through the variation of camera angle, focal length, selective focus, or camera movement. This can make a scene more interesting after it is edited. If the director is working from a storyboard, the videographer gives suggestions as to how the camera can be placed and moved to match the desired effect and look.

Audio Engineer

The EFP audio engineer is responsible for accurately recording sounds on the location shoot. Unlike studio audio engineers who have the equipment storeroom within easy reach, the field sound engineer, or sound recordist, must anticipate all sound requirements for the location shoot and pack the necessary items to accommodate them. Once on location, the audio engineer must live with the equipment decisions already made.

While studio sound engineers often have large, easy-to-read VU meters and high-quality control room monitor speakers to assess sound quality, location audio engineers often cope with tiny VU meters located on a portable audio mixer and a set of headphones. Since the camcorder is designed to be operated by one person—the videographer (or news videographer)—he

or she may have to assume the duties of the audio engineer. This may be easy when the production is very basic, but can be quite a burden on the videographer when the audio situation is complex. When more than one or two microphones are required, the person assuming audio responsibilities must set up the microphones with the use of a mixer and then provide one or two audio channels from the mixer to the camcorder for recording. Audio engineers sometimes record a separate soundtrack, called wild sound, on an audio recorder to be added in postproduction.

Lighting Director

Location shoots require a crew member who can provide lighting that will satisfy the basic needs of the camera and the aesthetic requirements of the script. On smaller crews, that job goes to the videographer, but as the size and complexity of the production grows, a separate crew member, the lighting director, can be an indispensable addition. The videographer may need to start blocking and shooting one location while the lighting director and crew start lighting the next location to move the production along at a quicker pace. The lighting director should not only have a thorough knowledge of lighting techniques and instruments but also a familiarity with the specific demands of the lighting situation and the electrical power capabilities of the locations.

Grip or Utility

In the film industry, almost every member of the crew has a specific job title that has evolved over the years. Jobs like best boy, gaffer, and key grip are lumped into one title for TV production: the grip. People from a TV studio background usually call them utilities. Unlike in the film industry, these grips or utilities can cover quite a broad range of jobs in the production unless otherwise limited by a union agreement.

On any given crew, one or more members function as a grip whose responsibilities are to hold, or grip, reflectors or lights, a shotgun microphone, the recorder, or any other piece of equipment that requires attention during the shoot. The grip is often an assistant or apprentice to one of the other crew members and should have a basic knowledge of the equipment—

that is, the grip should know the equipment by name and how to handle it. Because of the responsibility of holding equipment during the shoot, the grip should be steady and capable of moving equipment in and out of location as well as in and out of the vehicle used for transporting the equipment.

Talent

Selecting talent is a somewhat different chore from selecting other members of the team. Whereas other crew members are most often employed by the same company as the producer, the talent may not be. In a half-dozen different shoots, it would not be unusual to have a different main talent for each one. This may not be the case, however, for industrial video for training and demonstration purposes, or for internal public relations programs that have a regular host.

Talent may be selected by committee or by the executive producer, producer, or director. Talent can be locally acquired on location (that is, in the city you will be traveling to) or imported with the rest of the crew. One mistake often made by beginners is to select nonprofessional actors as talent because of their voice or overall appearance. This can be dangerous. Inexperienced talent often force numerous retakes, because they may be unable to take direction to correct mistakes. Sometimes nonprofessionals look terrific in person or in rehearsal but cannot adapt to the real situation when taping. The advice here is to stick to experienced professionals whenever the budget allows.

As in so many areas of today's TV production, many professionals are likely to be in a union or guild. This is very much the case with talent. Many professional performers are required to join either the Screen Actors Guild (SAG) or the American Federation of Television and Radio Artists (AFTRA). A requirement of membership is the commitment to never work without a union contract, even in a nonunion production. This means you will have to pay minimum professional rates (and maybe more) to have a union professional in your show.

Editor

The editor takes the original, or raw, footage that has been shot and, with the help of a script, reassembles the program into its proper order. Often the scenes are shot out of sequence and numerous takes are available for each scene. This allows the editor to use some creativity and professional skills to produce a finished master that is creative and visually pleasing. However, the master must also follow the accepted rules for keeping the flow of the program visually and chronologically correct, while conveying the meaning intended by the producer, director, and scriptwriter.

A good editor enhances the ideas of the people who wrote and visually interpreted the script without changing either its meaning or its effect on the viewer. When hiring an editor, look for three skills: a thorough knowledge of the software and computers involved, knowledge of the input and output players and recorders (and their formats), and, most importantly, a strong sense for how to tell a story visually.

Scheduling and Coordinating

Scheduling an EFP project is often a slow and difficult process. Since many crew members in EFP work have other responsibilities, and video equipment is constantly being used for a variety of projects, getting a full crew with all the necessary equipment sometimes seems like trying to carry all the unfolded laundry without a laundry basket. If you stoop down to adjust a scheduled shoot time for a critical crew member, you may find that you have dropped something else, such as the availability of a special camera or even the talent. Occasionally an unforeseen delay, albeit a short one, can cause a serious problem in postproduction, such as missing a scheduled visit to the editing suite of your choice. Computer scheduling programs like Microsoft Outlook can help with the scheduling process.

Factors to Consider

When creating your schedule, first consider the general categories of items to be scheduled. You have people, equipment, materials, and facilities or locations. Prioritize these items based on your lack of control over them, and schedule first the items over which you have little control. The logic here is that once you have locked into place those items that may have no flexibility, you can more easily schedule in the more flexible items. A couple of examples may help to illustrate.

First, your independent production company may have contracted to shoot a five-minute demonstration/sales video for a company that manufactures a farm implement that attaches to a small tractor. The implement removes weeds that grow between the rows of soybean fields. Obviously, the first thing to do is find out what a soybean is and where it is grown. If you are not from the Midwest, you may think that soybeans grow in health food stores. Fortunately, your client cannot only educate you about soybeans and the new product but also suggest an appropriate location, such as the client's own test plots, for the shoot.

Factors such as soil conditions, weed height, soybean height, and weather may dictate whether you can actually go into the field for a demonstration. In other words, you must know the details and limitations of your location. After all of these factors are considered, a window of time (for example, the last week of May) can be designated as the best time for the shoot to take place.

A second example probably represents a more common situation. An advertiser requests that your independent production company shoot a 30-second commercial featuring a new line of small kitchen appliances. Since the appliances require a precise setting and lighting situation, you decide that a studio is needed.

As is often the case with smaller production companies, you do not own a studio or a space large enough to house the necessary set and lights. In this case, you must find a studio that is affordable and technically acceptable. The studio must also be available at a time that will allow you enough postproduction time to have the commercial completed before the first scheduled broadcast date. Once you have the studio scheduled, you can proceed to schedule other items.

These examples were chosen because location or facilities are often the least available and not within the producer's control. However, any necessary item can have the least availability. Your talent may have only two days a month available for shooting; the digital Betacam HD camcorder that you need to rent may be in high demand and short supply; your whole team may have a sporadic schedule of shots for previously scheduled projects.

As a rule of thumb, you can expect to schedule the following categories of items (listed in descending order of scheduling difficulty):

1. Location or special facilities (studio, office building, yacht).
2. Special equipment (fog machine, fireworks, special spotlight).
3. Talent or crucial crew members (a famous spokesperson or star).
4. Postproduction time, facilities, personnel
5. Graphics, props.
6. Crew members for noncrucial assignments.

Keep in mind that for any given shoot, any or all of these can be difficult to schedule.

Guidelines for Schedule Making

There is no set formula to guide your schedule making, but here are a few hints that will come in handy when going about the chore:

- *Be flexible.* Do not allow your own inflexibility to create scheduling problems. Even if you do not like starting a project on Friday, it may be the best starting day when you consider the schedules of others.

- *Do not schedule too tightly.* Add time for reshooting or catch-up. If your shooting will be done outdoors, make sure you include some rain or snow dates.

- *Consult past schedules whenever possible.* How long did the same crew take for a similar project in the past?

- *Have contingency plans.* What is the probability of equipment failure? Are certain pieces of equipment prone to failure in the field? Make sure that equipment failure, crew no-shows, or talent problems do not prevent you from meeting your completion deadline.

Location Selection and Survey

In this phase of preproduction, the actual shooting location must be selected and investigated for specific information to facilitate the actual shoot. The script will probably guide you to a few choices for the loca-

(M) **MOTOROLA INC.**

VISUAL MEDIA PRODUCTIONS

LOCATION SCOUTING REPORT - Video

Project Number : ___ ___ ___ ___ ___ — ___ ___ ___ ___   Scouting Date : _____

Contact Person : _____   Phone : _____

■ ADDRESS OF LOCATION : _____

Directions/Parking ? _____

_____

_____

_____

_____

FEEL FREE
TO DRAW OUT
DIRECTIONS

■ SPACE REQUIREMENTS :

Number of Camerpersons : _____   Camera Positions : _____

_____

Descibe Shot/Activity : _____

_____

■ LIGHT REQUIREMENTS ;

Level Required : _____   Source of Light : _____

Ceiling Height : _____   Ambient Light : _____

Reflective Surfaces : _____   Sun Location : _____

■ SOUND :

Recording Sound : _____ ☐ Sync ☐ Wild   Potential Interference : _____

Ambient Sound Present : _____ ☐ Use ☐ Avoid

■ POWER :

Location of Outlets : _____   Capacity ? _____

Location of Circuit Breakers : _____   Tie In ? ☐ Yes ☐ No

Engineer/Maintenance Contact : _____   Phone : _____

Figure 6-2   Location scouting report used in corporate video. (Courtesy of Motorola, Integrated Information Systems Group, Visual Media Communications)

tion of your shoot. Many times the location is actually dictated by the script, for example, Walt Disney World, a particular shopping center, or the corporate president's office. In this case, you can avoid the selection process and go right to the scouting procedure.

When the script gives only a general description of the location (for example, the backyard of a suburban home or a classroom), you have to select a few possible locations and scout them with a visit to see if they will satisfy your needs. Beyond the general look or aesthetics of the place, each location that you intend to use must meet some specific requirements. You may want to find some forms that will prompt you to remember all of the variables that you want to consider.

During this visit, you may find it helpful to conduct a survey for later comparison with surveys taken at alternate locations. An excellent way to do this comparison is to use a digital still camera. Using these still shots, you can sit in the comfort of the office and discuss with other members of the team which site would be better suited to the production and what problems other members foresee. The following is a list of some of the questions you need to ask during the site survey or at least before the final decision is made.

Is the location accessible? A beautiful mountain meadow or an island in the middle of a lake may be aesthetically perfect, but if your crew can only reach it on foot, by canoe, or by specially equipped four-wheel drive vehicles, you should be prepared to pay for that or look elsewhere.

Can you get permission to use the site? The owner might let you visit but not necessarily bring your 10-person crew, equipment, vehicles, and the curious onlookers often attracted by the sight of a video camera. Permission in writing is the safest method. A check of local laws regarding shooting is necessary; a permit may be required.

Can you maintain the appropriate traffic control? Shooting on a street corner or side street may seem easy during a 7:00 A.M. visit, but how busy would it be if you shot at 11:00 A.M.? Sidewalks or even hiking trails can be full of curious people, or even not-so-curious people, who demand the right-of-way. Make sure that the owner, park officials, city, or highway police agree to let you divert traffic from your location. In many cities, permits are required to shoot on or near any public property. These permits may also require fees and proof of insurance coverage.

What kind of lighting do you have? Full sun can be as troublesome as no sun at all. You may need to add fill light to harsh shadows or shaded faces. If artificial light is preferred, can you somehow eliminate the unwanted light? Time of day may dictate your shooting schedule.

What are the sound characteristics of the location? Empty rooms without carpeting or draperies may have echoes. In most cases, adding sound is no problem, but taking away sound is nearly impossible. A too-noisy location is undesirable and may require highly specialized microphones. Again, try to find out what the location sound will be at the approximate time of day at which you will shoot.

Is electrical power available at the location? If not, you may merely need to pack some batteries. But if artificial light is required, you will have to generate your own AC power. This may be accomplished with a gasoline-powered generator, but it is another piece of equipment that adds its own bulk and weight, plus that of its fuel. Also keep in mind that video lights require *lots of power* and that the generators produce noise as well as power.

Is there an acceptable spot available for camera placement? Many panoramic views available to the scout may be unavailable to a cumbersome video camera with attached tripod and cables. Make sure that there is a safe spot for your three-legged friend.

Does the location allow convenient loading and unloading? Are the doors and hallways wide enough and the floor even enough to allow your crew to roll in the cases of equipment? Where can you park the equipment van? Inconvenient access can add unnecessary and costly time to your shoot.

Will the location be available at any time after the scheduled shoot? It does not happen often, but even professionals can lose, destroy, or record over raw footage before the edited master is completed. Clients or producers can change their minds about how the program should look and sometimes require a return to the location for a reshoot. Even if this is a rare necessity, it is a good idea to pick a location that allows a possible return for additional shooting.

What crew conveniences are available? Will the crew have to bring their lunches? They may need adequate water, bathroom facilities, shade, or a cool spot to rest. Full sun for a full day or no sun at all may lead to some very unhappy crew members. If talent has been hired to be on location, they may have special needs that require special facilities, such as a dressing room trailer parked at the site.

Will the shoot be sent via microwave or satellite to another location? Can the signal that you send to the other location be seen, or are there buildings, mountains, or interferences that may require special arrangements?

Is safety and security an issue? Can you physically watch all of your equipment (and perhaps all your people) to guarantee safety throughout your stay? How cold or hot does it get at the location? Does your insurance include coverage for shooting at the location or under the circumstances?

Graphics and Props Preparation

The preproduction stage is the appropriate time to order the graphics and other necessary materials so that they will be ready before actual production begins. For most productions, this will include artwork for studio cards that do not have to be recorded in a studio, photographic work for slides, film footage (for example, animation) or computer-generated animation, or graphics. In large production houses, most of these things are done in-house by staff artists, videographers, cinematographers, or computer specialists. Smaller production units often have to find specialists who can provide these materials as subcontractors.

This stage of the production process is the appropriate time to locate costumes, makeup accessories, set props, and other items necessary for the production. If sets or props need to be constructed, initiate the process at this point.

Clearance on Copyright Materials

If you expect your video project to really be yours after it is completed, it is best to make sure that all the material you use has been created by you or people who are working for you on the project. If you or one of your coworkers uses material owned by others, you may find yourself spending time with lawyers instead of looking for more video projects to produce.

The use of other people's material without their permission is a copyright infringement; if you are caught doing it, you have created a legal problem for yourself. The problem arises very often when copyrighted music is used without permission. Four simple approaches will help you avoid this problem:

- If you need music for your program and the music you choose is copyrighted, contact the copyright holder (the record company, music publishing company, or individual artist) in writing and ask for permission to use the material. In your request, be as specific as you can as to your intentions. Name the material, the excerpt (if appropriate), the program it will be used in, the distribution or exhibition plans, and any other relevant information. If you do this far enough in advance of your postproduction time, you may get an approval for use of the materials (referred to in the publishing business as "clearance").

- Use material that is in the public domain— material that has never been copyrighted or material whose copyright has expired. Material that has not been copyrighted is probably available from your local amateur composer or music student. They may have excellent material already composed or may be able to compose music tailor-made for your project. Material composed long ago, such as old folk tunes ("I've Been Workin' on the Railroad" or "Oh, Susanna") or classical music that could be performed especially for your project, is generally available for use, since the copyright has long since expired. (Bach and Beethoven are rarely offended when you use their material.)

- Purchase the material or subscribe to a library service that provides music or other material such as sound effects. These services work in two ways. One way allows you to use the material as often as you need to use it; you buy this privilege when paying for the material, and its use is at your discretion. A second type of service involves a needle-drop fee. Music library services provide you with the material, but you must pay when you use it. Hence, every time your "needle drops" on the record (also known as LPs, those big plastic platelike things used before CDs and DVDs) for actual use in a production, you owe the service a fee.

- Hire a musician or musical group that will use original compositions and perform them for you. Once you pay for this service, you should own the privilege of using the material.

Another consideration is that you have permission to use the images of people who appear on camera in your project. This can be accomplished by having those people sign a Model Release, in which they give specific permission for you to use their image in your project or program. More about this in Chapter 12, Copyright and Legal Issues.

Travel Planning

By definition, all EFP involves some type of travel. Some set procedures for travel will help you to cope with the trials and tribulations of constantly leaving your home base to get the work done. If the travel is local and requires only a reasonable amount of driving time, a minivan, station wagon, or hatchback automobile can possibly serve the needs of a small crew and a one-camera shoot.

Transporting Equipment

For out-of-town shoots, your transportation vehicle should have plenty of space for backup equipment, extra personnel, extra tape, hard-drive recorders or memory cards, and perhaps some test or repair equipment. If your shoot is three driving hours away from your studio or office, you certainly do not want to waste time sending the vehicle back for an extra battery, cable, or mic.

A van or truck might also allow you to bring a power generator when needed. Sometimes, renting the

appropriate vehicle enables you to bring along all the necessary equipment and personnel and prevents the need to hire freelance personnel or rent equipment at the location.

While EFP crews tend to carry their equipment in cases and use different vehicles for different shoots, an ENG crew usually has a dedicated vehicle with the equipment always stored in that vehicle. The typical news van has many built-in shelves and storage areas for the gear (including the camera) that enable quick and easy access. Most ENG gear is kept as ready-to-shoot as possible because of the ever-present possibility of spot news happening. In these situations, seconds can mean the difference in getting the shot or not. The camera system has to be in a constant state of readiness, so that you can just turn it on and shoot. This also means that the gear must be in a secured state while riding in the vehicle at all times. You cannot have equipment rolling around or falling over while you are driving. Careful thought has to be given as to how the gear will be carried. The goal is to get as much equipment in the van as possible, keep it readily accessible, and at the same time keep it safe under all kinds of driving conditions.

Equipment Cube

Whether you drive a car, truck, or other vehicle, you should know the volume and weight of your equipment before your shoot so that you can compare these figures with the available storage space and maximum load-handling capability of your vehicle. This information is probably available in the owner's manuals for your equipment. Before renting a vehicle for a shoot, you should find out how much cubic space is needed for your equipment. Make sure that when you reserve a rental car, you don't just say, "Give me a minivan or a full-size sedan." These terms mean different things to different rental companies. If your cubic feet demand requires a particular brand of minivan, make sure that you request it by name and explain why it is important that you actually get that particular vehicle. Full-size sedans can have widely varying trunk space. If the vehicle you get is too small, you will find that the crew does not like riding to the shoot with heavy equipment on their laps.

EQUIPMENT CHECKLIST

CAMERA

- ☐ Set up and registration
- ☐ Charged batteries
- ☐ AC power supply
- ☐ Camera control unit
- ☐ Distribution amplifier/equalizer
- ☐ Composite/component adapter
- ☐ Wide angle lens/adapter
- ☐ Filters
- ☐ Waveform and vector scopes
- ☐ Tripod w/head
- ☐ High hat
- ☐ Tripod wheels/dolly
- ☐ Boom/crane
- ☐ Steadi-cam/Tyler mount
- ☐ Suction mount
- ☐ Gyro lens
- ☐ Tripod adapter plate
- ☐ Lens cleaner and tissue
- ☐ Shipping case
- ☐ Weather protection

LIGHTING

- ☐ Open-faced lights
- ☐ Fresnel lights
- ☐ HMI lights
- ☐ Reflectors
- ☐ Silks/scrims/butterflies/flags
- ☐ C-stands
- ☐ Extension cords
- ☐ Blue gels or dichroic filters
- ☐ Colored gels
- ☐ Black-out cloth
- ☐ Grip equipment
- ☐ Sand bags/water bags
- ☐ Spare lamps
- ☐ Gloves

RECORDER

- ☐ Record/play test

- ☐ Charged batteries
- ☐ AC power supply
- ☐ Playback machine
- ☐ Color monitor/outdoor hood
- ☐ Coaxial cable/barrels
- ☐ RF cable
- ☐ Multi-pin cable
- ☐ Tape stock
- ☐ Head cleaners
- ☐ Shipping/carrying case
- ☐ Audio monitoring headsets

AUDIO

- ☐ Omnidirectional/shotgun
- ☐ Hand-held/lavelier
- ☐ Fishpole/boom
- ☐ Wireless
- ☐ Filters
- ☐ Format adaptors
- ☐ Mixer/stereo
- ☐ Cables
- ☐ Wind protection
- ☐ Sound panels

ODDS AND ENDS

- ☐ Duct tape
- ☐ Rubber mats
- ☐ Plastic tarps/trash bags
- ☐ Rope
- ☐ Contact cement
- ☐ Tool kit
- ☐ Aluminum foil
- ☐ Spring clamps
- ☐ Colored tapes
- ☐ Magic markers/pens
- ☐ Self-stick labels
- ☐ Chairs
- ☐ Food/water
- ☐ Talent make-up
- ☐ Hair spray

ADDITIONAL ITEMS FOR THIS SHOOT

Figure 6-3   Equipment checklist.

The process of determining the total cubic feet for your equipment can be achieved by simply stacking your equipment, which has been packed in its travel cases, on the floor in a compact manner and measuring the height, width, and depth of your cube. First, multiply height by width by depth to find the volume. Keep in mind that most rental cars, SUVs, and minivans don't have open cargo areas but simply areas where the back seats fold down but can't be removed. The odd spaces created by these folded seats can make loading equipment cases difficult and leave a lot of wasted space. Renting cargo vans is the best solution, but most of the time they are not readily available at airports.

Measuring for the equipment cube may seem time consuming, but it only needs to be done correctly once. New pieces of equipment can usually be added to the list without going through the cube procedure. After you know the amount of cubic space you will

A

B

Figure 6-4   (A) These soft cases are great for carrying your equipment around town, but they are probably not strong enough when checking the equipment as baggage on a plane flight.
(B) For any type of travel, your equipment should be packed well in protective cases; the number, size, and weight of the cases should be carefully noted.

need, it will be easier to select the appropriate vehicle for rental or purchase.

Air Travel

When the location is many miles away, air travel may be the only means of transportation. Because of the large expense involved, you are faced with some tough decisions. Should you bring a full crew and pay their airfare, lodging, and meals, or hire freelance professionals at the location? Should you bring your own equipment, pay for its transportation, risk its rough handling at airport loading and unloading, or pay to rent equipment at the location?

Both questions are complex and depend on the availability of qualified personnel and reasonably priced, dependable professional equipment. Keep in mind that renting equipment often means changing equipment or brands, and operating procedures may be different. Do this only if your personnel are experienced.

Whatever your decisions, make sure that you make your travel plans well in advance of your shoot date. Nothing is more aggravating than going through your travel decision-making process only to find that the vehicle you want to rent is not available or the flight you need is booked. Air travel reservations and tickets bought in advance of the shoot date often result in discount fares, which may allow you to bring the extra crew member or piece of equipment.

Travel Tips

Here are some travel pointers to consider before traveling:

Never put your camera, camcorder, recorder, or laptop computer in with the baggage or airfreight. Always hand-carry these items as carry-on luggage, and stow them either on the floor beneath your feet or up in the overhead bin. Several companies make padded, soft cases specifically to take the camera/camcorder on a plane as carry-on luggage. The camera and recorder are the most important pieces of equipment you have, and you cannot take a chance on them being dropped from the cargo bay door by a reckless handler, or left in Chicago when you've gone on to Los Angeles. You must also be prepared to *shoot* at any time before, during, or after the flight. You should have at least one battery, a tape or storage medium, and a mic—as well as the camera—with you at all times. In some cases, the aircraft is too small to allow storage on the floor or in an overhead compartment. When you must let the crew stow your camera in a luggage compartment, it may be very helpful to personally carry the camera in its case to the aircraft. Try to explain to the person loading luggage that it is an expensive and fragile professional camera. Try to convince them to load it last (and it will be unloaded first). When you arrive, try to connect with a baggage handler to hand you the camera before you go to baggage claim.

Send all of your cases through as luggage on your flight. Never ship any of your gear air freight unless you will not need it for awhile after you get where you are going. Air freight can take a full day or more to get there and doesn't arrive at the same terminal as you do.

Keep all your cases at a reasonable size and weight. Any cases larger than the biggest suitcase typically used by travelers, or any case weighing more than 70 pounds, can be rejected by the airline. This may mean more cases, but at least they will all be boarding the same flight as you.

Expect to pay an excess baggage fee for most of your cases. It is not unusual to have 15 or more cases with you for production shooting or extensive news shoots. It may cost more than sending them by freight (anywhere from $30 to $75 a case), but they will be there when you are. There often is no other option, especially for a traveling news crew.

Call the airline in advance to tell them what you are bringing. The airline may be able to help check the cases through and make better arrangements for your camera on the plane. They are used to dealing with TV crews.

Make sure everything is well packed and padded. As with the determination of your equipment cube, your regular set of gear needs to go through a packing/ padding determination only once. After that, you should have a set of pads that you use whenever you travel. If you think that this is not important, watch how luggage is loaded and unloaded from airplane cargo holds. It will renew your motivation to pack and pad your equipment well.

Make a list with brand names, model numbers, and serial numbers of everything you are taking. Leave one copy at home and keep one copy with you at all times.

Remember that thieves know what expensive video equipment cases look like. In a large airport, an inat-

tentive videographer can lose a case or two in a split second.

Have a Skycap help you whenever you can. This costs more money, but helps prevent theft and makes it easier to haul. This used to be easier than it is now. Because of heavy security, there are fewer Skycaps at airports. Make sure that you have the personnel to handle everything if necessary.

Get a car or van that you can work out of the whole time you are on the shoot. If the car is just big enough to hold the crew and gear with no room to spare, you might find yourself having to dig out equipment every time you need something. It may be better, though more costly, to rent a bigger vehicle or a second vehicle to give yourself some room to work. At least you will not be unloading the entire car at every stop.

Foreign Travel

Traveling outside the United States can be fun and challenging but also a major headache for those who are unprepared. Each country has its own way of doing things; many do not have the rights of a free press. Doing business as usual could land you in jail and, in some repressive countries, could actually get you in big trouble. These are not things to be taken lightly. Do extensive research regarding the countries you will be traveling in to see what media restrictions may be in place. Permits may be required to do any kind of professional photography, including news. Find someone who has shot in that country before and gain from his or her experience.

In addition to the political concerns that can be dangerous to your health, there are economic concerns. Most countries, including the United States, have import/export laws placing tariffs on certain high-quality photographic and electronic equipment. After going to certain countries and returning to this one, you will be asked to prove that the equipment you have is indeed yours and that you bought it here after paying the proper taxes. The best way to prove this is to have a **carnet**, a document recognized by the Customs Service that guarantees that the equipment is yours. You need a complete list of all your equipment with brands, serial numbers, purchase prices, and model numbers. You should have many copies of this list with you as you travel. The carnet requires the posting of a bond for this list of gear (up to 10% of the equipment's value). Although the document is recognized in many countries around the world, it is not recognized in all countries. The next best solution is to simply have the gear registered with the U.S. Customs Service. The carnet is for reentry to the United States, but some countries also take it as proof of ownership. If you are going to a country that doesn't accept a carnet, try to get in touch with their consulate here to make arrangements to get your gear in and out of that country. Always travel with as much documentation as possible. It is not unheard of to have gear confiscated or impounded for lack of documents. There are companies in almost every port, both here and abroad, that offer a customs-help service. These customs brokers are simply facilitators who, for a fee, can guide you through any customs clearance legally.

Press credentials are very useful in a foreign land. Officials at many entry points to a country are accustomed to seeing traveling news crews. Showing a press pass, even a hometown press pass, can prove effective. If your gear looks worn and has ID stickers of the station on it, few customs officials will question its origin. If it is EFP gear that looks new, you will need documentation. A letter from the production company or from that country's consulate introducing you is better than nothing. Always have a return ticket with you, even if it is for an incorrect date. Coming into a country with new or near-new video gear and a one-way ticket can send up a very large red flag. You may find yourself trying to spring your gear from the impound cage for the next few days.

Always have a sufficient amount of cash with you. It is amazing how many problems can be solved with the right amount of money in a foreign land. Credit cards, ATM cards, and traveler's checks may be fine in the hotel, but not elsewhere. Bribery is not a nice word in this country, but it is a way of life in many parts of the world. Gratuities may be a better word, but regardless of what you call it, you had better be prepared for it. Never let anyone see how much money you have, and never keep it all in one place. A healthy dose of paranoia and some preplanning can make your international trip a smooth and successful one.

After the crew has been selected, schedules have been created, locations scouted and selected, and necessary travel preparations have been made, it's almost

time to begin the next phase of the project, production. Before that happens though, you need to make sure that everything that you have planned will actually occur. One of the best ways to do that is to inform everyone involved in the production phase when the shoot will occur, where it will occur, and what will be needed for the shoot. Directors and production managers have to worry about two major ingredients for a successful production shoot: the people in front of and behind the camera. Getting the right people to the right location on time (and for the right length of time) requires a "meeting of the minds" between the director and the talent. Getting the right equipment and people to operate the equipment requires the production manager to schedule the equipment and the people for the shoot. Most of the problems that occur can be avoided by common sense; be clear to the staff about what is needed and when it is needed. One of the best ways is to communicate the requirements simply and noticeably. For example, the Call Sheet shown in Figure 6.5 is a commonly used form that lists all of the talent needed for a particular shoot. The top part of the sheet has spaces to list the unit of production, the day of the schedule (first day of four shoot days), the date of the shoot, the name of the production, the producer, picture title, and director. The next section lists the set, scenes, and locations for the talent.

The cast and day players are the people (talent) who must be at the shoot, and they are reminded what part they play, their makeup, the time they are needed, and other remarks about their role for that day. At the bottom, there is room to list the "Atmosphere and Stand-ins," the people who don't have speaking roles but must be on the set for "atmosphere," as "background" players, or to act as stand-ins for the stars during some of the initial rehearsals.

Similar sheets can be constructed for the crew to inform them where to be, when to be there, and what jobs they will be performing. An equipment "call sheet" is equally important, especially on complex productions that require very specific audio or lighting equipment. The point for all the paperwork is to help make a complex task involving many people, lots of equipment, travel, and lots of hard work as simple and clear as possible to everyone involved in the production. Once you have everything organized for the first

Crew Call

Date: _____
Time: _____
Unit: _____

Day ___ of ___ shooting days

Production/ Program Title:

Producer:

Director:

Set/Scene/Location:

_____/_____/_____

_____/_____/_____

_____/_____/_____

_____/_____/_____

Crew:

Figure 6-5   Forms like this Call Sheet keep everyone informed about the who, when, and where for an upcoming production shoot.

day of actual shooting, it's time to move from the pre-production phase to the production phase.

PART TWO: PRODUCTION/ SHOOTING ON LOCATION

Pulling up to the location of the shoot is when the moment of truth starts. The planning, preparation, and training are now going to be put to use. Now, more than ever, the main factors driving news (ENG) and production (EFP) are in play: *time* and *money*. News is done on a deadline, and production is done on a budget.

In either case, the goal is to stick with what you have learned. You must go about the act of shooting with deliberation: a conscious attention to the details of what makes a story work, what shots are necessary for editing, how much time everything is taking, and where everything is leading. This section of the chapter contains some of the general considerations that need to be dealt with in any location shoot. Each trip into the field will be different. Conditions and circumstances will be different, as will your goals. With a firm grasp of the basic elements of visual communication and the abilities of your equipment, you can execute any shooting assignment—news or production—with confidence.

The three most important points at the start of any location shooting are:

- You must have everything you might possibly need with you at the start of the day.

- You must adjust your needs to the limitations of the site.

- Stick to the plan.

It is expensive to reshoot after you have wrapped from a location.

ENG versus EFP

The differences between an ENG shoot and an EFP shoot can be enormous. The coverage of news events is largely unpredictable, and short notice is more common than advance notice. Therefore, the strategy for an ENG shoot is to be constantly prepared for almost any twist and turn in the situation. A news videographer never knows whether the next shoot will be a plane crash or a city council meeting. As he or she pulls up to the location a mental checklist needs to be done. Sometimes, with very little knowledge of the story or situation, the news videographer must make decisions that can affect the way the story is covered. Things as simple as whether or not to bring the tripod from the car can change the way the story is visually approached. Anticipation and instinct are two very valuable traits in a news videographer. Unfortunately, both of them tend to come with experience, rather than from a textbook. The best way to learn news shooting is to know the basics and just get out there and do it.

Most EFP situations involve following a master plan or script. There will always be unexpected problems, but for the most part, a production shooter will know everything that needs to be done far in advance. The shoot has been planned. The difficulties

during the shoot are keeping things on schedule and on budget while still achieving the producer's goals. Much of this section is aimed at the typical EFP shoot, but all the principles described here can apply to any form of shooting.

Setting Up

One of the first skills a good videographer needs to learn on location is how to imagine the site with all the equipment in place. "Loading in," as it's called, needs to be done with an eye to the finished setup. The camera location is always the very first thing to be determined. But moving a large sofa out of the way of the camera's spot can backfire if it's moved right to the place where the key light has to go. Upon arrival, the videographer must first envision the situation with everything set up, so that equipment can be quickly placed in the right spot the first time.

Figure 6-6   Equipment for a large news or production shoot can take up quite a bit of space. Having everything in cases can make travel and loading easier.

For EFP shoots, keep in mind that just having a crew show up for the shoot doesn't mean that anyone remembers what to do, or at least what they are supposed to do that day or on that shoot. It is a good idea to have a meeting just after making the initial on-site assessment to give out specific assignments. This division of labor will help avoid crew conflicts and also prevent people from standing around at the location. It will also help prevent having all the equipment cases piled right where you need to work. It is always a good idea to establish a staging area where equipment can be close to the final location without its being in the way.

Setting up for your shoot involves a number of individual tasks, some of which happen concurrently. Sometimes, as the scene is coming together, you will notice potential trouble spots. Before the work of the entire crew is wasted, you need to stop the setup and make adjustments. For example, a multimedia project about bicycle riding requires a mountainous terrain to help demonstrate the ruggedness of a new model mountain bike. The site survey and the preproduction process set the bike and a rider against rugged hills or mountains. On the shoot day, the hills are hidden by low clouds. Is there a better place for this shot now that the hills are gone from view? This decision needs to be made before everything is set up.

Initial camera placement is dictated by the type of shot that you want to obtain first. If you want to prevent the busy background behind your subject from being a distraction, you could keep the camera-to-subject distance long and shoot with a long focal lens. This will blur the background. A shot that requires showing quite a bit of detail of a complex object like an old coin needs to have the camera very close to the subject.

The appropriate, preferable location for the tripod is a level area, out of the way of traffic (both vehicular and pedestrian) and wind gusts or water spray. Use of a handheld camera requires that the location also be relatively flat to allow the camera operator to move around unimpeded. Other mounting options present a more complex preparation problem. If the camera is to be mounted on a crab dolly that will travel on tracks, this dolly unit needs a flat surface and plenty of space. You also must allow enough time for constructing the dolly's tracks. Other mountings, such as those on an auto for shots of a driver and/or passengers while driving, or shots of the scenery as the car passes by, take plenty of time and must be mounted carefully to avoid camera vibration while the car moves. In addition, if the car is moving at high speeds, the mount needs to be extremely strong and able to withstand high wind speeds without moving or perhaps getting blown off the car.

Sound and Light

Once the subject is placed and the camera location is chosen, lights and sound equipment can be added if necessary. If the subject is placed in natural light, you might have to add reflected sunlight for fill or use filter material to soften the light. A light reflector will help fill in harsh shadows or simply add more light to the subject. Artificial lights may be added if the available light is insufficient. Adding artificial light to natural light may require matching the color temperature to the existing light, usually 5600° K. This can be accomplished by using an HMI light or placing a color-correction gel (daylight blue) over a standard video light. Specific types of light mounts and light stands can be considered to give the desired lighting on the subject within other constraints, such as available power, available space, ability to reflect off surfaces, and so on. While lighting is attended to, other crew members can be attending to the audio needs of the production.

With any luck, a good scouting report has yielded a location selection that considers the ambient sound of that location and outside sounds such as traffic that might occur at varying times of day. A final assessment at the time of the shoot is always necessary. Things may be different. All too often, small but common things, such as occasional aircraft passing overhead or the all-but-unnoticed rumble of an air conditioner, can escape the location scout but become an extreme annoyance when heard on mic.

Microphone selection and microphone placement are critical procedures on location. Are they or their shadows in the shot? Can framing and lighting accommodate the mic placement demands? If microphone cables are placed across a place where people must walk during the shoot, care must be taken to securely tape the cables to the ground for safety and to prevent cables from being pulled out of the recorder, or microphones being yanked out of your shot because someone or something has caught the cable. They also must be kept away from power cords to reduce the chances of audio interference hum.

Basic Camera Setup and Prep List

- Connect camera to power supply or attach battery.

- Turn on power to camera.

- Remove the lens cap.

- Set focus to manual.

- Set exposure to manual.

- Set filter for indoor or outdoor light.

- Set lights, reflector.

- Set white balance (manually).

- Set subject or object, then adjust lights.

- Set for establishing shot.

- Zoom all the way into your subject/object and focus to get a sharp picture.

- Zoom out to your desired shot.

Location Integrity

Location integrity concerns the assessment and maintenance of the condition of the location at which you are shooting. Although your location scouting should give pertinent information, when you arrive for the shoot you once again have to ensure that the situation will be safe and then make sure the location is not damaged during taping. Everything from electrical shock hazards to the condition of the hardwood floors has to be considered. The shooting location has to be made safe for not only the crew but the public as well. Do any cables or cords run across pathways? If so, are they taped down? Is there sufficient distance between car traffic and the crew? Are all lights well secured and stands weighted down to avoid accidentally tipping them over? You should also consider things like slick flooring or the ability of the location's floor to support your equipment and crew. Crowding all the equipment and crew onto a small balcony to get the perfect shot of the sunset behind your talent might be motivated by aesthetic concerns, but if the balcony can't support the huge increase in weight it has to bear, the shoot could be a disaster.

One important goal in location shooting is to be able to enter the location with your crew and equipment, set up, rehearse, shoot, and wrap up without leaving a trace. It is the same kind of awareness that you would have when going backpacking or camping. You need to use the site, but not abuse it. Heavy, bulky equipment can cause damage to woodwork or even cut grooves in flooring. Hot lights set too close to delicate drapery can cause discoloration, scorching, or even a fire. Rolling or dragging your equipment across exposed wires can also create problems. It is always a good idea—if possible—to have thick blankets like those used by moving companies to place over floors and carpet or pieces of delicate furniture that are very near the equipment setups. Scratching an antique desk can take the profit right out of any shoot or stick the station with a hefty bill. That is why TV stations and production companies have insurance. Without it, your job or entire business could be in jeopardy.

Maintaining Control

Studios are designed the way they are to allow the television producer the ability to control almost all production variables. In addition to sound, light, camera placement, and availability, the studio usually is closely temperature controlled and is considered a restricted area to people not involved in the production. When you go to a remote site for your EFP shoot, your job is to try to control as many of the production variables as you can given the crew, budget, equipment, and time frame allowed for by the project. Again, selecting the right location will help you control the variables.

In any situation where you are acting as both videographer and director (and maybe producer, too) you need to be in charge at all times. You must watch over the entire site, looking for potential problems and safety concerns. If a grip or PA (production assistant) is no longer needed in his assigned role, reassign him to crowd control or to pulling camera cables. Unless you have large unionized crews, it's best to keep everyone working on some aspect of the production or site integrity the entire time they're on location.

In ENG, control may be nearly impossible to obtain. In general, a news shooter will only have to worry about two people: herself and the reporter. And this worry is usually to just stay out of the way. That involves constantly looking over your shoulder and from side to side. Shooting inside a factory with busy forklifts zooming around the plant floor can make for a dangerous situation. Shooting in a sports arena with many intoxicated fans can be just as dangerous. In each situation, you cannot control the environment, so you must have complete control of what you are doing. Tricks like setting up with your back against a wall or fence will protect that direction of approach from unwanted intervention and danger. By using site materials (chairs or tables, for example) or natural boundaries like walls or hedges, you can usually create a little "safe zone" for your setup. The more you can isolate yourself from trouble, the better the shoot will go. Of course, at times you will have to "wade in among 'em" to get the shots. In those cases, all you can do is hold tight to the camera and make sure any cables are closely controlled and not getting hung up on anything. And nothing upsets people more than getting their head banged by the battery on the back of your camera as you turn around too quickly in a crowd. Move with deliberate caution.

Continuity

When you have to shoot in more than one session you have to be concerned with **continuity**. This is a consideration for making sure that from one shot to the next, the important elements stay the same. In other words, your talent has to be dressed the same, have the same hairstyle, etc. For the general background of your shots, you have to be concerned with the appearance of the location. When returning to a location for a second time, you should be thinking about the placement of furniture, props, and all things that were in the shots during your first shoot. Editing together shots with slight background differences results in a jump cut. You should also be looking for differences in light. If you have used artificial lighting in the first shoot, then make sure that your lighting is exactly the same, especially on the faces of the talent, on the second and subsequent shoots. If shooting outdoors, the time of day becomes critical. You should not edit shots together that were shot at very different times of the day, because the color temperature will cause skin tones to

vary. Paying attention to continuity ensures that you can edit shots or scenes together that were shot at different times at the same location without creating jump cuts or leaving the audience wondering why the video just doesn't seem right. Often the responsibility for continuity falls to a **script supervisor**.

Backup Plans

Try not to go to any location without some type of backup plan. This may be necessary for a variety of reasons. Weather problems can force your shoot to a different location to record from a sheltered spot. Last-minute changes in personnel due to illness or conflicting scheduling can force you to rethink crew assignments. If your camera operator is a no-show at the last minute, who will be your backup shooter?

No matter what the plan is, in either news or production, you should always have a what-if scenario in the back of your mind. How can this shot be done while eliminating the offending element? You're set up in a good spot to get the candidate at the podium, but now the audience is standing on their chairs and you can't see the stage at all. How are you going to get the most dramatic part of this speech? You can run down to the front of the crowd, but how will you get the podium audio? Can you still see the politician from an angle that low? Never assume your first choice will work perfectly, especially in news. For EFP you will have more control—and, one hopes, more help—but you still need to have a plan ready when the situation goes awry.

Security

Shooting on location means that you leave the safety and security of the studio. When you go on location to shoot, you bring expensive equipment out into the open for people to see and perhaps give those that are criminally inclined an opportunity to steal it. Not only does theft of cameras and other equipment happen, it happens all too often. Professional camcorders can be sold quickly and often transported out of the country before they can be traced to the rightful owners. There are criminals in this country who travel to newsworthy events to see if an opportunity will arise to steal equipment. ENG often requires a news crew to shoot in a high-crime area, increasing the chances that thieves may see the equipment and try their luck. Although it would be rare for a camera to be stolen right off the tripod while the crew is working around it, the times when cameras and other equipment are being loaded and unloaded are the most opportune for thieves. The most simple rule of thumb for protecting your gear on location is to never let it out of your sight. If you're by yourself, that means taking the camera to lunch with you and even to the bathroom. You wouldn't leave a $10,000 diamond necklace lying on the back seat of your car while it's parked, would you? Many cameras are worth a lot more than that.

Your crew is also at greater risk on location. Muggings and assaults can happen, especially when newsworthy events are occurring and attention is focused on a particular action, but not necessarily the perimeter where the production crew is working. In ENG work, reporters and videographers are often in danger from other people, but also from the elements of the event itself. Shooting a forest fire, hurricane, or tornado presents obvious personal danger. News events like foiled robberies that result in hostage situations can lead to shooting, bombs, and other dangers. Covering wars, uprisings, or events like the riots that occurred in Los Angeles after the legal decision in the Rodney King case can put television production people in a situation where danger can come at any time and from any direction. In dangerous situations, the job of the EFP producer is to keep his crew and equipment safe. In ENG, the crew might only be the videographer and the reporter. These people must truly "watch each others' backs" while shooting.

It is not unreasonable for producers and even news crews to hire private security guards to accompany them into the field when the possibility of danger exists. In larger cities, production crews pay off-duty police to watch over the production.

Dealing with the Public

Remote shooting doesn't necessarily imply shooting at locations remote enough to be far from the public. This is especially true in ENG, where most of the stories involve people. On a large-budget EFP project, crowd control is often the responsibility of a crew member, such as the assistant director. Even if production permits don't require it, that person should get permission from the appropriate authorities to barricade streets or portions of streets to keep curious onlookers away from the shots. When this is not possible, a crew member should be asked to deflect passers-by and gawkers. The vast majority of the time, people who appear at the location are merely trying to satisfy their curiosity about what is going on.

Unfortunately, these folks and their questions (or their desire to be on television) can be time-consuming distractions and can jeopardize your ability to get the necessary shots. It is a constant job to find shorthand ways to fend off the curious (sarcastically referred to by news people as "lens lice") so that you can get the work done in a timely manner. It is never a good idea to be rude or curt with the public, no matter how obnoxious their behavior may be. It is not uncommon for people to vent their anger about the news media at you, even though you may be on a production shoot. Don't argue with them. Say you're sorry for the state of affairs in TV but you're powerless to change any of it. Acknowledge their complaint but don't enter a debate. You have work to do, and they have years of anger that won't be satiated in this situation. Avoid confrontation at all costs. This is one of those unforeseen factors that can change a shoot. One belligerent member of the public can shut down an entire production. You could be forced to move to another location or call the police.

Checklists

Shooting on location with portable equipment is a complex task that consumes considerable time and energy. You can easily make it an even harder task by trying to memorize everything that you need to do and bring to the shoot. Instead, make appropriate lists and notes to yourself (and others) during preproduction so that you can arrive at the shoot with everything and everyone that you need for the shoot. You can begin setup, rehearsal, and shooting without having to return to home base to get forgotten equipment, supplies, or even people. In EFP, the location shoots are often very different from each other. No two are exactly alike. Therefore, the equipment and facilities that you require for each shoot are probably somewhat different. Using the facilities sheet during each shoot helps you keep track of everything that you need for each shoot on location.

This sheet has been known for years as a "fax" sheet, but now that the electronic send/receive devices common to almost all offices are referred to as fax machines and people use fax header sheets with every fax sent, it is best to rename the facilities sheet to avoid confusion with a sheet used for electronic faxing. Using a checklist for equipment needs and facilities will save you time as the shoot goes along. "A gaffer's clamp would really solve this problem, do we have one?" Check the sheet.

You should also have checklists of shots needed for the day or location. It's easy to forget the cutaway of the sign after spending so much time on the talent's blocking and lighting. Even in news, it is a good idea to have a scratch "laundry list" of shots in your pocket. A quick meeting with the reporter at the start of the story can lead to such a list. The reporter goes off to gather facts and the videographer starts the methodical work of "knocking off" the list. There are always so many things to remember and deal with (like the public) that forgetting a very small but highly important shot can easily happen. If at all possible, make a list.

Recording

After taking into consideration all of the above ideas and concerns, it is now time to start recording. Keep in mind that all that has been discussed so far is actually there to ensure that the creativity of the shoot can happen in a safe environment free from unnecessary distractions—even if it's in the middle of utter chaos. By being acutely aware of all that's going on around you, you can now comfortably change your concentration to the real business at hand: shooting. Nobody ever said TV was easy.

Rehearsing

In EFP, rehearsals can begin as the camera, lights, and sound equipment are being set. This may involve a performer narrating, an athlete demonstrating a tennis swing, a chemist pouring liquid into a test tube, or even an animal performing a trick. The person who is directing the shoot should see how the subject will per-

form the desired action and make sure it is in keeping with the intention of the script. This is often a judgment call on the part of the director, because it is the director who has the most influence on the visual interpretation of the words and directions contained in the script.

This is the time when many problems make themselves apparent. Lights may need to be adjusted, the mic placement changed, or the entire shot scrubbed. Rehearsals can actually start before the talent or real subject is there. If you have any idea what the action will be, have a stand-in walk through the scene. They may be the wrong height or hair color, but seeing a body in the shot can get the scene closer to the final frame. There's a saying in the movie industry: "You can't light air." It means you can set up all the lights you want, but until there is an actual subject in the picture, you can't tell if everything is working according to plan.

Even in ENG, it's a good idea to rehearse such things as stand-ups or even to first walk through a handheld camera shot before recording it. You may find that the shot doesn't work and you can quickly move on to something else. Many reporters never "nail" the stand-up on the first try. Especially if the stand-up is going to take place as some background action is happening, a good rehearsal can save the shot. As the complexity of the shot increases, so does the need for rehearsal. The reporter may want to do the on-camera shot just as the train is pulling into the station. Walking through the shot while imagining the train being there may look silly to the watching public but could also mean the difference in getting this one-chance shot right or not getting it at all.

Shooting (and Reshooting)

As your finger is poised on the record button, there is one more checklist to be gone over. Is the camera white balanced? Is the focus set? Do you have enough recording time? Is the audio good or do we have a plane flying over? Are the batteries holding up? Are you comfortable? It doesn't do the scene any good if the camera operator is contorted around the camera and can't stand there for more than 30 seconds before fatiguing, or if the eye piece is not adjusted for your eyes. You should be at the point where everything has been dealt with and now, free from anxiety, all you have to do is just make the shot.

Your concentration can now turn to maintaining framing, following the action, and making sure the shot goes the way it was intended to work.

It is of crucial importance that you know what you have recorded once the shot ends. You may be surprised by how often your memory can conflict with what actually ends up on the recording. In the jostling of the crowd, how long was the candidate in the frame? You may think it was several seconds, but after reviewing the shot it might turn out to be only one or two seconds—not enough to be usable. Don't say you have the shot unless you are absolutely sure you have it. In EFP situations, you often have the luxury of playing the shot back in the field to check it. That, of course, presents another possible problem: after playing back a shot, you must make sure that you recue properly so that you don't record over previous material. In ENG you almost never have the ability to look at what you have done in the field. You simply have to know what you have or don't have recorded. That requires a rather intense level of concentration, often involving counting the seconds in your head to determine the length of shots.

A constantly revolving and evolving checklist of factors, such as camera wobble, framing, anticipation of action, the best focal length to use, editing considerations, and simply choosing which subject to follow, are all part of the creative process. Once again, that's why you can't be overprepared for any shoot. And news can be the most difficult of all to plan for. In the chapters on ENG and EFP styles, more specific information is given as to what kinds of shots and techniques various situations will require.

Wrapping Up

There are several pitfalls that you should think about when you begin to wrap up after your shooting is over. First, are you sure that you have shot everything that you will need? Less experienced videographers often make the mistake of leaving the location without getting all the shots necessary for the editor to put the story together. The shots most commonly left out are cutaway shots or transition shots used to cover some bad video. It is best to review your shots on a color monitor to make sure that all of your shots have proper color balance, exposure, framing, composition, and acceptable backgrounds. At this time it is a good idea to listen carefully to your audio. You may find that some of the audio is not clear, or that you picked up some interference. This is also a good time to record some ambient sound for use in editing. After you have completed this test of your recorded material (and have reshot anything that is not acceptable) you should begin to wrap up.

Start the process by turning off all of your video lights. The less you use your lights, the longer they will last, so turn them off as soon as you are sure they are no longer needed. Also, they must cool down before they can be removed from their mounts and put back into their cases. Next, if you are recording onto tape, remove all tapes from recorders and check to see if all tapes are properly labeled. Make sure you do this before the power to the recorders is cut off, because you cannot eject tapes without power to the machines. If you are shooting on hard drive or flash drive, make sure that your footage log is accurate. The next step is to turn off the camera and remove it from the tripod or mount. Put the camera in its case or in a very safe but visible place, usually on the floor. Remember not to leave the camera unattended, because this is the point in the location shooting process when cameras can be stolen. Your tripod or mount should then be taken down to traveling size and put in its case, if it has one. All connecting cables for signal and power should be properly coiled and stowed in the accessories case or bag.

At this point, it is appropriate to carefully remove all gaffer tape that you have used on floors, walls, or doors. You may have to remove any sticky residue that remains after the tape has been pulled off. Sticky residue on glass can be carefully removed with a razor blade. Floors, walls, and desktops can be cleaned with a mild solvent, but avoid using any liquid on wood surfaces if at all possible. If your light housings are cool to the touch, they should be lowered, then removed from their stands or mounts. Place the lights in their case, but remember that the bulbs are extremely fragile, especially when they are hot or even warm. Take down the light stands or mounts and place them in their case or secure them in the vehicle. All props and set pieces should be removed and placed in the vehicle. You probably should place your camera in the vehicle last so you do not have to put heavy equipment cases on top of the camera case.

Now you should have all the equipment loaded in the vehicle, and you can conduct a very careful visual survey of the location called the "idiot check." Check around power outlets for extension cords left behind. Was your equipment placed in more than one room at any time during the shoot? This is another good reason to have a staging area where equipment can stay when not in use. Check all rooms used for the shoot. And pick up all the trash generated during the taping, such as coffee cups and soda cans. If the site is as clean as when you first entered it, and the objects or furniture have been replaced in their original locations, ask the contact person to look it over. Let them know you have made every effort to return the site to its original condition. If they "buy" your cleanup, thank them for the use of the location (especially important if there is any chance that you might have to return to that location) and leave with peace of mind.

Even in the hectic pace of news, take the time to restore the site you have used to an acceptable condition. Your trash can be a very ugly reminder of why many people distrust or even hate the media. Sometimes, you may only have apologies to give for the trampled flowers, but make some type of effort to acknowledge your damage. Don't confuse arrogance with the rights of a free press. If you make a mess, take responsibility for it.

Whenever possible, take the time before you leave a location to make sure that you have gotten all of the shots that were planned on the shot sheet (or shot list).

This is also a good time to make notes on your video log about the quality of the scenes and takes. Write notes about which scenes or shots might require a reshoot or getting alternative footage. Once you leave the location, it will cost you time and money if you have to go back to it.

SUMMARY

Good video projects come from good planning and good execution. It has been said that in EFP, you should plan the shoot, then shoot the plan. In ENG, the situation is somewhat different, because there rarely is time to make a plan, so preproduction for news shooting has more to do with being prepared for anything and everything that can happen. Even though ENG is usually a bare-bones style of shooting, you must have a myriad of supplies and equipment with you or in your vehicle at all times. The ability to improvise will often come in handy.

EFP almost always starts with a plan. After a project is initiated, the preproduction process of goal setting, research, scriptwriting, crew selection, location selection, and materials preparation begins. Careful consideration must be given to travel of any kind, because it involves not only people, but sensitive and expensive equipment as well.

The culmination of the preproduction process is the actual production. The crew needs to unload the equipment with a special consideration for where the camera will be placed and how the location will be lit and the sound collected. When arriving on location, it is important to carefully note exactly what is there—the location of the furniture, plants, books, etc. It will be important after the shoot, when everything must be put back exactly the way it was before the shoot. Professional videographers always have a backup plan for any location and are always careful about security. Protecting your equipment from the elements and theft is important. Security also means making sure that your crew is safe at all times. Before you shoot, make sure that all of the variables that should be under control are under control. Consult your checklists for things you need to do before the shoot. If everything seems right, the actual shooting should occur and go smoothly. Remember, don't leave a location until you are sure that you have all of the shots that were planned and any shots that might help make a better video project. After the shooting, wrap up by removing all equipment and making sure that the location is in exactly the same condition as you found it.

7

Postproduction: Editing It All Together

After planning a project in preproduction and acquiring all the aural and visual elements during the shooting or production phase, it is time to edit everything together in postproduction. In this computer-based, **nonlinear editing (NLE)** age, many editors begin their work during the production phase, selecting and sequencing shots at the end of each day's shoot. Digital editing makes this possible because editors do not have to wait until all the film footage or analog videotape is complete. Instead, they can complete a digital sequence, save it on a computer, work another sequence, and then another, ultimately retrieving all the saved sequences and making some tweaks for the final edit.

Since the dawn of the 21st century, three digital NLE systems have captured most of the market for video postproduction: Avid, Final Cut, and Adobe Premiere. Each of these comes in different versions to meet different budgets: Avid Media Composer and Avid Express; Final Cut Pro and Final Cut Express; and Premiere Pro and Premiere Elements. To be sure, there are many other editors, such as Windows Movie Maker, which comes with Microsoft Windows; iMovie, which comes with Apple computers; Pinnacle, which Avid purchased; and Sony's products, including

Vegas Video. These are just some of the available video editing programs; by the time this book goes to print, there might be further buyouts and mergers, as well as new products.

While each editing program has its unique characteristics, all the programs share a common logic and use similar functions. In the first part of this chapter, "Technical Editing Basics," we examine the common ideas and steps for nonlinear editing, regardless of the hardware and software. It is beyond the scope of this section to train you on any one editing system; instead, this section is intended to be a companion as you learn the editing software available to you with that system's manual and tutorial, and maybe an instructor. While this section discusses digital nonlinear editing, we recognize that some editors continue to work with analog linear tape. For this reason, Appendix D provides a general discussion of analog tape-based editing.

In the second part of this chapter, "Creative Editing Basics," we explore the conceptual or theoretic principles of editing: the constructs of audiovisual storytelling. These concepts apply to all video editing, regardless of the linear hardware or nonlinear software used.

PART ONE: TECHNICAL EDITING BASICS

Telling a story effectively remains the objective of editing in the digital age. That was the goal in the first era of motion image editing: cutting and splicing film. That continued to be the intent in the second era: analog tape-to-tape editing. (See Appendix D.) In today's third era of digital NLE, effective storytelling remains the aim. To achieve a successful story in digital postproduction, a series of 11 logical steps is recommended:

1. Log
2. EDL
3. Capture
4. Import
5. Trim
6. Sequence
7. Layer
8. Effects
9. Mix
10. Render
11. Distribute

Log

During production (Chapter 6), you can begin to watch and log your footage immediately after you shoot it. Logging continues after you've finished shooting, until you have all your audio and visual elements logged. A **log** is a list of what you have acquired, with brief notes describing each item. You can create your log with simple pencil and paper or use any number of software programs to assist you. (See Figure 7-1.)

For your log, make a list of each shot or audio clip in order on each tape, disc, or drive. As you review your video and audio elements, note the timecode number if the element is on tape, or the filename if it is on a disc or solid-state card or drive. Briefly describe the shot, including the shot size (LS house, MS Bob, CU Carol, etc.), to help you make editing decisions later. Also, note any problems with the shot (out of focus, bad lighting, shaky, poor audio, etc.), or if the shot is good, and where you might include the shot in your final piece.

Edit Decision List

Having logged your video footage and sound elements, you can make decisions about how the project might edit together. You can create an initial **edit decision list (EDL)**, using pencil and paper to write down the shots and sounds in the order you think you might edit them, or you can use a software program to help you generate your EDL. (See Figure 7-2).

For the EDL, you select the shots from the log that you want and write them in the sequence they are to appear in the master edit. In addition to noting the length of each shot, you can keep a running sum of the overall length, or **total running time (TRT)**, to get an idea of how long the project will be. You can also note special considerations, such as transitions you plan to use, music clips you plan to lay under, and so on.

It is very valuable to create an initial EDL, because that focuses your thinking and helps you make some preliminary decisions before you sit down at the computer. The acronym EDL refers not only to this initial plan of editing, but also to the final list of edits after you have finished. This final EDL is valuable if you first edit an initial, **rough cut** of your project, and then use the EDL to make the **final cut**. A rough cut is a preliminary version of your project, without fancy transitions, sound sweetening, and other items that will be added later to give the project its final polish.

Sometimes, preliminary editing is done in an **offline edit** session. This term goes back to the days of videotape editing, but is useful in computer-based editing, as well. An offline editor typically uses low-resolution copies of the original footage to edit a rough cut, making the critical editing decisions (sequence of shots, trimming heads and tails, length, pace, etc.) without the added time and cost of rendering high-resolution files, transitions, audio mixes, and the like. The offline editor also generates an EDL to give to the online editor. The **on-line edit** session costs more than the offline session because of the advanced equipment and editing talent. Here, the editor uses the edit decisions from the offline session, but edits the high-resolution files for the final cut and includes transitions, effects, titles, full sound mix, and any other elements needed for the finished piece.

For many low- and no-budget ENG and EFP projects, including student productions, the offline

Log for Drive/Tape #	Name			Project	p.
No.	Filename or Timecode	Length mm:ss	Video shot size, subject, action, movement	Audio in- outcue	Comment
1					
2					
3					
4					
5					
6					
7					
8					
9					
10					
11					
12					
13					
14					
15					
16					
17					
18					
19					
20					
21					
22					
23					
24					
25					

Figure 7-1   A sample video logging sheet.

and online sessions are combined, with the editor making the initial edits from full-resolution files, adding effects, mixing audio, and the like as he or she works through the footage, using the preliminary EDL as a guide. Of course, many changes are usually made along the way as the editor tries different and better

EDL	Name				Project		p.
No.	Drive or Tape #	Filename or Timecode	Length mm:ss	TRT	Video Description	Audio Description	Comment
1							
2							
3							
4							
5							
6							
7							
8							
9							
10							
11							
12							
13							
14							
15							
16							
17							
18							
19							
20							
21							
22							
23							
24							
25							

Figure 7-2   A sample EDL sheet.

ways to cut shots together. In the computer world, editors can save projects at the end of their sessions and open them another day, changing them over and over until the editors, directors, producers, clients, and others are happy with the final project, or until the deadline hits.

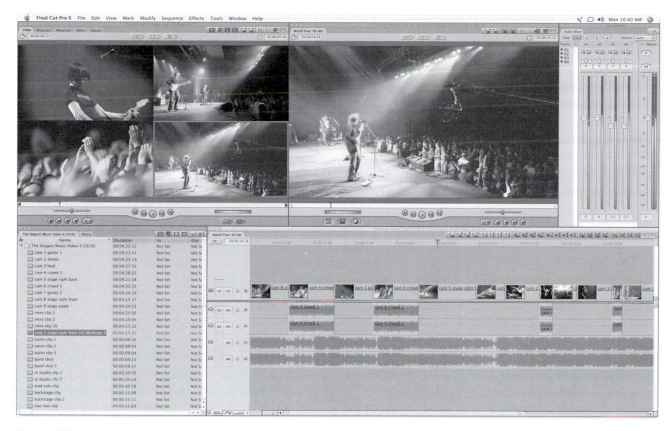

Figure 7-3   A screenshot from Final Cut Pro. In this arrangement, the clip storage area (browser) is bottom left; source monitor (viewer—here a quad split) top left; record monitor (canvas) top center; audio mixer top right; and timeline bottom center and right. (Courtesy of Apple)

Capture

With all the aural and visual elements assembled, and with a log and EDL to get started, the actual editing session (whether offline or online or combined) begins by capturing the footage onto a computer drive. If the footage was acquired on videotape, such as Mini-DV or DigiBeta, a VTR or camcorder must be connected to the computer, usually by **FireWire (IEEE 1394)**, **Universal Serial Bus (USB)**, or **Serial Digital Interface (SDI)** connections. If the source material is on a disc, such as Mini-DVD or Mini-CD, the disc must be placed in the disc drive. If the original files are on a **solid-state** medium, such as a memory card, Flash device, or computer drive, that medium needs to be connected to the computer.

After launching the editing software program, one of the menu items—often under the "File" menu—is to **capture**. Capturing is the process of transferring the footage from its acquisition medium to the computer drive from which you will edit. A capture window typically prompts you to name each file and to select a drive and folder to store the captured clips. Capture all the elements you plan to use in editing your project. Note that by logging your footage in advance, you can save time and drive space by NOT capturing the shots that are no good and that you do not plan to use.

Import

Once the footage has been captured onto your computer drive, you need to **import** it into the software program for editing. Some programs automatically import the clips when they are captured; others do not. Look for the "Import" command—usually under the "File" menu—which prompts you to go to the folder where you stored the captured clips. Click on the clips you wish to edit and import them. Most software interfaces have a clip storage area (bin, browser, or whatever your software calls it), which is a window that contains the icons and/or names of the clips you import. (See Figure 7-3.) Note that importing does not actually move a clip to a new place on the computer drive; it merely creates an icon in the software interface's clip storage area that "points" to the actual clip. Note that if you move that clip to a different folder or location on your drive, or if you rename it or delete it, the software will not be able to find the clip. When that happens, you will be prompted that the clip cannot be located.

Trim

Once you have imported the clips, you need to **trim** each one. Trimming refers to cutting the **head**—front or beginning of a clip—and **tail**—back or end of a clip—so only the frames you want are seen or heard in the final project. Most editing software gives you at least two ways to trim. One is to drag a clip from the bin to the play monitor (viewer, source, whatever). Usually at the bottom of the monitor window are buttons to click for the **in-point** and **out-point**. (See Figure 7-3.) The in-point is the frame on which you want the clip to begin playing in the final edit. The out-point is the last frame you want. Play the clip and click on the buttons for the in- and out-points on the frames you desire.

For example, imagine a clip that begins with some shaky footage as the camera operator attempts to pan and zoom onto a subject. Eventually, the shakiness stops and the subject is seen in a steady shot with good focus, lighting, framing, composition, and audio quality. After the desired soundbite, the subject ad-libs some irrelevant comments. You only want the part of this clip with the steady shot and the usable soundbite, so you mark the in-point for a frame AFTER the shakiness and BEFORE the subject speaks the soundbite. Likewise, you mark the out-point AFTER the soundbite but BEFORE the irrelevant ad-lib.

The second way to trim a clip is to drag it to the **timeline** (sequencer, whatever). (See Figure 7-3.)

Once the clip is in the timeline, you can move the cursor to the head of the clip, and the pointer changes to another icon for trimming. Click and drag forward, or right, to lose the unwanted frames: the shaky footage in our example. To trim the tail, place the pointer at the end until it changes to the trim icon, then drag back, or left, to lose the unwanted footage at the end: the ad-lib in our example.

Sequence

The timeline (sequencer, whatever) is the window you use to arrange the clips in the order, or **sequence**, you wish. If you trimmed a clip in the source monitor, you can simply click on that image in the monitor and drag it down to the timeline. If you already dragged the clip to the timeline and trimmed it there, it's ready to go. You can watch your edits as you build them on the timeline by looking at the record monitor (canvas, playback, whatever). (See Figure 7-3.)

Arranging clips is as easy as clicking and dragging on their icons in the timeline and dropping them where you want them. This works the same for both video and audio clips. Usually, you will experiment with different arrangements of shots, continuing to trim them a bit here and there until the sequence of shots plays back with a clear storyline and smooth flow. An important feature in most software programs is the "Undo" function, usually under the "Edit" Menu. When you trim or move a clip and decide you don't like what you've done, you can select "Undo" and voila, you are back to the way things were before you made the trim or move!

Layer

On the timeline, you can add more video and audio tracks. The new video tracks stack on top of the existing tracks, and the new audio tracks appear under the existing tracks. These multiple tracks allow you to **layer** new video and audio into your project.

Typical uses for multitrack layers of video elements are **matte** shots, which are images that **key** or **superimpose** one image into another. Another use is for **titles** that are keyed into other shots, such as **lower-**

thirds, which identify a subject's name on the lower-third of the screen. Typical uses for multiple layers of audio elements are to add sound effects and music tracks to dialogue tracks.

Effects

With the video elements trimmed and arranged, you might want to add some visual effects. These can include transitions between shots, rather than straight cuts, such as **fades**, **dissolves**, or **wipes**. Effects can also include **filters** that change brightness, contrast, and color. Other effects blur and distort video clips, or alter the original footage in all kinds of ways. Most software programs have an "Effects" menu under the "Window" or similar command. *Caveat editor:* just because your software allows you to add effects doesn't mean that you should. If your story is strong, your shots are good, and your audio is clean, you can communicate your message effectively—and even better—without effects. Use them cautiously, only when they truly contribute to the message. Consider the wisdom of Huell Howser, the producer and talent of a popular travel show in California, who states that whenever he sees lots of fancy effects he assumes the producer is covering for the story that's missing.

Mix

With the audio elements trimmed and arranged, you might want to make some changes to the aural clips. To **mix** them, you simply stack them on multiple layers. (See Figure 7-4). You want to **balance** the various audio clips so that the most important element—usually the dialogue—can be heard easily (foreground), with the other elements—usually sound effects and music—at a lower level (background). This is the same **figure-ground** principle used in composing visual images (Chapter 4); with audio, it is the primary sound and not the picture element that is the "figure" and receives foreground attention, while the other contextual audio elements are in the background. To adjust the audio levels, most software provides nodes (rubber bands, whatever) with which you can pull the audio level up or down. Typically, you place the cursor over the line in the middle of an audio clip, changing the cursor to a pointing finger, allowing you to click to create a node. Drag up for increased volume and down for decreased volume.

You might want to add some audio effects, such as **fades** and **cross-fades**, allowing the audio to come in or go out gradually rather than harshly. Other effects allow you to add **echo** or **reverberation**. **High-pass** and **low-pass filters** allow you to reduce frequencies at the low and high ends, perhaps to make a voice sound hollower and less resolute, as if it were coming through a telephone. **Notch filters** let you reduce a certain range, or notch, of frequencies, such as a 60 Hz electrical hum that might have been recorded inadvertently with the dialogue, or cut down **room tone** if the microphone was too far away from the subject. **Parametric** and other **equalizers** allow you to manipulate frequencies even more, such as boosting or lowering bass or treble frequencies in a musical recording.

Render

To see visual effects and to hear audio effects, you must **render** them by instructing the computer to create a new file with those effects. Unless a new file is created, the software can only play back the footage from the original file, which does not have the effects. Many editors render short effects as they work so they can double-check how they look or sound. For example, most computers can render a one-second fade or dissolve relatively quickly, or even show a common fade or dissolve in realtime without rendering. For longer effects, such as adding a sepia tone to a one-hour western to give it an old-world look, the editor often waits until the end of the day, saves everything in case the computer crashes, and then selects the "Render" or "Export" or similar command just before leaving, allowing the computer to render this large effect through the night.

However often you render or do not render, when the final project is complete on the timeline, you will likely want to render the final piece. Most software can play back the production from the timeline and even print it onto videotape from there. However, if the playback magnet or laser has to skip from one sector or drive to another sector or drive, that skip can appear as

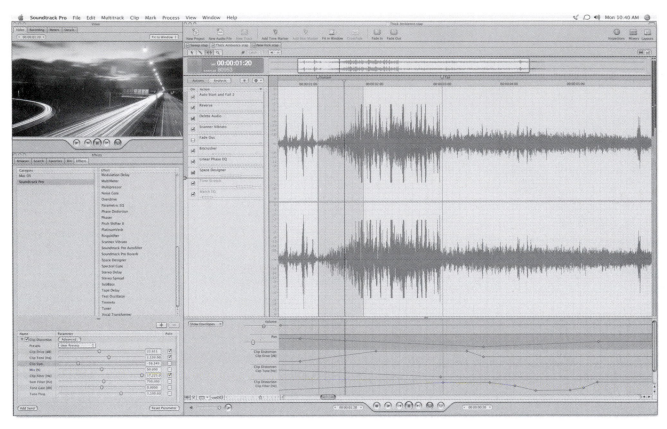

Figure 7-4   A screenshot from Soundtrack Pro. Multiple audio layers are stacked; the tracks of the stereo clip being edited are on top and have been expanded to show the waveform; and the nodes on the tracks below show the balance—when the level of each track is brought up or down. (Courtesy of Apple)

a glitch on the video. Is it best to render, or export, the entire project into a single file. That way, when printing to video, mastering to CD or DVD, or copying to another drive or solid-state medium, the playback magnet or laser only needs to read one file continuously.

Distribute

Once your final project is rendered, the last step in the postproduction process is to make it available for distribution so people can see it. A number of options are available. You need to consider cost, technology available to you, ease of accomplishing your final project format, playback technology available to your target audience, and other factors in deciding the best way or ways to finish your production for distribution.

Outputting to Tape   One distribution option is to print or export your project to videotape. Most soft-

ware programs have a "Print to Tape" or similar function—usually under the "File" menu—that lets you set things up, including a **leader sequence** (color bars, tone, slate, countdown), and then start a videotape recorder (VCR) or camcorder, which is connected to the computer, to record the project.

Authoring a Disc   You might also create a **compact disc–read only memory (CD-ROM)** or a **digital versatile disc (DVD)** with your production. (See Figure 7-5.) Using the disc authoring software on your computer, you can burn your video project file onto a disc, perhaps setting up the disc to start playing by itself (autorun) or even to display a menu with chapters and other selections for your viewers.

Posting on the Internet   The Internet offers a potential medium for distributing your project. Using the Web page creation software on your computer, you can create a homepage for your project, from which you can create a link to the video. Then e-mail the link

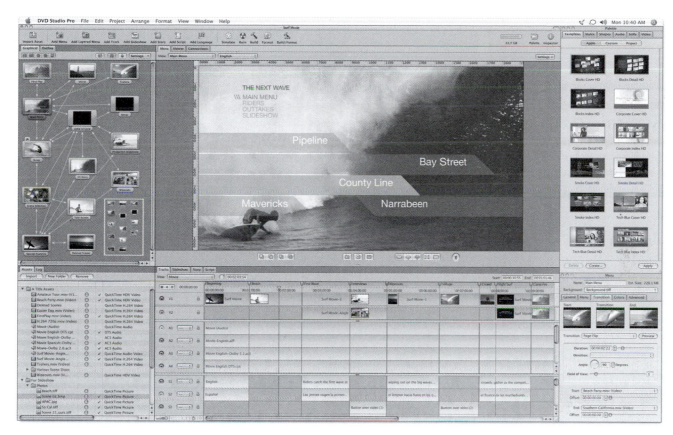

Figure 7-5   A screenshot from DVD Studio Pro. This is set up to author a DVD, including a menu that allows viewers to select certain segments by assigning them chapter markers. (Courtesy of Apple)

to everyone you know and invite them to watch your masterpiece!

Four media players have captured most of the market for playing video and audio files on the Internet: Windows Media Player, which comes with Windows operating software; Apple's QuickTime Player, which comes with Macintosh operating systems; Flash, created by Macromedia and owned by Adobe; and RealPlayer. There are other players, but these four dominate the market. Each offers a free player—for both Windows and Mac operating systems—that can be downloaded from its Web site. *Caveat emptor:* the Web sites naturally try to persuade you to purchase the full-blown version of each, with which you can create content and not just play it back. The free version is playback only; you may choose to buy the full version if you wish to use that software to compress your project for distribution on the Web.

Each media player uses its own compression **algorithm**—the mathematical formula for removing re-

dundant information from video and audio files to make them smaller and more suitable for sending and downloading via the Internet. Many content creators compress their files with at least two of the dominant media players—Windows and QuickTime—because these come loaded on every computer: Windows on PCs and QuickTime on Macs. Many use RealPlayer, as well, because of its popularity. Flash usage has grown in recent years because nearly every computer has it and because the popular video website YouTube (owned by Google) uses Flash. If you choose to use just one compressor, it is recommended that on the homepage for your project you let readers know which media player they will need to view your video, and provide a link to the Web site from which they can download the free viewer. For example, if you use Windows Media Player, you might direct Macintosh users to the "flip4mac" Web site to download the free software that plays Windows Media files within QuickTime.

Technical Concepts

When working with video, you can gain a better understanding of the editing process by familiarizing yourself with some key terms and concepts that explain video recording and playback. A solid grasp of the fundamental technical aspects of video should provide a good context for understanding what happens technically during editing.

Scanning

The chapter on video explains in detail how a camera converts light coming into the lens into an analogous electrical signal for recording. If it is a digital camera, it then samples that analogous waveform into a binary series of 1s and 0s. That signal is played back in the same way it was recorded: through a process of **scanning.** Three different scanning processes make up the global television and video market: the **National Television System(s) Committee (NTSC)** standard, used in the USA, Japan, and other countries; **Phase Alternation Line (PAL)**, used in Germany, Australia, and other countries; and **Séquentiel Couleur À Mémoire (SE-CAM)**, used in France, Russia, and other countries.

NTSC video is created by a **scanning beam** that traces out 525 lines on the face of a TV monitor. It does this in two moves, called **interlaced scanning.** (See Figure 7-6.) It scans first the 262.5 odd-numbered lines and then the 262.5 even-numbered lines. This entire scanning process occurs 30 times per second (actually 29.97 frames per second [fps] for historic engineering reasons that have to do with image stability when TV migrated from black-and-white to color). Thanks to our **persistence of vision**, this is fast enough to allow our eyes and brains to believe that we are seeing a solid, constant image.

Fields, Frames, and Segments

The complete scanning of either the odd or the even lines forms a half-picture known as a **field.** Two fields, when combined or interlaced, form a **frame** or complete picture. In some tape formats (e.g., older one-inch type C), a frame is encoded onto tape in one continuous line and is called a **nonsegmented format.** Other formats (e.g., mini-DV) that encode each frame

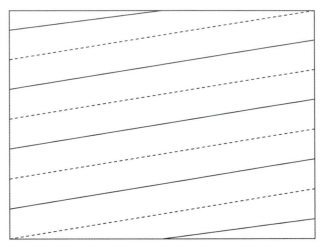

Figure 7-6   For interlaced scanning, the odd-numbered fields, represented here by solid lines, are scanned first, followed by the even-numbered fields, represented by dashed lines.

on a separate line are called **segmented formats**. (See Figure 7-7.) The nonsegmented format allows for some special effects, like noise-free slow motion or freeze-frame, without using a time-base corrector; segmented formats require time-base correction.

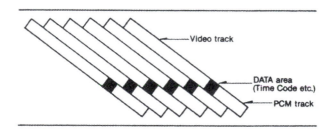

Figure 7-7   Segmented track pattern on a cross-section of mini-DV tape.

Tracking and Skew

When video is recorded on any tape format, it is recorded at a particular speed with the information placed onto the tape at particular locations and angles. The precise way in which the image is laid down on the tape is called **tracking**. Because each videocassette recorder (VCR) might have slightly different tracking from the next, the tape might play back differently in different VCRs, or "decks." Many VCRs have a control that allows the playback machine to track very closely to the way the original recorder placed the information onto the tape. Older videotape machines required you to set the tracking control (measured by a small meter) on your source and or playback machines to optimize tracking. Most current video decks have **automatic track finding (ATF)**, an electronic system that lets the machine adjust itself for optimal playback.

While tracking refers to the precise angle of each scan across the tape, **skew** refers to the tension of the tape around the video drum. Like tracking, skew can vary from machine to machine. As with tracking, older VCRs had manual skew controls, while today's machines adjust the skew automatically.

Digital Recording

Analog and digital are two ways of encoding information onto a storage medium. Conceptually, the difference between the two may be understood by considering analog to be a continuous process while digital is a discrete process. **Analog** videotape recording occurs when the recorder receives electrical signals that are converted from, and analogous to, the light and audio waves that the camera and microphone pick up when recording. The recorder continuously tries to make a copy of those signals.

Digital encoding breaks the electrical signals down into small "pieces" or **bits** and assigns a numeric description of the signal using 1s and 0s. This process is called **sampling**: taking a sample of each point along the analogous waveform and assigning that point a digital, or binary, code. (See Figure 7-8). The higher the sampling rate—that is, the more samples per second—the better: more points along the wave are used so they reproduce the original wave more accurately. The more bits used to code each point the better: more 1s and 0s give each point a more discrete, or unique, code. For example, many **digital video (DV)** formats can record audio with a sampling rate of 48,000 **Hertz (Hz)**, or 48,000 times per second, meaning that each second of the audio waveform is broken down into 48,000 unique pieces. Additionally, these formats can record at 16 bits, meaning that a string of 16 1s and 0s is assigned to each of those 48,000 points per second. This is a very high-quality sampling and recording rate—even slightly better than is necessary for human hearing.

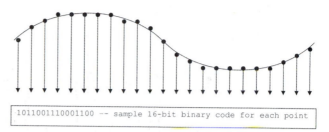

Figure 7-8   Sampling involves the selection of many points each second along a waveform and assigning each point a binary code of 1s and 0s; here, 16-bit sampling assigns a string of 16 1s and 0s to each point.

The device that samples the original analog waveform and converts it to a binary digital signal is a **coder-decoder (codec)**. Different digital video formats have different codecs, and the devices are built into the cameras. For example, the mini-DV codec compresses the digital signal by a ratio of 5:1 (more on compression in the next section). To convert video that has been recorded in an analog format (e.g., VHS), stand-alone codec boxes are available that can be connected to the analog videotape recorder (VTR) for input into a digital source, such as a computer, to record the converted signal at output.

Compression

Digital video requires many megabytes (MB) of storage space. Uncompressed, one frame of NTSC video needs about 1 MB. That means one second (30 frames) needs about 30 MB. Even a multi-gigabyte (GB) hard drive can fill up fast at those rates! For this reason, most codecs also **compress** the signal: they remove redundant information to reduce the file size. For example, if a newscaster sits in front of a still backdrop, that backdrop does not have to be recorded separately for each frame. Instead, the backdrop can be digitized once and the signal can be coded to include that same backdrop in each frame for however many seconds the clip lasts. Then only the newscaster's movements must be recorded for each individual frame, reducing the amount of digital information required for each frame while maintaining the image.

Compression may be either **lossless** or **lossy**. Lossless compression schemes reduce the file size without any loss of detail. In the previous example, if neither the backdrop nor the newscaster is recorded with any loss of resolution and at a full frame rate (30 fps), the compression is lossless. However, it is sometimes desirable to compress a file even more, particularly for delivery over the Internet to people who do not have very high-speed connections. To accomplish this, lossy compression is necessary: removing additional information to reduce the file size considerably. In our example, the newscaster's segment could be reduced from, say, a full DV 720 × 480 pixels to just 320 × 240 pixels. The number of bits recorded per pixel could be cut, reducing some color and brightness information. The frame rate could be cut in half to 15 fps, discarding every other frame so that the remaining frames each hold on the screen for two frame counts. The audio could be cut down by resampling from 48,000 Hz to 22,000 Hz, and the bit rate could be cut in half from 16 to 8. All this compression seriously reduces the file size, but on playback the viewers see a smaller, jerkier image with tinnier sound because both video and audio fidelity have been lost.

It should be noted that audio information does not require nearly the storage space that video information requires. You can download the audio file of a favorite three-minute song in a second, but downloading the three-minute music video of that song takes longer. Because audio requires less file space than video, compressing audio does not result in as much savings as compressing video. For this reason, some content creators choose to leave the audio uncompressed for full fidelity sound even when they compress video. That way, the viewers can at least hear high-quality audio even if they have to watch small, jerky video.

A number of different compression systems are available. New systems are constantly being tested to improve video quality while decreasing the space required after compression. Some still cameras that also record short video clips use a lossy compression system developed by the **Joint Photographic Experts Group (JPEG)** called **Motion-JPEG.** Common DVDs use a lossless scheme created by the **Moving Pictures Expert Group (MPEG)** called **MPEG-2,** which reduces video to about 20% of its original file size. That same group has developed a newer compression algorithm called **MPEG-4,** which is supported by all four Internet media players: MoviePlayer, QuickTime, RealPlayer, and Flash.

For video editing, most professional software offers a variable compression rate that allows for different levels of quality. A high-compression mode (smaller file size) is used for doing offline edits, which increases the speed of the process and reduces the amount of storage needed, but greatly lowers the quality. A low-compression mode (larger file size) is used for online editing where the edited master file is high resolution, suitable for broadcast or high-quality storage, such as DVD or professional digital tape.

Digital Videotape

A number of digital videotape formats are on the market, including DigiBeta, DVCam, DVCPro, and digital HDTV. While each has its unique characteristics, such as the width of the tape, the angle and speed with which the video head passes across the tape, the placement of the video fields on the tape, and the method for recording audio, all the formats share some common characteristics. Here we'll use one popular digital video (DV) format as an example to explore a bit more detail: **mini-DV.**

Mini-DV is the low-cost format of choice for many consumers, as well as prosumers and even some professionals. The audio and video recording is excellent and, as with all digital formats, tape dubbing has no **generation loss.** This format features a very small videotape cassette (the tape is just 1/4-inch wide, or 6 mm), thus allowing for very small camcorders. Tapes consist of a plastic ribbon covered with a metal oxide that is magnetized to record the digital signal. VCRs that play and record mini-DV range from inexpensive camcorders to sophisticated units with many features. (See Figure 7-9.)

Figure 7-9 This DV player/recorder has time-based stability and is used to feed digital nonlinear editing systems. (Courtesy of JVC)

Mini-DV resolution is 720 × 480 pixels. Scanning is interlaced. Audio may be recorded at different sampling levels, the best being 48,000 Hz at 16 bits. The mini-DV codec uses a 5:1 compression ratio, allowing just under five minutes of full-resolution video per GB. Mini-DV contains the typical information tracks of all videotape formats—audio, video, and control track—but also has a subcode and an Insert and Track Information (ITI) track. The subcode track contains information about timecode, date, time, and track numbers. The ITI area contains information that allows video insert editing. Audio information is stored in two ways: one way, **pulse-code modulation (PCM)**, offers CD quality, while the other, **linear**, allows audio dubs after the original video is shot. (See Figure 7-10.)

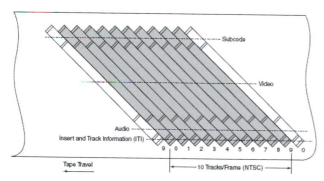

Figure 7-10   Track pattern on a cross-section of Mini-DV tape.

A higher-definition version of DV is available, **HDV**, which provides **progressive scanning** rather than interlaced scanning and the wider HD aspect ratio of 16:9 rather than the NTSC aspect ratio of 4:3.

Tapeless Recording

In addition to tape-based recording, tapeless recording systems are gaining popularity. Some cameras use **optical disc** recording, which burns the digital signal onto a disc with a laser light. For example, some photo cameras can record short, compressed video clips on mini-CDs. Some full-resolution camcorders record on mini-DVDs. **Solid-state** recording devices are also used. For example, some cameras record on memory cards or sticks. Some can be connected directly to hard drives. The advantage to solid-state recording is that

there are no moving parts that can wear down or break: no magnets pass across moving tape, and no lasers burn spinning disk surfaces. Because of the promise of longer-lasting hardware, many manufacturers began debuting solid-state recording devices for cameras in the early 2000s. As storage devices increase in capacity while decreasing in size and cost (a 2 GB USB Flash card the size of a keychain costs about $20 at discount stores as of this writing), solid-state recording will likely continue to replace magnetic tape and optical disk recording.

Nonlinear Editing (NLE)

Whatever the format for acquiring footage—tape, disc, or solid state—once it is in the computer, each shot is a separate file. Like a word processor that stores documents as separate files, these digital shots and sounds can be stored and retrieved easily and in any order, unlike a linear tape, which has to be shuttled back and forth to arrive at different shots. This ability to access shots randomly is called **random access**.

Nonlinear, random-access editing may be done in one of two different working environments: **stand alone** and **work group**. The stand-alone station is just that—an editor that is self-contained and can be used to edit all images into the finished product. Once all information and files are available at the station, a final cut can be put together by the operator. Stand-alone stations do not require network connections with other equipment, and therefore there is no need for network compatibility. A stand-alone system includes everything the editor needs: CPU, software, monitors, keyboard, mouse, and other peripherals for input and output, including tape decks, camera connections, and so on.

Work group editing requires workstations that are interconnected by some type of **local-area network (LAN)**. Video and audio workstations, graphics stations, digitizing stations, logging stations, character generation stations, and special effects and animation stations are all connected to allow multiple editors to access a centrally-stored data bank with raw video and audio that can be transferred to and from editors.

Whether stand alone or work group, the raw audio and video files can be edited using either **destructive** or **nondestructive** editing. In destructive editing, once a file is edited, it is saved in place of the original file. This is useful when storage capacity is limited and there is too little room to save both the original file and the edited version. However, if the editor changes his or her mind and wishes to retrieve the original file to make a different edit, it is too late. In nondestructive editing, the original file is maintained. The edited file is given a different name and saved apart from the original file. This is the preferred method because the original file can always be retrieved for editing anew. However, this method requires more storage capacity to keep both the original file and the edited file.

PART TWO: CREATIVE EDITING BASICS

In addition to understanding the technical editing basics of your video hardware and software, it is vital to know and apply the creative editing basics—the conceptual process of telling a story in images and sounds. You may think of each shot and each audio piece as a sentence or phrase. Just as we apply proper grammar when using language, a grammar of sorts exists in the assemblage of shots and sounds on the way to forming stories.

Everything in an edited piece should have a purpose and a relationship. Every shot is there for a reason; every sound is there for a reason. Every shot should be related to the shot before it and after it; every sound related to the video over it. Everything should work together to tell the story so that the product is greater than the sum of its parts.

Each shot must be in its position to meet an objective—to carry out a function. The story line must be advanced by the constant progression of video images (still or moving) and audio sounds (dialogue, music, sound effects). Editing is not just the butting together of shots; it is the creation of a story with a beginning, a middle, and an end, all working to communicate an idea or show an event.

Sequencing the Shots

Ideally, every grouping of shots, or **sequence**, should have an overall statement or idea. The viewer should come away with more than just the experience of seeing a collection of pictures—a slide show. There should be an understanding of the point just made. The idea might be as simple as a blood shortage at the Red Cross, but a random collection of shots on this subject adds nothing to a viewer's perception of the shortage. To the contrary, a well thought out ordering of the proper shots can convey much added information and understanding for the viewer.

Instead of random shots of the interior of the blood center, a careful selection can show the viewer what the script is conveying. A good four-shot segment on the blood shortage might consist of: (1) an opening shot of a nearly empty room of donors giving blood; (2) a medium shot of a nurse assisting a donor; (3) a close-up of a blood bag being filled at the end of a tube; and (4) a closing shot of a technician stacking filled bags in a large but empty cooler. This series shows how few people are giving blood and demonstrates that very little blood is on hand to give to hospitals.

Basic Sequence

A basic sequence is made up of a wide shot, a medium shot, a tight shot, and a cutaway. This is the minimum sequence, but the idea usually stays intact within many variations. This basic sequence translates into the following:

1. Establish what the viewer is seeing: wide shot.
2. Develop that idea by giving more detailed information: medium shot.
3. Emphasize the details: tight shot.
4. Add any related information, if necessary, to break the thought and prepare for the next sequence, perhaps using a cutaway.

Preparing for the next sequence, in most cases, simply means allowing for an unnoticed bridge of time in the telling of a story.

Sample Script and Photoboard

Consider the following script to open a soccer story, along with a **photoboard** (like a storyboard with photos) to illustrate the edits. (See Figure 7-11.)

(Fade in ELS soccer stadium with crowd nat-sound).

What draws people to soccer? Is it a large stadium? How about the National Anthem? Could it be a roaring crowd? Maybe it's the sheer action: running fast, kicking hard, making the goal. When it's over, one team leaves the winner, and one team leaves the loser, every time.

(Take shot of player with SOT.)

There can be two story lines here: the written story as it appears, and a visual story that can add even more information to what is being said. Read the script over to determine:

- The amount of on-air time you have to cover.

- The specific subjects that must be shown.

- The picture information that can be added to enhance the story.

Allowing time between question marks for a little natsound, the script could be about 25 to 30 seconds long. Considering that a shot needs to last 3 or 4 seconds for the viewers to process (with exceptions—shorter for fast sequences, longer for slow sequences), this means the script can be covered with about eight to ten shots. Let's consider eight possible shots; more can be inserted later for quicker action.

Each story for a TV newscast should start off with about two or three seconds of **pad**: video with **natural sound (natsound)**. Because the news is live, timing errors can be made on roll cues, which can cut off, or "clip," the first second or two before the roll-in goes out over the air. It is better to lose some natural sound than part of the reporter's audio track, which is essential to understanding the story.

In our example, a good opening is an extreme wide shot of a soccer stadium with natsound of a crowd. After a few seconds of pad, the natsound is brought down to **bed level** (background) and the reporter's voice begins the opening script. Shots two and three illustrate the reporter's speculation about the National Anthem and a roaring crowd. Shots four and five show

the action of the game. Shot six is the climactic close-up of a goal. Shots seven and eight bring closure to the sequence, contrasting the winners and losers.

Note a few other important elements in this sequence:

- It has a beginning that sets up the story—a question about soccer's draw, followed by a middle—some reasons for the game's popularity, and an end—winners and losers.

- The basic shot sequence is used, beginning with a (very) wide shot to establish the story, then moving to medium shots, followed by a close-up for the greatest detail at the most dramatic moment, and ending with two slightly looser shots.

- The closing two shots set up the contrast between winners and losers, showing the reveling winners in a group with their faces to the camera, while a member of the losing team stands alone with his back to the camera.

- The sequence comes full circle, beginning and ending with stadium shots, starting with the anticipation of a full crowd in an extremely long shot and ending with a tight shot of a lone player in a defocused, empty stadium.

- The guidelines for framing and composition are used. For example:

  - The rule of thirds and figure-ground principles are applied throughout.

  - Shot two uses selective focus and leading lines to draw attention to the last players in the line.

  - Shot two also shows the players looking screen right, using normal left-to-right screen direction, appropriate for the start of a game before the action begins.

  - Shots five and six reverse the screen direction, using right-to-left movement, reinforcing the drama of a competitive sport.

(PAD NATSOUND) What draws people to soccer? Is it a large stadium?

How about the National Anthem?

Could it be a roaring crowd?

Maybe it's the sheer action: running fast...

...kicking hard, making the goal.

(NAT SOUND UP)

When it's over, one team leaves the winner,

and one team leaves the loser, every time.

Figure 7-11 Photoboard of a possible opening sequence to a soccer story.

- Shots five and six also maintain consistent screen direction; that is, the goalie jumps screen left and the ball enters the goal screen left.

- Shots five and six also use diagonal lines to reinforce action.

- All the shots flow smoothly from one to the next, maintaining continuity with no jump cuts. In most cases, the cuts reveal new subjects. In one case—the goal—two shots illustrate (five and six). Here, the match-action cut (defined in the next section) would occur on the motion of the goalie jumping toward the ball and the ball hitting the net.

Think about these shots, cut on the words as illustrated in the photoboard, and see how they fit with the script. We have interpreted the script visually. We have captured the feel of the story. We have also added to the words by showing more than the words alone can reveal, such as the excitement of the goal and the contrasting images between winners and losers.

This combination of sequence and pacing is just one possible way to cover this script. As you work with the shots in the edit room, you might find that some will look better when allowed to run longer and others when used very briefly. No two editors will cut the story the same way. In effect, there is no single right way to do it. The only common denominator is that it should tell a compelling story that flows smoothly and can be understood by the viewers.

Match-Action Cutting

Within sequences of this type, there is a method called **match-action cutting** that can really make a sequence come alive. If the video was shot with this in mind, or if you as the editor are clever enough to see it in the raw material given you, match-action editing can help give dynamics to a story. The idea is to make it appear as though more than one camera is recording a scene and it is being edited live, as if you are switching between two cameras the way a director does in a studio.

To perform match-action editing in ENG or EFP, the photographer must separate the action into the different parts and then shoot each part separately. One example is the goal in our sample sequence above. (See Figure 7-11.) The cut between shots five and six is a match-action cut. In shot five, the goalie leaps to block the ball. On the motion of him in the air, a cut occurs to show a close-up of the ball hitting the net. Assuming the videographer covered the game with just one camera, the goalie's leap and the ball going into the net are actually two different shots at two different times, but by editing them together with a cut "on the action" the editor creates the illusion that this is one goal.

Another good example is a factory assembly line. A sheet of metal is taken from a stack, put into a drill press, drilled, removed, and put on a new stack. Each part of the process is broken down into different shots, each from a different angle and with at least some variation in focal length.

The shots are edited together so that the viewer follows the sheet of metal through the drilling process but from many vantage points instead of just one. The worker removes a sheet from the pile in a wide shot; on his action of swinging it into place on the press, you cut to a medium shot taken from the side of the press to see the sheet slide into position (it wouldn't be the same sheet, but they all look alike), and so on. As in the soccer goal example, the actual cut should be made on motion or movement, just after the movement begins. The human eye is programmed to track motion, so when a cut is made just after some motion begins, and that same motion continues in the next shot, our eyes follow the motion and we don't even see the edit.

For smoothly matched action, the edits must be precise. Each edit must be very accurate with respect to the action so all the movement appears continuous. The position of the subject in the last frame of the first shot must be the same (or appear to be the same) as the position in the first frame of the second shot. If an edit is not "spot on," it will look like a jump cut. The assembly line example is an easy one because the same thing takes place over and over; there is **repeated action**. It is harder to get the shots necessary for match-action editing when you have no control over the situation and things are not following a set pattern. For the soccer example, matching action is harder than for the assembly line; still, sports have regular patterns of play, making it possible for a thoughtful and quick sports shooter to shoot for match-action cuts.

Matching or repeated action exists in most things you shoot—look for it. If you are shooting in an office and one of the subjects answers the phone, talks, and then hangs up, perhaps another call will need to be answered. For the second call, choose a different angle and/or focal length. You could, say, match-cut a tight shot of the phone ringing to a wider shot just as the person picks up the receiver. A good editor sees the sequence and cuts it together to put life and interest in an otherwise dull office sequence. This can be done without staging the events; simply look for repeated action on the part of the subjects and anticipate where best to place the camera. Even in standard interviews, the establishing two-shot can have the interviewee in the exact same position saying something similar to the beginning of the soundbite. The edit from the two-shot to the talking head shot can be made into a match-action edit. It looks sharp, but it has to be done correctly. Watch movies to see how they use matched action and then look for examples of it in TV news.

Maintaining Continuity

Even in news shooting, like movie making, the visual story is often done in bits and pieces to be assembled later. The continuity of the finished product determines how well the viewer is able to follow the story. There are several aspects to maintaining good continuity when it comes to choosing camera angles and shot choices in the editing process.

The 180° Rule

The main element of continuity is the **180° rule**. A simple example of this is an interview for TV news or any two-person conversation in production or theatrical settings. In the theater, the audience stays on one side of the subjects. When you are shooting, the camera replaces the audience and therefore should always stay on one side of the action. Draw a line between the two people involved in the interview or conversation. All camera angles should be taken from one side of

that line or the other. You choose which side of the line to shoot from, but you must stay on only one side.

This line is sometimes called the **line of interest** or the **action axis**. The direction in which a person is looking determines a line of interest or axis of action, such as two people in an interview: they look at each other creating one line. All of your camera angles should be looking either up or down one side of that line.

For ENG and EFP videography, a line should be established in most shooting situations: meetings, speeches, concerts, protests, marches, sports, or simply any place where there is movement. If the subject does not determine the line, draw one where you will have the best background or lighting conditions and stick with it. Your wide shot not only establishes what you are looking at but also the relationships among the objects in the picture. These relationships must be maintained. People walking left should continue walking left in any shots that show them. The line rule keeps the relationships constant throughout your sequence of shots, no matter how many shots you use. (See Figure 7-12.)

For example, a speaker delivering a speech shot from the left side of the room (as you face the speaker) will be facing screen-right. Through the rest of the piece the speaker will always face right. A line of interest is drawn between the speaker and audience. The audience will always be facing screen-left. If you shoot all your shots with this in mind, any combination of shots can be edited together, and the audience will always appear to be facing the speaker and vice versa. The viewer is never at a loss to identify the relationships among the subjects.

Crossing-the-Line Editing

These points work well when the shots are done correctly and in a controlled situation. What if the shots were not done correctly, or the situation was uncontrolled and no line was ever established? The editor still must maintain continuity for a good, understandable flow of shots. By letting the line float but always keeping it in mind, the editor can move the camera angles anywhere if she does it carefully step by step.

The key to continuity is movement or direction, both actual and implied: the actual movement of a basketball team on the court or the implied direction

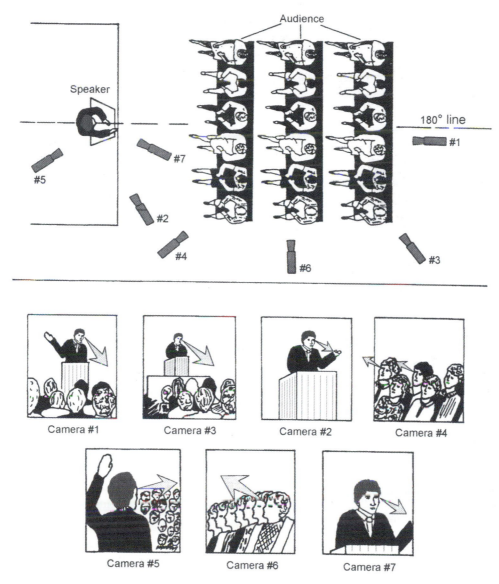

Figure 7-12   Camera placement and several sample shots for covering a typical speech. Here, the 180º line, or action axis, is between the speaker and the audience.

of a person sitting on a park bench. As long as it has movement or direction, any shot you start with defines your first continuity line—your line of interest. A good rule of thumb to get to the other side of that line in editing is to "turn" on one of these types of shots:

- A shot straight down the line of interest.

- A shot that literally moves across the line, taking the viewers along from one side to the other.

- A close-up shot.

- A wide shot that cuts to another wide shot with a different line.

In the example of the speaker and the meeting, a shot straight down the line of interest would come from the center-back of the room and have no movement or direction. This type of shot destroys the line started from the left side of the room and gives you freedom to reestablish a different one. You could also dolly a camera from the left to the right at the back of the room, visually taking the viewers across the line. You might also turn using a close-up: shoot a tight shot of the speaker facing left, then cut to a wide shot from the other side of the room so that the speaker is now facing right. You have crossed the line but not confused the viewer, because the speaker (the reference point) is in both shots. The dramatic change in focal length will mask any jump in speaker's position or posture. If you want to turn using two wide shots, you can shoot one from the left rear of the room and cut to a wide shot from the middle of the right side of the room. It is possible to turn and not confuse the viewer by using wide shots, because all the elements of the scene are present in both shots, although they are still very different.

For this crossing-the-line editing to work, the line cannot be crossed very often or the continuity will be lost anyway. As always, when you sit down to edit, look at all the shots available to you, not only for content but also for continuity. You should be able to separate shots into sequences by continuity, grouping shots with common lines of interest and identifying turn shots to cross those lines if necessary.

Continuity within Sequences

Continuity can be changed at the end of a sequence, but not in the middle of one. Each visual sequence, like a written paragraph, must stick to one subject. Within a sequence, every subject that has movement or direction must maintain that direction. To allow the viewer to understand that subject fully, each shot in the sequence must flow easily to the next shot. Each aspect of continuity must be maintained within the sequence.

Movement If the subject's direction or movement is to the right at the beginning, it should always be to the right throughout the sequence. Watch a good action movie and look for the direction of the subjects (cars, people, backgrounds). Look for the 180° rule and study how it is used. The continuity is usually very good in action movies. Also watch how they use turn shots to change the line.

Details Continuity also refers to other elements in the picture besides movement. Not only must directional and spatial relationships be maintained, but also the details within the sequences. An obvious example is the clothing a subject is wearing. If the subject has on a green shirt in one shot and a blue shirt in the next, but there is no implied change in time or place, then there is an obvious break in continuity. This also applies to the details of position and tone. You can't cut from a medium shot of the mayor slumped in his chair on the phone to a wide shot of him leaning forward drinking coffee, or from a tight shot of the councilwoman's angry glare on the podium to a medium shot of her laughing. They just don't fit together.

Background Objects in the background cannot move from one shot to the next because there will be a disruption in the sense of reality. For example, furniture in a room must stay in the same arrangement. Continuity means that background elements must remain the same within the framework of the story line. For ENG and EFP, many elements are not controllable, but you still must avoid very obvious breaks in continuity. In a story about a family moving out of their house, you would not show a scene with the father packing the last box in an empty room then cut to the mother packing a box with that same room half full.

Lighting The lighting within a sequence must also remain the same. Shots taken on a cloudy day cannot be intercut with shots taken in full sunlight. A dusk-to-night outdoor concert should not show the group playing at full darkness cut with shots of the audience in sunset lighting. The time difference is too great and noticeable to even the least discriminating viewer. TV viewers are all professionals at TV watching—they have been doing it almost all of their lives.

Establishing a Story Line

ENG and EFP productions tell some sort of story. As a videographer or editor, it is your job to make that story come alive and make it understandable within the confines of the script and the time limit. Many news pieces and commercials have no real visual story line, just a sequence of shots that show a particular subject. But whenever any action occurs or time obviously passes during a shoot, it can be put into story form. The script determines most, but not all, story lines in EFP. In ENG, the subjects themselves determine the story lines. Whenever you shoot or edit for either news or non-news, your goal should be to establish a good story line.

In the scriptwriting chapter (Chapter 5), we covered the elements of a basic story: a beginning, a middle, and an end. In visual terms, the beginning is like a wide shot; it establishes the primary setting, characters, and relationships. The middle is like a medium shot; it pulls the viewers into the story with more details that move the characters and events forward. The end is like a close-up; it drives home the main idea with the most intense or dramatic moments. Each of these three parts of a story can be conceived as consisting of one or more paragraphs, or segments. By visualizing each segment, you can shoot and edit a thorough, interesting, and satisfying story.

Visualizing Paragraphs

No set length or number of shots makes up any segment. The beginning may be just one shot or many. The total length of the story usually determines how long each segment will be. A 90-second story probably will not have a 30-second opening sequence. Once you have established a story line in your head or on paper, break it down into its beginning, middle, and end. Take each part and look for the visual paragraphs, or sequences, that make up that part. By organizing yourself before you shoot and edit, these visual paragraphs should come together in a flowing, descriptive story.

In many TV scripts, it is impossible to establish much in the way of a visual story line. Many pieces end up being laundry lists of shots or *wallpaper* jobs. The script has no real visual interpretation, except for the very literal. A story about banks that are in financial trouble may be made up of exterior shots of the banks named in the story. The news photographer and editor have little creative input on the story line. If the writer and photographer can work together as much as possible, some of these situations can be avoided or worked out.

The point is to strive for good TV—that mesh of good audio and good pictures that communicates the maximum information to the viewer. In following the script, strive for the best sequencing and story line. You have a good chance of communicating something if you can visually hold the viewer's interest. Sometimes pretty pictures are the best solution to the story

line problem if you cannot obtain sequencing within the confines of the script. In this case, each shot should be able to stand alone as a complete idea or picture.

Shooting without a Script

The biggest difference between ENG and EFP is the order in which the product is assembled. For EFP, you are shooting to a script, and it is easy to get what you need to cover that script. You go out knowing which pictures to get. For ENG, you are shooting for a script that has not been written yet. It is hard to second-guess how the final story will be structured, what parts will be included or left out, and what specifics will be written about. You must shoot to maximize the editor's latitude when the piece is edited. At the same time, you cannot provide too much material, because there will not be enough time to go through it all within the usual TV news deadlines.

Sometimes you must shoot for two or three different story lines because the outcome or direction is unclear as the story develops before you. At a certain location, the story might be the crowd at the beach, the heat, the traffic, the troublemakers, or people being turned away because the park is full. All of these elements, or only a few, can be included in one story, or you may concentrate on just one. The final script determines the type and amount of material that should be shot, but the final script does not materialize until long after the shooting is over. How do you cover all the possibilities and come up with good sequences and story lines but not overshoot?

The writer-producer is often not present when you shoot the video. However, if you follow the basic guidelines regarding what kind of shots to get, and keep in mind what it takes to edit a story, you should have the material for any good basic piece. If you look at each situation as a mini-story (beginning, middle, end) and shoot each situation as though it will be sequenced together (wide shot, medium shot, tight shot, cutaway), then you have covered all the bases.

By getting the minimum number of essential shots, you have covered the story and given the editor the basis for cutting to almost any script. Get the basic four-shot sequences first, just in case that is all you get. Extra shots or artistic shots can be taken only after the basics are recorded and time permits. If the editor is in a hurry, there must be places in the video where the basic shots can be found without much searching through shots that, while good, may be of lesser interest or importance to a basic story line.

Pacing

The last element in the relationship among shots in editing is the pacing, or timing, of the shots. The timing of each shot helps determine the mood of the piece. As a general rule, a shot less than two seconds long will not be consciously perceived by the viewer unless it is a very graphic or aesthetically simple shot. A shot longer than seven seconds with no movement is usually longer than the viewer's attention span. The average length of most shots in EFP and ENG is about four seconds. A zoom, pan, tilt, or action in the picture can allow a shot to run almost any length, depending on the mood you are trying to capture.

Ultimately, it is not a fixed number of seconds that is important. What counts is that the shot is on long enough for the viewers to "get" the information and not so long that it causes them to lose interest. So just when should you cut from one shot to another? The overarching answer is: *when the visual statement is complete.* That is, once the viewers see the expression on the face in the close-up, or note the object in the subject's hands in the medium shot, or recognize in the wide shot that the scene is set on a flooded street, it is time to cut to the next shot.

Editing for Dynamics

If all the shots are static with no camera moves, the pace of the edits will generally be quicker than if there are some camera moves or action shots. If you are cutting several static shots together, try not to make the edits on a predictable beat. Vary the time between edits to give the piece some dynamics of its own. Let wide shots stay up longer than tight shots. It is easy to see what is in a tight shot, but a wide shot usually contains more information that takes longer to perceive.

Zooms and pans must be allowed to run their course. Cutting in the middle of camera movement is most often uncomfortable to the viewer. By their nature, these types of shots should be going somewhere,

and cutting out early makes them unfulfilling to the viewer. Anticipation is created with no real payoff.

If movement is needed, but the entire shot is too long, it is better to start in the middle of the movement than to end in the middle. Let the shot finish. It is usually easier to see where the shot was coming from than not to know where it is going. It sometimes works just to use the middle of the movement, no start or finish, as long as you can tell what it is you are looking at, such as a long pan of rows of books. Seasoned videographers sometimes shoot camera moves three times: one with a slow pan or tilt or zoom, one with that same movement at a medium speed, and a third at a fast pace. This gives the editor a choice to select the camera move at the speed that best fits the pace of that moment in the story.

A camera move shot has a certain mood to it that may not fit with the rest of the piece. Camera moves are most often used to add dynamics to what editors and producers see as dull pieces. There is a fine line between adding editorial interest and false excitement. Camera moves can add complexity that you may not want to your piece, distracting the viewer from the subject at hand. That is why most new videographers are asked not to use zooms and pans until all other basics have been mastered.

Avoiding Predictability

While staying within the sequencing, story line, and continuity guidelines, try to vary the pace of the shots enough to avoid any predictability. The worst case is when the viewer can tell when the next edit is about to occur. The viewer should always be expecting more information (until the end of the piece) but should never be able to guess how or when it will come. As long as this anticipation is satisfied, and the viewer cannot predict the next edit, the edit pace is correct. A fast-moving story requires faster edits. A slow-moving story requires more time between edits. A good action piece can have quite a few short shots if they advance or enhance the action. In a fast-paced sequence, the shots may be shorter than three seconds, as short as 20 frames, but they must still be aesthetically clean enough so that there's not too much information and the viewer can perceive what is in the frame. This usually means using many close-ups and extreme close-ups.

Editing to Music

Cutting to music is a good example of following a pre-set pace. Most of the time, it does not look good to cut on the simple beat of the music because it is too predictable. You will have a better flowing piece if you cut on the back beat, but even then not on every beat. Use the edits to emphasize or punctuate the music, so that the cuts are not simply a tapping foot, blindly following the lead of the music.

Picking out one instrument to follow with the edits can give the edit pace a nice tie-in: the images will flow with the music but never be predictable. Sometimes, switching from one instrument to another for different parts of the song can add to the interest of the pacing. With the current abundance of rock videos, there are many examples of good editing to music. Take a close look. If you turn down the sound and watch the edits, you can get a feel for the dynamics of the editing without the music. Learning to feel the pace without audio clues is a good way to learn any style of editing.

Varying the Editing Speed

By changing the pacing of edits, you can change the whole mood of the piece. Switching from long-running shots to quick edits can heighten tension, action, excitement, or anticipation. Slowing down the pace can give a more relaxed feeling, an easier flow, or an emotional touch with the feeling of relaxation, serenity, or even sadness. Sit back and watch how your piece plays after you complete each segment. Do not just watch how the shots fit together, but watch how the piece feels as it moves along. Is it too fast or too slow? Does it convey the wrong mood? Does it flow as one unit, or is it simply a slide show?

Ask another editor to take a look at your piece. Sometimes you can be too close to your own work to give it an objective critique. Bad pacing can make a piece drag on forever or seem as choppy as rough seas. Good pacing can make a piece fly by while conveying much information, or touch the hearts of the viewers through its warm flow of images.

Comprehension

One of the biggest and most common mistakes made in all forms of video production is failing to perceive the finished product as a viewer would. The mistakes are often most noticeable in news stories. In the drive to make pieces exciting and dynamic for the viewers, the editors make use of every trick to keep the flow of images coming at a blinding pace. Fast cuts, zooms, and special effects abound. Music videos seem to be the standard by which stories are cut.

The problem with the music video style is basic: comprehension—and the lack of it. Music videos are cut the way they are so teenagers can see the same video dozens of times and still get something new out of them each time. The satisfaction gained from a single viewing is extremely low for that reason: the producers want you to see it over and over. The typical news story is just the opposite. By far, the majority of the audience sees a story one time and one time only. If there are any distractions at all while viewing the already short presentation, comprehension is thrown off. If there is no time allowed for absorption, what chance does the viewer have for understanding?

It is important that you, as the videographer-editor, make sure the edit pacing is right for the comprehension of the story as well as the dynamics of the story. Sometimes the rapid assault of images effectively conveys the emotion and content for which you are striving. But if there is more to communicate than that, make sure there is breathing space for the audience to take it in.

Adding Postproduction Value

Up to this point, we have been addressing the most used type of edit, the simple **cut**: an instantaneous transition in which the full frame of one shot replaces the full frame of the previous shot. However, editing software allows you to add other types of transitions and effects to your editing. The most common effect is the **dissolve** or **mix**, in which the two images are blended momentarily during the transition. Other effects are also available, such as **wipes** and **squeezes**, in which geometric patterns are used to replace one image with another or one image changes size or dimension, perhaps appearing to zoom into or out of the previous image.

In most video editing programs, you simply place two shots together on the timeline and then select the effect you want from some type of "Effects" menu. In some programs, you might place one shot on the "A" video track and the second shot on the "B" track. You then overlap the two shots by the number of frames you want the effect to last (e.g., 30 frames for a one-second effect), and drag and drop the type of effect over the overlapping edit.

The use of an A track and a B track has its roots in the early days of TV, when most news stories were cut on A and B film reels (or rolls). The A-reel had all of the pictures with the sound: talking heads, soundbites, stand-ups, and so forth. The B-reel had all the cover footage to be used over the reporter's voice track. The piece would then be assembled live on the air. It required the technical director to switch from one camera pointing at a film machine to the other and back at the proper times so that there was always a picture on the air. This led to the term **B-roll**, referring to all the shots without dialogue that illustrate what a speaker is discussing—the close-ups, inserts, cutaways, and so on that visualize a story. This technique was appropriately called **A/B-roll editing**. (See Figure 7-13). That same concept is found today in editing software that uses both A and B tracks on the timeline.

The Dissolve

Special effects can allow an editor to explore a whole new area of pacing and mood creation. The dissolve or mix can be a boon or bust to the finished piece. The dissolve is an excellent way of showing the lapse in time from one shot to the next. To go from the countryside in daylight to the city at night with a straight edit (or cut) would be rather abrupt, but a dissolve can make the transition smooth and even artistic. (See Figure 7-14.)

In many pieces, this way of showing the passage of time can aid in the telling of the story, because fewer shots are needed to make the transition. You can take a subject from one location to another with a simple dissolve instead of transition shots. In a long piece, it is a good idea to use both transition shots and dissolves for variety.

Figure 7-13   An editor operates an older A/B-roll editing system. Multiple VCRs and monitors are mounted in the racks. The edit controller, video switcher, effects generator, and audio mixer are mounted in the console. Today, all this equipment is replaced with a computer and editing software. (Photo by John Lebya)

When a piece calls for a slow-edit pace, a dissolve adds to the relaxed feeling and to the flow from one shot to the next. In going from static shot to static shot, such as shots of photographs from an old family photo album, the dissolve takes the hard edge off the edit and gives a desirable, fluid transition. For the artistic piece, the story on fall colors or the day in the life of a nursing home, the dissolve can add to the beauty of the shots or give a feeling of sensitive compassion.

The basic rules of editing should still apply, however. You do not dissolve between two shots that are very similar in composition. You still try to give variety to the shot selection and follow basic sequencing patterns. For a solo dancer on a stage, dissolves are desirable, but each shot should be as different as possible from the next. If the dancer is framed screen right in a wide shot, the next shot could be a medium shot with the dancer in the left part of the picture. In other words, do not overlap similar images.

Let the mood and pacing of the piece determine how long a dissolve should last. A duration of 30 to 60 frames (1 to 2 seconds) seems to look best for most uses. The slower the pace, the slower the dissolve. You must keep in mind, however, that making all edits into dissolves can make the piece boring and predictable.

Figure 7-14 A dissolve is used here to signify the transition of time from day to night. (A) Daytime shot of villagers outdoors. (B) Dissolve is half-finished (superimposition), blending the daytime and nighttime shots. (C) Dissolve is complete, ending on nighttime shot.

Try to have a good practical or artistic reason for each dissolve and any other effect you use.

The Wipe

Wipes come in a great variety; the standard left-to-right straight edge is the most common. (See Figure 7-15.) With digital effects, wipes can be as wild as you can imagine and the effects just as varied. Most of the literal graphic ones, like spinning stars or heart shapes, have little place in ENG, but have some application in EFP. The straight-line wipe is used in live newscasts to go from one story to the next without having to cut back to the set for the transition.

You very seldom see a wipe used in a produced news story. When it is used, however, its use is similar to that in the newscast itself: to go from one thing to something totally separate. If several pages of written information are to be put on the screen, a wipe is used to go from one page to the next, such as in election night tallies. Digital wipes, such as page or cube wipes, are very popular for this type of transition. The different types of wipes are often used in entertainment programs and commercials, to give the production variety and a jazzy look.

Compositing

Many software programs allow you to **composite**, or **matte**, images—to blend parts of two or more pictures to create new pictures. (See Figure 7-16.) You probably know that when you watch the weather announcer on your local news, that person is really standing in front of a screen (probably green or blue) and the imagery behind the person is placed there electronically. This is one common use of compositing, called a **chroma key**, in which a color (blue or green) is keyed out and replaced with something else—in this case the weather images. Other types of keys include **luminance keys**, in which brightness levels are used to insert other images, and **matte keys**, in which any of a number of items can be used, including selecting individual pixels.

Compositing is more likely to be used in EFP than in ENG. Because of journalists' ethical obligations of truth and accuracy, it is not usually acceptable to remove a person from one image electronically and insert that person into another image. Only in rare cases where a person really was in some situation or location, and the original photos or video sequences were

Figure 7-15 A wipe is used here to signify the transition from one location to another. (A) Golden Gate Bridge. (B) Wipe is half finished (split screen), blending the bridge and lighthouse shots. (C) Wipe is complete, ending on lighthouse.

lost or destroyed, could an argument be made for compositing that person into an image of that same situation or location. Again, the obligation is to represent

Figure 7-16 Compositing, or matting, is used here to blend two images. (A) Woman with megaphone. (B) Soccer team. (C) Composite image—the white background behind the woman has been replaced with the soccer team, and her image has been resized to fit better into the composition, creating the illusion that she could be a cheerleader for the team.

the truth of the story, so caution must be exercised not to distort any facts with fancy matting tricks.

In EFP, however, with the understanding that scripts are created to tell the clients' stories rather than to report the news, it is more common to see composite images. They can enhance a script with the viewers' understanding that the illusion of certain places and times is important to the story, even if the actual places and times cannot be photographed. For example, a corporate video might call for the company CEO to appear in a faraway location that the budget cannot afford. In this case, the CEO can be shot against a solid-color backdrop, and stock footage of the exotic location can be keyed in later, creating the desired illusion and saving a costly trip.

Editing Sound

Traditionally, sound editing has not been as complicated for TV as it has been for the movies. The poor quality of most older TV speakers and the conditions under which most people watch TV reduced the need for good sound. Today, however, sound editing is every bit as crucial as picture editing. Anyone can download high-fidelity MP3 sound files from the Internet, so why should TV audio be of any less quality? Additionally, today's big-screen TVs demand big sound from the speakers. With **high-definition television (HDTV)**, viewers expect high-definition sound quality. High-fidelity stereo mixes and 5.1 surround sound are the norm. Of course, these high-quality soundtracks might be mixed down to simple mono for playback on low-end systems, such as standard VHS tape machines, just as the high-quality images might be compressed for Internet or cell phone distribution. However, many clients want the original project to be mastered with the highest possible sound and picture quality so that high-quality copies can be dubbed for distribution in addition to any lower-quality versions.

Accurate Representation of the Event

The two sources of audio in ENG are the audio of the talent (news anchor or recorded reporter) and the sound accompanying the pictures. Because most TV news is based on journalistic standards, the addition of any other audio is frowned on. The addition of music is the only exception, although in some cases it is not desirable. Adding sound can be misleading, deceptive, and sometimes downright dishonest.

The most you can do in ENG is move the sound around from one shot to another, but the sound must accurately represent what you would hear if you were there. An example is a shot of a mine with a whistle blowing; the next shot is of miners filing out to go home. The sound of the whistle may not have been recorded at the same time as that shot of the mine, but it did blow while the crew was taping and it did signal the end of a shift. The sound was used correctly.

An example of sound used incorrectly is a shot of people at an accident scene and the news photographer running up to the injured on the ground while a siren is heard. The siren in this case was taken from a story shot last week and used to add a feeling of breaking news to the piece. The photographer actually arrived late. In this case, the siren should not have been used at all. It made the story into something it was not. If you did not get the sound at the location, you should not manufacture sound to make it appear as though it came from the location. If it makes the pictures seem different from what they really were, then the sound should not be added. Sound needs to depict what happened accurately.

Adding Sound for Effect

If you record an explosion from a mile away, it can take the sound of the explosion several seconds to reach the camera. Do you move the sound? For EFP the answer is simple, because any sound is fair game if it enhances the idea you are trying to get across. You would have to get very far out of line to violate the "truth-in-advertising" law.

For ENG the question is harder to answer. Years of Hollywood conditioning have made audiences expect to hear the sound at the same time they see the explosion. In real life, however, the sound and picture do not match. What do you do?

You can assume that sound and picture are in sync at the point of origin (the explosion site). The audio can be synced back up in editing if the shot contains the explosion as the only audio source. If, however, there are people in the foreground reacting to the explosion as it happens, their audio, and therefore the audio from the explosion, cannot be moved. Moving the explosion's audio would distort the people's reaction to it.

There is, nevertheless, room for creativity when it comes to audio in ENG. You can add sound where it is obvious to the viewer that the sound is added for effect. Shots of an abandoned school house with the sounds of a school bell and children playing can give a powerful emotional touch to the scene. It is obvious that no children have been there in decades, but the audio implies the rich history of the once thriving school.

Imagine a reporter doing a stand-up in front of a roaring water pump with a mic that does not pick up the sound of the pump because of its placement. You see the pump, but you do not hear it. By adding the background sound of the pump in editing, the shot seems to come together better. All the pieces fit and work together for the overall effect. These are just a few examples of adding sound to enhance ENG work, but you must use sound carefully. It is a fine line that separates enhancement from deception.

Avoid Abrupt Edits

In general, avoid abrupt starting and stopping when editing audio. Abrupt starts and stops are to audio what jump cuts are to video: they distract the audience. Even when audio must come in very quickly, a fast fade in is better than a full-volume take. A cut made in the middle of the bell's ring doesn't sound right. Either a quick fade-up or finding the natural starting point for the sound would be preferred. Audio cutoff is the same. Find a natural end for the sound or fade it out quickly. Background audio can come and go with the edit points as long as the audio is truly in the background. Every picture has a sound, unless it is a graphic or a freeze-frame. There is background sound for just about everything.

Natural Sound

A good news **package** opens with a picture that begins to tell the story or captures the viewer's attention. A reporter stand-up opening is often boring and gives the viewer little to look forward to. It looks like more news anchor and not more news. With an opening shot, there should be some good **natural sound (natsound)**.

Use with Opening Video A story on flooding might open with a shot of water flowing over a dam. The roar of the water is heard for a few seconds before the reporter's voice comes in. This breaks the constant flow of talking and can spark someone's interest to look at the TV instead of only listening to it.

Not only must the pictures be good, but the sound must also be good enough to make someone want to watch the pictures. Good use of natural sound can draw the viewer into the story and give the pictures that "you-are-there" feeling. This means you should open a story not only with the best picture you can but also with the best sound.

Use as a Transition You can use the natural sound of the pictures to break up paragraphs in the track, get into or out of **soundbites** or **talking heads**, and bridge a gap from one part of a story to another. To move from talking about people buying new homes to discussing the number of new homes being built, you could make the transition on a shot such as an electric saw (with the sound up full) cutting a board in front of new construction. After a couple of seconds of the saw, the reporter continues the story, now talking about all the new construction. Time limits can make this type of editing difficult, but if the story is well thought out, and the reporter and videographer work together on producing it, the end product will show the effort and have a greater impact on the viewer.

The "L" Cut

A popular form of creating an audio transition is to start the audio of the next shot (usually the beginning of a new sequence) under the current shot. This is called the **"L" cut**. On the editing timeline, it actually looks like a "lazy L" because the audio on the lower audio track begins ahead of the video on the upper video track. (See Figure 7-17.) For example, we see the building planner looking over the drawing for the new housing development as the reporter's track about the project comes to the end of a paragraph. While the planner is still on screen, we hear the sound of a buzz saw ripping through wood for about one second or so before the picture of that saw pops up and starts the next section of the story about construction. The au-

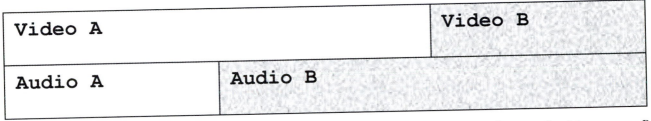

Video A		Video B
Audio A	Audio B	

Figure 7-17   A diagram of the "L" cut; here, the audio for segment B precedes the video by a few seconds, giving segment B the appearance of an "L" lying on its back.

dio pulls the viewer into the next sequence and softens the transition from one location to the other.

Room Tone

One thing professional editors always ask camera crews to get while recording interviews on location is **room tone**: the sound of the location without any of the subjects talking. In high-quality editing, where two soundbites are to be edited together, there might be a difference in the background noise from one bite to the next. To disguise that difference, some of the ambient sounds of that location can be laid in under the edit point to bridge from one shot to the next. This makes the audio edit sound more seamless.

Multiple-Source Audio Mixing

Every editing software program offers multiple channels of audio with which to work. One track is usually designated for the reporter's audio or dialogue and a second track for all natural sound and soundbites. If music is appropriate and desired, it goes on a third track. Additional sounds might require additional tracks.

Most editing programs offer enough audio tracks for ENG and EFP. Low-budget projects have many fewer audio tracks than professional movies, which can reach 100 or more channels. However, in the rare case that an ENG or EFP project requires more audio layers than are available in the software, the editor can use the methods of **laydowns** and **laybacks**.

In our example above, let's assume only two tracks are available in the editing program. The editor would decide which two audio sources were most important for determining the pacing and shot selection for the story. The story would be edited with just

those sources all the way to its conclusion. For this discussion, assume it is a reporter's voice track and the natural sound of the pictures that are laid down first. Wanting to add a music track under the entire piece, the editor would first take both of the audio tracks of the finished piece and do a **mixdown** or **laydown** by exporting the project as a new file with those two audio channels mixed. This mixed audio would then be laid back onto just one channel, leaving the second channel free to mix in the music.

Editing Methods

Many problems can arise in audio editing. An image you choose to accompany a soundbite turns out to be too short or too long. An audio clip of natsound does not match a picture. The reporter's voice is difficult to time with music fading to background. The best way to avoid problems is to plan the editing well in advance. Two methods, or approaches, to editing are useful to consider.

Checkerboard   One method is to edit only the principal images and sounds first for the whole piece. For ENG, this might be the reporter's talking head and some images that have natsound you plan to use "up full." After editing these primary shots and full-volume sounds, the video and audio tracks might have some blank spaces where you plan to fill in additional images and sounds to finish the story and give it its final polish. This pattern of a shot followed by a blank space (black on a videotape) followed by another shot followed by more black is sometimes called **checkerboard** editing. The idea is to edit only the major story images and sounds, and then go back and fill in the rest, including graphics.

The advantages of this approach are that you can:

- Make the most critical editing decisions first, followed later by the quicker decisions about filler elements.

- See what video and hear what audio stand on their own and identify what you will need to replace or enhance later.

- Time your piece before it is actually completed.

The disadvantage is that if you are facing a severe time crunch, you might still have blank moments of video or audio, or have incomplete graphic work, such as missing **lower-thirds**, when the project is due.

Section by Section A second approach to editing is to edit one complete section at a time. With this method, you include all the visual and aural elements as you go, finishing one part of the whole story before continuing to the next part. You leave no blank spaces, but complete the polished edit piece by piece.

The advantages of this method are that you can:

- Fine-tune each part of the story as you go, giving you the freedom to change any parts of the story as you come to them.

- Get a stronger sense of the overall visual style of the piece, including type fonts and colors for graphics and other elements.

- Skip over entire parts of the story and go straight to the end in the event of a severe time crunch, giving you at least some form of finished project to meet an air deadline.

The disadvantage is that it is too easy to get hung up on one little edit, such as the exact position of a graphic element or the exact number of frames for an audio fade-in, resulting in a loss of editing momentum and the ability to see the "big picture" of telling the whole story.

In reality, most editors use a combination of both checkerboard and section-by-section editing. Depending on the time crunch, the amount of A-roll footage versus B-roll footage, the editor's own working style, and other variables, an editor might start with a checkerboard, then come to a segment that he or she com-

pletes in its entirety, then go back to a checkerboard for another segment, and so on.

Music Editing When using music, it must be laid down first if any of the video is to be edited to the music. If nothing is to be in sync with the music, then it is best left until last so it is easier to mix it with other audio. Again, planning is the key.

Start by laying in the music. Next, lay in all the other audio that is to be up full (reporter's track, soundbites, and natsound with pictures) in the proper place. Finally, insert the rest of the shots, editing them to the music and any natsound, if appropriate or needed. Keep the music level up full when the music is the primary, or foreground, sound element, and fade the music underneath the other sound elements when they are foreground and the music is the secondary, or background, sound element (figure-ground principle). If planned properly, this method lets you edit to the music without affecting the placement of the rest of the audio so that the finished piece has all the elements timed perfectly.

SUMMARY

Editing can be every bit the creative challenge that shooting is. The best shooters are the ones who learn how to edit. Just as a shot can sometimes be improved by moving the camera just a few inches, an edit can sometimes be improved by changing the timing by just a few frames. The goal of the editor is to take the material at hand and make an understandable presentation: an interesting and comprehensible story. While all editors share that goal, the different methods and varieties of solutions are as expansive as the number of editors themselves.

Whatever their individual styles, all editors share an understanding of both the technical and creative editing basics. In today's NLE world, the technical basics include logging, creating an EDL, capturing audio and video clips, importing them into the software, trimming the heads and tails, sequencing the elements, layering additional audio and video tracks, adding effects (if appropriate), mixing the audio, rendering the final cut, and distributing the project by any of various media (e.g., tape, disc, Internet). The creative basics include how to sequence shots, maintain continuity, establish a story line, pace the edits, add postproduction effects (if appropriate), and edit sound. By understanding both the technical and aesthetic concepts and by following the guidelines put forth in this chapter, you can get started editing your project—the story you want to tell.

8 Video

LIGHT, LENSES, CAMERAS, AND RECORDERS

You can walk into almost any electronics store or large discount store and walk out with a really nice camcorder that will record directly to a DVD or a digital tape format for about $500. Can you start making video projects? Yes! Will they look professional, like we see on TV? Probably not! Although these cameras can get some great shots, most of them work with automatic features that prevent you from having control over the video. Also, unless you know about the basics of how the camera works and what the features can do for you, the video you shoot will probably look like it was shot by an amateur. Learning what equipment to use and how to use its features will help get you to the point of shooting truly outstanding video and making professional-looking projects.

Like any craftsperson or artist, a successful videographer wants the most information possible about the tools of the trade. Knowing how a piece of equipment works reveals its limitations and its possibilities. To become truly proficient at creating video, a TV videographer sooner or later has to learn the technical things too often left just to the engineers and maintenance staff. As camcorders move toward simpler and simpler operation, it actually becomes more important for the user to know how each part of the system works. Relying on the camera to do all of the thinking reduces the level of creativity by reducing the attention to detail. To master the craft—indeed, the art—of video, the videographer must master, and understand, the tools in every respect. This book will give the videographer a good start on the road to that understanding.

The medium of TV involves three basic forms of communication: sight, sound, and motion. The basic tools for creating these for TV are a camera, a recording device, a microphone, and a source of illumination. In Chapters 8, 9, and 10, the basic elements of each piece of field production equipment are introduced. This chapter discusses the camera, with its lens, and the recorder—the two most important elements in capturing sight and motion. Chapter 9 deals with microphones and recording techniques—the sound element. Chapter 10 presents light sources and their control—the one component necessary to accomplish any type of photography or videography.

Video: The Process of Image Acquisition

There is no end to the machines, gadgets, and accessories that a videographer can consider prized possessions on a shoot. There is a big difference, however, between a basic set of gear and the ideal set of gear. Although budgets will determine the type and quantity of equipment, there will always be several items that simply cannot be left out. These may be of the lowest or highest quality, but they constitute the minimum needed to do the job.

Today's TV videographers have a wide range of equipment available; therefore, it is hard to provide a definitive list. The list below will satisfy job requirements at the minimum standards of quality almost anywhere:

- Camera with lens.

- Videocassette recorder or digital recorder, either mounted on/in the camera or separate (stand-alone).

- Four to six hours of battery power.

- Tripod with fluid head.

- Set of three AC-powered (120V) location lights and AC extension cords.

- Camera-mounted light, with batteries and cables.

- Omnidirectional hand mic.

- Two-lavalier mics.

This chapter will introduce the reader to most of the basic forms of equipment used in portable video today. As more and more manufacturers and newly developed technologies enter the market, no one book can describe them all in detail. The following text will go through a basic description of how a typical device works. It is always a good idea to get the service and operating manuals for the equipment you will be using and read them thoroughly to truly understand that particular piece of gear. Today's marketplace underscores that thought. With a growing number of tape formats, recording formats, and delivery systems, a videographer can easily find herself in a situation where nothing seems compatible, where analog and digital are used side by side. Just keeping up with the changing technologies is a full-time job. Understanding them is a career. But the basics of what they do will always be the same.

Figure 8-1   The interior of a production van, viewed through the side door. Custom shelves are made to organize and store equipment.

PRINCIPLES OF LENS OPERATION

The lens of the human eye is a truly amazing mechanism for directing and focusing light on the light-sensitive rods and cones in the back of our eyes. In video cameras, the zoom lens tries to perform the same tasks. While our eyes have a single lens, video lenses are complicated devices with many individual pieces of glass that can be physically moved to direct, focus, and magnify the light from images in front of it. If the lens cannot focus properly, the picture is fuzzy; if it cannot transmit light efficiently, then the picture is dark or distorted.

Lens Components

No less valuable than the eye's lens is the lens on a camera. While most discussions of video equipment center on the camera and tape machines, the lens is a crucial part of the image-gathering process. A high-quality lens can make the best camera the best performer, and a poor-quality lens can leave the camera's picture out of focus and distorted. The eye has one simple lens that does amazing things. The camera needs several lenses, called **elements**, to duplicate the complex workings of the eye. Nonzoom lenses used in still photography are made up of as many as five elements in two groups that properly place an image on the recording surface or **focal plane**. A zoom lens, which is used on most TV cameras, has 13 or more elements.

A lens is basically two prisms joined together. If the prisms are joined at their apexes, they form a **concave lens** that refracts light out from the center. If joined at the base, they form a **convex lens** that converges the light to a single point.

Light refracted through a prism can be broken down into areas of different wavelengths. Even after prisms are joined to make lenses, small defects can cause aberrations in the sharpness and color of the image by not transmitting all frequencies evenly. By combining groups of concave and convex lenses and using special coatings, almost all of the defects of any single lens can be overcome. Such defects as **chromatic** and **spherical aberrations**, curvature of the field, distortion, flare, and astigmatism are all corrected by the many elements contained in the average TV lens. Each of the elements in the lens serves a specific purpose in controlling the quality and quantity of the visual information.

Focal Length

The distance from the optical center of the primary lens to the point where the light converges on the focal plane (the principal focal point) is the focal length of a lens. On professional TV camera lenses, the focal length setting can be read off the zoom portion of the lens. The focal length determines the **field of view** of the lens. A lens with a very short focal length has a very wide field of view and is called a **wide-angle lens**. A lens with a long focal length has a narrow field of view

and is called a **telephoto** lens. Focal lengths are measured in millimeters (mm). The average TV zoom lens starts at about 8 mm and goes to 100 mm or more. Focal lengths between 4.8 mm and 25 mm are considered to be wide-angle fields of view. From 25 mm to 75 mm, a lens is said to have a normal field of view, meaning that the lens sees things in a way similar to the way your eye does. From 75 mm to the longest focal lengths available, the lens has a narrow field of view, the image is magnified, and the setting is referred to as telephoto.

The field of view of a lens is often expressed as the horizontal angle of view and is measured in degrees. The widest setting of many professional lenses is about 8 mm. This focal length represents an angle of view of about 50°, which would have a view about 6 feet wide of a wall 6 feet from the camera. A wide-angle lens, about 5.5 mm, has an angle of view of about 75°, which sees an area 10 feet wide of a wall 6 feet from the camera. Similarly, a lens of 300 mm would have an angle of view of less than 2° and would cover only a span of about 1 foot of a wall 50 feet from the camera.

The advantage of a zoom lens over lenses of fixed focal lengths is that the focal length can be set at any point from 8 mm all the way to 100 mm, or whatever the parameters happen to be on that lens. We will say more about the zoom lens a little later. While fixed focal length lenses, sometimes called **prime** lenses, are generally of a higher quality than zoom lenses, they are simply not practical for most TV shooting styles.

Focus

Another set of elements in the lens determines the sharpness of the image sent to the **principle focus** or **focal plane**. These elements are usually at the front of the lens. By moving these elements further away or closer to the remaining elements, objects at different distances to the focal plane can be brought into sharp focus. The point of focus in front of the camera determines an area called the **plane of focus.** Almost all lenses have focusing marks on the barrel that read in feet and meters. If the focus barrel is turned in order to line up the number 10 on the focus mark, then the plane of focus is 10 feet from the camera (more precisely, from the focal plane of the camera). Often objects at other distances are also in focus with the barrel

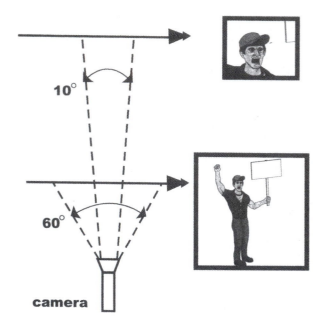

Figure 8-2   A wide field of view (60°) would see the subject head to toe. A narrow field of view (10°) would see only the head and shoulders of that same subject.

set at 10 feet. The range of acceptable focus in front of and behind the plane of focus is called the **depth of field**; on older 35-mm still cameras, this information can be read right off the lens for any focal plane setting. Video lenses do not have this convenience; the eye must judge what the range is. (See Figure 8-3.)

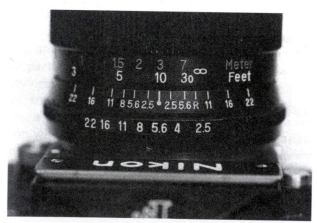

Figure 8-3   The still camera lens has its focus set at 10 feet and its f-stop at f5.6. The middle scale on the lens lets us read off the depth of field for those settings. At f5.6, everything from 30 feet to approximately 7 feet will be in focus.

Three factors have an effect on the depth of field for any chosen plane of focus: the focal length, the iris opening, and the distance from the camera. As the focal length increases, the depth of field decreases; as the iris is opened up, the depth of field decreases. (See Table 8-1.) As the lens is focused on objects closer and closer to the camera, the depth of field also decreases. The greatest depth of field occurs with wide-angle focal lengths with the iris opening very small and the lens focused at infinity. The shortest depth of field comes at telephoto settings, with the iris wide open and the lens focused at its minimum focus point.

Table 8-1   Factors That Affect the Depth of Field

Factor	Effect on Depth of Field
Focal length	As focal length increases, depth of field increases.
Iris opening	As the iris opening increases, depth of field decreases.
Subject to camera distance	As the distance from the subject to the camera increases, depth of field increases.

Take a video camera outside and play with the zoom and focus, first in full sun and then in deep shade. Notice how much more depth of field you have in the sunny areas, even as you zoom in. Also, notice how much easier it is to stay in focus when the lens is at its widest setting. As you begin to use a video camera more, you will get used to combining the effects of focal length, focus, and iris to achieve the results you want.

Although it is still rare to see an auto-focus function on a professional style camera, it is standard on consumer and **prosumer** (a more sophisticated or professional videographer, e.g., a wedding videographer) cameras. The auto-focus function can make shooting moving objects easier to keep in focus, but as we have mentioned earlier, a true professional likes to maintain as much control as possible over the tools. As anyone who has used an auto-focus camera can attest, the system doesn't always do what you want it to—a situation unacceptable to a professional.

The **hyperfocal distance** of a lens is the distance from the lens to the first point where an object is in focus when the lens is focused at infinity. When shooting

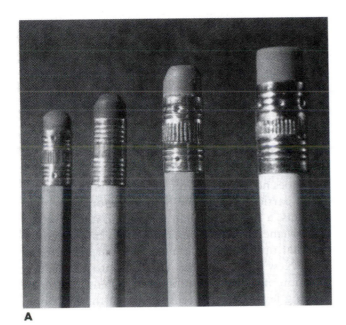 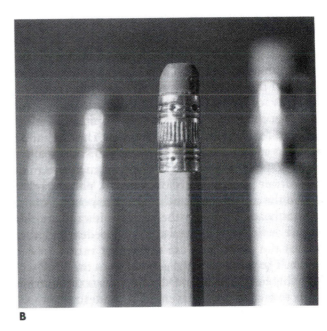

Figure 8-4 (A) Deep depth of field. (B) Shallow depth of field. Frame 1 was made with the iris at f22. Everything is the same in frame 2, except the iris is at f2.8. The same exposure was maintained by adding neutral density filters to the camera lens.

news or any uncontrolled action where there is little time or ability to focus properly, this number comes in handy. The number will vary depending on the iris setting and focal length, but at full wide angle, the iris settings will have little effect on the hyperfocal distance. This translates into the ability to focus the lens at infinity and know that everything at the hyperfocal distance or beyond is in focus.

MacroFocus

Although every lens can focus on infinity, each lens has a limit on how close it can focus. This varies from one type of lens to another and is called the **minimum object distance (MOD).** For a typical broadcast lens, the Canon HJ17eX7.6B, that distance is about 22 inches. Most typical TV lenses have a minimum distance similar to this. Therefore, to get a really close up shot of a small object, a very valuable feature to have on the lens is a **macro focusing ring**. The macro focus is usually a pull-out knob on the rear area of the lens barrel that allows a rotation of the rear elements inside the lens to change the focus distance. This macro focusing ring changes the MOD on the Canon HJ17eX7.6 lens from 22 inches to less than half an inch.

Figure 8-5 On this Fujinon lens, the small macro knob at the base of the lens must be pulled out slightly to allow its rotation.

It is possible to macro focus as close as the surface of the front element of the lens itself when it's at the wide-angle focal length. The macro focus can be used with the lens focused at any point and set at any focal length.

However, with the macro focus engaged, the focal length cannot be adjusted without disturbing the focus of the picture. In macro, a zoom lens in effect becomes a fixed focal length lens because of this limitation.

Creative videographers have found unlimited uses for the macro focus. The macro's effect on the front focus and zoom can be used to creative advantage. With a lens set in macro, any change of the focal length changes the point of focus, which gives you the ability to use the zoom to change focus. This abnormal behavior can lead to some very unusual shots. An understanding of the relationships among the various elements that make up a TV lens can lead to interesting shots that enhance the visual quality of the product.

Aspect Ratio

Even though lenses are round, the pictures they make are rectangular. The ratio between the width and the height of the TV picture is always the same. All analog TV cameras have an **aspect ratio** of 4:3 (or 1.33:1 in cinema terms): for every four units of width in the picture, its height will be three units. This limitation becomes most noticeable when, for instance, a videographer tries to shoot a still picture of a military officer printed in a book. The still photographer turned the camera on its side to get the portrait of the general head to toe. For the video camera to see this picture head to toe, extra space is needed on either side of the photo, because the aspect ratios do not match. The full shot of the general from the book will probably be just head and shoulders or a tilt up from boots to face to avoid empty or undesirable space on either side of the photo. Learning to see things as the video camera sees them means getting used to seeing everything in this 4:3 aspect.

Video shot for high-definition TV (HDTV) is in the 16:9 ratio. This wider ratio affords a picture that is similar to a 35-mm slide in shape. It is also closer to what we see in movie theaters. It is superior to the 4:3 aspect ratio because 16:9 is more like our normal human way of seeing things. Our field of vision is more rectangular than the old 4:3, which is closer to a square shape.

Iris

Every lens has an aperture for controlling the amount of light passed on to the focal plane. Just like the mechanism in the eye that controls the amount of

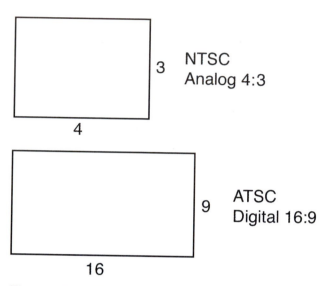

Figure 8-6   NTSC analog aspect ratio of 4:3, compared with new ATSC digital aspect ratio of 16:9.

light, this aperture is referred to as an **iris.** This control over light quantity is done by a series of overlapping metal leaves or fins that can be rotated one way to make the hole very small or rotated the other way to make the hole very large. The efficiency of a lens to pass light is referred to as its **speed.** A fast lens can transmit a large amount of light, whereas a slow lens transmits a much smaller amount of light. The speed is measured in **f-stops.** An f-stop is the ratio between the size of the aperture and the focal length of the lens. f-stops are a standardized way of measuring the passage of light on every lens; the numbers refer to a specific amount of light. A lens set at f8 gives the same amount of light no matter which camera or format of recording. The differences in lens speeds come from how wide the iris can be opened. The smaller the f-stop number, the more light the lens transmits. A lens that can go to f2 is not as fast as a lens that can go to f1.4.

Most lenses used for video shooting range from f16 to f1.8. Each f-stop shown on the lens represents twice as much light as the one before it, or half as much as the one after it. The f-stops would normally be f16, f11, f8, f5.6, f4, f2.8, f2, and f1.4. An iris at f8 lets in twice the amount of light as a setting of f11, but only half as much light as f5.6. If the exposure is increased by one stop, you are allowing in twice as much light. The smallest f-stop number tells you how "fast" a lens is. The typical lens mentioned above can only go to f1.8, which is only one-quarter of a stop faster than f2 and three-quarters of a stop, or 75%, darker than the next full stop of f1.4. A small increase in the fastest f-stop does not greatly affect the lens's ability to gather light, particularly in low-light situations. For most cameras, a lens faster than f1.4 would not show any improvement in gathering light. Each camera has an internal optical system; most of them are rated at f1.4. Newer ENG cameras have internal speeds of around f1.2. Lens makers are making lenses with speeds to match this, but both cameras and lenses of this type are very expensive. It does no good to place an expensive fast lens like an f1.2 on a camera that can only receive an f1.4 amount of light.

Video lenses allow the increase or decrease of exposures by fractions of stops because the iris is free moving (unlike a still camera) and can be set at any point within the range of the lens. At the stopped-down end of the iris (the smallest aperture), there often is a position labeled **"C"** for **cap.** When the iris is in this position, no light at all is being sent to the camera. This feature protects certain workings of the camera when not in use and also shows the camera true black. (See the discussion on black balance later in this chapter.)

Most lenses operate best at the middle range of their f-stops. The optimum is usually f5.6 and one stop up or down from there. Only in very controlled situations is it possible to always operate at optimum. At f5.6 the flaws that may be inherent in the lens will be at their minimum and all the lens elements will be performing at the best degree possible. The iris has an effect not only on the exposure but on the look of the shot as well. The f-stop setting is only one factor in setting up a shot and does not have to be dictated by lighting conditions.

Auto-Iris

All video lenses have servos that control the iris setting. A **servo** is an electronically powered gear that adjusts the setting. A switch can easily change the iris from manual to auto to allow the camera to set the proper exposure for you. This can be a help or a hindrance to the videographer. Another small button on the lens allows the operator to briefly put the lens into auto-iris only for the time the button is depressed. This method is generally the choice of most videographers, because it can set an exposure quickly but not stay in auto all the time, where it is likely to **roam**. Roaming is where the iris reacts to everything that comes into the frame. In a scene with much action or many camera moves, an auto-iris can fluctuate wildly as dark-clothed subjects and bright light sources pass through the frame. The result is an amateurish scene with an exposure that fluctuates from dark to light with every movement in the frame. Most scenes require only one constant exposure setting. Auto-iris also does not guarantee the proper exposure. It merely "averages" the scene exposure between the brightest and darkest elements. Auto-iris would leave the face of an interview subject wearing dark clothes shot against a dark background overexposed because of this. The videographer determines which element is most important (often the face of the subject) and exposes for that element. Once again, allowing a machine to make critical decisions can leave the videographer at a creative disadvantage.

Zoom Lenses

Many lenses used by still videographers and a great many cinematographers generally have a fixed focal length. Video cameras almost without exception have a **zoom lens**, a lens that can change focal lengths through a series of sliding elements within the lens. Zoom lenses permit changing the field of view without changing the point of focus or the aperture. Unlike the two optical groups that make up a fixed focal length lens, four different optical groups make up a zoom lens (see Figure 8-7):

- The **focusing group** gathers the light into a sharp, clear image.

- The **variator group** moves inside the lens to change the image size from wide angle to telephoto.

- The **compensator group** moves with the variator group to keep the image in focus and reduce aberrations caused by the first two groups.

- The **prime lens group** focuses the image on the recording surface, such as film or a TV camera chip.

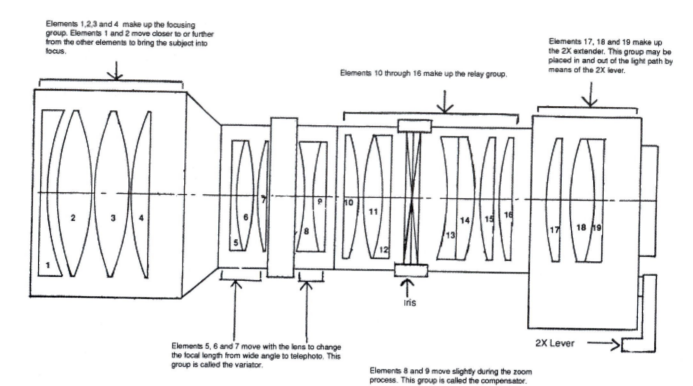

Elements 1,2,3 and 4 make up the focusing group. Elements 1 and 2 move closer to or further from the other elements to bring the subject into focus.

Elements 10 through 16 make up the relay group.

Elements 17, 18 and 19 make up the 2X extender. This group may be placed in and out of the light path by means of the 2X lever.

Iris

Elements 5, 6 and 7 move with the lens to change the focal length from wide angle to telephoto. This group is called the variator.

Elements 8 and 9 move slightly during the zoom process. This group is called the compensator.

2X Lever

Figure 8-7   Optical groups for a typical TV zoom lens.

When setting up a shot for proper focus, it is customary to zoom all the way into the object you determine to be the focus plane, focus the lens, and then zoom out to the desired focal length for shooting.

TV zoom lenses also come with a box of electronic servos formed into a hand grip and attached to the side of the lens. (See Figure 8-8.)

The servos drive a series of gears that turn the zoom barrel as well as the iris ring (mentioned earlier). A rocker-style switch on top of the hand grip controls the zoom servo, which allows you to move the elements continuously at speeds from a mere crawl to a fast snap zoom. The zoom and the iris can be operated electrically from a remote location with the proper cable and control unit.

With an extension cable, the zoom control can be operated from anywhere the operator wants within the length of the cable. On all lenses, the power zoom can be turned off, leaving the lens to manual control. By simply twisting the zoom portion of the lens tube, you can adjust the focal length or do zooms. This method of zooming generally cannot be done as smoothly as the power zoom, but can be done faster than most servos can operate. Zooms that are this fast

Figure 8-8   The typical TV zoom lens has a hand grip like this one with a rocker-style zoom control, a button labeled "RET" to see return video from the deck (either from confidence heads or on playback), a switch to select auto/manual/remote control for the iris and a button to set camera exposure if the iris is in manual control.

are generally not used except as special effects or in certain types of sports coverage. An adjustment within the zoom-control housing can change the speed range of the power zoom.

The range of the zoom can vary greatly from one lens type to another. Old consumer camcorders have a 6:1 or 8:1 zoom ratio. If the widest focal length is 9 mm, then the longest is either 54 mm or 72 mm, respectively. The zoom ratios for professional lenses are more often 14:1 or as high as 22:1. Lenses are often referred to as a "14✕" or a "20✕" or whatever the multiplier is for the maximum focal length. Sometimes the multiplier is followed by the minimum focal length. The Canon HJ17eX7.6 lens has a 17:1 zoom ratio, and a 7.6 mm minimum focal length. This tells us that the maximum focal length for that lens is 17 × 7.6 mm, or 129.2 mm. When the range extender (✕2) is added, the maximum focal length doubles, yielding a focal length of 258.4 mm. Professional lenses with focal length ratios as high as 30:1 or more are made, but these require extra support brackets to attach to the camera. At such extreme focal lengths, it becomes very hard to maintain a steady picture on a lightweight camera even on a typical tripod, but especially when handheld or on the shoulder.

The widest focal length available on a zoom lens is about 4.8 mm, which is considered an ultra-wide-angle lens, but this lens does not have a large zoom ratio. Most professional wide-angle lens zoom ratios are about 10:1. Consumer and prosumer camcorders have lenses with greatly enhanced zoom ratios compared to older cameras. A ratio of 400:1 is not uncommon. Most of this high ratio is not made by the lens itself but done electronically by digitally magnifying the picture in the camera. Most of these camcorders have built-in image stabilizing devices to remove the annoying shake from the shots, but these devices generally only help a little. The best advice here is to avoid using the digital zoom feature. Besides the inevitable camera shake, the image is often grainy and not of professional quality. (See Figure 8-9.)

A common feature on TV zoom lenses is the **2✕ range extender.** This small device, which is part of the last elements at the rear of the lens, has a lever that can be moved to a 2 position; this drops an optical system into the light path, effectively doubling the focal length at which the lens is set. (See Figure 8-10.)

The zoom can continue to be used with the extender in place, but all focal lengths will be doubled. In effect, a lens that ranges from 10 mm to 100 mm would become a 20-mm to 200-mm lens with the ex-

A

B

Figure 8-9   (A) The birdhouse was shot by an optical zoom. The birdhouse is in sharp focus. (B) The birdhouse is about the same size, but was shot with a digital zoom and lacks sharp detail. Whenever you can get a sharp picture with the appropriate sized subject or object using the optical zoom, it is best to avoid using the digital zoom.

tender in place. In the highly competitive news business, this addition to the lens is an absolute must. It is less important for field production, because the 2 range extender slightly degrades the quality of light passing through it. Whenever the 2 range extender is engaged, the amount of light passing though it is reduced by about one-half (the equivalent of losing one f-stop) and the sharpness of the image is reduced by a sometimes noticeable amount. This makes the extender of limited use in low-light situations. If the

Figure 8-10   The lever on the back of this lens can be moved for the "×1" or normal position to the "×2" or double position.

highest technical quality is required, use of the 2 range extender is not recommended; it should be considered only if it would enhance the value of the shot.

A minor drawback of zoom lenses is that they lose some light at the very end of their focal length range. For example, the Canon HJ17eX7.6 zoom lens has a maximum relative aperture of f1.8 from 7.6 mm to 97.5 mm, but at 130 mm the maximum aperture is only f2.4. In low-light situations, this sudden darkening of the picture at the very end of the zoom can be noticeable. Therefore, for high-quality work, it is best not to use a zoom at the end of its range. Using the auto-iris can make up for this effect as long as there is enough light to set the exposure in the middle of the f-stop range.

When the lens is zoomed all the way in, it is nearly impossible to get a steady picture. Any small movement of the camera will be greatly exaggerated by the long focal length; this makes steady telephoto shooting off the shoulder next to impossible. Today, many **image stabilizers** are available to take the shake out. Some are part of the lens itself, and others fit onto the front of many normal zoom lenses. Most modern home camcorders have similar devices built into them. One drawback to their use is the difficulty in **panning** (moving the camera left or right) or **tilting** (moving the camera up or down). These types of actions must be done slowly, or the motion control device overcompensates for the movement. Nevertheless, image stabi-

lizers can produce spectacular results compared to ordinary zoom lenses.

Light Quality Control

The elements of the lens combine to make the sharpest image possible with the smallest loss of brightness at the focal plane where the image will be recorded onto a light-sensitive medium. Because lenses are sealed units, the operator has no control over how well the lens works inside. The last layer of quality that the manufacturer puts on the lens is a special coating on the glass. This coating helps with color reproduction and aids in correcting many minor flaws in the ability of the glass to transmit a sharp image. Special care must be taken when cleaning a lens so as not to harm this coating.

The best way to insure against damage to the front element of your lens is to always keep a clear filter or a **UV (ultraviolet) haze filter** on the lens. Many TV stations have a rule that a camera never leaves the station without one of these filters on the lens. Neither filter has any noticeable effect on the picture quality or the amount of light transmission; they merely serve to protect the front element from scratches, dirt, and other problems that could cause costly repairs or lower the quality of the lens.

One of the most common problems in maintaining picture quality is glare on the lens from light sources. At certain angles to a light source, light rays reflect off the front element, causing a glare across the lens surface. This glare reduces the contrast of the picture as well as its sharpness. Just as our hands often function as a sunshade for our eyes when we look in the general direction of the sun or any bright light, the camera lens needs the same protection to work at its optimum. The sunshade or **hood** that comes with the lens is an absolute must to prevent direct light from striking the front element. As the light source comes closer and closer to the camera's field of view, it becomes increasingly difficult to protect the lens. Glare is actually the worst when the light is just outside the shot. You may find yourself using your hand to shade the light from the lens. Once the light source is in the shot itself, there is little that can be done. When a light is in the shot, the glare is reduced, but other effects called **flares** (circular patterns of reflections in

Figure 8-11   Lens flare from the sun.

the lens) can be just as objectionable if not used in an artistic fashion. (See Figure 8-11.)

Accessories

Many attachments are available to enhance lens performance. Many videographers like to take shots at more than the shortest focal length allowed by their standard lens. Although changing to a wide-angle zoom lens is probably the best way to get a wider angle shot, it is also time consuming to change the lens, not to mention the inconvenience and expense of having a second lens available. A wide-angle **retrozoom** is another set of optical elements that can be mounted on the front of most professional zoom lenses. This attachment works like the 2 extender, only it decreases the focal length by multiplying them by around 0.8. This would make a normal lens 6.4 mm instead of 8-mm and allows zooming and focusing as normal. The other way to get a quick wide-angle shot is to attach a single-element wide-angle adapter. This curved lens either clamps or screws onto the front element of your normal zoom lens, much like a filter. The drawback here is that the picture can be focused only with the macro-focusing device, thus preventing the use of the zoom: the lens becomes a fixed focal length rather than a variable focal length lens.

There are teleconverters that look and work like retrozooms to make objects even larger. Teleconverters multiply the image size (commonly by about 2.8 times the image size). One drawback of both the retrozoom

and the teleconverter is the added weight on the camera and lens itself. This can put added stress on the camera body at the point where the lens is attached.

Close-up lenses or **diopters** are single-element attachments that reduce the minimum focus distance of the lens. They also reduce the maximum focus distance so the lens can only be focused on objects close to the camera. Diopters come in different strengths, such as 2, 3, and so on. A strong diopter on a good lens will allow a camera to zoom in to the mint date on a dime so that it fills the entire picture. One drawback to diopters is that they require more light than a typical shot. A diopter will somewhat degrade the sharpness of a lens in high light levels but will *greatly* reduce the sharpness in low light with the lens iris wide open.

Filters

The clear glass and UV filters mentioned above are just two of the many types of filters available for a video camera's lens. Most lenses have a threaded lip on the front element onto which a round filter or filter adapter can be screwed. The common diameter for video lenses ranges from 49 mm to 77 mm, although filter size may vary from one type of lens to another. Some lenses have no threads on the front element and require an adapting ring that clamps to the outside of the lens barrel. Most filters are threaded on both sides so that they can be stacked or combined with other attachments. Generally, no more than two filters can be used at one time without the filter edges showing in the corners of the picture. This is called **vignetting** and may also be caused by other factors, such as a poorly aligned lens. Many videographers always leave the clear filter and add any other filters on top of it to make sure that the front element stays protected at all times.

Two other types of filter mounts are available for professional use: the round non-threaded filters and the film-style square filters, such as the 2 × 2 inch, 4 × 4 inch, and the 6 × 6 inch. These filters require special adapters, which are made for every lens. With the larger unthreaded filters, it may be necessary to obtain a larger sunshade for the lens to avoid glare problems. The square filters are generally used with a **matte box**. (see Figure 8-12.) A matte box is a rectangular, tapered box that looks like a bellows and attaches to the front of the

Figure 8-12   This simple matte box attaches directly to the front of the lens. It has two slots for 4×4 filters and has a "French flag" fixed to the front for added light flare protection.

lens in such a way that the lens can be focused without rotating the matte box.

A series of slots at the back of the box permits the use of up to three square filters. These filter slots may be rotated independently of the lens to orient the filter as desired. (See the discussion of star and graduated filters below.) The rest of the box acts as a sunshade for the filters. The matte box is the most versatile and effective system of using filters with the lens, although it may be too cumbersome for most ENG work and some EFP shooting where weight and maneuverability are important considerations.

Filters fall into three broad categories:

- Color enhancement.

- Diffusion.

- Special effects.

Color enhancement filters can be used to change the perceived color of light used in a particular shot. This type of use is generally unnecessary because of the white balance circuit in the video camera, but they can be used to achieve very controlled, known artistic results.

Diffusion filters reduce the sharpness and/or contrast of the picture. They are often used to give a film look to the video or to soften skin-tone detail.

Special effects filters do everything from creating multiple images to split-screen fields of focus. Many of the effects created by these filters can also be done electronically in post-production. Some of the new digital cameras can create these effects internally. It is a good idea to shoot a scene calling for filters at least once without filters, so that the producer or editor has the choice of using or not using the effect. Today, as more and more editing is done digitally in non-linear systems, the need to use filters in the field has been greatly reduced. Many of the same effects can be done more easily in the computer without permanently changing the original image.

The following is a partial list of the more popular filters used in TV work. Most are used for EFP shooting or for feature stories in ENG. They are not recommended for general news use. Most of these filters come in different degrees of effect, rated from 1 to 5. A number 1 filter has only a slight effect, and a number 5 has the maximum effect.

Sepia Effect Filter   This filter gives the scene a warm brown tone, similar to that of old photographs from the turn of the century. It can be used to imply a look back in time.

Enhancing or Warming Filter   This filter creates a warm look by selectively improving the saturation of reds and oranges, with little effect on other colors. It is used to bring out better skin tones on light-complexioned subjects and give dark-skinned subjects a deeper, richer color. It is also good for the fall color shots of autumn.

Polarizing Filter   This filter reduces glare and reflections on surfaces, such as glass or water, in the picture, while saturating colors and darkening in the blue of the sky. The polarizing filter is made to turn in its housing to achieve the correct angle to the reflections. As you turn the polarizer, watch the effect in the viewfinder to find the optimum orientation. It can make white clouds really stand out from the blue sky or take away annoying reflections from car windows.

Fog Effect Filter   This filter creates the look of real fog in the scene. The effect is most noticeable in overexposed areas of the picture or around light sources in the shot. It can add a dreamlike quality to scenes or give atmosphere to interior scenes. (See Figure 8-13.)

Figure 8-13   These before and after shots show the effect of a fog filter that adds a fog effect and lowers contrast.

Contrast Control Filter This filter lowers the contrast in the picture and mutes the colors. It lightens black areas and reduces the density of shadows, so that more detail can be seen in the shadows without affecting the white areas of the picture. It is a good filter for scenes where shadows are particularly dark, and can help give video a film look.

Double-Fog Effect Filter This filter combines a soft fog with a heavy low-contrast effect that allows a sharper image than fog alone. It is particularly good to reduce the effects of overexposed windows in interior shots without adding a dense fog look to the picture.

Diffusion Effect Filter This filter uses a slight ripple effect in the filter glass to reduce the sharpness of the picture without creating a foglike effect. It is often used to hide skin blemishes or wrinkles from the camera and looks good in backlit situations. It also causes a halo effect around light sources in the shot.

Softnet Filter This filter uses a net material between laminated glass to create a soft diffusion without the halation, or blurring, of highlights in the shot. The net comes in several colors, allowing multiple effects from one filter: black net leaves the dark areas dark; white net lowers the contrast as it diffuses; red net warms the colors of the scene; skin-tone net enhances skin color.

Dot Filter Instead of a net to cause the diffusion in the picture, this filter glass is covered by thousands of dots in varying sizes (similar to a paint sprayer mist). It comes in white, black, and skin tone. The filter is similar in effect to the net filters, but without the slight star effect on highlights.

Star Filter This filter has engraved lines that form a grid on the glass surface. The grid causes highlights, such as the sun, candles, and headlights, to appear starlike. The grid comes in different sizes from 1-mm to 4-mm spacing; a 1-mm grid has the longest rays and a 4-mm grid the shortest. Star filters also come in varying numbers of points; stars with 4, 6, 8, or 12 points can be created. These filters can give a glamorous quality to pictures with highlights in them, making them sparkle or helping reduce the sharpness of light sources (by using a 12-point 4-mm star) without affecting anything else in the picture. They are also free-spinning within their housings so the points of the star can be rotated to any angle.

Split-Field-Effect Filter This filter is basically a close-up lens cut in two. It allows you to have a close object in the bottom half of the picture and a faraway object in the top half of the picture, all in sharp focus. The one-half close-up lens is a fixed-focus element; this means that the lens must be focused first on the background and then the foreground object, or the camera must be moved in or out until that object is also in focus. This filter creates the ultimate depth-of-field lens, where everything from just in front of the lens to infinity is in focus.

Graduated Filter This filter contains the effect only in one-half of the filter, while creating a smooth transition from that effect to clear near the middle of the filter. Graduated filters come as sepias, corals, oranges, and neutral densities. They are generally used over the sky portion of the picture to change the color of the sky without changing the color of subjects on the ground. They can create the look of a sunset sky without turning the ground pink too. The neutral density filter can be used to gain an even exposure on the sky as well as the ground on overcast days. The filters work best in a matte box setup, where they can be positioned at just the right place in the frame without adjusting the shot.

A problem of some filters with nets and dots is that the diffusion material can sometimes be visible in the picture. This can easily happen when the lens is wide and at maximum aperture. The net or screen can be faintly visible across the entire picture. A good way to avoid this is to get filters that fit behind the lens. For video cameras, this would mean having them in the filter wheel of the camera. If this is not possible, it may limit the use of some filters to smaller apertures or longer focal lengths so that they will not be seen.

Digital Effects

Most consumer and prosumer cameras come with the ability to perform digital effects that were previously only available through the use of a special effects generator (SEG).

Compared to older cameras, newer video cameras seem like computers with the ability to capture video as well. New video cameras can take an image captured by the camera and process it in a number of ways. Some examples of digital effects common in video cameras are:

- Negative image: the color and brightness of an image are reversed (e.g., light to dark).

- Monochrome: color is removed from the picture to yield a black-and-white image.

- Sepia: the image has all color removed except for the sepia (brownish) color, which gives the illusion of old footage or an old movie.

- Solarization: the image is intensified and brightened to make it appear as if it is an illustration.

- Mosaic: a tiled effect is derived from the original image.

- Keying: parts of a frame can be replaced with parts of other frames (e.g., a person inside a studio can be made to appear as if the person is outside or at some other location).

- Still shots: many consumer video cameras have the ability to take still pictures and combine them with video footage.

Although these effects are handy when they are available in the camera, and can make home videos more exciting, most professionals wait for the digital effects to be added in postproduction. If you add effects to the original footage as it is shot, you will not be able to go back to the footage and use it in "normal mode." Special or digital effects are not used when gathering footage for ENG use. As with many automatic features available on video cameras, digital effects might be best left in the "off" position, unless there is a compelling reason to use a particular effect. Digital effects can call attention to themselves, detracting from good videography and distracting the viewer. Again, it is probably best to make decisions about digital effects after the original footage is shot, when time can be spent viewing the footage and deciding which effects should be added during editing.

Interchangeable Lenses

Most cameras on the market are designed for use with specific lenses. A lens for a Sony camera cannot be put on an Ikegami camera unless it is modified at the factory. Some models of cameras may share the same lens specifications, but they are the exceptions. Each camera manufacturer has a different design for the way a lens works with its internal focus plane. And every camera must be shaded to any lens (that is, adjusted to the light characteristics of the lens) that is being used on it to achieve the optimum quality. One very popular video camera that allows interchangeable lenses is the Canon XL-2. (See Figure 8-14.)

Care and Cleaning of Lenses

Dirt is the great enemy of lenses, and it does not take much to get a lens dirty. In addition to the huge amount of dust in the air, there is always the chance that something will come in contact with the lens and smudge it, such as your hand or fingers. For the lens to work at its optimum, it must be free of all dirt and smudges. Loose dirt or dust can be blown or brushed away with the proper tools, but not wiped away. Touching the lens with dry cloth or tissue may actually grind the dirt into the glass. For loose dirt, a soft photo brush and an air blower can be used. Simple squeeze-style blowers or air-in-a-can can be purchased at any photo store.

Do not, however, blow air from your mouth. If the squeeze-style or other type of blower does not clean the lens, switch to a liquid cleaner. Always try to use a cleaner made to be used on high-quality glass. Lenses, and even some filters, can be very expensive. A deep scratch or other blemish can require an equally expensive trip to the factory for regrinding, recoating, or replacement. Most photo stores sell lens-cleaning solutions along with tissues to wipe the lens clean. A homemade solution of a few drops of dishwashing soap and distilled water works as well as some commercial products. A very clean, soft, lint-free cloth can also be used instead of the photo tissues. There are also products on the market that have premoistened towelettes in individual packets specifically formulated for cleaning lenses.

No matter what you use, the method should be the same. Never use more fluid than you need and never grind the pickup material (such as a tissue) into the lens. Always use a circular motion and try not to go over the same part of the lens more than once if you can help it. A good cleaner used sparingly will do the job, and any excess will evaporate quickly. Never use plain water; it has too many mineral deposits in it and does not evaporate quickly enough.

Keep a cap on the lens at all times when the camera is not in use, such as when it is in transit, in storage, or in any hazardous environment (a desert or beach, or in windy conditions). Often the dirt on your lens will not be visible in the viewfinder. Visually inspect the cleanliness of the lens often. The time when dirt really stands out is when there is any glare on the lens or a highlight, such as the sun, in the shot. While a little glare and the sun may be part of the shot, any dirt on the lens will stand out and result in an embarrassingly amateurish shot. The time to find out that you have a dirty lens is not in the middle of a shot where you pan past the sun. It might have been your only chance to get that shot.

Modern professional TV lenses are made to work in the harshest environments. This does not mean that the nonglass parts never need cleaning. The rotating barrels of the focus, zoom, and iris all must be kept clean. Wipe the lens free of any dust and dirt as often as possible. Use a compressed air blower to get in the small places, possibly with the help of a soft brush such as a toothbrush. Never use water to clean the lens. Never use any cleaner that has oil in it. All the moving parts of the lens and servos are on sealed bearings and need no further lubrication. If they are stiff to use, they are dirty, not in need of an oiling. Make sure the gears and teeth of the lens barrel are always clean and free of dirt and dust. Most lens units are considered waterproof, but are really just water resistant. If exposed to excessive dampness, they may short out, or dirt may collect in the condensation and foul the servos at a later time. If the lens does get a bad drenching, allow it to dry out completely by putting it in a sealed plastic bag with silica gel or another desiccant (a substance that absorbs moisture).

Check the tightness of all the accessible screws on the lens (including the back of the lens) as well as the lens control unit on a weekly basis. Like most TV equipment, any repair work or extensive servicing should be done by experienced people. If you wish to do more than the very basic care, have someone with more experience show you the right way to do it. The final word on lens care is to know the lens's factory service center nearest you. Most offer overnight service or even loaner lenses; they can certainly help you over the phone with small problems. Keep a heavily used lens in top-notch shape by having a factory overhaul every two years.

VIDEO CAMERAS

A current-model portable video camera barely resembles the huge, heavy studio camera of TV's early years, because of the numerous design changes made over the years. But the color video camera of the earlier days of TV had to perform the same basic functions as to-

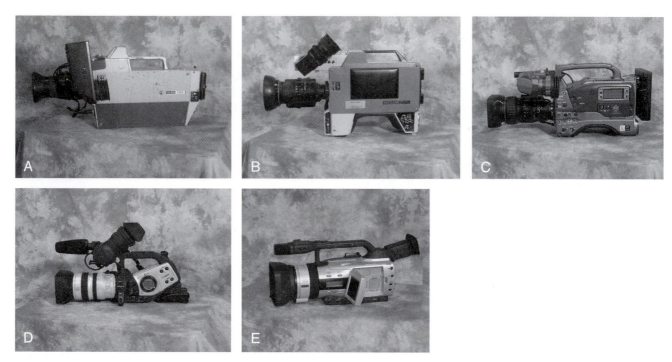

Figure 8-14 (A) This Ikegami ITC 350 camera was popular in the very early days of portable video. (B) The Ikegami ITC 730 camera was in common use in the 1980s. Both Ikegami cameras were heavy and used vacuum pickup tubes. (C) A JVC solid state minDV camcorder manufactured in 2000. It was smaller and lighter than the vacuum-tube cameras, but produced a high-quality image. (D) A Canon XL2 miniDV camcorder. Note the much smaller body and larger lens. This camera can accept a wide variety of lenses, shoot at varying frame rates, and produce a high-quality image. (E) This Canon Gl-2 camera is a prosumer model that has three chips and many features similar to larger professional cameras. It can take still pictures and perform numerous digital effects. Unlike professional cameras, it features an LCD swing out monitor.

day's cameras: light filtering; the separation of white light into red, blue, and green; image sensing; and signal processing. Today's cameras are simply smaller, lighter, and more accurate.

Camera Basics

We have now taken the light that makes up a real image, traced its progression though the lens, and seen how the lens may manipulate it. It is now time to transform that image into a form we can use.

In a film camera, this would be as simple as having a light-sensitive material on a celluloid backing exposed to the image. The camera would simply be a means to move and position the film. For a video camera, recording the image is a more involved and complicated process. The inside of a TV camera is filled with circuit boards and other wiring, with at least a dozen places to make adjustments. Since making a

change in any one of the adjustments causes a change in the remaining unadjusted areas of the camera, the proper equipment and the proper training are required of anyone who touches anything on the inside. Unless an experienced maintenance person has shown you how to make adjustments inside your camera, do not try it.

In the new world of digital cameras, making adjustments is considerably easier. A digital camera is software driven. In older cameras, adjustments were made by turning tiny screws. In today's digital cameras, they are made by calling up menus in the viewfinder screen and using buttons to raise or lower selected values (see Figure 8-15). If you don't like the way your changes look, you can always go back to the default settings and start over. Anyone can play around with the camera parameters and be able to reset the camera to its normal setup.

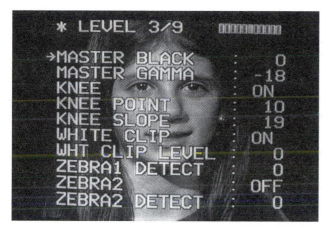

Figure 8-15   This is one page of a setup menu on a digital video camera. Buttons or other controls on the camera allow you to scroll through the pages and the individual menu items to change their values.

Filter Wheel

As it comes from the lens, the first thing an image passes through in a broadcast-quality camera is a filter wheel. This wheel (sometimes two wheels) contains typical photographic filters, just like those on the front of a film camera lens. (See Figure 8-16.) Normally, there are three types of filters in the wheel: clear, color correction, and light reduction. The electronics of a camera are similar to a roll of film: film has a specific speed or level of sensitivity to light, known as the **ASA** (from the American Standards Association), and is designed for a specific color of light. All TV cameras are

Figure 8-16   The front of this professional camera has two filter wheels. Here, they are set in the "1" "B" combination.

made to work their best with light at 3,200° K (Kelvin), the color temperature of typical TV lights.

Shooting a scene lit by TV lights is done with the filter wheel dialed to the clear (3,200° K or indoors) position. If the shoot is outdoors in sunlight, then the filter wheel is turned to a daylight or 5,600° K position. This filter is nothing more than an orange-colored filter designed to convert daylight color temperatures to that of tungsten (TV lights). A similar filter used with film cameras is the 85B. Video cameras can be balanced to any light temperature, but assume it is operating at its factory-designed optimum (or preset) of 3,200° K. As the amount of sunlight increases, a video camera can increase shutter speeds to regulate the amount of light it receives if the range of the iris has been exceeded. This usually has an adverse effect on any movement in the picture, however. The most effective way for a video camera to handle high brightness levels is to simply select a **neutral density filter (ND)** on the filter wheel. In single–filter wheel cameras, NDs are usually combined with a daylight color-correction filter.

The standard one-wheel camera has four positions on its wheel:

- Clear—(3,200° K) used for interior shoots, or exterior at night.

- Daylight—(5,600° K) used outdoors in moderate amounts of sunlight intensity or in shaded areas.

- Daylight +1/4 ND—used for open sunlit areas on clear days.

- Daylight +1/8 ND—used for very bright daylight scenes, such as a sunny day at the beach or the ski slopes.

A 1/4 ND allows 25% of the light to pass through it without affecting it in any other way. A 1/8 ND allows 12.5% of the light to pass through. Although each camera model has different nomenclature or different combinations in its filter wheel, they all operate on the basic principles stated above. These filters allow a camera to shoot in any typical lighting condition.

Prism

The light forming the image passes through a prism after going through the filter wheel. Unlike most consumer and low-end industrial cameras, which have only one pickup device, a professional camera will split the beam of light into its three **primary additive colors** for TV, which are red, blue, and green. These are not the **primary subtractive colors** for mixing colors; red, yellow, and blue are the colors for mixing paint and should not be equated to the primary additive colors (for mixing light) in any way. The way a TV camera arrives at all the colors of the rainbow is considerably different from the way an artist does on a canvas or even from the way a filmmaker does in making a color print. The camera prism delivers a very pure blue, green, and red picture to three targets or light-sensitive surfaces. These three colors can be recombined later to represent the true colors of the object being photographed. It is the intensity of each TV primary color that determines the true color when the information is recombined into a video picture.

Charge-Coupled Devices

In the 1980s, cameras were designed to use **charged-coupled devices**, or **CCD**s, from the older methods of using light-sensitive tubes. The CCDs became known simply as chips. After about 1990, camera manufacturers stopped making cameras with tubes, because the chip technology far surpassed tubes. Many problems that were inherent in tubes, such as **smear, lag,** and **burn-in,** were eliminated by the use of chips.

Most chips are rated by the number of **pixels** each chip has. Each pixel is like a grain of emulsion on a film; the greater the number of them present, the sharper the image. The more pixels present on a chip, the more sensitive the chip is to light. Newer cameras can almost see in the dark. They are capable of making good pictures in no more light than that of a single candle. This is something a tube camera could never do.

Video Signal

Electronic impulses from the chips are sent on to the rest of the camera, called the processor. Much of the camera's insides make up the video processing unit of the camera. This complex series of boards and circuits shapes the video image into its many parts, mainly **chroma** (color) and **luminance** (brightness). Before that information leaves the camera, it can be recombined into one **composite** signal or left separate in its **component** state to be recombined later. Component video carries the chroma and the luminance or brightness signal in separate wires. (See Figure 8-17.)

Figure 8-17 These two wires are commonly used to transfer component and digital video. On the right is an S Connector; on the left is a 4-pin FireWire connector.

Fields and Frames

The images of the video signal are relayed in a similar manner to that of film. Each video image is just like a frame from motion picture film. Video is recorded at a rate of 30 frames per second, however, instead of 24 frames like the movies. Each video frame is made up of two fields, sometimes called odd and even. These fields are essentially half pictures that are combined through a process called interlacing.

NTSC, PAL, and SECAM

Whether a video signal is component or composite, it is based on a reference system. In the United States the reference system is called the **National Television Systems Committee** or **NTSC**, which was set up by the federal government. Only a few other countries use the NTSC system, most notably Canada, Mexico, and Japan. NTSC has 525 lines of resolution and scans at 59.85 fields (29.97 frames) per second. Common practice for discussing frame speed is to round off to 30 frames per second. One drawback to the NTSC system is that it allows the viewer at home to adjust the color on their TV set. This led NTSC to be jokingly referred to as "Never Twice the Same Color." Having no guarantee that the viewer's set is properly adjusted can mean a great deal of loss for the artistry of video.

The other two reference systems in the world are the PAL and SECAM standards. **Phase Alternation Line (PAL)** was developed by Germany, England, and Holland in 1966. PAL has 625 lines of resolution and scans at 50 fields (25 frames) per second but does not have color controls on the TV receivers like NTSC. Consequently, PAL has less color distortion than NTSC, but because of the slower scan rate, many NTSC viewers see PAL pictures as flickering too much. In 1962, France introduced the **Séquentiel Couleur À Mémoire** (SECAM) system, which was later adopted by the Soviet Union and several other European countries. SECAM has 625 scanning lines at 50 fields (25 frames) per second, like PAL.

These three systems are not compatible with each other. A special device is necessary to translate one system to another when making dubs.

Digital Video

The system adopted by the United States, Canada, Mexico, South Korea, and other countries is referred to as ATSC, for the Advanced Television Systems Committee that helped develop it. Digital video's aspect ratio is 16:9, wider than the NTSC 4:3. The system is capable of producing 1,080 lines of resolution; far more video information than the 525 (480 displayable) lines in NTSC. The 1,080 resolution is only one version of digital television, which will also support SDTV, standard definition television (480 or 576 lines), or EDTV, enhanced definition television (720 lines).

In digital video, images and sound are captured using digital sampling technology, delivering a movie-quality experience, multicasting and interactive capabilities. The Federal Communications Commission (FCC) has mandated that all television stations must broadcast in digital video beginning February 17,

2009. The FCC made this decision to improve the technical quality of broadcast television because digital video:

- Is free of ghosts and snow.

- Allows multicasting (several channels of programs instead of just one).

- Can be compressed and stored easily.

- Allows multiple generations of copies without noticeable decline in quality.

Digital video also differs from analog video in the way the picture is shown on the screen. Digital video can use progressive scanning, while analog video only used interlaced scanning. In progressive scanning, the image is displayed on a screen by scanning each line (or row of pixels) in a sequential order rather than an alternate order, as is done with interlaced scanning. Progressive scanning scans the image lines (or pixel rows) in numerical order (1,2,3) down the screen from top to bottom, rather than in an alternate order (lines or rows 1,3,5, etc. followed by lines or rows 2,4,6). Progressively scanning the image onto a screen every 60th of a second, rather than using "interlacing" alternate lines every 30th of a second, produces a smoother, more exact image on the screen that is perfectly suited for viewing fine details, such as text. Progressive scanning is also less susceptible to image flicker, which is common with interlaced scanning.

CAMERA FUNCTIONS

On the outside of every professional-quality camera are the operational controls. These switches and buttons are the primary means of controlling the electronics inside the camera. Each model and each camera manufacturer can have widely varying controls and placement of controls on the camera body. (See Figure 8-18.) Although cameras generally don't have many switches, just one of those switches being in the wrong position can affect the quality of the video or even prevent the camera from operating.

Figure 8-18   All of the camera function switches are located on the lower front and side of this professional camera.

Power Switch There is always a main power switch on the camera that sends energy to all parts of the camera or camcorder. Another switch on the camera may control the power to the record device and also acts as a power saver to the camera itself. This switch can be a three-position switch: Standby, Save On, and On. **Standby** is used when you do not need to operate the camera but want to start up the camera suddenly. A trickle current from the power source keeps the circuits warm and allows the camera to be ready to shoot in just a couple of seconds when it is turned on from the standby position. **Save On** gives you a picture in the viewfinder, but if the camera is hooked up to a VCR, it prevents the VCR's tape servo motors from coming up to speed, thus saving power. If you try to record when the camera is in this mode, it will take a couple of seconds for the VCR servo to come up to speed before the recording can begin. In a news situation, this is clearly a disadvantage, but if you are spending quite a lot of time lining up or waiting for a shot, this function lets you work with the camera picture without running the deck battery (or camcorder battery) down until you need to roll. But more importantly, if the servo is left running without recording, you are needlessly wearing down the video record heads and the drums of the tape machine and running an increased risk of damaging the tape itself. Digital recorders do not need this function because very little power is needed to keep the DTE recorder or flash memory recorder ready to record. The **On** position is when everything is up and

ready for instantaneous recording as soon as the button is pushed.

Camera/Bars Switch This switch makes the output of the camera either the picture or the color bar generator contained within the camera.

Gain Switch Most cameras offer the user three choices of gain in the sensitivity of the chips. Gain, which is measured in decibels (dBs), is usually left at zero or normal for most shooting but can be raised as high as 48. To raise the level of exposure if the lens is wide open, you can shift the gain switch by one position. Under extreme low light, you can go to the last position of the gain switch. Each position increases the sensitivity of the chips by the amount labeled on the switches or on some cameras by the amount you have predetermined. Gain increases also increase the **picture noise** (graininess). Although some newer cameras can boost the gain up to 48 dB, even an 18-dB picture gain is not considered to be of broadcast quality unless it is a news shot under terrible conditions. Even a 9-dB gain can be objectionable in some news and almost all EFP situations. Use gain only when you cannot get a picture without it.

White Balance Button To allow the camera to work under any type of light, each professional camera has a white balance circuit. By showing the camera something white (zooming in on a white card, wall, or paper) and pressing a button or flipping a switch, the camera sets the reference volts on each chip to make a white picture with that color of light. An indicator in the viewfinder tells the operator when the white balance is done (usually in two or three seconds, or less). Some cameras also show you what the color temperature is on completed white balance.

Some cameras also have a **black balance** switch to set the black reference in the camera. This is done automatically in most cameras, but heat can affect the black balance. If your camera has a black balance, you should use it every time you white balance, or any time the atmospheric (hot/cold) temperature changes even if the light does not. A good camera should white balance under most colors of light when the proper filter wheel is dialed in. Again, in consumer and prosumer cameras, the white balance function can be automatic. That is great for saving time and avoiding mistakes, but it once again relinquishes creative control to the machine and can lead to subjects being shot in the wrong color.

White Balance Channels Many professional cameras have three channels of white balance circuits from which to choose. The first two are normally called "**A**" and "**B**." They both work the same way and allow you to balance for two scenes. If a shot requires you to follow a subject from a sunlit area to a room lit with only incandescent light, you can set the white balance on A for daylight and the B for incandescent. As you follow the subject from one room to the other, only a quick flip of the switch is needed to maintain the proper colors. The third position is **Preset**. This setting puts the camera in its factory-preset white balance of 3,200° Kelvin, the TV lights' normal color temperature. The camera now acts like a film camera with a constant color reference (that is, it is the same as using a selected film stock); any correction for color temperature has to be done by means of filters in or on the camera or on the lights themselves.

Shutter Selection Many cameras now have variable shutter speeds, much like film cameras. The normal shutter speed of a video camera (usually an electronic shutter) is 1/60 of a second. Speeds of 1/125, 1/500, and 1/1000 of a second are usually available. These additional shutter speeds allow the camera to do certain special effects or let the operator shoot at low f-stops in bright light, but they are not useful in most situations. The most common use is in an isolated sports camera. The faster shutter speeds allow for brilliantly clear and sharp slow-motion pictures and freeze frames of fast-moving objects. The trouble is that when these pictures are played at normal speed, they appear to stutter or strobe on the screen. You should only use the faster shutter speeds for shots to be played in slow motion or frozen, or for shots with little movement.

Clear Scan

You may have noticed that when computer screens are shown on video, they often have an annoying flicker or rolling, as though the horizontal hold is broken. Computer monitors, unlike NTSC TV sets and monitors, do not scan their CRTs at the same rate as normal television (59.85 Hz). They can scan at rates both higher and lower than that of video. Many professional cameras can change their own scan rates to match any

computer monitor by use of a selection switch, usually as part of the shutter switch, called **clear scan.** This option allows the camera to show very clear, flicker-free computer screens. Matching rates to some monitors with really low scan rates can leave the camera's ability to shoot moving subjects greatly reduced, and any movement by the camera such as a pan will result in blurred pictures.

Monitoring the Picture

Up to this point we have only discussed the inner workings of the camera and the means of controlling those functions. Now it is time to see the results of what the camera is doing, starting with what the camera sees and analyzing the quality of the video output.

Viewfinder In some early video cameras, the viewfinder was simply a glass window with some crosshairs in it. The operator never even looked through the lens. Today's cameras have high-resolution video mini-monitors as viewfinders, and some are in color. Because the picture appears after it has been processed, the operator sees just what the recorder or any output destination of the camera sees. The viewfinder has brightness and contrast controls that need to be set at proper levels. The contrast control should be turned up all the way, and the picture quality should be adjusted by the brightness knob only. A good picture should show whites as white and any deep shadows as a rich black.

Most cameras have a considerable amount of information available to the operator in the viewfinder. Some information is contained in the picture itself, such as the zebra striping. The **zebra bars** that appear over parts of the picture are a graphic display of the exposure level. Most cameras come from the factory with the zebra bars that can be set at levels between 70% video, or 70 **IREs** (Institute of Radio Engineers' standard measure) and 100 IREs of video; this means that any portion of the picture with an exposure of 70 units or above, as measured on a waveform monitor, will have these stripes. This measure, 70 units, corresponds to the proper exposure of skin-tone highlights on a subject with a light complexion or the proper exposure of a white piece of paper. If a person's face is the part of the picture that needs proper exposure, then the zebra bars should appear over the brightest highlights on the

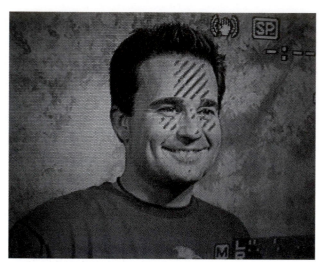

Figure 8-19   Zebra bars appear on the face of the subject as seen through the LCD viewfinder of the camera. These bars are set at 70 IREs, and their appearance on the highlight areas indicates proper exposure.

face, usually the cheeks and center of the forehead. (See Figure 8-19.)

Many videographers prefer that skin tones be more in the 55- to 65-unit range to avoid that *video* look, and they back the iris off (reduce the exposure) just until the zebra bars are removed from a face. Some videographers prefer to set the zebra pattern at 100 units to better see overexposed portions of the picture, especially when people are not in the shot. In analog recording, any portion of the video picture at 100 units will have greatly reduced definition and appear **washed out**. Video above 110 IRE will be seen as simply a white glow. For digital recording, anything above 100 IRE will lose all detail and turn to that white glow. Zebra bars can be set at any level by a service person, and many cameras can show two different sets of zebras at the same time: one a standard crosshatch at 70 units, and the other a square mosaic set at 100 units.

Other warning lights or indicators show low battery power, end of tape/memory, low-light levels, which filter is in use, and if the shutter speed is other than normal. By holding down the **RET** button on the lens control unit, you can show return video in the viewfinder. This return video may be the confidence playback function of the deck while the actual recording is being made (on some camcorders), or the scene played back from its recorder or other source if the camera is connected to it by a multipin cable.

LCD Viewer   Consumer and prosumer cameras now come standard with a fold-out liquid crystal display (LCD) viewer. This display, although somewhat low in resolution, provides the videographers with a good color picture of the shots as they are recorded. The LCD displays are thin and consume a small amount of power compared to a standard cathode ray tube (CRT) monitor. When shooting with the LCD display in use, the viewfinder is often disabled. This may cause problems for some videographers who do not get too close to the camera because of their vision, because the image may appear fuzzy. This alters shooting style a bit, especially for those experienced shooters who are used to direct contact with the viewfinder. Instead of pressing an eye to the rubber cup to see into the viewfinder, the videographer has to view the LCD viewer at a distance of 6 inches or more. LCDs will show all of the same information that can be seen through the viewfinder.

Color Bars   The color bars are the most common reference point in any TV work. Most professional cameras have a switch that turns on a color bar generator and feeds the color bars to the camera output. This internal color bar system is essential to track down any problems in the video system, because it is such a known reference. If the color bars do not look right, nothing else will.

Associated Test Equipment

Waveform Monitor   A waveform monitor is needed to make adjustments on the electronics of a camera. (See Figure 8-20.) Generally, only camera maintenance people use this device, but the data it provides are needed for any high-quality work with cameras, recorders, digital devices, microwave or satellite transmitters, or time-base correctors. This monitor, sometimes just called a scope, is the window to the inner parts of the video signal. Any problem with the video signal can be found by analyzing the different information available from the waveform monitor. A videographer who wishes to truly master a video camera should learn to read and use the waveform monitor.

Hooking a camera up to a monitor and experimenting with exposure should give some information on how a video signal works and how to recognize problems in the camera.

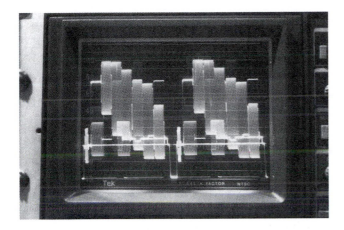

Figure 8-20 The waveform monitor shows what color bars look like when everything is working properly. This picture looks at both fields of one frame of video and shows both chroma and luminance.

Vectorscope The vectorscope also checks the color or chroma of the TV signal. (See Figure 8-21.) If reds in the picture do not look right, this scope can identify whether it is the operator's eye, the TV set, or the camera that is wrong. The waveform monitor and vectorscope are the two most important means of analyzing the quality of your video signal.

Figure 8-21 This vectorscope shows how color bars are represented when the video signal is optimum.

Color TV Monitor The most common, but technically weakest, form of monitoring the video picture is the color TV monitor, which can be a plain TV set. It is good for showing composition to others such as the director, producer, or reporter. Unless the monitor has been carefully set up and adjusted, and view-

ing conditions are optimal (no glares or high room light, for example), any other information such as true color reproduction or even exposure cannot be judged from the picture on the screen. The viewfinder and the waveform and vector monitors are the most accurate indicators.

A color monitor is also good for the cameraperson to use as a viewfinder on lengthy shoots when the camera is in a fixed place on a tripod. The strain on the eyes, neck, and back can be greatly reduced by having a conveniently placed monitor (to line up and maintain the framing). Although the most common type of monitor used for this purpose had a cathode ray tube design, their heavy weight and bulky size became much less popular when newer flat-screen monitors became available.

Maintenance To maintain your camera, protect it from shock and keep it clean. There is virtually nothing inside a camera that the typical operator can repair or adjust. Take good care of the camera and notify qualified maintenance personnel if there is a problem. It is the operator's job to keep the outside of the camera in the best possible shape. All screws, especially those holding the side panels in place, must be checked for tightness on a regular basis. Protect the camera from the elements as well as from bumps, jolts, and drops. Although most cameras are somewhat water resistant, none of them are waterproof. A rain jacket, a plastic protector shaped to fit the camera and keep moisture out, is an absolute must if you are shooting outdoors.

Troubleshooting You must be able to tell when something is not right with your camera. When your car makes unusual noises, you bring it in for a mechanic to check it out. When your video camera starts giving substandard pictures or strange colors, have a technician test it. Sometimes a thorough checking by the camera operator can isolate problems to certain areas of the camera, which can lead to a very simple operator-capable fix. A switch in the wrong position is the most common error. Know where all switches should be set, and check them first in case of trouble. Check your power source. Put up color bars and see how they look. If the bars look good, then you know the problem is not in the output of the camera, but in the input before the image gets to the video processor section of the camera. Unfortunately, most internal problems cannot be fixed in the field. Identify a good maintenance person or factory service center if you do not have an in-house repair facility or when you are out of town.

VIDEO RECORDERS

Cameras designed for portable video (excluding Webcams) have some type of video recording device as part of the design. While it is easy to see the unit as one piece of equipment, it is necessary to think of each component as separate. Cameras are combined with digital videocassette (miniDV or DVCPro), DVD, hard drive, or flash memory storage.

Videotape recorders are used in a wide variety of applications. The major differences among the various decks stem from the format of the videotape and the application for the deck. Portable recording devices must be constructed to be lightweight, to run on batteries, to withstand temperature variations, and be somewhat protected from dirt, dust, and water. Professional-quality decks feature high resolution, good picture stability and color, the ability to encode or record a number of different types of information like time code, and a multitude of inputs and outputs to accommodate any situation.

THE FORMAT WARS

In what has become a dizzying array of formats, the selection of a tape machine has moved from what just a few years ago was two or three choices to now over a dozen. In 2000, a survey conducted by a video trade publication found that 50% of people shooting and/or editing video—across all fields of use—were using the Betacam SP format. S-VHS was the next most popular. Only about 28% were using digital formats in some capacity. As of 2007, that has changed dramatically. Most professional shooting is done using Digi-beta, DV-CAM or DVCPRO. Now the question is not whether shooting is done in analog or digital, but whether it is done in standard definition or high definition.

In the early days of videotape, the standard was a two-inch reel-to-reel tape developed by Ampex. The recorder was as big as a desk, and editing was accomplished by using a magnifying glass and a razor blade. It was never practical for field use. A one-inch tape format (known as type C) was developed, and it became the studio standard for many years. It had very good resolution and allowed special effects like slow motion without distortion. This one-inch type C format had very limited use in the field. Although portable one-inch decks were made, they were just barely portable and certainly not dockable with a camera. They were usually mounted on a cart and could not be subjected to any movement, such as being carried, while recording.

Because of the size of the tape, the amount of storage space it required, and the cost of the tape, other, more practical formats were developed.

From its introduction in 1982 until just a few years ago, the Sony Betacam dominated the professional world of videotape for portable recording. But as video slowly converted to digital, a host of new formats arrived on the scene. It is unlikely that all of these formats will survive over a great length of time. Conversely, it is likely that more formats (and recording media) will be introduced in the near future. If this process of advancing technology follows the computer world, then any prediction today as to what the future will bring will be wrong. No one knows the future. The only thing you can say for certain is that the future is digital. The following is a brief rundown of the formats in use, past and present.

Older Formats: Hi8, S-VHS, and 3/4-Inch SP

The biggest revolution in the video world came when broadcast-quality equipment became available to the average consumer. By the mid-1980s, the average citizen could produce a TV program that was equal to the technical quality of broadcast quality. The Hi8 and Super-VHS (S-VHS) formats had the minimum 425 lines of resolution necessary to be considered broadcast quality. In the early 1990s, network news turned to these formats during the Persian Gulf War because of their small size, light weight, and relatively high quality. Parts of one episode of a popular TV sitcom, *Growing Pains,* were shot on Hi8 without any consciously noticeable dip in quality. Both the Hi8 and S-VHS formats came in models that featured all the options of a professional format in a slightly larger package than the regular consumer models, and both made dockable decks that could go on camera heads designed to be used with higher quality formats.

The **3/4-inch U-Matic** format was the standard of the portable video world for more than a decade and was the first easy-to-use format that allowed nonbroadcast users the ability to shoot and edit in a format that was relatively inexpensive. The quality approached "broadcast quality" when the format was enhanced to U-Matic SP using metal tape. However, this format was quickly replaced in the professional world when higher quality formats (e.g., Betacam) emerged. U-matic machines are no longer being manufactured. Because of the vast libraries of 3/4-inch tapes in the world, playback machines in U-matic format stayed around for a long time, but the machines are scarce now because both the tapes and the machines are bulky and the quality cannot compete with newer formats.

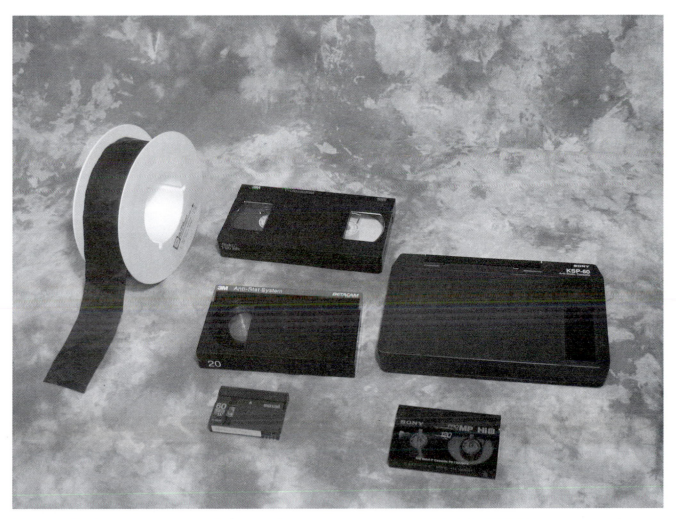

Figure 8-22 Video tape sizes: upper left, two-inch reel-to-reel; upper center, 1/2-inch VHS/S-VHS; center, 1/2-inch Betacam; lower center, miniDV; lower right, Hi8.

Standard Analog Videocassette Formats: Beta SP and MII

In 1982, Sony developed a 1/2-inch videocassette format for broadcast use from their Betamax consumer format. The new format was introduced as part of a one-piece camera recorder unit they called a **Betacam.** The term went on to mean the Beta format for professional use, as opposed to home-use Beta tapes. Many people still mistakenly refer to any professional camcorder as a "Betacam," whether it is made by Sony or not. The original Betacam format is no longer made and was replaced by Beta SP. Like 3/4-inch SP, this format enabled the use of the older format tapes but greatly improved the quality of the video when metal particle tape was used.

Another 1/2-inch tape, the M format, was introduced by Panasonic in the mid-1980s, about the same time as Beta. It was an offshoot of VHS but never developed a professional following. In 1987, the **MII** format was introduced to compete with Beta SP. MII also makes use of 1/2-inch metal particle tape, but uses a cassette shell unique to its format, unlike the Beta tapes, which still use the original Beta cassette shell. Blank Betamax tapes purchased at the local discount store worked in a professional Beta machine. The M formats, which never found a wide following, are no longer manufactured. Panasonic has replaced them with digital formats.

Digital Formats: D Series, Digital Betacam, Betacam SX, DV, DVCAM, DVCPRO, and Digital S

While digital tape is definitely the tape of the future, no one standard has come to the forefront to dominate the industry. As you'll see in the descriptions of the different formats that follow, confusion is the best way to describe the situation. As we will keep mentioning in this book, it is unlikely that all—or even many—of these formats will survive. Just like the MII format, rising technologies will overtake the weaker, less popular forms. But for now, below is a thumbnail sketch of what's out there today.

Many postproduction (editing) facilities have been using digital recorders for some time to create the edit master. Earlier 3/4-inch cassettes and the later models with 1/2-inch cassette tape systems were made by both Sony and Panasonic and designated by a "D-x" notation (e.g., D-1, D-2, and so on); these have generally replaced the one-inch type recorders. These machines are still primarily used in studios, and not taken into the field.

Standard 1/2-Inch Formats

In 1993 Sony introduced the **Digital Betacam** format, using a discrete cosine transform (DCT) recording technique referred to as the ITU-R 601, with a 2.34:1 compression ratio and a recording data rate of 127.76 Mb/s (megabytes per second). The resulting files are similar to JPEG files in the computer world. This format is often referred to as Digi-Beta, and it is commonly in use for broadcast and cable/satellite program work. One version of this format came as part of a one-piece all-digital camcorder, the BVW-D700. In late 1996, Sony also introduced another digital format, **Betacam SX,** which used 10-bit MPEG-2 digital encoding with a 4:2:2 sampling rate, 10:1 compression format, and an 18 Mb/s data record rate. MPEG-2 is the digital method used in most digital editing and all digital transmission. The 4:2:2 sampling means that for every four luminance samples taken, two red samples and two blue samples are also taken. This format was particularly interesting to news departments, because the signal can be transmitted via microwave at two times normal speed, thus redefining transmission time. Sony also introduced yet another format called MPEG IMX as an edit format, but not for field use. Also, JVC introduced **Digital S**, also known as D-9, which is based on their S-VHS system and has an eight-bit 4:2:2 sampling rate in a dual-DV recording format (two DV chipset processors used in tandem) and a 50 Mb/s data rate.

The 6.35-mm Tape Formats

In the 1990s, the consumer and lower-end professional or industrial market transformed to a digital format called **DV,** using a smaller tape width of 6.35 mm. DV refers to a specific method of recording a digital signal on the tape, similar to JPEG files but differing from other files like MPEG-2 and DCT, a format de-

Figure 8-23   These two camcorders are small in size, sell for less than $500, and feature both optical and digital zooms.

veloped by Ampex. All DV formats use an eight-bit 4:1:1 sampling rate in which only one red and one blue sample are taken for every four units of luminance, a compression of 5:1, and a data recording rate of 25 Mb/s.

The camera and lens will always outperform the recording device, regardless of the format. There is no question that the DV-formatted camcorders look better than their Hi8 and S-VHS cousins. Nevertheless, DV, made by both Sony and Panasonic, has become the format of choice for consumers, prosumers, and budget-minded professionals. The development of this format—especially mini-DV cassettes—has led to the design of camcorders so small they fit into a shirt pocket, and has brought professional quality to almost any user for a reasonable price. DV has become as generic as the old VHS format.

Sony introduced its DVCAM version of DV to appeal to the industrial or prosumer market. The major difference between DVCAM and Standard DV is a larger spacing of the recording tracks (called track pitch), which requires the tape to run at a faster speed. This change is a benefit in editing, because it enables more accurate edits and fewer audio problems.

Panasonic's upgraded version of DV is the DVCPRO. Its real difference from DV is the double tape speed, which has a better tolerance of tape drop out. Unlike the larger professional formats, DV tapes

can be recorded and played in different manufacturers' machines. Sony's DV and DVCAM can be played in Panasonic's DV and DVCPRO decks, and vice versa. For all practical purposes, there is no quality difference among any of these four formats. DVCAM and DVCPRO are better formats for professionals, because of the increased editing capabilities and other added features of their respective machines, but the actual quality of the recording is the same.

Panasonic has also taken the DVCPRO to a new level with their AJ-HDX900 DVCPRO HD camcorder. This camera is designed to provide global content providers (digital cinematography, cable and television program production) with a moderately priced camcorder (under $30,000) that can produce HD images in any of eleven video formats.

If you are confused about formats, don't worry—most people, even professionals, are also confused. The marketplace for format choices is very confusing. The one thing to carry away from this discussion of tape is their compatibility (or noncompatibility). Close attention must be paid as to where and how the material on a recorded tape is to be used. How many points of transfer or translation is that tape going to have to go through? In the transfer/editing/transmission/storage process, the different machines or systems handling the signal can go from eight bit to ten bit, DV to MPEG-2, 25 Mb/s to 50 Mb/s, and so on and

Figure 8-24 This Panasonic AJ-HDX900 camcorder brings HD recording within the reach of many video professionals.

vice versa, with the resulting picture ending up worse than an old analog picture.

It would be a disservice to the reader to try to predict which if any of the current formats will survive or dominate in their current form. The acceptance of digital format acquisition methods at the professional level has slowed somewhat because of the above-stated confusion and the mismatching formats. It is likely, however, that we will see videotape replaced with several types of random-access media at some point during the next few years. Only then will video be truly digital, free of the limitations presented by the moving parts and mylar-based tape inherent with the use of videotape. The only thing that is certain is that many of the functions of the recording device will remain the same.

Digital Video Recorders

After years of dealing with a multitude of clumsy and sometimes annoying videotape formats, a huge change seems to be occurring. Three types of digital "tapeless" recorders are available for professional, prosumer, and consumer use. Direct to DVD, hard drive (also known as DTE or Direct to Edit), and flash card recording are quickly becoming commonplace. Many camcorders, especially at the consumer level, record video directly to a mini DVD disc. DTE recorders can record video

onto a small hard drive similar to an iPod. Flash memory recorders can record video onto flash cards similar to those found in digital still cameras.

DVD Recorders DVD recorders are now common in many camcorders. A DVD recorder allows digital recording, random access, and easy editing. These camcorders are consumer or prosumer level and do not seem to be good enough for professional work. Hitachi hit the market first in 2000 with the DZ MV100, which features MPEG-2 compression, basic editing tools, and easy navigation for both playback and record. The recording is made onto a mini-DVD disc (8 cm in diameter, about 3 inches) and can be played back on any DVD machine. One of the criticisms aimed at these camcorders has been the lack of a FireWire output to allow easy input to a nonlinear editor, but this connectivity issue has recently been addressed by the manufacturers.

Figure 8-25 This Sony camcorder records directly to a DVD.

Hard Drive Hard drive digital video recorders, known also as **DTE** or **Direct to Edit** recorders, are small devices that feature a hard drive (e.g., 40 GB) and resemble an iPod. Video is recorded onto and from the recorder by using a FireWire cable that can pass audio, video, time code, and other control information. These recorders are designed to facilitate "direct to edit" by allowing the easy transfer of video to a computer equipped for nonlinear editing. Recording on this type of device allows the user to begin editing without capturing, file transferring, or converting the video files.

Figure 8-26   Small digital recorders like this one mount easily on a video camera and replace bulky videotape recorders. After recording video in the field, this recorder can be directly connected to a nonlinear editing system using FireWire. These devices are also known as DTE (Direct to Edit) recorders.

The device acts as an external hard drive (which it is) and can be accessed easily from the computer.

Flash Memory   Some newer camcorders have entered the market with the ability to record directly to a solid-state memory card. Similar in size and shape to the PCMCIA cards commonly used in laptop computers, this storage medium is neither tape nor disc. The Panasonic P2 card is really four SD flash memory cards combined into one larger card. The advantage is that it has no moving parts and is not sensitive to extreme temperature, vibration, or shock. The manufacturers claim that the cards are rewriteable up to 100,000 times. Since flash memory cards do not use tape, they are not susceptible to tape dropout, making flash memory cards a clean edit source. Shots can also be arranged into folders, making editing easier.

Time Code

One of the most important pieces of information in video recording is the time code or **TC**. Similar to edge numbers in film, the time code allows each frame of the video to be numbered. In whatever machine a tape is played back, scenes or shots can be referred to and

Figure 8-27   This Panasonic camcorder records video on a P2 memory card (lower right), which can be inserted directly into a laptop for editing.

located by their time code number. In older professional analog machines, time code is recorded like an additional channel of audio on the videotape. It has a separate track and its own space on the tape. This type of encoding is called **linear time code (LTC)**. On newer tape formats, there is also a form of time code recorded in the picture portion of the video signal. The numerical information is added to the vertical interval space left as the tracing beam shuts off to return to the top of the picture. This channel of time code is simply called **vertical interval time code (VITC)**.

Time code in a professional machine can be recorded as either drop frame or nondrop frame. Because video in NTSC is recorded at 29.97 fps, numbering each frame will not be an accurate counting of the time of the recording. A one-hour recording will have 1 hour and 8.6 seconds of time code. Drop frame TC skips two frames every minute, except every tenth minute. This allows the counting of frames to meet the real time of the recording.

User bits are stored in yet another portion of the video signal. They can store characters of the alphabet as well as numbers. Whatever is entered into the user-bit channel will be recorded within every frame of video, just like time code. Once set, user bits do not advance or change as the recording takes place. Each frame has the same information. That makes user bits a good way to label tapes. The operator's name, initials, date, or unit number can be placed in this channel to aid in cataloging later. The limit, however, is eight characters.

On machines that allow it, one of the more popular uses for vertical interval time code is as a clock. While linear time code is usually set on **Record Run** so the numbers only advance when the tape does, VITC can be set on **Free Run** so the numbers continue to advance no matter what the VCR is doing. The VITC can be set in sync with any clock, such as a wristwatch. Many news videographers set the VITC in sync with their reporter's watch. In this way, a reporter can take time code notes using the time of day while the videographer is shooting. During a long interview, soundbites can be noted easily without looking at the recorder. Later in editing, the reporters can simply have the editor switch the playback machine to VITC and search quickly for the sound or shots referred to in their notes. This can save valuable minutes when editing under deadline pressure.

Professional camcorders and decks always have TC in and out ports. On multicamera shoots, one camera or deck can be designated as the master TC source and feed the other units—a process called slaving—so all the tapes will have the same TC while recording. This makes the editing process much easier by allowing the editor to sync up the same scene shot from different cameras and intercut them as if the scene were being edited live at the location.

One disadvantage of the newer DV formats at the prosumer level is the inability to customize time code. Although most recorders have TC, it cannot be set by the user and has no separate in and out ports. Each tape put into the machine starts at 00:00:00, and the machines don't allow multiple recorders to be synchronized to the same time code during recording. But the good news is that all DV formats have time code, and it can be read by almost all nonlinear editing systems.

Typical Control Functions

Standard video recorders operate in the same manner as audiotape recorders. There are positions for play, record, stop, fast forward, rewind, and pause. Later model VCRs had a search function that allows the operator to scan the pictures on the tape at a fast rate with

the machine in the pause or play mode. Some older models of video recorders have an audio dub function that allows the recording of audio on only one of the audio channels (usually channel 2) as long as there is video already recorded on the tape. The small video recorders or decks that fit on the back of, or are included in, a professional camera have fewer functions than the stand-alone models. Although many of these onboard decks have a complete function panel, it is usually covered by a door and rarely used by the operator. These types of decks are generally thought of as record-only decks because of their limited functions for other uses. The play function on the typical nondigital onboard broadcast-quality videotape deck only played the tape back in the viewfinder, and required a playback adapter unit in order for the picture to be seen outside the camera. Professional nondigital onboard decks and one-piece camcorders often could not record a video signal from any source other than the camera. That limitation usually meant that a second deck was needed in certain situations. Onboard digital decks allow the recording of other signals in addition to the camera and play back recorded video in full color without an adapter.

Typical Inputs

The functions of analog dockable tape decks or built-in tape recorders are very limited and thus have fewer input points. They accept video only from the camera to which they are attached, but they do permit audio to be recorded either through the connectors in the back or from the camera's own mic. Professional onboard tape decks have input/output points for time code to allow one deck to be "slaved" to another deck or source to share a common time code.

A typical stand-alone analog videocassette recorder can receive a video signal in one of two connectors: via the **BNC** connector, which carries a standard composite video signal, or via the multipin cable connector, which carries a component signal. The origin of the acronym BNC is often debated, but one popular theory is that it stands for **"Baby N Connector."** This name comes from a similar connector used during World War II by the Navy.

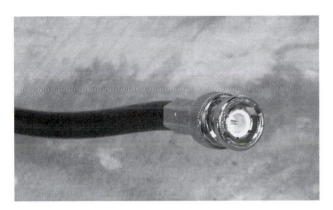

Figure 8-28   A video cable with the BNC connector.

Most one-piece camcorders also have an input point for **genlock**. This BNC connector is used to link the unit to other machines or cameras to synchronize the timing of the video signals. This is necessary whenever more than one camera or recorder is used together or used as part of a live transmission.

The multipin connector on most professional decks is the 27-pin Beta connector. This connector supplies component video to another machine, either another deck or an edit machine. On prosumer models, this connection is usually an S-video connector, which again supplies a component signal.

Digital decks have an additional input/output (I/O) port for delivering an all-digital signal of not only the video but the audio as well. It's called **FireWire** or **iLink** and is often referred to by its more technical name, IEEE-1394. (See Figure 8-17.) The information can flow in either direction, so the port can be used for playback, recording, or editing.

Typical Outputs

The video output of a stand-alone VCR usually comes from three types of connections and forms. Component format decks have a multipin connector that allows the video signal to stay in its separated state as it leaves the deck for another source that can handle component video. The next output is the NTSC composite signal that comes out of a BNC connector. On lower quality machines, this signal may come out of an RCA-style plug.

The standard male XLR connector provides the audio outputs of all professional decks. Switches on some

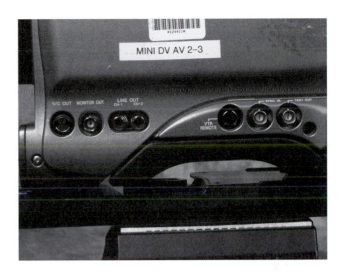

Figure 8-29   Typical outputs on a professional video camera.

decks allow the mixing of the output of both audio channels into just one connector for more flexible uses. The audio output levels can be controlled on each channel separately, and the signal usually comes out at line-level impedance (See Chapter 9.) Less expensive decks may havpe RCA or miniplug connectors to get audio from the deck. There is always a socket for a headphone or ear piece to monitor the sound recording and playback; it is commonly a 1/8-inch miniplug. Some decks have sockets for both.

Camcorders also have an output for the time code, which works both as the video is being recorded and on playback, and a BNC (video connector) output for a TBC (time-base connector used to correct minor playback problems), if one is used. A switch called **confidence playback** on some professional videotape decks permits the audio and video to be monitored while it is being recorded. The audio confidence, delayed by about one second, can be heard on the headphone output only. The video confidence can be seen on any of the video outputs of the deck or in the return position through the camera's viewfinder. Meant only to serve as a quick check on whether something is indeed being recorded on the tape, the video confidence picture is black-and-white and of poor quality in appearance. The same is true of the audio confidence: the quality is poor, but it shows that something is being recorded. Confidence playback is often used to spot check the recording in progress and ensure there is no head clog or other failure of the system. It makes no sense to waste time shooting if the machine is not working properly.

Onboard Decks

Many professional camera systems come as true one-piece camcorders. These machines make it easy for one person to shoot from the shoulder and eliminate one cable (to the deck) and one battery. These analog decks are not made to play back video without the use of a playback adapter. They can play back the recording "in the camera" to check to see if something was recorded or to review what was recorded, but it will only be in black-and-white and the signal doesn't leave the camcorder without the playback adapter. Because of this, there are no output connectors on these decks except for a headphone, a time code BNC (for jamming or inserting time code to another deck), and a video BNC out for use with a monitor that only shows the camera output, not the recording. A multi-pin plug on the deck allows it to be attached to the playback adapter. Dockable decks do not have as many functions as the stand-alone VCRs, but they record with the same level of quality. With an added adapter, record-only dockable deck can be converted into a stand-alone decks and used with a multi-pin cable or BNC coax cable to record from the camera or any other video source.

Meters

The audio record levels are always visible on analog **VU (volume units)** meters or the newer style LED peak meters on the deck. The meters, calibrated from 20 decibels to 0 decibels in the green, and 0 to 3 decibels in the red (for analog meters), indicate the strength of the audio signal. A good recording should have the loudest passages or sounds peaking at 0 dB, with most of the signal around l0 dB. If the meter needle goes above 0 dB into the red, it may mean that the audio is being recorded with distortion. The ability of a deck to record audio over the 3-dB level is called **head room.** Some machines have little or no head room and distort any sound "hotter" or stronger than 5 dB. Others can

handle signals up to nearly 10 dB without distortion, although the sound may be somewhat compressed. For digital recording, the audio has no head room. Anything over 0 dB is distorted.

Figure 8-30   This display panel on a professional camcorder shows audio level at –4 dB.

One of the meters usually has a scale to read off video signal strength as well. This is usually a short green line. When the meter select switch is in the video position, the needle should be somewhere on that green line. A dark picture can give the needle a low reading, and a very bright picture a high reading. If no video is present, the needle does not register. A third scale is there to measure recorder battery strength. A **Batt Check** button shows the relative strength of the battery. Most battery scales are not calibrated; the needle position means something only if you know what a fresh battery reading looks like on that particular machine.

Warning Lights

Every video recorder has warning lights or some method of indicating to the operator that something has gone wrong or needs checking. The most common of these is the **tape-end warning.** When the tape is in the last two minutes of record time, this light flashes and an audio warning can be heard over the headsets but nowhere else. This method of alert is the same for all the warning functions. Other warnings usually include **RF** or **Clog** (no video being recorded),

Servo (VCR receiving poor video signal), **Dew** (excess moisture inside the machine), and **Battery** (battery's power nearing end). The newer digital recorders have fewer exposed moving parts and are less susceptible to these problems. The most common warning for these devices alerts the operator to the amount of record time remaining.

Time Base Correctors

The complicated electronics of TV operate on very precise timing for the various functions involved in creating the TV signal. Any time two or more signals are mixed, such as videotape mixed with live pictures from the studio during a live newscast, the timing of their electronic functions must be in sync. The **time base corrector (TBC)** is one way to bring the video in sync with the broadcast signal of the TV station. It also improves the stability of the picture by replacing the control track of the video with a newly generated one, thus eliminating any errors or defects in the original information. The functions of the TBC are becoming almost invisible to the user and are simply part of the machine.

Maintenance

As with a camera, there is very little you can do to fix a video recorder unless you have been trained in a factory-sponsored school or by experienced technicians. Like any other piece of equipment, the video recorder must be treated with respect. Do not let it get dirty; if it does, clean it as soon as possible. Do not let it get wet, and keep it away from harmful environments, such as cigarette smoke. For news use, the deck will go into some of the worst imaginable conditions. If the deck is not at its top performance level, it is not likely to bring home good-quality video. The best professional decks are made to take abuse, but up to a limit. The best protection for stand-alone recorders is a cloth carry bag custom made to fit the deck. This offers not only protection from dust, dirt, water, and shock but also a good shoulder strap and plenty of pockets for carrying extra equipment, such as a spare battery, tapes, or audio gear.

Most VCR manufacturers recommend using a cleaning tape on a regular basis. This tape cleans the machine's video and audio heads of any dirt particles that may interfere with the recording process.

Digital recorders should be treated with great care. Their small size makes them susceptible to being dropped, submerged, or otherwise abused. Since they are sealed, digital recorders are not user serviceable. The best way to protect them is to handle them carefully and keep them dry, fully charged, and out of the hot sun. Just like a hard drive or memory card, the material on them should be downloaded to maximize the capacity of the device for your next shoot.

Troubleshooting

There is always a time when things simply do not work. Traditionally, one of the most likely things to fail is the tape machine. Because of the highly accurate moving parts and their exposure to the environment when tapes are changed, the tape deck is subject to more wear and tear than the other equipment. A mental checklist should be second nature to anyone using a portable VCR in the field. On such a complex machine, the solution to a problem can be easy if you know where to look for the cause of the trouble.

The most common reason a recorder or camera will not work is also the simplest: no power. It is often easy to tell when there is no power present, but a drained battery can sometimes work some functions but not others. Check the battery first. In tape decks, the most common problem is the tape itself: is the record tab in place? (If not, the machine will not record.) Is the tape being threaded? (If not, it may not be seated properly in the tape carriage.) Is the tape rewound? Once these things are checked out, the problem may be in the circuits that control the mechanics, sometimes called the machine's logic. Shutting the power off to the deck for a minute or two may clear the logic circuits and allow them to reset. The last area of possible trouble is the mechanics of the deck. A dirty pinch roller can cause the tape not to thread properly. Most problems such as this, however, require a trip to the maintenance department. In the digital tapeless recorders, memory must be managed to provide enough space for recording.

You should know the position of every switch on the deck for every function you wish to use. You may never use some of the switches because of the type of work you do, but if they are in the wrong position for some reason, they may prevent the correct operation of the machine. *Study the manuals for your equipment carefully.* It is not uncommon to have just the playback function of a deck fail, so in certain circumstances, you may want to play the tape back on another machine, just to be sure. Very little field repair work can be done on a video recorder, although one easy fix is to clean the clogged video heads. They can be easily unclogged without a trip to the shop, even if a head-cleaning tape is not available on location. A new, unused tape can be played or fast-forwarded in the clogged deck. The rougher surface on the new tape can often break the clog loose.

BATTERIES

More power-efficient cameras and decks with higher capacity battery technology have considerably reduced power worries in recent years. Most people are familiar with lead-based batteries, like those in our cars (wet cells) or flashlights (dry cells). The standard alkaline dry cell–type of battery is rarely used to power a large piece of equipment, because it does not pack enough punch per ounce of battery weight; also, it generally cannot be recharged. The most popular source of battery power over the past 20 years has been the **nickel-cadmium (Ni-Cad)** cell battery, which gives quite a bit of power for its size and weight and can be recharged many times before wearing out. Today, new technologies are changing the once-heavy batteries into fairly light, compact units. Like the technology used in cell phone batteries, many battery styles are going to nickel metal halide (NiMH) versions. Their power-to-battery-weight ratio makes them a good choice for field use. Additionally, lithium ion technology is also being used in battery production, replacing a Ni-Cad-type battery weighing several pounds with one that weighs several ounces, yet gives the same or even more power.

The battery's power output must match the power requirements of the equipment to which it is hooked. A 30-volt power belt made for portable lights would fry a 12-volt system camera. In today's world of camcorders, one battery generally powers both units. The most popular is the clip-on **brick** battery, a generic name for any cube-style battery. The 18.2- or 14.4-volt capacity of these batteries gives them the reserve power to operate the equipment at its rated volts (12 volts) for the maximum amount of time without harming them.

Battery capacity is rated by **ampere hours (Ah).** The typical brick battery has a rating of 4 Ah; that is, it can deliver one amp of power for four hours. Your camcorder's manual will tell its power consumption and how many watts the camcorder uses, say, 18 W. Amps are watts divided by volts. In this case 18 watts ÷ 12 volts = 1.5 amps; this means that a 4-Ah battery should run the camcorder for a little longer than 2.5 hours (1.5 amps = 2.7 hours). Of course, the exact time will vary depending on the age of the battery and the operating conditions. Older batteries tend to "fade" and have less capacity than newer batteries. Also, batteries that are operated in extreme cold or hot conditions may not work as efficiently as those operated in more moderate temperatures.

Various types and sizes of packaging are generally used for the batteries used in today's video productions.

Recharging

Many professional videographers will state that a successful field shoot depends upon batteries and their ability to accept and hold a charge. This requires some knowledge about battery care.

The first step in proper battery care starts with proper recharging. A Ni-Cad battery should always be fully drained before it is recharged. Many new charging systems on the market finish draining half-used batteries and condition them before recharging. If the charger does not do this, try to discharge the battery fully without overdraining the battery to avoid what is called a **memory**. A battery will memorize the amount of power it is accustomed to giving. If the battery is always only half drained when recharged, the battery will learn to have only that amount of power. NiMH

Figure 8-31 Three different batteries. (A) a battery commonly used for miniDV camcorders; (B) the "snap-on" battery commonly used for professional video cameras; (C) an older style "slide in" battery still used in cameras, recorders, and monitors.

and lithium batteries do not have memory problems. It is important to know that Ni-Cad batteries cannot be recharged on a charger designed for NiMH or lithium ion batteries. Use only the charger that is designed specifically for your batteries; otherwise, the batteries will be damaged or ruined.

The two types of battery charging are fast and slow (trickle). A fast charger works only on batteries designed to be fast-charged and takes about 1 hour.

The slow charger usually takes about 12 to 14 hours to fully charge a battery. Most chargers will prevent overcharging and automatically switch to a maintenance cycle once the battery is charged. At 14 hours per charge, one charger is needed for every battery in everyday use. The charger must also match the battery. While many types of batteries are made to fit the same brackets, they do not necessarily work on the same chargers. Make sure your batteries and chargers are compatible. The newer types of batteries (referred to as "digital batteries") are charged on smart systems that allow fast charging times and self-diagnosis of battery condition.

Life Span

The order of battery use needs to be rotated so that no battery gets more use than the others. This makes the batteries reliable to the same degree; one should not wear out while others go without any usage, which can also be harmful. A professional battery should be able to undergo hundreds of recharges before the drop in capacity makes the use of that battery too impractical. The life of the battery may be extended by regular checks on the condition of the individual cells within the battery. A bad or weak cell can hasten the demise of the other good cells by shifting too much of the load over to them. Unfortunately, this check can only be done by trained maintenance personnel.

Proper Care

Batteries are very susceptible to temperature, both hot and cold. The ideal temperature for a battery is about 75° Fahrenheit, but as temperatures drop below freezing or go above 100° Fahrenheit, the ability of the battery to deliver power starts to fall off rather quickly. In very hot climates, or when batteries are left in the car for long periods of time, a cooler with a no-leak ice pack is a good way to ensure fresh batteries. The reverse is true for very cold weather: keep the batteries as warm as possible. Temperature also comes into play when recharging the battery. Never try to recharge a frozen or a blazing hot battery. Always allow the battery to reach a normal temperature before putting it through the rigors of charging. Once charged, the typical battery has a shelf life of about two days at full capacity. After that, it will start to lose about 5% of its power every week; the decay accelerates as time goes by. If the batteries cannot be left on a trickle charger, their shelf life should be kept in mind. When using lithium ion batteries, it is wise to charge them the night before a shoot.

TRIPODS AND CAMERA-MOUNTING DEVICES

Professional portable cameras are designed so they can be used on the operator's shoulder for handheld photography. Although this is essential, it is not the optimum way to use the equipment. Most professional uses of portable cameras and camcorders involve a tripod mount. The tripod raises the production values of photography more than any other element except lighting. Nothing says "amateur" more than handheld shaky shots.

Fluid Heads

Most professional tripod heads involve a combination spring/fluid mechanism for giving **pans** and **tilts** a smooth motion. The fluid acts as a dampening agent to resist movement so that the camera does not simply jerk up and down or to the side. There are two adjustments for the fluid (one for tilt and one for pan) that can make the resistance as heavy or as light as the operator likes. There are also locks for the pan and tilt to keep the camera in one place without drifting. A third function on the head is the **counterbalance**, which adjusts the internal springs to the exact weight of the camera.

To make a fluid head work, the camera's center of gravity must be perfectly balanced on the head. To do this, the head itself must be leveled (using the plumb-bubble bullseye found on the head), the pan and tilt locks must be off, and the pan and tilt friction must be

Figure 8-32 This standard professional tripod and head has two-stage legs, a midlevel spreader, and a shoulder strap for easy carrying.

set at the lightest setting. There should be an adjustment on the quick-release plate to slide the camera back and forth to get its center of gravity over the center of the head so the camera stays level without touching it. Lock the sliding plate in this position. A good fluid head should permit you to tilt the camera forward and back with minimal friction dialed into the tilt function, and you should be able to take your hand off the camera at any angle and have the camera stay in that position without drifting. If it does drift, it means the spring portion—the counterbalance—of the head is not adjusted properly. The head must be rated for the weight of the camera. If the camera is too heavy or too light for the head, all the functions of the head will

Figure 8-33 Fluid heads like this model help the camera operator get smooth pans and tilts. The bubble indicates when the head of the tripod is level.

be of little value. Trying different levels of friction can help you find the point where the camera can make very smooth movements with little effort.

Tripod Legs

The days of the wooden tripod or sticks are long gone. Most tripods today are made of alloys, graphite, aluminum, or carbon glass, and are very lightweight. The lightness is a great asset for the news crews, but weight can be helpful to stabilize the camera, particularly on windy days. Never trust a tripod to hold your camera up in a strong wind or in any situation where things are likely to bump into it. Lightweight tripods are made to help the operator, not to take the responsibility for holding the camera. If you walk away from the camera, make sure that the camera cannot fall, or take it off the tripod and set it on the ground until you return. Anchor weights or sandbags to hold the tripod firmly in place are always worth using.

The best tripods have a two-stage leg deployment that can go from a height of about 26 inches up to around 6 feet. The length of each leg can be set separately so the tripod can be used on uneven surfaces with minimum leveling at the head. Most leg designs make use of the spreader, or spider, to keep the legs from sliding out from under the camera on slick

floors. These spreaders have an adjustable span to bring the legs in closer, spread them further apart, or be removed entirely in difficult situations.

Dollies

A dolly is a movable device that allows you to mount the camera on it and shoot steady video while moving. The simplest form of a dolly is wheels on the tripod legs. While this type of dolly may be good for some basic moves, it is hard to control and almost impossible to steer once movement starts. Many dolly platforms are made to use a standard tripod attached to them. The most common dolly, a **doorway dolly**, accommodates any tripod but is small enough to fit through most doors. This dolly has large inflated tires that give a smooth ride over fairly flat surfaces. For uneven or rough surfaces, the tires can be replaced with special wheels that run along rails laid on the ground.

Figure 8-34 The dolly on the left (A) can be used on most smooth surfaces; the dolly on the right (B) uses a portable track system to ensure smooth camera movement. (Courtesy of Indie-Dolly Systems)

This type of dolly obviously takes time to set up, and any dolly usually requires a second person to push it. On larger dollies, like the **crab dolly**, the operator sits on the dolly itself while the built-in tripod raises or lowers the camera hydraulically.

Homemade or common items can be used to make a dolly without much cost or hassle. The most popular is the wheelchair. While the operator sits in the chair with a shoulder-mounted camera, another person can easily roll the chair. Wheelchairs are good for minimizing shocks due to pavement irregularities, because their wheels are large. They are also handy because they can fold up and fit in the trunk of a car to get to the location. Another possibility is the typical grocery store cart. Industrial carts (like the ones you might use at Home Depot or Sam's Club to move large purchases) can work well. Shooting from a slow moving car can work for tracking shots, but don't even think about shooting while driving unless you can remote control the camera. Shooting through a car window can be difficult because of reflections off the glass. Try not to touch any vibrating surface while shooting. Although it may seem like a good idea, avoid shooting from the back of a pickup truck. If the truck moves with any speed at all, the camera and the operator are at high risk. Just about anything with wheels can be made to work in certain situations; just consider safety in addition to aesthetics.

Cranes and Booms

The crane shot is a favorite of the movie industry. The shot starts out high and wide as the camera slowly descends to eye level in the middle of the action. On a **crane,** the operator sits on a platform that is raised or lowered at the end of a long arm. A **boom** has the camera remotely mounted on an arm. All camera functions, such as pan, tilt, zoom, and focus, are done at the base of the boom arm. The smaller versions of these booms are very popular in video field production and can be operated by one person.

Cranes and booms can also add an incredible amount of production value to the shoot by moving the camera through a space where no person could go, such as sweeping over the heads of the crowd.

Steadicam

The **Steadicam**® revolutionized the handheld camera. One of its first uses was for shooting the 1976 motion picture *Rocky* with a film camera. Subsequently, it has been used extensively with both film and video cameras. This complex system of counterbalanced arms is connected to a harness worn by the videographer, with the camera mounted at the end of the armature. Al-

Figure 8-35   This portable boom or jib can be operated by one person. A monitor located at the base shows the operator what the camera sees. (Courtesy of Stanton Video Services, Inc.)

though it is rather strenuous to operate, the Steadicam combines many of the effects of the dolly and crane to achieve an incredibly stable picture, even with the operator running over obstacles or down stairs. In the professional model, the camera operator can view the picture on an LCD screen mounted near the bottom of the mount. A video screen mounted in the arm near the hand grip allows the operator of the Steadicam JR to see the picture from the camera, no matter which way the camera is pointed. A new, smaller version is made specifically for EFP. It is lighter and easier to use, but still takes a considerable amount of practice to learn. Many smaller and less-expensive versions of this camera mounting system can be found for home or industrial use.

A

B

Figure 8-36   (A) The Steadicam Flyer model is a professional mount worn by the camera operator and can get great shots even when the camera operator is moving. (Courtesy of Alan Lifton; photo by Julie Bergman) (B) The Steadicam JR is designed for consumer or prosumer cameras, and can be held by the camera operator.

Car Mounts

Shooting in or into moving cars can be very troublesome. If the camera must be mounted outside the car, a suction device with a camera attached grips the hood or door. This mount can provide some dramatic angles, but safety lines should always be used in case the suction doesn't hold. Sets of bars and clamps that fit almost every car are also available; these allow a camera to be placed almost anywhere.

Aerial Mounts

Shooting from aircraft can be very limiting because of the air turbulence and the vibration of the engines. Even in a helicopter, the picture really only looks steady on the wide shots. As soon as the videographer zooms in, the viewer can see the chop of the ride. One commonly used mount for aerial photography is the **Tyler Mount,** which functions as a Steadicam in the air. Attached to the frame of the aircraft, this mount removes the vibrations and minor bumps of the ride and lets the camera produce a steady picture, even at long focal lengths. The aircraft must be approved for using it, but the Tyler Mount offers excellent aerial photography.

Several devices available today mount externally onto aircraft that contain the camera in a large spherical housing. The direction and zoom of the camera are controlled remotely by an operator from inside the craft. Freeway chase videos, which have become common news video, especially in large cities, were made by helicopters all using some form of external mounted camera stabilization system.

Special Mounts

Many types of mounts can be made with a little ingenuity. The key is making them strong enough to hold the camera and withstand other forces. If you can think of a place to put the camera, then someone can surely devise a way to get the camera there. (Remember, however, that anything attached to the outside of an aircraft would have to have FAA approval.) With the advent of new color cameras called lipstick- or cigar-cams that are the size of their namesakes, it is

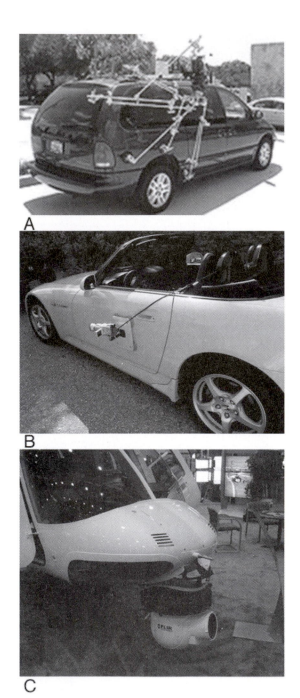

Figure 8-37   (A–B) The car mounts allows a camera to be mounted outside the vehicle to get shots of chase scenes and for shooting objects in front of the camera car. (C) The aerial mount on this helicopter allows a camera operator to control the camera from inside the helicopter. This particular camera and mount system is for an infrared camera, which will get usable images even when shot at night with almost no light on the subject.

possible to put a camera just about anywhere. A lip-stick-cam can be placed at the end of an audio boom to get shots from odd places, such as holding the pole with the camera out of one moving car to shoot another car. You can move the camera from the wheels, up the side, over the hood, and then raise the camera to let the car speed on past under the camera.

The key to mounting any camera is always safety—for the camera, the operator, and any members of the crew or public. Mounting a camera on a roller coaster might seem like a good idea, but only if you have taken into account the G-forces of the ride. Is the mount strong enough to withstand being whipped around at several times the force of gravity? It could be a life-threatening disaster to have the mount break and the camera sent flying in the middle of the ride. Safety first.

Miniature Cameras

One of the great benefits of the new DV format cameras is their small size relative to their quality. Where at one time mounting a Betacam in a difficult situation would be time consuming and possibly dangerous, a small DV camera can be placed with ease and secured safely. Through the use of fiber optics with these small cameras, cameras can now be hidden on a person. No longer is a bag or briefcase necessary; the camera lens can be hidden in a pair of sunglasses and the recorder hidden in a jacket pocket. Many of the numerous poker shows on television use miniature cameras mounted within the customized arm rests of the poker table. These cameras give the audience a view of the players' "hole" cards, which are dealt face down. Other applications include hidden camera shots during investigative reporting in ENG work.

SUMMARY

Creating professional-looking videos requires the videographer to know about the equipment. This chapter discussed the basic components needed for professional video production in the field using portable video equipment.

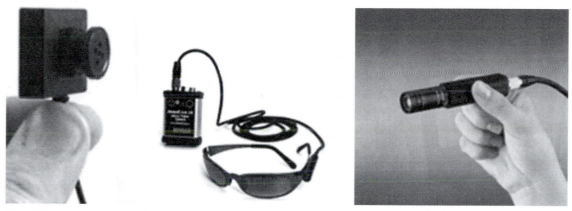

Figure 8-38 The camera on the left is a button camera, which can be worn as part of the camera operator's clothing. The camera in the center shoots video from the frame of the sunglasses. The camera on the right is called a "lipstick camera" because of its size and shape. (Photos courtesy of Jones Cam, Elmo)

Video cameras have complex lens systems that are capable of collecting, magnifying, and controlling the light that goes through them. Lenses can be set wide to get a shot with a long distance from left to right or at telephoto to get a magnified shot that has a short distance from left to right. The amount of light that passes through the lens is controlled with the iris control. Some cameras have auto-iris controls, but these should only be used in special circumstances, because they restrict control over the light entering the camera in a way that may not be appropriate for the shot. Lenses can be adapted to special situations or yield special effects when fitted with a variety of filters added to the front of the lens.

Video cameras, at first equipped with vacuum pickup tubes, now have solid-state devices to change a light image into an electrical signal that can be processed in the camera and then sent to a recorder or monitor. Most consumer and prosumer cameras can perform a number of functions automatically, but professional cameras allow the camera operator to switch off these functions to allow manual control of the video being recorded.

Video recorders are changing from analog videocassette recorders to digital videocassette recorders, hard drive recorders (Direct to Edit), and flash memory recorders. The newer recorders are smaller and higher quality than the older analog versions. In addition, both DTE and flash memory recorders save time by allowing immediate editing after shooting. Video formats have changed from analog to digital, and there are numerous choices available. The use and care of batteries, tripods, and various camera mounts was also discussed in this chapter.

9 Audio

So you've got a camera and you are ready to make some terrific videos. That's great, but one of the biggest mistakes that beginning videographers make is forgetting the importance of audio. Whether you are shooting news, a corporate video, or a dramatic scene for an entertainment show, nothing undermines the quality of your production faster than bad audio. The sound that accompanies your video has to be clear, clean, and appropriate for the video that you are shooting. This means that attention needs to be paid to sound and how you collect it. This chapter will take you through the basics of what you need to know about collecting sound for your video and the importance of understanding microphones.

Microphones (mics) are the first link in the technical chain that forms an audio production. The choice, placement, and quality of the microphone help determine how strong this link will be. Capturing good audio is essential to video projects; therefore, it is important to understand how your tools, microphones, work. Microphones have existed for more than 100 years. The first was used in Alexander Graham Bell's telephone to change audible voice signals into electrical energy. It was a simple and inexpensive carbon microphone sensitive to the frequencies of sound typically generated by the human voice.

MICROPHONE STRUCTURE

A **microphone** is a **transducer**, a device that changes energy from one form to another. Microphones change sound or acoustical energy into electrical energy, or more specifically, sound waves into electrical signals. Sound waves strike the microphone's **diaphragm** and the microphone's **element** translates that mechanical energy into electrical energy. The diaphragm is the part of the microphone that moves when it is struck by sound waves. The element, which is connected to the diaphragm, is the part inside the microphone that translates this movement into an electrical signal.

Four basic designs have been used for microphone elements over the years: **carbon, ceramic, dynamic,** and **condenser**. The first two, carbon and ceramic, were used in early mics, but they are rarely used in professional audio work today. The latter two, dynamic and condenser, are the microphones of choice for almost all professionals. Because each element has unique electrical and sonic properties, knowing the differences between them will help you choose the right mic for the job.

MICROPHONES AND AUDIO-RECORDING TECHNIQUES

Dynamic Microphones

Dynamic microphones have parts inside them that physically move when struck by sound waves. This movement creates an electrical current, which becomes the audio signal. Although various companies have manufactured many different variations of dynamic elements, there are two general classifications: the moving-coil type and the ribbon, or velocity, type.

Moving-Coil Microphones

Most moving-coil microphones are made up of a Mylar diaphragm attached to a coil of wire called a voice coil, which is suspended within a magnetic field. As the term *dynamic* implies, dynamic elements are designed to allow movement. A moving-coil element consists of a finely wound coil of wire suspended in a magnetic field. When the diaphragm is struck by sound waves, the coil moves within the magnetic field. The movement within the magnetic field induces voltage fluctuations in the coil, which becomes the output signal.

A moving-coil microphone is the most widely used in professional audio applications for several reasons:

- They have a very good frequency response, similar to what our ears hear, and can gather audio from many different kinds of sources. A common frequency range for a professional dynamic mic is 40 to 15,000 Hz.

- Generally they are the most ruggedly designed mics available: they are shock resistant, unimpaired by most temperature extremes, insensitive to extremes in humidity, and can withstand high sound pressure levels without overloading.

- They DO NOT require an external power source (known as phantom power, +48 volts).

- They are generally inexpensive.

Ribbon, or Velocity, Microphones

Another dynamic microphone similar to the moving-coil mic is the ribbon, or velocity, mic, in which a thin ribbonlike piece of corrugated metal is positioned between the poles of a magnet. When struck by sound waves, the ribbon vibrates between the magnetic poles, causing a small voltage in the ribbon that becomes the audio signal. Because the ribbon is flat, it is sensitive to sound pressure striking it directly from either the front or the back. Ribbon mics were used extensively in the 1930s and 1940s in studio-produced radio. Although they are very sensitive and have a very good high-frequency response, their drawbacks include shock sensitivity, fragility, and noncompact size. Ribbon microphones are rarely used in professional video production, but recording engineers find them useful under certain circumstances for their unique frequency response.

Condenser Elements

Condenser microphones have a thin diaphragm that serves as one plate of a capacitor. Capable of storing electrical charges, a capacitor is an electrical component with two electrodes, two plates of metal (+ and –), separated by a small distance. Unlike the dynamic element, which makes use of electromagnetism to generate an electrical signal, condenser mics operate on a principle known as variable capacitance. The diaphragm and the backplate act as the electrodes of a capacitor.

When sound waves strike the diaphragm, the distance between the two electrodes changes, producing a change in capacitance of the element. This results in a very small signal voltage that becomes the audio signal.

The quality of a condenser mic depends on the design of its capsule, which is the condenser element and its acoustic system or housing. The capsule plays a major role in how the mic responds, not only to different frequencies but also to different directions of sounds.

A condenser microphone requires two additional features to produce its audio signal. One is an impedance-converting amplifier that converts the signal to low impedance to enhance signal quality. The other feature is a power supply. DC power is required to charge the capacitor element or, more specifically, to

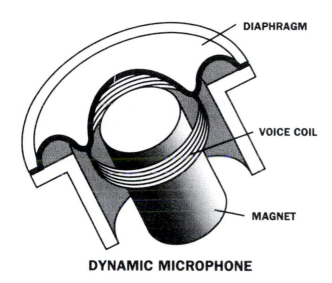

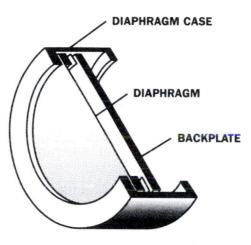

Figure 9-1   Diagrams of dynamic and condenser microphones. (Courtesy of Shure Brothers, Inc.)

polarize the two plates of the capacitor and provide power for the amplifier circuit inside the microphone.

In an electret condenser microphone, a more recent condenser microphone design, the voltage needs of the mic are smaller. The diaphragm is made of a dielectric material that is capable of permanently holding a charge. The power supply is needed only for the pre-amplifier. A good electret condenser mic should hold its internal charge for 10 years or more, but will eventually wear out. A disadvantage of this type of microphone is its inability to respond to the higher frequencies.

The power that a condenser microphone requires to operate is commonly called **phantom power**, or +48 volts. It is referred to as phantom power because the power is supplied to the microphone along the same wire that carries the audio signal. Recording consoles, field mixers, and high-quality ENG/EFP cameras are capable of supplying phantom power. However, this is not the only way condensers can be powered. Many condenser microphones are equipped with space for a battery inside the mic that will supply the power for the element and amplifier, or an external box can be inserted on the microphone cable that produces +48 volts along the mic cable. Very high-quality recording microphones come with a specific power supply for the microphone, providing the utmost efficiency for the microphone's design and performance.

Considered the mic of choice for accurate sound recording in professional work, condenser microphones are very sensitive and have excellent frequency response. One drawback is that they are more expensive than their dynamic counterparts; a second is that they require a power supply. A battery does not at first seem like a serious drawback, but when you are in the field, providing power to a mic can become a problem if you are not prepared. Finally, condenser microphones are sometimes too sensitive for extremely noisy situations or sudden loud noises, and are sometimes inappropriate for outdoor use.

SENSITIVITY

Microphones are also categorized by their sensitivity— their ability to reproduce sound in several different ways. A microphone's sensitivity to sound is its ability to hear quiet sounds, or its ability to produce a relatively high voltage level at its output. A microphone's directional sensitivity is how well a microphone hears from different directions, and its frequency response is a measurement of the mic's ability to pick up sounds of differing pitch or wavelengths.

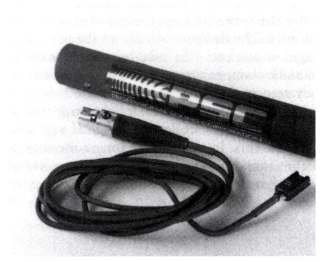

Figure 9-2   (A) This lavaliere mic has a detachable power supply allowing it to be used with a wireless transmitter. (B) The rear of this camcorder features XLR audio inputs and a slide switch next to the tally light that allows a condenser microphone to receive 48V of power.

Sound Sensitivity

Microphone sensitivity is defined as the amount of electrical signal a microphone produces from a given input sound source. Different mics have different sensitivities; some mics simply put out a stronger signal than others. Sensitivity is determined by measuring the microphone's electrical output when the mic is placed by a sound source of a known intensity or pressure. At first it may seem that the more sensitive a mic is the better, but experienced audio production practitioners realize that good audio production consists of the absence of sounds you do not want to hear as well as the presence of sounds you do want to hear. Overly sensitive mics can be just as much a problem as those that are insensitive.

Directional Sensitivity

Microphones have different abilities to pick up sound from varying directions. A **polar response** chart is a representation of the pickup pattern, or polar pattern, of a particular mic. The mic's polar pattern determines where sounds can originate and still be transduced into an electric signal. Manufacturers usually provide polar

response charts to provide technically accurate information about the pickup characteristics of individual microphones so that the end user can understand the directional characteristic of the microphone and place it accordingly in practical use. These standardized charts depict the angle of sound sensitivity relative to the element of the microphone and sound pressure levels. In effect, they show how a mic will respond to sounds that come from various angles and at various levels of sound pressure. The head of the mic is at the center of the chart. Sounds coming from the top, or 0°, are called **on axis** and those from the side, or 90°, **off axis**.

A microphone's ability to gather sounds at various degrees off axis is what determines how directional the mic is. The further the distance from the tip of a mic, the less the sound level is transduced. On the chart, this is shown by the concentric circles around the tip of a microphone, which represent sound levels that decrease in intensity as you go away from the mic. These charts are especially helpful because there are many variations of the general pickup patterns. Also, many mics have slightly different patterns at different frequencies. In addition, there are some hybrid and altered versions of the standard patterns. (See Figure 9-3.) Three major polar patterns describe professional mics: omnidirectional, unidirectional, and bidirectional.

Omnidirectional

Omnidirectional mics are capable of picking up sound equally from all directions. The omnidirectional pickup pattern can be imagined as a three-dimensional sphere with the microphone's diaphragm in the center. If you place an omnidirectional mic in the center of a circle of people, the sound level coming from any of those people should be almost identical to the others, assuming that they are all equidistant from the mic and all persons are speaking at about the same level. The mic's diaphragm can react to sound pressure changes equally from all directions. However, an omnidirectional mic does tend to be more directional at higher sound frequencies; it is best to point the mic in the direction of the primary sound source to be recorded. In other words, even for an omnidirectional mic, sound on axis will tend to be of better quality than sounds off axis.

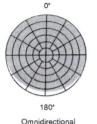

0°

180°

Omnidirectional   Unidirectional Cardiod   Supercardiod   Hypercardiod   Bidirectional

Figure 9-3   Polar response charts for various microphone types. The shaded areas show where sounds can be picked up by the microphone.

Unidirectional

Unidirectional mics are capable of picking up sound from only one direction. The unidirectional pattern can be imagined as a heart-shaped sphere originating at the microphone's diaphragm. Unidirectional mics use a pressure-gradient device and/or reflectors to achieve this directional characteristic. These mics can respond to differences in audio pressure between the two faces of its diaphragm (the pressure-gradient device), or they can achieve directionality by the use of a reflector. Some designs use a combination of these methods. Directional mics are good at reducing background noise from two sources: (1) off-axis sounds and (2) excessive reverberation (usually found inside small rooms). They can also be placed at a greater distance from the sound source while maintaining their frequency response and sensitivity. These are the mics of choice in stereo recording, because of their ability to give a sense of sound location.

Cardioid/Supercardioid/Hypercardioid   When pressure-gradient and reflector designs are combined in one mic, the resulting pattern is called a cardioid. **Cardioid microphones** are unidirectional and pick up sound primarily from one direction. The word *cardioid* comes from the shape of its response chart, an inverted heart-shaped pattern. Cardioid microphones pick up sounds almost entirely from the area directly in front of the mic and almost nothing from the far sides or rear, which makes them very desirable in noisy situations. The three basic patterns are cardioid, supercardioid, and hypercardioid.

Each pattern has the same characteristic of rejecting sounds from behind and to the sides of the microphone, yet there are some imperfections. As the polar

Figure 9-4   An Electro-Voice® RE-10 dynamic supercardioid microphone. The ribbed shaft aids in the directionality of the microphone.

pattern is narrowed to achieve more directionality in front of the microphone (supercardioid and hypercardioid), the mic's sensitivity to sounds directly behind it increases. This is the trade-off for being able to focus only the sound directly in front of the microphone, and is generally not a problem.

Ultradirectional More directional than the hypercardioid, the **ultradirectional** or **shotgun microphone** uses an entirely different capsule design to achieve its special purpose. The shotgun mic allows even greater distance between mic and source and greater rejection of off-axis sounds. The design is simply a tube with the diaphragm at one end. The tube has slits in it covered by an audio-dampening material to ensure the full frequency response of the on-axis sounds. This allows sound to enter the tube from straight on (parallel to the tube or on axis), while reflecting off-axis sound through the slits. In general, the longer the tube, the more directional the shotgun mic is, and the further away the sound source can be. Because its polar pattern is more sensitive to a wide range of frequencies, it is more directional for higher frequencies than for lower ones.

The shotgun is the workhorse microphone of ENG and EFP work. For the stand-alone newsperson, a shotgun mounted on the camera is the primary source of natural sound and sometimes even interview sound. A two-person news crew uses the shotgun for almost all sound gathering. In EFP production, the shotgun is often boom-mounted for precise sound gathering in the studio and on location where hidden mics are not possible. When using a shotgun microphone, it is critical that the user wear headphones that monitor the microphone's signal, as a small error in aiming, or placing, an ultradirectional microphone can produce a big change in audio quality.

Bidirectional

A bidirectional microphone picks up sound equally from only two directions. Resembling a figure eight, its pickup pattern is achieved in mics that are purely pressure-gradient devices (no reflectors used). The most common of these mics is the ribbon mic. One of the oldest mic designs around, the ribbon mic is still widely used today in radio and studio work. Larry King has made the ribbon mic familiar to a new generation of TV viewers by using a silver old-school ribbon mic as his desk mic and logo on *The Larry King Live* show on CNN. If you interview someone who is at the same but opposite distance as you are from the mic and who speaks at about the same volume, a bidirectional mic will be equally sensitive to both voices and eliminate any side audio. This assumes that your locations are at the correct angles relative to the mic.

FREQUENCY RESPONSE

The goal of a sound technician is to accurately capture the sound source for reproduction. This requires a microphone capable of picking up the entire frequency spectrum of the sound waves that strike the mic's transducing element. A mic used for picking up conversation needs to be sensitive to the frequencies of the human voice, a range of about 100 to 10,000 Hz. A mic used in a sound studio for picking up the sounds of a piccolo must accurately transduce frequencies as low as 500 Hz and as high as 15,000 Hz. Although the construction and pickup pattern of a mic may qualify it for a particular application, it should not be used unless it has the appropriate frequency response capabilities.

Most professional-quality microphones can reproduce sounds within a frequency range of about 500 to 15,000 Hz. A chart like Figure 9-5 can show a mic's frequency response or sensitivity to various frequencies of sound.

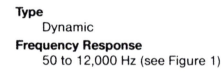

Type
  Dynamic
Frequency Response
  50 to 12,000 Hz (see Figure 1)

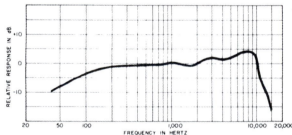

Figure 9-5   Frequency response chart for a dynamic microphone. (Courtesy of Shure Brothers, Inc.)

Ideally, the microphone will have a flat response curve, which implies that the mic is equally sensitive to all frequencies in its range, but this is rarely the case. The most common weakness in mic frequency response appears at the upper end of its frequency range, where the response curve drops off considerably, demonstrating an inability to reproduce sound waves at high frequencies. This drop off is present at low frequencies, but is not quite as common and often less important. Many mics are designed with special characteristics to slightly alter their frequency response.

It is common to have a mic with a **bass rolloff switch** of some sort, allowing the user to purposefully deemphasize frequencies at the low end of the audio spectrum. This helps correct the proximity effect, or the tendency of unidirectional and bidirectional mics to emphasize the bass or low-frequency response when the sound source is close to the mic. Bass rolloff can also be useful to eliminate troublesome environmental noise like airconditioners, footsteps that can shake a mic stand, clothes rustle, or the rumble of a distant train. (See Figure 9-6.) Other mics used in vocal work sometimes have a **presence boost** in the upper midrange to enhance the voice. These features also help add brilliance, clarity, and general intelligibility to the sounds recorded.

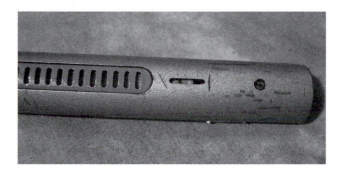

Figure 9-6 The bass roll off switch is located below the ribs, near the bottom of the shaft of this mic.

IMPEDANCE

Microphones can also be differentiated by several technical factors. One factor, **impedance**, is very important, because selecting the wrong impedance mic can cause immediate and sometimes serious problems. Other factors, like output noise and maximum sound pressure, are important only in very specific situations when the production requires specific sound pickup other than typical voice or music, or in situations with a lot of interfering signals or sounds.

Microphone Impedance

Microphone impedance refers to the amount of resistance a signal encounters in a microphone circuit. The more impedance in a circuit, the less signal will flow out of it. Therefore, all other things being equal, low-impedance microphones produce more signal than high-impedance microphones.

Most professional mics have low impedance, which allows long audio cable runs without significant loss of signal. Their higher level of signal relative to high-impedance mics gives better rejection of hum and other types of interference. Also, low-impedance mics are compatible with almost all professional audio and video equipment.

Although impedance levels are rated as high or low (corresponding to the designations high Z or low Z), mics can be found that are somewhere in between. Table 9-1 lists typical microphone impedance levels and their corresponding measurement in ohms, the unit of electrical resistance.

The impedance of most professional mics is usually 150 ohms; it is measured as –60 dB, which is referred to as **mic level**. After an audio signal has been passed through a mixer, recorder, microwave transmitter, or any other processing device, the signal coming from that device is usually sent at a medium impedance of 600 ohms and is measured as 4 dB, which is referred to as **line level.** When audio signals are called high or low in professional situations, that usually means the line level is high (more signal) and the mic level is low (less signal). In other words, a mic level signal is weak and a line level signal is strong. For a mic level signal to reach line level, it must be amplified, which occurs when the low-impedance signal is processed by a mic pre-amplifier.

Table 9-1 Typical Microphone Impedance Levels and Their Corresponding Measurements

Rating in Ohms	Impedance Level
38 to 150	Low
600 to 2,400	Medium
9,600 and above	High

Overload

When mics are bombarded with more audio signal than they can process accurately, the mic is overloaded. Dynamic mics are very hard to overload. They have very low distortion across their entire 140-dB dynamic range. The same cannot be said for condenser mics. At high acoustic levels, the output signal of the capsule can overload the impedance converter circuit in the microphone. Some mics have built-in **pads** (an inline device that can change the signal that passes through it) that can reduce the signal level, sometimes at the cost of adding noise to the sound, thus reducing quality.

The sound recordist must also be cautious not to overload the microphone preamplifier that boosts the electrical signal for recording. If a grating or distorted sound is heard that is not an accurate reproduction of your sound source it must be determined which link in the chain is overloading. It could be caused by the microphone or the mic preamplifier, or by the mic cable being broken.

OTHER FACTORS

Besides the major considerations of element construction, pickup pattern, frequency range, sensitivity, and impedance, several other factors should be considered when selecting a microphone. Hum and radio frequency interference, signal-to-noise ratio, output noise, clipping level, and maximum sound pressure are often specified by the manufacturer. Some of these factors are critical for broadcasting applications, but are not as important in other applications.

SELECTION AND PLACEMENT

Now that the numerous characteristics of microphones have been explained, it is appropriate to discuss how to use this information to complete the processes of mic selection and mic placement.

Choosing a Mic

Mics have varying elements, pickup patterns, frequency responses, impedances, appearances, applications, and special accessories, such as built-in filters. In addition, some mics even have a personality—a sound different from other similarly constructed or designed microphones. Because of the variety of choices, it

seems that the selection process could be lengthy and complicated. Fortunately, this is not usually the case. Most audio production facilities have a finite selection of mics available for production work. This selection consists of representatives of the different types of mics available: omnidirectional, unidirectional, dynamic, condenser, and so on. Not many production houses would stay in business if they decided to buy an additional microphone whenever the producer or production manager decided that a different mic might be somewhat better than those already owned. High-quality microphones are expensive. Good-quality microphones can often yield high-quality sound in a variety of situations, and many good mics often overlap each other in what they can do well. For example, a cardioid mic is best for many interview situations, but an omnidirectional mic might work just as well if you can keep the extraneous noise in the room low and keep the omnidirectional mic close to the source.

Four factors should be considered when selecting the best mic for a production:

- What are the general production goals, such as what is the end product supposed to be, how will it be distributed, who will the audience be, and what quality level should be obtained?

- What is the sound source that is being captured? Is it a voice, a specific musical instrument or group of instruments, or environmental sounds? How loud is the source and what frequencies is it producing?

- How much control will there be over the sound environment?

- How many sound sources are involved in the production?

- Will the mic be on camera? If so what are the aesthetics of the mic?

Placing a Mic

When placing a microphone it is critical to understand the mic's polar pattern, its directionality. The sound recordist must point the microphone in the proper direction and also place the microphone in the proper proximity to the sound source so that the mic can produce a useable electrical signal. The microphone's sensitivity characteristics are seriously considered when placing a mic. An understanding of a mic's sensitivity, polar pattern, and frequency response affect where the recordist will place a particular microphone in relation to the sound source.

Not only must you choose a mic based on its design characteristics but also based on where the mic must or can be placed. Limitations such as personnel, budget, time, boom shadows, and environmental concerns can dictate which mics you can use and where they can be placed. Knowing how to place a particular mic helps you to identify whether a particular mic is right for the job and can make the difference in capturing usable or unusable audio.

STYLE

Of all the equipment manufactured for the reproduction of sound, microphones display the widest range of appearance and design. Although there are many different brands of audio recorders, they vary only slightly in appearance. Microphones can range in size from a lavaliere, sometimes smaller than a dime, to a shotgun mic more than two feet long, to a studio overhead mic the size of a large grapefruit. Because microphones vary extensively in size, weight, appearance, and application, knowledge of these factors provides a better understanding of how to use microphones and select the one appropriate to the task.

Figure 9-7   Various shapes and sizes of handheld mics.

Handheld Microphones

The handheld mic category is the broadest of the style categories. It is not a question of which mics are in it but which ones are not. A typical handheld mic found throughout the world today is the Electro-Voice 635A.

Figure 9-8   Rugged mics commonly used in portable video productions: (A) Electro-Voice 635A, and (B) Shure SM58.

This omnidirectional dynamic mic is so rugged it could be used as a hammer. Built to last a lifetime, it is the generic and general-purpose mic. The mic is small enough to fit in a hand and light enough not to be a strain. Most handheld mics are similar to the 635A in appearance. They have a relatively small head or capsule for the diaphragm at the end of a four- or five-inch shaft. Handheld mics can have any polar pattern, can be either dynamic or condenser, and can have various quality levels. Another example of this type of mic is the Shure SM58.

A handheld mic is generally used by a singer or someone addressing the camera or interviewing a subject. Because it is easily manipulated, it is good for gathering sound quickly from multiple sources, such as when a reporter doing an interview points the mic at the person talking with little effort or even walks the mic closer to the source. Almost all handheld mics are made with a pleasing appearance so that they will not be distracting on camera. Handheld mics can be mounted on a desk or floor mic stand. In ENG work, where speed can be the overriding factor in getting the job done, the handheld mic is indispensable because of its versatility despite any limitations. However, the disadvantages are limited pickup range and sound quality that is not always optimal.

Mounted Microphones

Mounted mics can be one of two types, studio or shotgun mics, and are designed to be supported by a mechanical system such as a desk stand or overhead boom.

Studio mics are designed for the highest quality sound reproduction. Because appearance is not important, these mics may be larger than those that appear on camera or on a speaker's podium. The on-camera or podium mics are sometimes referred to as desk mics, but are still designed for studio use only. Studio mics are not moved often, especially not when sound is being recorded. Many have solid or integral micattachment devices or specialized shock mounts that reduce low frequencies traveling into the microphone from the stand. These specialized mounts must be used on mic booms and floor stands.

Shotgun mics are generally not meant to be handheld. You can mount a shotgun mic in any of three primary ways: (1) on a camera, (2) on a studio boom or stand, or (3) on a portable boom called a **fishpole.**

Both studio and shotgun mics require a fair degree of isolation from mechanical noise, that is, noise caused by handling or brushing up against something. A good camera mount for a shotgun has a rubber pad in the holder surrounding the mic to cushion it from shock. A boom usually has a suspension system of heavy-duty rubber bands, a shock mount, so that the shotgun literally floats within the holding bracket.

Generally, shotguns are not meant to be seen by the camera, so their appearance does not matter. They can gather quality audio at a distance from the sound source. Because they are so directional, a boom allows the operator to position the mics at the best possible angle to get only the desired sound while keeping the mics out of the shot.

The disadvantage of mounted mics is their need to be fixed to a certain location. The most widely used mic system in professional video production, the fishpole shotgun, is fixed to the fishpole and requires a full-time operator. If the shotgun is fixed to a camera, it cannot always be at the right angle to cut out unwanted background noise or to capture the sound source desired; it will gather any and all sounds in front of it.

Figure 9-9   (1) This microphone is mounted on a fishpole that can extend to a long length, which helps to get the mic close to the sound source while staying out of the shot. (2) Sometimes the soundman is required to be in an unusual place to get the mic positioned correctly for good sound while still being out of the shot.

Lavaliere Microphones

Lavaliere or mini-microphones became quite popular when TV presented new problems for audio production professionals. The mics used on TV had to sound good, and they also had to have an acceptable appearance on camera. The lavaliere mic was an answer to this appearance problem. Designed to be worn by the person whose voice is to be recorded, lavaliere mics (also called lavs or lapel mics) are quite small and unobtrusive. Lavs are usually condenser microphones, although there are some dynamic lavs. All condenser lavs need a power source to work, but dynamic lavs do not.

The microphone head or capsule is at the end of a long, thin cable run from the power unit. Most lavs

Figure 9-10   A Sonotrim lav with windscreen and attaching devices surrounding it.

use standard AA or batteries but they can also be powered by the camera or mixer using phantom power. The end of the power unit acts as the connector end of the mic with the standard male XLR receptacle. Lavaliere mics are almost always constructed with an omnidirectional pickup pattern, because the sound of the human voice emanates from the mouth in an omnidirectional pattern as the head turns during speaking. Designed to be worn either against the clothing of the person or beneath an article of clothing, such as a tie, scarf, or shirt, lavaliere mics are designed with a built-in boost in the high-frequency range because the sound reaching the mic may be filtered by the cloth and cause higher frequencies to be missed. For live TV, two of these mics are often placed on the same tie clip in a technique known as **dual redundancy** to provide a backup if one fails.

SPECIAL APPLICATIONS

In addition to the considerations of structure, sensitivity, impedance, and style, the type of application for the mic may influence which mic is best for your audio needs. Special application microphones have been developed to meet the needs of some atypical applications.

Performance Microphones

Microphones designed for performances will usually have special characteristics or devices built into them to suit the needs of audio performers. Consider the needs of a performer like Shakira. Because of her bouncing, swinging, and jolting style of singing, she needs a mic that will take some abuse. First, her mic should have a shock mounting that dampens the noise created from rough handling. She would also need a mic that would withstand the explosive wind and breath sounds generated from her movement and her style of singing. Mics designed for this purpose have a special filter called a **pop** or **blast** filter that will stabilize the diaphragm, thereby minimizing the distortion and allowing truer sound reproduction. Performance mics are often used at very close range. Anyone who has seen rock stars perform on TV knows that they practically swallow the mic as they sing. Mics used for this purpose must have the characteristics that enhance the singer's vocal qualities, sometimes including a bass rolloff feature to minimize a booming low-frequency sound or a boost of the upper midrange frequencies. Another common design feature of performance mics is the ability to reject background noise to permit a higher amplification level for the desired sound before getting audio feedback in the system. For artists who prefer holding their microphones, lightweight mics are a necessity.

Multiple-Application Microphones

Some microphones are now designed and marketed to be used in a wide variety of applications. These mics are designed so that they are able to provide different pickup patterns in different situations. The mics designed in this way are also known as convertible or system mics. These mics often come with several attachments that allow different configurations for various applications. Some mics change configuration by the flip of a switch. Essentially, this type of mic can function as an omnidirectional or unidirectional mic, or even one or more variations of the special cardioid patterns to provide the pickup abilities of various types of shotgun mics. As with any multipurpose tool, this type of mic may not be as good in any one configuration as the best mic of that type. However, this slight trade-off of some excellence for versatility is a worthwhile one for many users with limited budgets but a wide range of audio pickup needs.

Headset Microphones

Headset microphones are mounted on a bracket with one or two earphones attached. This headset is worn on the head of announcers in both radio and TV. Their use in TV can be seen most often in sporting event announcing and network reporters on the floor of the political conventions.

The headset mic has a mini-boom that holds the mic in place very close to the announcer's mouth. This is especially important in situations where the announcer may have to turn his head to follow action or receive information from another person. This mic can have either a dynamic or condenser element. Its pickup pattern is cardioid, because the important sounds are coming from one source, the announcer's mouth. A popular variation of this mic is the micro-headset mic. This type of mic has also become very popular with on-stage singers, especially those who incorporate lots of movement into their acts.

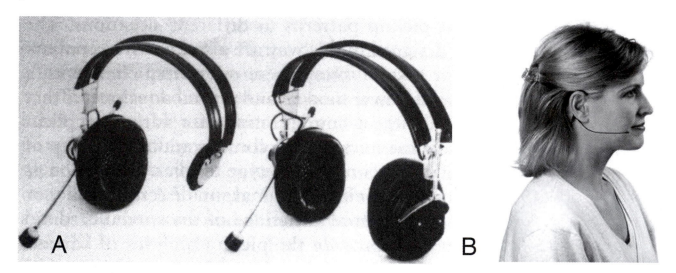

Figure 9-11   (A) Headset mics like those used by sportscasters. (B) This small and lightweight mic fits under and around the ear. Because it is almost invisible, it is more appropriate for on-camera use.

Surface-Mount and Pressure-Zone Microphones

Surface-mount and pressure-zone microphones, also called boundary mics, are usually used in situations where two or more people are the source for audio to be recorded or broadcast, and these people are positioned in front of a flat surface such as the floor or a table.

These microphones are commonly seen on either side of a politician on the clear plastic rectangles that appear on camera. These rectangles are teleprompters that display the text of the politician's speech but cannot be seen by the audience. In most cases there is a main microphone in front of the speaker and the microphones on the rectangles are used for redundancy

and sound support for the main microphone and/or to add room tone.

The polar pickup patterns of these mics are somewhat different than conventional mics. The mics come with both omni- and unidirectional patterns, but only one hemisphere of the omnidirectional sphere or unidirectional heart shape is available.

When this type of mic is unidirectional, it can be used to isolate a particular vocalist or part of a musical group. It can also function as a single instrument mic, for example, for a bass drum, by placing the mic on the floor directly in front of the instrument.

You can create your own boundary mic with mics you already have. By taking a hand mic or lav and laying it parallel to the floor or any boundary surface,

Figure 9-13   A wireless microphone system can consist of any standard mic connected to a small portable radio transmitter.

Figure 9-12   Two examples of pressure zone microphones.

pointing it to the center of the sound source, and raising it just slightly (1 or 2 mm) off that surface with a bit of tape or something else small, you can achieve a close approximation of an actual boundary mic.

Wireless Microphones

In many production situations, a standard microphone with a cable is not appropriate. Cables are not attractive on camera and can cause the talent to fall. Sometimes, production personnel or others at the location can trip on an audio cable, causing injury or pulling the cable out of the equipment it is connected to. The wireless microphone, often referred to as a radio-frequency (RF) mic, frees the person being mic'd from the tether of an audio cable, which is often aesthetically undesirable or downright impractical in film or TV shots.

The belt pack radio transmitter, used for lavaliere microphones, is attached to the person being mic'd. A plug is attached directly to the mic or other audio source and sends the radio signal encoded with the audio information to a receiver. The standard receiv-

Figure 9-14   This Lectrosonics UHF wireless set has two transmitters: a plug-on and a belt pack (only one can be used at a time). The receiver is a diversity type with two antenna systems.

ing distance is usually no more that 100 feet, but with a very good system the receiver may be at a location up to one-quarter mile away. Some handheld microphones have the transmitter built into the mic shaft itself.

Although wireless mics are essential in location TV work, they should be treated with caution. A great many factors can arise to interfere with the signal. This is particularly true in urban environments, where various electrical sources and other RF signals from standard broadcasting and point-to-point communications generate radio-frequency interference.

RF mics come in two frequency ranges: VHF (very high frequency) and UHF (ultra high frequency). Years ago, VHF frequencies (174 to 216 MHz) were very popular because they worked fairly well and were cheap to buy. But they were also very susceptible to interference of all kinds. Toward the end of the 1990s, the entire radio frequency spectrum was reshuffled by the FCC to accommodate digital TV and a host of new users. Most frequencies common before 1990 are no longer available today. Some older RF mics are not legal under the current FCC rules for frequency use. For that reason, most wireless mics sold now are in the UHF frequency range (450 Mhz and above). They provide much better range and reliability than earlier systems, but they do cost more. When you buy a professional wireless mic, you will be asked where the mic will be used to help ensure that you will not be using a frequency that many others in the same market will also be using. A mic bought in Phoenix for use in that market may not work well in Los Angeles. Production crews traveling around the country often carry wireless systems that can change frequencies to adapt to the local airwaves. These wireless mics are called **frequency agile**. Even with these, if more than one set of wireless mics are being used, the soundperson must take care to make sure the frequencies are spread out from one another to avoid interference. A large production or a network news crew may use up to eight wireless mics at one time. Keeping them all clear can be a headache, especially when traveling.

One of the biggest causes of interference is reflected radio waves from the transmitter striking the receiver at different times, just like reflected audio waves cause echo. The path between transmitter and receiver must be as clear of obstructions as possible, especially anything made of metal. To further improve your chances of getting a good signal, make sure the receiving and transmitting antennas are parallel; in other words, one cannot be horizontal while the other is vertical. Also, be sure that they are not curled or bunched up if they are the soft type.

One type of wireless that cures some of the interference problems is the **diversity** system. In effect, in this system each transmitter has two receivers. The system switches seamlessly to whichever receiver has the best signal so there is no interruption of the sound.

Getting the signal into the typical wireless **belt pack** transmitter (the type most commonly used) is not as easy as it might look. Each brand of transmitter has its own special cable connector for its associated microphone, and it is not usually compatible with anything else. You will need an adapter cable that goes from a female XLR to the particular transmitter's connector type to attach a different microphone to it. Because most wireless situations call for the use of a lav mic, it is beneficial to have one wired to plug directly into the transmitter. Some transmitters, called **plug-ons**, can be plugged directly into an audio line or the bottom of a mic. They are more bulky and cannot be hidden on a person as easily as the belt pack can.

ACCESSORIES

Differing applications and locations demand that microphones be flexible enough to be positioned in various places under numerous conditions. Many accessories are available to the audio technician for mounting the mic and ensuring that quality sound can be gathered under adverse conditions.

Mounts

Microphones are not freestanding instruments and require a device or mounting system to keep them secured in place. For interviewing or sound collection on location, this is most often accomplished by simply holding the mic in hand. Most mics are shipped with a **mic clip.** The mic clip allows the mic to be attached to a microphone stand. Many mics will fit in a standard mic clip, like the one supplied by Shure with their SM57. But many mics have very customized designs and the mic clip that is supplied by the manufacturer is a must have if you are going to use the microphone. Mics with smaller shafts need their special mic clip, and highly sensitive recording mics and shotguns must use their custom shock mounting devices so that they may be attached to a mic stand.

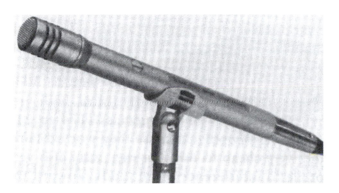

Figure 9-15 Mic clasp for attaching a mic to a stand. (Courtesy of Shure Brothers, Inc.)

Acoustic Filters and Windscreens

Some microphones are designed to cope with problems inherent in close mic'ing. Inexperienced announcers and people who are being interviewed may pop their *P*s, speak too loudly or forcefully, or blast the microphone with too much sound. Many mics now have pop-and-blast filters built into them to correct these problems. These filters are contained inside the mic housing; the sound must pass through them before striking the diaphragm. Some pop filters are designed for use in front of the mic rather than inside it. These filters, made of a mesh material, can be positioned between the speaker/singer and the mic and are common in recording studios.

Windscreens are foam-rubber-like casings designed to fit over the top of a microphone. Almost all hand mics, lavalieres, and headset microphones can be used with windscreens to reduce the sound made by air currents

or wind. The effectiveness of this type of windscreen can vary greatly depending on the nature of the mic. In general, the more directional a mic is, the more susceptible it is to wind noise, and the harder it is to protect. Because shotgun mics are the most affected by wind, a simple foam windscreen is not enough to achieve quality audio under windy conditions. For optimum sound, a shotgun is used in a basket-type windscreen called a **zeppelin.** This device surrounds the mic with a space of dead air while allowing most audible frequencies to pass through. (See Figure 9-16.)

AUDIO CABLES AND CONNECTORS

To complete the technical chain of an audio system, the signal must get to a recording device through an electrical interface: a cable and its connectors.

Balanced and Unbalanced Lines

An unbalanced line is the type of audio line found in most consumer-level audio products, such as home camcorders and cassette recorders. The cable consists of a single conductor carrying the positive signal and a shield carrying the negative signal of a circuit. While this type of line is fine for most consumer needs, it is limited to cable lengths of less than 10 feet to maintain quality and can be susceptible to outside

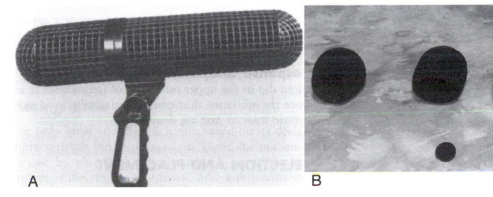

A   B

Figure 9-16 (A) A zeppelin system is used for cutting down wind noise. (Courtesy of Light Wave Systems, Van Nuys, CA) (B) Various windscreens. The windscreen at the right would fit a shotgun mic; the small windscreen below fits a lavaliere mic.

electrical interference, especially in cable lengths of more than 10 feet. This type of line is not recommended for any professional use. Unbalanced lines often have to be used on camcorders that have a mini-plug external mic input.

In a balanced audio line, the mic signal is carried by two leads instead of one. The shield is the ground so that the conductor leads are completely isolated from other electrical components. A balanced line is far less susceptible to RF interference and ground loop hum found in unbalanced lines. If you must connect a balanced line to an unbalanced line, it is best to have a one-to-one isolation transformer between the two. This device keeps the ground loop of the unbalanced line from inducing hum or noise in the balanced line.

Connectors and Adapters

The standard connector for balanced audio lines is the three-contact **XLR** type, sometimes referred to as a **cannon connector**. The input end of an XLR cable is always a female connector (receptacles for the connector pins), and the output end is always a male connector (the connector pins). A microphone always has a male connector. The XLR connectors are the only type used in professional audio recording but may not be the only types encountered in field production or news gathering.

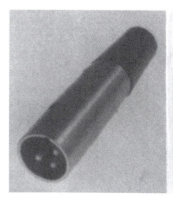

Figure 9-17 Audio balanced line (XLR) connectors. On the left is a male connector, on the right is a female connector.

It is typical in ENG work to be asked to record audio sources from a wide variety of systems in the field. A good audio kit should include adapters to tap into

Figure 9-18 Three popular unbalanced audio connectors: from left to right, 1/4-inch phono plug, RCA type, and 1/8-inch mini-plug.

The most common is the 1/4-inch phono plug. This plug comes in balanced (stereo) and unbalanced (mono) versions. In most cases, you will not need a stereo signal. This 1/4-inch connector is the most common way to tap into a house **public address (PA)** system or audio mixing board not designed for video production. The output of such systems is usually labeled "monitor out" and is typically mono at mic level, but it can be line level or even a nonstandard level. Many video supply companies sell adapters that are 1/4-inch phone (stereo or mono) at one end and XLR at the other.

Other connectors that you are likely to encounter in the field are the 1/8-inch or mini-plug, the RCA-type connector that your stereo uses. While adapters are available to convert these plugs to XLR, it is quite easy to make up short cables with the different types of connectors at each input end and an XLR at the other.

Signal Loss in Audio Cable

A mic level signal is able to travel up to 200 feet or more with insignificant loss of signal strength. On very long runs, a loss of some audio frequencies may occur as well as an increased susceptibility to hum or electrical interference. For long distances, it may be necessary to amplify the audio with a mixer near the source end to deliver enough signal strength to the cable destination. By amplifying the signal to line level from mic level, a higher quality signal with less hum can be transferred over a greater distance.

Phase

If the polarity of the audio cables or mics used in a single system does not match, the signal may be out of phase and cause the cancellation of some frequencies or the entire signal itself. This can be a very tricky problem to track down without the use of a volt-ohm meter or a cable tester. While this problem is not common, it is possible. If you find a cable or source that is out of phase, a small in-line adapter can reverse the phase (polarity) of the audio line, or you can rewire the cable or connector.

Filters and Pads

A variety of in-line filters and pads in barrel style are available that aid the audio-gathering process. These items can be invaluable in getting the most out of your mics and overcoming weak points in your audio system. One common style is a barrel shape, which allows you to put the filter or pad in the audio line at any point where there is a connection.

Switchable Attenuator Pad. A switchable attenuator pad reduces impedance by 15, 20, or 25 dB to avoid overload distortion at the recorder from too strong a signal. It also comes in handy for matching audio signal strengths.

Line Adapter. A line adapter is a 50-dB attenuator that reduces line level to mic level. Whereas the output level of many mixers, VCRs, recorders, and amplifiers is at line level, many recorders and most wireless transmitters only accept mic-level input.

High-Pass Filter. A high-pass filter reduces bass and rumble by rolling off or cutting out the low frequencies. It allows high frequencies to pass through the circuit and reduces the low frequencies. This filter is good for reducing air-conditioner noise and wind rumble.

Low-Pass Filter. A low-pass filter reduces hiss by rolling off or cutting out the high frequencies. It allows

the low frequencies to pass through the circuit and reduces the high frequencies.

Presence Adapter. A presence adapter gives a slight boost in the upper midrange of frequencies to enhance the quality of the human voice.

Response Shaper. A response shaper puts a slight dip in the upper midrange of frequencies to reduce the sibilance that can sometimes be present in certain mics or mic'ing situations.

Handheld Microphones

A handheld mic is often the easiest to use. You simply pick it up and point it at the source of the sound. Singers, TV evangelists, used car salespersons, and TV reporters often use handheld mics, which are made for gathering audio close to the source. Meant to be seen on camera most of the time, handheld mics do not require a boom person or as much time and hassle to put in place as a hidden lavaliere would require. There is just one hard and fast rule: they must be within about one to two feet of the source of audio. Some handheld mics are shock-mounted within their outer shell to withstand rough handling without creating excessive mechanical noise. The Electro-Voice RE-50 is an internal shock-mounted mic well suited for ENG work.

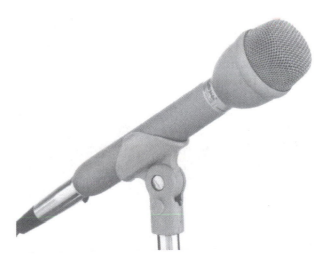

Figure 9-19 This RE-50 mic is designed to reduce wind and popping noise and features an internal shock mount to reduce handling noise. (Courtesy of Electro-Voice, Inc.)

A news photographer working without a soundperson may have no choice but to give the reporter a hand held mic to gather almost all the audio, especially for interviews and stand-ups. The handheld mic allows the reporter to place the mic where it can get the best sound. If the news crew is talking to a gathering of steel workers outside a closed factory, the reporter can maneuver the mic to whichever person is talking while being able to bring the mic back to record the questions as well. This approach can be problematic, because without a shock-mounted mic, the sound of fidgeting fingers on the mic can be very distracting.

In EFP work the handheld mic is used more often as a prop and not out of necessity, as in ENG. Because the quality of the audio is more important in EFP, it is not a good idea to leave the handling and placement of the mic in the hands of the talent. That is why most EFP crews have a soundperson. Some talent, such as a used car salesperson, likes to have a mic to hold onto like a security blanket. It may in fact be just a prop, with the actual sound being recorded by an unseen mic. If you have time, budget, or personnel, there are usually better ways to get that audio in many situations. The best exception to this rule is in the case of singers, but even they are now using the newer micro-headset mics (such as those Madonna and Garth Brooks have used) to free their hands for instrument playing or dancing.

Even when a handheld mic is used on a floor or desk stand, it still must be within two feet of the sound source to obtain good-quality sound. As the mic is placed further from the sound source, the risk of the audio sounding hollow or having an echo is increased. For a news conference at which several speakers are seated at a long table, using more than one mic is a good alternative. It is best to follow the rule of three to one in the placement of the mics, however many people are present. This principle says that for every unit of distance between the mic and the audio source, the distance between mics should be at least three times greater. The greater the directionality of the mic, the less chance of phase problems from reflected sounds or multiple mics.

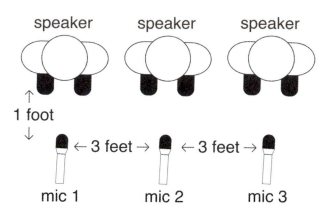

Figure 9-20   Three to one rule: if Mic 1 is one foot in front of speaker 1, Mic 2 should be three feet from Mic 1.

Camera-Mounted Microphones

The best mic to mount on a camera is the ultradirectional type, although any type of mic can be used. A shotgun microphone will pick up audio mostly from the camera's field of vision. Sounds that come from the sides (outside of the picture) are not picked up nearly as well. Even in highly directional mics, there are still **flanges (off-axis lobes)** of sound pickup to the side and rear areas of the mic. Although those flanges are not as sensitive as the on-axis lobes of the polar response chart, they may still pick up some unwanted sounds, such as the reporter whispering in your ear next to the side of the mic while you are shooting.

Sound gathered at the camera is usually referred to as **background (BG) audio.** Most producers refer to it as **natural sound**, or the sound the camera naturally hears. It is the most valuable sound an ENG person can get. Natural sound is what makes many pictures come alive. Having it can mean the difference in keeping your job or losing it. Some news photographers try to use their camera mic to do reporterless interviews. Under certain time pressures or acoustic conditions this may be acceptable, but most of the time it is not. The photographer places the camera (and therefore the mic) as close to the subject as possible to reduce the amount of background noise (unwanted audio) from this interview, so the person sounds more on-mic. The net effect here is okay sound, but a picture that has its perspective (and therefore its subject) distorted. It can make people's heads and their features seem enlarged or out of proportion. Of course any mic can be used to gather natural sound or BG, but for one-person crews, the camera mic is the standard tool for achieving that end. Camera-mounted mics can also be used to collect **room tone**. Room tone is the sound of the room without any speaking or other sounds made by the talent or the crew. It may include the sound of an air conditioning system, the buzz from fluorescent lights, or just the outside noise that leaks into the room. Room tone is essential in the editing process, so always take a few moments with the entire crew on set to call for quiet and record 10 to 30 seconds of room tone.

Boom Microphones

Although most microphones can be placed on a boom, the most common one used on booms is the shotgun. The portable boom or fishpole allows its operator to place the mic in the optimum position to gather the best audio. This is a common way for production crews and larger news organizations to gather audio in the field. Good teamwork between the photographer and the soundperson can keep the mic out of the picture but in the right place to get the best audio. The task of the boom operator is to keep the desired sound source on axis while aiming the mic away from other distracting sounds. In the case of the reporter interviewing people on the street, a fishpole can be used by an audio person to do what a handheld mic does, only without the mic being seen. This gives a more natural, realistic look. The audio person lines the mic up with the person's mouth at an angle to avoid having it also pointed at, say, the street or an idling car at the curb. Most of the time the mic is at waist level, as close to the person as possible and pointed up. The fishpole can also be held above and pointed down to the audio source, but this increases the possibility of reflected sound being gathered if the ground is a hard surface, such as concrete. (See Figure 9-9.)

Lavaliere Microphones

Lavalieres, lavs, or mini-mics can be the best sounding but most frustrating mics to use in field productions. They are by far the most susceptible to mechanical noise caused by material rubbing against the mic or the cable. Extra care is needed when using this type of mic. The most common use of a lav is on someone's tie, jacket lapel, or shirt. The most common lav clasp is the alligator clip. You simply clip on to any edge or fold of material. The two most common mistakes in using lavs are not hiding the mic cable and not properly securing it.

Viewers are often distracted when they see people being interviewed on TV using a lav that is simply hanging from the front of their clothes. It looks sloppy and inappropriate. This leads us to another problem. It is natural for everyone to move somewhat during a conversation. If the mic is placed incorrectly or the cable is not secured, a little movement translates into a horrendous scratching sound called mic rustle.

You must use considerable care when choosing where to attach a mic to a person. Look for a spot that is not distracting to the camera and will not be brushed against by any part of the person's clothing or jewelry. Next, make sure the cable is fastened down so that it cannot pull on the mic. The easiest way is to loop the cord to the back of the alligator clip and pinch it with the material used to hold the mic. The other way is to use a fabric tape or a similar product such as surgical tape (from any drug store) to tape the cable to the inside of the clothing or even the person's skin. For an active subject wearing a lav, using both procedures is highly recommended.

Many other devices are available for attaching lav mics. The second most popular is the pin or "vampire" clip. This holder attaches to the cable and has two fine stick pins that catch the subject's clothing. It is used extensively when hiding the mic under clothing. Care must be taken not to damage the material or stick the subject with the sharp pin.

Because lavs are so small, most EFP users prefer hiding them in the person's clothing. This is not an easy job, but the results are well worth the effort. This mic placement can make everyone wearing one sound good without seeing the mics. This is especially true in a dramatic production, where seeing the mic can ruin the mood. There are many ways to hide a lav that is often no bigger than a small pea. The dangers are clothing rustle and muffling. The mic capsule must be as unobstructed as possible, even if it is already under the clothing. The mic must be taped down with sev-

Figure 9-21   A front and back view of how to properly attach a lav mic to clothing using an alligator clip. It not only dresses the cable but hleps dampen cable noise.

eral inches of tape between clothing layers, with the capsule taped on both sides and with only the grill area of the capsule left exposed. If the mic goes between clothing and skin, the mic can be taped directly to the skin using surgical tape or the equivalent. Sometimes a little funnel made of tape or even very soft leather can be fashioned to shield a hidden mic from rustle. This process is tricky and may take some trial and error to perfect.

Wireless Microphones

The distinguishing factor about a wireless mic is not the mic, but the means of transmitting the audio from a mic to a receiver at the recorder. Of all the types of mics, using a wireless has the most dramatic results. Wireless mics allow the audience to hear someone perfectly as though they are "up-close," even though they are obviously some distance from the camera or are

moving about the set or location, without seeing a microphone or cable in the shot.

Combining the use of the wireless with the hidden mic can truly free up your subjects to be as natural as they can be. Wireless mics have become so popular in all forms of EFP that most producers simply will not work without them. They have become as important as, if not more important than, boom mics to get high-quality audio without a mic being on camera. A wireless mic allows the talent to roam the location cable free, to turn backwards to the camera while still being on-mic, and to have close-in mic sound. With extensive use of wireless mics, a production can take on a more natural sound, as if the viewer were actually there.

The use of wireless mics has also made quite a difference in news gathering. Veteran news producer Ray Farkas made extensive use of wireless mics on stories for the networks and other news outlets. Farkas was the pioneer in using wireless sound and leading photojournalism into a new sound era. By eliminating the boom mic and placing the camera and crew a great distance from the subject, Farkas was able to relax the video subjects so completely that they forget they are wearing a mic and being videotaped. The results became known as the "Farkas interview," an interview that is not only more conversational in tone but actually looks like the viewer is eavesdropping on a private conversation. This technique can make a simple news story more compelling to watch and more convincing. Although no staging is allowed in journalism, the obvious presence of camera, lights, and mics can make an interview look more like a TV show than a slice of real life. Farkas's highly stylized technique may not suit all or even many of the traditional looks of TV news, but it does represent what attention to the audio-gathering process can do for editorial content.

Even without the more complex uses that Farkas has developed, the wireless is an invaluable tool for any everyday news crew. Besides wiring a subject for better natural sound or walking interviews, the wireless can be plugged into PA systems or placed on podiums at meetings and gatherings so that the camera can go anywhere within the location and still have a house audio feed. The wireless can be quickly and easily placed anywhere within a scene to get a close-in presence to the sound.

Even if you cannot plug in directly or put the mic at the source of the audio at an event that has a PA system (**public address** or **house sound**), you may be able to place the wireless directly in front of the PA speaker. The audio is not as good as a direct feed, but if the sound system does not have excessive buzz or hum, you can still get house sound. The small size of wireless transmitters allows you to place the mics just about anywhere. If you are shooting a long line of Super Bowl ticket buyers, you might simply set the wireless on the counter at one of the ticket windows. You could then make a shot from anywhere around the window and still have great audio from the activity there. One shot may be from the end of the line with the window in the background as the viewer hears the conversation at the window. This helps focus the viewer on what is taking place. The technique may also be as simple as putting the mic at the stream's edge for a wide shot of a beautiful valley as canoeists pass through it. The camera is up on the side of a small hill, but the audio is of the water flowing in the stream below and the sounds of the canoeists as they pass through the shot. Syn-

chronous sound that you could not get with the mic at the camera position can now be gathered with creative use of the wireless. This simple and subtle use of close-in sound can make a good video story into a great one.

MONITORING, MIC PRE'S, MIXING, AND STEREO

After you have selected the appropriate mic, mount, filter, and screen, and achieved proper placement, you need to consider other aspects of the sound-recording process. Multiple microphones for any given sound situation require combining signals, called **mixing.** To ensure that your sound is appropriate for your situation, you must also learn to monitor the sound. A brief mention is also made here about stereo-sound recording and microphone preamplifiers.

Figure 9-22 The safest way to get good audio when shooting video is to use headphones to monitor the sound.

Monitoring

While the performance of your equipment may be well known, you cannot really know if everything is working properly unless you actually hear what you are getting.

A good pair of headphones is absolutely mandatory for any audio or ENG/EFP person, and at least a good ear piece is essential for a one-person operation. Without hearing what you are getting, an unheard problem can make all your efforts worthless. Most professional VCRs offer a confidence playback head in the audio-recording circuit. This system allows you to actually hear the sound on the tape after it has been recorded while you are still recording. The playback head passes over the tape about one second after the record head lays down the audio. Because of this delay, confidence audio sounds weird because it is out of sync with what you are seeing. Most videographers and audio persons only spot-check the confidence circuit occasionally during the recording process because of the distraction. Newer digital recorders do not have this feature and require direct monitoring.

It takes some practice to "hear" audio. Even with a good set of isolation headphones, it is hard to separate the audio you are monitoring and the sounds that are bleeding through the headset. If the headset is turned up too loud, you may think the background noise is excessive when in reality it is not. It takes the experience of doing field recordings and playing them back in the studio to become comfortable with knowing what you're getting on location.

Microphone Preamplifiers

When a microphone is plugged in to a camera or a mixing console it is always connected to a microphone preamplifier (or mic pre). A mic pre is a special electronic circuit that amplifies the low-voltage, low-impedance signal of a microphone to the appropriate level for recording. ENG/EFP cameras come with an adjustment for audio gain. This is the preamplifier adjustment. All mixing consoles and field mixers have multiple microphone pre-amplifiers. It is important to take care in adjusting the microphone preamplifier as this is the most likely source for audio distortion if it is turned up too much, or too much gain is added to the incoming signal. As a general rule, adjust the micpre so that the loudest sound does not distort and your average level approaches zero on the audio meters.

Mixing

The last stage that the audio signal is likely to go through is some form of mixing before it is recorded. To mix audio, it first needs to be monitored. Whenever more than one mic is being recorded on a single audio channel, it is best to use a mixer to make sure each mic can be separately controlled to ensure the best blend of audio sources.

Popular professional, portable mixers have three or four input channels, filters that will cut out certain audio frequencies, a tone generator, two output lines, and a master output volume control. They can take line or mic-level impedance inputs and send mic or line level out. They can also feed phantom power to condenser-type mics on any channel. Most importantly, they are usually stereo, with each channel capable of being panned right or left. This ability lets the operator place only the audio of channel 1's input on the channel 1 output by panning channel 1 to the left. Panning channel 2's control to the right would place its audio on the channel 2 output only. Additional channels can also be panned to either output channel. The audio person then has the flexibility of isolating or combining signals to the recording tracks in the camera.

Figure 9-23 This small but versatile audio field mixer can be powered by three AA batteries and is used for EFP or ENG sound recording for video.

These portable mixers are very popular for use with camcorders. Two record channels on the recorder can be set up with a tone signal from the mixer; the input volume adjustments can be made at the mixer, and no further attention is required at the camera. In some cases, the sound person will use a wireless mic to send the output of the mixer to the camcorder, thus allowing the photographer to roam freely while the audio person can go wherever the best sound-gathering location is.

Stereo

Stereo audio is most common in performance videos and is not practical for most ENG and EFP shoots. In EFP production, stereo sound is usually added in post-production, where the variables are controlled and the source material is dependable. Such factors as the mics used and critical mixing techniques make stereo recording a very demanding job in the field. More effort is required at the time of recording than most productions can afford—and typical news gathering will never allow the time needed for stereo recording.

SUMMARY

Professional videographers know that the quality of the video project depends not only on the pictures, but also on the sound. Collecting sound for your video work is important—audiences know when the sound is not right. Selecting the best mic and using proper technique will help to make your video project look and sound more professional.

Microphones have been used in electronic media for over 100 years, beginning with Alexander Graham Bell's telephone in 1876. Although many advances in mic structure and design have occurred, the mic's basic function of collecting accurate sound has stayed the same over the years.

Microphones used in most professional situations have two types of construction: dynamic and condenser. Dynamic mics generate sound when sound waves strike a moveable coil of wire inside the mic, creating a small electrical signal. Condenser mics have a positive (+) and a negative (−) electrode inside of them. When sound strikes one of the electrodes, the distance between the two electrodes changes resulting in a small electrical signal. In both of these designs, the small electrical signal becomes the sound signal. Microphones can also be differentiated by their impedance (resistance to signal flow) and their style (e.g., handheld, lavaliere, stand mounted) Some microphones are used for special applications, such as when you are trying to collect audio from a moving singer/performer, multiple speakers, or in situations where microphone cables won't work and a wireless mic is needed. There are a variety of cables and connectors that can be used in video production work, and selection of the appropriate equipment requires knowing the application and the advantages and disadvantages of the connectors. Most mics are designed to be placed and used in specific ways, so knowing how these mics work and how to place them on location will help you to collect accurate and appropriate audio. The best way to ensure that you are collecting good audio is to always monitor your audio. In the field, make sure that you wear headphones connected to your recorder to guarantee that the sound being recorded is the sound needed for your professional production.

10

Light: Understanding and Controlling It

If you ask an experienced photographer or videographer what the key to creating good images on film or video is, they will probably tell you it is the control of light. In both film and video, the images are made by light reflecting off of the subject of the image. Manipulating light for the camera is truly an art, and one that is crucial for high-quality video.

Lighting is probably the most overlooked, misunderstood, and feared aspect of ENG and EFP. Very often, light kits are low-priority items in budgets for field gear, and subsequently, especially in days of lean budgets, well-equipped light kits are never purchased. Existing kits often go for months without replacement bulbs, again a result of the low priority assigned to lighting in the field. In ENG, lighting that goes beyond a camera-mounted light and one basic light for live shots doesn't always happen. Today's cameras boast of their low-light capabilities, creating the impression that lights simply aren't needed anymore. That impression, coupled with the limitations of trunk space, crew members, and setup time, means that even for EFP the portable light kits are often left at the station, in the studio, or in the vehicle. And that is a huge mistake.

It seems odd that lighting equipment gets such casual treatment; after all, without light there would be no photography—video or otherwise. Especially when using relatively inexact video cameras, you must pay constant attention to the lighting factor to produce a realistic image.

Portable video practitioners may treat lighting casually because much of their work is done outdoors. Available sunlight provides enough light to allow the video cameras to see the desired scene and record the action. But seeing is not always good enough. With some additional lighting effort and consideration, the camera will not only see the scene and the action, but it will also detect additional mood, dimension, interest, focus, and indeed understanding in a good video segment.

This chapter looks at the very nature of light. Its qualities, its quantities, and the instruments that create and shape it are all discussed in this chapter. We will also discuss the basics of lighting theory and technique and how they relate to the content of all video productions—both ENG and EFP—to go beyond simply making the subject visible to the camera.

PART ONE: THE PHYSICAL PROPERTIES OF LIGHT

What Is Light?

Without light, there would be no picture. A good knowledge of the physical and artistic characteristics of light is a prerequisite of understanding TV photography in any form.

Photons and Light Waves

Light is just one part of the total electromagnetic radiation spectrum, but, unlike other forms of this type of energy, light is visible radiant energy. Actually made up of very small energy particles called **photons,** light follows the common rules associated with all wave physics. The big difference between light and X-rays or radio waves is light's inability to penetrate solid objects. Light is easily deflected. In fact, except for the light source itself, reflection is the only way light can be seen. Shining a bright light into a dark night sky produces no evidence of that light from the side or below, unless some dust, fog, or other material crosses the path of the light and reflects it. Light is visible only when we see its effect as it strikes an object.

The photons released by the light source all travel in a straight line away from the source at the same speed. The sun is the best example of a light source. Points at the same distance away from any side of the sun receive the same amount of light.

Photons travel in that straight line until they encounter something. In space, that may be quite a long time, but once they reach Earth, it doesn't take much to start blocking them. Our atmosphere, which is actually very thin by the standards of physics, blocks a great deal of sunlight striking Earth. Some of the light is absorbed by the air and converted into heat; some is reflected by the air, which is the source of our beautiful blue skies. The same is true as light strikes the surface of the planet. Everyone notices that a black car sitting in the sun gets a lot hotter than a white car. The black car is absorbing the light and its energy, while the white car is reflecting most of it. Photography concerns itself with both the reflected light and the absorbed light. Knowing that light always travels in straight lines and how light is absorbed or reflected is the key to understanding so much of modern photography and the way today's video equipment works.

Spectrum

Like all electromagnetic radiation, light can be classified by its wavelength or frequency. In addition to its speed (186,282 miles per second), light waves can be measured in units called **nanometers (nm)**. Visible light, or white light, contains all the wavelengths between 400 and 700 nm. Wavelengths shorter than 400 nm go from ultraviolet and X-ray to gamma and cosmic (the shortest). Wavelengths longer than 700 nm go from infrared and radar to broadcast signals such as TV and radio transmissions (the longest).

Shining a light through a prism reveals the various frequencies that make up that light; these frequencies are bent at different rates according to their wavelengths. The resulting light on the other side of the prism appears as a rainbow. This represents the spectrum of frequencies contained in that light. In nanometers, the colors in the rainbow range from violet (~400 to ~430 nm) to green (~492 to ~550 nm) to red (~647 to ~700 nm). Lights that have a continuous spectrum have all of the wavelengths between 400 and 700 nm present. Not all light sources have continuous spectrums, and not all wavelengths within any spectrum are present in equal amounts. Sunlight has much more energy in the shorter wavelengths (blue, indigos, and violets), whereas filament light (such as the common household lamp) has more energy in the longer wavelengths (oranges and reds).

The Color of Light

Our brains adapt to the colors and light that our eyes see. We tend not to notice the difference in the relative colors of light sources. The light in our homes at night seems to be the same color as light in our yards at noon. To an optical prism or an "objective" camera, the color of light in those two situations is very different. Taking still photos on film indoors at night using just the lamps in the room for light results in pictures tinged with orange. The film, which is balanced for outdoor use, is designed to recreate realistic colors only in daylight. A video camera operates in much the same way as photographic film. We need to understand what color the video camera is set for and adjust it when the color of light for our shooting is different than the "default" setting. Thus, the understanding of light is crucial for us to create the end product with accurate colors that we desire.

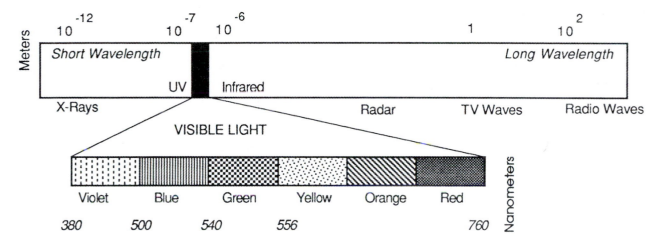

Figure 10-1   Although the visible light band is narrow, within this band are differences in wavelength that determine the color of light. (Graphic courtesy of Manny Romero)

Primary Additive Colors

The color emitted by a light is referred to as its **hue** or **tint**. When all the wavelengths are combined, we get white light. But when only specific individual colors (frequencies) are combined, the result is yet another color. For example, combining a pure green and a pure red light produces yellow light. Within the visible spectrum, red, blue, and green are known as the **primary additive colors**. Combinations of these three colors in various ratios can be made to create all other visible colors. This gives a very basic explanation of why three-chip cameras divide the light coming through the lens into red, green, and blue. Mixtures of the information from these chips can be regenerated into the full-color image the camera is shooting. If these primary colors of light are combined in equal amounts, the result is white light.

Subtractive Primary Colors

The primary colors that an artist uses for painting or that a lab uses to make a color film photograph are magenta (reddish blue), cyan (blue-green), and yellow. These three primary colors are called the **subtractive primary colors**. Mixing materials such as dyes or pigments of these colors will yield different results than mixing the colors of light. Mixing the three subtractive primary colors of magenta, cyan, and yellow paint together yields black, not white.

Color Temperature

Although our eyes generally perceive most light as being white, it generally is not, technically speaking. Although the additive properties of a light's spectrum allow objects of any color to be perceived correctly once our eyes and brain have made the necessary adjustments, the amounts of each frequency in the spectrum may vary by quite a bit. Light sources with a predominance of higher frequencies (more energy) tend to be blue, and those with lower frequencies (lower energy) tend to be red. Thanks to Lord Kelvin (who first defined the absolute temperature scale in 1847), we have a very convenient way of quantifying the color of a light source. The **thermometric** scale he invented is used to measure the temperature of a light source in degrees of Kelvin (K). This measurement is known as the **color temperature** of the light. Low temperatures (around 2,000° K) are very red, and high temperatures (around 9,000° K) are very blue.

Because all artificial light is created by heating or applying energy to a known material, such as a tungsten filament inside a light bulb, it is possible to pre-determine the color temperature of that source.

Indeed, even the sun acts as a huge filament burning at a constant temperature. This consistency allows a videographer to judge with some certainty what color of light exists within any scene.

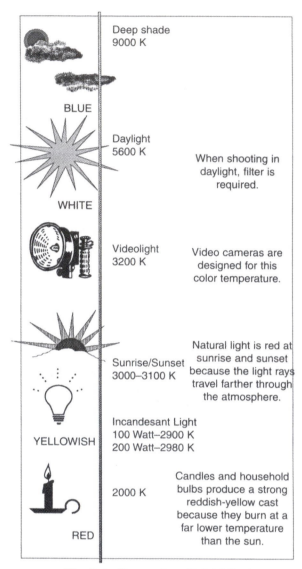

Deep shade
9000 K

BLUE

Daylight
5600 K

When shooting in
daylight, filter is
required.

WHITE

Videolight
3200 K

Video cameras are
designed for this
color temperature.

Sunrise/Sunset
3000–3100 K

Natural light is red at
sunrise and sunset
because the light rays
travel farther through
the atmosphere.

Incandesant Light
100 Watt–2900 K
200 Watt–2980 K

YELLOWISH

2000 K

Candles and household
bulbs produce a strong
reddish-yellow cast
because they burn at a
far lower temperature
than the sun.

RED

The Color Temperature (Kelvin) Scale

Figure 10-2 This represents how video cameras respond to different kinds of light. (Graphic by Manny Romero)

The Direction and Size of a Light Source

Two additional factors that determine the quality of light are its direction or angle to the subject and scene and the spectral quality or harshness of the light source. Again, our eyes tend to make up for a lot of the things the camera simply cannot do. We see in stereo, creating three dimensions, so depth perception is generally not a problem. The camera does not. And, for the most part, we see details equally well in the shadows of a scene or face as we do in the areas that are lit. Again, the camera does not.

The Angle of Light

In the two-dimensional world of the TV screen, the only way we can perceive depth—the third dimension—is by the shadows present. The shadows or dark areas of the picture convey a multitude of information about the subject or scene. Shadows can let us see the texture of a surface. They can give us the time of day or even the season of the year. They can relate the mood of the situation. They can define the area of main interest within the frame. But above all, they define the space we are seeing.

With the source of light behind the camera and very close to the lens, a scene is almost without shadow. This look is referred to as **flat lighting**. It is hard to perceive depth, texture, or spatial relationships in the picture. As the light source moves away from the lens, we start to see how the shadows fall both on the objects creating them (attached shadows) and on their surroundings (unattached shadows).

These shadows are the chief determinant of the quality of light. When any great videographer refers to the quality of light, he or she is talking about the direction of the light or, more simply, the shadows created by it. Flat lighting of an area of a scene or a face within a scene may be desirable at times, but flat lighting an entire scene should be avoided. Later, we will discuss the manipulation and meaning of shadows in more depth, in the section on lighting styles and technique (part three of this chapter).

Hard and Soft Light

It is impossible to describe the quality of light without talking about both the shadow and its edge: the area of transition between what is lit and what is not. One simple factor determines the difference between hard and soft light: the size of the source in relationship to its distance from the subject. This factor is often referred to as a light's ability to **wrap**. Hard light is created by very small sources of light as seen from the area being lit.

The sun is an excellent example of a hard source. It may be many times the size of the Earth, but because of its distance, it appears to us as a very small object. The shadows created by it on a cloudless day are razor sharp. As you look at your own shadow on the pavement, you see a perfect outline. Now, let a small cloud move in front of the sun. The sun is no longer—technically speaking—the light source: it is now the cloud. To us, the cloud is much larger than the sun. Now look at your shadow on the ground. It's fuzzy and the shape is ill defined. We now have an example of a soft light source. That fuzzy nature of the shadow is the result of the light wrapping around the object (you). The source is larger than the subject—either wider or taller or both. That defines soft light.

Keep this distance relationship in mind as you go through the rest of the chapter, and certainly when you are on location setting up lights. Lighting instruments that are called soft lights are only soft at certain distances from the subject. A soft light set up 30 feet from the subject is not going to be nearly as soft (have as much wrap) as when that light is 10 feet from the subject.

The Quantity of Light

Intensity

The intensity or amount of light has traditionally been measured in units of **foot-candles (fc)**. One foot-candle is the amount of light given off by *one candle, one foot away*. Today, it is common to see the units of light quantity being expressed in **lux**. One lux is the amount of light at one meter from a candle. One foot-candle equals about eleven lux. Because foot-candles are still the more common way of measuring light in this country, we will continue to use the term in this book. However, when you see a camera's low-light performance ratings listed by its manufacturer, it will be in lux (the Canon XL-2 lists 10.5 lux as minimum illumination, but recommends 100 lux minimum), because most cameras are manufactured in countries that use the metric system.

Light Meters

Light meters are indispensable in film work but are rarely seen on a video shoot. This is because almost all video cameras come with auto-iris controls and many videographers adjust light based on what they see in the monitor or viewfinder. However, one way to judge your camera's performance and your light's settings is to measure it with an incidence light meter (one that measures the light falling on an object and not reflected from an object). Try all the different lights in your kit one by one and measure the foot-candles at various distances and angles to the light. You will quickly see how much light is given off and how the lights can be aimed or manipulated to put the desired amount in the desired place. You will also see how much light your camera needs to make a good picture. This experiment is particularly good for adjustable lights.

The meter can check the ASA rating (the speed) of your camera or show how many foot-candles it takes to get a good exposure at different f-stops. To do this, set up a gray scale in the light you wish to use. If you don't have a gray scale, use a plain gray card of any form, or even a dull white one in its place. Zoom the camera in so the card fills the frame. Put the camera in auto-iris mode and read the f-stop off the lens. Now measure the amount of light falling on the card with the meter. Adjust the meter's ASA setting until the amount of light measured gives the same f-stop that the camera shows. That will be the ASA rating for that camera when it's on the filter you currently have dialed in. An advanced professional can use a light meter to light a scene without the camera present, to light by a certain formula (e.g., a key/fill/back ratio of 2:1:1) without a lot of trial and error, or to achieve a certain amount of light to work the lens at a specific f-stop (e.g., 200 fc on the subject requires an f8). The light meter can be invaluable in doing site surveys when looking at the quantities of available light.

The Inverse Square Law

A lamp placed near us gives off a certain amount of light. If the lamp is moved closer, there is more light; if the lamp is moved away, there is less light. The actual relationship between distance and illumination is often critical in location video work to achieve the desired quantity of light on a subject. This relationship is described by a law of physics known as the inverse square law, which states that the amount of light diminishes by a factor equal to the inverse square of the distance change. When the distance between a light and the subject is doubled, the amount of light falling on the subject is reduced to one-quarter of the original amount. As an example, if a light placed 10 feet from the subject produces 100 fc, moving it back to 20 feet away would result in the subject's foot-candles being reduced to 25 (a distance change by a factor of 2; square that to get 4, and then invert it to get 1/4, thus one-fourth the amount of light). If you move the light to only 5 feet from the subject, you would get 400 fc (a distance change factor of 1/2; square that to get 1/4, and then invert it to get 4, or four times the amount of light).

This relationship is of particular importance when lighting subjects that move around within a scene, such as a walking stand-up by a reporter or other on-camera talent. As the subject moves closer to the camera, he or she is also moving closer to the light. If the light is already close to the subject, that distance might be cut in half during the walk. As we have just seen, that would increase the amount of light on the subject by four times from the start of the walk to the end of it. The result is not an aesthetically pleasing picture. One way to minimize this effect is to have the lights set as far as possible from the area of the walk. If the subject started at 50 feet from the light and moved to 40 feet from it, the multiplying ratio would only be 1.6 times the amount of light at 40 feet—a much better, and more acceptable, rate of change than four times the brightness. We'll discuss other solutions to this problem later in this chapter.

Absorption and Reflection

Earlier, we talked about light's ability to be absorbed and reflected by different colors. These characteristics now come into play when dealing with quantities of light. It is virtually impossible to light a black object. The more light you put on it, the more light is absorbed. What you will quickly notice in doing such an exercise is that it's the reflected light that we really see. If the black object has a shiny surface, we'll see the light's glare. The object never gets any brighter as we

add light, but the glare gets worse. The reverse is true for white objects. A small amount of added light shows up right away: it's almost all being reflected by the surface and the white color.

These properties of light have to be considered when lighting a scene or subject. A dark wood-paneled room is going to require more light to give a good image than a room with white plaster walls. But there is more to absorption and reflection than just the color of the surface. Factors such as texture and the angle of the incoming light can change things dramatically.

Texture

A very smooth surface will reflect more of the light striking it than a rough surface. The light striking a very smooth surface is efficiently absorbed by the color and reflected back. As the surface of the object becomes rougher, more and more of the reflected light is restriking raised areas of that surface as it's bouncing up from the recessed areas. The overall amount of reflected light is therefore greatly reduced. If you have a scene with red velour curtains and vinyl seats of the same tone of red, the seats are going to appear much brighter than the curtains. The added texture of the velour is absorbing more of the light.

Angle of Incidence

Another law of physics that applies to lighting is the one governing reflection. As we learned earlier, light travels in straight lines, much like a bullet. As a beam of light strikes a surface, some of it is absorbed and turned into heat, and some is radiated back from the pigment of the surface revealing its color. Some of it is reflected in the form of what we called **glare**. The smoother the surface, the more glare you will get. Unlike the portion of the light coming back as the color of the object, glare is somewhat subjective in where it comes from. A smooth surface acts like a mirror. The light striking it is reflected at a predictable angle. If the beam of light strikes the surface at an angle of 45° measured from the surface in the direction of the light source, the beam will be reflected at a 45° angle to the surface measured from the opposite direction on the surface. Here is a rule of physics that will always help you with lighting: **The angle of incidence (incoming**

light) is equal to the angle of reflection (outgoing light). (See Figure 10-3.)

This law of physics will come into play in almost every lighting setup you do. You may have placed the light in the perfect place to create the perfect shadows but discover that the surface of the object being lit is producing nothing but glare in the direction of the camera. What to do? By remembering the relationship of the light source and where the reflection will be visible, you can readjust whichever element is easiest to eliminate from the picture. In other words, move the light to send the reflection to a point other than at the lens, slightly change the position of the object, or move the camera location or height.

Light Source

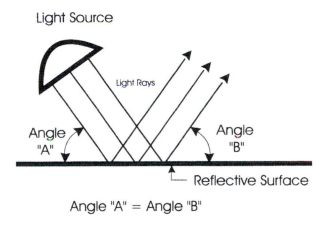

Figure 10-3   Light is reflected at a predictable angle.

Glare can also work in your favor. Let's go back to that black object we were trying to light earlier; let's say it's a statue of a black cat. By placing one light behind the statue, we can create a glare around the edges of it, giving it form and separating it from the rest of the picture. Now by placing a white surface such as an art card at the side of the statue, the card's reflection on the surface of the cat will be seen by the camera. That reflection will show the contours of the statue. The cat will appear to be lit, but in reality it was all done with simple reflections.

To summarize, the quality of light is dependent on two things: color and shadow. Just as the video signal is divided into chrominance and luminance, light is also divided into its color and black-and-white elements. Color (quality of light) depends on which sources you use and what, if any, filter you place in

front of them. Shadow (quantity of light) depends on the size of those light sources and where you place them. As you go about the job of dealing with light, you should always keep these two factors separated. Each must be dealt with in its own way.

PART TWO: CREATING LIGHT

Light Emitters

Even though today's cameras can shoot in nearly any type of light, not all light sources will produce the quality of light you desire. With an understanding of each type of light source, you will be better able to judge the performance of your camera, particularly when it comes to reproducing realistic colors.

The Sun

The single best source of light for portable video, the sun, is also the cheapest and, in many locations, the most readily available as well. The sun can be the hardest light source to manipulate, but usually helps make the subject's skin tone appear natural. This is not surprising, because the sun is our natural supplier of light—the light by which we judge reality. Almost everyone has bought clothing in an artificially-lit store only to perceive its color quite differently in the sunlight. Mismatched sock wearers often realize the color disparity only after the sun reflects off the socks. Since the sun follows its own schedule, it is necessary to go to great lengths to control sunlight.

As Edison and other early filmmakers quickly discovered, the sun is a great source of illumination for making movies. Unfortunately, this cheap and easy source of natural light has some annoying qualities in addition to the beneficial ones. First, it is not always visible in the daytime. Clouds, smog, mist, trees, buildings, mountains, billboards, and even large people can prevent sunlight from reaching the subject of the video camera. Second, the sun changes position in the sky continuously throughout the day. As the sun moves, color temperature changes. At early morning, the sun rising in the east strikes the subject in a scene at a low angle. Despite having a constant color temperature before it reaches Earth, sunlight displays varying color temperatures at different times of the day. In the morning, when the sun is low in the sky, its light must travel through a great deal of atmosphere to reach your position. The sun's shorter wavelengths are absorbed faster than the long ones, thus leaving only the redder frequencies. If there are few pollutants or dust particles in the air, the sunrise will be a beautiful yellow or gold color. With dirty air, the rising sun first shows up as a red disc on the horizon, giving the scene a pink glow. By noon, the sun is shining almost straight down. The amount of atmosphere it is going through is considerably less. Midday light has regained those bluer frequencies to the point where they dominate. In early morning, sunlight measures about 3,500° to 4,500° K. Noontime sunlight is 5,600° K or higher, and in the late afternoon, the color temperature is similar to early morning (although often a bit lower), about 2,500° to 3,000° K. Sunsets are often more red than sunrises because of atmospheric changes created by the midday sunshine adding more moisture and dust to the air. This low-angle sunlight yields less light than the higher-angle sunlight characteristic of midday.

Color temperature changes occur throughout the day: You need to white balance every time anything changes, not only for time of day but also for such things as clear or cloudy skies. The same idea holds true for white balances in sun and shade. This is where many new videographers make mistakes. The temperature on the sunlit street may be 5,600° K, but in the deeply shaded courtyard of the apartment complex, the indirect daylight can be 6,500° to 7,500° K—very blue. Without correction, your video will be very blue, too. Many videographers prefer to balance their camera for 6,500° K and not change it as they go from full sun to full shade. Color reproduction in the shade will read true and the colors in full sun will appear slightly warm, which can be good for skin tones and take some of the coldness out of direct sunlight on the subject.

Because of these differences in the angle of the sun and the quality of light at different times of the day, when more than one shot is required to complete a particular scene, it is best to shoot the scene at the same time of day with similar amounts of cloudiness. Many directors of TV commercials favor the early morning light (one hour after sunrise) because of its

golden glow and will shoot an entire commercial with that type of light. Other directors and videographers prefer the last hour before sunset (both are referred to as the **golden hour**). This may require several shoots at that location on successive days. Some videographers attempt to manipulate the overall light appearance by performing the white balance procedure while the camera is aimed at a light blue card. This procedure tends to give the video that golden hue. The color of the scene can also be manipulated by filters on the lens, just as in film photography. Despite the fact that early morning and late afternoon color temperatures are lower in degrees Kelvin, it is incorrect to call the reddish-orange color at 3,000° K cooler than the noontime blue of 5,600° K. Although videographers refer to blue and green as cooler colors, and gold, red, yellow, and pink as warmer, the technical concept of color temperature needs to be separated from the emotional response to colors. The term **warm light** refers to a cool-color temperature or a slight pink or golden look. **Cool light** refers to a warm-color temperature or a slight bluish look.

Traditional standards of photography contend that sunlight reflected off objects yields the most natural (and hence most eye-pleasing) light. Therefore, objects or subjects need to be placed in such a way that sunlight is reflected from them into the lens. This can be accomplished most easily by positioning the camera between the sun and what is to be shot. If the subject is between the camera and the sun, there are two possible results: a strongly backlit shot or direct sunlight shining into the lens. Both effects can be undesirable if handled incorrectly by a novice camera operator; however, as we'll see later, they can be used to great advantage by a skilled operator.

Artificial Light

The two broad categories of artificial light sources are incandescent and fluorescent. While most modern video cameras can white balance for these types of sources, they are inconsistent in color temperature and therefore unreliable to a professional video maker. The light from typical office ceiling fluorescents is highly diffused but "top heavy." It eliminates the shadows necessary to give subjects the appearance of depth, leaving only the shadows of the eye socket on a subject—not a flattering appearance. Light from typical house lamps is usually too dim and, like the fluorescents, not the optimum color. For these reasons, common incandescents and fluorescents are usually avoided in portable video, if at all possible.

Today's low-light cameras allow the videographer to shoot almost anywhere without the need for additional lighting, but they still do not satisfy some of the basic needs of high-quality photography. For a news videographer, shooting with available light is a major blessing, but just helps somewhat for a discriminating videographer in EFP or for stylized ENG work. We come back to the definition of photography: manipulating light, shadow, and color to achieve a specific artistic or editorial result. Professional video practitioners use specially designed lights that give a better color temperature for more natural skin tones (either 3,200° or 5,600° K) and enable them to have control over light quality and intensity.

Incandescents

Incandescent lights make use of a filament, usually made of tungsten, to create the light. Whereas it is easy to measure the temperature of the light coming off a known material, other factors can greatly change the ultimate color of the light. For example, ordinary household bulbs give off light that is about 2,800° K. Because of their design, these bulbs vary greatly in their color temperature. As the atoms of tungsten are given off when the filament is heated, they stick to the inside of the glass bulb. Over time the glass darkens and the color temperature drops. Other factors, such as whether the glass bulb is clear, frosted, or tinted, can change an incandescent lamp's color.

Tungsten/Quartz

Professional tungsten halogen or quartz lights are the most common light sources used in video production.

Although they use a tungsten filament within a halogen-filled sealed quartz globe to produce light, these professional lights are quite different from common household light bulbs. They are often simply called tungstens. In video production, tungsten, quartz, or halogen all refer to the same type of light.

Tungsten filaments give off a very constant 3,200° K over their life span, which may only be around 75 hours of use. Most tungsten bulbs are used in some sort of housing that enables the user to control the light.

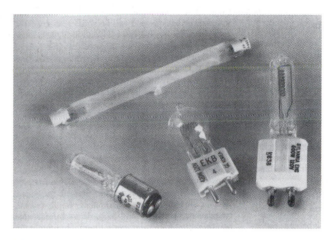

Figure 10-4   Some common tungsten bulbs used for video lights.

One form of the tungsten bulb comes with its own reflector and focusing lens. This type is called a **parabolic aluminized reflector (PAR)**. It is often referred to as a **sealed beam** light. Unlike the bare-bulb tungsten lights, PAR lights can come in different color temperatures, such as daylight (called a PAR 64), for use outdoors.

Lamps

The bulbs used for professional lighting are often referred to as lamps or globes. They come in a variety of shapes and sizes; they can be 110, 220, 30, or even 12 volts, and the globe can be clear or frosted. They are usually described by a three-letter code such as DYS, which refers to a 600-watt, 120-volt bulb with a particular connecting pin configuration.

Lamp handling requires a note of caution. Lamps become extremely hot during use and remain hot for some time after operation. They should not be handled when hot; not only can they cause severe burns, but the lamps are also extremely fragile when hot and that causes the filaments to break easily. Lamp handling, even after a cooldown period, must be done with care. Handling a lamp with bare hands can leave a slight oil deposit on the quartz glass that will hasten the lamp's burnout. The area of glass that was touched can be weakened, leading to a possible bulb explosion when the lamp is turned on. If lamps must be handled, do so with cloth or plastic gloves, but only when the lamp is cool. It is wise to carry some heat-proof gloves in your lighting kit to avoid any possibility of burns or lamp-glass contamination from the oil on your skin. Some companies will supply you with small plier-type tongs designed for lamp removal and installation.

Spare lamps are always necessary. Every light kit should have them. Even though most lamps are rated for about 75 hours of use, a burned-out lamp after fewer hours is not uncommon—often occurring in the middle of a story or production shoot. Make sure the replacement lamp is designed and rated for the housing into which you are putting it. If you replace a burned-out lamp with one that has a higher wattage rating, you may damage the housing or even start a fire. Using a replacement lamp with a lower voltage rating than is required can cause a nearly instantaneous burnout of the new lamp.

Fluorescents

Fluorescent bulbs, part of a larger group of lighting devices called gas discharge lamps, give off light by electrifying a metal vapor inside a glass tube. Contacts at each end of the tube allow electricity to flow through the gas, causing it to glow. Much like filament lights, many differences exist between consumer tubes and those used in film and TV production. A consumer-grade tube's color temperature may vary from brand to brand, but most are around 4,200° K. The real problem with fluorescent lights is their spectrum. Unlike the smooth mix of frequencies from a filament bulb, fluorescent tubes often have a higher degree (a spike) of green in their output and can actually be missing some frequencies altogether. While our eyes compensate for this, the camera does not. Video shot with fluorescents can give a very ghastly green pallor to the skin tones. White balancing may not fully compensate for this effect because of the missing hues and large amount of green in the light. Professional tubes compensate for this and can come in either 3,200° or 5,600° K, which will match the professional tungsten lights or daylight, respectively. The consumer versions of these lamps are called warm white (about 3,200° K),

cool white (about 5,600° K), and daylight (about 6,500° K). If you're doing quite a bit of shooting in a space that has fluorescent fixtures, you may want to change the bulbs to one of the color-correct ones.

Color-Correcting Fluorescents

Because the typical fluorescents found in the home and office can vary greatly in color temperature, great lengths are taken to avoid them or correct them in color-critical productions. Professional lighting handbooks have long charts and tables to deal with the wide variety of these lamps in correcting them to different film stocks. There are specially designed filters called minus green gels that can be put over fluorescent bulbs to reduce the green spike in their spectrum. A plus green filter can be placed over tungsten lights that, when used with a matching lens filter, allow the camera to compensate for the added green of the fluorescent light.

Mixed Light

Situations with mixed sources of light can cause problems. Imagine the face of a subject whose right side is lit by a tungsten-halogen lamp and whose left side is lit by a fluorescent bulb. If the camera is set for 3,200° K, the right side would look normal and the other side could be a sickly greenish blue. Because the video camera compensates for only one color temperature at a time, it is best to avoid mixed lighting situations. In the above example, it would be best to turn off the fluorescent and add tungsten-halogen light to the left side of the face. This may not always be possible, however, because some lights must stay on to prevent disruption of others (such as shooting at just one desk in a large office workspace).

The biggest advantage of modern video cameras regarding color temperature is that they white balance under any light if the lights are evenly blended. As long as the scene has a consistently even mix of any number of light sources that are within a limited range, the picture should be close to the true colors. When the mix changes because the distance from any of the light sources varies, the ratio of relative intensities changes, such as when the subject moves closer to the windows in a fluorescent-lit room. Mixed-light white balancing

Figure 10-5   The top picture shows a small fluorescents kit for field use. The lower picture shows a fluorescent that can be used with a variety reflectors to guide the light.

works best when each light source is about the same intensity and close in relative color temperature. It is hard to mix tungsten and daylight (3,200° and 5,600° K), but tungsten and household incandescent or fluo-

rescent are much closer in temperature (3,200° and 2,800° K or 4,400° K). In our example of the face above, a possible solution would be to get the tungsten light on the face from directly in front of it. Although fluorescent light would still be mixed in, the resulting white balance would reveal fairly true colors. The background will be a different story. The face would look good, but someone sitting behind the subject at another desk would have that green cast to their skin tone and possibly to the entire background of the scene as well. One trick is to use as little tungsten light as possible on the subject, thereby reflecting more of the fluorescent light in the white balance. The tungsten is just enough to give some red hues to the skin and minimize the greens without throwing the background too far out of color balance.

Carbon Arcs

The most famous light in Hollywood is the big carbon arc light, which has been used on movie sets ever since filmmaking was invented. These large round lights, called studio arcs, are intensely bright and use two carbon electrodes and high, direct current voltage to create an arc between them. The important word here is large. The arc lights still used today are very big in size and weight and produce not only large amounts of light but also large amounts of heat. They are mostly used outdoors in movie productions and seldom used in video production.

Hydrargyum Medium Arc-Length Iodide Lamp

Another type of arc lamp uses alternating current instead of direct current. The most common arc of this type is the **hydrargyum medium arc-length iodide (HMI)** light. The light is created by a mercury arc between two tungsten electrodes sealed in a glass bulb or globe. HMIs are a daylight temperature light. As they age, the temperature tends to decrease, however. A new light may be as high as 6,000° K, but a very old bulb may be as low as 4,800° K. HMI lights have been very popular in filmmaking and are becoming very popular in video as well. Unlike tungsten lights, there is much more involved in HMI operation. (See Figure 10-6.)

HMI lights take a very large amount of power to start the arc in the bulb, up to 60,000 volts for the one-second starting surge. After the surge, it takes about one minute for the light to come up to operating strength and color temperature. HMIs operate using a 220-volt AC circuit and require a ballast not only for the starting surge but to regulate the voltage to the lamp. Each light runs at a specific voltage, and no two bulbs operate at the exact some voltage. The ballast for most small HMIs, such as the kind you would use for a video production, runs on a normal 110- to 120-volt power supply and increases the voltage to 220. Even though HMI lights can be small enough to use on top of the camera, the ballast must be attached to the light, usually by a cable. Some mini-HMIs are available that have built-in ballasts and can be powered by the camera's battery just like a normal tungsten camera light.

Ballast comes in two forms, magnetic and electronic. The older magnetic styles are very heavy and bulky, even for a small 200-watt HMI. The more modern electronic solid-state ballasts are very lightweight and compact but still make the smallest HMIs more space consuming than tungsten lights.

HMI lights have many advantages. Because the light is at sunlight temperatures, color perception is at its best. They come in sizes ranging from 28 to 12,000 watts. You get much more light from an HMI lamp than from a tungsten lamp of the same wattage—roughly five times as much, in fact. A 1,200-watt HMI puts out the equivalent of 6,000 watts of incandescent light in a similar fixture. The lights may cost more to buy, but they are cheaper to run per foot-candle of light output, a major consideration if only a limited amount of power is available. HMIs also come in a DC-battery version for portable use. HMIs come in almost any type of housing, so there are few situations where they cannot be used.

Industrial High-Intensity Discharge Lamp

High-intensity discharge (HID) refers to another type of arc discharge that produces light through vapor or gas pressure in a glass globe. The three most common types of HIDs are mercury vapor, metal halide, and sodium vapor. For video use, the metal halide is the only

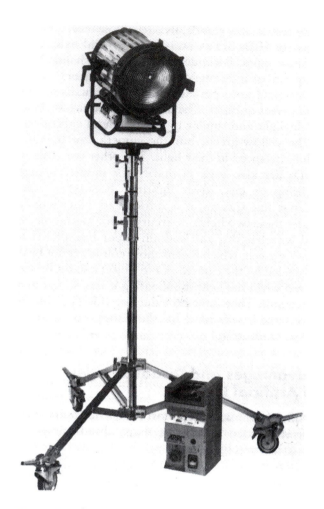

Figure 10-6   HMI light. (Courtesy of Arriflex Corp.)

one of interest. Metal halide lights are used in sports stadiums, parks, airports, and malls to light large areas at night. The color temperature is closest to daylight and similar to HMIs. Metal halides tend to be yellow-green, but the camera can be easily white balanced in their light. The other two types of HIDs are also used primarily for industrial night lighting or city street lighting. Because of their strange line spectra, it is difficult to white balance under these two lights. Mercury vapor has no blue or red wavelengths, and sodium vapor has almost no blue or green, which means those colors cannot be reproduced by the camera (a red object cannot be seen as red when the light illuminating it has no red in its spectrum). They have no value for video production and make it very hard for the camera to reproduce colors accurately.

Advantages and Disadvantages of Artificial Light

Artificial light is, for the most part, a necessary evil in portable video. There are many disadvantages to using artificial lights:

- Expense.

- Weight and size.

- AC power requirements necessitating extension cords.

- Excess heat.

- Artificiality or sickliness of subject's appearance if the subject is not properly placed and the camera is not white balanced.

- Artificial light draws lots of current and can blow fuses or trip circuit breakers.

This might seem like enough reasons to justify leaving the light kits in the studio, but there is one compelling reason to bring them: if you do not, you will miss quite a few important shots. Even today's video cameras are not sensitive or accurate enough to allow us to always use available light.

There are also more subtle reasons for using artificial light:

- You must often add light to maintain a realistic appearance; existing light may create an unrealistic appearance on the camera, and you must compensate with added light to make the subject appear more normal on tape.

- The existing light may be undesirable: too harsh in some areas, too dim in others. Added light can give the proper balance.

- Added light can enhance the shot aesthetically. You can highlight important visual elements and deemphasize the less important ones.

- You may sometimes want to create an artificial environment to achieve the mood of the story. This is particularly true in EFP work, especially when making commercials or dramatic presentations. Though less common in ENG, creating the environment with the addition of artificial light is as old as filmmaking itself.

In many shooting situations, the light kit helps the portable video cameraperson achieve proper exposure and maintain the necessary control over the environment. Artificial lights are tools that a good ENG or EFP practitioner uses to help get the shot that will make the video piece a professional product both for exposure and for creative reasons

Lighting Equipment

Lighting equipment comes in three categories: housings, mounts, and modulators.

Light Housings

To gain control over artificial light sources, the bulb must be housed in something more than a simple socket. The light housing or fixture provides the primary control over how the light reaches the subject or scene. The housing can direct, focus, or limit the illumination coming from the bulb. The housing can also dissipate the heat a bulb produces. Almost every year, new and improved housings are developed. The lights available in 1980 seem old and outdated when compared with the lights available in 2007. Like cameras and VCRs, lighting equipment changes with new designs and improvements. On the other hand, the basics have not changed in decades. A light made in 1950 still has plenty of uses in today's digital video world. This is another reason that lighting equipment is the best investment you can make: it simply never loses its usefulness despite all the new designs entering the marketplace.

Light housings fall into two broad categories: floods and spots. Although dozens of variations exist within these two groups, a few simple types usually account for most lights available in a typical video production.

Floodlights

Floodlights are the simplest of all lights. They provide even illumination of wide areas. The flood's primary use is to provide overall illumination for a scene or to fill shadows created by other lights. The housings are simple, with little means of controlling the light.

Scoops   The most basic floodlight is the **scoop**. (See Figure 10-7.) As its name implies, the scoop is simply a large metal bowl, 8 to 18 inches in diameter, with a bulb in the bottom of it. Because of its size, although it weighs practically nothing, a scoop is mostly used in studios. The lights just take up too much space in a vehicle and on location. However, they are cheap. You can get the type that has a traditional screw-in socket, the same as a household socket, and use *photoflood* bulbs purchased online or at a camera store. These bulbs come in 3,200° and 5,600° K colors and up to 500 watts in power.

Broads   **Broad** lights have a small reflector behind a linear-filament (or tubular) bulb. (See Figure 10-8) They are usually between 250 and 1,000 watts. Broads are easier to control than scoops. Most have small **barndoors** to regulate the light spread. The light from a broad is fairly hard, producing well-defined but low-density shadows. Because of their small size, broads can be easily placed anywhere in a room as long as there is no danger of heat damage to the surroundings. Small broads are often called **nook lights** and used to light backgrounds.

Floodlight Bank   This light is made up of several sealed-beam-type lights in a rectangular housing. The overlapping of the lights creates the soft effect of a floodlight. Sometimes called **modules**, they can contain from 4 to 12 lamps, usually laid out in banks that can be switched on individually. They are also referred to by the number of lights in the module, such as a **ninelight**. Only one version of this type of light is used in most location video productions, because the size and power requirements are too great for small-scale location shooting.

Spotlights

Spotlights are used to light specific areas of a scene. These lights can be easily controlled and focused. Traditionally, the main source of illumination in most scenes is provided by a spotlight of some sort. The sun is the best example of a spotlight. The opposite of floodlights, spots use a very compact source of illumination to produce well-defined, dense shadows. A spot

Figure 10-7   Scoop light.

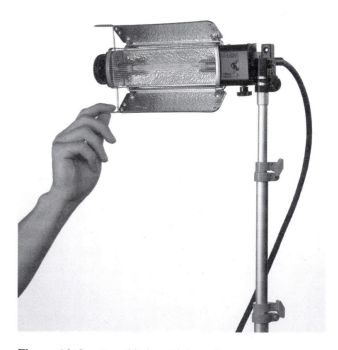

Figure 10-8   Broad light with barn doors.

is made up of a small bulb and some form of parabolic-shaped reflector to concentrate the radiant light into a direct beam.

Open-Face Spot The **open-face** spot is the most commonly used light in all of video production, because it is the most economical and efficient light to use. (See Figure 10-9.) Almost all open-face spots have the ability to focus from a spot position (called "pinned") to a flood position. The focus ability is accomplished by moving the bulb closer to the internal reflector (flood) or away from the reflector (spot). This takes the bulb into and out of the reflector's parabolic focal point. While the flood position is not as even and uniform as that of a broad or other floodlight, this housing allows most users to get double duty out of one light housing. The disadvantage of this type of light is the quality of its light pattern. The light beam is uneven in intensity, and the lack of a focusing lens can prevent getting distinct, hard-edge shadows. For most work in EFP and almost all work in ENG, these drawbacks are minimal.

Fresnel Spot The **Fresnel** spot (pronounced fre-*nell*) can also be adjusted from spot to flood like the open-face lights. But it differs from the open-face light in two ways: a Fresnel has a glass lens at the front through which the light passes and a different method of focusing the light. Unlike the open-face light, for which changing from spot to flood is achieved by moving the bulb closer or further from the reflector, the Fresnel light moves the bulb and reflector closer or further from the lens as a single unit. A Fresnel also allows a much narrower spot (around 10°). The focus of the lens gives shadows created in the light beam a hard, well-defined edge but leaves a softness to the outer edge of the overall beam, so that the blending of several lights to cover a large area is possible without unevenly lit spaces. Fresnels come in tungsten and HMI sources and range from 100 to 10,000 watts. The one disadvantage is the loss of light because of the lens. A 1,000-watt Fresnel only puts out the light equivalent of a 650-watt open-face light. However, this system is designed for maximum light control.

Ellipsoidal Spot The **ellipsoidal** spot (sometimes called a **focal spot**) is the most specialized in its application. Here, the lens moves back and forth in front of a fixed bulb and its ellipsoid-shaded reflector to focus the edges of the light pattern on a particular surface.

Figure 10-9 A Lowel Pro light. The dial allows the open-face light to be focused.

Figure 10-10 An LTM Pepper light with a Fresnel lens and barndoors.

The light is intense and directional. Often stencils (called **gobo patterns**) are inserted in the light housing to throw a well-defined shadow (such as those created by venetian blinds, prison bars, or tree limbs) on the surface of a wall. (See Figure 10-11.) Generally, this type of light is too expensive, big, and limiting to use for portable video. It is usually used in theater productions and dramatic applications in the studio, *but* if you have the time and budget, it can add greatly to the look of your field productions.

Several companies make projection lenses that attach to Fresnel-type lights making them an ellipsoidal spot. This relatively inexpensive solution can add greatly to the production values of any shoot by allowing the videographer to project symbolic patterns on surfaces.

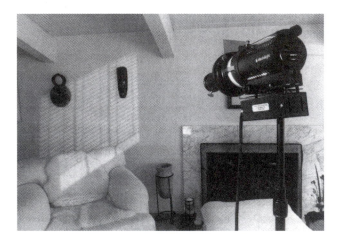

Figure 10-11   A Dedo light with projection lens. The window-blind pattern or gobo gives the effect of sunlight coming through a window.

Mounts

Most TV studios have a system of crosshatched pipes suspended from the ceiling called a **lighting grid** on which lights are hung. Lights designed for studio use ordinarily have a C-clamp for this application. In the field, lights are most often attached to tripod stands, some of which have small wheels to allow for easy repositioning. Lights made for stands have receptacles that fit over the standard 5/8-inch stud on the top of tripod stands called **kit stands** (compact) or **baby stands** (heavy duty). Larger lights, like many HMIs, have a 1 1/8-inch stud on the light and slip into a re-

ceptacle at the top of large stands called **rollers, juniors,** or **combos**.

Gaffer Grip   Small lights are more flexible than large lights to mount, since their weight does not require a sturdy tripod. Small lights, such as open-face spotlights, are often attached to poles, cameras, or kit stands, or on items like shelves and bookcases by means of a large clamp called a **gaffer grip.** (See Figure 10-12.) Some companies offer wide varieties of clamps, mounts, and special poles for securing lights in the field.

Grip Arm   There are many variations of this device in lighting. A standard **grip arm** is a metal rod that attaches to a stand by means of a **grip head** and is used to hold other light modifiers. These arms can be of various lengths and flexible instead of rigid. (See Figure 10-13.)

If you have ever seen a production lighting crew at work, or even a network news crew, you would have seen a box containing a multitude of clamps and other devices made to mount lights and accessories in just about any fashion anywhere. It's called a **grip kit**. Such things as C-clamps, pipe clamps, door brackets, furniture clamps, vice grips, putty knives, and more, all with the standard 5/8-inch stud attached, can be found in the box. A good location crew—even if that's just you—should be able to set up lights using something other than the standard kit stands. In a room where the camera may be panning 360°, or there are too many toddlers running about, you may need to mount the lights out of the camera's view and harm's way using the furniture or other stationary objects as stands. (See Figure 10-14.)

In a situation in which there are excess crew members, it may be possible to have a crew member, or **grip,** hold a light for you while you are shooting. It is not recommended, because the lights get hot and the holder often cannot hold the light steady, but if all else fails, have a crew member don the heatproof gloves, avoid puddles of water, and stand as still as possible.

Gaffer Tape   The most popular item to have in a grip kit is **gaffer tape**. Lights (if you're careful) and grip equipment can sometimes be taped to poles, trees, or equipment cases with gaffer tape. Gaffer tape is usually silver or black (preferred) and, although it is sometimes referred to as duct tape, it is not the same thing. Gaffer tape is expensive and has a cloth backing, and while it has good bonding strength, it is much easier to

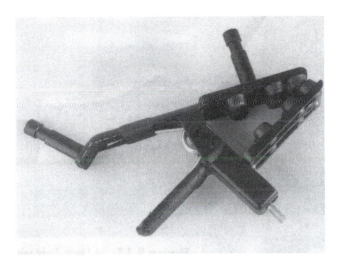

Figure 10-12   An alligator or gaffer clamp with two light studs attached.

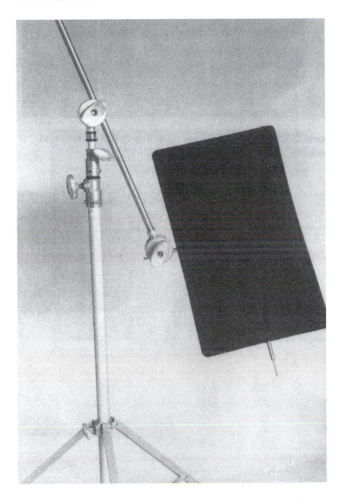

Figure 10-13   A grip head and arm attached to a light stand and holding a flag or solid gobo in place.

remove than duct tape. Gaffer tape is strong, but not nearly as reliable as the gaffer grip. Exercise a considerable amount of caution when using tape to mount lights. Do not forget that lights generate heat on all sides. They can scorch paint and material and can cause a fire. Falling lights break and often explode. If you stick tape to anything, you'd better be able to remove it without removing part of what it's stuck to. Good tape may stick too well to most surfaces. Removing it may also remove paint, wallpaper, floor tiles, or even wood veneer. Removal may leave tape gum deposits on the surface. The owners of the property may not take kindly to your ruining their decor.

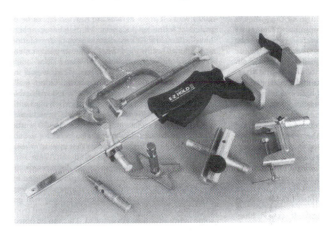

Figure 10-14   Just some of the many clamping devices or "grips" used to attach lights to almost anything.

Modulators

Although some lights have built-in adjustments to allow for focusing the light beam, many that are used for field production do not. When using remote lighting, you must have control over both the amount and size of the light beam. You must also control where the light does and does not fall on the scene you are lighting. In addition to selecting the appropriate fixture for size and function, you must often use additional equipment to maximize light control.

Shaping the Beam

Barndoors   The **barndoors** are rectangular pieces of metal (both two- and four-door) with hinges and are attached to the front of lights to direct the light beam more selectively. Barndoors give you control to prevent light from falling on areas that do not require it or areas that simply should remain in shadow.

Snoots Shaped like a tube or coffee can, a **snoot** contains the light beam in a narrow, circular pattern. Barndoors can be added to the front of the snoot to further control or shape the light. They are useful for lighting very selected areas far from the light itself.

Gobos The **gobos** are similar to barndoors in that they shade or deflect light away from areas that should not be lit. The most popular form of **gobos** is called a **solid** or **flag.** They are commonly rectangular pieces of metal or black cloth in a frame that may be attached to a light mount such as a stand with the use of a grip arm. They are not attached to the light itself. Gobos come in a wide variety of shapes and sizes. Small round ones are called **dots** and **targets** and are used to shade areas within the light-beam's pattern instead of at the edges. Narrow ones are called **cutters**, **fingers**, and **sticks**; these are used when a long, thin shadow is needed in the scene. As they increase to a size big enough to control large light sources such as windows, they are referred to as **teasers**. They are also referred to by where they are placed, such as **toppers, bottomers**, and **siders**. Gobos or flags are the most effective way of controlling light in the cramped spaces of location-shooting, but they usually require more time to set up than the videographer has to spend in ENG situations. A thick black aluminum foil, known as black wrap, is also used to shape light by deflection.

Shaping the Quantity

Dimmers In the TV studio, lights can be dimmed by use of **faders** (lighting controls that electronically reduce light output), but those are rare in most ENG and EFP situations. Some manufactures make field faders or **dimmers** that work with lights up to about 1,000 watts. Larger devices are just too big to be of practical value on location. Many videographers have fashioned their own dimmers out of items found at the local hardware store. Consumer-grade extension cord dimmers made for table and floor lamps can handle lights up to 300 watts, which would include many used in location lighting. Other wall-mounted household dimmers can be wired with cable and made to work as a dimmable extension cord, with careful attention to safety standards. These homemade dimmers

can handle lights up to 500 watts. Carrying consumer dimmers is also good for reducing the output of any table lamps that appear in your shots, which are often too bright.

A word of caution about using dimmers to cut down the amount of light: if the output is reduced by more than 20%, you will notice an appreciable drop in the color temperature of the light; they will get very red. You might also notice a buzzing sound from some lights after they are dimmed. This can be objectionable if the mic picks up the sound. Also, standard dimmers designed for incandescent lights do not work on HMI lights, although many HMI lights have built-in dimmers.

Scrims A wire-mesh screen called a **scrim** can be used on the front of a light to effectively reduce the amount of light from that instrument.

Figure 10-15 A Pepper light with scrims and a gel holder. A half double scrim is on the light.

Scrims come in predictable strengths labeled single (cuts the light by one-half stop) and double (cuts one stop). They also come as full and half. The full covers the entire light and the half just half the light. The half is used to even out the amount of light falling on surfaces that are at an angle to the light. If you wish to throw a slash of light across the wall in the background of a shot, and the only place for the light to be placed is off to the side of the room, you line up the light to form the slash. However, the part of the slash closest to the light is a lot brighter. To even it out you need to position a half scrim over the light with the wire mesh on the side of the light closest to the wall. You have reduced the closest half of the beam, now leaving the entire slash of an even intensity across the wall.

Screens and Nets Similar to scrims, **screens** and **nets** (both refer to the same item) are used out in front of the lights, as opposed to attaching onto them. Made of either metal or fabric mesh, they also come in full and double strengths (again, one-half and one stop, respectively). They are either square or rectangular and usually held in frames, with the smaller ones being open ended or held in a three-sided frame. This reduces the chance of seeing the shadow of the frame when it only partially covers a light. Like gobos, nets are held in place by grip arms or similar means.

Neutral Density One way to reduce the amount of light coming from a fixture is to place a **neutral density (ND)** gel in front of the light. This grayish gel is calibrated to know exactly how much light each one is cutting. The three most popular grades are referred to as N3, N6, and N9. N3 (1/2 ND) allows a 50% transmission of light, which is a one-stop reduction. N6 (1/4 ND) has only a 25% transmission, or two stops less light. And N9 (1/8 ND) has a 12.5% transmission, or three stops less light.

These gels do not diffuse or change the color of the light in any way. ND gel also comes in large sheets and rolls for covering windows in rooms or cars to reduce the light coming through those windows and to match interior light levels. ND gel can also be combined with color-correcting gel to match interior light temperatures as well.

Shaping the Quality

One of the quickest and easiest ways to increase the quality of light is, as we learned earlier, by increasing the size of the source. There are many ways of doing that.

Umbrella Lighting The most common way to produce a very soft-quality light is to attach an umbrella to it. Umbrellas are a must in any portable lighting kit. They are attached to the light housing so that the light is aimed directly into the umbrella. (See Figure 10-16.) The light housing is aimed away from the subject, but the shiny underside of the umbrella reflects the light onto the subject.

Broad lights make the best umbrella sources, but spotlights in a flooded position can be used. The re-

flective surface then returns the light past the housing and onto the subject. Umbrellas are made with silver reflective surfaces to bounce the light, but some are made of silk so the user may face the umbrella in either direction to get reflected light or diffused direct light. Others have a blue reflective surface to turn tungsten light into a daylight color.

Soft Boxes Several companies make boxes that cover almost any light fixture. They have a diffusion material over the front of them to soften and increase the size of the source. Generally referred to as **soft boxes**, these tools are very common in both the film and video industries. Their design allows them to be more easily controlled than other forms of soft light by attaching **baffles** (rigid material attached to the front sides of the box that help shape the light beam) and **egg crates** or **louvers** (a grid of material placed over the front of the diffusion surface that contains the spread of the light by forming the beam into a shaft of light).

Figure 10-16   Broad light with an umbrella.

The next position for diffusion is *just* in front of the light. By stretching diffusion over the front of the open barndoors, or on a small frame made to fit close to the light, the effective source can be made larger still. But with this arrangement, it is now harder to contain the light's beam. Remember, too, that anything that comes in contact with a light must be made of fireproof material.

Figure 10-17   The Lowel Rifa light comes with a soft box to diffuse light.

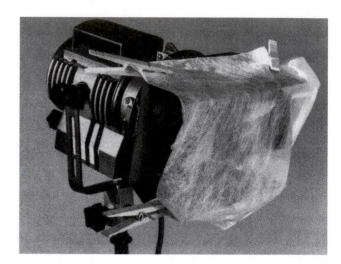

Figure 10-18   Spun glass can be stretched across the front of a light and held in place by clothespins to create a diffused light source.

The actual diffusion material is usually some type of flameproof gel, spun glass, or frosted glass. Frosted glass is usually placed over the opening of the light housing. Its use is limited in field production because of its breakable nature. Several companies make a multitude of diffusion materials. Don't be fooled by some of the names, such as **tracing paper, soft frost,** and **shower curtain**. These products are designed to be used with hot lights. Do not use homemade or nonprofessional materials anywhere near a light. Some of the most popular materials are **opal**, **tough frost**, **tough spun** (spun glass), **216**, and **brushed silk**. Competing companies can have different names for the same material.

Silks and Butterflies Just like the cloud over the sun, the further out front the diffusion material is from the source, the more diffused the light. **Silks** have the same type of frames used by nets and gobos, either three- or four-sided. Silks are a very white silk material

that passes light at a known rate. A full silk transmits 50% of the light. They also come in half, quarter, and eighth strengths. When the size of a silk becomes larger than a 4-foot square, the silk is usually called a **butterfly** (6-foot square) or **overhead** (12-foot square or more). These larger sizes need to be attached to more than one stand and, if used outdoors, carefully weighted to avoid wind gusts blowing them over.

Reflectors Unlike flags, **reflectors** have a light-colored surface that reflects light into desired areas rather than blocking it from certain areas. Reflectors can be stiff boards, metal, or even light-colored cloth, and can come in sizes ranging from a six-inch square to panels six-feet square. Far and away the most popular form of the reflector is the circular flex-type cloth using a highly reflective silver material on one side and a bright white material on the other. These reflectors can be mounted, but are generally handheld by the cameraperson or other crew members and are usually used to reflect light onto nonmoving subjects, such as a reporter appearing on camera. No lighting kit should be without this inexpensive but invaluable tool. (See Figure 10-20.)

White Cards One of the simplest forms of bounced light comes from the common picture-mounting material called **foamcore**. This is a thin layer of Styrofoam sandwiched between two layers of very white, heavy paper to form rigid cards in sizes ranging from a couple of feet square to six- by eight-foot sheets. These

Figure 10-19   A full, open-ended silk used to soften and reduce the direct sunlight falling on the subject.

inexpensive cards can be cut to size, mounted by almost any means because they weigh nothing, and used to reflect any light source from tungsten to the sun.

Walls and Ceilings Finding material to bounce light off is easy to find. Start by looking around the room you will be shooting in. Because white is the most popular color for most walls and ceilings in both homes and offices, they make good bounce surfaces. Of course, any surface can be used to reflect light to some degree. The one word of caution is to be conscious of the color of the surface. A light blue wall will reflect that blue onto the subject. Try to always use just white surfaces, and always remember to white balance for that bounced light: it will not be the same temperature as the direct light.

Figure 10-20   A collapsible reflector provides enough light to fill in the subject's shadows.

Shaping the Color Quality

In addition to changing the *amount* of light that comes from an instrument, we can also manipulate the *color* of light by placing a colored, heat-proof, cellophane-like material over the front of the lighting instrument. This modulator is called a **gel** and is common in EFP work. Many lights have **gel frames** that attach to the housing. Color gels can be divided into two categories: *color correction* and *color elimination*. The most common correction gel used in video production is the **daylight blue**, which converts tungsten light to a daylight temperature.

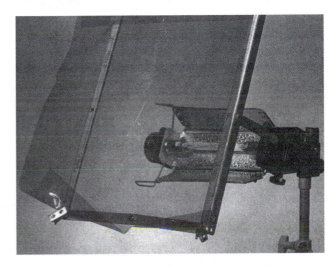

Figure 10-21   Light with daylight blue gel in frame.

Daylight blue gel is often called a **CTB (color temperature blue)** and comes in several strengths: full, half, quarter, and eighth. Another use for this gel is matching the color temperature of a TV screen. Most color TVs have a temperature of nearly 9,000° K. For the camera to see true colors on any TV set picture in the shot, you will need to correct any lights you're using to a high-color temperature (or make the TV's picture very red to compensate for the lights). A full CTB gel on a tungsten light will raise the temperature of the light to match daylight.

Another popular and useful gel is the **CTO (color temperature orange)**. It also comes in various strengths. This gel shifts the light from high temperatures to low. A full CTO changes daylight to a tungsten temperature. This gel can be used on HMI lights to match tungsten ones or used in large sheets to cover windows converting the daylight streaming in to the same color as your video lights. Most often, this gel is used in lower strengths to simply warm the light after you have white balanced for the uncorrected sources. By white balancing for the main light in the scene, you can add a quarter or eighth CTO to give skin tones a slightly redder (warmer) tone.

Color-elimination gels remove all or most of the color from a light source except the color of that gel. A green gel casts only green light (unlike CTOs and CTBs, which only shift the temperature of the light). For instance, a primary-green gel covering a light allows the transmission of virtually no red wavelengths. A white sign with red lettering will appear as a green sign with black lettering under this light. The red pigment contains no green and therefore can't reflect that color, and the green light is simply absorbed and leaves the lettering to appear as black. This type of gel can come in any color or shade of color. Except for the primary-color gels, most color-elimination gels do transmit a little of all wavelengths so objects will retain some of their natural color. Using a light-green gel (nonprimary) on lights used to illuminate foliage in the shot can make the leaves stand out without discoloring areas around them too much.

Some Technical Considerations

Nothing is worse than setting lights for a shoot only to have them suddenly go out due to a blown fuse. If you're in a commercial building, that event cannot only be bad for you but for other tenants, workers, and customers. To add to the misery, you may not know where the circuit board is located, and it may take a maintenance person to open it. Valuable time can be lost and bad feelings can start to grow. Before you attempt any location lighting, you must have a thorough understanding of the amount of power required and whether or not you have that amount available for use.

Volts and Amps

Most of the lights you will be using out in the field run on 110 to 120 volts AC—normal household current. Only battery-powered lights use direct current (DC), which is why the bulbs from indoor lights are not interchangeable with battery-powered light bulbs. You should be able to figure out how much current is needed to power your indoor lights. The amount of current available is measured in amperes (amps) and multiplied by volts, giving you the power expressed in watts. The equation would therefore be:

watts = volts ✕ *amps*

It can be remembered as: **W**est **V**irgini**A**. Because each of your lights has a watt rating, you can figure the amps needed for each light. This equation would be:

amps = watts / volts

To build in a safety factor, it is a good practice to use 100 as the voltage, even though it may really be 120. Any long extension cable runs can increase the amount of amps and, unless you figure that in, put you in danger of an overload. If you wish to put up two 600-watt lights in a room, you would divide 1,200 watts by 100 volts to find that 12 amps of power are needed to safely run the two lights.

Most homes and offices have electrical outlets divided into many separate circuits. In an older house, each circuit may be only 15 amps, yet have several outlets (in different rooms) on that circuit. Most modern homes and offices have more circuits with fewer outlets per circuit, and each circuit has 20 amps. This means you should never have more than 2,000 watts on any one circuit. Finding more than one circuit may be difficult. The first place to start is by finding the circuit breaker box for the area you are working in—a good idea if you plan on using more than one light. The circuits may be labeled in the box. If they are not, and you need more than 20 amps, try to find outlets as far from each other as possible to increase your chances of getting two separate circuits. Make sure that you have some heavy duty extension cords to route your lights to other circuits. Also, you should check to see if anything else is being used on the circuit you are using. A coffee maker in use can limit the amps available to you. If you know you will be working in an older home where fuses may still be in use, have spare fuses available.

Avoiding Overloads

For on-location shoots that require a lot of power, you may want to rent a generator. Many types of generators made for TV and movie work can supply power with little or no noise. Electricity is dangerous, and should be dealt with accordingly. Make sure all fixtures are grounded, do not stand in water while touching anything connected to the power, and do not overload any system you are using. Some lights are only meant to be used with bulbs under a specific wattage. Many extension cords are made to carry only a certain number of amps. The length of the cable also determines how much of a load can be carried. A 2,000-watt light with 200 feet of cable would need an 8-gauge wire (sometimes just called #8). The lower the number, the *more* amps it can carry. A 500-watt light could use a 16-gauge cable to go 100 feet. The more wattage you use, the smaller the gauge number should be; the longer the cable run, the smaller the gauge number. Note that the smaller the gauge number, the thicker the cable. All the cables should be three-wire cables. An overheated cable or light housing can easily start a fire.

PART THREE: BASIC LIGHTING TECHNIQUE

The Starting Point: Exposure

In every shooting situation, indoors or outdoors, the first thing a good videographer looks at is the amount of light available. There may be enough to shoot in or you may need to add some of your own. How much is enough? Relying on auto-iris to set your exposure can lead to some undesirable shots. Knowing how to set the proper exposure on any scene without the help of the automatic functions is a requirement in the professional world.

Base Lighting

One of the drawbacks to early video photography was that the video camera required a large amount of light to record a good image. Unlike film cameras that can use extremely light-sensitive film stock, or developing procedures that maximize a small amount of light, the light sensitivity of video cameras was limited by the quality and sensitivity of the pickup tube, a component not subject to easy replacement or change. Therefore, the first requirement in video lighting was to provide the camera's pickup tube with a quantity of light large enough to enable the camera to function properly. This minimum level is called the **base light**.

Today's CCD chip cameras require very little base light to make a good picture. However, "very little" does not mean no light. Base light should be thought of as the minimum light required for shooting. The scene always looks better, especially in EFP work, if the light levels are somewhat above the base. The first requirement in lighting a scene is to make sure you have enough base light on every area of the scene for which you wish to see detail. Areas with less than base light (like shadows) appear gray or black in the picture, which may be desirable. By knowing your camera's ASA or lux rating, you can determine the base-light level in foot-candles or lux for any f-stop you use. Lux is a measure of light quantity used in countries that use the metric system and has become the standard measurement for judging video camera sensitivity. **10.74**

lux is equal to 1 foot-candle. A typical professional digital camera available for ENG or EFP applications, the Sony DVW790WA, requires 2,000 lux at f9 for an acceptable image. (Less light is required if you use a lower f-stop setting.)

Finding the Correct Exposure

Exposure is both a scientific and subjective point. A light meter can show you how much light you have on your subject and therefore help guide you to the proper exposure. You can put the camera on automatic iris and let it tell you what the exposure should be. But just as filmmakers decide *what* subject and *where* to measure the light to achieve the end result they want for the film's look, a videographer must also choose to go beyond the auto-iris to get aesthetically pleasing results. The proper exposure for a piece of white paper shot full frame may be without argument, but the correct exposure of someone sitting in front of a window may be quite subjective.

The problems of not enough light are easy enough for most beginners to notice. The low-light picture is muddy, dull, and seems to be of all the same shade of gray in the viewfinder. Most of the newer portable cameras have a signal of some kind that alerts the camera operator to a potential low-light problem. This indicator is sometimes a **light-emitting diode (LED)** that glows when there is insufficient signal level output from the camera. A slightly different version of this type of indicator is a white line across the picture that indicates either too much signal (requiring a reduction in iris opening), a proper operating range (requiring no iris setting change), or too little signal (necessitating an increase in iris opening or a general increase of light on the scene). Many other aids that help find the right exposure are visible in the viewfinder of different cameras, such as the zebra stripes in all professional cameras.

The problems of too much light being let into the camera can be difficult for many first-time video shooters. They may think the picture is better when everything is bright and you can see details in all the shadow areas of the picture. It usually is not. *Overexposure usually shows up as the loss of detail in the brighter areas.* Areas of the picture or subjects within the picture that become overexposed start to lose texture and

definition. The writing on a white piece of paper starts to disappear as the paper is overexposed. If that paper is on a desktop in your shot, you may indeed have to overexpose it to get the proper exposure for the entire picture. As we shall see a little later, it's the contrast ratio that helps determine what the proper exposure should be.

Use of High Gain

Use of the high-gain circuit increases the sensitivity of the pickup device, thus increasing the range of light in which the video camera can supply an image. However, use of this additional amplification enhances the noise, or graininess, in the video as well. The resulting picture often appears somewhat grainy, and darker areas of the frame are muddy and have confetti-like specks of color. Scenes or stories shot in high gain that are edited or duplicated on a linear editing (analog) system will suffer noticeably, because some video information (and thus quality) is lost in the process.

Obviously, some ENG stories must be shown despite minor video flaws. Unfortunately, too many important news stories occur at night. Shooting these stories requires as much boost to the lighting situation as possible. The 12- or 30-volt battery-powered portable light that is often used gives acceptable illumination only on subjects 6 to 20 feet from the camera. When shooting outdoors at night, these battery-powered lights offer only a little help on large scenes, but they are still necessary. The 6- or 9-dB gain is quite often used when more light is needed but cannot be added. Because of the graininess of the resulting video image, the 12- or 18-dB gain should be used only on very important shots that cannot be done any other way. Some new professional digital cameras have gain controls up to +48 dB, which should only be used for very special shots in very low light situations.

These large gain enhancements may be used at night to record objects at a distance or in special situations—for example, when the lights would interfere with the actions of a SWAT team's operation, or when shooting a nature film about nocturnal animals. The resulting video will be noisy and the video level (the amount of video signal) will probably be low, but there is a common procedure to improve the look of the picture. When the tape is played or edited, the chroma level can be lowered on the shots done at low light and high gain. Lowering this level causes the colored, confetti-like speckles in the darker areas of the picture to lose their color. This technique produces a nearly black-and-white picture, but since our eyes see very little color at night, the loss of some chroma is not objectionable. However, the brighter areas of the picture retain some chroma, and the perception of overall noise in the picture is greatly reduced.

Contrast Ratio

Unlike the human eye, video cameras are severely restricted in their ability to perceive large variations of brightness within a given scene. When extremely bright objects are framed with very dark objects, many video cameras do not reproduce details well in either the light or dark areas. Excessively bright areas, such as a pure white shirt, may tend to glow and appear otherworldly. Very dark portions of the screen may be muddy and lack detail, resulting in an unappealing, two-dimensional image.

In an overall scene, most video cameras can properly show bright areas that are no more than 20 times brighter than the darkest areas of that scene. The typical film used in motion pictures has a contrast range of about 200:1, and our eye sees at about 1,000:1. This is the primary reason that film looks better than tape. In a film shot, the brightest part of the frame can be 200 times brighter than the darkest part and the detail in both areas should be visible. This allows very dramatic lighting to heighten suspense and drama. Our eyes see the best of all and are able to see very bright and very dark objects in the same "frame." As technology improves the contrast range of video, the quality of the look will increase dramatically. But for the present, it is still a good rule of thumb to stick with the 20:1 rule for video contrast. For example, if when using a reflective or **spotlight meter** you measure the reflected light from the brightest area of the picture and it is equal to 400 foot-candles, then any area of the picture reflecting less than 20 fc of light is beyond your camera's contrast range (400:20 is equal to 20:1).

A piece of typical white paper reflects 60% of the light that strikes it, whereas black paint reflects only 3%. White plaster, however, reflects 90%. If you have 200 fc of light falling on a white plaster wall in a scene, it will reflect 180 fc. A dark brown chair in that scene reflects only 6 fc, which is beyond your 20:1 contrast range. If you expose for the wall, the chair becomes underexposed, even though the same amount of light is striking it. *Therefore, you must keep in mind not only the amount of light striking the objects, but also their ability to reflect that light.* Going back to our earlier example of the white paper on the desktop, if the shot is of a person sitting at a dark wood desk in a dark suit, then the proper exposure for the overall shot would have the paper overexposed, because it falls outside the contrast ratio of the main subject. The darker areas would need to be seen more than the paper.

These considerations demonstrate why it can be very difficult to expose for two subjects in the same scene when one is in the shade and one is in the sun. When using a TV camera, you try to expose for the brightest area, but the difference in brightness between objects in both sun and shade can be well over 200:1. Exposing for the brightly lit person sends the other into darkness, and exposing for the darker one causes a total loss of detail in the bright one.

In a practical sense, videographers must watch out for bright/dark combinations in every shot. The contrast ratio problem becomes more apparent when the brightest and darkest areas of the scene are right next to each other or where one is much larger than the other. If your subject is wearing a bright white shirt and dark trousers, suggest lighter trousers or a pastel shirt. White blouses can be less harmful to the overall look if partially covered by a scarf or jacket. A small area of overexposure is much less noticeable.

A dark-skinned subject can present problems to a video camera operator. A light-colored shirt and light background can make a proper exposure difficult. In daytime shooting, extra light is often necessary to brighten the subject's facial features. You must pay close attention to lighting and background to avoid having a dark-skinned face blend in with the background.

Do not forget that an extremely dark or extremely light portion of the screen can often be compensated for by an iris adjustment. The problem arises when two extremes appear in the same shot. If you cannot get detail in both areas of the picture at the same time, find a way to adjust the shot to reduce the amount of too light or too dark areas, or adjust the lighting to reduce the contrast ratio. (See Figure 10-22)

In ENG work, you are often forced to work with shots that have more than a 20:1 contrast ratio. An example might be an interview with a tall plane-crash eyewitness wearing a hat on a heavily overcast day. The white sky reflects large quantities of light, but the shaded face of the subject reflects very little light. The contrast ratio between sky and face will be far in excess of 20:1. The iris must be pushed, or opened, beyond what the overall picture requires, to get the face to show on tape with some detail. In this case, the background will be overexposed. If the background is overexposed, the edges of the subject's face may be undefined, making the subject look abnormal.

Figure 10-22   In this scene, the proper exposure for the overall frame leaves the subject in the dark. Light should be added to the subject.

There are some possible solutions in this case, however:

- Try to find a dark background—for example, against a wall, fire truck, or tree.

- Frame the subject's face as tightly as possible to reduce the amount of background in the shot, thereby reducing the overall contrast in the shot.

- Anticipate these conditions and use a camera-mounted battery light with a dichroic filter

(converts 3,200° K light to 5,600° K) to brighten the face. Even without the filter, the extra light on the subject's face will help the contrast, despite being too red; for ENG work, a reddish face is certainly better than no face at all.

In ENG, if you do not get the shot, a competitor probably will. It is your job to find a way to make the shot work with few technical distractions. In some ENG situations, you may have to shoot despite adverse lighting conditions, because the story is too important to miss. The audio may be usable, even if the video is not. As chip cameras get better, it is possible to drive the contrast to greater extremes and not have the picture look bad. In fact, in many EFP projects, overexposure of certain areas of the frame is a specific style. Overexposure can be used as a creative force if done with purpose. A shaft of sunlight coming through a window can blow out (overexpose) part of the picture or even part of the subject to show the intensity of that light or draw the viewer's attention to the light and thus to the subject.

Increasing the Quality through Contrast

The flat lighting created by the light very near or on the camera puts no shadows on a subject's face, nor does it show tone differences on a subject's face. After a tape with this type of lighting is dubbed (copied) in an analog system (nondigital), the resolution begins to decrease and, because there is no contrast to the subject's features, the face begins to disappear completely. The face washes out and has no texture or features. Historically, news stations often aired third- or fourth-generation analog dubs. The quality of these was already lower than the original tape, and if the lighting is very flat the picture would have almost no detail.

High-quality professional video cameras can "see" a 100:1 contrast ratio or more, but tape limitations and a 10:1 home TV set contrast ratio force the videographer to keep contrast ratios low. Most home TV sets have only a 10:1 ratio because of high levels of room light. This is one more reason for keeping the lighting ratios within about 20:1 for the overall scene, and even less for the subject itself—but *some contrast is always necessary.* There should be light and dark areas in the picture and the topography of the subject's face must be clearly distinguishable. Having shadows—the modeling effect—adds texture and more of a three-dimensional feeling to a picture, which makes it is easier to see on the home screen and therefore easier to watch.

There are some things you can control so that the picture showing at home is as close as possible to the way things are. For example, you may think you are changing the picture too much by setting up several lights. You probably are not, however, if the end result is a picture with light levels high enough to properly expose the picture, a contrast ratio in the proper range, and a picture that looks natural and pleasing to the viewer. Because the camera does not see things in the same way you do, you must help it to see that way by adding or adjusting lights.

The Art of Casting Shadows

You should now know what light is, how it travels, what creates it, and the tools for controlling it. Now you need to know how to use light to your advantage beyond just providing enough light for the camera. Too often, ENG and even some EFP shooters rely on just a camera-mounted light to give them exposure. This is certainly necessary in adverse conditions, but it lacks character and artistic purpose. The purpose of good lighting is to cast shadows. The absence of shadows—flat lighting—adds nothing to a viewer's visual understanding of the shot or scene. The world around us is literally defined by shadows. Without them we could no longer see depth or texture. We couldn't even tell the time of day without a watch. During a shoot, you will need to light many different scenes indoors and outdoors, both to control contrast for the camera and to help the viewer better see what story the pictures are telling. Although each lighting situation is unique, there are some fundamental guidelines you can follow that will help you light any scene.

Basic Theory

The History of Lighting

Most of what we know about lighting comes from a single period of art history. A painter named Caravag-

gio in the early 1600s developed a style of painting that used shadows to express depth on the two-dimensional canvas. An admirer of his went on to perfect this style and become one of the most famous painters in history: Rembrandt van Rijn (1606–1669). This painter from the seventeenth century created a way of working with light and shadow that transcended its own time and medium and survived well into modern times. The technique is called **chiaroscuro**, an Italian word meaning "light–dark." Rembrandt's paintings have very clear—but not necessarily visible—sources of light that only illuminate selected parts of the frame. Even his outdoor scenes make use of clouds and their shadows to provide areas of light and dark within the picture. Rembrandt's style depicted light sources as being natural. Light in his paintings—as in life—could only come from a naturally-occurring source. No one has ever found a better way of lighting since. There are three main characteristics of chiaroscuro lighting, as discussed below.

The Source and Intensity of Light There is only one apparent light source that selectively lights only parts of the scene. The overall illumination is low—called low-key lighting—and the overall background is darker than the subject of the shot.

Shadow Direction and Fall-off Dense, attached shadows make the direction of the light readily apparent. The quick fall-off or diminishing of the light's intensity before reaching the background allows darker areas of the frame to dominate, thus directing the viewer's eye to the lighter areas, that is, the subject.

Object Texture This highly directional light source accentuates the texture and form of objects in the frame. Faces, clothing, furniture, walls, and even dust in the air take on a three-dimensional quality.

Chiaroscuro lighting can convey both high and low emotional intensity. The quantity of dark and light areas helps determine what the perception will be. This type of lighting uses a low-key technique, usually a Fresnel spot with barndoors, and very little fill. The background is usually lit with other very directional, narrow beam lights to control the amount of the scene receiving light. Chiaroscuro lighting intensifies the three-dimensional properties of the subjects, clarifies the space around them, and gives an emotional quality to the scene. The particular emotional quality should be selected based on the subject you are photographing in ENG work and on what the script calls for in EFP. Each lighting setup should have a predetermined goal beyond making a good exposure for the camera. Chiaroscuro lighting is the basis for almost all the motivational lighting you will do.

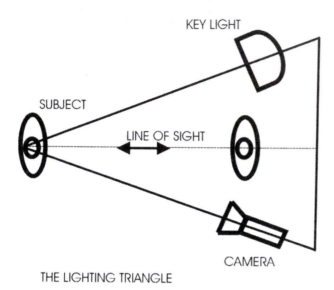

KEY LIGHT

SUBJECT

LINE OF SIGHT

CAMERA

THE LIGHTING TRIANGLE

Figure 10-23 This is the basic lighting triangle formula that will give a chiaroscuro look. This idea can be applied to almost any situation.

The Rembrandt Way

Chiaroscuro lighting is now more popularly known as **Rembrandt lighting**. There are a few simple tricks to getting the flavor of the master in anything you light. By sticking with these principles, you can't go wrong. As we said, after nearly 400 years, nobody has come up with a better way. These five points can be used as a guideline to Rembrandt lighting:

- Place the key light, or angle the subject, so the shadowed side of the subject is closest to the camera (so it appears the subject is looking into the direction of the light but not at it).

- Move the subject away from the background.

- Look for a dark background.

- Make the subject the brightest and/or biggest area of the shot.

- Have the darkest area of the background directly behind the subject.

This theory can work for everything—not just for setting up lights but in simply positioning subjects in any shot. Our plane-crash witness mentioned earlier can have a chiaroscuro feel by positioning his head in the shot against the dark foliage of a tree and having him face in the direction of the flashing fire truck lights. The red lights become the subliminal key light source giving texture to his face, even though they do not overpower the diffused daylight. The dark tree makes his face the brightest area of the picture. This is simple and quick, yet it meets the artistic standards of Rembrandt on a very basic level.

A

B

Figure 10-24 (A) A simple example of Rembrandt lighting: dark shadows and background, with a single motivating light source opposing the direction of the subject. (B) The lighting setup used to create the Rembrandt scene.

A   **B**   **C**

Figure 10-25   (A) Key light only. (B) Key and fill light. (C) Key, fill, and back light.

Zone Lighting

Along the same lines as chiaroscuro lighting, **zone lighting** selectively lights only certain areas of the picture, which are divided into zones by distance from the camera. This is usually the foreground, midground, and background. The subject is usually in the midground. Each of these areas is lit separately, with dark or shadow areas separating them. This technique helps to create a three-dimensional look and draw the eye to whatever you wish to emphasize in the frame.

Formal Lighting

Three-Point Lighting

The technique of three-point lighting has been used for years in both professional TV and photography studios. It is based on the principles of chiaroscuro, but doesn't try to disguise the artificiality of the light. This method of lighting is simple but effective for many situations that call for lighting a particular subject or object. Three carefully placed directional lights—the key light, the fill light, and the backlight—can light a subject in a way that provides an appropriate level of base light for the video camera; gives sufficient shadow for definition of shape, size, and texture; and separates the subject from surrounding objects and the background. The three-point technique is appropriate in most ENG or EFP situations to satisfy basic lighting needs. Figure 10-25 displays the same shot under three different lighting conditions.

Figure 10-26 gives guidelines for light placement in a situation in which the subject is facing the camera.

Key Light   As the name implies, the **key light** is the most important light and is, therefore, placed first. The key light should be the brightest and most directional. A key light placed on the camera-subject axis (right over the top of the camera) produces a very flat, shadowless picture. In most cases, this is not flattering to the subject.

Start with these guidelines for placing the key light:

- Place it anywhere from 10° to 90° off the camera–subject axis, depending on the effect or look you are creating.

- For a subject not facing directly toward the camera, focus the key light on the opposite side of the subject's face from the camera position.

- Elevate the light above the subject at about a 45° angle from the camera-subject plane.

The key light creates a strong shadow, sometimes called the **draw**, on the subject's face. This is known as the **modeling effect**. The photographer is responsible for bringing the viewer's attention to the most important aspect(s) of the screen. Since the audience is naturally drawn to the brightest part of the screen, and since the key light illuminates an area so brightly, the key light is used to focus the viewer's attention. For subjects not looking directly into the camera, the key light should be the light that the subject faces toward, but not at—thus, the short side of the face (the side away from the camera) is lit by the key. Focusing the key light on the long side of your subject (the side nearest the camera) makes it seem like the subject is looking away from the light. This gives the appearance of subject discomfort or avoidance, which can be misleading, distracting, or unpleasant for the viewer. It also casts the draw, or shadow, out of view for the camera, thus losing the three-dimensional effect.

Fill Light   The next light to set when using the three-point lighting technique is the **fill light**, located at an angle about 10° to 45° from the camera on the opposite side of the camera from the key. Again, the light should be placed above the subject to give a more normal appearance. In studio TV, the fill light is often a scoop or a Fresnel spot adjusted to give a wide or flooded-out beam. These types of lights are preferable because they are less harsh and soften shadows created by the key light without eliminating them. Unfortunately, portable kits rarely contain scoops or other diffused lights. Typically, portable kits have small spotlights without lenses. Since the key and fill lights are usually of equal strength in portable kits, the fill is often placed at a slightly greater distance from the subject, resulting in a less intense light for fill (remember the inverse square rule!).

Many portable kits have adjustable lights that allow the light to be pinned to a narrow beam to give sharp, bright light or flooded to give a softer, less bright light. For example, the fill light could be set at a distance from the subject equal to the key light and set in the flooded or wide position, and the key could be pinned. *As a general rule, your key light should be twice as bright as your fill (a 2:1 ratio), but a key that is four times as bright as the fill (a 4:1 ratio) is not uncommon.* The combination of properly set key and fill lights should give enough base light for the video camera to operate at an acceptable level and create a perception of depth, giving your subject a three-dimensional quality.

Backlight   The third light in the three-point lighting technique is the **backlight**. The primary purpose of this light is to separate the subject from the background by highlighting or framing the subject with a rim of light. The backlight is most often a spot, both in the studio and in the field. It is focused on the back of the subject and aimed so it's not shining into the camera lens. Barndoors are a must on backlights. The

light is placed directly opposite the key light, behind and above the subject at an angle of about 45°. It is not unusual for a backlight to be as strong as the key light for a key–fill–back ratio of 2:1:2. A more subtle 2:1:1 is the most common choice. Because the effect of a backlight as seen from the camera position is more reflection than illumination, the strength of the backlight must be considered in relationship to the subject or object being lit. A person with golden blond hair will reflect a great deal of the backlight toward the camera, so only a little is needed. A person with a lot of very black hair can absorb a great deal of light and may need a very strong beam from the backlight. There's a saying among cinematographers that a backlight should be felt and not seen. It is best to judge the strength of the backlight with your eyes and get the brightness just to the point where it is noticeable.

Adding to Three-Point Lighting

Other light placements are common in the photographic world, and a good TV videographer should take advantage of their availability. With a minimum of setup time, you can properly light most ENG and EFP assignments using the basic light kit. Three lights are more than adequate to light any medium-sized meeting room or interview. With the addition of a couple of extra lights and some accessories, creativity need not take a back seat to expediency.

Background Light   The **background light**, or fourth light, is often used to locate the subject in the set, that is, to show the relationship of the subject to the background. The placement of this light can vary, but the idea is to illuminate part of the background to show its texture, shape, and depth relative to the subject. It may be extra trouble to purchase, carry, and set a fourth light, but it becomes very important when you must videotape a subject with dark hair or a dark shirt against a dark background. The fourth light can give the viewer a better understanding of volume of the location that is shown within the shot.

One way to use a background light is to light the area directly behind the subject if the subject is centered, or on the empty side of the frame if the subject is not centered. But it should not light the entire background, only a portion of it. Many times a well-placed background light can be substituted for a back-

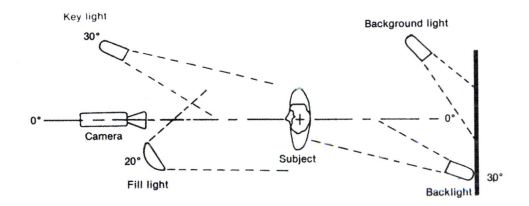

The standard three-point lighting setup with an added background light.

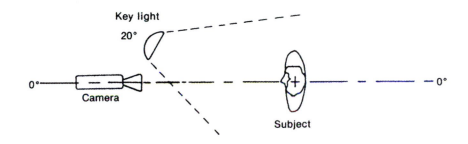

A single light source should be near the camera and flooded as much as possible.

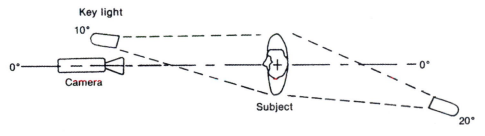

When only two lights are used, the combination of the key and back is effective.

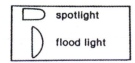

Figure 10-26   Light placement when the subject faces the camera.

A   **B**   **C**

Figure 10-27   Some examples of interview lighting using the three-point lighting principle: (A) a single hard source creates a serious tone, (B) a single soft source creates a more relaxed feel, (C) a soft key light and a backlight create and easy but formal look.

light to achieve subject/background separation. This is also the light that can add special effects to the scene. For example, you can make the background interesting by using a cookie or another shadow-forming device placed in front of a narrow-beam background light. A very common technique in movies is to use a Venetian or mini-blinds effect. A slotted pattern on the background light gives the effect of window light coming through blinds. The light serves its purpose by giving highlight and detail to the background while also making it seem natural. Experiment with background lights using different patterns and also different directions.

Kicker Light   An additional light often used in EFP is the **kicker light**. It is a light set from a low angle to the side of the subject and slightly behind. Its purpose is to highlight the subject's hair or face. The kicker is often used in hair product commercials to add a glamorous look. In drama scenes, the kicker is used to denote time of day. A very soft, flat kicker on an actor's face represents early morning or late evening, while a hard, spotted kicker says midday.

Eye Light   In some dramatic EFP presentations, you can use a small, highly directional light to illuminate a subject's eyes. The **eye light** is usually a lower wattage lamp aimed at the eyes from the camera position. It is used to direct audience attention to the facial expression of the subject. This light in a more subtle form is sometimes called an **obie light**. The name comes from the silent movie star Merle Oberon, who had her cameraman use a light mounted on top of the camera to shine directly on her face and nowhere else. This flattened her lighting and minimized her wrinkles. Today,

the eye light or obie is used to fill shadows in facial creases and give a reflective sparkle in the subject's eyes.

Lighting with Color

For most work in EFP and ENG, keeping the color of light the same from all sources in a scene is the standard. However, for creative work, you will find yourself mixing colors of light more and more. By knowing what color any particular light source is, you can predict how it will look on the screen when added to your shot. If you are doing an interview inside a room during the day, but for some reason you wish it to look as though it were night, you may light the subject with tungsten, balance for that, and let some daylight spill into the background. The area lit by sunlight will appear blue, similar to that of moonlight (as used in TV and movies), especially if the daylight is of a much lower intensity than your key light. You may use daylight from a large window as your key on a subject, but tungsten as the backlight to give the hair a warm glow. Once you have mastered the idea of color temperature, you can balance the camera for any key light and paint the rest of the picture with color created by temperature or gels or both. You will quickly find that the use of CTO and CTB on backlights, background lights, and even kickers gives your pictures a creative edge.

Natural Lighting

As cameras have gotten better and better over the years, popular lighting styles have changed. No longer

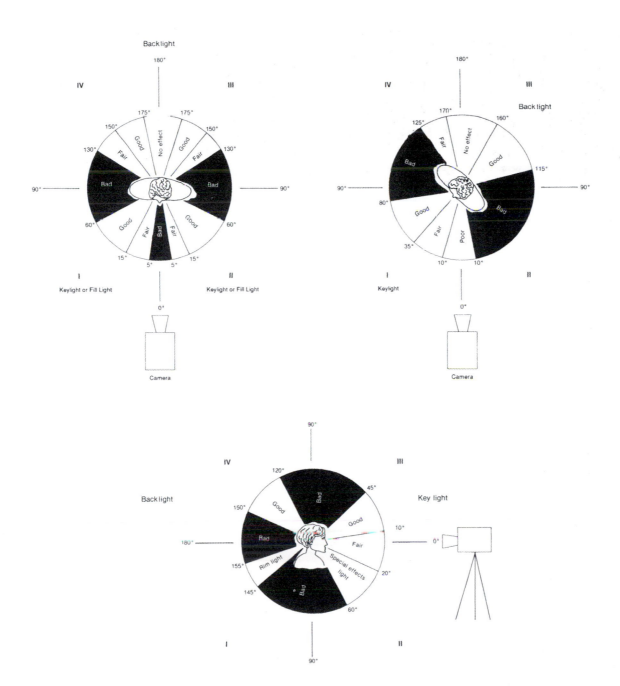

Figure 10-28 Use these lighting zones as general guidelines. They may not apply to recreating natural lighting, special effects, or creative lighting, but do deal with formal portraiture lighting.

is it necessary to bombard a subject with a huge amount of light to get proper exposure. Artificial light has become something that is simply added and manipulated primarily to suit the needs of the videographer, not the camera. Three-point lighting looks like something from the studio. Since location shooting is

all about being on location and having it look that way, finding alternatives to this formal approach to lighting would only make sense. Using some of the techniques mentioned below, you can create a pleasing natural light with soft shadows that meets your lighting requirements without disturbing the natural look

Figure 10-29   Putting light on the background opposite the subject adds interest, separation, and motivation for the key light and the mood.

Figure 10-30   The kicker gives a stronger jaw line and a more natural look.

of your location shoot. It also takes you a step closer to the style of the master, Rembrandt.

Adding to Existing Light

Too often, hundreds of pounds of delicate lighting equipment are bounced around in a truck then laboriously set up, only to result in a scene that looks as if it could have been shot in the studio. The addition of artificial lighting often gives an artificial look to a remote scene and destroys the natural appearance of a location setting. If the subjects can easily perform or be interviewed in the studio, why bother hauling out the remote equipment? One reason for a remote shoot is to preserve the natural environment of the subject. Some-

times there is the need for minimum base-level lighting. Some situations simply demand additional light. The best way to fulfill the technical requirements of the video camera is to *add* to the existing light without overpowering it. Unlike studio scenes, in which three-point lighting is the standard, many locations only need to have the existing light levels raised to produce a pleasing, well lit scene.

Preserving Color Temperature   By taking what you learned about color temperature, you can size up the color of any scene. Whether it's daylight streaming through the windows (5,600° K), ambient reflected daylight coming in (6,500° K), or just household lamps (2,800° K), you should now know how to adjust your lights to match the natural light in the scene. You may wish to use the natural light as the key and use your lights as the fill, back, or background sources.

Preserving a Natural Look   To preserve the natural look of the location, keep the direction of the natural key light the same as it was without enhancement. If there isn't enough natural light to satisfy base requirements, add your light source near to or in line with the existing light source. If your additional lighting produces shadows that are too dark, fill light may be necessary. The fill light should be as subtle as possible, such as using bounced light, but bright enough to fill the shadows. Many times, the light at the location is nondirectional or flat, as in an office building, so the additional lighting you provide should also lack directionality for the most part—that is, it should have no shadows. In these situations, it is necessary to find natural elements of light and dark to gain a three-dimensional look.

Creating a Natural Look

Soft Lighting   Except for standing outside in the sun, humans are almost never seen in any kind of direct light. We don't put spotlights in our homes or offices that shine in our faces. So any time we light someone like that, the visual message is artificial and conspicuous. The goal of a natural look is a type of lighting simply referred to as **soft lighting**. Shadows are undefined or have very hazy, soft edges. It is hard to recreate this type of light with standard lighting equipment alone. You can create soft light effects using hard lights by adding umbrellas, boxes, or a diffusing material, such

Figure 10-31   To create a natural look, this interview setup was done with two lights. The key light was a 3 × 3-foot foam core with a 1,000-watt broad light bounced off it, and the backlight was a 100-watt Fresnel. The window light was blocked by a Duvetyne curtain to allow the use of uncorrected tungsten lights and to allow the camera to use a larger f-stop. The slower lens setting allowed better use of the practical, or incandescent, light on the table and a more out-of-focus background.

as spun glass, in front of them, or by bouncing the light off another surface such as we discussed earlier in this chapter. Larger diffusing material can even be hung from the ceiling in front of the lights to produce a wall of light. Any of these methods will yield a natural soft light on the subject or scene, but you must remember that the amount of light reaching the subject will be greatly reduced and the color temperature lowered by the diffusing material. Light from an umbrella source is only one-half to one-third of what it would be if the light came directly from the fixture.

Bouncing light is the best method of adding soft light in situations where the room is small. If a room's ceiling is light colored, relatively smooth, and no higher than 8 to 10 feet from the floor, you can aim a light at the ceiling and the reflected light will enhance the base illumination level. Almost any type of light can be used for this purpose, but very weak lights will lose much of their lighting power before reaching the subject. How much of the ceiling you light can make a big difference in the resulting look. Lighting only a small portion can produce a very "top-heavy" light with dark eye sockets on any subject too close to that part of the room. Lighting the entire ceiling is better most of the time, but you have to make sure the direct light doesn't hit the walls or it will show up in the shots.

Direct Light   You can also achieve a natural look with direct lights. By aiming them not into faces but from

other directions or onto other parts of the scene, the direct light will create its own ambient or reflected light. As an example, a person sitting at a desk can be lit from behind by a strong direct light in the kicker or backlight position. The light can look like daylight from an off-camera window (very strong), or light from an unseen lamp (diffused) hitting the subject. As that light also hits the desk top, some of it will be reflected back onto the subject, or you can add more fill of your own. In Figure 10-33, the key light—the direct light—is actually behind the subject, which is not an abnormal scene in real life.

Figure 10-32   The only light source for this scene is from behind the subject. Reflected light from the book and table fill the subject.

Backlight There is an entire theory of natural lighting that uses a key behind the subject; it's called **backlighting**. This type of shot creates difficult problems for cameras and videographers, but the results are well worth the trouble. This style is used most often outdoors, using the sun as the backlight key. To make the shot work, most of the objects in the shot need to be backlit as well. A subject with too much of the background directly lit may not show up well on camera. This type of backlit scene may need to be done with a manual iris to achieve the proper exposure on the subject. Most backlit scenes will have an area of overexposure. When using this style, try to overexpose as little of the picture as possible. In both ENG and EFP applications, a backlit shot can produce warm or pastel colors and good textures as long as the background is also shaded and as little as possible of the sky is in the shot. This effect may be desirable for many reasons—for example, to soften the features of a subject's face.

Figure 10-33   With the subjects backlit and against a dark background, you can expose for the softer reflected light.

A backlit scene is lit with ambient or reflected light—nature's soft light. This reflected sunlight tends to be more blue than direct sunlight, but white balancing in this reflected light corrects the problem. In effect, by using this reflected light you are getting the best qualities of sunlight without the drawbacks. You can get great skin tones without the horrible dark shadows caused by harsh, direct sunshine.

At certain angles, sunlight can reflect off an object's surface, creating glare. This is when backlighting can

be troublesome. Paved surfaces such as concrete can be very hard to include in backlit shots. That is why in backlit TV commercials they wet the streets down with water to darken the surface. Wet concrete actually reflects less light as long as there are no puddles.

Lens flares, caused by backlights striking the lens, could be desirable. The rows of flares created by the light can be used to add dynamics to the shot and help emphasize the sun or light source. A story on solar power practically requires a shot of the sun, and such effects can add interest.

Source Lighting

Source lighting is the best possible natural lighting; you see it most often in the movies. All the artificial light sources are cleverly placed so the viewer is unaware that any are used. The scene looks as though it is lit only by the natural light sources in the picture or perceived to be just outside the camera's view; this is why it is called source lighting. This is modern-day chiaroscuro lighting.

It may actually take many lights to make a scene appear as though it has no added light. A room with windows should look as though the only light comes from those windows. To make a scene look like this, you can use artificial lights to fill in the shadows or accent certain highlights (thereby controlling the contrast ratio).

You can also use artificial lights to make the lighting appear as though it is coming from table lamps in a room, the light from a fireplace or candles, or any natural light source that happens to be there. These natural sources of artificial light are called **practicals**. They generally do not provide the amount or quality of light necessary for shooting but simply provide the motivation for how a scene is lit. It is helpful to the viewer if the light source is incorporated into the shot or shown in a setup shot so that there is at least a subliminal awareness of where the light is coming from—but it's not necessary.

Balancing the lighting contrast ratio of the subject in the room to the daylight in the windows can be very difficult in source lighting. In EFP work, as in the movies, large sheets of neutral density gels can be taped to the window to cut down on the amount of light coming in. These can also be combined with color-correction gels

Figure 10-34 Natural light, like the illumination provided by the windows, is what photographers and videographers seek to recreate.

Figure 10-35 Cameras used for news gathering should have a camera-mounted light available. Usually, these small lights run on 12 volts and can receive power from the camera battery.

to bring the color temperature down to the temperature of tungsten, if that is easier than changing all of your artificial sources to daylight temperatures. It will take some practice to become proficient at balancing contrast ratios, but you can follow these rules to start:

- Choose a natural light source and make it your key light.

- Color correct so all light sources match (if desired).

- If the key is too weak, add light from the same direction as the key, and light only the areas originally lit by the natural key.

- Add fill light to bring the contrast ratios down.

- Make sure the shadows caused by the fill lights are not evident in the shot; only the key light and effects lights should produce any noticeable shadows.

Lighting on the Run

News videographers will often use a small spotlight mounted on the video camera to provide enough light to properly expose the subject or scene being shot.

This method is usually used outdoors at night when no other light source is available.

However, it can also be used when the subject is moving in low-light situations and the videographer must keep the subject lit. This technique is also used in crowded situations when stationary light placement is impossible and in rushed situations in which the videographer has only enough time to shoot the scene and move on to the next location or get back to the station.

Speed is very important in many ENG situations. The run-and-gun method of news coverage requires a news videographer to have that camera light in place at all times so that subjects can be grabbed at a moment's notice for a quick shot off-the-shoulder interview or "bite." If there is no light, or if existing light is poor, the camera light or **sungun** is the best chance for a proper amount of illumination.

Using a Camera-Mounted Light

It has many names: sungun, peewee, beanie, headlight, Frezzi, or news light. But those terms all refer to the same thing: the camera light. Although the camera-mounted light is expedient, it has both practical and aesthetic drawbacks and is therefore not recommended for general EFP work. These lights can be as inexpensive as $20, or you can pay more than $500 for a professional version. There is an art to using one, but be forewarned:

- Any light mounted close to the lens of the camera will shine almost directly into the eyes of the person being interviewed, causing that person to squint or be uncomfortable. Often, the subject will turn away from the camera because of this.

- The light may be reflected off the subject's skin or glasses, causing a hot spot in the picture.

- A camera-mounted light aimed directly at a subject will yield a flat, washed-out image that prevents the desirable depth effect that can be obtained from three-point or natural lighting.

- The light used on a subject close to a background (such as a person against a wall) may cast an undesirable shadow on the background surface.

- The camera light can create overexposed foregrounds and underexposed backgrounds.

The older style 30-volt power belt for a 250-watt portable light lasts only about 15 to 20 minutes. Today, many camera lights run off the same battery that the camera is using. They are also 12-volt lights and generally no more powerful than 20 or 25 watts. Some are as high as 75 watts. Since the average camera uses about 20 watts of power, using a 20-watt sungun attached to it will drain your battery twice as fast as shooting without the light. A 75-watt light will drain it three times as fast. If you do much shooting early in your workday using that light, you may not have batteries available for later shots. A videographer working a night shift may have only two or three batteries to use, so it is important to conserve them and use AC lights whenever possible. It is advisable to use a separate battery belt for the sungun if possible. A 12-volt belt can run a 20- or even a 75-watt light for a long time.

If a dichroic filter is available for your battery light, daytime shadows on subjects can be filled with that light if the subject is close enough. A reporter standing in the shade, or backlit, can be helped out with a battery light and a dichroic filter. The effective distance for this application is only about four feet in open shade, so its use in this way is limited. And since most 12-volt lamps are 25 watts, they are ineffectual compared with direct sunlight.

Many videographers add a bit of diffusion to their sunguns to help minimize their harshness. The diffusion gives a more even spread to the light beam. This also allows the camera light to be used as a colorizing fill light. In fluorescent situations, for example, a little boost from a diffused sungun can give the subject a better skin tone and fill the eye socket shadows without washing out the entire shot or drawing attention to the fact that light was added.

A recent innovation in camera-mounted lights has come from a light that is a small panel of LED lights. These small but potentially bright LED light panels come in both flood and spot styles and can be either 3,200° K or 5,600° K. One model even has infrared lights for shooting in darkness, another model is shaped in a ring and can be mounted with the camera lens in the center.

One-Light Setups

Speed can be absolutely crucial in the news business. A good videographer is always looking for shortcuts to quicken the pace of production while at the same time keeping a competitive edge. The biggest drawback to the camera light is the look: it is expedient, but it also screams "down and dirty." To avoid this look, many videographers have set up a one-light package they can easily carry with them and set up quickly. An example of a basic one-light package is a single-light with an umbrella (to diffuse it), a stand, and an extension cord. The umbrella light gives a pleasingly soft high-quality light that can be easily directed. You can create soft-edged shadows or place it over the top of the camera to simply raise the base light of a scene. Even in the most rushed setups, the light works well because it can be placed almost anywhere. Using one light in this way may cause flat lighting in some situations, but if all you need is base illumination, you've got it, and this technique is still a step above the sungun look.

Light as an Editorial Tool

Just as the painters of the Renaissance found, light can be used for so much more than mere illumination. Light, or more accurately the shadows it creates, can tell us so much about a scene. Even in news situations, the videographer still needs to interpret and communicate what he or she sees using the camera and all the tools at hand. A common question asked at lighting seminars is, "How would you light that shot?" The answer is often: "Show me the script first." Lighting must match what's going on in the scene whether it's news, commercial, or fiction.

High Key/Low Key

Lighting styles fall into two broad categories: **high key** and **low key**. High-key scenes are bright with a low contrast ratio. They have few shadows, and any modeling is very subtle. This type of lighting is usually thought of as upbeat, happy, positive, successful, and energetic. It's the lighting of comedies. Low-key scenes are mostly dark, with many dense shadows and little fill light. The key light seems to be the only light being used. This lighting is thought of as serious, sad, concerned, negative, failing, and low energy. It's the lighting of dramas.

The best place to see examples of these two types of lighting are on the network news magazines like *Dateline*, *20/20*, and *60 Minutes*. A story about a swindler and his victims will have most of the interviews done with dark backgrounds and subjects with well-defined attached shadows modeling their faces: the serious, somber tones of low-key lighting. A story profiling a popular singer will have interviews with bright lighting, very thin shadows, and bright backgrounds (usually looking out windows): the cheery, glowing tones of high-key lighting.

Time of Day

One of the oldest tricks of lighting is to show time of day. The long shadows of early morning and late afternoon are unmistakable. Add color to them—gold for morning and orange for evening—and no one will miss the meaning. This not only applies to outdoor shots but, more importantly, to indoor setups. By

A

B

Figure 10-36 (A) Here, the interview is lit in a high-key fashion and conveys a somewhat neutral tone. (B) In this photo, the interview is lit in a low-key style. The dark areas dominate and create a serious mood.

placing a light outside a window, shining it into the room at a low angle, and adding color, you can achieve the "time of day" effect quite easily. You can also keep the light in the room and, by adding gobos in the shape of windows, create both the look of window light and the time of day.

Mood Lighting

Once your basic lighting setup is completed, use the remaining time before the actual shooting to experi-

Figure 10-37   By adding a light outside the window at eye level, this scene appears to take place in either early morning or late afternoon light. Coloring the light can determine which it is: gold for morning, orange for evening.

ment with mood lighting. By simply modifying the setup, you can easily manipulate the mood of the shot. When lighting in the field, do not forget that adding light to a scene starts to change the mood of the scene. The more subtle and indirect the lighting, the more natural people tend to appear and behave.

The mood you are trying to convey in the shot will dictate the type of lighting for the shot. Imagine that you must shoot an interview with a welfare mother in a darkly lit apartment. The easiest way to bring up the base light level would be to use the camera-mounted light. But a sungun interview with bright light shining in the woman's eyes would look like a harsh, uncaring invasion by the media into the woman's life. If that's the look you want, okay. But you can make a better shot while more accurately portraying her situation. You can shoot this interview using just one light, but its placement is crucial.

One possible solution might be to place a diffused light at a 90° side angle to the camera. Attach barndoors to the light or flag it to keep the light off the background behind the woman so it remains dark. The dreary apartment retains its character and the woman is lit, but she is less likely to be distracted by the light. Your audience will focus on the woman and her story, rather than the bright lights in her eyes or a distracting background flatly illuminated by the camera-mounted light. The subtle lighting allows the woman to be the

most important element in the story, not the expensive equipment that has intruded into her life, or the furniture or belongings behind her. The strong shadows on her face convey the serious tone of the subject matter. Good lighting is lighting that is not noticed. Good lighting techniques enhance the mood and bring out the subject for the audience. Good lighting does not challenge or distort the existing mood of the scene or direct attention from the subject.

There are many styles to creative lighting. Most are derived from master painters—like Rembrandt—whose work can be seen in art history books or art museums anywhere. If you want to be more than just a basic videographer, you need to study the styles that make up the creative world of lighting.

Directing the Viewer

Across the broad range of lighting styles, there is one element that should always be present: showing the viewer what's important. Most of the time, the important part of the shot will be the subject. It can also be any aspect of the frame you wish to draw attention to. By only lighting selected areas of the frame, you show the viewer which elements you want them to notice. The subject, such as the interviewee, is the obvious choice, but additional aspects such as background items can add both to the editorial meaning and the aesthetic value of the shot.

An interview with the CEO of a large corporation can be enhanced by shooting him or her out in front of the desk rather than seated behind the desk. The shot at the desk would leave little background to be used in the frame, and thereby eliminate added visual editorial content. By placing him or her in a chair far from the desk—but with the desk in the background—you can shoot the CEO with a close-up and have a pertinent element still visible. Selectively lighting the desk and its large chair to make it stand out while leaving the remainder of the background dark will emphasize the CEO's powerful position. The audience will see, literally, the position of power (the large desk and chair isolated by the light), while at the same time seeing the CEO in a close shot. You have maximized the information given to the viewer visually while the viewer listens to the dialog.

As you set up for a shot, look around for elements that can add to the understanding of the picture. Even in noninterview shots, look for items that are important to the story. Selectively, even if subtly, make them brighter than the rest of the shot. A story about a teenager's success on the baseball field might contain a shot of his room with a wall of trophies. You should find a way of lighting the trophies (light from a window?) while letting the rest of the room remain at least slightly darker. Even a wide shot of the room will immediately show off the trophies to the viewer. With today's fast-paced editing and limited screen time for any one shot, no matter which form of media, this added visual emphasis helps the viewer understand the scene quickly and easily.

Figure 10-38 Highlighting an object in the background can be both editorial (the object is part of the story) and artistic (the object adds a dynamic to the frame design).

To Light or Not to Light?

Because of time constraints of ENG work, news videographers repeatedly face the dilemma of mood preservation versus mood contamination. In ENG you don't have the time to recreate the mood with better lighting, but the existing light levels or color may just not be quite right. When do you forgo the existing mood and turn on the lights? Only experience can answer that question. Fortunately, new cameras and lenses are being introduced that require lower baselight levels than their predecessors, which should allow news lighting in the future to continue to become eas-

ier and more subtle. In the meantime, one good rule of thumb for natural-light interviews is to shoot when you see the whites of your subject's eyes. If there is not enough existing light to see the white areas of the eyes as white and not a dark gray in the viewfinder or LCD viewer, then you need to add more light. Keep in mind that this is a very general rule. Once again, contrast will be your most important factor. Contrast will determine separation of subject and background. Often the subject is too dark or too backlit against a bright background; you will be unable to see their eyes clearly. You may be able to overexpose the scene but still not see their eyes. More light must be added to the scene to keep the subject from appearing corpse like or as a silhouette—effects you do not want, except in special situations. Decide what the subject of your shot will be, then expose for it. If the rest of the scene is overexposed, add light to your subject so you can close down the iris a bit for the overexposed portion or just change the shot.

Adding a decibel boost (gain) will increase the sensitivity of the pickup device, thereby increasing the range of light in which your camera is effective. This should only be done in the most extreme cases. If a decibel boost gives that added detail to a shot to be able to see the subject, then do it. Remember that every decibel boost increases the noise or graininess of the picture. At 18 dB, the picture quality is quite poor. Any decibel boost for EFP use is strictly out, except for nature programs when shooting nocturnal animals. Only in very desperate ENG situations should you use this gain switch for signal boosting. Choose to use it very carefully.

SUMMARY

Regardless of the lighting style you choose, approach the setup with the following principles in mind:

- Survey the available light, subjects to be lit, and lighting equipment on hand.

- Decide on the appropriate color temperature.

- Consider light direction and balance.

- Light for your wide shot first, then your tight shots.

- Build your lighting by setting one light at a time:

  - Start with your key light; place and adjust it with no other lights on until you are satisfied with the results.

  - Place and adjust your fill light; make sure that its placement and intensity are acceptable for the situation.

  - Complete the basic setup with a backlight.

  - If necessary, add background lights and/or a kicker, eye light, or special-effects lights.

When you build your lighting setup one light at a time, problems surface early and can be more easily corrected without the confusion of other lights in wrong positions.

Keep in mind that turning on *any* light can change everything. You may have contaminated the scene.

The choice then becomes how much effort you put into rectifying the damage.

In EFP situations the script will always determine the solution. You are satisfying a client, and your lighting has to do that as well. How well you light will determine how well you are communicating the ideas of the client through the script. The end justifies the means. To compete in the world of production, you need the highest skill levels you can possibly obtain, and lighting will be the highest skill of all.

For news, the answers are not at all obvious. The camera light says "news crew," so the viewer knows there's a news videographer there taping the scene. But that light causes some people to act unnaturally, appear unnatural, or even perform for the camera. If you choose not to use the light, it may yield more "real" results. Turning out all the existing lights in an office and setting up your own to selectively light certain areas for emphasis may be problematic, but doing so may also lead to a better communication of real information. Lighting is a production variable that takes time, effort, and experience. Lighting skill and technique enhances your video and can give it a professional look. Patience, experimentation and hard work can make lighting a strong part of your video skills.

11 Budgeting and Pricing

If you have been reading the chapters of the book in order, by now you should be familiar with the process, equipment, and techniques of producing a video project on location. You should know the differences between the processes for projects in ENG and EFP, the personnel involved, and the methods of telling video stories in each of the styles. What you probably don't know about is the business of portable video. This chapter will provide a lot of what you need to know in case you actually want to make money with your video skills.

Whether you are in broadcasting, in-house corporate video, or independent entertainment production, one of the first and most basic principles of video is that it is a business. Your work can be aesthetically superb, but if you do not know how much it cost to produce, or if you cannot price it to make a profit, you may soon be out of a job or out of business.

Budgets are statements of business goals in financial terms. One of the goals of a video project is to complete it for a designated amount of money, based on the best estimate of costs by the people making the budget. Budgets help keep video producers on target—they provide a disciplined approach to communication problem solving. They also help measure performance. In the business world, a corporate video that truly gets the job done for $1,000 is better than a video that does it for $2,000. In the entertainment world, a program that can be shown on a variety of channels and is not "time sensitive" can be worth tens of thousands of dollars or more to the producer.

Most business or corporate managers see the use of industrial video as an added cost, while most videographers and producers see it as a good investment. This difference of perspective is common throughout the industry. The best argument for using video is that it tells the necessary story and generates the desired effect more convincingly than other methods. In broadcast news operations, video can deliver the news stories from the field faster and cheaper than film. In the corporate world, video can deliver a message about a new benefit, procedure, or product more quickly and effectively than other methods. For example, a corporation with a new health benefit option that cuts health costs to employees may want the president of the corporation to deliver the message to encourage employees to choose the new option and to enhance the image of a compassionate and concerned chief executive. The options available for delivery of the message include (1) a brochure with a picture and a message from the president, (2) a visit from the president to all branches of the corporation to personally deliver the message, or (3) a video of the president's message delivered to all branches of the corporation.

A simple cost analysis may reveal that the brochure is the least expensive of the options. But a good video manager may easily make the case that brochures are often read once, if at all, and then thrown away by most employees. A face-to-face video from the president may be viewed several times, especially when the specific details of the new health plan are explained. The video can be used for other public relations purposes, and the costs are relatively low. The president only has to do a good job delivering the message once—and it doesn't even have to be in one take. Editing can help make the president's message perfect, and then the entire corporation sees an excellent delivery of the message every time the tape is shown. Obviously, the expenses incurred by the travel of the president and any assistants would probably exceed the cost of the video. Also, travel for this purpose would take the president away from other important tasks.

The size of the budget may not necessarily be the best indicator of the quality of the resulting video project. Creativity and skill can often substitute for dollars in a budget. This is especially true in corporate video, where entertainment value is secondary to effectiveness.

Constructing an elegant set would enhance the aesthetics of a scene, but may not help the audience remember the purpose of the video. The same is true of elaborate computer graphics and digital effects. These may be both beautiful and exciting, but may not contribute directly to the effectiveness of the video project. This logic may apply to many aspects of the production. Big-name talent may be recognizable, but are they credible to the particular audience? A supermodel like Tyra Banks may look great in your video, but is she credible when demonstrating and discussing a new high-powered multimedia computer? How about Jessica Simpson—would she be better or could a high-profile professional football player do a good job? A local public school teacher with knowledge and confidence about using computers may be more convincing, and certainly less expensive, for getting the audience to focus on the goals of the video.

Big budgets can give you more flexibility because you have the option of high-priced talent, fancy post-production work, or a large crew. But solving a problem with video is similar to other problem-solving situations: throwing money at the problem may help, but can be expensive and does not guarantee anything. For example, large-area lighting that requires numerous lights and people to set them may not be much better than a lighting strategy that relies on close-up lighting with a standard portable light kit. Creativity and skill can often compensate for a low budget or help achieve budget reductions in one aspect of production because of budget overruns in other aspects of the production.

ENG AND EFP

The biggest differences between ENG and EFP emerge in the pricing and costs of portable video. Generally speaking, strict adherence to a budget is necessary in EFP work, but only marginally important in ENG work. A big-budget EFP project usually results in a high-quality video piece, while the quality of ENG stories may have no direct relationship to the amount of money spent shooting them. EFP work usually begins when a budget is approved, but ENG work begins whenever an event worth covering is imminent, or an issue worth showing and discussing surfaces.

Electronic News Gathering

A majority of ENG work is shot and edited by news department employees in broadcast TV stations. The footage is owned by the station and is almost always shown during the station's own newscasts or the newscasts of stations owned by the same group. Usually, these stories are not marketed to any other users.

A story or event coverage is sometimes sold to another broadcaster or news programmer (e.g., another TV station, or CNN). The sale may occur on a per-piece basis, or it may be part of a contractual agreement for numerous stories on one or more topics over a period of time. Video may also be traded for other services or video.

Prices for this type of ENG product may fluctuate wildly. The key determinants of price are the importance (news value) of the piece (which may depend on the importance of the event), the length of time it will be available, and how many other ENG photographers obtained similar footage. The price range may begin as low as $50 for a short piece of moderate interest, and increase to thousands of dollars for dramatic footage in high demand.

Many ENG stories sold by TV stations are sold to that station's network, or, if the station has no network affiliation, to a news service or state or regional cooperative. These stories are sometimes made available to other members of the group or network via some type of closed-circuit, satellite-distribution system or broadband server feed.

Cable News Network (CNN) has become the leader in acquiring and distributing video news from every corner of the world. Because of CNN's arrangements with various TV stations and foreign networks, they are a 24-hour per day trading service for news pictures.

Freelance ENG photographers, sometimes called "stringers," shoot news stories and cover events for a variety of buyers. These professionals, like their counterparts in EFP who do freelance work or have independent production companies, are often found in larger markets or locations that tend to generate many news stories, such as state capitals.

Because most ENG stories are not shot to be sold, most pieces are not budgeted as in EFP work. Local news budgets are not broken down by story. A news director for a TV station looks at ENG costs by a time unit (such as a typical broadcast week or month) that includes the salaries of the photographer, editor, and reporter, knowing that maintenance and overhead expenses are met by other departments. Most often, the only factor that varies in the budget is the cost of overtime payments. News departments do create emergency funds in case of big, expensive stories to keep the station on a relatively stable and predictable budget.

Electronic Field Production

Whether you are the manager of an in-house video production unit in a corporation or a manager/owner of a small independent production house, knowing the worth of your video product is the key to staying in business. Knowing the worth of your product helps you to charge your clients reasonable prices while allowing you to make a fair profit. The profit allows you to reinvest in your future through the purchase of new production or business equipment, or to provide special benefits such as bonuses to employees for high-quality work.

Costs in EFP production are somewhat different from those in studio TV. In EFP work, the setting does not come to you; you must go to the setting. This often generates large expenses for transportation of

equipment and personnel. Because of the extensive handling that portable equipment receives, all equipment requires more frequent maintenance.

If videotape is still being used for the project, costs in are higher in EFP than in studio production. Film-style shooting of EFP requires many takes of each scene, resulting in a minimum of two to three times more tape than studio work. In addition, most tapes shot in the field, whether for ENG or EFP, are edited before being shown. Far less editing occurs in studio work, but studio costs are generally higher because of overhead expenses, such as rent or mortgage payments and regular utilities expenses. Also, the crew is usually bigger in studio television.

In-House versus Independent Production Units

When video services are needed, an individual can do the work or a professional can be hired. When a corporate entity has repeated need for video services, it may decide to start its own video production unit or contract with an outside production business, often referred to as an independent production house. Going outside the company, or "outsourcing," has become increasingly common since the late 1980s, when the need for sophistication in the video product became more important than saving money by doing a lower quality job "in-house."

In-House Production Unit

The purpose of establishing an in-house corporate video production center is to provide the corporation with a much-needed service for less money and more control than contracting outside the firm. Almost always, the size of this unit grows or shrinks in a way that corresponds to the corporate need for the service and the health of the business environment. The corporate video production unit receives money in two general ways: (1) by charging the in-house customers for services rendered (sometimes referred to as a chargeback), or (2) by a direct flat-rate budget based on projected expenses.

Chargeback The first method simulates an independent production unit in the marketplace. In-house clients go to the video manager and agree on the services to be rendered by the video unit and the cost of those services. The payment is made through some type of interdepartmental transfer. Often when this type of system exists, the video manager competes with other media or even with outside production units.

This keeps the pricing structure of the in-house unit very realistic. A good production team can do well in this system by keeping busy and providing excellent services at good prices. This system forces the video unit to earn its salary; in other words, the only financial support it receives is obtained directly through the amount of work it does.

Flat rate A second method for financing an in-house video production unit is through some type of annual or flat budget. The production unit is automatically funded on a year-to-year basis without actually charging the in-house client on a per-piece basis. Variations on these two basic funding systems are common. Video units may receive some type of annual budget and may charge certain in-house clients for some kinds of services. In-house units that usually work on a chargeback basis may perform some services or provide services to in-house clients without charge.

Regardless of what type of financial system the company uses, it is essential to know the costs of providing necessary services to your clients. Because managers of corporate video units that receive annual funding are expected to provide the production service on the given budget, the manager should know how much work can be done with a given finite budget to avoid operating at a deficit. Unrealistic prices by a video unit on a chargeback system either result in a noticeable deficit or a surplus that might anger the in-house clients.

Independent Production Unit

Independent production units produce a wide variety of video projects for corporate and entertainment purposes and generally have more freedom in their pricing. The only limitations are the goals set by the production company's owners and managers and the need to make enough money to stay in business. Often, the marketplace exerts a great deal of influence on the price. The general rule is that the price is set at what the market will bear. This is directly related to competition; numerous competitors lead to lower prices.

This is not to say that quality and reliability are not pricing factors. High-quality work and a high degree of reliability are certainly worth a higher price, but competition limits your pricing range and flexibility. Too much competition often leads to underpricing and cutting corners to get the job done. Too little competition might prevent your prices from having credibility. Without any competition, your client has no point of reference on prices. Keep in mind that few clients actually understand and appreciate the time, equipment, and labor required to produce a professional-quality EFP video project.

CREATING AN ACCURATE BUDGET

The secret to creating an accurate budget is understanding all the possible sources of costs for the production. Most production units have some type of guide or budget sheet that lists possible costs for productions based on those done in the past by that unit. As new sources of cost are incurred, these new sources are added to the list.

These costs can be broken down into categories to help the organization of the process. Various strategies and systems exist. For many, especially smaller operations and most in-house corporate video units, the categorization follows a more generic approach that would be typical of any business that sells a product. The categories typically found in this system include materials cost, services cost, labor cost, and overhead cost.

A tradition handed down from the movie industry regarding budgets consists of two very general categories: (1) creative and executive talent and production, and (2) postproduction and related expenses. This system uses the terms "above the line" and "below the line."

Line Costs

Budgets for large-scale productions in both the film and broadcast industries have traditionally delineated costs in a specific way. The first classification consists of costs encountered in securing the story rights and script, the development costs, intellectual property costs, the producer and producer's immediate staff, the talent, the director, and the costs for travel and fringes (fringe benefits) of these people. These costs are referred to as above-the-line costs.

Typical Above-the-line Costs

- Story and Writers

- Producer and Staff

- Director and Staff

- Cast (talent)

Costs associated with above-the-line people are listed and tallied on a budget sheet. Then a thick black line is inserted, and the costs associated with below-the-line people are listed and tallied under it. That line is sometimes facetiously referred to as "the demarcation line between power and no power."

All other costs directly incurred by the production are categorized together (though listed separately) and referred to as below-the-line costs. These are for materials, services, labor, and so forth—costs not included in the above-the-line category. The below-the-line costs are sometimes categorized by the stage in the production process (for example, pre-production or post-production) in which they are incurred. Commonly included in these costs are: equipment rental, wardrobe, props, insurance, fees paid for locations, and editing costs.

Typical Below-the-line Costs

- Camera

- Sound

- Script Supervision

- Electrical

- Set Construction

- Set Dressing

- Props

- Wardrobe

- Makeup and Hair Special Effects

- Transportation

- Location Expenses

- Stock Footage

- Licenses

- Insurance

- Legal Fees

- Editing

- Postproduction Sound

- Graphics

- Music Visual Effects Dubbing

- Publicity

The above-the-line costs and below-the-line costs are combined with the indirect or overhead costs to give a grand total. Although this budgeting procedure works for major studios, it is not as functional for smaller operations that have not had as much budget and budget-tracking experience.

Budgeting for Smaller Projects

Most video projects do not even approach the size, scope, or costs of a feature film; therefore, the above/below the line method is not appropriate for most video project budgets. The following method is more appropriate for most video projects, from student projects up to large-scale corporate or independent program video (e.g., low-budget reality show). This method combines areas of major costs—materials, ser-

Budget		Show Name
ABOVE THE LINE		
1001	PRODUCERS	
1002	DIRECTOR & WRITER	
1003	TALENT	
	TOTAL ABOVE THE LINE	
PRODUCTION		
2001	PRODUCTION STAFF	
2002	GENERAL & ADMIN	
2003	CREW	
2004	LOCATION	
2005	EQUIPMENT	
2006	ADDITIONAL EQUIPMENT	
2007	TRAVEL	
2008	CATERING	
2009	STOCK	
2010	TRANSPORTATION	
2011	WARDROBE	
	TOTAL FOR PRODUCTION	
POST PRODUCTION		
3001	EDITING EQUIPMENT	
3002	EDITING LABOR	
3003	SOUND	
3004	CLIPS & STILLS	
3005	GRAPHICS PACKAGE	
3006	MUSIC	
3007	MISC	
	TOTAL FOR POST PRODUCTION	
MISC.		
4001	MISC., ETC	
	TOTAL FOR MISC.	
	SUBTOTAL	
	CONTINGENCY (5% BELOW THE LINE)	
GRAND TOTAL (4 SHOW NOT INCLUDING BREAKAGE & ACCELERATED COSTS)		

Figure 11-1   This is a budget summary form for a television show or feature film that has general costs broken down into Above The Line, Production, and Post Production categories. (Courtesy of Steve Paskay)

vices, labor, and overhead—to give an accurate picture of the costs of producing video projects of small to moderate size.

Materials

Some materials for video projects, such as lamps, set or scenery construction, and materials used for graphics preparation (slides, graphic cards, cue cards), are expected to provide only one usage. For every project that requires a script, a certain amount of paper and office forms are used. Other materials may have some leftovers or reusables, but it is not safe to expect this to occur. Include the full cost of these materials in your budget.

Typical materials costs include the following:

- Videotape

- Audiotape

- Memory and software

- Film stock (slides, still, movie)

- Set construction (lumber, paint, nails)

- Graphics materials (markers, paper, paint, photocopies)

- Tools (purchased for a specific project)

- Props (furniture, equipment for a specific project)

- Miscellaneous (gaffer's tape, special adapters)

The videotape, audiotape, and other storage media used in the project may or may not have later use. Some of it will not be recycled: for example, the edited master will remain in use only for the project for which it was purchased, or at least until the client is thoroughly satisfied with the finished program. However, some of the raw footage shot on location may come in very handy for future productions that require a specific shot or cutaway from that location or type of location. It is sometimes amazing how creative and resourceful video people can be if reusing video or audio can save a return trip to a location. If you keep these things in mind, you can be more accurate when assessing your materials cost for storage media.

Services

This cost category includes the services purchased specifically for the project that are not provided by in-house personnel or equipment. When you must rent a vehicle, do a special effect at another facility, or cater meals at a location, categorize these as services costs. A slightly different type of cost that falls under this general category is the cost incurred when you must use copyrighted materials and pay a fee for that privilege.

Typical services costs include the following:

- Rental of equipment/vehicles

- Rental of locations

- Rental of facilities (e.g., post-production)

- License fees (music, stock photo/slides, or video)

- Catering of meals

- Security

- Parking fees

- Permits

- Outside contracts (security, construction)

- Production of graphics materials or special effects

- Duplication (DVDs, etc.)

Labor

The general definition of labor costs is the total cost of all hours (or days) spent by all employees involved in a project. Assigning exact costs for this category is most accurately done after the project is completed. However, you must try to predict exactly how many hours or days a key crew member like a director will or can spend on a given project. The price for the project is often needed well ahead of the project's completion—usually before the project is even begun.

Typical labor costs include the following:

- Executive producer

- Producer

- Director

- Writer(s)

- Researcher(s)

- Assistants

- Camera operators

- Video recorder operators

- Engineer(s)

- Lighting director

- Art director

- Grip(s)

- Production assistants

- Editor

- Office staff

Labor costs call for accurate predicting if your production is to be successful. To budget for the cost of a director on a project, you must try to get an accurate picture of how much effort will be required. Predictions are most accurate when two types of information are available: (1) the number of hours spent by your director on a similar project, and (2) the number of hours generally spent by other directors on similar projects or similar amounts of work. Very simply, once you have predicted the amount of time, multiply this figure by the director's unit rate. The unit rate is determined for any convenient length of time (for example, hour, day, or week) by dividing the director's total pay for a known period by the appropriate number of units.

For example, your director earns $4,000 per month. What are the unit rates for each day or hour worked by the director? The following equation will give the daily unit rate (we assume here that each month has 20 workdays):

> Daily unit rate = total monthly salary divided by the number of workdays per month:
>
> $4,000 per month @ 20 workdays per month = $200 per day.

To find the hourly unit rate use this equation:

> Hourly unit rate = daily unit rate divided by the number of work hours per day:
>
> $200 per day divided by 8 work hours per day = $25 per hour.

NOTE: On larger productions, or when freelance help is hired, the number of work hours is usually 10 hours, but longer days are not uncommon.

The hourly rate should be multiplied by the projected number of hours that will be spent by the director on this particular project. This procedure needs to be repeated for all persons involved in the production.

For most union or personal service contracts, there is a base-pay unit, usually set at one full day. Along with this rate for union and nonunion people are overtime and other compensations agreed to by employee and employer. In some cases, flat rates can be negotiated.

Once the labor costs for all production personnel are added, you then have a general idea of what the actual costs will be. This first sum is merely the dollar amount that will be going directly to the employees. What must be added to this direct payment is the amount that your company pays for employee benefits, such as life insurance, hospitalization, retirement, or bonuses.

These fringe benefits can add anywhere from 30% to more than 100% of the cost of the work to your direct labor costs. These added costs are almost always associated with full-time employees. Failure to include these costs will cause you to underestimate your overall costs, which may result in underpricing your product and lead to some red ink. When using contract or freelance help, fringe benefits are not involved.

Overhead Expenses

Overhead expenses are those expenses generally associated with being in business. Typical overhead expenses include the following:

- Salaries (nonproduction)

- Benefits (for full-time employees)

- Office/studio space rental

- Utilities (heat, light, water, telephone, Internet service)

- Dues (professional organizations)

- Subscriptions (magazines)

- Licenses (software, stock footage, music)

```
                              BUDGET


Production Requirement                 Rate          Budget

A.   Production Operating Expenses
 1.  Off-Line Editing (Rough Cut)                  $ 10,000
 2.  On-Line Edit                                  $  6,000
 3.  Equipment Rental                              $ 14,000
 4.  Video Tape Stock                              $     800

Production Operating Expenses Sub-Total            $ 30,800


B.   Professional Services
 1.  Computer Animation & Graphics             $   3,000
 2.  Archive Research & Purchase               $   1,000
 3.  Music Composition & Audio Production       $   3,000

Professional Services Sub-Total                    $  7,000


C.   Personnel
 1.  Producer/Director
       Pre-Production (5 days)      $    100    $     500
       Shoot (10 days)             $    250    $   2,500
       Post-Production (10 days)   $    250    $   2,500
 2.  Audio/Engineer (10 days)      $    200    $   2,000
 3.  Dir. of Photography (10 days) $    250    $   2,500

Personnel Sub-Total                                $ 10,000


D.  Travel/Scouting/Meetings
 1.  Hotel                                     $   2,400
 2.  Ground Transportation                     $     500
 3.  Meals                                     $     450
 4.  Telephone/Fax                             $     500

Travel/Scouting/Meetings Sub-Total                 $  3,850


E.  Talent & Rights
 1.  Writer                                    $   1,000
 2.  On Camera/ Voice talent                   $   1,000

Talent & Rights Sub-Total                          $  2,000


TOTAL BUDGET                                       $ 53,650
```

Figure 11-2   This budget for an in-house industrial video project shows per-day and project costs for personnel in Section C. (Courtesy of VAS Communications)

- Reference/library materials (books, sound library, graphics clip art)

- Equipment depreciation (office/production equipment)

- Maintenance (janitorial, grounds keeping)

- Miscellaneous (donations, gifts)

Certain kinds of labor costs may also be associated with overhead. Salaries of others not directly involved in the project (a secretary, for example) can be included in labor costs if the employee spends an easily definable amount of time on the particular project be-

ing priced. Often, this is not the case, and the project is merely assigned a portion of this type of office salary in the overhead cost. Equipment depreciation costs may also be included in a general category of overhead expenses. Without going into great detail or accounting theory, depreciation can be thought of as the value that your equipment loses as a result of use and aging. For example, if a high-quality digital camcorder costs $60,000 and is expected to last 5 years, the cost of owning and using the camcorder can be calculated as $60,000 divided by 5, or $12,000 per year.

There are numerous ways to deal with these costs, but for use in pricing your product, follow a simple procedure in which you ascertain a unit rate of overhead costs in the same way you obtain a unit rate for labor costs. Total the previous year's overhead costs and then divide that total by the number of working or operating days:

$$\frac{\text{Total Previous Year's Overhead Costs}}{\text{Number of Operating Days}}$$

The result is a daily overhead cost. This daily cost, or a fraction thereof, should be added to other costs.

Keep in mind that this cost may fluctuate from year to year. If you are aware of definite fluctuations in overhead that would change the overhead unit rate in your current year, you should adjust the figures accordingly. Salary raises or bonuses for office or executive employees, increases in utility use or rates, or changes in tax rates can influence current overhead expenses.

If you think that changes like those mentioned above have occurred, you can adjust the unit rate by first adjusting last year's total overhead expenses by the amount of the expected changes. Another method is to calculate your overhead cost more often than once per year. A quarterly assessment of overhead costs will sometimes help to keep your unit rate closer to reality.

When the four general cost categories (materials, services, labor, and overhead) are added together, you have a total cost for the project. This is also the price at which you (or your company) break even with no financial loss or gain. But if your price is set to break even, chances are that your department or company

will lose money. As unforeseen expenses always crop up, it is good business policy to add something to your total cost to provide for a rainy day.

If you include another factor—profit—in your pricing formula, you will help guarantee that you will be able to meet any cost overruns and perhaps save some money to buy more or better equipment in the future.

BUDGET TRACKING

The best way to give accurate prices for your video work is to have accurate information regarding the actual costs. You can do this by keeping accurate records of expenditures for the projects your company produces. This recordkeeping or bookkeeping process is called budget tracking.

This procedure allows you to compare the projected budget for a video service with the actual cost. By making this comparison, you not only can assess your ability to cover your incurred costs and attain your desired profit amount, you also can gain valuable data for pricing future projects. If you track your budgets after you make them, you can easily evaluate your ability to predict costs. This procedure is a relatively easy one to establish.

First, whenever you give a budget estimate for a project, make sure that it includes a dollar amount for

Table 11.1 Budget Tracking

Cost Category	Budgeted	Actual	Difference
Materials			
Videotape	$450	$275	$175
Set	$150	$175	($25)
Paint and lumber	$85	$80	$5
Total Materials	$685	$530	$155
Services			
Van rental	$150	$150	$0
Special effects	$250	$350	($100)
Costume rental	$75	$75	$0
Total Services	$475	$575	($100)
Total			$55

all possible items within each of the cost categories (see Table 11-1). Set up this budget breakdown so that each cost item has a line with at least two columns: one for the budgeted or predicted cost, and a second for the actual cost.

A third column might also be included for cost overruns—when actual costs are more than the estimated costs. Or the third column may be used for budget surpluses—when the actual costs are less than the predicted costs. This third column is derived by subtracting the actual cost from the predicted cost. The sum of the positive and negative numbers in the third column will give you a report on your pricing accuracy: a positive number shows that you have safely assessed your costs and have some money left over to contribute to profit (as in the example shown in Table 11.1); a negative number means that you have underestimated costs and you may have to use money initially earmarked for profit to pay for the costs of producing the project.

Computer Assistance

Just as computers and computer programs have become essential for business managers to organize, track, project, and plan in their areas of responsibility, these new technologies are helping EFP producers with the planning and business aspects of portable video production. (See Figure 11.3.) Computer programs created by video professionals allow producers and their staffs to generate budget figures in standardized categories in very short periods of time, whereas the tedious paper-and-pencil method formerly took days. This type of program also allows the individual producer to create special tailor-made budget categories.

This type of software can also perform budget tracking. After a final budget for a project is entered, expenses are entered as they are incurred, either at some regular interval or at the end of the production. This program allows you to quickly recall the amount budgeted for a particular category of expense, the number of expense entries in that category, and the remaining balance. The program also allows you to update the budget when hourly or unit rates change.

EFP Pricing Formula

Every production situation brings a unique problem to the person who must accurately assess costs and set prices. This section presents a general formula for the identification and categorization of costs associated with EFP video projects.

A combination of five factors is necessary to set the price for an EFP video project. The first four factors are materials, services, labor, and overhead costs. These can be combined into one major category of cost:

$$
\begin{array}{c}
\text{Materials Cost} \\
\text{Services Cost} \\
\text{Labor Cost} \\
\underline{\text{Overhead Cost}} \\
\text{Total Cost}
\end{array}
$$

These four, when combined and added to the fifth factor, profit, yield the formula for price:

$$
\begin{array}{c}
\text{Total Cost} \\
\underline{\text{Profit}} \\
\text{Price}
\end{array}
$$

or

$$
\begin{array}{c}
\text{Materials Cost} \\
\text{Services Cost} \\
\text{Labor Cost} \\
\text{Overhead Cost} \\
\underline{\text{Profit}} \\
\text{Price}
\end{array}
$$

The fifth factor, profit, is considered separately because the amount of profit is often under the control of the price setter. Profit is the amount of money you want to make over and above all of your costs for the project. Profit may be used for reinvestment in equipment, facilities, real estate, bonuses, or simply to build the company's cash reserves. A closer look at these factors gives a better understanding of the role each plays in price setting.

The profit factor in the pricing formula is often the most difficult to quantify. How much money do you want to make on a project? Enough to buy dinner? Enough to buy new editing software? Enough for

FILM PRODUCTION COST SUMMARY

Bid Date: **February 1, 2006** Actualization Date: **March 22, 2006**

Production Co.:	**Easy Production Services**	Agency:	**Big Fees R Us**		Job# **fs-21**
Address:	**123 Easy Street**	Client:	**Isnot Purina**		
City, State:	**New York, NY 10002**				
Telephone No.:	**(212)555-1212**	Product: **Happy Dog**			
Prod. Contact:	**Tiffany Goldwyn**	Agency Prod.:	**Ima Bigego**	Tel: **555-1212**	
Director:	**Steven Smileberg**	Agency Art Dir.:	**Oso Talentless**	Tel: **555-1213**	
Dir. of Photography:	**Haskell Camera**	Agency Writer:	**Pickle Kipling**	Tel: **555-1214**	
Set Designer:	**Robert DeSign**	Business Mgr.:	**Bean Kounter**	Tel: **555-1215**	
Editor:	**Mary Clipncut**	Title:	**The very Best!**	No. **2**	Length **:30**

No. Pre-Prod. Days: **0**	Pre-Light/Rehearse	1. **"He's so happy now"**
No. Build/Strike Days: **0**	Hours: **0**	2. **"All the fleas jumped off!"**
No. Studio Days: **0**	Hours: **0**	3. **"Cute little pit bull"**
No. Location Days: **0**	Hours: **0**	4. **"Look at what he rolled in!"**
Location Sites: **Grand Canyon**		5.
		6.

SUMMARY OF ESTIMATED PRODUCTION COSTS		ESTIMATED	ACTUAL
1. Pre-Production and Wrap Costs	Totals A & C	$40,286.95	$42,836.14
2. Shooting Crew Labor	Total B	$34,972.65	$30,910.49
3. Travel and Location Expenses	Total D	$20,330.30	$20,000.49
4. Props, Wardrobe, Animals & Handlers	Total E	$5,050.00	$5,150.44
5. Studio and Set Construction Costs	Totals F, G, & H	$57,239.74	$54,782.82
6. Production Equipment Rentals	Total I	$20,575.00	$20,710.47
7. Stock and Processing 35 Cass Digi-Beta (:30)	Total J	$5,425.00	$5,115.00
8. Miscellaneous Costs	Total K	$10,150.00	$5,878.84
9. Insurance at: 6 %		$11,641.78	$9,441.00
10.		$0.00	$0.00
	Sub-Total Direct Costs:	$205,671.43	$194,825.69
11. Production Fee: 21 %		$61,884.01	$49,884.67
12. Directors' Creative Fee	Total L	$85,500.00	$84,702.00
13. Talent Fees and Expenses	Totals M & N	$28,698.66	$29,139.64
14. Editorial and Finishing:	Total O, P & Q	$60,315.70	$60,502.23
15.		$0.00	$0.00
	Grand Total:	$442,069.80	$419,054.23
16. Contingency at: 10 %		$44,206.98	$41,905.42

Comments:

Locations as specified: Grand Canyon. Flagstaff, Arizona (30 miles away) is nearest airport.

This sample budget courtesy of Easy Budget. (800)356-7461 Sales@easy-budget.com
http://www.Easy-Budget.com

Figure 11-3   This sample production cost summary can be used for film or video production and shows both estimated and actual costs.

a new video camera? Enough to pay off your mortgage? Obviously, the amount of profit is related to the total cost of the project. It would be great to make $800 profit on a project that involves only $200 of real cost, but this percentage of profit is rare in everyday business.

A good manager would not settle for a $50 profit on an $8,000 job unless there were some unusual circumstances. A $50 profit for that much expense is too much work and too much risk for such a small profit.

The base profit percentage in the production business is about 20%. In other words, you can usually add 20% of the total cost as the profit factor in your pricing formula (or multiply total costs by 1.2).

Some projects may justify a higher profit figure. Low-priced jobs usually have a minimum dollar amount included for profit. Some projects may be risky, require crucial deadlines, or present difficult or unpleasant conditions. If any of these conditions are present, a 25 to 50% profit margin may be quite reasonable.

You may feel you should do certain projects for reasons other than direct economic gain. These are the jobs that may enhance your credibility, give you desired publicity, give your creative desires a boost, or simply give you a shot at working for a highly desired clientele. Foregoing profit even in these cases may not be necessary, but it may ensure that you get the job because you are the lowest bidder.

In some instances, you may want to take on a video project at a loss, even if the client is not a highly desired one. For example, the price structure in a voluntary loss situation may look like this:

Materials cost	100
Services cost	50
Labor cost	100
Overhead cost	50
Total cost	$300

The above figures are the costs for a small video project (for example, a public service announcement or commercial). If the client pays only $275, you are left with a negative profit of $25. For what reason would you undertake this project?

A quick look at the cost of being in business can shed some light. Some costs, such as labor and overhead, are incurred whether you have a project to do or not. Your overhead costs are fixed, and your labor costs might come from full-time employees who get paid whether they have a project to do or whether they are reading magazines in the office. If you do not have a project, you still have some costs:

Labor cost	100
Overhead cost	50
Total cost	$150

If you do not take on this project, you still have to pay $150 in costs. By taking on the project, you cover most of your costs and lose only $25 instead of $150. Besides, it is better to have your employees gaining experience in video production instead of in magazine reading.

This policy of accepting negative-profit jobs is risky. If client X finds out that client Y paid less for a similar job, the integrity of your rate structure may suffer and you may have to continually justify your prices to clients. Except for highly unusual circumstances, it is best to take on jobs at your normal profit rate.

ENTRY INTO THE VIDEO MARKETPLACE

The above discussion makes the assumption that you are already in business and have the equipment or procedures to obtain the equipment you need to produce portable video projects. Many new entrants in the field of portable video decide to be in business for themselves and try to acquire the equipment and related materials and people necessary for them to conduct business. This can be a daunting and dangerous endeavor. The cost of obtaining the equipment is quite high. A full traveling kit for high-quality professional EFP work, which includes a professional camcorder, light kits, wireless mics, audio accessories, cables, cases, and a two-wheel hand truck to carry the cases, can easily cost $150,000. This estimate does not include a vehicle to transport the equipment or personnel, nor does it include any studio facilities or editing facilities. Although computer-based nonlinear editing systems are not expensive (often $4,000 or less), video recording/playback machines and other pieces of equipment can bring your total to $200,000 or more. Obviously, this kind of capital outlay prevents many new video professionals from casually entering the field of high-quality production.

Leasing

Some of this initial cost outlay can be reduced by leasing or renting some of the equipment. You may find that it is much more realistic to lease a camcorder for $400 or more per day than to purchase a new one for $60,000. Extended leases that are not on a day-to-day basis may reduce your per day cost. Like all leases, you don't really own the equipment; the leasing company does. At the end of the lease period, you must return the equipment or buy it from the company. This can be problematic when unexpected business comes your way.

Using the Web for Video

The World Wide Web offers some relatively new opportunities for video producers to improve their business. The first opportunity is that a video producer can market his or her services using a typical Web site home page to display a resume both in text and audio/video formats. The site can also be used to store drafts of work for clients. After these rough-edit drafts are posted on the Web, clients can have easy access to them. By showing the client a draft copy, the producer can gain valuable insight into what the client expects in the finished product. This procedure saves the video producer time. By posting the video on the Web, the producer need not travel to the client with a tape or have the client come to the producer. The client views the video when convenient and can give immediate feedback via e-mail.

Examples of scripts, storyboards, and actual projects can be seen or played when prospective clients go the Web site. Obviously, the Web site is a 24-hour-per-day marketing tool that can reach many people from all parts of the world.

Video Producers as Hosts   The use of the Web for video production business is still in its infancy. People who shoot video professionally are just starting to explore the video applications available on the Web. At present, bandwidth problems prevent easy distribution of full-frame, full-motion video on the Web. Video professionals are cautiously approaching business on the Web, due in part to video quality issues. One business that has emerged is the video professional using the company Web site as a host for all work done for all clients. By providing this service, the clients need not be Web "savvy" because the work is exhibited from the same source from which it is produced.

Being Realistic

It may be best for you to start your business at a smaller level and build up to a more professional or high-end level *after* you have gained experience and a strong track record or reputation. Instead of a state-of-the art camcorder, you may opt for a low-end professional or industrial digital camcorder. Instead of an extensive light kit, you may choose to start with a much smaller kit that is very flexible and can adapt to many lighting situations. An extra video recording deck may be nice, but when it is absolutely necessary, you can rent one. Top-of-the-line wireless microphones are the best for most situations involving soundbites from subjects, but you can also get less expensive wireless mics and supplement them with some good-quality cabled mics.

The point here is that you must avoid overextending yourself financially. Portable video may be your life's desire—your ambition is to shoot terrific video and produce video projects that are both aesthetically pleasing and entertaining to your audience. Unfortunately, if you decide to go into portable video as an independent businessperson, your work must produce enough money to pay the bills and your salary. This reality has resulted in many individual and small business failures. The rule of thumb is to make sure that your equipment is the best that your business can justify economically.

SUMMARY

After reading this chapter you should know about the budgeting differences between ENG and EFP. Generally, ENG stories are not budgeted by story, and decisions about which news stories to cover and how to cover them are dictated not by the budget, but by the importance of the story. EFP projects, however, are almost always controlled by a budget. Whether you are producing a pilot program for a cable channel or an informational video project for a corporation, the budget dictates the scope of the project. Individual decisions such as what kind of sets can be built, who can be hired as talent, or where to go on location to shoot the project are guided closely by how much money is available in the budget.

There are two general kinds of EFP production units: in-house and independent. In-house units are found within a company or corporation. These units are there to further the goals of the company and usually produce projects for the parent company only. Independent production units can have a variety of different clients and produce many different kinds of projects: entertainment, instructional, motivational, documentary, etc.

Large-scale video project budgets are often broken down into above-the-line and below-the-line costs. Above-the-line costs are those associated with the producer, director, writer, and talent. Below-the-line costs are those costs associated with shooting, gathering sound, lighting, editing, wardrobe, sets, props, etc.

Creating a budget for smaller video projects requires identifying all sources of cost for the project. One way of categorizing the costs is to separate the costs into the categories of materials, services, labor,

and overhead. If you are pricing a project for a client, you should also add a percentage of the cost for profit. Many people who attempt to go into the video production business often do so without really understanding the large outlay of money that accompanies this type of business. Often, it is best to lease or rent equipment that will be only used occasionally. Knowing the real costs of video production is the single best step that you can take to help you price your projects appropriately to help you stay in business.

12 Laws, Ethics, Copyrights, and Insurance

One of the best aspects of producing portable video is that a large number of people might see your work. In fact, when you are on location, some people might even see it while you are shooting. This exposure is a blessing for videomakers in added recognition, and the high profile can also be a blessing through higher ratings, more sales, a larger corporate budget, and so on. But with the two rewards of exposure and money can come some very substantial legal problems. For those who plan to produce video programs or segments, a cursory knowledge of how to protect yourself from legal entanglements and your material from being stolen or misused is as necessary as any shooting or editing techniques.

Most videographers encounter two major areas of the law: the right to privacy and the right of ownership, or copyright. The former is the most common problem in ENG and the latter in EFP. Either issue can certainly create more trouble than you would suspect. The safest thing to do before shooting anything, whether news or not, is to be sure not only of your rights but also of the rights of everyone or everything that appears in your video or has anything to do with it. This sounds complex, but the level of complexity is somewhat a function of the amount of money involved. A student project only seen by a class or school can do many things that a multimillion-dollar network

TV show could never dream of doing without having every legal *i* dotted.

DEFAMATION: LIBEL AND SLANDER

A major concern of all ENG and EFP production is **defamation of character**. Defamation occurs when a person is wrongfully portrayed in a negative way so that his or her good name and reputation are harmed. Defamation is usually divided into two categories. The first is **libel**, defined as defamation through *recorded* means. Libel law stems from the practices of early print media and gives some protection to citizens against journalists or other writers simply publishing words that harm their reputations. Libel law has since been extended beyond the "printed word" to include the "recorded word." The electronic media are subject to the same laws as the print media regarding libel.

The idea is that, whether published printed words or broadcast recorded words, the journalist has time to consider how the subject of a story is being portrayed. The story is constructed with forethought; there are options regarding how to portray the subject. If that subject is falsely portrayed in a harmful light, whether on television, radio, the Internet, or in a newspaper or magazine or pamphlet, the author (writer, producer, etc.) and the news organization may have libel charges brought against them.

For example, the entertainer Carol Burnett sued the tabloid magazine, *The National Enquirer*. The magazine published a story indicating that she was an alcoholic. She is not. While this particular magazine is not considered to be journalistic, but rather a "fluff rag" not to be taken seriously, Ms. Burnett sued because the story hit too close to home. Some in her family suffered from a history of alcoholism—a history which she had broken—and she felt the magazine had gone too far. While simple inaccuracies occur from time to time, and can be overlooked or corrected with an apology, this incorrect information hurt Ms. Burnett's good name and reputation, and she believed the magazine needed to be held accountable. Ms. Burnett won the lawsuit.

The second category of defamation is **slander**, defined as defamation through *spoken words*. Slander is not considered as harmful as libel. Libel is more serious because it involves time and thought; the reporter deliberately writes or records harmful words about the subject. In contrast, slander occurs without much thought or deliberation. A person might say something harmful on the spur of the moment, but the words are not necessarily carefully chosen nor knowingly intended to be part of a permanent record, such as a newspaper or television broadcast.

For example, in 2005 during a live NBC telecast to raise funds for relief efforts for the victims of Hurricane Katrina, singer Kanye West suddenly stated, "George Bush doesn't care about black people." This statement was considered merely slanderous, not libelous. West, together with actor Mike Myers, was reading a script from a prompter. The script contained no wrongful and harmful words against the President (if it had, that could have been considered libel). The rapper went off script to make his assertion. Moreover, the telecast was live, so the producer could not have been expected to delete the statement. For these reasons, the rapper's unexpected opinion was considered slanderous but not libelous. The President chose not to bring charges against the rapper (perhaps because Presidents are always subject to people's outbursts of opinion).

PRIVACY VERSUS THE RIGHT TO KNOW

One of the basic rights of all Americans is the **right to privacy**. This right normally derives from the **Fourth Amendment** to the Constitution, which states:

> The right of the people to be secure in their persons, houses, papers, and effects, against unreasonable searches and seizures, shall not be violated, and no warrants shall issue, but upon probable cause, supported by oath or affirmation, and particularly describing the place to be searched, and the persons or things to be seized.

This right "to be secure" has consistently been interpreted to mean that people have a right to privacy in their homes and other nonpublic places, as well as a right to safety. This right applies to those whom you might want to record for a story as much as it applies to you.

Balancing each person's Fourth Amendment right to privacy is the media's **First Amendment** right to report. The First Amendment reads:

> Congress shall make no law respecting an establishment of religion, or prohibiting the free exercise thereof; or abridging the freedom of speech, or of the press; or the right of the people peaceably to assemble, and to petition the government for a redress of grievances.

This right to freedom of speech and freedom of the press has consistently been interpreted to mean that news organizations have the right to print or broadcast the news without fear of censorship, even if a report puts a person in a negative light—as long as it is true and relevant. Remember that libel occurs when that negative portrayal is *wrong*. If the report is true, the news organization may have a defense. The next section explores the media's defenses against libel. Non-news organizations, such as entertainment companies, also have a First Amendment right to script their stories without fear of government censorship. The legal concerns of non-news organizations will be explored in the subsequent section.

ENG: News Productions

Broadcast journalism has a great many freedoms under the law that other types of video production do not enjoy. How the end product is used is very crucial to the rights of the makers as well as the subjects. Because news is a public service, and the right of a free press is guaranteed, there are very few ways to stop someone from covering an event or showing a particular picture or scene on a newscast. However, if the news staff does not understand the subtleties of balancing free speech against people's right to privacy, the results can range from loss of prestige to high-priced civil suits. Being wrong can be costly to you and to your employer. When a case of libel is brought against a news organization, the defense—if there is one—usually falls into one or more of four categories: (1) the public's right to know (2) truth (3) consent and (4) public property. Additional factors can influence each case, as well: (5) context, (6) public figures, (7) trespassing, (8) hidden cameras, (9) names and numbers, (10) police orders, and (11) other things to know.

The Public's Right to Know

The courts have made it very clear that the public's right to know is one of our most secure freedoms. This right generally applies to anything that could be considered interesting to the public, is in the public eye, or affects any portion of the populace. The public's right to know allows the news to show the victim of a car crash, the President on vacation, or the unsanitary conditions inside a poorly run meat-packing plant. However, this does not mean a news broadcast has the right to libel or slander someone or otherwise misrepresent the pictures shown or the words read.

For example, some years ago Las Vegas singer Wayne Newton sued NBC News for linking him to known organized crime figures, thereby damaging his public image. He alleged that NBC's combination of words and pictures created a defamatory impression. Newton won a large judgment ($19 million) in a local court, though a higher court later lowered the amount. NBC argued that it had a legitimate reason for doing a story about Mr. Newton because he is a public figure. However, Mr. Newton was able to demonstrate that the story was false and, moreover, that the reporter knew it was false.

Truth

The best defense against a libel suit is that the information you have presented is the truth. If you are doing your job properly and not misrepresenting the facts, this should be easy when producing news. In 1996, ABC News learned the hard way that news coverage cannot be deceitful in any way. As part of their investigation into unsanitary conditions at a popular food market, an employee of ABC applied for and got a job at the market using a false resume. A jury found ABC's allegations of unsafe practices in the store to be true, but gave an extremely large settlement to the store's management because of the deceptive way ABC uncovered the story. The end does not justify the means, and a jury can drive that point home in a big way.

Related to truth, another defense is to present a story as opinion. For example, news organizations regularly conduct public polls to gauge the public's opinions on a variety of issues. If a poll reveals that, say, a majority of Americans believe that a certain actress did not deserve to win an Oscar for best actress in a particular movie, the poll can be considered newsworthy because of the prominence of the actress and the Oscar awards. Although this poll might hurt the actress' feelings and possibly even cause her to lose an audition or two (though the added publicity might actually increase her auditions), she would not be likely to file any lawsuit because the news organization only reported public opinion. If the news organization itself chooses to state an opinion, then that opinion must be labeled as such. If in print, the opinion piece should appear on the opinion page; if broadcast, it should be labeled as commentary.

Regarding the defense of truth, sometimes a reporter might be asked to reveal his or her sources of information so that the accuracy of that information might be evaluated. Most states have **shield laws** that protect reporters from revealing their sources. (See Figure 12 1.) Sometimes reporters stand behind those laws; sometimes not. A very famous case of the former—*not* revealing a source—was *Washington Post* reporters Bob Woodward and Carl Bernstein not revealing the identity of their source, known as "Deep Throat," during their investigative reporting of the Watergate scandal in the Nixon White House. They promised this source they would not reveal his identity while he was living. However, in 2005 he chose to go public on his own and the world learned that Deep Throat was (William) Mark Felt, an Associate Director of the FBI during the Nixon administration.

A very famous example of choosing to *reveal* a source occurred in 2004, when CBS news anchor Dan Rather reported a story that President Bush had been given preferential treatment to get out of duty when he was in the Texas Air National Guard. The story was based on documents attributed to Bush's commander, Jerry B. Killian. However, the documents proved to be after-the-fact recreations; that is, forgeries. With the source's permission, Mr. Rather revealed that the source of these documents was former Texas Army National Guard officer Bill Burkett. Burkett argued that the documents were "like" the kind of special handling that Bush received, but the damage was done. It is worthwhile to note that even though Mr. Rather revealed his source, with the source's permission and confession that the documents were not authentic, damage to Mr. Rather's reputation still occurred. *Caveat reporter:* get the facts right. Having a source fall on his own sword after the fact does not substitute for a reporter's obligation to tell the truth.

Ethics

The obligation to be accurate requires special consideration of **ethics**. Ethical concerns stem from the branch of philosophy that explores choices of right and wrong. Entire books have been written about journalistic ethics. For this brief review, let us oversimplify and state merely that sometimes, even if a story might be true, it might not be right to report it. Tabloid journalism serves as a timely example. In fact, it can be argued that what separates the tabloid magazines and TV shows from mainstream journalism is ethics. If a prominent Hollywood couple splits, that might be accurate, but is it prying into their personal lives to report the details of their breakup? If a male

politician is photographed kissing another male politician on the lips, is it right to report a story that implies he is gay? If he is an elected official, the news organization can argue that the public has a right to know about the kiss and its implication. At the same time, if the politician chooses not to reveal his sexual orientation, and the kiss only implies but does not prove any orientation, the politician can argue that this photograph is **intrusion on seclusion**, more commonly called **invasion of privacy**.

A special area of ethical concern is **staging**. This refers to arranging the elements within the frame for your story. For EFP production, especially fiction, this is not a particular concern because viewers understand that each scene is scripted and carefully arranged (blocked) within the context of the set, whether that set is constructed (e.g., in a studio) or actual (e.g., a student's apartment).

For ENG and nonfiction, however, staging is of greater concern because of the obligation for accuracy. To be sure, the images must be framed and composed well, so a little arranging of the scenery for the sake of good lighting and composition is usually allowable. However, it is not permissible to change the scene to the extent that the truth of the situation is manipulated. Consider the example of a news package about a local company charged with giving a kickback to a local politician in exchange for getting a government contract. The CEO denies the charges and agrees to let you record an interview with him in his office. When you arrive, you notice that his desk is positioned in front of a window in a way that you will shoot against the window, resulting in too much bright contrast from this back light. You explain this to the CEO and he allows you to pivot his desk in a way that you can shoot without the bright window and its contrast problem. This would fall in the realm of ethical staging; you're not misrepresenting anything, but only making a furniture adjustment for the sake of lighting.

Now let us pretend this company has a photo in the lobby that depicts the CEO shaking hands with the politician in question when the politician toured the company the previous year. You decide to remove that picture from the lobby and put it on the wall in the CEO's office behind his repositioned desk so that the picture is seen prominently in the shot. (This is a hypothetical example, so let's not be concerned that the

CALIFORNIA SHIELD LAW
Cal. Const. article 1 § 2(b)
Cal. Evidence Code § 1070

THE BASICS
The California Shield Law provides legal protections to journalists seeking to maintain the confidentiality of an unnamed source or unpublished information obtained during newsgathering.

WHO IT PROTECTS
The Shield Law protects a "publisher, editor, reporter, or other person connected with or employed upon a newspaper, magazine, or other periodical publication, or by a press association or wire service" and a "radio or television news reporter or other person connected with or employed by a radio or television station." The Shield Law also likely applies to stringers, freelancers, and perhaps authors

WHAT INFORMATION IS PROTECTED
? The source of any information. There need be no assurance or expectation of confidentiality.
? Unpublished information
  • Specific information obtained during newsgathering but not disclosed to the public
  • Includes "all notes, outlines, photographs, tapes or other data of whatever sort"
  • Includes newsgatherer's eyewitness observations in a public place
  • Applies even if published information was based upon or related to unpublished information
? Protects only information obtained during newsgathering

WHAT IT PROTECTS FROM
The Shield Law only protects a journalist from being adjudged in contempt by a judicial, legislative, or administrative body, or any other body having the power to issue subpoenas, for the failure to comply with a subpoena. The Shield Law does not protect the journalist from other legal sanctions. Thus the Shield Law generally does not apply when the journalist or news organization is a party to a lawsuit and other sanctions are available.

EXCEPTIONS
? The Shield Law is a provision of the California Constitution. Therefore, there are no statutory exceptions.
? However, the California Supreme Court recognized a situation in which the Shield Law provides only qualified, not absolute, protection from contempt:
? When the information is sought by a criminal defendant or upon cross-examination by the prosecution if the journalist has testified for the defendant. In this circumstance, the defendant's federal 6th Amendment right to a fair trial preempts the state constitutional shield law. *Delaney v. Superior Court*, 50 Cal. 3d 785 (1990); *Miller v. Superior Court*, 21 Cal.4th 883 (1999); *Fost v. Superior Court*, 80 Cal. App 4th 724 (2000).
In this situation, a journalist may be subject to contempt for not disclosing information if:
  1. The defendant demonstrates a reasonable possibility that the information with materially assist the defense; and
  2. The defendant's fair trial rights outweigh the journalist's rights. In deciding this, a court will consider:
    A. The degree of importance of the information to the defendant
    B. Whether the information is otherwise available from another source and the defendant has attempted to obtain it
    C. If testifying would hinder the newsgathering ability of the reporter
    D. If the information is confidential or sensitive
If the court does order disclosure of the information, it must:
  1. Give the reporter 5 days notice before a contempt citation will be issued
  2. Issue a written order
? Disclosure of information under these conditions does not constitute a waiver of the right to assert the Shield Law for the same information in the future

What are the legal threats to a journalist protecting the identity of sources and unpublished information?

1. Contempt of Court
This is primarily a threat when the journalist is not a party to the lawsuit but is seen as a source of information by one or both of the parties. A judge may issue a contempt citation against a journalist for failing to comply with a subpoena issued in the action requesting disclosure of the information. Contempt may involve jail time and/or monetary fines. There are two kinds of contempt:
a. Criminal: Punishes one for not obeying a court rule or order
    ? may result in up to 6 months in jail
b. Civil: Designed to coerce one to comply with the court's order
    ? may result in unlimited jail time
? In California, an unlimited civil contempt citation may be switched to a limited criminal contempt citation upon a finding by a judge that:
(1) The journalist has a clearly articulated moral principle; and (2) Jail will not induce compliance with the court's disclosure order.
In re Farr, 36 Cal.App.3d 577(1974)

2. Liability
When a journalist is a party to an action, typically defending a defamation or privacy action, information may be sought by the opposing party through the rules of discovery. Judges can impose monetary or procedural sanctions for failure to comply with these rules. Moreover, when disclosure of information may be necessary in order to defend oneself, a judge can prevent one who refuses to disclose the information from asserting that defense.

TIP:
Be careful not to disclose unpublished information inadvertently. You may waive your rights under the Shield Law by disclosing information in conversations or telephone calls, with the investigators or the parties' lawyers, even if it is never published.

THE "REPORTER'S PRIVILEGE"

THE BASICS
The Reporter's Privilege is a non-statutory doctrine that also offers protection to those seeking to protect the identity of confidential sources and unpublished information. The Reporter's Privilege is recognized in most federal and many state courts including California.

WHEN TO USE IT
The Reporter's Privilege should be invoked in situations in which the Shield Law does not apply, such as:
  • Federal Law or the law of a state without a shield law applies
  • The threatened sanction is something other than contempt
  • The one seeking protection is not one to whom the Shield Law applies

HOW IT WORKS
The Reporter's Privilege is a qualified, not absolute, privilege in all situations. In California, a court will only require a newsgatherer to reveal sources and unpublished information if:
  1. The information is relevant and goes to the heart of the plaintiff's claim
  2. The plaintiff has exhausted all other alternative means of obtaining the information
  3. The plaintiff's need for the information outweighs the public interest in protecting confidentiality, including, for example, the need to protect whistleblowers; and
  4. The plaintiff has made a showing of merit of the case (in libel cases, present evidence of falsity) *Mitchell v. Superior Court*, 37 Cal.3d.268 (1984).

Most Federal courts apply a similar test.

WHAT TO DO IF:

1. You receive a call from a prosecutor or a defense lawyer asking you about a story you have written.
    1. Be careful not to disclose any unpublished information. You may waive your right to use the Shield Law for that information.
? If you are threatened with a subpoena,
    1. End the conversation
    2. Call your lawyer

2. You are *not* a party to a lawsuit and you are served with a subpoena requiring you to appear in court.
    1. Contact your lawyer
    2. Appear in court and assert the Shield Law or Reporter's Privilege. You should not just ignore the subpoena
? If you are ordered to disclose the information, request a written decision and delay of five days before a contempt citation is issued

3. You are *not* a party to a lawsuit and you are served with a subpoena requiring you to provide information directly to the parties.
    1. Contact your lawyer
    2. Assert the Shield Law or Reporter's Privilege in a letter to the parties
? If the parties persist, consider bringing a Motion to Quash Subpoena to the court

4. You *are* a party to a lawsuit and you are served with a discovery request seeking the identity of a confidential source or unpublished information.
    1. Object to the discovery on the basis of the Reporter's Privilege

A POCKET GUIDE TO
PROTECTING UNPUBLISHED INFORMATION AND CONFIDENTIAL SOURCES

A SERVICE OF
THE FIRST AMENDMENT PROJECT
SOCIETY OF PROFESSIONAL JOURNALISTS (Nor. Cal.)

HOW TO USE THIS GUIDE
This pocket guide is intended to be a quick reference and provide general information to journalists and citizens. It addresses some common problems, but does not substitute for research or consultation with a lawyer on detailed questions. This guide current as of September 16, 2004.

FOR MORE INFORMATION OR HELP:

FIRST AMENDMENT PROJECT.....................510/208-7744
www.thefirstamendment.org

CALIFORNIA FIRST AMENDMENT COALITION...415/460-5060
www.cfac.org

Funding provided by the Sigma Delta Chi Foundation of the Society of Professional Journalists

Figure 12-1 A two-sided brochure of California's shield law.

CEO would never allow this—pretend you get away with this when he steps out and he doesn't notice when he returns). This would be an example of unethical staging because you are now misrepresenting the situation. You are implying guilt—which has not been de-termined—by associating the CEO with the politician in this picture. The truth is that this picture is not even in the CEO's office (you had to move it from the lobby); it was taken during a company tour a year ago (the occasion is not known to have had any financial implications); and the existence of this picture alone in no way means the CEO gave the politician a kickback (lots of CEOs have pictures with lots of visiting politicians). In staging a scene, the ethical question to ask is whether or not the truth of the event is altered when you rearrange elements. If the truth of the situation remains, you may rearrange for the sake of image and sound quality; if the truth is altered, you may not.

One special case of staging involves **reenactments**—recreating scenes that were not recorded by using available accounts of what happened. No doubt you have seen reenactments of crimes, for example. No one was present with a camera to record the crime, so the TV producer recreates the crime according to available testimony, police records, and whatever other evidence is available. Because television is a visual medium, dramatizations such as these are acceptable, as long as they depict what is known without knowingly falsifying the truth. As you know from watching reenactments, they are labeled as such. Either a host or narrator announces that the scene is not the actual event but has been staged, or the word "reenactment" or "dramatization" or something similar is keyed over the scene, at least for the first few seconds. Again, the ethical obligation is one of truth—being honest with the viewers by letting them know they are watching a staged recreation of an event.

The same consideration applies to **file footage** or **stock footage**—scenes from an archive or a library of already-recorded footage—that you might use to add a visual element to a story, even if the footage is not from the event being reported. Label the video as such. For example, when the news media report a story about a famous sports player, and there is no current footage available, they use stock footage of that sports figure from some previous event. For the sake of truth, the words "file footage" or something similar appear over that clip to let the viewers know the video is not from the story being reported, but is used only to show visually the person who is the subject of the current story.

Consent

In addition to truth and the ethical considerations it brings, another defense against potential libel is **consent**. If a person consents to appear in your news report, then you have a right to use that person's image and whatever he or she says. For EFP non-news stories, as will be discussed later, it is always best to get a written consent form from each person you record. In contrast, for ENG news stories, written consent is not usually necessary because there is precious little time to get it and because the agreement to be interviewed (for print or broadcast) is normally considered to be **implied consent**. That is, when someone agrees to let you set up a camera and microphone and interview him or her for a news story, you can safely use sound-bites from that interview, as long as you do not deliberately edit things to present a falsehood (e.g., removing the word "not" from an accused person's statement, "I did not commit this crime").

In addition to agreeing to be interviewed, a **public forum** presents another type of implied consent. When a person agrees to appear at a **privileged event**—an event that is open to the public or at least open to credentialed journalists (whether or not it is held on public or private property)—that person's agreement to appear implies consent to be recorded. For example, universities love to invite their famous alumni to return to campus to speak with students. When an alumnus agrees to appear at the student union to give a talk and answer questions, that appearance is a public forum. The person knows that he or she may be recorded. The news media have a right to record the event and use sound-bites in their newspapers and newscasts, if those bites are deemed newsworthy.

Returning to the topic of ethics, remember that even if a subject has given consent and an item in a story is accurate, it might not be right to publish or broadcast that item. For example, Texas Tech University basketball coach, Bob Knight, is famous for his outbursts. Years ago, when he was the coach at Indiana University, CBS reporter Connie Chung interviewed him, as well as other celebrities, for a special report on how famous people deal with stress. With the lights, camera, and microphone all on him, Mr. Knight made a statement to the effect that he believed stress is like rape; if it's inevitable, one should relax and enjoy it. Immediately he realized the damning nature of what he said, even though he was trying to be funny, and retracted the statement, asking Ms. Chung to edit that out. What do you think she did? She aired it, of course. Would you have done the same thing?

Pro argument for using the soundbite: Mr. Knight had implied his consent by agreeing to be recorded; he said what he said; and that kind of soundbite gets ratings. Con argument: Mr. Knight immediately acknowledged that he had misspoken; he requested that this statement not be used because he did not mean it—that is, it was not an accurate reflection of his thoughts; and the soundbite was irrelevant to the story because he does not actually believe it—he was just trying to be funny and realized the statement was not humorous. After the story aired with the soundbite, Mr. Knight considered filing defamation charges against CBS and Ms. Chung, but in the end, he decided to let it go. The bottom line is that he said what he said during an interview to which he had consented (besides, it was neither the first nor the last time he uttered a controversial statement).

Public Property

A reporter has a right to report what the average person can see and hear from the vantage of **public property**, including streets, sidewalks, parks, lobbies of government buildings, and so on. (See Figure 12-2.) When a celebrity becomes engaged in a scandal, reporters typically camp out on the sidewalk or street outside that celebrity's home. They do not have a right to intrude on that person's private property without his or her consent (Fourth Amendment), but they can report from the adjacent public property (First Amendment). They may interview any passersby about the story. They may also photograph what the naked eye can see from the public vantage point. That is, they may use a normal angle lens (e.g., 35 or 50 mm) to shoot what the unaided eye can see, but they may not use a telephoto lens (e.g., 100 mm or more) to zoom in and record something on the private property that the unaided eye cannot see—that would be prying (intrusion on seclusion).

There are exceptions to this, such as celebrity stories in which the public's right to know might sometimes allow the use of a zoom lens. For example, when a President retreats to his favorite vacation spot, we sometimes see fuzzy pictures of him relaxing in the sun, riding horses, playing golf, and the like. Sometimes, news organizations send reporters in helicopters to get a birds'-eye view of a story. Again, the

"I don't care if your uplink is on North Pole public property -- the public does _not_ have a right to know if I wear boxers or briefs!"

Figure 12-2   A cartoon lampooning public property and the people's right to know.

videographer can shoot what the unaided eye can see from the helicopter, or perhaps even zoom in if warranted. For example, freeway chases are usually shot from a helicopter with the lens zoomed in to isolate the suspect's car on the road, but that road is public property, so this is allowed.

Sometimes people have the misconception that they have a right not to be recorded at all. For example, a storeowner might see a news photographer taking pictures and order the photographer to stop. If the photographer does not, the storeowner might call the police, even though there are no legal grounds for doing so as long as the photographer is on public property. If the photographer is not harassing the owner or creating a public disturbance, any action against the photographer by the owner could end with the owner going to court, not the photographer. As long as a photographer is on public property, practically the only reasons that can prevent video recording are public safety or risk to national security.

Exercising the right to take pictures can be overdone. For example, news organizations often hire helicopters with photographers to fly over celebrity weddings to get images. In a case such as the one of Madonna's wedding some years ago, the resulting air show with its noise spoiled the ceremony and became almost as big a story as the event. Unfortunately, celebrity status brings attention. Everyone would agree that the helicopters were an invasion of privacy, but any news show or newspaper would pay to have the pictures because the public really wanted to see that wedding. This does not make it ethical, but the public's right to know is a powerful force, and, in this case, it did make it legal.

Context

Being in the news media does not give you the right to **misrepresent** what you see or imply criminal wrongdoing without reasonable proof. You may not fabricate facts or use a shot from one event and imply that it represents another event. The context in which the scene is used must reflect the reality of the situation at the time of shooting. While most problems of misrepresentation or accusation come during editing or because of narration used over the pictures, the videographer should still be aware of any potential problems.

Here is a typical situation in which you could find yourself when shooting news. Suppose the assignment is to shoot people smoking in a public restaurant for a story on a proposed change in smoking laws. The owner of the Dinner Bell Cafe has agreed to let you shoot there. With the owner's permission, you do not need the consent of each individual patron. However, it is considered polite and ethical to seek permission of any customer that your camera approaches or anyone who needs to be lit by your sungun or stand light. If you can make the same shot using your zoom lens and existing lighting, then you need not ask them. Let's suppose that you shoot the cafe when it is lit well enough for you to shoot with natural light, and you do most of it on a tripod from the sides of the room so that many of the diners do not even notice your presence. The video airs on the news and one of the shots depicts an easily recognizable couple who is having an affair, which is discovered only after they appear on the news. The two sue the station for airing their pictures.

Is the station liable? No. The station cannot be held responsible. The couple may sue the restaurant, but they have no legal grounds for suing the broadcaster. If the story was about people having affairs and they showed this couple, it would be quite different. Even if it were true, it would be an unjustified invasion of privacy, unless the story was actually about that particular couple. This is why footage of people apparently committing crimes shows their faces covered by a video blur or mask so that they are unrecognizable. These people have not yet been convicted of any crimes. The safest way of dealing with questionable situations is to apply a good measure of caution. Do not say or imply anything bad about someone unless you are prepared to defend that accusation in court, or you know for certain on advice from an attorney that you are within your rights.

Public Figures

The really gray area of the privacy issue concerns people who can be considered public figures: politicians, movie stars, business leaders, and so on. The media camped outside Michael Jackson's ranch during his trial for child molestation. They could not have done that to just anyone. As a popular entertainer, Mr. Jackson put himself in the public spotlight and yielded most of his right to privacy to the public's right to know. There is still debate as to whether that media stakeout was ethical, but it was legal. The unfortunate part of this area of the law is that not all public figures attain this status by choice. Some are the innocent bystanders caught up in events not of their making. The victims of crimes and disasters, relatives of the famous, and even witnesses to events can suddenly find themselves the center of media attention—and powerless to do anything about it.

In addition to a somewhat reduced right to privacy, celebrities have an additional **burden of proof** if they believe someone has defamed them: **malice aforethought**. That is, a celebrity must demonstrate that the alleged defamer acted maliciously, with actual intent to harm, in publishing or broadcasting a defamatory story. A non-celebrity must only show that the defamer cannot demonstrate evidence of truth. For example, if you (assuming you are not famous) are wrongly accused in a news story of committing some felony crime, you may have a case for a libel lawsuit (depending on a whole mix of other variables, of course, such as actual damage—the particulars to be decided by legal counsel). For a celebrity, however, the mere fact the story was wrong is usually not sufficient for a libel case; the celebrity must demonstrate—in addition to actual harm—that the defamation was planned with malicious intent.

Trespassing

In the pursuit of an important story or shot, many news shooters have found themselves breaking other laws. The most common is **trespassing**. A property owner is powerless to stop a news crew from shooting while the crew remains on public property. However, this does not apply to private property, where the crew members cannot only be removed but also arrested. Trespassing charges are seldom filed against news crews for two main reasons. First, property owners usually do not want the added publicity or hassle. Second, courts are generally sympathetic to the media if the story is in the public interest.

The public's right to know is an area of the law with wide latitude for abuse by the media. The news technique made famous by *Sixty Minutes*, where the shooter and reporter barge into a private place and thrust the camera into the face of the accused, is a prime example. The reporters fire accusations at the accused who screams for them to leave while covering his or her face. This approach produces very dramatic pictures and can make any subject look guilty. *Sixty Minutes* does this successfully because the producers are *very* sure of the person's guilt or inability to prove innocence. However, this *is* trespassing.

Most trespassing by news crews goes unnoticed until after the fact. The trespass might be as simple as a photographer hopping a farmer's fence to get a better shot of a beautiful sunset, or as serious as sneaking into a building to show that foreign workers removing asbestos are not provided with protective clothing and masks. The former is done out of the innocence of the story; the latter, out of the public's right to know that people are being unfairly exploited and their lives put at risk. In both cases, the photographer could end up in jail. The charges may later be dropped or the fine, if any, inconsequential. Regardless of the reason for the trespass, you may experience at least some trouble.

In the majority of cases, the trespassing videographer would be ordered to leave and that would be the end of it. There are cases, however, when just the opposite can happen. The videographer shooting the sunset could be held at gunpoint by an angry farmer tired of too many vandals. The farmer can make the videographer wait until the sheriff shows up. When you are an uninvited interloper, you increase the chances of being in the wrong place at the wrong time.

A law that makes it an acceptable risk for so many news crews to trespass is the one against robbery. If you are caught taking pictures on private property, the property owner can order you to leave, or even detain you until the police arrive, but cannot take your camera or any of your other possessions because this is your property. Taking it against your will or by threat is defined as robbery. It does not matter that you are on someone else's property; your things, including the images recorded on the tape or disc or chip, belong to you or to your employers, who have you as their representative.

Unfortunately, just as the law often allows you extra leeway in cases of trespass, it also tends to allow leeway to angry property owners who may destroy your tape-disc-chip or damage your equipment. You might be told that pursuing any charges against the property owner is inadvisable because there is very little to gain from it. You can easily appear to be the bad guy breaking the law or harassing the property owner. You must weigh the worth of what you are trying to do against the risks you are taking. The laws do not bend in your direction only.

Hidden Cameras

A common technique for taking news pictures on private property, where the owner would not allow a crew access, is to use a hidden camera. Today's micro-cameras, which record near-broadcast quality images on mini-DV tape cassettes or small memory cards or microchips, can be hidden with ease in handbags, briefcases, or even under clothing. (See Figure 12-3.) With the use of fiber-optic lenses, miniature color cameras can be placed almost anywhere. For this type of setup, a wide-angle lens is often no larger than a small button and can easily look just like one. Fiber optics enable the camera to be placed some distance from the lens in the same way that a microphone is run by cable to a recorder.

The use of a hidden camera is as old as photojournalism. News organizations and law enforcement agencies have set up sting operations using cameras concealed behind false walls or two-way mirrors to capture subjects doing everything from selling phony

Figure 12-3   A pinhole camera about the size of a button can be easily hidden. (Courtesy of Spy Gadgets)

health insurance to planning murders for hire. In 2006, *NBC Dateline* produced a series of investigative reports about men soliciting sex from minors via the Internet. The news crew caught many perpetrators on hidden video when they appeared at a house, thinking they were going to a rendezvous with an adolescent. After discovering a crew from NBC, the men left, only to be greeted on the street by local sheriffs with waiting handcuffs.

While such uses often lead to arrests and even jury investigations, this does not mean that the accused are always found guilty. John DeLorean, a flamboyant automobile executive, was recorded by hidden camera purchasing cocaine. He was acquitted of the charges despite the video evidence. The jury thought he had been pressured into buying the illegal substance by government agents. If it had been a news crew doing the secret recording and DeLorean suing them, it could have cost the news organization millions of dollars to be wrong. You must make sure the law is on your side before you engage in or make public your investigative activities.

The most common situation involves going onto private property to show illegal or questionable activity in cases where the visible presence of a camera would cause the activity to stop. The videographer usually uses the disguise of an interested party to the

activity, for example, a spectator at a pit bull dogfight or a buyer of child pornography. Making use of a wide-angle lens, the hidden camera can merely be pointed in the direction of the activity to show an overall view of what is happening. This use of video can be quite dangerous. Before engaging in any risky form of photojournalism, you should consider what the worst possible outcome might be and how you can minimize your risks. In some cases, it could cost you your life.

Because this technique pushes the limits of the right to privacy, the laws concerning the use of hidden cameras can vary from state to state. Check with your state's attorney general's office before using a hidden camera on private property; check with your lawyer before airing any part of it. Both the context in which the video is used and the way in which it was obtained can determine liability in any criminal or civil complaint. At least one state in the Midwest has made it illegal to use such a camera to record on farms after reaction to the use of hidden cameras by the news media in response to animal rights groups who were protesting the treatment of livestock. Disguised protesters and TV journalists in that state were visiting "puppy mills" to expose the horrible conditions under which the dogs were bred and raised. The resulting public outcry did not lead the state to clamp down on the offending "mills" but rather on the journalists. Laws that restrict journalism are almost always tested in the courts, and this example points out the complexity of interpreting the right of privacy versus the public's right to know.

Names and Numbers

Another aspect of privacy involves information. Credit card numbers, tax returns, addresses, social security numbers, and bank account and telephone numbers cannot be made public by the news media. Showing an audience this type of information without good cause can be a serious violation of the right to privacy, even for people who fit the category of a public figure.

The U.S. Post Office has one hard-and-fast rule: you may not show the names and addresses of any letters or packages in a photo because that is not public information any more than the parcel's contents are; it is meant only for the sender and the addressee to know. This situation would also exist in a department store if you were shooting a story on consumer credit. You cannot show someone's credit card number on the screen. In both situations, there are ways to get all the shots needed, including extreme close-ups, without violating anyone's rights. It might be part of a story to show the destination of mail. By carefully arranging the letters in a pile, you can have successive letters stacked so that only the city line of the address can be seen. Without the name and street, the city cannot be linked to any one individual. The same can be done with credit cards. By asking the customer to hold the card with a finger covering the name and part of the card's number, a viewer would have no way of getting the name and credit number to misuse.

Anytime you shoot names and numbers, you must pay special attention to the rights of the people associated with them. Sometimes the most innocent situation can lead to a nasty legal conflict. If you are in a real estate office doing a story on home buying, and you shoot a close-up on some bid papers, you might inadvertently show the name of the bidder. If other business associates see the story and confrontation results in a deal falling through, you might be sued for invasion of privacy. Permission was never given to make the deal public, and the bidder was not a public figure.

Regardless of the situation, you must always consider how much personal information you might be revealing about someone, especially if that person has nothing directly to do with your story. The safest thing to do is never to show anyone's name or personal identification numbers unless you have permission or that information is already public knowledge, such as the address of a criminal charged in a serious crime. The fact that someone's name and number are listed in the phone book does not give you the right to use this information, unless that particular person is the subject of public interest.

Police Orders

Sometimes police officers try to stop news photographers from recording crime or accident scenes, and even threaten the shooters with arrest. The shooters usually comply; it makes sense to maintain good media–police relations, not to mention to avoid going to jail. But the shooters often attempt to find ways to circumvent the officers' orders for the sake of the story; they need to get some footage. Usually, the photographer simply backs away and uses a telephoto lens to continue shooting. Nonetheless, the threat of arrest is real, although officers know charges are unlikely to be filed against the photographer; the police usually release the shooter after a short time.

The official reason for detaining the photographer can simply be interfering with a peace officer. This offense can be hard to prosecute, but it gives the police legal grounds to lock a shooter in the back of a squad car. The reality is that most police know that keeping the photographer locked up until the event is over accomplishes what they want: no pictures. If you are threatened with arrest, believe the officer regardless of your opinion about your rights.

There are times when the police and the media seem to be at cross-purposes, and you must take extra care to make sure you are not pointlessly exercising your rights at the expense of good police work. One of the reasons police often do not want pictures at the scene of a crime is to prevent valuable evidence from becoming common knowledge. Only the criminal, the police investigators, and the prosecutor should know the details of the crime scene until the trial. This eliminates the innocent but disturbed individuals who confess to the offense, or false witnesses who come forward to throw off suspicion from someone else. If the police are sure that only the real criminal would know certain details about the crime scene, then the fakers can easily be spotted.

The greatest problems arise when the police do not make clear their reasons for denying pictures. The public's right to know can be on a collision course with the ability of the police to do their job. If the news organization has established good relations with local law enforcement, most problems will not arise. One part of the constitutional responsibility of a free press is to question authority. This aspect of journalism can put you at odds with the police. In the absence of a good working relationship, the news media can hamper an investigation with aggressive coverage. Knowing where the line is between your rights and the duty of the police to protect the public can be almost impossible. You must decide in a split second whether the shot is worth the chance of getting arrested. Sometimes you have to lose a battle to win the war.

Part of your duty to serve the public's right to know is to be able to do just that: inform the public. The police or any other agency or organization might try to stop your coverage for any number of reasons. It is your job as a journalist to decide if their reasons are valid (not showing a rape victim), are simply self-serving (no bad publicity), or are an attempt to cover up wrongdoing (the police using excessive force). If you are locked in a squad car, you will not be able to make any decisions or take any pictures. Your most important goal is to keep shooting video without getting arrested. You can be a very powerful person with your camera, and with that power comes a great deal of pressure to direct what you do or do not do. Remember that without your camera, you are powerless. Many people will want to censor what you are shooting.

Other Things to Know

Almost all TV stations have lawyers who scrutinize pictures or scripts that might lead to legal problems before the material is aired. Of course, there are always times when a lawyer is not available for this purpose, so there are a few other useful things for you to know. If you, as a news photographer, know that something you are recording could result in a potential legal problem, try to head off as much as you can in the field while still covering the story. If some people really do not want their pictures taken and they are not directly part of the story, do not shoot them. Avoid problems that serve no purpose in the story. If you know that the video you are shooting is for a story on couples having affairs, then you should provide plenty of shots of couples where the audience would have no way of identifying them. Shoot only their clasped hands; shoot them out of focus; use a potted plant in the foreground to block the view of their faces; shoot them from behind; do not let the particular cafe be recognizable in the shots; and so on. This makes the job of the editor easier and adds another layer of safety to keep you and the station out of trouble.

At the same time, you should not censor yourself so heavily that you cannot get the job done or get all the pictures you need. You have to rely on the other people involved with putting the material on the air. You might not always be the best person to make the decision on what to show or how to show it. Unless you know for a fact that you cannot show something, or you were given explicit instructions on how to shoot it, do the shooting with several options in mind. Trust the editors and the news management to make the best use of the pictures. After all, the pictures are not public until they are aired. You can shoot anything, but you cannot always air everything. If you at least avoid the obvious problems (e.g., showing the faces of undercover police officers), other problems can be dealt with in postproduction by not using the shot or by applying special effects.

EFP: Non-News Productions

Any video product that does not fall under the category of news does not enjoy the same latitude regarding privacy. With the backing of the Fourth Amendment, violating someone's right to privacy can quickly lead to the courtroom. The way the courts interpret privacy laws is much stricter for non-news productions than for news. Even if the method of shooting and the presentation are the same as news, if the videographer is not shooting for a news organization, there are some restrictions on "free press" rights. These restrictions have to do with: (1) profit and publicity, (2) content, and (3) the intended audience.

Profit and Publicity

Most non-news production is done not to serve the public but to serve the producer or subject of the video. Because these parties are benefiting from the video, they are not allowed to do so at the expense of someone else's rights. Non-news production normally brings to mind commercials or entertainment and informational programs, but it also includes areas like public service announcements, charity promotions, and business presentations. Although an organization might be nonprofit, and its 30-second video spot shot for free, the organization still benefits from the publicity. People see the spot and donate money to that charity. While a community service might be important and have the best community needs in mind, the organization is not allowed to invade anyone's privacy. It is easy to see that showing the face of a down-and-out person on Skid Row in a paid commercial for a trade school without permission is violating a right to privacy for simple monetary gain. It might not be as easy to see that the same shot in a public service announcement without permission still violates this same right, but it does.

Content

Even with permission, you cannot use a person's image in any way you please. It is not acceptable to misrepresent what you are doing. If you ask permission to photograph someone and give either a direct answer or implication of how the pictures will be used, and then use the pictures in a totally different manner (e.g., showing the person in a negative way), you could still be in for a big lawsuit. Also, unlike news, the plaintiffs in cases like this tend to be more aggressive because they can argue that the producers exploited them for money, rather than using their images for journalistic reasons. A news organization might be able to show that the misuse of the picture came about by error due to the rush to meet a deadline, which resulted in the material not being double-checked. An EFP production company does not have the problem of on-air deadlines only hours from shooting because it has the time to make sure that everything is right and within legal bounds.

In this discussion of content, **humor** deserves special mention. In a nutshell, in the context of humor, anything goes. A political satirist can get away with saying the most outrageous things about politicians, without a grain of truth to any of it, because the satirist is clearly making the statements for the purpose of comedy. An actor on a comedy sketch show can portray, say, the President in an outlandish and negative way because the portrayal is clearly in a humorous context. Jon Stewart can take a paparazzi photo of a famous actor or actress and twist it to the extreme, making a statement that is at once absolutely ridiculous and downright hilarious, because it is understood that Mr. Stewart's television show is meant to be humorous; after all, it airs on Comedy Central.

The legal theory here is that media organizations have a First Amendment right to free speech, and any attempt to censor humor is a violation of that right. In a nonfictional context (e.g., news, documentary), where informing the public is the primary objective

(entertainment might be secondary), there is an expectation of truth and accuracy. In the context of comedy, entertainment is clearly the objective, not information, so exaggeration and untruths are accepted for the sake of laughs. For example, Vice President Dick Cheney was involved in an unfortunate incident in 2006: he mistakenly shot and wounded a hunting companion while quail hunting in Texas. While news organizations strove to learn the details of the accident to report the facts, pundits and cartoonists strove to parody and exaggerate the incident for the sake of entertainment, often portraying the Vice President in brutal ways. (See Figure 12-4.) Because the context could be demonstrated to be humorous satire (e.g., Jay Leno is a known comedian), the Vice President had no legal right to attempt to file any defamation charges.

Mr. Vice President, the quail are over there.

Figure 12-4 A cartoon lampooning Vice President Dick Cheney, after he accidentally shot and wounded a hunting companion in Texas.

Intended Audience

The greater the number of people who see your product, the more you need to make sure that every little legal detail is properly handled. In the case of a student video, the rights of some subjects can be overlooked because only a very small number of people will ever see the video. A student is generally allowed to gather video in the same way as a news crew, even without a press pass. Context can be overlooked because no one outside the class will see the video. It is similar to art students copying a great painting for a class project; inside the classroom, the use is educational and non-profit, and therefore acceptable, but any use outside the classroom is illegal. If a student video is only screened in class, it is unlikely there are any rights issues. But if that video is submitted to a contest where it will be screened and judged, the student had better be sure the rights of everyone in that project, from the actors who appear on screen to the musician whose music is on the soundtrack, are not violated.

Most corporate videos are not too concerned with the right of privacy in their video presentations if the intended audience is only the workers within the company. Just as in the student video example, the size of the audience is small enough that any infractions of the law will more than likely go unnoticed. The key word here is "unnoticed." As a corporate video producer, you might record in public areas and never get permission to use people's pictures in your presentation because they and anyone who knows them will probably never see the end product. Of course, there is a remote possibility that someone portrayed in a negative fashion will find out and sue.

Caveat producer: the feeling that if your audience is small enough you need not worry at all about anyone else's rights can lead to real trouble. Sometimes this belief can work, but the one time that it does not, it could cost the company or you a fortune. The key to this issue is that the image of a person who has not given permission for its use must be recognizable in a video. If the shot is wide enough or done from behind or lasts such a short time that the subject cannot be recognized, then a charge of invasion of privacy will be hard to justify. Still, unless you know for certain that no one you are shooting will complain or even find out how their pictures are used, you had better secure an okay from all parties involved in any recognizable on-screen appearance. Take a stack of **consent forms**, sometimes called "talent" or "performance" release forms, whenever you shoot and ask everyone in the video to sign one. (See Figures 12-5 and 12-6.)

COPYRIGHTS

A TV news photographer can shoot almost anything and air it. But an editor cannot take just any source of video and insert it into a news story. One TV station cannot simply record another's newscast and use video from it as its own. Nor can segments of any other program or movie be used in its news stories unless it is used by permission of, or by purchase from, its owner. For non-news production, without the "run and shoot" requirement that is often necessary for breaking news stories, copyright considerations are even more stringent. Because non-news production usually allows more time in the schedule, some of that time should be used for proper acquisition of copyright permission. For these reasons, it is important to know the basics of **copyright** law—statutes that recognize people's right to own material they create. Also, **trademarks**—graphics that others own, such as corporate logos and cartoon characters—are protected similarly to copyrighted works.

Violations

One of the most common copyright violations is the use of movie clips in news stories. Without the permission of the owner or copyright holder of the movie (the studio or producer), you cannot use any part of a movie in your news story. If, however, the studio has sent you a video press kit made up of the trailer and several clips from that film, you can use the pictures in any news story where they would be appropriate. By sending you the press kit, the copyright holder has in a sense given you permission to use the film clip. The same rule applies not only to ENG, but to EFP and, really, to any TV show or program.

Often TV stations in smaller markets break the copyright rules because no one from the movie or TV industry will see the story. This is similar to making copies of your favorite movie and giving them to your friends. It seems innocent, but it is illegal. The FBI warning at the head of each video applies to all TV producers and news people, as well as to the public. If you want people to respect your right of ownership for what you produce, you must respect their rights.

Performance Release

CALIFORNIA STATE UNIVERSITY, FULLERTON

In consideration of my appearance
and/or creative work on the program
(print title or producer's name)_____,
and for no subsequent remuneration,
I (print name)_____,
on behalf of myself, my heirs, executors, administrators and assignors, do hereby
authorize in perpetuity California State University, Fullerton to use live or
recorded on tape, film, computer chip, or other media, my name, voice, image,
performance, musical composition, written work and/or other material therein for
display and/or transmission, in classrooms and theatres, over any distribution
systems worldwide including theater, broadcast, cable, and/or the internet.

I further agree on behalf of myself and those stated above that California
State University, Fullerton may also use my name, likeness, and biography for
publishing and promoting broadcasts and other associated uses.

I warrant and represent that all material furnished and used by me on any
such programs is my own original material, or material which I have full authority
to use for such programs. Furthermore, I agree to indemnify, defend, and hold
harmless the State Of California, the Trustees of the California State University,
and California State University, Fullerton and its employees, officers, directors,
and/or agents for any and all claims, suits, or liabilities arising from my appearance
and the use of any of my materials, name, likeness, and/or biography.

Signature_____ Phone_____

Address_____

Email_____ Date_____

If signatory is a minor:

Signature of_____ Phone_____
legal guardian
Printed name of legal guardian_____

Address_____

Email_____ Date_____

Figure 12-5 An example of a university's performance release form. If a subject completes a release form, there is less chance of being sued for unauthorized use. Forms like these are used extensively in non-news productions.

PERFORMANCE RELEASE

I hereby assign all rights for the sound and/or image recording made of me this date,

_____, to (producer's name or program title)_____,
and I hereby authorize the reproduction, sale, copyright, exhibition, broadcast,
cablecast, webcast, and/or any and all other means of distribution of said recording
without limitation and in perpetuity, with no subsequent remuneration.

If adult: If minor:
Signature_____   Guardian_____

Figure 12-6   An example of a simplified performance release form. Short forms like these are often used when there are many subjects in a shoot.

If you are caught using parts of movies or TV shows without permission, the owner can charge you a rental or licensing fee that can be as high as several thousand dollars a minute for what you used, plus residual payments to those who worked on the show.

Fair Use Rules

The news media, and to some extent non-news organizations, can use limited copyrighted material without permission in some special cases. By invoking the **Fair Use Clause** of the 1976 Copyright Act (Title 17, Ch. 1, Par. 107), it is possible to use some protected material in your production, either ENG or EFP. The Fair Use Clause reads:

Notwithstanding the provisions of sections 106 and 106A, the fair use of a copyrighted work, including such use by reproduction in copies or phonorecords or by any other means specified by that section, for purposes such as criticism, comment, news reporting, teaching (including multiple copies for classroom use), scholarship, or research, is not an infringement of copyright. In determining whether the use made of a work in any particular case is a fair use the factors to be considered shall include—
(1) the purpose and character of the use, including whether such use is of a commercial nature or is for nonprofit educational purposes;
(2) the nature of the copyrighted work;
(3) the amount and substantiality of the portion used in relation to the copyrighted work as a whole; and
(4) the effect of the use upon the potential market for or value of the copyrighted work.

The fact that a work is unpublished shall not itself bar a finding of fair use if such finding is made upon consideration of all the above factors.

In brief, fair use is determined by one or a combination of four factors: purpose, nature, amount, and effect.

- If the *purpose* of the usage is nonprofit (you do not charge viewers or make any money from the creator's work) and/or educational (you show the work for instruction), this might be fair use. For example, teachers are permitted to show movies within the confines of their classrooms for discussion and learning; a trickier question is whether or not they can post movies on their course Web sites because the movies could be downloaded once they are on the Web, even if the sites are password protected.

- If the *nature* of the work is intended for research or comment or some similar objective, this might be fair use. For example, many organizations, including the government, produce their own **video news releases (VNRs)**—short video "news packages"—and send them to broadcast stations in the hopes they will use them to fill their news programming. The objective is free publicity in the form of a soft news story about the organization, so the nature of a VNR lends itself to fair use (though defamation laws restrict you from editing the VNR to put the company in a negative light).

- If the *amount* of the copyrighted work you use is minimal—some interpretations suggest no more than 10% of the whole—that might constitute fair use. For example, for research purposes, an Internet radio station might put 20 seconds of a 200-second song on its Web site, and then invite listeners to play the music and respond to a survey about whether they like or dislike that music.

- If the *effect*, or impact, of your use of someone else's creation presents even the possibility of economic harm or loss of value (e.g., a lost sale), that is NOT fair use; for fair use to be claimed, there can be NO potential for any loss of market or value. For example, a student newspaper creates a movie review link to its Web site and places downloaded trailers of the movies that are reviewed on that site. The trailers have the potential to entice people to purchase tickets to, and DVDs of, those movies, so this might be fair use because there is not likely to be any economic harm to the films' producers.

Authors' disclaimer: It is impossible to cover the full gamut of fair use in this brief section. The examples above are in no way legally binding; they are presented merely as illustrations of the types of uses that might be considered fair use, if certain conditions are met. Many variables come into play regarding fair use. Before assuming that using some part of someone else's creation is fair use, you should always consult with an **intellectual property (IP)** lawyer—someone trained in the intricacies of copyright law. The money paid to a good IP attorney can save you many times that amount in a fine if you violate copyright law. In other words, if you implement any of the examples in the previous paragraph, or similar uses of protected work, do not assume your use is fair until an expert has assessed all the variables of your case. This discussion of fair use is illustrative, not legal, so you cannot use it in your defense if you are found to be in violation of copyright statutes.

Permission

For non-news production especially, it is always best to acquire copyright permission. To be sure, many students use actors in their productions without thinking to get signed talent release forms from them, or the students use favorite songs in their projects without obtaining the rights to use those songs. As long as these projects are not seen outside of the classroom, this usage is normally considered legal because the projects are created for educational purposes only. However, as soon as students submit their projects to competitions and festivals, they are in violation of copyright laws because wider audiences will now see the work. Moreover, if a distributor happens to be at a festival and wishes to buy a project to sell to movie theaters or television stations or take direct to DVD, money is now involved, and all copyright permissions must be renegotiated (assuming the initial permission was for nonprofit student use only). Everyone who holds rights to any part of the student project, such as the actors who performed and the musician whose music is used, will want his or her cut of the paycheck.

For this reason, it is wise for students producing EFP stories (fiction or nonfiction) to get in the habit of always taking talent release forms with them when they shoot and having everyone on camera sign them. Additionally, it is wise to ask your musician friends to compose original music for your piece, and have them also sign a release form. Failing that, use royalty-free music clips. Your school probably owns a **music library** or two that you can use without paying royalties, or you can use the free **music loops** that probably come with your video editing software, or you can search the Web for royalty-free or **public domain** music (discussed later) that you can download and use for free and legally. In the latter case, be sure to verify that any music you download really is free and legal and that the Web site is not simply advertising free downloads to get you to visit that site without actually having the right to give you those downloads. The issue of copyright on the Web is discussed in a subsequent section.

News production has a bit more leeway regarding fair use than does non-news production. The First Amendment is interpreted to give news organizations the right to report stories because the public has a right to be informed. A good example of a time when news has more freedom to use copyrighted material than non-news is when a famous actor dies. Non-news productions may not use clips from that actor's films without obtaining all the necessary permissions from the copyright holders. News organizations, however, are permitted in their obituaries to use clips from that actor's work without first getting copyright permission. The law allows any material that is directly related to the telling and understanding of a story to be used in that telling. Especially at the network level, such use is carefully scrutinized to make sure it is not abused. Fair use material is generally limited to one-time use only, and it does have to adhere to a strict and direct relationship to the subject of the story. Showing a scene from *The Da Vinci Code* in a feature story about a local woman who claims she is part of the secret society depicted in the film would not qualify as fair use. But a story about a major scandal concerning the making of the movie (there are none as far as we know) could allow the news organization to use clips without permission.

In stories involving controversy, it is often best not to make the video being fair used too prominent in the piece. In other words, the clips should not "wallpaper" the package. A good method of distancing the material from your original portions of the story is to play the fair-used material in a monitor and then shoot the set as well as the video so it is obvious that the video is being copied and not simply used as normal B-roll. While fair use can shield a news organization from copyright fines, it cannot shield them from lawsuits trying to assess damages. The suits can fail in court, but the cost of simply defending against them to that point can be more trouble and costly than paying off the copyright holder.

Piracy

The day after Christmas 2004, a giant tsunami inundated a number of coastal cities and villages around the Indian Ocean. Some people—mostly vacationers in Sri Lanka and other places—turned on their camcorders and recorded giant waves of water flooding over and around trees, streets, buildings, and people. Within a day, nearly every TV news outlet in the world was running this footage. How did so many get access to it so quickly? Some bought it. Others took it form the Internet or from satellites without paying for it.

The age of satellite transmission has not only made it easier to get images from one place to another, but it has also made it easier for more people to have access to these images. Unless a signal is scrambled, anyone with a satellite dish and the proper tuner can tap into any channel on the satellite. Because so many different organizations use the few satellites available for occasional use, scrambling has not been a practical method of protecting news material. Entertainment outlets, such as HBO or pay-per-view shows, control one particular channel on the satellite for extended periods of time, or even own a particular channel. They can easily have their signals scrambled to protect against piracy.

News professionals have traditionally shown a low concern for piracy because the ease of accessibility and speed of delivery are always more important. Journalists in the past have generally respected each other's rights of ownership, even when they share the same satellite channel. It is not unusual to see NBC, CBS, ABC, FOX, and CNN stories all being fed one after another on a single channel from the satellite. Sometimes only their mutual cooperation allows any network to get material from a distant location in a timely manner. Unfortunately, the expanding number of news organizations has made the competition to get exclusive pictures more important than ever. The expanding market for the pictures has also made the ability to keep them exclusive harder and harder.

A picture taken by an NBC affiliate can be sent via satellite to the NBC network in New York, which can in turn send the picture to all NBC affiliates across the country on their regular news feed by satellite. One of the affiliates that receives the feed might have a contract to provide pictures to CNN News and uses the shot in a story sent to CNN. CNN puts the story on its feed to all its subscribers. One such station happens to be a CBS affiliate, who repackages the story and sends it to CBS network in New York. In the evening the shot appears on both NBC and CBS. If the special group-owned stations' news services contain affiliates of all three networks, the picture can end up on every news show in America. The lightning speed of satellite delivery makes each of these transfers possible and explains how one picture can make it to every TV channel in the country in a few short hours without openly breaking any copyright laws (individual agreements notwithstanding).

The case of the Indian Ocean tsunami is more complex. The magnitude of the wave and its destruction made it a major news story. Some who paid for footage alleged that the video never made the legal rounds and was simply stolen off satellite feeds or from Internet sites. Others alleged that the story justified nonpaying use of the video under the public's right to know. This example demonstrates that once pictures start to travel from one station or from one company (a broadcasting company can own stations with different affiliations) to another through network or smaller news service feeds, be they via satellite or the Internet, the copyright laws can be stretched to the limit. Today, this issue of pirating video is even more confusing because full-motion, full-frame video is easily accessible via high-speed, broadband connections to the World Wide Web. Because the Web is digital, any news video put on a Web site by a news service (e.g., CNN, MSNBC) can be easily downloaded by unscrupulous individuals, edited for their own purposes, and then resent or "Webcast."

Exclusivity

Because of the way business is generally done in TV news, it can be almost impossible to keep a particular picture exclusively in your organization if the picture is of great interest to the public. However, if proper legal precautions are taken and the pictures are tightly controlled, you might be able to maintain exclusivity. It can be easier to control pictures not produced by members of your station or company. Previous agreements can make pictures shot by staff members available to other members of the group or company

automatically. An independent producer or freelance photographer might offer you exclusive pictures, and as part of the agreement to let you air them, the pictures come with tight restrictions on their use. The famous Zapruder film showing the assassination of President John F. Kennedy is not the property of the public or any news organization. It requires special permission from the owners to air it, and you must comply with many restrictions in its use. As in any legal contract, you are bound by the agreement you have signed, and it can take precedence over other agreements. The agreement might say that only your station and not other parts of your network or group can air the video.

Bugs

One way producers keep track of their video and avoid any unauthorized use is by marking the video as theirs. In a manner similar to putting a brand on cows, videomakers can "brand" their footage. In TV terms, this is called a **bug**, also known as a **watermark**: a small logo or abbreviation, much like the rancher's brand, is superimposed in one corner of the picture when the video is dubbed or transmitted. While it is widely used in news throughout the world, it is most common in sporting event highlights. Instead of recording hours and hours of sports, a local station can simply contract with an authorized highlight producer. Several times a day this company feeds by satellite condensed highlights of all the important sporting events of the day. All the video has a bug in the corner of the screen to identify the origin of the pictures. If the bug should appear on another station or anywhere else that has no agreement with the producer, then legal action can be taken to stop this activity.

Courtesies

The easiest way to get other people's material is simply to ask for it. For pictures that are not controversial or have little competitive advantage, most stations or producers allow their use if the owner of the video gets an on-screen credit. This credit is somewhat like the bug, only larger. Usually displayed across the bottom of the screen, it reads, "Video courtesy of (producer's name)," whether it be CBS News or Paramount Pictures or John Doe. You must obtain permission to use this method of protection.

The use of the "courtesy" is usually granted by verbal agreement and not written up or signed. If you or your company has a reputation for honesty in this type of agreement, then getting permission is usually quite easy. But when the video is very important, it is more difficult to get permission for use in this way.

There is a point where the escalation of fighting within the media to keep exclusive rights to something does slow down. News organizations that happen to get video of a dramatic or history-making event when others did not might indeed share the pictures with or even without a credit because they feel the public, not just their viewers, must see it. A private party might not feel that sense of duty to inform the public and reserve the rights to the pictures, as in the case of the Zapruder film.

Pool

In some situations, only one camera is allowed to enter a restricted area, or there is only enough room for one camera. In the course of daily news coverage and during large national stories, this situation arises time and time again. The solution is to form a **pool**. One camera goes, but its video is shared among all interested organizations. If you have ever seen the President of the United States outside the White House, you would have noticed a small band of press people who have a slightly closer position than the larger group of press. This small group is the White House Pool. These few TV cameras are from the major news sources, but the video from each of them is made available to anyone who wants it. Because every TV news photographer covering the President would want this front-row advantage, it would be a madhouse of pushing and shoving without the pool arrangement.

The most common use of pools in the TV news industry is in the courtroom. As in the example of the President, it would be too disruptive to have many cameras in court. Usually one person or group in every market coordinates the pools to make sure the burden of having to do the extra work involved (wiring a

courtroom for sound, providing a multiple outlet box, or making dubs) gets handled fairly. Often the pool photographer cannot be in position in the hallway to get the crucial just-out-of-court statements by the defendants. In these cases, it is common practice for non-pool photographers to let the pool organization use their hallway interviews.

Some situations in the field can require the videographers present to form an impromptu pool on the spot, without the time or ability to check with management before doing so. An example might be a group of shooters at the command post of firefighters battling a raging forest fire. The commander is going via helicopter to see if the fire lines are holding in a remote village cut off from the usable roads; one seat is offered for a videographer from the group. In this situation, the videographers present would decide among themselves who is the best to go. The video is then dubbed either at the site later or at the station. The group can enter into an agreement on the ownership of the footage independent of any outside input.

This ability gives the shooter in the field the power to negotiate access to restricted or dangerous areas. Setting up a pool so that footage can be shared and no other cameras need to access the site makes dealing with the media just that much easier for the emergency services people. If the media can be satisfied with one photographer, then it becomes an easy solution to a growing problem: throngs of photographers all wanting pictures or, worse yet, trying to sneak their way into very dangerous situations. Once a deal is made, all parties must abide by the agreement or the possibility of it working out again in the future will be jeopardized. The emergency agency cannot let anyone else into the area, so the pool photographer must make the video readily available to any news organization actively covering that event.

Certain restrictions apply if the organization allowing the pool is made fully aware of them and understands them. The pool may be restricted to only those present at the time of departure or to those there by the time of arrival back from shooting. In this case, a news organization that showed up several hours late, or simply did not send anyone to the site, would not have a right to the shoot. Usually, any media outlet trying to cover the event, whether present at the time the pool was formed or not, gets a share of the footage.

Public Domain Materials

Many portable video producers need to obtain video or audio but cannot aquire it through their own shooting, or they require music but have no musicians on staff to compose or perform it. There is an answer to this general and widespread problem. An abundance of film footage is available that can be used because its copyright has expired. Many films are sold on videocassette or DVD in discount or grocery stores for less than $10. Often, these films no longer have copyright protection, and a video producer may use this footage as desired. Buying these videos from the grocery store can be convenient, but the quality derived from an old VHS copy might not be acceptable. Companies exist that can, for a reasonable fee, supply a copy of the material you need in the format of your choice.

Music or soundtrack material is similarly obtained. Excerpts from some old radio shows are often available at a very reasonable price. Sound quality is always an important criterion for the decision to use this type of material. If you have a musician or vocalist available, you might choose to have a fresh version of a song produced for you. This can yield a high-quality soundtrack, but the producer must either obtain permission from the publisher or use music that is not copyright protected. Material in this category, both audio and video, is referred to as being "in the **public domain**," meaning that it is owned by the public in general, or includes traditional songs that might never have been copyrighted. For example, your musicians could perform songs like "Turkey in the Straw" or "She'll Be Comin' Round the Mountain" without fear of copyright problems, but, strangely enough, not "Happy Birthday." Classical music has this benefit as well, but not other artists' performances of classical works, because their performances are their property even if the music is not.

If you choose to use copyrighted music, you might find that the copyright holder has an organization that will provide assistance in obtaining clearance and collecting fees. For much of the popular music recorded in the last 40 years, this organization is either Broadcast Music Inc. (BMI) or the American Society of Composers, Authors, and Publishers (ASCAP).

Additionally, anything for which the government—federal, state, or local—holds the copyright is in the public domain. Tax dollars fund government, and taxes are paid by the public, so the public has already paid for any materials copyrighted by the government. This means you can use any print and audiovisual materials owned by any level of government. For example, if you wish to use clips from government propaganda films during the great wars of the last century, you may do so without obtaining any copyright permission. You should note, however, that the source from which you obtain government-owned material might charge you a material and/or processing fee. If you contact NASA, for example, and request a copy of some rocket-launching footage, NASA might charge you for the cost of finding the footage in its archives, copying it to the format you want (e.g., DV, MPEG-2), and shipping it to you or posting it at a Web site for you to download. Similarly, libraries with government archives may charge you fees for their work in getting the material you request. Also, keep in mind that footage *of* the government might not be owned *by* the government. Again, the Zapruder film is an example. The footage is of an American President at a privileged incident open to the public (a car ride along a street), but the film was not shot by a government-hired filmmaker; instead, a private citizen recorded this famous and tragic scene and his estate continues to own the rights to it.

COPYRIGHT GUIDELINES FOR THE WEB

The responsibility for following copyright law falls on the user of other people's material, regardless of the means used to obtain that material. This includes the World Wide Web. Because it only takes a click or two of a mouse to download text, graphics, photos, audio, or video, some mistakenly believe they can take whatever they find on the Web and use it however they wish. This is not the case. Recognizing that the current copyright law, enacted in 1976, was inadequate to address the slew of problems caused by the digital distribution of content on the Internet, Congress passed the **Digital Millennium Copyright Act of 1998 (DMCA)**. The DMCA does not replace the **1976 Copyright Act**, which is still in force; rather, it attempts to address "a number of other significant copyright-related issues," particularly those dealing with digital content in the age of the Internet. The following are some guidelines to use when getting material from the Web:

- Works on the Web are considered copyrighted as they are created, even if copyright is not claimed in the material.

- If you use other people's Web content, you can be sued even if there is no money involved. This is especially true if the usage damages the profitability of the original material. The famous Napster case illustrates the general concept. Napster distributed copyrighted audio material via a system of **peer-to-peer (P2P)** information sharing. Numerous musical groups and their publishers claimed that this activity limited the profitability of the original product. The legal system determined that Napster's activity was a violation of copyright law. In 2001, Napster was ordered to cease and desist, though it emerged again in 2003 as a legal file-sharing service under its new parent company, Roxio. Since then, a number of other court cases have continued to examine the legality of P2P file sharing of copyrighted material.

- Material that was originally posted on an electronic mailing list is not in the public domain unless specifically stated by the originator of the material.

- Copyright holders do not have to defend themselves or their material because it is protected, unless permission is granted for the material's use.

- Copyright violation is a crime that can result in monetary fines, and some violations can be treated as felonies.

- Reposting or reusing material that was received in an advertisement or promotion has the same protection as other material, unless permission is granted for its use.

PROTECTING YOUR WORK

A common violation of copyright laws occurs when protected material is copied and used improperly. This law concerns all videocassette recorder (VCR) and digital video recorder (DVR) owners, as well as Internet users. Material recorded off the air or from cable TV or from the Web can be used for personal viewing. The user can even copy the material for his or her own viewing or listening, or to preserve the original recording. However, no part of the recording may be used in any other way, such as editing a clip and putting it into another production. Also, copies may not be made and distributed to others.

After putting many hours and dollars into an original creation, it would be quite annoying to have your work stolen by unscrupulous video producers who decided that it was easier to use your video than to produce their own. This is difficult to prevent; a copy of your video can easily be duplicated, especially if it is in a digital format. But you may be able to be compensated for this theft. Copyright law provides legal protection for your work as well as others' work. Intentional theft of your copyrighted work can be penalized with very stiff fines of up to $100,000. Criminal penalties (e.g., a jail term) can be levied as well. Accidental use of copyrighted material carries penalties of $500 to $20,000 per incidence of such use.

Obtaining Protection

Protection of your creative work is guaranteed by law. Whether or not you register your work with the Copyright Office, it is your intellectual property. A good way to ensure this and to protect your work in the event someone else uses it is to register your work with the U.S. Copyright Office in the Library of Congress in Washington, D.C. You can obtain all the information and forms you need on the Web. Go to the U.S. Copyright Office forms site at http://www.copyright.gov.forms/. The site lists the different types of material that can be copyrighted and provides links to forms that can be filled out and returned to the office. Audiovisual creations are considered for copyright purposes to be performing arts (PA), so Form

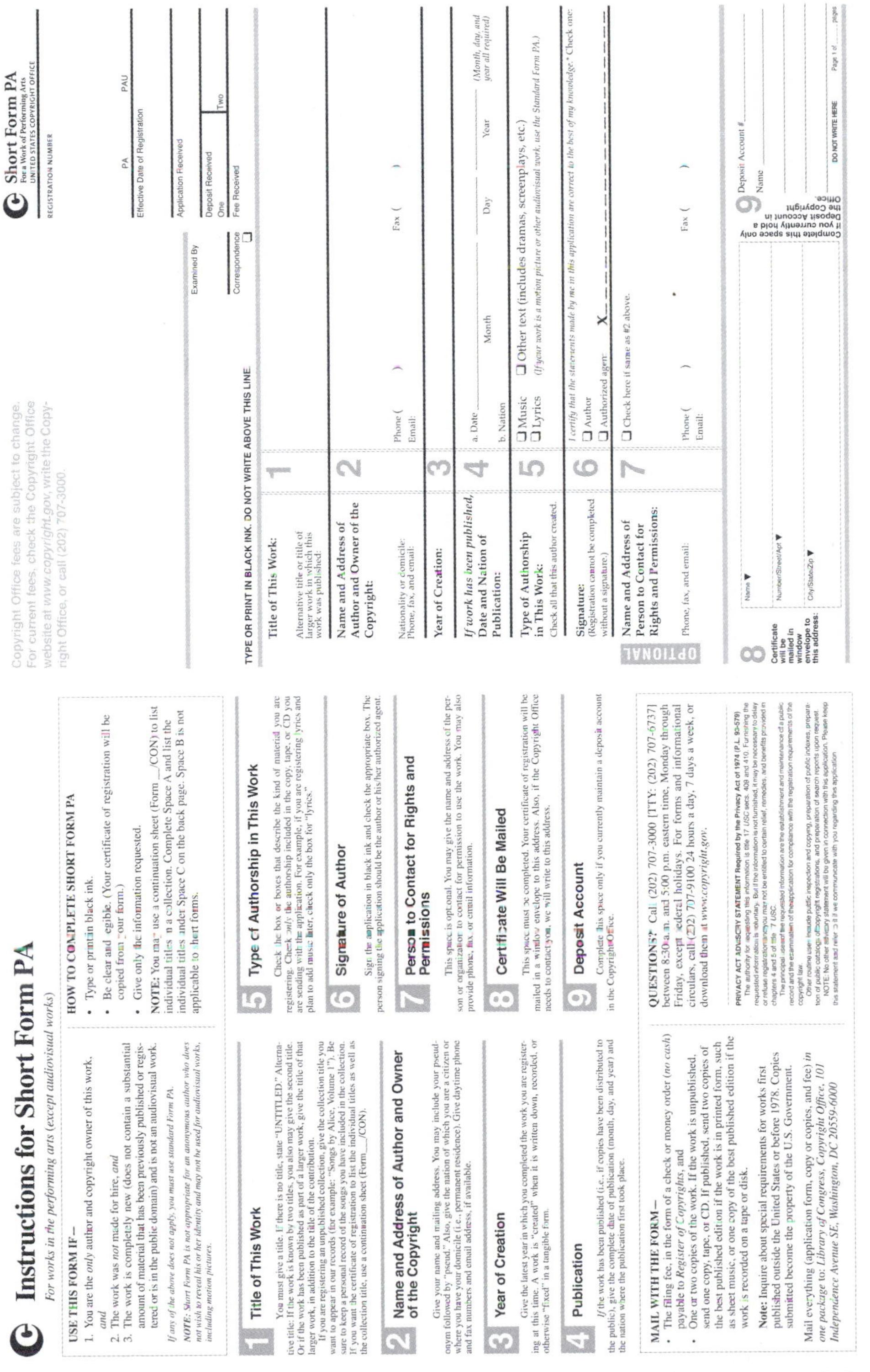

Figure 12-7   Short Form PA is used to obtain copyright protection for works of performing arts, including most video productions, created by a single author. When more than one person shares the copyright, the regular Form PA is appropriate, which can be downloaded from http://www.copyright.gov.forms/.

PA is most likely the one you'll use, and if you are the only author, you can use the easier "Short Form PA." (See Figure 12.7.) Each form comes with line-by-line instructions to help you fill it out. For voice information about copyright registration, you can call 202-707-3000, or you can call the copyright hotline at 202-707-9100 and ask that an application form be sent to you. Forms can also be obtained by fax. The application form registers your copyright, along with the appropriate fee ($30 at the time of this writing) and a copy of your work or two copies if it is already published. The office will send you a certificate as proof of the registration.

Alerting Others of Protection

Perhaps the most effective way to discourage others from unauthorized use of your work is to indicate that you hold a copyright on the work. This is simple and straightforward. If you want to copyright a video, simply put the word "copyright" with your name and the year on the label. The Copyright Office recommends that you include this information in the video itself. The abbreviation "Copr." or the symbol "©" can also be used. For written work, the notice of copyright should appear on the first page. The copyright notice protects you in the United States. To protect your work in other countries, add the words "All Rights Reserved."

Scope

What aspects of your creative project can be copyrighted? The complete project can certainly receive this protection. Some components of the project can also be protected. The entire script and the music and/or audio track are also subject to copyright protection. Any portion of these aspects of the work is protected as well. But it is important to note that the *idea* for the video project cannot be copyrighted. Others may use your basic idea and produce another project. In fact, they can obtain their own copyright protection for their work.

Copyright law protects only *tangible* products; that is, copyright can only be claimed for something in a produced or published form. Intangibles, such as ideas that do not exist on paper or in some recorded form that a person can see or hear, may not be copyrighted. For example, you might have an idea for a great video project—a short drama set against the backdrop of illegal immigration. To claim copyright, you need to write that idea down, at least in the form of a simple treatment if not an actual script—a written product that describes your characters and story. This written expression of your particular approach to the idea can be copyrighted, but not the idea itself. In other words, the idea of a drama dealing with illegal immigration can be used by anyone, but the specific way you have expressed your particular treatment of that idea cannot be used by others without your permission, at least not legally, if you have written it in a tangible form. Another video producer can take your basic idea but must express it differently in his or her take on illegal immigration. If the methods are too similar, you may be able to sue the infringer for monetary damages.

INSURANCE

No matter how many precautions you take, something always goes wrong. Most of the time the problem is simple, such as a broken cable or a camcorder that will not thread the tape. The delays and breakdowns can cost the ENG producer a shot or cost the EFP producer money. Sometimes people can be injured by a falling light or a business can suffer losses due to a water pipe you broke. You can violate someone's rights even without turning on a camera. In the case of physical injury, your troubles can skyrocket. As an employee, you might not have to worry about the ultimate outcome of such events because your employer is covered by insurance. If you are a freelancer or working as an independent contractor, however, you should protect yourself with insurance.

Comprehensive Liability

Everyone doing business needs some type of protection in case of accidents. When you are in an automobile, you might, through no real fault of your own, cause someone to be injured or even killed. This is why you need car insurance. You need insurance at work for the same reason. Working for a TV station or corporation, you usually can rely on them to have such insurance. A news photographer who causes an accident (such as setting up a light that eventually falls on someone) would be able to turn to the company for protection against a lawsuit. A freelance photographer hoping to sell a video would be responsible and held liable for the injuries.

Anyone making videos on their own for news, production, and other uses needs to understand **liability**. Suppose you agree to shoot a public service announcement (PSA) for a charity at a very wealthy person's mansion. A light falls, starting a fire that gets out of control and burns the house to the ground along with its priceless art collection. If the owner does not sue, then the insurance company will. Without insurance, you could lose everything you own and end up in personal bankruptcy court for a simple one-hour PSA shoot.

In recent years, the average coverage for an independent videomaker was $1 million in liability insurance. This amount covers most common claims filed as a result of property or bodily injury or death. This sounds like a great deal of money, but if you look back at the burned-down mansion example, you can see that even this might not be enough. More than likely, though, it would be more than enough for any problems you would normally encounter. One million dollars' worth of coverage can cost several thousand dollars a year in premiums, but if you want to stay in business, it is a necessary cost.

Comprehensive liability insurance is required if you want to do any recording on public property that requires a permit. Many rental companies require it before renting you equipment. Even production companies asking you to work as an independent contractor want you to have liability coverage. Everyone who has anything to do with you, your equipment, or the location in which you are shooting, wants some assurance that they will be protected in case anything should happen and you are found at full or partial fault. Not having liability insurance can cause prospective video clients to take their business elsewhere.

Equipment Loss or Damage

When you work for yourself, people routinely want to know if you have appropriate loss or damage coverage and the means to cover any damages you might cause to the equipment you are using. The bank might still own part of your gear, and if you rent, the rental house owns the gear. If your $30,000 camera should fall from a tripod and topple over a second-story balcony, then you would want some means of replacing it without a second mortgage on your house. If you rented the camera from a rental company, the company would also want to know about your coverage.

If you are using equipment owned or rented by your employer, then you need not worry about who pays if something happens, but only about preventing something from happening. People working as independent contractors more than likely would own their own equipment, or rent or borrow it. A freelance videographer can invest anywhere from $10,000 to $200,000 in a set of broadcast-quality gear. Having insurance can mean the difference between losing everything, including your ability to make a living, and going on to the next shoot.

Rental Floaters

A good insurance policy not only covers anything you own but also any equipment you need to rent. This additional rental coverage, known as a **floater**, covers you in case anything should happen to the rental gear while it is in your possession. Each floater is issued for a certain dollar maximum; it is priced according to how high the coverage is. If you are renting a high-end high-definition camera, then a $100,000 floater would probably be enough. The amount must be high enough to replace, at current cost, all the equipment rented at any one time. The floater also needs to be made out to the company or person from whom you are renting the equipment before you take the gear. You will need a floater for each company or person from whom you rent. Most insurance companies charge a fee for each company named, and a copy is sent to that company. A floater is usually good for one year, no matter how many or how few times you need it.

Rental houses can offer insurance on the spot to qualified renters who do not have a floater. The cost of this type of insurance is usually 10% of the rental fee. You can also get an uninsured renter's policy if you rent equipment you own to other people. This type of coverage would be added to your own equipment loss policy and would not only cover you in case the person damaged your gear but also in case of that person's inadequate coverage.

Restrictions

In almost every policy, there are exceptions to what is covered and when it is covered. For example, some policies might not cover your equipment if it is stolen from inside a vehicle. Others might not cover injuries that happen from operating or riding in a boat or airplane. By reading the fine print, you can discover any number of things that a particular policy does not cover. You might find that the videotape or the memory card or the disk in the camcorder is not covered, but the recorder is.

Other Coverage

You can get insurance for just about anything concerning video production. As the cost of the project increases, a small expense for some protection in an uncertain world is usually a good idea. The average coverage required for the video business is aimed at protecting people from getting hurt either physically or financially. Many exceptions to the coverage are things that can hurt you if you are the producer of the project. For a price, you can get things like cast insurance for your production. This covers any additional expenses incurred because the person appearing in your program or segment cannot finish the project due to sickness or injury.

You can insure the project for the cost of producing it so that if it is stolen everyone can still get paid. You can even insure the camera against failure in case you miss the shot because a chip goes bad. Other coverage includes sets, props, and even the wardrobe of the people appearing on camera. If you are working with any union or guild contracts, they can require special cov-

erage. While most of these extra types of coverage are out of the budget range for small video productions, anyone dealing with large amounts of money for an increasingly complex production should consider them. This type of coverage usually is required when people have invested money in your project and want some guarantees of at least seeing the project finished in case something goes wrong. There are several special types of coverage that all videomakers might consider as their budgets grow.

Errors and Omissions

A special type of coverage called **errors and omissions (E&O)** can protect you from an oversight in the use of copyrighted material. You might think you have received licensed permission only to find out after the production airs that the person who gave you the rights did not own them. This coverage protects you from this and also covers plagiarism, unfair competition, libel, breach of contract, and invasion of privacy. Any complete production that you plan to sell or syndicate for public viewing often requires this type of insurance before anyone will buy it or show it.

Workers' Compensation

Should you be in charge of a production large enough to hire people to work, many state and federal laws determine how much protection you must give employees. **Workers' compensation** insurance is required in most states for anyone with employees or independent contractors. This coverage provides medical, disability, or death benefits to any cast or crew member who becomes injured in the course of their employment. This coverage is needed in addition to normal liability insurance.

Completion Guarantee Bond

A **completion bond** (usually 1 to 3% of the production budget) is used to guarantee that the video project you have agreed to do will get the funding necessary for completion. When independent producers finance a project with a bank, a company, or a group of investors, the financers often ask for this type of policy to protect their investment from poor budget planning on your part or for some other reason. The bondholder is saying that the program will be made so that it will at least have a chance to make money or otherwise satisfy those concerned.

Producers' Insurance Policies

Almost all the above-mentioned types of coverage can be combined into one blanket policy, referred to as a **producers' insurance policy (PIP)**. PIPs come with different combinations of coverage to fit almost any type of production. You can often design your own package to fit the exact needs of your project. By working with an insurance company experienced in the film and video industries, you can tailor the coverage to suit your budget as well as your risk.

The cost of any insurance coverage is dependent on several factors. The higher the budget, the higher the insurance costs. The ceiling of the policy also determines the price: a $10,000 floater costs less than a $50,000 one. The amount of the deductible can change your premiums. Some deductibles are rather high, but the annual premium is significantly lower. Most small independent videographers and producers have year-round policies that cover all the work they do in that year (within the limits of the policy). You can often determine the cost of insurance before you actually have to buy any special coverage for a particular production. PIP premiums are usually based on the cost of the project and run between 2 and 4% of the total budget. With extra coverage, a long shooting schedule, or any hazards, the cost can be as much as 10% of the project's budget. For small productions, the cost often ends up being 10% of the budget because the premiums cannot go below certain minimum amounts. In some cases, the insurance might be the major cost of the shoot if you are doing things on a shoestring.

The more you have to interact with the public or any public agencies, the more you need to know about insurance. Even if you do not have the coverage, knowing what you are not covered for can be a great help. Having insurance takes some of the risk out of what you are doing. Many people, especially at the low end of the budget scale, go without any coverage. They have chosen to assume all the risk themselves. Most of the time they play the odds and win. You should always step back and ask yourself what would happen if something should go wrong. It might be a risk you are no longer ready to take.

SUMMARY

As producers of both ENG and EFP video, you must know the basics of the legal, ethical, copyright, and insurance issues. You may not defame a person, wrongfully harming his or her good name or character, either by recorded means—libel—or by spoken words—slander. If you are accused of defamation, your defense typically falls into one of four categories: the public's right to know, truth, consent, or public forum. Even if a story is determined not to be defamatory, ethical considerations might suggest that it still not air; just because it *can* air legally doesn't always mean it *should* air ethically.

ENG shooting is understood to be news, so an agreement to appear implies consent for use. EFP shooting rarely has implied consent, so talent release forms are recommended, and even required in the case of financial backers wanting to know the production will not be sued. Humor presents a special category of shooting in which the satirist is free to use just about anything in any way he or she wants, as long as it is clear that the intent is humor. Public figures also present a special category because people want to know about the lives of the rich and famous, and video producers want to provide those stories. Public figures are more likely to tempt shooters to trespass to get a shot that will sell; however, shooting must remain on public property. Without consent, shooting on private property is trespassing. Even so, for a celebrity to claim defamation, he or she must usually demonstrate malicious intent in addition to falsehoods and damage to character.

Copyright is an area of special legal concern, particularly in this age when just about all text, graphics, photos, audio, and even video are digital and accessible via the World Wide Web. As easy as it is to download others' work, copyright law does not permit you to use it without obtaining permission from the copyright holder, sometimes for a fee. Four categories of special limited use, known as fair use, allow you to use copyrighted material without permission: (1) purpose—you make no money and you use the work for education, research, and the like; (2) nature—the work is intended for commentary, criticism, and so on; (3) amount—you use only a small portion, usually 10% or less; and (4) effect—your use does not harm the potential market or value of the work. Any other use without permission—unless the material is in the public domain—is considered piracy, no matter how hard or easy the work is to obtain. Piracy can result in very stiff penalty fees and even jail time. Copyright law protects not only others' works that you might wish to use, but it also protects your work against piracy by others.

Insurance is an important consideration for all video productions. While producers of no- and low-budget projects often forgo insurance because of the cost, it is important to consider that cost against the potential loss in the event of personal or property damage or lost or broken equipment. You can purchase insurance to cover just about anything, from broad umbrella policies that insure against liability, to workers' compensation policies, to policies for specific equipment, to policies that insure against unforeseen legal problems (e.g., unintentional copyright infringement), to completion bonds that guarantee backers that your project will be completed. Some insurance companies offer producers' insurance policies (PIPs)—packages that include any combination of, or all, the various types of coverage to meet the specific needs of a production.

13 New Trends and Technologies

The future of ENG and EFP video production is solid state. In the previous edition of this text, that sentence read, "The future of video is *digital*." Clearly, the digital future has arrived. Today, ENG and EFP are not only digital, but the industry is now moving rapidly toward a tapeless environment. Rather than acquire footage with cameras that record on videotape, there is considerable incentive to shoot directly onto solid-state devices that record the digital video and audio files onto microchips. To be sure, many shooters continue with digital tape formats, such as mini-DV or Digital Beta (DigiBeta). As of this writing, digital tape still offers unparalleled storage for the price. A mini-DV tape can hold one hour of good-quality footage (720×480 pixels, 29.97 fps) for under $5. Because the mini-DV format requires about one gigabyte (GB) of storage for each four to five minutes of video, that same hour of footage requires 12 to 15 GB of solid-state storage, which can cost more than $100 if stored on individual Flash drives, though the cost is lower if the storage is part of a large-capacity drive (e.g., a 250 GB external drive that costs about $250, or $1 per gig, as of this writing).

In addition to digital tape, some camcorders record directly on discs, such as mini-DVDs. These have an advantage over tape in that the user can place the discs directly into the disc drive of the computer for playback and editing. In contrast, tape requires that a playback device be connected to the computer, and then the footage has to be captured to the computer's drive via a FireWire, USB, or similar connection.

While we acknowledge that tape and disc recording are still much in use, the future will eventually be solid state because the cost of high-capacity microchips continues to plummet. An example of how prices continue to fall is the USB Flash drive—that little keychain gadget on which you can carry your files, plugging it into any USB connector in any computer. (See Figure 13-1.) These devices have been on the market for a few years, with the first 128 MB Flash drives costing over $100. Today you might carry in your pocket a multi-GB (that's GB, not MB) Flash drive that costs you less than $50. Microchip storage capacity continues to increase while the price continues to decrease. This can only mean that more and more camcorders will shoot directly onto microchips, bypassing tape and discs.

The incentive to migrate to solid-state recording—once the price point for mega-GB chip storage rivals tape and disc storage—are the advantages that direct-to-chip recording offer:

- There are no moving parts. No plastic tape wraps around video drums and presses against magnets; no disc spins with laser light burning micro-holes onto its surface. Fewer moving parts result in fewer malfunctions.

Figure 13-1   A miniature USB Flash drive like this, the size of a key, holds 2 GB and costs under $20.

- A computer can recognize the chip as just another drive, be it a USB Flash drive, a memory card or stick, or an external hard drive. This means the footage does not first have to be captured onto a drive through a cable before it can be viewed and edited on the computer. Eliminating the time needed to capture video is a strong incentive to go solid state.

- The life of a microchip is longer than the life of a plastic tape or disc. While the cost of a mega-GB or terabyte (TB) external drive is currently too great to use for long-term storage—few companies can afford to archive closets full of $1,000 drives—the cost will continue to drop. Footage archived on solid-state devices will last longer than footage archived on discs or tapes (in theory, anyway—solid-state archiving is too new to have been field-tested over decades).

FORMAT WARS

The industry will continue to fight format wars. The authors wish they did not have to make this prediction, but alas, the past and present inform the future, and the past and present of video production include battles over video formats. Perhaps you have read about the marketplace duel between Beta (Sony) and VHS (JVC) 1/2-inch videotapes for home recording in the 1970s. VHS won, even though Beta had better image resolution, because VHS tapes could be slowed down to record up to six hours (good for sporting events). As digital video moved into the market in the 1990s, a slew of formats appeared with names like D-1, D-2, D-3, D-5, M-II, and the like, which have been forgotten. Mini-DV became popular with its 1/4-inch (6-mm) microcassettes, but even then Sony developed another DV format (DVCAM), as did its rival Panasonic (DVCPRO). On the Internet, you can watch video wrapped in the Windows Media codec (Microsoft), in the QuickTime format (Apple), in the Real-Player version (RealMedia), in Flash (Adobe)—which used to be for animation but is gaining ground for video—or even in other Web-based players, such as DivX. Today, manufacturers are ready to cash in on high-definition (HD) video, but will the format be 720 progressive lines (720p), 1080 interlaced lines (1080i), or perhaps 1080p, all of which are available? Maybe the high-definition version of digital video, HDV, will emerge the winner because of its lower price. Will HD programs be stored on HD-DVD or Blu-Ray discs, or will distributors have to offer both? (See Figure 13-2.)

For consumers, it would be a joyous day if all the manufacturers could cooperate on one standard. However, while standardization would simplify life and eventually lower costs for consumers, the manufacturers all want their own versions of things to become the default marketplace standards, just as VHS tape was in the 1970s. Because manufacturers, and not consumers, make the equipment, the marketplace will unfortunately continue to see a variety of formats all vying for supremacy ... and our dollars. The result will continue to be slower-than-necessary migration to the newest formats, as has been the case with high-definition television (HDTV); developed decades ago, HDTV still does not have much market share, though it is increasing. Why does the lack of a single format lead to this slow development? Money. Consumers hesitate to buy a technology if they fear it will become obsolete in a short time. Just ask those who bought Beta tape decks in 1976.

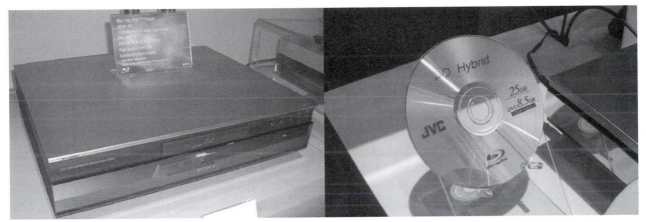

Blu-Ray deck and disc

HD-DVD deck and discs

Figure 13-2   Rival high-capacity DVDs vie for market supremacy: Blu-Ray and HD-DVD. (Courtesy of Blu-Ray, Sony, JVC, Toshiba, and Mitsubishi)

BUYING EQUIPMENT

Staying exposed to current technology will always be important for equipment purchases. It is important for ENG and EFP producers to stay at least somewhat familiar with new video production equipment. It is not essential, or even possible, to keep up with each and every innovation or product change that surfaces from the myriad companies that sell equipment. However, it is wise to have at least a basic understanding of what is available for three reasons:

- New equipment might be available to enhance the performance of the equipment you already have (e.g., lenses that can improve the image quality of your existing cameras).

- You might be asked to make a recommendation for a major piece of equipment, and selecting a soon-to-be-obsolete format or technology might make you look less than knowledgeable (e.g., buying mini-DV when HDV might serve your company's purposes better for only a little more money).

- Generally, newer equipment not only offers higher quality but is often more economical to use, less expensive to maintain, and more durable than older equipment (though nothing beats an old Sony 3/4-Umatic deck for durability).

Keeping current with new trends and technologies in video, including postproduction editing and multimedia distribution hardware and software, will help you make better recommendations for future purchases and prepare you for changes in production and editing techniques. For example, as more and more corporations invest in wide-screen LCD or plasma monitors for their conference rooms, you might consider a camera that gives you the option to shoot in the 16:9 aspect ratio, in addition to the 4:3 aspect ratio, for those occasions when you are hired to produce a corporate video that will be shown on a wide screen. (See Figure 13-3.)

Figure 13-3   As wide-screen LCD and plasma TVs, such as those on display here at the NAB 2006 conference, become more commonplace, ENG and EFP producers will be asked increasingly to shoot and edit in the 16:9 aspect ratio. (Courtesy of Panasonic)

CAMERAS

Cameras will continue to increase in image quality and decrease in size—up to the point where they are too small to be operated. The biggest changes in cameras for the foreseeable future concern not only the migration to tapeless recording, but also the image quality and camera size. The solid-state CCD image sensors in most professional, standard definition (SD) cameras can provide more than 850 lines of resolution and the capability to shoot with just a fraction of a foot-candle. High-definition (HD) cameras, of course,

record even more lines. In other words, professional cameras can outperform the playback equipment.

Camera size and weight continue to decrease while quality increases. In fact, many consumer—and even some prosumer—cameras are so small that they cannot be shot from the shoulder and must be held with one hand in front of the operator's face. While this allows people to shoot for long periods of time without fatigue, getting a steady shot without a tripod is more difficult. Camera manufacturers have partially solved this problem by incorporating image stabilization circuitry into the camera to help get steadier shots. This technology senses camera movement and digitally adjusts the pixels to narrow the range of that movement.

Cameras the size of shirt buttons have been marketed that have a fairly high degree of quality and are used by ENG operations and news feature programs that try to bring the "inside story" to the viewers with hidden camera shots. (See Figure 13-4.) This type of camera is really just a lens and a little bit of circuitry to transmit the image to a nearby receiver, hidden in a bag or behind a wall or in a truck or someplace similar, where the image is amplified and recorded. For full camera-recorder (camcorder) units, the size will need to be big enough to hold steady and operate easily, while the image resolution will continue to increase and price will continue to drop. (See Figure 13-5.)

EDITORS

Video editing programs will continue to offer more features for less money. This no-brainer prediction is simply the reality of a free marketplace. With "the big three"—Avid, Final Cut Pro, and Adobe Premiere—continually vying for greater market share, along with the smaller players—e.g., Windows Movie Maker, Apple QuickTime, Sony, Roxio—each must necessarily offer more for less to remain competitive. Buzzwords for marketing features include:

- *Real-time editing:* watch effects like wipes and dissolves when playing from the timeline, instead of having to render them before viewing.

Figure 13-4   Micro-cameras like this one, the size of a plug, can be easily hidden for surveillance or other shooting, while still offering acceptable image quality. (Courtesy of Spy Gadgets)

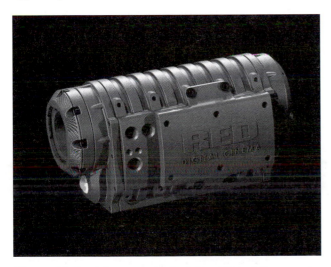

Figure 13-5   This unit, the Red One Digital Camera, debuted in 2006, offering up to 4 K resolution (approximately 70-mm film) for a price under $20,000. (Courtesy of Red One)

- *Multi-camera editing:* sync and play multiple video streams from multi-cam shoots and edit "on the fly" as the various angles play simultaneously.

- *HD-compatibility:* edit both SD and HD video, but be sure to check *which* HD formats are compatible.

- *EDL creation:* generate an edit decision list using the timecode numbers encoded in the video frames.

- *5.1 audio*: get surround-sound capability with noise reduction technology.

- *Royalty-free sound effects and music loops:* get audio files for sound and music with the software for you to use without having to obtain and pay for additional copyright permission.

- *More bells and whistles:* enjoy ever-improving features like digital vectorscopes, waveform monitors, and audio meters and mixers, as well as more and fancier wipe patterns, title fonts, color manipulation, and so on.

MONITORS

Monitors will continue to be flat screens that come in all sizes, from super-size to pod-size. It is becoming increasingly hard to find a computer monitor that is not a flat screen. Flat panels take up less space than older monitors, and they provide very high image quality. The deep **cathode ray tubes (CRT)** of yesteryear are vanishing in place of **liquid crystal displays (LCD)** and **plasma** screens. This is not only the trend for computer monitors, but for television sets, as well, not to mention camera phones and pod-sized MP3 audio and MP4 video players. To be sure, discount electronics stores still sell very inexpensive CRT television sets for those who want a small and cheap TV. But the more expensive and larger flat screen models will naturally come down in price, and flat-screens will eventually be the norm even for smaller screens. Whether a gigantic monitor for a home theater, or a mid-sized monitor for a standard living room, or a computer monitor for a desktop or laptop, or a teeny monitor for a pocket-sized phone or other gadget, consumers want their image monitors to be flat and to come in any size they want. They want their super-sized Super Bowl and they want their pocket-sized podcasts. (See Figure 13-6.)

Figure 13-6   This video camera cell phone has a one-inch-wide screen for playback. Contrast this with large, wide-screen TVs, such as those shown in Figure 13-3.

SPEAKERS

Ditto audio speakers. As with image monitors, audio monitors (loudspeakers) will continue to improve in quality and be available in all sizes. The little earphones that connect to your iPod provide sound with greater fidelity than did the full-size speakers on your grandparents' first TVs. In contrast to tiny earphones, gigantic speaker systems are available for home theaters that boast all the latest surround-sound features and **tweeters** (for high-range frequencies—treble) and **woofers** (for low-range frequencies—bass). Of course, speakers of every size and price exist between the extremes. As with image monitors, consumers want their audio monitors to give them superlative quality and to come in any size they want. (See Figure 13-7.)

Figure 13-7   The earphones hanging down from an MP3 player contrast in size to the home-sized speaker.

DIGITAL TV

Broadcast transmission continues to move from the analog to the digital spectrum. In 1996, the U.S. Congress mandated that broadcasters give up the current spectrum of frequencies used for analog television (VHF) and switch to a new spectrum using digital broadcast signals (in the UHF range). Every station was originally to have been broadcasting digitally by 2006; however, the realities of format wars, prices, and the like kept this from happening. The current moving-target deadline is 2009, though few in the industry believe even this is possible, so the deadline is likely to be extended again.

Added to that are the problems with the **digital television (DTV)** transmission standard chosen by the FCC. The United States is the only country in the world to have chosen a standard called "eight discrete amplitude level vestigial side-band" or **8-VSB**. The Advanced Television Systems Committee (ATSC), established in 1982, decided this standard. However, that technology was rejected by the Digital Video Broadcasting Group (DVB) established by European countries and the Japanese government. The Europeans went with a system called DVB-T, which is based on a transmission technology known as "coded orthogonal frequency-division multiplexing," or **COFDM**. The Japanese adopted a system based on COFDM technology called "integrated services digital broadcasting," or ISDB. The advantage of COFDM over 8-VSB is that it spreads the signal over a large number of carriers to reduce the chance of a common signal interference called **multipath** or reflection. In contrast, 8-VSB uses a single carrier and consequently suffers from problems of signal interference. Both the European and the Japanese systems have been up and running for years already. In the United States, only a few consumers—the "early adopters"—have true DTV (and not simply a DTV converter connected to an older analog TV).

While it is not necessary for anyone but broadcast engineers to know the physics behind these DTV transmission systems, it is useful to know their names. Videomakers in the current world of standard definition television already know the names of the three global standards: NTSC (America, Canada, Japan, others); SECAM (France, Russia, others); and PAL (Germany, Australia, others). So too in the digital world, it seems we will all have to know the names 8-VSB and COFDM, and be able to convert our programs from one format to the other for different markets.

Wouldn't it be great if the whole world just adopted one standard? Cherry-picking from the best on the market today, we would recommend these standards, all of which are currently available:

- *Image:* 1920×1080p square pixels (16:9 aspect ratio).

- *Frames per second:* 24 (looks more like film and requires less storage than 30 fps).

- *Compression:* MPEG-4 AVC (the "advanced video coding" version of the MPEG-4 algorithm, using a standard called H.264)

- *Color:* xvYCC (broader color range for hi-def TVs than the current color standard—BT.709-5)

- *Audio:* 48K 16-bit stereo (the human ear can't hear any better than this), and 5.1.

- *Transmission:* COFDM (less interference than 8-VSB).

- *Storage*: Blu-Ray discs (higher capacity and faster data rate than HD-DVD discs).

A single standard that incorporates these already-available formats might be expensive at first, but if it were standardized, the price would drop.

What theory will guide the future of DTV? Is it the "Field of Dreams" theory: build the DTV network and consumers will come? Or is it regulation theory: Congress must mandate that the FCC select a single standard that incorporates the best options available—or at least the most politically expedient? Or is it marketplace theory: eventually the issue of DTV and HDTV standardization will sort itself out based on what consumers prefer?

HIGH-DEFINITION TV

High-definition television (HDTV) will continue its slow pace of development as more considerations are worked out, such as standardization, cost, and consumer habits. The high definition in HDTV comes from its having many more pixels than standard definition television (SDTV). An SDTV image is about 640 by 480 pixels, or 307,200 individual points of light (DV is 720 × 480, PAL and SECAM have a bit more than NTSC). In contrast, an HDTV image is about 1920 × 1080 pixels, or 2,073,600 individual points of light. In rounded numbers, HDTV, with more than 2 million pixels, offers image resolution that is almost seven times sharper than SDTV, which has just over 300,000 pixels. Note also that the aspect ratio—the ratio of width to height—in SDTV is 4:3 (640:480), where HDTV is wider, with an aspect ration of 16:9 (1920:1080). With its greater image resolution and wider aspect ratio, HDTV offers an image much closer to 35-mm film than does SDTV.

HDTV currently requires about a 19 megabyte-per-second (Mbps) transfer rate, compared to SDTV, which requires only about 4 Mbps. For over-the-air transmission, this requires greater bandwidth than is currently available on the VHF spectrum. This is one reason why the FCC assigned all new spectrum space in the UHF band for TV stations to transmit digital television (DTV—see above). The new spectrum allocations have sufficient bandwidth to transmit HDTV.

However, the FCC did not actually mandate that a broadcaster transmit an HDTV signal in the new DTV frequency assignments. The rules only state that programming has to be at least as good as NTSC. Because NTSC only requires about 4 Mbps, while the new bandwidth for each station can accommodate about 20 Mbps (HDTV-capable), a broadcaster can actually choose to transmit about five or so SDTV signals simultaneously in the new spectrum. Those signals need only be digital rather than analog. This means television station managers can transmit five or so digital programs in their new bandwidths, which means five or so times the revenue streams from advertisers, and perhaps transmit one HDTV signal only for mega-programs, such as championship sports tournaments (e.g., World Series, Super Bowl), high-profile live events (e.g., Oscars, Emmys), and other high-spectacle occasions that viewers are most likely to demand in high definition (e.g., IMAX movies converted for HDTV, Prince Charles's eventual coronation as King of England). In addition to transmitting five or so simultaneous SDTV signals, some broadcasters are experimenting with other uses for their new, wider spectrum space, such as broadcasting voice and data (telephone and Internet service), interactive-enhanced programming (e.g., horse wagering), and the like. (See Figure 13-8.)

As broadcast stations and networks wrangle over the myriad problems facing them, computer makers

Figure 13-8   This field report from a horse racetrack is produced by TVG, the Television Gaming Network—a 24-hour horse-racing channel that offers interactive wagering via three technologies: remote control, telephone, and the Internet. (Courtesy of TVG)

have integrated HDTV into their hardware by turning PCs into HDTV receivers. At a fraction of the cost of a new HDTV television, a simple card can be installed in the computer and the consumer is DTV-ready on a platform already used in a digital world. The reception problem of the DTV signal is still there, but the investment is relatively minor, and the technology is ready to go. But how many people are willing to sit at their desks to watch TV instead of in their living rooms? The bottom line is that while HDTV technology has been available for decades, other variables are still being worked out, such as standardization, cost, consumer habits, and so forth. While more homes adopt HDTV sets each year, these variables must still shake down before HDTV is truly available for the masses.

STREAMING VIDEO

Video streams on the Internet will continue to increase, both in quantity and quality. With fast Internet connections available through digital service lines (DSL), cable modems, integrated services digital networks (ISDNs), wireless high-fidelity (WiFi), and the like, home computers are capable of both watching live video pictures and downloading video programs with relative ease. Anyone with one of these fast ramps onto the information superhighway can log onto MSNBC.com, CNN.com, or any of the many online news services and watch any story on a computer. Or they can go to Ifilm.com, Atomfilms.com, or any of the online entertainment video services and do the same. The consumers can pause, rewind, and play the video multiple times. Where once viewers might have missed a line or fact or gag and never been able to recover it, they can now replay the story as often as they like to "get" what they missed.

As of this writing, the image quality for streaming video is usually only about 320 × 240 pixels (1/4 screen), and it usually plays at 15 frames per second instead of the full frame rate of 30 fps. Obviously, video can stream at any image quality and frame rate, but many providers select 1/4 screen and 15 fps to keep the file sizes manageable and not overload the Internet pipeline or viewers' computer capabilities. However, as program suppliers invest in servers with ever larger capacity, as Internet service providers (ISPs) develop faster distribution networks, and as consumers pay for more and faster video on the Web, image resolution will move upward. Full-frame SDTV or DV images, already available through many services, will be the next norm, followed by HDTV. All this, and the stories, are available on demand for anyone at anytime, not just for those sitting in front of their TV sets at 6:30 P.M. for news or Wednesday evenings at 9:00 P.M. for *Lost*.

A CAUTIONARY NOTE

Just because the technology can, doesn't mean the producer should. It is worth mentioning that all these new technologies are not as benign as they might seem. As digital effects become more and more sophisticated with the addition of faster and more powerful computers, reality and technology are being blended into a seamless picture. While this is great fun for commercial and entertainment videomakers, it can lead to real moral and ethical problems for news and documentary creators. If you can make it happen in the computer, why not? A subtle manipulation in a picture can be made to look so real that it could fool anyone. People can be placed in a scene that they never attended with the look of total reality. If just one case of this type of manipulation occurs in the future, it may cost the entire news industry its credibility with the public, just as its attempt to use recreations in newscasts did in 1990. The practice was halted almost immediately, but the damage it caused was real and lasting.

Ethical considerations remain paramount for the future. Misrepresenting truth in news or documentary remains unacceptable. In entertainment videos, while there is more leeway in what can be manipulated, no harm should ever be done to those involved. No one should ever be exposed to actual hurt or danger. Even when a program engages in misrepresentation for the sake of drama or comedy, as a number of reality shows do, full disclosure is still required at the end—both for those involved in the shooting and for those watching the end product. Participants and viewers alike deserve to know what the true objective of any program is.

SUMMARY

The future of ENG and EFP video production is solid state (tapeless). In this digital era, the industry will continue to fight format wars over acquisition, storage, and distribution. Staying exposed to current technology will always be important for equipment purchases. Cameras will continue to increase in image quality and decrease in size—up to the point where they are too small to be operated. Video editing programs will continue to offer more features for less money. Monitors will continue to be flat screens that come in all sizes, from pod-size to super-size; the same for audio speakers, from tiny earphones to large boxes. Broadcast transmission continues to move from the analog to the digital spectrum. High-definition television will continue its slow pace of development as more considerations are worked out, such as standardization, cost, and consumer habits. Video streams on the Internet will continue to increase, both in quantity and in quality. Yet, with all the wonder of digital technology, video creators must exercise caution: just because the technology can do something doesn't mean the producer should do it. Ethical concerns must still be at the heart of every production.

Glossary

Italicized terms within the definitions may be found elsewhere in the Glossary.

180° rule An imaginary axis of action running between the main subjects in a setting, such as a two-person interview; for continuity, all camera angles should be on the same side of the line

30° rule When shooting different *setups* of the same subject, separate each camera angle by at least 30°, without crossing over the 180° line, to maintain *continuity*

8-VSB Technology for digital television transmission that uses a single carrier for each signal, selected by the USA; compare with *COFDM*

A/B-roll editing Analog editing system in which shots from two different tapes are edited together; the A-roll has the shots with sound elements and the *B-roll* has the non-dialogue shots that visualize the story

above-the-line The personnel costs and expenses involved with securing a script and the rights, a producer and the staff, the talent (performers) and the director

action axis See *180° rule*

algorithm Any mathematical formula for *compressing* digital files by removing redundant information

ampere A measure of the amount or volume of electrical current

ampere hours A way of rating a battery according to how much electrical current it can generate over a period of time

analog An electrical waveform that represents the original light or sound waveform; contrast with *digital*

angle The location of a camera relative to the camera's subject

ASA A rating of the ability of photographic film to record light, as determined by the American National Standards Institute; the higher the rating, the less light is needed to record an image

aspect ratio The relationship of the width of a TV screen to its height; for standard NTSC television it is 4:3, but digital television is capable of having a 16:9 ratio

assemble A type of edit that transfers all information from the source machine to the editing recorder; it is similar to a *dub*

asymmetrical balance Composing an image with objects of different shape, mass, weight, color, contrast, line, and texture on opposite sides of the screen; contrast with *symmetrical balance*

audio-limiter switch   Control that prevents the recorded audio signal from becoming distorted because of too much signal strength

auto-iris   A feature on video cameras that allows the exposure to be automatically set by the camera

available light   The natural light in a scene; the light that exists before additional light sources are added

background light   A light illuminating the background of a scene or shot; it is usually the fourth light in a lighting kit.

backlight   A directional light used in three-point lighting; it is placed in line with the camera, but positioned behind and above the subject and aimed at the back of the subject's head and shoulders

balance   Adjusting levels in an audio mix so the most important element—usually dialogue—is at the foreground, and other elements—usually sound effects and music—are at the background

balanced audio input   An input into an electronic device that accepts signals with two conductors of equal voltage; used in professional work to ensure a better signal

bandwidth   (1) The measure of the capacity of a data line
(2) The difference between the upper and lower frequency limits of an audio or video component

barndoor   A rectangular piece of dark metal attached to a light to modify the direction of the beam, often used around a light in a set of four

bass/roll-off/switch   A microphone switch that prevents the microphone from reproducing low-frequency sounds below a certain set level

batt check   A control that when depressed or engaged gives an indication of the amount of remaining power of the battery in use

bed level   Background level in audio; secondary sounds are "bedded" underneath primary sounds so the primary sounds can be understood

behavioral effects   Changes in the things people say and do as a result of viewing a video program; see *cognitive effects* and *emotional effects*

Betacam   A professional 1/2-inch component video format from the Sony Corporation that was most popular with professional ENG operations in the 1980s

Betacam SP   The improved Betacam format, which replaced Standard Betacam; SP stands for "superior performance"

bit   One piece of binary information (1 or 0, on or off) in a digital file

bite   A piece of video of a person speaking in which their audio is heard clearly; also called a sound bite

black bursting   Recording a tape with a pure black signal (a control track, but no viewable picture); usually used for insert editing

blocking   The talent and camera movements specified by the director for each scene

BNC connector   A connector with a twist lock or positive grip feature used with single conductor video cable

boom   A pole (often extension type) mounted on some type of tripod base used as a microphone mount that can bring the mic close to the subject without being in the picture; see *fishpole*

bottomers   A flag used below a light source to shade the lower portion of the scene

bounced light   A diffuse, indirect light that reflects onto a desired subject; see *reflector*.

B-roll   Footage used to illustrate a story; the close-ups, inserts, cutaways, and so on that demonstrate what the speaker discusses

brick battery A powerful rectangular battery usually used to supply DC current to a video camera

broad light A rectangular video light that casts bright light over a large area

budget tracking A record-keeping process in which one records actual expenditures from a production and compares them with the projected expenses

bug A small logo or abbreviation that identifies the source of the video being shown, usually located in one corner of the picture.

burden of proof The plaintiff has the responsibility to demonstrate wrongdoing, while the defendant need only demonstrate reasonable doubt in the plaintiff's case

burn-in The image retention by a pickup tube, caused by shooting a very bright object or by aiming the camera at a static scene for a long period of time

butted Two scenes edited together without the benefit of an electronic transition such as a *dissolve;* sometimes called a straight cut

camcorder A one-piece combination video camera and recorder

camera control unit (CCU) An electronic device used to properly set up and maintain the quality of a video camera's image

cannon connector A high-quality multi-pin connector with a positive lock feature used for audio input and output; see *XLR connector*

canted camera A tilted camera angle in which the horizon line is not level, but appears at an angle

capacitor An electrical device used in condenser microphones that stores an electrical charge

capture Transferring video and audio from the acquisition medium, such as tape, memory card, and the like, to a computer hard drive for editing

cardioid A microphone pickup pattern that resembles a heart shape; a mic with this pattern is also known as unidirectional, and is most sensitive to sounds in front of it

cathode ray tube The electron gun in the back of a conventional TV screen or monitor that fires electrons at the pixels on the screen to produce an image; also known as a CRT

CD-ROM Compact disc, read-only memory; a CD-ROM stores approximately 640 MB, and is often used for software and other file distribution

centrifugal force The force that tends to pull a thing outward when it is rotating rapidly around a center; this force may affect the operation of some videocassette recorders if they are physically moving while recording

checkerboard Editing technique in which the primary elements, such as talking heads and soundbites, are laid down first, with blank spaces between them to be filled later by the secondary elements, such as *B-roll* shots and natsound; contrast with *section by section*

chargeback The amount paid by one unit of a corporation to an in-house production unit for services rendered on a piece-by-piece basis

charge coupled device (CCD) An imaging device made of solid-state microelectronics that changes light into an electrical signal; used in place of a vacuum *pickup tube*

chroma key Type of composite in which a color backdrop (usually green or blue) is *keyed* out and replaced with other imagery, as in most weather segments of newscasts

chrominance The combination of the red, green, and blue information in video

cinéma vérité A portable shooting style developed in France in the 1950s that popularized handheld camera work

clearance   The permission granted by a copyright holder to allow use of copyrighted material

cleared frame   Transition shot in which either the subject leaves the frame of the first shot before the edit, or the second shot begins without the subject in the frame

climax   Most dramatic or intense point of a story at its end; the conclusion that resolves the plot/s and rewards the viewers, followed by a *denouement*

clogged heads   A condition that occurs when minute pieces of dirt or magnetic particles from the videotape attach themselves to the video head of a VCR and cause poor-quality recording or playback

close-ended question   A question that can be answered with one or two words, such as "yes," "no," or a number (e.g., "How long have you worked here?"); does not elicit a full, expository answer; contrast with *open-ended question*

close-up lenses   Lenses designed to allow focusing on an object located a very short distance from the front of the lens

close-up shot (CU)   A shot in which the subject is framed tightly; for example, when a person is framed from the neck up; used to reveal detail and emotion; also called a tight shot

coax   Wire that carries audio and/or video signals; the wire has one central conductor and a braided shield for grounding that surrounds it

codec   (1) An abbreviation for compression/decompression of information
(2) A software program that can convert the data from a video project to a much smaller file

COFDM   Technology standard for digital television transmission that divides each signal across multiple carriers for less chance of *multipath* interference, selected by Europe and Japan; contrast with *8-VSB*

cognitive effects   The changes in knowledge as a result of viewing a videotape for training purposes; see *behavioral effects* and *emotional effects*

color   *Chrominance*—the control on a TV set that varies the amount or intensity of the chroma information

color enhancement filters   A piece of glass or a gel that functions to brighten (or increase the saturation of) the colors of the subject being shot

color gels   Cellophane material placed in front of lights to alter the color of light that reaches a subject or object to be shot

color temperature   A measure in degrees of Kelvin of the tint or wavelengths of a light; helpful in color balancing between shots; a light with high color temperature is blue; a light with a lower color temperature is red

color temperature blue (CTB)   A color-correction gel that, when placed in front of a light, raises the color temperature of that light toward the blue (daylight) end of the scale

color temperature orange (CTO)   A color-correction gel that, when placed in front of a light, lowers the color temperature of that light toward the red (tungsten) end of the scale

comet tailing   The smearing of light that occurs when a bright image source is moved across a darkened background

compensator group   Two lenses in a typical zoom (compound) lens

complementary colors   Opposite colors on the color wheel; theyt stand out more vividly when adjacent on the screen

completion bond   Guarantee that a production will be finished, usually one to three percent of the budget

component recording A recent development in videotape recording in which the color information is recorded separately from the brightness and synchronization information

composite video Luminance (brightness = Y) and chrominance (color = C) are recorded together in one signal; this yields a less resolute image than *component video* (Y/C)

compositing Blending parts of two or more images to create a new image; replacing parts of one picture, such as a solid color background, with another picture; see *matte*

comprehensive liability Insurance that protects the holder against financial costs if any kind of damage occurs, such as when shooting in a studio or on location, with personal or employee or rental gear, and the like

compression The reduction of size or value of a signal

condenser The transducing element in a microphone that generates electrical signals as a result of changes in capacitance between the diaphragm and the backplate

consent Permission given by a subject to appear in a story; EFP generally requires written consent, while ENG generally uses *implied consent*

consent form Legal document signed by those giving permission to appear in a production or to use something they created, such as music, artwork, and the like

continuity Logical flow of shots edited together with no *jump cuts*

contrasting colors See *complementary colors*

control track Track on videotape that carries the sync pulses that keep the tape stable during recording and playback

control-track editing In analog systems, using the control track signals to sync up the play and record decks; contrast with *time code editing*

contrast ratio The relationship between the brightest portion and the darkest portion of a picture (for example, 20:1)

convertible or systems mic A microphone that can be modified in shape, pickup pattern, or sensitivity to accommodate various audio situations

cookie A metal sheet with a pattern cut-out that is used to project light patterns on floors, cycloramas, and so on; also called a cucalorus

corporate video Video for non-broadcast purposes; used mainly by private enterprise, government, non-profit organizations, and associations

copyright The right held by all to own the rights to any tangible works they create in any medium, such as video, audio, print, art, digital program, and so on; all copyrighted material is *intellectual property*

crab dolly A movable camera mount that can be steered and is designed to allow the camera operator to sit on the device to operate the camera

crane Camera mount that allows the unit to be raised or lowered, similar to a *pedestal* but offering greater range for height and depth

cross-dissolve See *dissolve*

cross-fade Transition between audio clips in which the sounds are momentarily blended, usually for a second or more; analogous to a *cross-dissolve* in video

cut A signal or command to stop cameras and tape during a production; see *take*.

cutaway Shot related to, but slightly away from, the action being recorded; often used to cover unsatisfactory parts of a scene or interview

cutter A narrow *flag*

daylight blue A full CTB gel that, when placed in front of a standard video light, gives off light similar to sunlight or daylight in color

defamation of character Portraying a person in a harmful and negative way; see *libel* and *slander*

demographics Quantitative, objective, measurable variables of an audience, such as age, gender, income, and education level; contrast with *psychographics*

denouement Moment after the *climax* of a story that brings the tension back to normal, shows a glimpse of the future, and adds finality to the story

depth perspective Use of the *z-axis*, including fore-, mid-, and background elements, to create the illusion of three dimensions on a two-dimensional screen

depth of field The area in front of the camera where all objects appear in focus

destructive editing Edited digital file replaces the original, saving drive space but making it impossible to restore the earlier files

dew Moisture that may form or condense inside a camcorder or VCR due to environmental conditions; when dew is sensed inside of a VCR, a sensor may light, warning the user that the VCR or camcorder will not work

diaphragm A moving part of a microphone; see *element*

diffuser A piece of material (glass, fiberglass, cloth) that reduces the intensity or amount of light from a source and makes it less harsh; it may also be placed in front of a camera lens

DigiBeta Digital Beta; a popular professional *digital video* format that uses 1/2-inch tapes

digital Binary code of 1s and 0s, sampled from an analog waveform, that represents the original light or sound waveform; contrast with *analog*

digital service line (DSL) Communications line, usually fiber optic, that carries any number of digital signals, such as telephone and Internet

digital television (DTV) Any TV format that is digital, including *standard definition* and *high definition*

digital video (DV) 1) Generally, all digital formats for video, such as DV, mini-DV, DVCPRO, DVCAM, HDV, *DigiBeta*, and so on
2) Specifically, the *mini-DV* format

digital versatile disc (DVD) Stores approximately 4.7 GB, often used for movie distribution

Digital 8 A digital video format available to consumers; it uses 8 mm videotape

digital effects Special effects for transitions, such as picture compression, tumble or page peel, accomplished by the digital encoding of the video picture to be manipulated

digital video recording A method of recording a video signal that changes the signal into bits of data stored as numbers (0 and 1)

diopter A single lens designed to magnify an image

direct address The subject (e.g., news reporter, narrator) speaks directly to the audience through the camera lens

director The person who translates a written script into a video program

dissolve A transition in video where one video source is faded out while another is simultaneously faded in; see *fade*

distant learning Instructional TV that uses two-way communication over a distance, often accomplished by microwave or satellite transmission

distribute Making a product available to others; mastering and shipping tapes, CDs, or DVDs; or copying projects to hard or portable drives; or posting on the Internet

distribution amplifier Hardware that receives a video or audio signal and improves it by boosting and/or equalizing it before sending it on

divine proportion See *rule of thirds*

DMCA Digital Millennium Copyright Act of 1998; expanded the Copyright Act of 1976, clarifying issues relating to digital copying

dolly Forward and backward movement of the entire camera unit, moving closer to and away from the subject

doorway dolly A small platform on wheels, used to carry a camera on a tripod and small enough to fit through an average doorway

double fog filter Lowers the contrast of the overall scene, but only looks like fog over the very brightest areas

downlink Receiving a signal from a satellite down to a station on the ground

draw The shadow on a subject created by directional light

DVD See *digital versatile disc*

DTV See *digital television*

dual redundancy Two small (tie-clip) microphones placed on a single clip to provide a backup mic if one fails while recording

dub A copy ("dupe" or duplicate), or the process of copying a video- or audiotape, see *assemble*

dynamic A description of a shot or edit that shows movement, power, strength, or energy

edit To put together, rearrange, or eliminate segments of video or audio information on tape

edit control unit (ECU) Machine used to control the play and record decks, as well as set up and execute the edits, in an analog video editing system

edit decision list (EDL) 1) Notation of the aural and visual elements (tape segments, computer files, etc.) selected for inclusion in the final edit, written in sequence
2) Computerized final list of edits generated by the *off-line editor* to give to the *on-line editor* for the final edit

EFP See *electronic field production*

electronic field production (EFP) Portable video for non-news applications.

electronic news gathering (ENG) Portable electronic journalism

element A basic moving part of a microphone that generates the basic electrical signal

emotional effects A desirable effect of a video project, in which the audience experiences feelings as a result of viewing the video

ENG See *electronic news gathering*

errors and omissions (E&O) Insurance against oversights in obtaining copyright permissions

ethics Branch of philosophy exploring choices of right and wrong

extender A device used on a zoom lens that can double the focal length of the lens

exterior shot (ext.) Transition shot, also an *establishing shot*, that shows the outside of a building or location; contrast with *interior shot*

extreme close-up (XCU) Very tight shot showing only detail, such as facial features

eye level   See *normal angle*

external time code   Time code sent to a VCR that is generated outside the VCR

eye light   A small light used in dramatic shots to illuminate the subject's upper facial area.

fade   Gradual change from a video source to a black screen, or vice versa; see *dissolve*

faders   Sliding rheostats used to adjust the volume in audio, the intensity in lights, *or* the mixing of two video signals

Fair Use Clause   Copyright Act of 1976, Title 17, Ch. 1, Par. 107, outlining four conditions under which small portions of copyrighted work may be used without first obtaining permission: purpose, nature, amount, effect

fast lens   A lens capable of gathering a *large* amount of light; a lens capable of an f-stop of 1.4 would be a fast lens in comparison to one that was only capable of an f-stop of 4.0

fat side   The side of the face most visible to the camera; also called the long side; see *short side*

feeders   Microwave-equipped trucks used in *ENG* to relay video and live pictures back to the station

field   One-half of a complete TV picture, that is, 262.5 scanning lines, see *frame*

figure-ground   1) In video, the main visual element (the figure) dominates the picture, and the other elements (the ground) provide context
2) in audio, the main aural element—usually dialogue—is at the foreground, and the other elements—usually sound effects and music—are at the background

file footage   Film and video scenes already recorded and stored in archives or libraries, which producers may retrieve—either for a fee or not—for production use; also *stock footage*

fill light   Light used to soften the shadows caused by the *key* or main directional light

film style   A type of portable production that uses a single camera and often uses many takes of a scene for later editing

filter   Cellophane, glass, spun glass, or similar material used in lenses, cameras, or in front of lights that somehow modulate or change the light passing through them

final cut   Master edit; the final project with all video and audio elements completed; contrast with *rough cut*

FireWire   *IEEE 1394*; one of three main types of connections to transfer digital files between computers and peripherals, such as video cameras, used mostly in consumer and prosumer products; the other two are *USB* and *SDI*

First Amendment   Constitutional Amendment that guarantees the right of free religion, speech, press, peaceful assembly, and redress of grievances

fishpole   A hand-held extension pole used to get a microphone close to a subject. See *boom*.

flag   A solid or opaque light modulator used to direct light or create shadows.

flat   An upright square or rectangular frame covered with cloth or other material that can be painted for a scenic effect.

flat lighting   A type of lighting that does not yield shadows; often created with non-directional lighting or soft light from the camera position.

flatten   Visual effect of objects appearing closer than they are when seen through a telephoto lens, reducing *depth perspective*; see *compression*

flat rate   A nonvariable payment made on a regular basis; for example, a regular payment made to an in-house media production unit for services rendered

floater An insurance policy that provides coverage for rented production equipment

flooded (1) When an adjustable or focusable spotlight is in the least focused position
(2) When a scene is lit with a large quantity of nondirectional light

floodlight A video light that produces a diffuse, wide beam of light

fly away Portable satellite uplink system, which can be folded and transported in a trunk or checked as airline baggage

focal length The distance from the optical center of a lens to the point at which the light rays converge on the face of the image sensor; determines field of view

focal plane The point at which the light rays that pass through a lens converge and are in focus; when in proper focus, this point falls on the image sensor

focusing group The front three lens elements in a compound zoom lens, which determine the position of the focal plane

foot-candle (1) A measure of the amount of light used in countries that have not adopted the metric system
(2) The amount of light given by one candle one foot away from it

forced perspective 1) Use of a wide-angle lens to exaggerate *depth perspective*
2) Creating lines on a set or in a frame that are not parallel but converge toward a *vanishing point* to give the illusion of depth

Fourth Amendment Constitutional Amendment that guarantees "the right of the people to be secure in their persons, houses, papers, and effects"

frame One complete picture in video, equal to two *fields,* that is, 525 scanning lines; see *field*

fringe benefits Items used to pay employees other than salary or wage dollars; for example, health insurance

f-stop A designation of the size of the *iris* opening in a video lens

gaffer grip A device used to hold equipment in place

gaffer tape A wide, strong tape used to hold various pieces of equipment or wire in place

gel A cellophane-type material placed in front of a video light that changes the color of the light

gel frames A frame used to hold gel in place in front of a video light

generation loss Reduction in quality of an *analog* recording each time a copy is made; some signal information is lost and some noise is added with each successive copy

genlock A timing signal that allows the synchronization of two or more video sources

golden rectangle See *rule of thirds*

graphic card An art card, especially prepared for use in a video production, that conforms to the aspect ratio and other restrictions of TV

grip A person who helps carry and place equipment

gyro A stabilizing device on the lens to reduce the shakiness of telephoto shots or pictures taken from aircraft or other unstable locations

hard news A news story that is serious, timely, and deals with important issues in society; for example, crime or politics

HDTV See *high-definition television*

head The front portion of a clip, usually containing a slate and the seconds before the action begins, which is trimmed off in editing

head light   Slang term for a camera-mounted light

head room   (1) In video, the amount of space from the top of the subject's head in a shot to the top of the frame.
(2) In audio, the ability of a recorder to accept a degree of over-modulated signal without distortion

helical scan   Diagonal scan of a magnet across the surface of videotape, made possible by slanting the drum that carries the video magnets, resulting in better image quality than a straight vertical scan; also known as a *slant-track scan*

hertz (Hz)   A unit of measurement for frequency, equal to one cycle per second

high angle   The camera is placed above the subject—the height looks downward, making the subject appear smaller and weaker; contrast with *low angle* and *normal angle*

Hi8   A videotape format that uses 8 mm metal particle tape and features high-resolution and high-quality audio reproduction

high-definition/high-density television (HDTV)   A recently developed TV format that yields a higher-resolution picture due to an increased number of scanning lines per frame.

high-definition digital video (HDV)   A simulated high-definition format with progressive scanning and a wide-screen 16:9 aspect ratio, based on the standard definition DV format

high-intensity discharge   A type of mercury or sodium vapor arc discharge lamp that uses a low amount of electricity, but generates a large amount of light

high-key lighting   Lighting that is bright with a few shadows; used when an upbeat mood is desired

high-pass filter   Hardware or software that allows high frequencies—treble—to pass through, while dampening or eliminating mid-range and low frequencies—bass

hook   Aural and/or visual element at the open of a project to capture the viewers' interest and make them want to stay for more

hot   (1) A video picture with too much light
(2) Any signal whose level is too high

house sound   Sound that is available from the audio board of the "house" (the theater, concert hall, etc.)

house sync   A synchronization signal created by a sync generator for the purpose of having all equipment in a production facility use the same timing

hyperfocal distance   A measurement from the lens to the closest point that an object will be in focus when the lens focus ring is set at infinity

IEEE 1394   See *FireWire*

image stabilization   Technology that senses movement in a camera and adjusts to compensate and reduce shakiness; see *gyro*

impedance   The opposition or restriction to the flow of current, usually measured in ohms

incandescent   Lamps that give off light when they glow from electrical current passing through a filament located inside a vacuum

implied consent   In ENG, when a person agrees to appear in a story, that appearance is considered to be evidence of the person's consent, implied without the need for an actual written consent form; in contrast, EFP generally requires written consent

in-point   Frame of a video clip that you mark as the first frame to be shown in the final edit; compare with *out-point*

insert edit   A type of edit that replaces only the desired information, such as video-only or audio-only; contrast with *assemble edit*

insert   A type of *edit* in which video, audio, or both are put into an existing video piece

integrated services digital network (ISDN) Communications network that allows high-capacity data transfer at speeds much faster than traditional telephone networks

intellectual property (IP) Any and all copyright-protected material

interference Static and break-up that occurs when one RF signal crosses another signal at the same frequency

interior shot (int.) Shot that shows the inside of a building or location; contrast with *exterior shot*

interlaced scanning Process of tracing the odd lines first, then the even lines, in video recording and playback; contrast with *progressive scanning*

interrupted feedback (IFB) Communications system in which on-camera talent wears an ear-piece to receive directions from the director or producer in the control room or central station while on the air

intrusion on seclusion See *invasion of privacy*

internal optical system In almost all video cameras available now, a prism block that separates the white light into red, green, and blue light before the light strikes the image sensors

internal time code An electrical signal generated by a VCR that labels each frame of videotape it records

Internet A worldwide computer network in which information can be stored and retrieved by users

invasion of privacy *Intrusion on seclusion*, occurs when a person's *Fourth Amendment* right to security in his or her home or other personal arena is violated

intranet An in-house computer network used by corporations in which information can be stored and used by in-house users

inverse square law The rule that the amount of light that falls on an object decreases by the square of the inverse of the distance from the light to the object; if the distance from the light to the subject is doubled, the amount of light falling on the object is one-fourth the original amount of light

iris The adjustable diaphragm inside a lens that varies the amount of light that enters the camera; the aperture

JPEG Joint Photographic Experts Group; developed the JPEG still image format and Motion-JPEG video format

jam sync Synchronization signals sent into camcorders and VCRs from one central source

jump cut An uncomfortable edit juxtaposing two shots that do not go together smoothly; for example, a medium shot to a medium shot of the same subject with little difference between them

key Process of replacing one part of an image with another, or matting images together, using luminance, chrominance, alpha channels, or other options to select the part of the image to be replaced

keystoning Framing a shot so that parallel lines become diagonal, converging toward a vanishing point to create depth

keyframe An image used as a reference for a video clip

key light (1) A directional video light used to focus attention and give proper shadow and contrast to a subject
(2) The main source of illumination

lag The after-image seen trailing a moving object on screens

lamp A bulb for a video light

layback Taking a laid-down or mixed-down audio track and placing it back on one channel, freeing up other channels for more sound elements

laydown See *mixdown*

layer Process of adding multiple video or audio tracks to an editing project

L-cut Editing technique in which the audio of a shot precedes that shot, coming in at the end of the previous shot before the cut

lead room (space) Same as *look space*, but used when a person is moving left or right, rather than just looking in that direction

leader sequence Series of information at the start, or head, of a video project; typically bars and tone, followed by a slate and a countdown

leading lines Lines in an image that lead the eye to the main element

liability Responsibility for damage to property or equipment or injury to others; for purposes of insurance and the law, liability must be determined when damage occurs for the appropriate person/s to be assessed charges

libel *Defamation* through recorded means, such as print or video; considered more serious than *slander* because forethought is given to recorded words and images

linear Audio and video segments are recorded and retrieved in sequential order, rather than by *random access*

lead-in A news anchor's introduction to a story

LED (light emitting diode) A small light (usually red, yellow, or green) used as an indicator light

lens flare When a strong light shines directly into a lens, an optical distortion can be seen, often appearing as a series of pentagons; this problem can be avoided by changing the camera angle or deflecting the direct light

lighting grid In a TV studio, a cross-hatch system of bars mounted below the ceiling that allows the mounting of video lights

lighting panel The electronic device in a TV control room or studio that allows connection for, and control of, the lighting system

line (1) One of 525 scanning lines in a video picture
(2) In audio work, a level of signal that has been amplified and is higher in level than a signal from a microphone
(3) In a TV control room, the signal path that leads out from the switcher to the transmitter or videotape recorder—the on-air signal

line level A signal level in audio that is amplified and therefore stronger than a microphone-level signal

line of interest Sometimes called the stage line or the *180° line*, it is a line drawn through a scene to maintain continuity of screen direction when editing together shots taken from different angles to the subject,t by keeping the camera always on the same side of that line; two people talking to each other create a line of interest drawn from one person to the other that extends to infinity in both directions

lip-sync The accurate or synchronized combination of sound and picture, especially matching words with a talking person

live In *ENG* work, a shot from the field that is transmitted back to the TV station and broadcast as it is being photographed

live on tape A method of recording a program on videotape where the program is performed as if it were done live, all in one take, with no editing

low-key lighting Lighting that creates strong, well defined shadows used to create a serious or even somber mood

liquid crystal display (LCD) Technology that produces an image on a flat screen without shooting electrons from a cathode ray tube; most flat screens are either LCD or *plasma*

local area network (LAN) A system of interconnected computers with a narrowly-defined range, such as within a single building

log List of all aural and visual elements (tape segments, computer files) acquired for a production, including location information (time code, file name) and a brief description of each sound and video piece

long shot (LS) See *wide shot*

look space (room) Same as *lead room*; for asymmetrical balance, the space in front of a subject's eyes as the subject looks left or right, usually about 2/3 of the screen when the subject is positioned on 1/3

lossless Type of *compression* that does not lose detail, retaining the full resolution or fidelity of the original file; lossless files are compressed, but are larger than *lossy* files

lossy Type of *compression* that loses detail, sacrificing some resolution or fidelity of the original files for the sake of smaller file sizes; lossy files are smaller than *lossless* files

low angle Camera is placed below the subject—the height looks upward, making the subject appear larger and powerful; contrast with *high angle* and *normal angle*

low-pass filter Hardware or software that allows low frequencies—bass—to pass through while dampening or eliminating mid-range and high frequencies—treble

luminance key Type of composite in which a brightness level is keyed out and replaced with other imagery

luminance The brightness information in a TV signal and picture

macrofocus A focusing ring at the rear of the lens element that allows the focal plane to be brought very close to the front element

macro ring/macro lever The device on the barrel of the lens that engages the macrofocusing capability of the lens

malice aforethought *Defamation* with actual malicious intent; knowing that a story item is wrong and harmful and using it, nonetheless; especially necessary to demonstrate in cases of celebrity libel

master shot Overall shot of a scene; wide shot used to establish setting and character relations, usually recorded first, followed by a series of different "setups," including medium and close-up shots; see *establishing shot* and *wide shot*

match action Type of *continuity* edit in which shots from multiple angles are cut together so that the finished piece looks like one continuous action; subjects must repeat action for each camera angle; cuts are usually made on motion, causing the viewers' eyes to follow the movement across the edits

matte Type of *composite* in which any of a number of picture elements can be *keyed* out and replaced with other imagery

male A type of plug with prongs or pins designed to fit into a corresponding socket

matched action A technique in which one camera is used to shoot the same action from different angle,s and the raw footage is edited to give the appearance of multiple cameras shooting the action at one time

matte box A rectangular bellows-shaped hood that fits over the front of the lens to aid in shading the lens and to serve as a holder for large filters that do not attach to the lens.

media player A program that plays back audio or video from the Internet

medium shot   A relative description of a video shot, usually framing a subject from waist up

mic level   150 ohms, the standard impedance level of a professional microphone

microphone   A device for translating sound energy into electrical energy for amplification or recording purposes

miniboom   A small crane-like arm used for camera mounting

MiniDV   A digital video format available to consumers through a number of different manufacturers; the cassette size is considerably smaller than VHS or 8 mm cassettes

mix   The combination of two or more signals

mix select switches   Levers on a VCR that control which channels of audio are to be monitored

Mobile TV   Video sent to cell phones

modeling effect   The effect of showing depth and texture by creating shadows with directional light

modular camera   A portable video camera that allows for a variety of on-board videocassette recorders to be attached, or for others to be connected by cable

modules   A rectangular light made up of rows of individual *PAR* lights

moire   The rainbow distortion seen on videotaped subjects with a very small, repeated geometric pattern, such as a tie with very thin, evenly spaced stripes

mix-minus   Audio technique in which the audio operator sends the mixed audio signal to the on-camera or on-mic talent, but subtracts the talent's own live audio from the feed

modem   Technology that allows a computer to connect to the Internet via a standard line, such as cable TV or telephone

Motion-JPEG   Video format developed by the Joint Photographic Experts Group

MPEG   Moving Pictures Expert Group; developed the MPEG video formats, including MPEG-2 for DVDs and MPEG-4 for the World Wide Web

moving-coil   A type of microphone transducer that has a coil suspended in a magnetic field; a *diaphragm* reacts to sound pressure and displaces the coil in the field to create an electrical current, often referred to as a dynamic microphone.

multipath   Signal interference when common carriers using the same frequency cross electromagnetic paths

music loops   Clips of music that can be used in editing programs as the basis for creating soundtracks; usually public domain clips that come with editing software or that may be downloaded

multi-pin cable connector   A cable plug designed to connect a single cable containing many smaller individual wires that must always stay insulated from one another.

natsound   Natural sound; ambient sound in exterior settings, which can be recorded purposefully for editing later or mistakenly if the microphone is not placed close enough to the subject; analogous to *room tone* in interior settings

needle drop fee   A cost incurred when using a copyrighted musical piece for production purposes

negative motion   Movement along the *z-axis* away from the camera; contrast with *positive motion*

neutral density gel (ND)   A gray gelatin filter in varying densities that cuts down the amount of light without affecting any other characteristics of the light source

nickel-cadmium cell   A rechargeable battery unit made from nickel and cadmium; often referred to as a "NiCad"

non-destructive editing Edited file is saved as a new file, allowing retrieval of the original file, but requiring additional drive space; contrast with *destructive editing*

non-linear editing (NLE) Computer-based editing that allows *random access* of files, drag-and-drop sequence creation, digital manipulation of audio and video, and so on

normal angle Camera is placed at or about *eye level*— the height approximates how most people see each other; contrast with *high angle* and *low angle*

notch filter Hardware or software that allows a single frequency or range of frequencies to be selected for boosting or dampening

non-segmented videotape A type of videotape recording format in which information for one entire frame is recorded by one head without being broken into two parts, allowing for easier special effects, such as slow motion or still frame

NTSC (National Television Standards Committee) The U.S. government group formed in 1953 to set standards for TV's video signal

off-axis A sound source coming from some place other than where the mic is pointed

omnidirectional A microphone that receives sound equally well regardless of the direction the mic is pointed from the source

on-axis Sound coming from directly in front of the microphone

off-line edit *Rough cut;* usually created from low-resolution copies of the original files, without transitions, effects, sound sweetening, and the like, used to make decisions regarding what video and audio segments to use in the final, *on-line* session

on-line edit *Final cut;* created from original files, including transitions, effects, sound sweetening, and all that is needed for the polished master version

open-ended question Question that elicits a full, expository answer, such as "What do you like most about coming here every day?"; requires more than a "yes" or "no" response; contrast with *close-ended question*

optical disk A recording and storage medium that uses plastic disks onto which digital information is burned with laser light

out-point Frame of a video clip that you mark as the last frame to be show in the final edit; compare with *in-point*

over-the-shoulder (O/S) Two-person shot in which the camera is placed behind one's shoulder, resulting in the shoulder and back of the head in the foreground and the other person's face in the background

overhead expenses Costs incurred as a result of being in business, such as rent and utilities, but not directly related to a video production

P2P Peer-to-peer; an information-sharing network, such as the first Napster, in which individuals host and retrieve files among themselves, rather than paying another service

package News story that is pre-recorded and edited for insertion in a live newscast

pad Two or three seconds at the open of a news package with natsound only, used if the roll cue during a newscast is late and the first seconds are cut off

pan Horizontal pivoting movement of a camera left and right

parametric equalizer Hardware or software that allows a variety of frequencies and ranges to be manipulated

PAL (Phase Alteration by Line) The video signal standard set by Germany, England, and Holland in 1966

parabolic An inward curved reflector that focuses the light or sound it receives to a single point in front of it

parabolic aluminized reflector (PAR) A sealed-beam light with the bulb built into a reflector at its focal point, such as the headlights of a car

party colors A slang term for colored gels that change a light source to a single color of light, such as deep red, forest green, and so on

pedestal A device for mounting a camera that allows the unit to be raised or lowered, similar to a *crane*, but offers a more limited range of height and depth

persistence of vision Phenomenon by which the brain holds a visual image for a fraction of a second, allowing us to perceive motion when a series of sequential images is played rapidly (e.g., 30 fps video, 24 fps film)

perspective Apparent distance between subjects in a shot, exaggerated with a wide-angle lens and *compressed* or *flattened* with a telephoto lens

photons Units of energy that make up light waves

pickup tube An imaging device of vacuum tube construction used in video cameras to change light into an electronic signal

phi Greek letter for 1.618, the aspect ratio of width to height believed by classicists to be ideal for paintings

photoboard Similar to a *storyboard*, with photographs to illustrate each shot

pinned A position on an adjustable video light that yields its narrowest beam; the maximum reading that a needle-type meter can show

pixels The extremely small light-sensitive surfaces that make up the image-recording area of a charged couple device (CCD); the more pixels, the sharper the image will be

plasma Technology that produces an image on a flat screen without shooting electrons from a cathode ray tube; most flat screens are either plasma or *LCD*

plumb-bubble bullseye A circular container with a single bubble in a liquid; when the bubble is in a ring painted on top of the container, the device (tripod, camera, and so on) is level to the horizontal plane

plumbicon tube A vacuum tube designed to produce a video picture using a lead oxide coating on its light-sensitive surface

podcast An audio or audio and video file that is downloadable from an Internet site

pool One or only a few cameras cover an event, but other organizations are allowed to tap into the same feed, making the video from a restricted area available for wider distribution

polar pattern A diagram of a microphone's sensitivity or pickup capability

polarizing filter A glass filter over the lens that reduces glare and reflections by preventing certain angles of reflected light from passing through it

portable Refers to production equipment that can be easily transported to an on-location shoot; implies that it can be run on direct current or battery power

Porta-pack The first portable video system developed by Sony that used a reel-to-reel VCR and a black-and-white camera

positive motion Movement along the *z-axis* toward the camera; contrast with *negative motion*

post-production The last stage in the process of creating a video project; the stage in which editing is accomplished

pre-production The first or planning stage in the process of creating a video project

pre-roll A few seconds, usually five, that a video clip is rewound prior to the desired *in-point*, allowing the clip to play up to full speed before the edit point

presence boost An audio filter that emphasizes frequencies in the upper midrange, around 5 kHz, to enhance voices

press pass Identification card given by officials to media reporters and their crews, allowing them access to otherwise restricted events

primary additive colors Red, green, and blue. A TV camera reduces a picture to varying amounts of these three colors to make up the chroma segment of a video signal.

prime lens A fixed focal length lens.

prime lens group The series of lenses at the rear of any type of lens that focuses the image onto the recording surface.

prism block A device in a video camera that consists of several prisms that split the incoming light into its red, green, and blue components and guides the light to the appropriate chip.

privileged event Event that might be a *public forum* or might at least be open to credentialed journalists, giving them the right to cover it for a story

processing amplifier A device to boost a video signal with control over the strength and black level of that signal (similar to brightness and contrast controls).

producer The person in charge of a production.

producer's insurance policy (PIP) Blanket insurance that can be tailored for each production to combine all the necessary insurances in a single policy, usually two to four percent of the budget, though there are minimums

production The middle stage in the process of creating a video project when images and/or sound are recorded.

progressive scanning Process of tracing all lines sequentially, used in some versions of advanced and high-definition TV; contrast with *interlaced scanning*

prop An abbreviation for property used on the set of a video shoot or scene.

prosumer Professional-consumer; video cameras and equipment in the mid-level price and quality range between high-priced professional gear and low-priced consumer gear

psychographics Qualitative, subjective, descriptive variables of an audience, such as lifestyles, values, attitudes, interests, and hobbies; contrast with *demographics*

public domain Any creation in any medium that has no copyright or for which the copyright has expired, such as video and audio files, that may be used without obtaining any rights

public forum Event that is open to the public and, therefore, open to journalists who have a right to cover it for a story

public property Publicly held land and assets; journalists are allowed to report from public property as long as they don't pry into private property, such as using an overly-long zoom lens

pull *Zoom* out

pull-ups Subtractions or changes done to an edited piece of video causing a change in the total length of the piece.

pulse-code modulation PCM; audio recording that embeds the digital audio signal as pulses within the video scans; used in many digital video formats

push *zoom* in

quality light By professional consensus, light from a very large source that produces soft-edged shadows

quality of light A measure of both the color temperature and the harshness or softness of the light source

random access The ability to retrieve information from any point in a system without having to search through or scan information in a linear fashion; also known as *non-linear*

raising stakes See *rising action*

reaction shot A type of *cutaway* shot in which a person's or persons' response to an action is shown, as in a crowd's response to a fight

real-time switching The changing of video sources done *live* or when a program is recorded live on tape

re-enactments Type of *staging* in which an entire scene or event is re-created; generally permissible as long as truth is maintained and the scene is clearly labeled as a dramatization

record and playback controls The buttons to put the VCR in either the record or playback mode

reflector Hard or soft surface covered with a highly reflective material to redirect light to fall on a desired area

registration The alignment of the three color *image sensors* in a video camera to give one full color image

Rembrandt lighting The style of lighting made famous by the Dutch painter and characterized by the use of alternating areas of light and shadow in his scenes; creator of the *modeling effect*

remote An on-location shoot that relays a signal to another location, such as a broadcast station

repeated action Movement that is repeated for each new camera angle in shooting, allowing for match action cutting in editing

resolution A measure of sharpness or clarity in a video picture

retrozoom A multi-element glass lens that attaches on a zoom lens to decrease the focal length throughout the zoom range; a wide angle attachment

reverberation Creating *echo* by copying sound waves and delaying them behind the original waves, resulting in a second occurrence of the sound, usually at a lower level, a fraction of a second or more after the original sound

reversal A type of *cutaway* shot in which the listener is shown; often used to maintain *continuity*, as in an interviewer listening to an interviewee's response

RF Radio frequency; any frequency in the electromagnetic spectrum used for audio and/or video signal transmission

right to privacy Derived from the *Fourth Amendment* that guarantees security, people's personal property and belongings are considered to be private and not available for public scrutiny without permission

RF interference Noise in a video signal caused by unwanted broadcast signals (often from AM radio signals)

rim light Similar to *backlight,* only striking the subject from a lower angle; also called edge light

rising action Increasing the drama or intensity of each segment progressively throughout the middle of a story; also known as *raising stakes*

roaming Having the automatic iris constantly changing due to a portion of the scene fluctuating in brightness

rocker-style switch A long switch operated with a finger at each end and the axis of the switch in between; as the switch is rocked downward in the front, the servo runs forward; as the switch is rocked down at its rear, the servo reverses direction

room noise See *room tone*

room tone Ambient sound in interior settings, which can be recorded purposefully for editing later or mistakenly if the microphone is not placed close enough to the subject; analogous to *natsound* in exterior settings; also known as *room noise*

rough cut First edit; video shots and main audio elements are laid down in sequence, but no transitions, effects, audio *mixdown*, or other steps that come later in the *final cut*

routing system A system that allows the video and/or audio signal to be channeled or directed to multiple locations by cable

rule of "three to one" or rule of thirds When lining up a shot, it is aesthetically more pleasing to have the major elements in the frame fall on lines created by dividing the screen in thirds both horizontally and vertically

sampling Converting an analog waveform to a digital file by selecting many points each second along the waveform and assigning a discrete, binary code to each point

saticon A type of *pickup tube* used in industrial-quality and some professional-quality video cameras

saturation The amount of overall color in a picture

scanning Breaking an image into individual pixels of light for recording and playback

scanning beam Hardware that traces the pixels and lines on the screen of a TV monitor

script Written text that serves as a blueprint for production, including settings, action, characters, and dialogue

scoop A type of artificial light that provides generally diffuse light for fill purposes

scrim A piece of metal screen material placed over a light to reduce its output; see *diffuser* and *filter*

SDTV Standard definition television (NTSC)

SECAM (*Séquentiel couleur à mémoire*) The 1962 TV signal standard developed and used in France.

section by section Editing technique in which an entire section is fully completed with all aural and visual elements before editing the next section; contrast with *checkerboard*

segmented video A videotape format in which two (or more) video head passes are necessary to record a *frame* of video

servo A small electric motor used to turn a set of gears

sequence 1) A grouping of shots and/or audio clips 2) The process of arranging clips in order by dragging and dropping them onto an editing software interface timeline

Serial Digital Interface (SDI) One of three main types of connections to transfer digital files between computers and peripherals, such as video cameras; used mostly in professional products because of its high bandwidth and transfer rate; the other two are *FireWire* and *USB*

set shot A steady shot, usually 10 seconds or longer, recorded in the middle of action, used to give the videographer a momentary break from shooting and the editor some steady footage for editing; also known as *static*

setup Each new camera position during a shoot, such as O/S, medium, and close-up; might require modifications to lighting, microphones, and even "cheating" talent positions for optimal framing and composition

shade (1) To prevent light from falling on a certain area (2) To remotely set the iris and black levels of a camera

shaky camera Having too much movement of the camera while recording

shield laws Laws in place in most states that protect journalists from revealing their sources of information; considered necessary for a truly free press

shoot The actual production work of a video project

short side The part of the face least seen from the camera position; generally, the side of the face lit by the *key light*; see *fat side*

shower curtain A slang term for a heavy plastic fire-proof diffusion material used over a light source

siamese A single cable that bundles both an audio and a video line

siders Flags that are used to the side of a light source

signal-to-noise ratio A ratio that compares picture strength to noise strength; the higher the ratio, the better the picture

single-element wide-angle lens A glass lens that fits on a zoom lens to reduce the focal length to one specific wide angle focal length; thus, the zoom elements cannot be used with it in place.

skew The tension of videotape around the video drum

skew knob On older-style VCRs, this control would manually adjust the tension of the videotape across the playback heads

slander *Defamation* through the spoken word; not considered as serious as *libel* because less forethought occurs when someone speaks "off the cuff"

slant-track scan See *helical scan*

sliding element A group of lenses within a complete lens that is able to move closer to or further from the other lens groups

slow lens A lens whose iris does not open very wide and thus does not let very much light pass through it

smearing An undesirable aspect of a video picture with too much gain; smearing appears as colors trailing or flaring off of objects in the *frame*

SMTPE time code See *time code*

snap zoom A very fast-changing zoom, accomplished by manually rotating the zoom control with a quick wrist motion

soft frost A type of diffusion gel used over a light source to soften the harshness of the light

soft light (1) A large diffuse light source that creates soft-edged shadows
(2) A light fixture designed to create soft-edged shadows, sometimes called a soft box

softnet filter A very fine net material within a glass filter used over the lens to soften the look of a scene

soft news Stories that are not breaking and do not have an immediate impact, but are important nonetheless, such as features about people, interesting places, and the like; these stories are typically entertaining in nature, have a longer "shelf life" than *hard news*, and can air at anytime within a week or month timeframe

solid state Device that records directly on a microchip with no moving parts, such as computer drives and memory cards

soundbite A sentence or more selected from a recorded interview for inclusion in a story; the recorded words used in editing

special effects filters Glass filters on the lens that manipulate the image's color, focus, or position

speed A photographic term for describing how sensitive a lens or chip is to light

split-field effect A filter on the lens that changes the plane of focus for only one-half the picture

spotlight A directional, often adjustable, type of artificial light source for video

squeeze Digital effect in which an image is reduced in size and placed within another image, such as a graphic over-the-shoulder of a news anchor, or a picture-in-picture image

staging Rearranging elements or events for a recording; generally permissible for improved lighting, image composition, and sound recording, as long as the truth of the situation is maintained; generally not permissible if the truth is altered

stand-alone Editing system that is self-contained for use by a single editor working alone; contrast with *work group*

standard definition SDTV, SD; NTSC video resolution, including 640x480 or 720x480 pixels, with interlaced scanning, all offering the narrow-screen aspect ratio of 4:3; contrast with *high definition*

stand-up A shot in which a reporter or other on-camera hosts stands in front of a selected background to report a story, talking directly to the viewer

star filter A glass filter in front of the lens with a screen material in it that makes highlights such as light bulbs appear pointed like stars

static See *set shot*

sticks Slang term for a tripod

stock footage See *file footage*

stopped down To have the iris at a very small opening or even completely closed

storyboard Series of panel illustrations with descriptive text of both video and audio, used in pre-production to visualize the shots and accompanying audio in a project

superimpose Process of blending two images so the full image consists of two partial images; technically, a "half dissolve"

streaming Playing sound and/or video in real time as it downloads over the Internet, rather than storing it in a file for later playing

studio arcs Large carbon arc lights used in movie production

studio pedestal mount A professional, heavy-duty mounting system with wheels for studio cameras; it can only be used on very smooth surfaces

subtractive primary colors Magenta, cyan, and yellow used in paint mixing and color photo printing to obtain all the other colors but not used in video recording

sungun A small battery-powered light, usually camera-mounted

switcher A device to combine or switch video signals and special effects from a variety of sources into one video output

symmetrical balance Composing an image with objects of similar shape, mass, weight, color, contrast, line, and texture on opposite sides of the screen; contrast with *asymmetrical balance*

sync generator An electronic device used in a video studio that gives timing pulses to the cameras, VCRs, and all other pieces of equipment that need to be time-coordinated

tail Back portion of a clip, usually containing the seconds after the action stops, which is trimmed off in editing

take An individual shot or scene, usually one of several; an instantaneous change from one video source to another; see *cut.*

talent The persons who are performing in front of the camera

talking head   A shot of a person speaking, usually a static head-and-shoulders or head-only shot; generally slang for an interview shot

tapeless environment   Shooting, editing, and mastering without tape, using solid state or other media instead (e.g., DVDs)

teasers   Large black flats used to prevent light from falling on certain areas.

telecine   A device that transfers film or slides to video, consisting of a film projector, slide projector, video camera, and multiplexer; a device to direct projection into a video camera lens; also called "film chain" or "film island"

teleconverter   A multi-element glass filter that fits onto a zoom lens to increase its focal length while still being able to zoom.

three-act structure   Basic story pattern, including a beginning, a middle, and an end

tilt   Angling the camera either up or down.

time base corrector (TBC)   An electronic device that corrects for speed and mechanical errors in a videotape machine, giving the videotape a broadcast standard horizontal sync

time code   The numbering system for every frame of video, in hours:minutes:seconds:frames, embedded with the signal on tape and in digital video files; also known as *SMPTE timecode*

time code editing   In analog and digital systems, using the time code signal to sync up play and record segments or files; contrast with *control-track editing*

timeline   1) Part of video editing software's interface in which clips are dragged and dropped into the desired sequence, usually along the bottom part of the monitor
2) Schedule for completion of a project, with allotted dates for pre-production, production, and post-production

toppers   *Flags* used above a light source

total running time (TRT)   Sum of all segments of a project; overall length in minutes:seconds

track   1) A type of shot in which the entire camera unit follows a subject laterally (left and right), same as a truck
2) A set of rails that can be laid over bumpy flooring or terrain to achieve smooth camera movement
3) The portion of a videotape surface or editing timeline dedicated to recording or sequencing an element, such as a video track or audio track
4) A reporter's narration laid down on the audio track for editing a news package

tracing paper   Slang for a heavy, paper-like diffusion material used in front of a light source

tracking   The speed and angle at which the videotape passes the video heads, often adjustable during playback to maximize picture quality

tracking knob   A manual adjustment when playing back a videotape to align the video heads of a VCR with the video tracks laid down on the tape

transition shot   A shot used to bridge two video segments that otherwise might not smoothly connect

treatment   A preliminary synopsis or storyline that describes plot, characters, setting, and so on, for a forthcoming script

trim   Cutting the head and tail of a clip to get rid of unwanted footage and keep only the frames desired for the final edit

truck   Left and right movement of the entire camera in order to move laterally with the subject, accomplished by mounting on some type of device with wheels or on tracks

tweeter   Speaker designed especially for high frequencies, or treble

two-pronged question A question that elicits a two-part answer, usually a short factual statement followed by an expository comment, such as "How many years have you worked here, and what is the most unusual thing you have seen?"

tungsten-halogen lamp The standard light source for film and video production using a tungsten filament inside a sealed glass globe; it gives off light at 3,200° Kelvin

two-X range The range of focal lengths created on a zoom lens after the 2X extender is used

U-Matic format The first color video cassette format developed by Sony for use in the field; often referred to as 3/4-inch because of the tape's width

U-Matic SP format An improved version of the original U-Matic format, using metal particle tape for better sharpness and color; SP means superior performance

umbrella A device shaped like a regular rain umbrella that is mounted on a portable video light; the reflective underside of this umbrella reflects a diffuse light on a subject

unit rate The amount of cost incurred in a particular time frame; for example, the cost per day of owning a portable camera

Universal Serial Bus (USB) One of three main types of connections to transfer digital files between computers and peripherals, such as video cameras, used mostly in consumer and prosumer products; the other two are *FireWire* and *SDI*

uplink Transmission of a signal from a station on the ground up to a satellite

UV Ultraviolet

vanishing point A point on the horizon or outside the frame where parallel lines when viewed at an angle in a shot seem to converge

variator group The lens grouping within a zoom lens that changes image size by moving toward or away from the main lens groups

vertical interval time code The series of numbers stored in the vertical interval of a video signal that mark each frame of that video so those frames can be cataloged for later reference

video digital effects A sophisticated video manipulation that allows the video picture to be compressed, flipped, tumbled, and so on

video level control A device that can adjust the amplification of a video signal either up or down

video news release (VNR) A *soft news* package produced by a corporation and made available to news and other organizations for telecasting in full or in part

video processors Electronic circuits that control the amount and quality of all the components of a video signal

video switcher An electronic device that allows an individual to select among many video inputs

viewfinder A small black-and-white TV monitor with an eyepiece used by the camera operator to see what the camera sees

vignetting Dark areas in the corners of a picture caused by lens problems, e.g., the lens not being properly lined up with the camera's internal optics system

voice coil A small wire coil used in a microphone to transduce sound into electric energy so that it can be recorded

voice-over (VO) Narration from an unseen person, usually recorded in a separate session from visual shooting

VU meter A device to measure volume units of audio on a tape machine or sound mixer/amplifier.

watermark   Partially transparent logo, usually of a broadcast station, inserted over a corner of a video segment or program to show whose property it is; also known as *bug*

whip pan   Very fast pan in which the camera is "whipped" quickly to the left or right; used to follow very fast action, though not recommended because of the difficulty of framing

wide angle lens   A lens with a large field of view and focal lengths starting around 5.5 mm for video lenses

wide shot   A camera shot with a short focal length and, therefore, a wide field of view that includes a large amount of the area in front of the camera; also called a long shot

wipe   Transition between two video shots in which one image replaces the other in some type of geometric pattern, drawing attention to the transition itself, usually signifying a major change of topic, time, or place

wireless high-fidelity (WiFi)   High-speed broadband technology that transfers data via radio frequencies rather than cables or wires

woofer   Speaker designed especially for low frequencies, or bass

work group   Editing system that is networked for multiple editors to access all files; contrast with *stand-alone*

worker's compensation   Insurance coverage for medical, disability, and death, provided by employers for their employees

World Wide Web   The portion of the Internet that allows use of graphics, audio, and video information

wrong-field edits   Edits made when the edit machine mistakenly cuts from a position or negative field of one shot to the like field of the next shot, thereby breaking the required pattern of alternating fields

x-axis   In image composition, the dimension of width, in addition to the *y-axis* (height) and *z-axis* (depth)

XCU   An extreme close-up video shot

XLR connector   The standard three-contact plugs used in all professional sound work, originally the part number of this type of audio connector by the Cannon Company and sometimes still called cannon connectors

y-axis   In image composition, the dimension of height, in addition to the *x-axis* (width) and *z-axis* (depth)

z-axis   In image composition, the dimension of depth, in addition to the *x-axis* (width) and *y-axis* (height)

zebra bars   Diagonal white lines superimposed over parts of the picture that have a certain level of video signal and can only be seen in the viewfinder; many cameras have the zebra bars set at 70 units of video, which aids the operator in determining proper exposure

zip light   A type of soft light fixture in metal housing

zoom control   The device that operates the zoom servo to determine the direction and speed of the zoom

zoom lens   A lens capable of changing focal lengths without affecting the plane of focus, thus allowing continuous change in image size from widest to narrowest field of view, with no other adjustments needed

zoom ratio   This ratio compares the longest focal length to the shortest, such as 120 mm to 10 mm, or 140 mm to 10 mm; often expressed in ratio form, for example, 12:1 or 14:1; also known as the zoom range.

Bibliography

Books

Aesthetics

Arijon, Daniel. *Grammar of the Film Language*. Boston, MA: Focal Press, 1976.

Douglass, John S., and Harnden, Glenn P. *The Art of Technique: An Aesthetic Approach to Film and Video Production*. Needham Heights, MA: Allyn & Bacon, 1996.

Lester, Paul M. *Visual Communication: Images with Messages 4th Ed*. Belmont, CA: Wadsworth Publishing Co., 2006.

Ward, Peter. *Picture Composition*. Boston, MA: Focal Press, 1996.

Zettl, Herbert. *Sight, Sound, Motion: Applied Media Aesthetics*, 3rd ed. Belmont, CA: Wadsworth Publishing Co., 1999.

Audio

Alten, Stanley R. *Audio in Media*, 5th ed. Belmont, CA: Wadsworth Publishing Co., 1998.

Bartlett, Bruce. *Introduction to Professional Recording Techniques*. Indianapolis, IN: Howard Sams & Co., 1987.

Clifford, Martin. *Microphones*, 2nd ed. Blue Ridge Summit, PA: Tab Books, 1982.

Huber, Miles. *Microphone Manual: Design and Application*. Indianapolis, IN: Howard Sams & Co., 1988.

Budgeting/Business

Marsh, Ken. *Independent Video*. San Francisco, CA: Straight Arrow Books, 1974.

Van Deusen, Richard E. *Practical AV/Video Budgeting*. Boston, MA: Focal Press, 1984.

Wiese, Michael. *Film & Video Budgets*. Studio City, CA: M. Wiese Productions, 1995.

Corporate Video

Dizazzo, Ray. *Corporate Media Production*. Boston, MA: Focal Press, 2000.

Gayeski, Diane. *Corporate and Instructional Video*, 2nd ed. Englewood Cliffs, NJ: Prentice Hall, 1991.

Hausman, Carl. *Institutional Video*. Belmont, CA: Wadsworth Publishing Co., 1991.

Directing

Blumenthal, Howard J. *Television Producing and Directing*. New York, NY: Barnes and Noble Books, 1987.

Cury, Ivan. *Directing and Producing for Television: A Format Approach*. Boston, MA: Focal Press, 2006.

Hickman, Harold R. *Television Direction*. Santa Rosa, CA: Cole Publishing Co., 1991.

Kennedy, Thomas. *Directing Video*. Boston, MA: Focal Press, 1989.

Documentary

Kriwaczek, Paul. *Documentary for the Small Screen*. Boston: Focal Press, 2003.

Editing

Anderson, Gary. *Video Editing and Postproduction: A Professional Guide*, 4th ed. Boston, MA: Focal Press, 1999.

Browne, Steven E. *Nonlinear Editing Basics: Electronic Film and Video Editing*. Boston, MA: Focal Press, 1998.

Ohanian, Thomas, A. *Digital Nonlinear Editing*. Boston, MA: Focal Press, 1993.

Reisz, Karel and Millar, Gavin. *The Technique of Film Editing*. Boston, MA: Focal Press, 1986.

Rubin, Michael. *Nonlinear 4*. Gainesville, FL: Triad Publications, 2000.

Schneider, Arthur. *Electronic Postproduction and Videotape Editing*. Boston, MA: Focal Press, 1989.

Electronic Media

Medoff, Norman, and Kaye, Barbara. *Electronic Media: Then, Now, and Later*. Boston: Allyn and Bacon, 2005.

Framing and Composition

Gross, Lynne, Froust, James, and Burrows, Thomas, *Video Production: Disciplines and Techniques*, 9th ed. New York, NY: McGraw-Hill, 2005.

Katz, Steven D. *Film Directing, Shot by Shot: Visualizing from Concept to Screen*. Studio City, CA: Michael Wiese Productions, 1991.

Mamer, Bruce. *Film Production Technique: Creating the Accomplished Image*, 3rd ed. Belmont, CA: Wadsworth Publishing Co., 2002.

Millerson, Gerald. *Television Production*, 13th ed. Boston, MA: Focal Press, 2000.

Zettl, Herbert. *Television Production Handbook*, 9th ed. Belmont, CA: Thomson Wadsworth, 2006.

Legal

Blue, Martha. *Making It Legal*. Flagstaff, AZ: Northland Publishing Co., 1988.

Goldstein, Norm. *The Associated Press Stylebook and Briefing on Media Law*. Jackson, TN: Perseus Books Group, 2006.

Miller, Philip H. *Media Law for Producers*, 4th ed. Boston, MA: Focal Press, 2002.

Overbeck, Wayne. *Major Principles of Media Law, 2007 Edition*. Belmont, CA: Thomson Wadsworth, 2006.

Pember, Don R., and Calvert, Clay. *Mass Media Law, 2007/2008 Edition*, 15th ed. New York, NY: McGraw-Hill, 2007.

Trager, Robert, Russomanno, Joseph A., and Dente Ross, Susan. *The Law of Journalism and Mass Communication.* New York, NY: McGraw-Hill, 2007.

Lighting

Brown, Blain. *Motion Picture and Video Lighting.* Boston, MA: Focal Press, 1996.

Carlson, Verne and Carlson, Sylvia. *Professional Lighting Handbook.* Boston, MA: Focal Press, 1985.

Hunter, Fil, and Fuqua, Paul. *Light: Science and Magic*, 2nd ed. Boston, MA: Focal Press, 1997.

LeTourneau, Tom. *Lighting Techniques for Video Production.* Boston, MA: Focal Press, 1987.

Lyver, Des. *Basics of Video Lighting.* 2nd ed. Boston, MA: Focal Press, 2000.

Millerson, Gerald. *The Technique of Lighting for Television and Motion Pictures*, 3rd ed. Boston, MA: Focal Press, 2001.

Ritsko, Alan J. *Lighting for Location Motion Pictures.* New York, NY: Van Nostrand Reinhold Co., Inc., 1979.

News

Cremer, Charles F., Kierstead, Phillip O., and Yoakam, Richard D. *ENG: Television News and the New Technology*, 3rd ed. New York: McGraw-Hill, 1996.

Hausman, Carl. *Crafting the News for Electronic Media.* Belmont, CA: Wadsworth Publishing Co., 1992.

Orlik, Peter B. *Broadcast / Cable Copywriting*, 7th ed. Boston, MA: Allyn & Bacon, 2004.

Ryan, Michael, and Tankard, James W. *Writing for Print and Digital Media.* New York, NY: McGraw-Hill, 2005.

Stephens, Mitchell. *Broadcast News*, 4th ed. Belmont, CA: Thomson Wadsworth, 2005.

Tuggle, C.A., Carr, Forrest, and Huffman, Suzanne. *Broadcast News Handbook: Writing, Reporting, Producing in a Converging Media World*, 3rd ed. New York, NY: McGraw-Hill, 2007.

White, Ted. *Broadcast News: Writing, Reporting, and Producing*, 4th ed. Boston, MA: Focal Press, 2005.

Postproduction

Alten, Stanley R. *Audio in Media*, 7th ed. Belmont, CA: Wadsworth Publishing Co., 2005.

Browne, Steven E. *Video Editing: A Postproduction Primer*, 4th ed. Boston, MA: Focal Press, 2002.

Compesi, Ronald J. *Video Field Production and Editing*, 7th ed. Boston, MA: Allyn & Bacon, 2007.

Gross, Lynne, and Ward, Larry. *Digital Moviemaking*, 6th ed. Belmont, CA: Thomson Wadsworth, 2007.

Katz, Steven D. *Film Directing, Cinematic Motion: A Workshop for Staging Scenes.* Studio City, CA: Michael Wiese Productions, 1992.

Zettl, Herbert. *Sight, Sound, Motion: Applied Media Aesthetics*, 4th ed. Belmont, CA: Thomson Wadsworth, 2005.

Production

Compesi, Ronald. *Video Field Production and Editing*, 6th ed. Boston, MA: Allyn and Bacon, 2006.

Gross, Lynne, Foust, James, and Burrows, Thomas. *Video Production: Disciplines and Techniques*, 9th ed. New York, NY: McGraw-Hill, 2005.

Gross, Lynne, and Ward, Larry. *Digital Moviemaking*, 6th ed. Belmont, CA: Wadsworth, 2007.

Lyver, Des. *Basics of a Video Production Diary*. Boston, MA: Focal Press, 2001.

Mathias, Harry and Patterson, Richard. *Electronic Cinematography*. Belmont, CA: Wadsworth Publishing Co., 1985.

Musburger, Robert, and Kindem, Gorham. *Introduction to Media Production*. Boston, MA: Focal Press, 2004.

Schroeppel, Tom. *The Bare Bones Camera Course for Film and Video*, 2nd ed. Miami, FL: Tom Schroeppel, 1982.

———. *Video Goals: Getting Results with Pictures and Sound*. Miami, FL: Tom Schroeppel, 1987.

Shook, Frederick. *Television Field Production and Reporting*, 3rd. ed. New York, NY: Longman Publishers, 2000.

Smith, David. *Video Communications*. Belmont, CA: Wadsworth Publishing Co., 1991.

Utz, Peter. *Today's Video*. Englewood Cliffs, NJ: Prentice Hall, 1987.

Zettl, Herbert. *Television Production Handbook*, 7th ed. Belmont, CA: Wadsworth Publishing Co., 2000.

Programming

Perebinossoff, Phillipe, Gross, Brian, and Gross, Lynne. *Programming for TV, Radio, and the Internet*. Boston, MA: Focal Press, 2005.

Technology

Beaulieu, Mark and Okon, Chris. *Demystifying Multimedia*. San Francisco, CA: Vivid Publishing, 1993.

Grant, August, and Meadows, J., eds. *Communication Technology Update*. Boston, MA: Focal Press, 2004.

Writing

Aristotle. *Poetics*. 335 BCE. G. F. Else, trans. Ann Arbor, MI: University of Michigan Press, 1970.

Dancyger, Ken, and Rush, Jeff. *Alternative Scriptwriting*, 5th ed. Boston, MA: Focal Press, 2006.

Egri, Lajos. *The Art of Dramatic Writing*. New York, NY: Simon & Schuster, 1960 (originally published 1946).

Field, Syd. *Screenplay: The Foundations of Screenwriting*, rev. ed. New York, NY: Dell Publishing, 1984.

Friedmann, Anthony. *Writing for Visual Media*, 2nd ed. Boston, MA: Focal Press, 2006.

Garvey, Daniel, and Rivers, William. *Broadcast Writing Handbook*. New York, NY: Longman, Inc., 1982.

Hilliard, Robert L. *Writing for Television, Radio, and New Media*, 8th ed. Belmont, CA: Wadsworth Publishing Co., 2004.

Hyde, Stuart. *Idea to Script: Storytelling for Today's Media*. Boston, MA: Allyn & Bacon, 2003.

Meeske, Milan. *Copywriting for the Electronic Media: A Practical Guide*, 5th ed. Belmont, CA: Thomson Wadsworth, 2006.

Periodicals and Web Sites

Associated Press. http://www.apbroadcast.com/.

Digital Content Producer, Millimeter, & Video Systems. http://digitalcontentproducer.com/.

Digital Video. CMP Media, 600 Harrison St., San Francisco, CA 94107.

Digital Video Editing. http://www.digitalvideoediting.com/.

DV Magazine. http://www.dv.com/.

Film & Video. http://www.studiodaily.com/filmandvideo/.

Macworld. http://www.macworld.com/.

PC World. http://www.pcworld.com/.

Res. http://www.res.com/.
A Short Course in Digital Video. http://www.shortcourses.com/video/.

Studio Monthly. http://www.studiomonthly.com/.
Videography. P.S.N. Publications, 2 Park Ave., Suite 1820, New York, NY 10016.

Videomaker. Videomaker, Inc., 290 Airpark Blvd., Chico, CA 95926. (http://www.videomaker.com/).

U.S. Copyright Office Forms. http://www.copyright.gov/forms/.

Wex. http://www.law.cornell.edu/wex/index.php/Media.

Writers Guild of America. http://www.wga.org/.

Format Guidelines for Screenplays

Here are the main elements of the screenplay format. Following these elements is a sample script, *Writer's Block*, which demonstrates most of these guidelines. For more detailed information, please consult the Writers Guild guidelines or any of the many books on screenwriting.

Margins Margins should be one inch on all edges of the page, which means that the left margin should be one and a half inches to account for the half inch lost to "brads" (used to bind long-form scripts, one in the top hole and one in the bottom hole).

Type The font should be pica, a typewriter word indicating a serif, fixed-width font of 10 characters per inch. On most word-processing programs, including Microsoft Word, this is the Courier New font, set at 12 point, which is 10 characters per inch.

Page Numbers Beginning with *page 2*, number each page in the top right-hand corner, followed by a period.

Page Breaks Avoid breaking pages in the middle of dialogue lines. If this happens, allow extra lines at the bottom of the page so the next page begins with the character's name, followed by his/her dialogue.

FADE IN Always begin with "FADE IN": at the left margin, ALL CAPS, followed by a colon and a triple space.

Slug The slug gives the setting in abbreviated form, written in ALL CAPS. Every change of location or time requires one. Always begin with either "INT." or "EXT." (abbreviations for "interior" and "exterior," followed by a period). Next is a one- or two-word description of the location, such as "BEACH," "LISA'S KITCHEN," or something similar. Follow this with a space, a hyphen, another space and then either "DAY" or "NIGHT." Some writers use "MORNING," "LATE AFTERNOON," "DUSK," and the like, but it is preferred that you use only "DAY" or "NIGHT." Then, only if necessary for the story, describe the more precise time in the action line that follows, after a double space.

Action This sets up the scene. Keep it brief. Include only the information that is necessary to tell the story. The details of props, wardrobe, makeup, and so on are best left to the design team. Name the characters who appear in this scene, and *if it is the first time they appear in the script*, CAPITALIZE THEIR NAMES. Also CAPITALIZE MUSIC, SOUND EFFECTS, and VISUAL EFFECTS, such as CAMERA MOVES. Single space the action line, but follow it with a double space.

Character Write out the name of the character who speaks in ALL CAPS. Indent to about two and a half inches from left margin.

Parenthetical This is a one- or two-word description of how the character says the line, such as "(angrily)." Use this very sparingly, only when truly essential. If your script is written well, a good actor will provide a good line reading without prompting. Parentheticals should be in lowercase, in parentheses, single spaced below character line, about two inches from *both left and right margins* (about five spaces left of character line). One type of parenthetical is "(Continuing)"; use this when a character's dialogue is interrupted by an action description and the same character who was speaking before the interruption continues speaking.

Dialogue Write the words that the character speaks in upper/lower case, single-spaced below the parenthetical (if used) or the character line. The dialogue lines should be indented about one and a half inches from *both left and right margins*, making dialogue appear about three inches wide in the middle of the page.

Transitions These indicate the type of effect used to go from one scene to another, such as a dissolve or wipe. Write these sparingly: the director decides the transitions. You need not write "CUT" because a straight cut is the most-used transition and it is assumed, unless a different transition is indicated. If you indicate a transition, such as "DISSOLVE TO:," put it on the *right* margin, in ALL CAPS, followed by a colon, double spaced below the previous line. Double space again for the next slug line.

FADE OUT Always end the script with "FADE OUT." in ALL CAPS, followed by a period, on the *right* margin.

Shorthand
(O.S.): Off screen; used when a person speaks, but is not seen, as on the other end of a telephone. (O.S.) appears on the character line after the name, such as "MARK (O.S.)."

(V.O.): Voiceover; used when a character speaks what is in his/her head, such as narration, flashbacks and dream sequences. Also appears on character line, such as "LISA (V.O.)."

(beat): A pause. Use sparingly: actors will know when to pause in a well-written script. Format "(beat)" as a parenthetical (lowercase, in parentheses, single spaced below character or dialogue line, indented about two inches from left margin—about five spaces left of character line).

Ellipsis: Three periods with spaces between them . . . used when a character does not complete his/her dialogue . . .

Three dashes: - - - (with spaces between them), used when a character's dialogue is cut off by another character - - -

Underlining: Use underlining to add emphasis to words in dialogue, such as "I never saw you before." Use it sparingly, though: actors will know what words to emphasize in a well-written script.

ANGLE: This is a modified slug line used to indicate a change of camera perspective within a scene. Format as a slug line: at the left margin, in ALL CAPS, with a double space above and below. If necessary, describe the specific angle in an action line.

CLOSE ON: This is another modified slug line used to indicate a close-up on some person or object, such as "CLOSE ON LISA."

INSERT: This is another modified slug line used to draw attention to something within a scene, such as "INSERT—NOTEPAD."

POV: Point of view; this is another modified slug line used to indicate a camera perspective of what a character sees, such as "LISA'S POV."

FADE IN:

INT. OFFICE — DAY

LISA sits at a desk in front of a computer. THEME MUSIC plays.

NARRATOR
Welcome to Writer's Block, the program that helps aspiring authors break through those lapses in creativity and "get into the zone."

ANGLE ON LISA

NARRATOR
(Continuing)
Take Lisa, for instance. She's about to finish writing the greatest corpo-rate video script ever, only she doesn't know it yet. That's because she's suffering from writer's block. Oh, it's not that she isn't creative; it's just that she loses so much time trying to make her script conform to the correct screenplay format.

THEME MUSIC ends.

Lisa
(Screaming)
Arghhh! I hate this! Every time I get a good idea, I have to mess with these margins and I lose my concentration!

HEAVENLY MUSIC begins to play. ANGEL MARK floats down to Lisa.

NARRATOR
Today is Lisa's lucky day! Mark is here to save her with a brief handout on how to format a screenplay!

LISA
Who are you?

MARK
I'm Mark, and I'm here to save you with this brief handout on how to format a screenplay!

LISA
Where have I heard that before?

MARK
The narrator just said it.

LISA
Oh. Say, isn't formatting screenplays hard?

MARK
I'm glad you asked that, Lisa. Many people think so. But that's not the case! This brief handout gives you a quick guide on how to set things up.

Mark gives Lisa a handout. A MAGIC SOUND EFFECT is heard.

MARK
(Continuing)
The standard scriptwriting font is Courier New 12 point. A slug line states a location and time briefly, in all capital letters, beginning with the abbreviation for either "interior" or "exterior," followed by a one- or two-word location, such as "Lisa's office," followed by a dash and either the word "day" or "night."

LISA
So that's what a slug is.

MARK
An action line briefly sets up the scene and describes any activity or movement, such as "Lisa sits at a desk," or "Angel Mark floats down." Action lines are single spaced, though they are two spaces below slug lines. Action lines use regular lower-case letters; however, the first time a character appears, that character's name is capitalized. Music, sound effects, and special visual effects are also capitalized.

LISA
That seems easy enough.

MARK
For dialogue, the character's name is two lines below the action line and indented about two and a half inches from the left margin, spelled in all capital letters. One line below the character line, the dialogue is written, single spaced, indented about one and a half inches from both the left and right margins, making dialogue lines appear about three inches wide in the middle of the page.
LISA
I'm beginning to get it.

MARK
There are other formatting conventions, too, and they are all spelled out right in this handout. Now you can keep those creative ideas flowing without thinking that formatting is hard!

SAPPY MUSIC plays.

LISA
Oh, thank you, Mark! You saved my writing career.

MARK
Think nothing of it, Lisa! I do this every day.

LISA
My hero!

FADE OUT.

B Format Guidelines for Two-Column Scripts

Although the screenplay format discussed in Appendix A is used widely today for much film and television writing, it is useful to know the two-column format, as well. This format is used for some multiple-camera productions, as well as for many advertisements and corporate and instructional videos.

Unlike the screenplay format, which is governed by fairly precise guidelines that have evolved since the beginning of moviemaking, the two-column script format has only a few guidelines, and there are even exceptions to these. However, some conventions have emerged as fairly standard. The conventions presented here are suggestions; it must be understood that each client may require different format standards of the writer. Following these guidelines is a sample script, *Writer's Block*, which demonstrates most of these elements.

Margins/Font The standard font and margins for all scriptwriting should be used. Margins should be one inch on each edge of the page. The font should be pica, a typewriter word indicating a serif, fixed-width font of 10 characters per inch. For most computer programs, the pica font is 12-point Courier, the font used in the sample script. The standard font and margins were agreed upon because early scripts were typed in pica with one-inch margins, and each script page was about one minute of program time. That standard is still used today.

Header Each page should have a header that contains at least the page number at the top right margin, perhaps followed by a period, as in screenplays. Additional header information varies from client to client and may include titles, slugs, names, clients, dates, and so on.

Columns The video column is on the left; the audio column is on the right. The shot descriptions in the video column should be aligned horizontally with their corresponding sound or dialogue in the audio column.

Column Labels The columns may have "VIDEO" and "AUDIO" headings on each page, and these may even be underlined, though none of this is necessary. The suggestion here is that the columns are obvious *without* headings, and because headings require extra space in the header, they may be eliminated.

Dividing Line Some two-column scripts have a solid, vertical line dividing the video and audio columns. This stems from the days of typewriters, when each sheet of paper came with underlined column headings and a dividing line to assist writers in typing the columns correctly. It is suggested here that this dividing line is *not* necessary, especially because computer software aligns the columns neatly and automatically.

Capitalization   A recommended convention is to CAPITALIZE every word that is NOT SPOKEN. This includes everything in the video column, as well as character names, music, and sound effects in the audio column. Words for performers to speak are written in regular upper- and lowercase letters. This is done because: (a) research shows that it is easier for performers to read upper-lowercase letters than ALL CAPS, and (b) capitalizing all nonspoken words helps distinguish them from dialogue.

Video   The video column should contain descriptions of each shot. Typically, these consist of: (a) the shot size—LS, MS, CU, etc.; (b) the subject of the shot—BOB, CHAIR, PHOTO, etc.; (c) action or blocking notes—SHE STANDS, HE CROSSES, SHE POUNDS HER FIST, etc.; (d) special camera movements—ARC, DOLLY, ZOOM, etc.; and (e) visual effects—SMOKE, FLASH OF LIGHT, MORPH, etc.

A note on shot descriptions.   Unlike in screenplays, where shots must be spelled out (e.g., "close-up") because readers may not know production shorthand, abbreviations (e.g., "CU") are acceptable in the two-column format, because readers are typically involved in the production (though there are exceptions).

A note on spacing.   Video descriptions may be either single or doublespaced. Double spacing is preferred for production scripts because there is more room for changes and notes. Singlespacing is acceptable for nonproduction uses, such as "spec" scripts and publication. Doublespacing should be used between different shots and between different elements within the same shot, such as between a description, action, or camera movement; example:

```
LS VICTORIA AT WINDOW

SHE LIFTS A CUP TO HER LIPS

AND SIPS GENTLY

ZOOM IN TO CU VICTORIA
```

Figure B-1   *Audio*   The audio column contains: (a) characters, (b) dialogue, (c) music, and (d) sound effects (SFX).

As noted in the entry on capitalization, the dialogue should be written in regular, upper and lowercase letters, while everything else should be written in ALL CAPS.

Additionally, some writers place music and SFX cues in parentheses and underline them in order to make them *really* distinguishable from dialogue. This goes back to the days of radio scripts, when the convention was to write sound cues in ALL CAPS, (in parentheses), and underlined; for example:

```
(JAZZ MUSIC FADES IN)

(SFX: DISTANT GUNSHOT)
```

Characters   Character names may be centered over their respective dialogue, or they may appear on the first line of dialogue, followed by a colon. Here, the latter option is recommended because it saves a few lines of space; for example:

```
JOSEPHINE: Good morning, boys!
```

Also acceptable:

```
JOSEPHINE

Good morning, boys!
```

Spacing   Dialogue may be either single or double spaced. Double spacing is preferred for production scripts because there is more room for changes and notes. Single spacing is acceptable for non-production uses, such as "spec" scripts and publication. In any case, double spacing should be used between different characters and between sound cues; for example:

```
JOSEPHINE: Good morning, boys!

Say, where were you yesterday?

LANCE: (Embarrassed) Uh, that's

really none of your business.

(SFX: TIRES SCREECHING)
```

Punctuation   Punctuation is used sparingly in video and audio descriptions because they are abbreviated. Only dialogue is fully punctuated.

How to Format a Two-Column Script in Microsoft Word Using the "Tables" Tool

The "Tables" tool (not the "Columns" tool) in MS Word may be used to format a two-column script. The following tutorial may help. The sample script accompanies the tutorial.

1. Document.   Open a document in MS Word. Set your font as Courier New 12 point. Set your margins at one inch.

2. Header.   Under the "View" menu, select "Header and Footer." You may create any header you want, but for now, write your name, then tab over to the right margin and select "page number" (click on the "#" icon), and for fun, follow this with a period, the way they do in screenplays. If the letters are not already in 12-point Courier, highlight them and make them such. Close the header.

3. Tables.   On the top tool bar, select the "Insert Tables" button (the one with the icon of a page with multiple rows and columns; do *not* choose the icon with two columns, which is the "Insert Columns" button—that's for newspaper-style columns). Click on the button and drag down and to the right until you have a 1×2 table.

4. Video.   Your cursor should now be at the left margin of the left column—the "video" column. Select CAPS LOCK because you want to type everything in this column in ALL CAPS. Type:

```
FADE IN: <return twice>

LS OFFICE INT. <return twice>

LISA AT DESK IN FRONT OF
COMPUTER
```

Notice how "COMPUTER" wraps to the next line automatically. Also, if the letters are not already in 12-point Courier, highlight them and make them such.

5. Audio.   Now press TAB to jump to the right column. Your cursor should be at the left margin of this audio column. You want to open with some theme music, and then bring it under the narrator's (abbreviated. "NARR") dialogue. Select <u>underline</u>, then type:

```
(THEME MUSIC UP & UNDER)
<unselect underline> <return
twice>

NARR: <unselect CAPS LOCK> Wel-
come to "Writer's Block," the
program that helps aspiring au-
thors break through those lapses
in creativity and "get into the
zone."
```

Notice how the words wrap automatically.

6. New video.   Press TAB and you'll jump back to a brand new cell in the video column. Press RETURN to double space below the previous line. Select CAPS LOCK again, and then type the new shot, action, and camera movement:

```
MS LISA <return twice>

SHE FRANTICALLY STRIKES KEYS
AND MOVES THE MOUSE AT HER
COMPUTER <return twice>

ARC AROUND LISA
```

7. New audio.   TAB over to the new cell in the audio column. Unselect CAPS LOCK. Press RETURN once to double space below the previous dialogue and to line up the new dialogue with the video description. Continue typing the narrator's dialogue until the next video shot.

8. Continue.   TAB back to the video column, and continue on until you have finished the sample script.

9. Page break. Your page may break in the middle of a line of dialogue. This is usually something to avoid, so simply press RETURN enough times to make the page break just *before* that line of dialogue. Remember to do the same in the video column, so the video description stays aligned with its corresponding audio. Alternately, you can select the entire table, select "table" in the menu and then "table properties..." select the "row" tab and uncheck the box next to "allow rows to break across page"—then you don't have to do all the extra returns.

If the dialogue is fairly lengthy, you may *not* want to do this, but allow the page to break the dialogue and write in "MORE" at the end of the first page and "CONTINUED" at the start of the next page, the way they do in screenplays.

10. Save/print. Save the document and print it. How does it look?

Note on boxes. If Word puts boxes around each cell of your script table by default, you want to clear those boxes. Use "Select All" to highlight your entire script. Then click and hold on the "Outside Border," or "Box," function at the top of the Word toolbar. Drag down to the "Clear Box" and select that. The box lines should disappear from your script.

Note on spacing. If you wish to double-space your entire script, simply select double spacing for the document (select "Format" from the menu, then select "Paragraph..." to set double spacing); then you don't have to press RETURN twice between shots.

Note on macros. If you are a sophisticated Word user, you may create your own macros to do the capitalization and double spacing automatically within the cells.

FADE IN: LS INT. OFFICE LISA AT DESK IN FRONT OF COMPUTER	(THEME MUSIC UP & UNDER) NARR: Welcome to "Writer's Block," the program that helps aspiring authors break through those lapses in creativity and "get into the zone."
MS LISA SHE FRANTICALLY STRIKES KEYS AND MOVES THE MOUSE AT HER COMPUTER ARC AROUND LISA	Take Lisa, for instance. She's about to finish writing the greatest corporate video script ever, only she doesn't know it yet. That's because she's suffering from writer's block. Oh, it's not that she isn't creative; it's that she loses so much time trying to format her script into two columns!
CU LISA	(FADE MUSIC OUT) LISA: (Screaming) Arghhh! I hate this! Every time I get a good idea, I have to mess with these margins and I lose my concentration!

DISS TO: LS OFFICE INT. ANGEL MARK FLOATS DOWN TO LISA	(HEAVENLY MUSIC UP & UNDER) NARR: Today is Lisa's lucky day! Mark is here to save her with a tip on how to use Microsoft Word to format a two-column script!
MS 2S MARK & LISA	LISA: Who are you? MARK: I'm Mark, and I'm here to save you with a tip on how to use Microsoft Word to format a two-column script! LISA: Where have I heard that before? MARK: The narrator just said it.
CU LISA	LISA: Oh. Say, isn't Microsoft Word just for regular word processing?
CU MARK	MARK: I'm glad you asked that, Lisa! Many people think so. But here's my tip: you can use the "Tables" tool to format two-column video scripts! Allow me to demonstrate.
MS MARK, LISA, & COMPUTER MARK LOADS SOFTWARE	(SFX: SOFTWARE LOADING) (FADE MUSIC OUT) MARK: (Continuing) It's quick and easy to use, just like all of Microsoft Word's options.

CU POV COMPUTER SCREEN TWO COLUMNS APPEAR MARK BEGINS TO WRITE	You just select a one-cell by two-cell table, and you have two columns. You type your video shots in the left column... I use the convention of all capital letters... then you tab over to the audio column and write your sound cues and dialogue. When you select "tab" again, you're back at the left margin in a new video cell. LISA: Goodness, that's easy! MARK: It certainly is. Now you can keep those creative ideas flowing without worrying about aligning your columns!
MS MARK & LISA	<u>(SAPPY MUSIC UNDER)</u> LISA: Oh, thank you, Mark! You saved my writing career! MARK: Think nothing of it, Lisa! I do this every day.
LS OFFICE INT. MARK FLOATS AWAY	LISA: My hero! (MUSIC UP & OUT)
FADE TO BLACK	

C Storyboards

A script describes the action of a production; a storyboard shows it. Along with the script, a storyboard is a valuable instrument for planning, shooting, and editing a program. It is a tool that allows clients, producers, directors, writers, designers, crew members, and talent to visualize a scene or program before shooting begins, and to have a visual reference during production and postproduction. Experience shows that time invested in storyboarding is time saved in shooting and editing.

Storyboards consist of two parts: sketches and written descriptions. Each shot in a scene or program requires a new sketch, or panel, in a storyboard. That is, every time the director plans to cut to a new angle or image, that new angle or image is drawn. Drawings may range from professionally drawn, full-color pictures to rough pencil sketches with stick figures. Written descriptions consist of abbreviated summaries of both the video and audio for each panel.

The video description includes four possible items:

- Shot size (e.g., LS, MS, CU).

- Subject (e.g., man, woman, tree).

- Action (e.g., walking, fighting, standing next to fire).

- Any camera moves or special visual effects (e.g., pan, dissolve, explosion).

The audio description includes three possible items:

- Dialogue (incues and outcues are acceptable when the dialogue is lengthy).

- Sound effects (e.g., gun shot, door closing, tires screeching).

- Music (e.g., slow classical, trumpet fanfare, up-tempo rock).

It is important for both the creators and readers of storyboards to understand the conventions of this communication tool. First of all, aspect ratio is important. Standard television screens are four units wide for every three units high, or 4:3 (1.33:1). High-definition television (HDTV) and film screens are wider, ranging from 1.78:1 (HDTV, 16:9) to 2.44:1 (Cinerama). In all cases, the image is wider than it is tall, and the storyboard panels are sketched accordingly.

There are different types of transitions between shots, and these make up a second convention. The most common transition is a straight cut or take, where one image instantly replaces the other. Because this is the most used transition, it is assumed on a storyboard: the word "cut" is *not* written. However, if a different transition is used, such as a dissolve (momentary blending of the images) or a wipe (one image pushes the other off the screen in a geometric pattern), this transition is written in the description part of the storyboard.

A third convention consists of shot sizes. The three most common are "LS" for "long shot" (head to toe), "MS" for "medium shot" (waist up), and "CU" for "close-up" (shoulders up). There are some variations of these: "ELS" for "extreme long shot" (subject appears small relative to surroundings), "MLS" for "medium long shot" (knees up), "MCU" for "medium close-up" (chest up), and "ECU" for "extreme close-up" (face or eyes only).

A fourth convention regards some types of framing. Two common abbreviations are "2S" for "two-shot" and "3S" for "three-shot," when two or three people appear on the screen, respectively. When one person is on screen, it is *not* necessary to indicate "one-shot," and when *more* than three people appear, "group shot" or a similar term may be used. An additional abbreviation is "O/S" for "over-the shoulder shot," when two people are positioned fore- and background so the one in the background is seen over the shoulder of the one in the foreground, as in Figure C-1. (Note: O/S—see the slash—should not be confused with O.S.—see the periods—which stands for "off screen." O.S. is used for dialogue that a character speaks when that character is off screen, or not in the frame. This is different from "V.O."—voiceover—which is used when an off-camera announcer speaks or when the thoughts inside a character's head are spoken.)

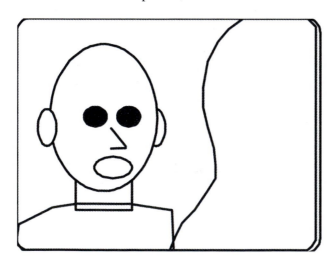

Figure C-1   O/S MCU to man.

A fifth convention is image composition, especially the "rule of thirds." According to this guideline, if the screen is divided into imaginary thirds both vertically and horizontally, the most important information appears *not* in the center of the screen, but at the intersections of the thirds, or on the lines between those intersections (called the "dynamic axes" or the "golden mean") In Figure C-2, a close-up reveals the eyes—the most important elements—not in the center, but "at the thirds."

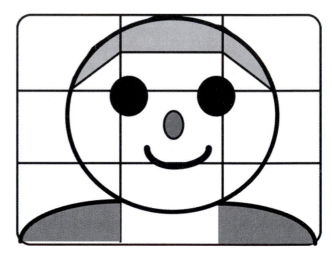

Figure C-2   Rule of thirds.

A sixth convention concerns the movement of a subject within the frame. This is indicated by a broken arrow inside the panel that indicates the direction of the movement. The example in Figure C-3 shows a long shot of a man walking screen right.

Figure C-3   LS man walks screen right.

A seventh and final storyboard convention deals with movement of the camera itself. A tilt is upward and downward movement of a *stationary* camera. A pedestal or crane is upward and downward movement of the entire *camera head*. Both tilts and pedestals (or cranes) are indicated by a solid, vertical arrow outside and to the right of the panel. The arrow indicates the direction. The example shown in Figure C-4 depicts either a tilt or pedestal (crane) down. The written description clarifies.

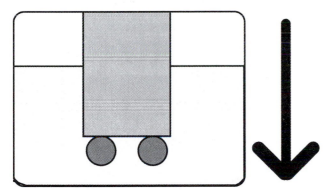

Figure C-4 The written description clarifies if this is a tilt or a pedestal down.

A pan is left and right movement of a stationary camera. A truck is left and right movement of a camera head. Both pans and trucks are indicated on storyboards by a solid, horizontal arrow outside and below the panel. The arrow indicates the direction. The example in Figure C-5 shows either a pan or truck to the left. A written description would, again, clarify which. An arc is a semi-circle around part of a subject. It involves trucking and dollying simultaneously. An arc is indicated as a pan or truck: a solid arrow outside the panel. The written description explains that it is an arc.

A zoom is the change of a lens's focal length to make objects appear closer or farther away. A dolly is the forward and backward movement of the whole camera, either closer to or farther away from the subject. Both zooms and dollies are indicated by a solid, diagonal arrow inside the upper right-hand corner of the panel. The arrow indicates the direction. A box with dotted lines inside the panel indicates the area to be revealed in the tightest part of the shot, either at the beginning or at the end of the zoom or dolly. The example in Figure C-6 depicts either a zoom out or dolly back. A written description would again clarify which it is.

Figure C-5 This is a pan or truck left.

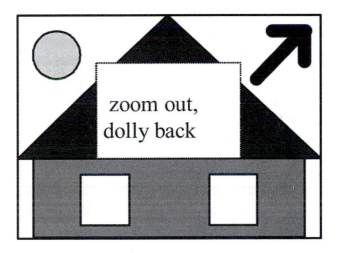

Figure C-6 This is a zoom out or dolly back.

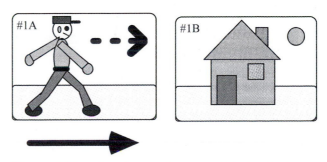

Figure C-7 The subject walks screen right in 1A; the camera pans right to the house in 1B.

Sometimes a camera movement, such as a zoom or tilt, reframes an item within the image, such as in the above example of a zoom out or dolly back. At other times, a camera movement ends on a new image that was *not* in the first frame, such as in the example in Figure C-7 that reveals a man walking, then the camera pans to the right—away from the man—to a house. When this is the case, both the beginning and ending images are storyboarded. But instead of numbering the sketches sequentially (e.g., 1 and 2—which indicate two separate shots), the sketches are given the *same* number followed by sequential *letters* (e.g., 1A and 1B—which indicate a continuous shot).

Figure C-8 is a blank storyboard page that may be photocopied and used in planning.

STORYBOARD   Project _____ Name _____ p. _____

Description should include both video and audio. Video: shot size, subject, action, and camera moves/special effects, e.g. *LS woman running, zoom to CU woman as fire explodes.* Audio: dialogue (incue and outcue if lengthy), sound effects, and music (if any), e.g. *"Hi, honey, I'm home," sound of door closing, up-tempo jazz.*

#____

#____

_____   _____
_____   _____
_____   _____
_____   _____
_____   _____
_____   _____
_____   _____

#____

#____

_____   _____
_____   _____
_____   _____
_____   _____
_____   _____
_____   _____
_____   _____

Figure C-8   A sample blank storyboard page.

D Analog Tape-to-Tape Video Editing

While nonlinear video editing in the digital environment is commonplace today, its roots go back to linear editing in the analog environment. Analog videotape editing, in turn, has its roots in film editing. A brief look back at the technology of editing can give you a better understanding of, and appreciation for, digital editing.

The very first recorded motion images were short movie clips on single rolls of film from inventors like Thomas Edison and the Lumière brothers in the 1890s. Soon, they and others discovered that they could cut and splice different pieces of film together to tell longer, more complex stories. The technology of cutting and splicing improved throughout the century that followed and continues today.

At the midpoint of the 20th century, with television the most popular medium of mass communication in the 1950s, inventors sought ways to record the electronic TV signal differently from the chemical process of film. In 1956, the Ampex Corporation introduced a large, reel-to-reel tape format called "Two-Inch Quadruplex," or just "Quad." The tape was two inches wide; four magnetic heads recorded four tracks of information (hence the name Quad) as the tape moved from a supply reel past the various recording and playback heads onto a take-up reel. This became the broadcast standard in control rooms for over a decade (it was too large to be practical in the field).

Next came one-inch Type C video: a full inch narrower. Other advances in technology allowed special

Figure D-1 The top picture shows a "cuts-only" 3/4-inch U-matic editing system with a remote edit control unit (ECU). The bottom picture shows an "A/B roll" editing system with two player VCRs that send the signal through a time-base corrector (TBC) and switcher then to the recorder VCR; the switcher receives video from the two player VCRs, an effects generator, and a character generator.

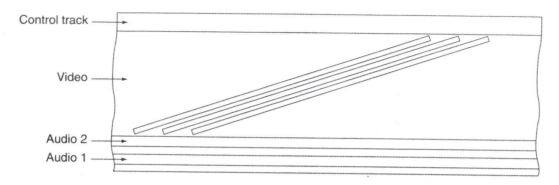

Figure D-2   Video slant track and audio linear track patterns on a cross-section of 3/4-inch U-Matic cassette videotape.

effects with this tape format, such as slow- and fast-motion and freeze-frame. As good as it was, Type C still required an operator to thread a supply and take-up reel, limiting its use for field recording.

Along came cassette formats in the 1970s. A format called 3/4-inch **U-matic** was a standard for field recording into the 1990s. (See Figures D-1 and D-2). The tape was only three-quarters of an inch wide, making it practical to enclose the reels into a single cassette, and the tape threaded itself automatically in a U-shape around the video drum inside the machine when it was loaded (hence the name 3/4-inch U-matic). Additionally, the video drum was slanted, allowing the magnets to pass diagonally across the tape's surface to record the image in a **helical scan** or **slant scan**. This diagonal scan allows more of the tape surface to be used for recording than does a straight vertical scan, resulting in a higher quality image. For this reason, helical scanning continues to be used for all small-format videotape recording, including **digital video** (DV).

Another popular cassette tape format was Betacam and, later, its improved version, Betacam SP, which is still used today. "Beta" for short (not to be confused with Betamax, the failed consumer Beta format that lost the market to VHS in the late 1970s) is better in quality and higher in price than 3/4-inch. It uses tape that is just a half inch wide and plays at a higher speed for greater video fidelity. (See Figures D-3 and D-4.)

A variety of other professional and semi-professional videotape formats have come and gone. Some can still be found in archives.

In addition to these formats, a variety of consumer videocassette formats were developed to be easy to use, inexpensive, and of good quality. Consumer formats

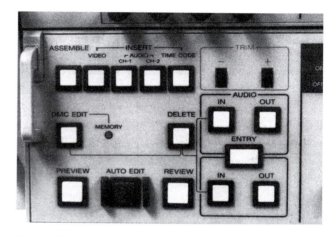

Figure D-3   The edit control buttons on a Sony BVW-75 Beta SP studio recorder. (Courtesy of Sony Corp.)

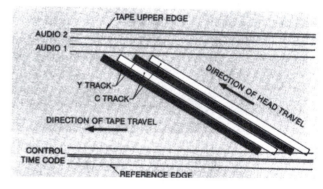

Figure D-4   Video and audio track pattern on a cross-section of 1/2-inch Betacam SP videotape.

generally have fewer lines of resolution and poorer color reproduction than professional formats. The first home video format, *Betamax*, debuted in 1975 and soon became obsolete. It was technically superior to its rival, *VHS*, which debuted in 1976, because Beta had a more stable and resolute image by moving the tape at a higher speed than VHS. However, Beta lost the format war for a number of reasons. For one thing, VHS could be slowed down to record six hours instead of two hours (but at lower quality), making it preferable for sporting events and other long-form programs. For another, the Matsushita Corporation, which invented VHS, licensed it to other companies, so multiple manufacturers produced VHS VCRs and tapes, driving the price down through competition. Sony did not license its Betamax format.

Other, improved consumer and **prosumer** (professional-consumer) tape formats in the 1980s and 1990s included Super VHS (S-VHS), the smaller 8-mm format, and its improved version, Hi-8, which offered not only improved image quality but improved audio quality with a **pulse code modulation (PCM)** recording system that yields two tracks of near-CD-quality sound. (See Figure D-5).

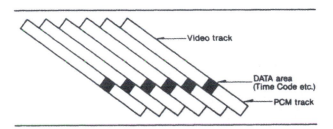

Figure D-5 Video and audio track pattern on a cross-section of 8-mm videotape.

The older videotape formats recorded **composite video**, a process by which the luminance (brightness, denoted by the letter Y) and chrominance (color, denoted by the letter C) portions of the signal were recorded together on one pass of the magnet, or one track per video field. Sometimes the two signals would interfere with each other, causing a loss of picture resolution. Later formats, including Betacam SP, MII, and others, record **component video**. This process uses two different tracks, or passes of the magnet: one for luminance and a separate one for chrominance. Sometimes called Y/C for short, component images are superior to composite images (assuming other variables are the same, including lighting, contrast, number of scanning lines, etc.), because the separate tracks keep the two signals from interfering with each other.

The process of editing analog videotape differed from today's digital nonlinear editing in technology, but not in concept. A source deck played the tape with the raw footage, and a record deck recorded the part of each shot determined by the editor. The two decks were cabled together via an **edit control unit (ECU)**. Many different models of ECUs existed, but they shared the same basic operation. A shuttle allowed both tapes to be cued to the frame on which the edit was to be made. Other controls might allow effects to be added, such as freeze-frames, colorization, posterization, and so on. Sometimes audio controls were on the ECU as well; other times, the audio controls were on a separate unit.

After cueing the source tape to the beginning frame of the desired edit and the record tape to the desired frame to lay down the edit, the editor pressed a "preview" button. This rewound each tape five seconds—a process called **preroll**—then played the tapes, using the five second preroll to sync them up so a glitch-free edit could be seen at the edit point when both "decks" were fully up to speed. The editor could then trim the in-points and out-points, if necessary, and preview again until satisfied. Once satisfied with the edit in preview, the editor would press the red "edit" button (at least it was red on every model of ECU I ever saw) to lay down the edit.

Editors could do either an **assemble edit** or an **insert edit**. Some of the nonlinear editing software programs continue to use this terminology. In an assemble edit, every part of the signal from the source tape was transferred to the record tape: video, both audio channels, and the control track signal. This was useful for quick "down-and-dirty" edits when a piece needed to be cut together in a hurry. It was also used to copy an entire program. However, assemble edits would break into any existing footage on the record tape, causing a glitch on the **control track**—the track that carried the pulses to keep things playing in sync—at the point the assemble edit ended. (See Figure D-6).

For an insert edit, the video only, or just one or both of the audio channels, could be replaced without the others. This allowed new video to be edited over existing audio, and vice versa. (See Figure D-7). For example, a talking head narrator could be laid down first, and then just video **B-roll** shots could be edited over parts of the talking head while leaving the voice

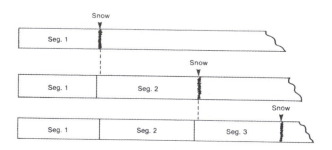

Figure D-6   In an assemble edit, all the information for a tape segment is copied from the source to the record tape, including the control track, which results in a glitch, or snow, at the end of each edit.

track unchanged. Or an off-camera narrator's voice could be recorded and laid down under existing video. To accomplish an insert edit, the editor first had to **black the tape**: record a steady black signal in a VCR for the entire length of the tape. This process laid down a control track, which was necessary because the individual audio and/or video signals in an insert edit were synced to that unbroken control track. Insert editing was preferred because it gave the editor the most control to drop in audio and/or video segments. However, it took more time than assemble editing to make these more discrete edits, and it also required the time

necessary to black a tape first—in real time (i.e., 60 minutes for a 60-minute tape).

Simple ECUs used **control-track editing**. They would sync up the control tracks on the source and record tapes to make the edits. While simple in cost and concept, the edits were not exact. Most control-track edits could slip up to four frames, meaning the edit could come in as many as four frames ahead or behind the desired edit point. While four frames aren't much for many edits, for some edits that loss of precision could be the difference between a good or a bad edit.

More sophisticated ECUs allowed for more precise, frame-accurate, **time-code editing**. Time code, developed by the Society of Motion Picture and Television Engineers (SMPTE) and, therefore, sometimes called SMPTE Time Code, is the numbering system for every frame of video in a production, noted in hours:minutes:seconds:frames. In the analog days of videotape, more sophisticated cameras recorded a time code signal, and more sophisticated editing systems edited with it. In today's digital world, every camera and every editing software program comes with time code capability. The time code signal is recorded on a separate track of videotape. Older analog ECUs had a switch to select either control track or time code editing, with time code preferred for tapes that had time code recorded on them.

Control Track		
Video Track Seg. 1 Interview	Video Track Seg. 2 B-roll	Video Track Seg. 3 New Video
Audio Track 2, Seg. 1 from Interview		Audio Track 2, Narrator
Audio Track 1, Sound Effects	Audio Track 1, Music at Bed Level	

Figure D-7   In insert editing, the control track remains unbroken while new video and/or audio segments are added.

In the digital world, hardware and software consistently read the digital signals to keep everything playing in sync. Back in the analog days, this was not the case. One tape might be recorded at a slightly different speed than another. The precise pixel on which the scanning began on one video source would not match the same pixel on another source for editing. All these sync problems required the video signals from all sources to be processed through a **time-base corrector** (**TBC**). This device takes the output signal of each video source and corrects it to a standard synchronization signal. Timebase correction is built into digital cameras and editing software.

Digital nonlinear editing systems allow editors to experiment with greater ease and speed than ever before. This is due in part to the speed with which digital files can be manipulated in computers. It is also due in part to the creators of digital systems, who learned from their analog predecessors. Aware of the problems that analog systems had to overcome, such as synchronizing multiple input sources, making frame-accurate edits, and matching the look of images across edit points, the creators of digital systems built these capabilities right into the hardware and software. Indeed, today's digital editing owes a great deal to yesterday's analog editing.

Of paramount importance, though, while recognizing the evolution from analog to digital editing, is understanding that the conceptual aspects of editing remain the same. No matter whether images and sounds are cut together in a computer or on tape or on film, the know-how to assemble footage into a well-told story is really what matters. Just about anyone can be trained on what buttons to push or what icons to click. Of greater value is the videomaker who knows what constitutes a great edit aesthetically, regardless of the technology used to make that edit.

Index